PORTER
ROCKWELL
A Biography

Pictured on front cover:

U. S. Marshal Pistol — Model 1842 is a .54 caliber pistol, with a smoothbore percussion lock, designed to be used as a club after firing. It has an attached swivel-ramrod for re-loading on horseback.

PORTER ROCKWELL

A Biography

Richard
Lloyd
Dewey

Illustrated by
Clark Kelley Price

PARAMOUNT BOOKS • *NEW YORK*

Library of Congress Cataloguing in Publications Data

Dewey, Richard Lloyd.
    Porter Rockwell: a biography

    Bibliography: p. 539
    Index: p. 575
    1. Rockwell, Orrin Porter, 1813-1878. 2. Mormons — United States —
Biography. I. Dewey, Richard Lloyd II. Title.

Library of Congress Catalog Card Number 65-063355
ISBN: 0-9616024-0-6

Paramount Books
Box 379
Seaford, New York 11783

First printing, May 1986
Second printing, June 1986
Third printing, November 1986
Fourth printing, March 1987
Fifth printing, November 1988

Printed in the United States of America

*To Richard Hyde Dewey and LeClaire Grant Dewey,
the world's finest parents*

Orrin Porter Rockwell
Courtesy of Church Archives
The Church of Jesus Christ of Latter-day Saints

Hawken Rifle

This is a copy of an earlier J and S Hawken, manufactured approximately 1845 to 1855. As one of the many St. Louis rifles manufactured by Hawken, it was adopted for plains and mountain use by civilian trappers, scouts, and hunters. The caliber varied, usually 40-50 caliber. Its rugged stock has smooth contours. It was a plain, unadorned, utility rifle, and had a reputation for accuracy and dependability.

Orrin Porter Rockwell
Courtesy of Utah State Historical Society

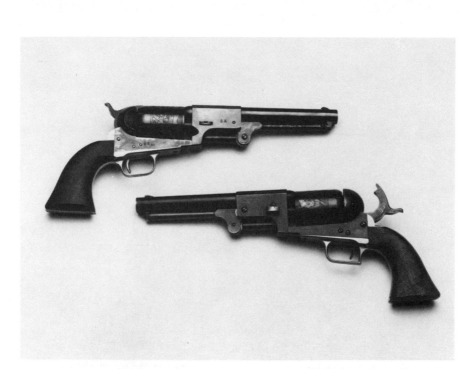

2nd and 3rd Model Dragoon

Made by Sam Colt in Hartford, Connecticut and introduced about 1849, this .44 caliber pistol was a direct outgrowth of the Mexican War. When the military realized single-shot pistols were ineffective, they adopted multiple fire weapons for their increased fire-power during skirmish actions. Previous to these multiple-fire weapons, single-shot weapons were more often than not fired once, then employed as a club, rather than re-loading in battle. This weapon changed the history and art of the skirmish. As a six-shot revolver, the multiple-fire capability of this weapon led to the demise of the sabre. Generally, two of these weapons were carried in pommel-holsters, draping over the front of the saddle.

Orrin Porter Rockwell
Courtesy of Utah State Historical Society

Colt Navy

Introduced in 1851 and often called the 1851 Colt, this weapon was a lightened, civilian version of the 3rd model dragoon. It was reduced to about two and one-half pounds from the nearly four pound Dragoon pistol. The Colt Navy was a .36 caliber, six-shot weapon, very popular during the two decades it was manufactured. It was mostly used during the Civil War and was a favorite of the cavalry. The weapon was also used for law enforcement. Rockwell owned at least one Colt Navy.

Muskatoon

The 1851 Springfield entered Utah with Johnston's Army and was employed by dragoons — horseback infantrymen — and by (the separate) cavalry units. This weapon is a short version of the longer arm used by foot troops. It was not preferred for civilian use because of its incredibly large (.58) caliber. It has a saddle ring, for fast-action horseback shooting, and was known for its rugged construction.

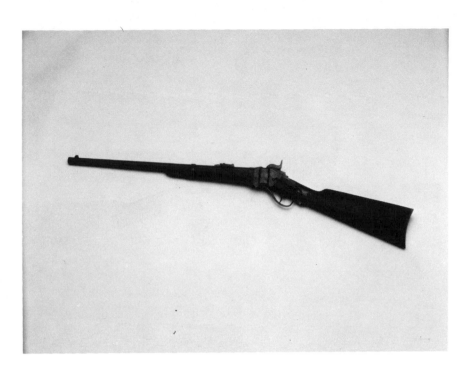

Sharps Rifle

This is a .53 caliber breechloading carbine, used with loose powder and ball or combustible cartridge single shot, and was popular during the Civil War. The Sharps was second in popularity during the Civil War only to the Spencer repeating carbine which utilized self-contained metallic cartridges. It was developed in the late 1840's. Adopted by the military in 1859 (pictured is a Model 1863), it was used extensively in the West as the one weapon most responsible for the near extinction of the vast herds of bison roaming the plains. As a long-range hunting rifle, the greatest expansion of the weapon to the West came after the Civil War. It was replaced by repeaters in the mid-1870's, Rockwell's final years. The Sharps was one of the favorite hunting rifles due to its legendary accuracy. It is the weapon from which the term "sharp-shooter" was derived.

Model 1860 Colt Army Model

As a .44 caliber, six-shot, single action percussion revolver, the 1860 Colt Army was one of the most popular contract handguns used during the Civil War, and a favorite of lawmen and outlaws during the settling of the West because of its reputation for dependability. A favorite phrase of Rockwell's was, "God created man, but Colonel Colt made them equal."

Acknowledgments

The author credits numerous individuals and institutions for the production of this work. For their generous time and making available research materials he extends appreciation to the staff of the Harold B. Lee Library at Brigham Young University — and in particular the Special Collections Department, under the direction of Chad J. Flake; to the Church Historical Department at Salt Lake City — in particular the Archives Section — which released for the author hard-to-access material; to the Utah State Historical Society; to Richard Horsely of Provo, Utah for his aid in tracing certain hard-to-find resource material; to Ty Harrison of Sandy, Utah for leads; and to John Rockwell of Lehi, Utah for both leads and family information. Special thanks is extended to the two pioneers of research on Porter Rockwell, whose monumental works will never go unappreciated. Nicholas Van Alfen introduced his master's thesis on Rockwell in 1938, listing numerous original sources which the author has relocated; and certainly Harold Schindler, for his book, *Porter Rockwell: Man of God, Son of Thunder,* must be recognized for greatly expanding Van Alfen's list with numerous additional sources and for devoting his life to such research. From the sources these two pioneers, and particularly the latter, have located and quoted from (enabling the author to find and, in many cases, expand the quotations) the author has re-interpreted many of the sources — and many historical points — before adding sources of his own. Respect for these pioneers, however, in the author's eyes, remains almost idolatrous, after spending years on this project himself.

For aiding manuscript preparation the author extends appreciation to Michael A. Fitzpatrick, Crickett Goodsell, Amy Clegg, Charles Larson, and Lloyd Weenig. For other production work, Lee Ann Hooker and Dorothy Chase. For proof-reading, to R. Vernon Ingleton. For editing, and a marvelous job at that, Wallace R. Johnson.

For design, Stephen Hales and Richard L. Anderson; for typesetting, Blake and Joan Penrod; for photography, Earl Roberge, Thomas Jay, and W. Mike Nielson; and for illustrations, Clark Kelley Price, a truly remarkable western artist, and one of the nation's finest.

Joseph Smith, 1844
Photograph of painting in possession of RLDS Church

Brigham Young, December 12, 1850
Copy of a Daguerrotype taken by Marsena Cannon

PORTER
ROCKWELL
A Biography

I

The mists of summer hovered above freshly plowed New England fields as, one week into the new season, a child was born. The heat of the rising day, June 28, 1813, cast holographic images through the meadowlands of Belcher, Massachusetts — of dancing angels and devils that would haunt Orrin Porter Rockwell the remainder of his days.

His parents, Orin (with one "r") and Sarah Witt Rockwell, were unaware of the effect on mankind that not only their child, but that of which their distant cousins would have; yet Abraham Lincoln and Ulysses S. Grant would never meet the son of this farm family, although they would indeed hear of him in later years.

His middle name, "Porter" was the one by which his associates would usually refer to him. And the lad's surname was worthy of respect. Windsor, Connecticut had probably been the first stop-off point for the family line, which could be traced to William Rockwell, the family's first immigrant and a deacon from Dorchester, England. (See Note 1 for genealogical details.)

Leaving a solid, respected reputation,[1] Porter's parents shoveled up their grundle of nine and moved to Manchester, New York in 1817.

In 1819 the family of Joseph Smith, Jr. moved just one mile from the Rockwell farm,[2] and soon the two families united[3] in a lasting friendship, but from it would arise a controversy that would sweep both hemispheres . . .

These early ties began in Porter's obscure farmhouse where his family and the Smiths burned numerous midnight pine torches, enraptured by young Joseph's account of seeing an angel and receiving golden plates, written, as Joseph asserted, by ancient prophets of America to supplement the Bible.

Porter was, in fact, so engrossed by Joseph's declarations that, according to Elizabeth Roundy to whom Porter later related his childhood experience,[4] he "begged his mother to allow him to sit up and keep the pine torch burning, their only source of light in the evening." Porter became so convinced of his new friend's account that he worked daily, after farm chores, picking berries and chopping firewood by moonlight, "giving the money to the Prophet to help print the *Book of Mormon*."

Although several years his senior, young Smith paved a similar road of pain and pertinacity which Rockwell would follow faithfully. At age ten Porter broke his leg. A Palmyra doctor attempted straightening it but managed to leave Porter with one leg shorter than the other. Joseph likewise had suffered from incompetent physicians, with leg bone disease and excruciatingly painful operations to scrape away the infection, and was left like Porter with a tell-tale limp that would mark his walk for a lifetime.

On April 6, 1830 Joseph formalized The Church of Jesus Christ of Latter-day Saints. In his journal Joseph records his parents being baptized, "and about the same time . . . Orrin Porter Rockwell."[5]

Porter's brother-in-law records Mrs. Rockwell was baptized the same day as Joseph's parents,[6] and soon three other Rockwells were baptized: Peter, Caroline, and Electa.[7] Porter's father would wait another two years for no recorded reason.[8]

The small church mushroomed in size, and to everyone's surprise Joseph received a certain revelation that directed several of the Saints to Kirtland, Ohio, preparatory to a major exodus from

New York.[9] The term Saints, as Joseph explained, meant mere disciples, or church members as, he defined, was used in New Testament days, rather than a revered saintly status; yet the word alone accounted for some of the persecution Joseph's people would receive in New York.

Porter's family, meanwhile, remained with the Fayette Branch in New York[10] until Porter's father decided to join the move.

That move came the following year, in which Porter's father followed Joseph's mother — an obviously dominant and powerful woman — who led not only the Rockwell family but a total of 80 Saints by steamboat down the Erie Canal towards Buffalo, New York, and then on to Fairport, Ohio.[11]

On the journey westward their boat was momentarily caked in by ice. Joseph's mother records, "At this, Porter Rockwell started on shore to see his uncle. His mother endeavored to prevent him, but he paid no attention to her, and she then appealed to me, saying, 'Mother Smith, do get Porter back, for he won't mind anybody but you.' I told him that, if he went, we should leave him on shore, but he did as he liked."[12]

Porter always did as he liked. Several other lads followed him until Lucy Mack Smith reprimanded them as well, and they returned to the boat.

But Porter just kept going. He presumably journeyed alone to his uncle's, and then traveled on to Ohio where he rendezvoused with his parents.

Shortly after their arrival in Ohio Joseph received another revelation — now instructing the Saints to gather in Missouri.[13]

Porter, age 17, obediently followed his Prophet. He moved with his parents from Ohio to Jackson County in Western Missouri.[14] Arriving there, Emily Austin explains, "We now resorted to flat boats to take us up the river to the mouth of Big Blue, in Jackson county, and to the ferry landing, and here we disembarked and our journey was ended, except a few miles by land into the country."[15]

With his journey ended Porter settled on a farm in the autumn of 1831, twelve miles west of Independence,[16] and here he worked side by side with parents and family, where an even stronger unity developed. Meanwhile, less than a mile west of the courthouse, Joseph chose a site where the Mormon Temple would be built.

Porter and the other Saints hoped this would be their final resting point.

Though Joseph's duties kept him separated from his childhood companion, Porter and Joseph never loosened their loyalty. Porter continued farming while Joseph presided over the church from both Independence, Missouri and Kirtland, Ohio.

Smith soon returned to Ohio and secured a printing press. A Mormon newspaper would begin grinding out issues at Independence.[17]

The Mormons in Missouri, meanwhile, spread themselves throughout Jackson County in various small settlements, under the direction of seven high priests, and purchased land from the U.S. Government at $1.25 per acre. While it was too late in the year to plant crops, the Saints built cabins all winter, receiving sustenance from a diet mainly of beef and cornbread.

During this winter Porter began courting Isaac and Olive Beebe's daughter Luana. Porter was so taken by her, in fact, that, after completing farm chores, he'd trek the long country roads into the city each evening.

And his tenacity paid off. On February 2, 1832 they were married.[18]

Meanwhile, the church continued growing in Missouri. Ohio Saints slowly made the exodus west, yet to Joseph's consternation a number of the "lukewarm" remained in Kirtland and eventually left the kingdom.

Reinforcements from converts, however, most notably from the Mid-West, poured into Missouri and made up for the loss. 900 Saints gathered at Independence by the summer of 1832, and Porter's home was cited for church leadership gatherings by elders and high priests.[19]

Porter's popularity among the Saints came largely from his new occupation . . . operating a ferry on the Big Blue River. Fellow Mormons were enchanted by his sense of humor, and they trusted his loyalty to church leaders — a loyalty which was to become legendary. Soon a church conference was even held on his ferry.[20]

But his first real troubles also began with this occupation. Porter was charged for operating a ferry without a license, although a grand jury discharged the allegation when it failed to return a true bill.[21] Nonetheless, it was a foretaste of the drama which would characterize his future.

And soon that drama came. The local Missouri populace became disenchanted with "this strange, new sect," a disenchantment that quickly flowered into full-fledged jealousy of the Mormons' industriousness. When the local ministry joined the action — some having watched their congregations defect *en masse* to the Mormons — the earth began to rumble.

A small core of anti-Mormon leaders propagandized throughout the communities, organizing a ragtag band of oldtimers — vigilantes really — to purge the countryside of these undesirables.

Then a new group formed at Independence, with other elements of society . . . the more respectable middle-class. Having gathered such a distinguished crowd, the local ministry felt they'd accomplished the first stage of their design.

As the meeting progressed, however, an unplanned obstacle emerged. Someone started passing bottles around. And the carefully orchestrated gathering soon degenerated into a whiskeyfest, whereupon most of the mob staggered away, stoned.[22]

Porter's closest neighbor, David Pettegrew, kept a most enlightening personal history, complete with vivid extracts. One novel observation explains a reason for the growing opposition: "The gathering of the saints continued, brethren came in daily from all parts of the United States, and this began to raise some excitement amongst the people opposed to our Church. The gift of tongues, I think, was the cause or means of the excitement. When they heard little children speaking tongues that they did not themselves understand, and knew also that those children could not have acquired the different tongues by learning, a Mr. Pool of Independence, when hearing some of these children speaking in different tongues, observed that he understood the tongue they spoke. It was the Delaware tongue, and he believed that this Book of Mormon was true because these children had never learnt these different tongues that we now hear them speak. Some of the local, anti-Mormon lawyers observed that if we did not put a stop to such things and suffer it to go on, all Independence will believe."[23]

In addition to a somewhat self-righteous attitude that certain of the Saints portrayed — in direct disharmony with Joseph's admonitions — the Mormons brought much of the persecution on themselves with their simple lack of tact: William W. Phelps, for example, the editor of the church newspaper *Evening and Morning Star*, published an article, "Free People of Color," promoting, in a sense, abolitionist doctrine.[24]

This particular incident was the spark that lit the keg.

The Missourians immediately released a manifesto to "rid our society" of the "deluded fanatics."[25] Another mob formed, this one more formidable, and leaders made certain whiskey would not be distributed. Nearly 500 locals met at the courthouse where they were lathered into a frenzy.

Pettegrew records, "This first mob part I saw were going by my house on their way to Independence to a great council held there, as to how and what should be their decision as regarded the Church of Mormon. They had a solemn and determined look. I saw several women in their company who seemed to be more interested in mobbing than their husbands. I remember very well that for two or three different days of their appointed meeting that it rained in torrents and I never heard in all my life such terrible thundering — the earth fairly shook, and during these heavy rains and storm I saw women returning home with their husbands from the mob meeting seeming perfectly satisfied with their day's labor. Although the lightening would flash so vividly as almost to blind, the thunder rolling over their heads and it looked as if heaven had opened its fury upon the earth, yet these persons went on regardless of all."[26]

They declared the Mormons must sign in writing a promise to leave the county, and that the Mormon newspaper close. They also demanded all Mormon-owned stores cease business, and for no additional Saints to settle in Jackson County.[27]

A dozen Missourians delivered the ultimatum to six local Mormon leaders. The reply was that the local Mormons would have to consult with church officials in Kirtland, and that it would take three months to receive an answer.

When the dozen Missourians galloped back to the mob with this report, the mob went into a rampage. Impatient for an immediate settlement on the matter they galloped into the woods searching for Mormon property. They discovered the home of

William W. Phelps and thoroughly vandalized it, then galloped about the countryside, searching for the Mormon newspaper press. They finally discovered it and tore it apart, then galloped off to the home of the bishop, Edward Partridge, and another Mormon, Charles Allen, whom they pulled from their homes and tarred and feathered,[28] "upon the public square, surrounded by hundreds of the mob."[29]

Porter, meanwhile, had been peaceably operating his ferry, when this same evening a dozen Missourian passengers suddenly whirled on him and warned him to "deny" the church or they would tar and feather him as well. Rockwell apparently said nothing. Once ashore they left without paying.[30]

This was Porter's first brush with the Missourians. And its psychological impact more than likely affected his complex personality. In his short life he had demonstrated a tendency for defiance, but one can only guess at the rancor brewing within now as he watched the Missourians gallop away from his ferry, laughing. The prophet of his boyhood had taught him to "love thy enemies," but Porter now faced Joseph's doctrine head-on, and probably found it distasteful.

The night finally ended. As the next day dawned, the Saints sought redress from the government. State officials assured them they would "look into it." Riding out to inspect the damage done to the Phelps' home, the Lieutenant Governor of Missouri, Lilburn W. Boggs, surveyed the scene, shook his head, and uttered a remark that quaked the Saints: It would probably be best if the Mormons simply left the territory.

Less subtle caveats came from night-riding mobocrats, armies of Missourians who now began riding through the streets of Independence, warning Latter-day Saints to leave the county or be flogged.

But the Saints would not budge.

So they were given an ultimatum . . . they had until January 1, 1834 for half their number to leave, and April 1 for the rest to go — or else! Meanwhile, mobbers moved in hundreds through the streets under a red flag[31] in token of blood.[32]

But even at this the Mormons decided to resist. In obedience to government officials' recommendations and in defiance of the mobbers' ultimatums, the Mormons declared they would fight the mobs with the law. They petitioned Governor Daniel Dunklin to raise troops to help protect them, "that we may sue for damages for the loss of property, for abuse, for defamation."[33] They also accused local government officials of treason against constitutional guarantees.

But Dunklin refused to protect them. In a letter written to a friend, Dunklin confesses, "I have no regard for the Mormons as a separate people; and have an utter contempt for them as a religious sect . . . "[34] (See Note 2.)

The mobs saw the Saints were not leaving, and when they learned they were actually fighting back with legal actions, they were enraged. And once again began to swarm.

On Halloween night, 1833, they lit on the Mormon "Whitmer Settlement."

Porter watched, defenseless, as nearly 50 Missouri mobocrats swept through the village and destroyed over a dozen homes. He also witnessed his brother-in-law, George Beebe, and his neighbor, Hiram Page, tied to a tree and whipped.[35]

Others were flogged senseless while their wives looked on.[36] At the home of David Whitmer, mobocrats could not find Whitmer, but grabbed his wife by the hair and pulled her out, screaming, then demolished the cabin.[37]

The Missourians rode off, ecstatic, screaming victory chants into the chilled, evening air.[38]

The next day the Saints were in a panic. They knew what had happened the night before was merely a foretaste, and now throughout the county each Saint wondered if his property would be hit next.

They were also in a scattered situation, their settlements extending east ten or twelve miles. "What to do for safety they knew not," reports the *Times and Seasons* in 1839. "To resist large bodies of the mob . . . appeared useless, and to gather together into one body immediately was impracticable for they had not in any one place houses to dwell in, or food for themselves and stock. A consultation was held near Independence by some of the principal men of the church to see what was best to be done; it was concluded to obtain peace warrants if possible against some of the principal leaders of the mob . . . They then went to a magistrate and applied for a warrant but he refused to grant one."[39]

Nightfall was closing in. The Saints knew Missourians would attack . . . but the question was where. Meanwhile, "the streets were filled with mobbers passing and re-passing, threatening the saints in different directions with destruction . . . "[40]

That night, as expected, the mobocrats gathered together in droves. The plan was to attack a small Mormon community called Colesville, and make it such an example of their ferocity that all the Saints of Missouri would literally beg to leave.

At Colesville, however, the Mormons were prepared . . . much to the Missourians' chagrin. Two Missouri spies preceding the mob had been sent to the village where a Mormon named Parley P. Pratt caught sight of them and shouted a warning to the village. Pratt was then clubbed by the two Missourians — until other Mormons came to his rescue — and the two spies were apprehended. The main force of mobocrats, realizing their plan had gone awry, abandoned the attack and the two mobocrat prisoners were released.[41]

Back at Independence, however, the Mormons were not so well-prepared. Mobocrats moved on the town, attacking, plundering, demolishing Mormon homes. David Pettegrew details the scene: " . . . they threw down some houses and shot at Sister Shurwood and several other sisters as they were running in a cornfield. I distinctly heard the reports of their guns. They broke into Brother Bennett's house and jerked his gun out of his hands and broke it in pieces over his head . . . "[42]

Meanwhile, at the Big Blue River, Missouri horsemen converged on another Mormon settlement. Porter was busy manning the ferry when the mobocrats reigned in at his father's cabin. Stripped to the waist and smeared in warpaint, they terrorized Porter's mother and eldest sister.[43] The mobocrats demanded Porter's father to come from the house, but Mrs. Rockwell claimed he wasn't home, and the mobbers left.

The mobbers then found one Mormon octogenarian, David Bennett, ill and unable to move. They beat him up, then shot him in the head. Miraculously he lived, but they galloped away and left him for dead.[44]

In the onslaught of destruction several Mormons decided to defend themselves . . .

They soon gathered in a cluster and galloped off towards the disturbance. The mob saw them coming and fired on them — but the Mormons fired back. One Missourian was shot in the thigh, and because of his screams the mobbers panicked and galloped away, now frenzied, frustrated, and frothing like a pack of wounded wolves.[45]

With fury they retaliated and went on a pillaging spree. They discovered Porter's home,[46] where neighbor Pettegrew reports, "They threw his house down, or all they could, cut open feather beds, destroyed all of his furniture and all they could lay hands on. Sick as I was, I mustered strength enough to go over to Brother Rockwell's the next morning and saw the destruction by the mob."[47]

The evening was finally over, and the Missourians cantered off into the night.

Not quite knowing what to do next, the next day two Latter-day Saint committees appealed to circuit judges. All they could obtain, however, were arrest warrants, "but it was too late to do anything with them, for the whole county was getting up in arms . . . " reports *Times and Seasons.*[48]

The night previous, three Latter-day Saints had caught a Missourian, Richard McCarty, pillaging a store, "and although seven persons testified against him, he was acquitted without delay."[49] The pillager then counterfiled. One John Corrill was baffled at the irony: "Although we could not obtain a warrant against him for breaking open the store, yet he had gotten one for us for catching him at it."[50] The judge, Samuel Weston, it turns out, had been a signer of the manifesto against the Mormons. And the three Saints were now herded off to jail.

Now, certain Missourians friendly to the Saints advised them "to leave the State immediately, as the wounding of the young man on Saturday night had enraged the whole county" against them; and it was a common expression among the mob that Monday, in two days, the 4th of November, "would be a bloody day."[51]

Next day, November 3rd, the mobbers somehow secured a

cannon.

Then, November 4th, the inevitable happened. "A large mob collected at Wilson's store, about a mile west of Big Blue."[52] They rode to the Big Blue River and took siege of Porter's ferry, "driving the owners away with threats of violence."[53] Porter watched hopelessly as the mobocrats kept his ferry under siege, while others galloped back to Wilson's store. There, two children informed the mobocrats that 19 Mormons were marching on the Big Blue Village to defend fellow Mormons against the Missourians.[54]

From Wilson's grocery, a combined army of 50 mobocrats charged off to ambush the 19 Mormons.

Spotting the coming army, the 19 defenders slipped into cornfields. The Missourians searched the fields, strong-arming Mormon women and children to help with the hunt.[55]

But then came a twist the Missourians had not expected . . . 30 other Mormons suddenly appeared. Because of their frenzied search, they had not seen this second Mormon force approaching behind them and had left themselves wide open.

A number of the arriving Mormons had seen their homes unroofed in recent days and were hot for revenge.

As the mob realized their predicament, they panicked and opened fire — but the Mormons would not flee. They simply stood there, taking the gunfire, and none would drop. Then they began advancing on the Missourians . . . slowly at first . . . and then they broke into a charge.

Although only 17 Mormons possessed guns,[56] they managed to frighten off the Missourians — two of whom were killed by gunfire — Thomas Linville and Hugh L. Brazeale. Porter later testified he had heard Brazeale, a local attorney, brag, "With ten fellows, I will wade to my knees in blood, but what I will drive the Mormons from Jackson County."[57] A number of horses were killed and five or six additional Missourians wounded.

Meanwhile, only one Mormon dropped from Missourians' bullets.[58]

The Missourians were humiliated. Having been scattered by a smaller Mormon force, they now held meetings and formulated another plan. This time they would fight back in an altogether different manner . . . one the Saints had seen before, but never with such intensity that would now be unleashed . . . a mode of warfare that would in fact haunt the Saints for decades:

Wild rumors. Mobocrats now sent messengers to inform all of Missouri that the Mormons had ransacked Wilson's store and shot his son, had attacked Independence, had allied themselves with Indians, and that the combined force was now planning a complete massacre of the entire state of Missouri.[59]

The defeated mobocrats hoped the governor would actually call the militia against the Saints.[60]

That same night, the three Mormons who had been jailed on the storebreaker's countercharges, John Corill, Isaac Morley, and Sidney Gilbert, found themselves in the courtroom when news of the wild Mormon/Indian war reached town. "This so enraged the crowd that were in attendance at the trial that a rush was made for the prisoners to kill them."[61] But the sheriff and a few friendly Missourians managed to escort the three through the broiling mob, back to their cells.[62] Later that night the sheriff released the three prisoners, sneaking them just outside city limits to confer with Mormon leaders. The three prisoners informed their leaders of what they had witnessed at the courthouse: that a rumor had enraged the Missourians and that because of it all Jackson County Saints had best flee for their lives, as it was obvious at this point property "was no object."[63]

The Mormon leaders agreed with the plan, and the sheriff escorted the three prisoners back to jail. Outside jail, however, a mob was beginning to form. Immediately it spotted the coming prisoners and opened fire.

Two of the Mormons dove for cover.

The third, A. S. Gilbert, simply stood there, paralyzed with fear, and took the gunfire. Two shots were fired at him point blank — but miraculously missed,[64] though he was knocked down by the barrels' exploding impact. The sheriff grabbed him and dragged him into the building, beating off the mob. The two other prisoners also fled into the jail.

When stories of the joint Mormon and Indian insurrection reached the governor, he believed them. Immediately, he sent the Jackson County militia to "rescue" Independence: Colonel Thomas

Pitcher, another signer of the Missourians' manifesto, was placed in command of the Missouri force, and now drove his troops forward to engage the Mormons head-on. Other Missourians "took their arms and started for Independence," with such conviction that early the next morning "there were hundreds there ready for war."[65]

But this time the Mormons were prepared and armed. They had just received news of the three jailed Mormons and their reaction was furious. 200 Saints now mounted up and rode forth to Independence to free their brethren from jail.

Unknowingly they rode directly towards the Missouri militia . . . who were now coming down the same road, straight towards them.

The face to face, man to man confrontation would occur just around a woodland bend . . . and, although no positive reports substantiate it, Porter Rockwell likely rode at the forefront . . .

II

Riding towards the enemy, Mormon leader Lyman Wight learned a fact which changed his plans.

He learned the three jailed Mormons had been freed. He also heard Mormon leaders had decided to evacuate the county. Thus, rather than continuing the march, Wight dispersed his army into the woods.[1]

And just at that moment the Missourians arrived.

Their leader, Colonel Pitcher, realized the Mormons had no intention of fighting now and decided to play upon their naiveté. He met with Wight to talk "peace terms," and shrewdly confessed that he and fellow Missourians had been at fault for all their prejudice, and now suggested that the Mormons, as an act of good faith, deliver their arms to the militia.

The Mormon commander agreed, but only if the militia would disarm the mobocrats as well. Of course Colonel Pitcher agreed, and then took the Mormons' weaponry.[2]

As the militia dispersed, the mobocrats rejoiced. They saw the Mormons defenseless now, and immediately launched an unabashed orgy of destruction.

In freezing November temperatures the Saints fled for safety.

Many were caught, tied, and flogged, while others were shot running from the whip. Others, ill and aged, died from the cold. Families were scattered in the confusion. Parents were lost from their children.

Lyman Wight, the once-proud leader of the potentially powerful Mormon army, found himself not only disarmed now but personally hunted by Missouri mobocrats. He also witnessed 190 women and children driven 30 miles across a prairie "thinly crusted with sleet, and I could easily follow on their trail by the blood that flowed from their lacerated feet on the stubble of the burnt prairie."

He further reports, "I was chased by one of these gangs across an open prairie five miles, without being overtaken, and lay three weeks in the woods, and was three days and nights without food."[3]

At this point David Pettegrew adds, "The mob now started towards my house and I made all haste for home and when I arrived I found the mob had driven my family into the streets, and were driving the brethren out of their houses and homes, placed them in the public road and told them to leave. If not, they might look for immediate destruction. 'If you do not flee for your lives,' said they, 'your God damned noses will smell hell.'

" . . . I now saw my family in the streets houseless, we must go or die. I bid them to march on as well as they could. I then returned to my house, endeavoring to take what I possibly could with me. No one can tell, or imagine, the feelings of my heart upon re-entering, in that once . . . cherished home. I looked around to see what I could take with me. The Book of Mormon, my Bible, a razor and a decanter of composition which my wife had requested me to bring were all I took. After leaving everything I bid farewell to my home and hastened to overtake my family. I found them placed in wagons as they were still sick. My wagons and animals were not home and, of course, they had to be left . . .

" . . . we travelled south, nothing but the canopies of Heaven for our covering, the earth for our beds, and in a large open prairie we saw daily companies of armed men as we passed along . . . the third day we came to a cave, where we found shelter . . . This cave was about fifty feet long and from sixteen to eighteen feet wide, and deep, solid rock overhead. The bottom was composed of small stones. The mouth of this cave fronted towards the northwest, and the cold winds had a fair chance at us. We experienced a very severe storm while in this cave and the sick suffered dreadfully."[4]

Times and Seasons continues, "Two of these Missouri companies were headed by Baptist preachers. The Reverend Isaac McCoy headed one about seventy . . . They broke open houses and plundered them . . . "

Four old Mormons sought to stay until the spring thaw. "These veterans," reports *Times and Seasons,* "the youngest of the four being 94 years of age, were assailed by a mob party, who broke in their doors and windows, hurling large stones into their houses . . . and thus they were driven from their homes, in the winter season. Some of these have toiled and bled, in the defence of their country; one of them (Mr. Jones) served as life guard to General Washington in the revolutionary war."[5]

In this tornado of violence Porter helped Luana gather what belongings he could, and helped his family flee to the shore of the Missouri River. And there they waited for churning waters to calm.[6]

Since the ferry was inoperative, over a thousand Mormons were stranded at the shore. Most of them stood day and night beside campfires, seeking to survive on what food they could find.

Undoubtedly this aggravation affected Porter's perspective, a painfully pessimistic outlook that would affect future choices — despite a naturally cheery demeanor that was purportedly his dominant characteristic. Waiting impatiently to cross the river, and, like the others, now thoroughly demoralized, Porter and his fellow Saints waited day after day for freezing rains to cease and for the river to calm. Finally, after a week of escalating hopelessness, a small miracle occurred. Parley P. Pratt describes what he witnessed: "All the firmament seemed enveloped in splendid fireworks, as if every star in the broad expanse had been hurled from its course, and sent lawless through the wilds of ether. Thousands of bright meteors were shooting through space in every direction, with long trains of light following in their course. This lasted for several hours, and was closed only by the dawn of the rising sun. Every heart was filled with joy at this majestic display of signs and wonders."

When the river calmed they crossed the waters into Clay

County,[7] but the scenes to follow left little over which to rejoice.

Emily M. Austin records their arrival: "[We] had already arrived and more were on their way ... we lived in tents until winter set in, and did our cooking in the wind and storms. Log heaps were our parlor stoves, and the cold, wet ground our velvet carpets, and the crying of little children our piano forte; while the shivering, sick people hovered over the burning log piles here and there, some begging for cold water ... "[8]

As if these problems weren't enough, a "peace committee" of twelve Jackson County mobocrats ferried across the river to meet with the Saints. In brazen fashion, they now sought legal titles for the property the Saints had left behind. The Mormons refused the committee's bold requests.

On their return across the river, the Missourians' ferry sprang a leak and seven drowned. Joseph summarized, "The angel of God saw fit to sink the boat ... "[9]

Anti-Mormons of course summarized otherwise. Some later claimed an angel named Porter sunk the boat.

While most of the Saints had fled directly to Clay County with Porter, some fled first to Van Buren County before joining the main group at Clay. David Pettegrew reports the problems facing one such smaller group:

"We remained in Van Buren County until the last of February. Our sufferings were to that extent that my pen cannot describe them. While residing in Van Buren County a mob made its appearance for the purpose of still driving us on ... Mr. [John] Cornet told me if I did not leave this place immediately he would spill my blood. I told them of the property I had left in Jackson County and that I was very determined not to dispose of my farm; that I left the country, although I was destitute of means, provisions and all the necessaries of life, and that the weather was extremely cold, the snow deep and my family barefooted. My wife told them that we had been robbed of everything ... 'You wish us to turn out in this cold and deep snow, that we may freeze' ... They then accused us of being British Tories ... We had given them no cause to believe anything of the kind, and their imagination had gone far beyond their reason. I told them that they could bring no charges against me, and why they should still continue that persecution I would be pleased to know, but it was all to no purpose, they were enraged and told us to leave immediately ...

"My wife and myself had gone over to Mr. Hartely, who was a [non-Mormon] friend of ours. As we came near the house we saw a large company of horsemen at his house, and on coming up we found them to be a mob party on their way to tear down our houses. Mrs. Hartely was quarreling with them in our behalf. She was a noble-hearted woman, kind and generous almost to a fault. She told Mr. Langly that if he unroofed our house that she would accommodate us in her house, and Mr. Langly told her if she did so he would tear the roof off her house. 'Mr. Langly,' said she, 'poor dog that you are, talking about pulling the roof off my house, you poor, miserable wretch, the only thing you possess in this world is a little sugar tail filly. You can't raise corn enough to feed your chickens. Go home, and attend to your own business and you will do a great deal better, and if you ever put your foot in my house again I will be the death of you.' She struck several over the head with her broom.

" ... I was obliged to leave my family in care of Mr. Hartely, who promised me he would do all in his power to care for them.

"I then made my escape across the Missouri River and there waited for the arrival of my family. They were a long time coming as the mob did everything in their power to prevent my family from joining me, but my wife managed to get away unobserved, and I rented a farm in Clay County ... "[10]

Nearly all the Saints were now in Clay County, and Porter's former neighbor, Pettegrew, details his experience there: "The majority of the people looked upon us as a poor deluded people, and thought many of us were Christians and honest. When any of them were sick they would send for us to sit up and nurse them, and they thought a great deal of the Mormons. When the cholera made its appearance amongst them, they would invariably call upon us to take care of the sick and would shed tears when we would leave them and beg us to remain, as though we could save their lives ...

"At the time the cholera was raging in the county, Judge Cameron would spend a great deal of his time with me. He had resigned the gambling table and now wished to instruct himself upon religious matters, and he was very much afraid to die. He told some of the brethren that he believed I was a good Christian, but when the cholera subsided I did not see him so often, though he was still very friendly to me and my family and did many favors."[11]

For a time the people of Clay County received the Saints warmly.[12] Porter probably sought the peace of a simple farm life, yet within three years the Mormon leaders would once again stir up the local populace. Slavery flourished in Clay County, and because of the Saints' criticisms, David Pettegrew found himself recording, "The old feelings and excitement of Jackson County now began to show itself in Clay. It was first started by the ministers of the gospel such as Edwards and Balden, Baptist ministers, and others soon followed. They soon had the people to arms and . . . We were now forced to take up arms in self defense. The excitement had got to its highest pitch and their head men such as Judge Cameron, Judge Birch and others made several speeches to the people, which seemed to allay somewhat their excitement. They came to the conclusion to give us Caldwell County and that we should live there by ourselves, and thither we moved. The land we had purchased we had to leave unsold . . . Although some of the people believed that we were a persecuted people, that we were an innocent and unoffending sect, yet they dared not express their sentiments. After settling my business I followed the rest of the Mormons to Caldwell County. I purchased a farm at Government price and, highly delighted with the prospect before me, I soon built me a house . . . "[13]

In 1836 Porter and Luana also gathered their belongings and moved to Caldwell County. Meanwhile, Porter's sister Electa fell in love with a Missourian, and Porter likely watched with dismay as she married the Clay County resident in January, 1837.[14]

All the while, his preoccupation seemed to be his family. Luana had delivered their first child, Emily, January 31, 1833, in Jackson

County, a year before their expulsion, and she now gave birth to their second, Caroline Stewart Rockwell,[15] shortly after their arrival in Caldwell County. Due to family ties, he named his first two children after his sisters.

Finally, Porter seemed to have his wish . . . a serene farm life. By the spring of 1838 he and the Saints were again flourishing. They had established themselves in the western section of the county, in a land parcel far away from outsiders and the trouble they had invariably brought. And they named it, appropriately enough, Far West. The town soon had 150 log cabins and more than a handful of stores.[16] A foundation for a temple site had been excavated, and the city was ready for immigrants.

Among the new immigrants from Ohio would be the Prophet. Before his move to Caldwell County, however, Joseph had led 204 Mormon soldiers from Ohio in an attempt to redeem Jackson County and set the Mormons back on their property. But Zion's Camp, as the army was called, had met with disaster; this, according to Joseph, because of the unrighteousness which had prevailed among army personnel: back-biting, apostasy, complaining, and rebelliousness. As an apparent punishment, the Lord saw fit to curse the company with an epidemic of cholera, as Joseph explained, and 14 soldiers died. The miserable excursion over, having never reached Missouri, Joseph led them back to Ohio.

Here the Prophet met with even greater dissensions. He saw the failure of the Kirtland Safety Society, the collapse of the local banking system, and several associates once close to him now seeking his blood, swelling the ranks of the apostates and sending him fleeing to Far West.

To Joseph's consternation, numbers of the Ohio dissenters actually followed him to Far West.

Joseph's patience in the new land, just as in Ohio, was tried, but this time he moved swiftly, excommunicating once-close associates now possessed by greed and lust for power: John Whitmer was one of the first, then W. W. Phelps for misuse of church funds and Oliver Cowdery for "urging vexatious law suits against the brethren" and for an apparent attempt at counterfeiting. Two days later he disfellowshipped David Whitmer and Lyman E. Johnson.

But Joseph's major thorn was another close associate. B. H. Roberts tells the tale most accurately: "Sometime in June Elder Sidney Rigdon delivered what was afterwards called his 'Salt Sermon,' because he took as a text:

"'Ye are the salt of the earth: but if the salt have lost his savor, wherewith, shall it be salted? It is thenceforth good for nothing, but to be cast out, and to be trodden under foot of men.' (Matthew 5:13)

"The doctrine of the text the speaker applied to the dissenting brethren and intimated that the 'trodden under foot of men' should be literal, much to the scandalizing of the church, since the dissenters made capital of it to prejudice the minds of the non-Mormons of the surrounding counties. This, unfortunately, was followed shortly afterwards by a communication drawn up by Elder Rigdon, it is said, and addresssed to the leading dissenters . . . commanding them to leave Caldwell county within three days under penalty of a 'More fatal calamity' befalling them if they refused to depart. The document was signed by eighty-four men [and not to his credit Porter's name appears 69th] . . .

"These dissenters, or some of them, were accused of crimes, with stealing, with being associated with counterfeiters . . . " continues Roberts. "But if these accusations were true, they constituted crimes which lay open to the law, and should have been punished by the law. Those eighty-four citizens of Caldwell county were not justified in taking the law into their own hands and under threats of vengeance driving these dissenters from Far West, for that was the effect of these threats. The dissenters took hasty departure, late one afternoon in June, leaving their families to follow them, which they afterwards did."[17]

From there the dissenters understandably took their problems to the local Missourians, fanning the flames of hatred even higher.

Several Latter-day Saints formed a secret band to retaliate against the apostates. This band of Saints determined to fight local Missourians and even assassinate church members whom they found in disagreement. Lorenzo Dow Young has left the most telling account of this episode and the involvement of one Sampson Avard: "In the latter part of the summer, I found he was in Far

West among the Saints holding secret meetings attended by a few who were especially invited. I was one of the favored few. I found the gathering to be a meeting of a secret organization of which, so far as I could learn by diligent inquiry, he was the originator and over which he presided. At one of these meetings he stated that the title by which the members of the society were known, 'Danites,' interpreted meant 'Destroying Angels,' and also that the object of the organization was to take vengeance on their enemies. Avard considered it the duty of the members to pursue them to the death, even to their homes and bedrooms. At different times new members were sworn in by taking the oath of secrecy and affiliations. The teachings and proceedings appeared to be wicked, blood-thirsty, and in direct antagonism to the principles taught by the leaders of the Church and the Elders generally. I felt a curious interest in these proceedings and determined to hold my peace and see what would develop.

" ... From the meeting I went direct to Brother Brigham and related the whole history of the affair. He said he had long suspicioned that something wrong was going on but had seen no direct development. He added, 'I will go at once to Brother Joseph, who has suspicioned that some secret wickedness was being carried on by Dr. Avard.' Dr. Avard was at once cited before the authorities of the Church and cut off for his wickedness. He turned a bitter enemy of the Saints."[18]

Enemies of the church, of course, claimed Mormon leaders had organized the Danites. Many of the enemies, but not all, were embittered ex-Mormons who, then and later, produced some widely-accepted works, including James H. Hunt (*Mormonism; Embracing the Origin, Rise and Progress of the Sect, With an Examination of the Book of Mormon; also, Their Troubles in Missouri, and Final Expulsion from the State*),[19] T.B.H. Stenhouse (*The Rocky Mountain Saints: A Full and Complete History of the Mormons, from the First Vision of Joseph Smith to the Last Courtship of Brigham Young*),[20] John Whitmer (*History of the Church of the Latter-day Saints From 1831-1846*)[21] and his affidavit in *Document Showing the Testimony Given Before the Judge of the Fifth Judicial Circuit of the State of Missouri, on the Trial of Joseph Smith, Jr., and Others, for High Treason, and Other Crimes*

Against That State, February 15, 1841; Copy of the Testimony Given Before the Hon. Austin A. King.[22] Sampson Avard's affidavit in the same publication,[23] Oliver Cowdery (*Defence in a Rehearsal of My Grounds for separating Myself from the Latter Day Saints,*[24] although recent research suggests this document is a forgery, probably first published in 1905; see end of Note 3), John Hyde, Jr. (*Mormonism: Its Leaders and Designs*),[25] William A. Hickman (*Brigham's Destroying Angel; Being the Life, Confession, and Startling Disclosures of the Notorious Bill Hickman, the Danite Chief of Utah*),[26] John Corrill (*Document etc.*),[27] John Cleminson (*Document etc.*),[28] William Swartzell (*Mormonism Exposed, Being a Journal of a Residence in Missouri from the 28th of May to the 20th of August, 1838*),[29] William Hall (*The Abominations of Mormonism Exposed; Containing Many Facts and Doctrines Concerning That Singular People, During Seven Years' Membership With Them; From 1840 to 1847*),[30] John C. Bennett (*The History of the Saints, an Exposé of Joe Smith and Mormonism*),[31] John D. Lee (*Mormonism Unveiled*),[32] and Reed Peck (*Mormons So Called*).[33]

An amusing angle to the distortion was the willingness with which the Saints "used" the rumors. Oliver Boardman Huntington joked to his journal, "This society of Danites was condemned by the public like the rest of Mormonism; and there was a great [concern] about the Danites, all over the county and among the army; but who and what they were no one was any wiser for anything they heard; and as many stories were in circulation, the most horrid and awfully distorted opinions their minds could imagine, and they all thought that every depridation was committed by the Danites; Danites, awful Danites; every mobber was afraid of the thoughts of one of them awful men.

"And if they were to see a man of their own acquaintance, and were told in confidence he was a Danite, they would even shun his company and conversation. Such being their opinion and belief of the Danites, and we knowing it, concluded to make the best of it."[34]

Joseph confides in his journal: "The Danite system alluded to by Norton never had any existence. It was a term made use of by some of the brethren in Far West, and grew out of an expression I made use of when the brethren were preparing to defend themselves from the Missouri mob, in reference to the stealing of

Macaiah's images (Judges chapter 18) — If the enemy comes, the Danites will be after them, meaning the brethren in self-defense."[35] This single reference had been so twisted and magnified out of both context and proportion that church enemies made a crusade of it against the Mormons, and felt "Danites" were behind every mysterious occurrence for decades afterwards.

Twenty years later Brigham Young referred to them, simply to make a point, seeking to frighten away outlaws with his wry exaggeration: "If men come here and do not behave themselves, they will not only find the Danites, whom they talk so much about, biting the horses' heels, but the scoundrels will find something biting their heels."[36]

Sampson Avard was the first to contact the Missourians. Before the Fifth Circuit Court of Missouri he claimed, "I consider Joseph Smith, jr., as the prime mover and organizer of this Danite band."[37] Avard had been the first to be excommunicated attempting to start the band, despite his claims. The "Danites," meanwhile, were tagged with several names: Brother of Gideon, Daughter of Zion, Destroying Angels, Thresher, Big Fan, and The Sons of Dan.

The most revealing information on the secret society, however, was recorded further by Joseph in his journal. (See Note 3 for details.)

Porter, meanwhile, continued his faithfulness to the church. On July 6, 1838, at Far West, Missouri, he was ordained a Deacon, the first of four possible steps in the church's priesthood.[38]

Despite the slander, the Saints overall enjoyed serenity for a time, but this calm turned out to be just another lull before a storm . . .

Only this one was political.

As a voting bloc the Mormons were now considered hot property. And just before elections the Missourians began lobbying for their vote. This much-longed-for attention came to the Saints despite a reported incident by enemies that 20 Saints had driven Missourians from Mormon-owned land. (The story went that Missourians attempted to settle the Saints' property, and in anger the Mormons reacted; twenty gathered themselves into a vigilante-style posse and rode forth, snapping whips at the

Missourians' feet and driving them away.)[39]

From this rumor alone some Missourians were fused and ready to explode, but their public servants kept them at bay, desperately seeking the Mormon vote.

Then one afternoon the storm broke. Taking the Saints completely by surprise, the Missourians' hostility burst forth on — of all days — election day. That morning a candidate for office, William Peniston, had made an inflammatory speech against the Saints, seeking to prevent them from voting if they came to the polls. Interestingly, Peniston had been among those who'd curtsied to the Saints during the campaign, but now, finding he was unpopular, decided to lash back.

After his speech, whiskey was passed around, and the scene was ripe for action. As the first group of Mormons rode up to the Gallatin polls,[40] a drunken Missourian named Dick Weldon swaggered up to a Mormon. What happened next set in motion events that would sweep the Mormons and Missourians into a virtual war . . .

Inflamed by Peniston's speech, the drunken Weldon told the Mormon, named Brown, "The Saints are not allowed to vote in Clay County no more than the damned Negroes."[41] Weldon then reared back his fist when another Mormon, Perry Durfee, caught Weldon's arm.

Durfee was knocked down, and several Missourians pounced on him with boards and clubs. Durfee screamed for help.

Five infuriated Mormons ran into the mob, knocking and punching their way through towards Durfee, sending a dozen Missourians sprawling.

When one of the Saints became isolated in the mob, twenty Missourians turned on him with knives . . . but he took off running.

Another Mormon, the seventh of the party, grabbed a board and charged the Missourians. In awe they stared as he whacked away at the mob, purportedly sending all twenty to the earth.

As it happened, a handful of Mormons thus rescued Durfee from a glut of soused Missourians. One of the Mormons later confides, "I felt the power of God nerve my arm for the fray. It helps a man a great deal in a fight to know that God is on his side."[42]

The Missourians watching were struck with amazement. Less

than ten Saints had stayed off 50 to 100 Missourians, and, incredibly, the mob panicked and broke into a run.

But news of the event ran even faster than the Missourians . . .

Stories of the incident roared through the state like prairie fire, and the anger of the Missourians now began billowing toward a darkening sky.

Meanwhile, news of the episode spread with equal speed to Joseph at headquarters — an express rider galloped in the report to him, and because of expected reprisals, he organized 20 horsemen. He then personally led his platoon down the road to Daviess County, and rendezvoused with another Mormon group. From there they galloped to the home of the local justice of the peace, Adam Black.

The Prophet, one witness explains, "politely requested him to sign an agreement of peace."[43] Black wrote one up, claiming he would "support the Constitution" and not instigate further violence against the Saints.[44]

After Joseph rode away, Black all but laughed at the Saints. He mounted up and rode off to the Missourians, telling them he'd just been forced to sign a pledge, and then wrote up a warrant for the arrest of Joseph for "harassment."

Word of Black's version of the story shot through the settlements and made its way to the new governor of Missouri. Lilburn W. Boggs would not stand for a judge in his state to be terrorized by a local religious zealot, and immediately ordered 400 militia to capture the Prophet. Word additionally went from the governor's office that recruits were needed. As a result, mobocrats from 11 counties joined forces and galloped off to support Justice Black. While the governor supposedly feared Joseph would resist arrest, he likely cared less about Joseph's arrest than simply about frightening the Saints into leaving the state altogether.

But Joseph countered his move. As mobocrats waited for arms to arrive, the Saints ambushed a supply wagon filled with guns intended for the mob.

The strategy back-fired, as this only aggravated their mania.

Boggs was now out for blood.

In a frenzy he ordered the militia to destroy all Mormon resistance.

Missouri settlers began attacking Mormons at DeWitt, a village

50 miles outside Far West.

Joseph called for reinforcements to aid the community, but it was too late. Missourians surrounded DeWitt and entrenched themselves before Joseph's reinforcements could arrive. And from their breastworks, the Missourians issued an ultimatum.

But the Mormons refused to leave town, so the Missourians held the community under siege.

Meanwhile, across the county on the following day at the village of Adam-ondi-Ahman, Mormons were hitched to trees and flogged, and left tied and bleeding for their wives to cut down.

Back at DeWitt, the Mormons still under siege finally realized their hopelessness and surrendered.

October 12th was the day the Saints trudged from town with few belongings, and made their way towards the Mormon stronghold at Far West.

Arriving at Far West they discovered Joseph planning to defend Adam-ondi-Ahman, not knowing it had already been attacked. (When Joseph's troops did arrive, they found the community literally destroyed. Aside from the men who'd been flogged, cattle had been scattered, farms burned, and two Mormons taken prisoner and ridden out of town on a cannon.)

As if Joseph's problems were not complicated enough, two Apostles, Orson Hyde and Thomas B. Marsh, apostatized from the church. In anger they went to the Missourians and signed an affidavit that sent them gnashing. They claimed the Danites had "passed a decree that no Mormon dissenter should leave Caldwell county alive," and that they "proposed to start a pestilence among the Gentiles . . . by poisoning their corn, fruit, etc." and that they planned to destroy the towns of all Missouri resistors, and eventually "make it one gore of blood from the Rocky Mountains to the Atlantic Ocean."[45] Joseph defended himself against the charge, labeling it as pure slander, but it was too late — the Missourians were up in arms. They next re-doubled their efforts to rid themselves of the Saints — and now rode forth every evening through Mormon settlements, burning, plundering, killing cattle, and carrying off prisoners.[46]

Local ministers, meanwhile, screamed anti-Mormon invective from the pulpit. One Methodist minister, Samuel Bogart, found himself a militia captain and claimed he would shower Far West "with thunder and lightening." His plan would begin at Crooked River, he said, but the Saints soon learned of the plan.

Brigham's brother, Lorenzo Dow Young, reports his astonishment: "Perhaps I had slept two hours, when I was awakened by the bass drum sounding the alarm on the public square. I was soon out to see what was the matter. There were five men on the ground, of whom I inquired the cause of the alarm. They informed me that two of the brethren had been taken prisoners by the mob on Crooked River, tried by a court martial that day, and condemned to be shot the coming morning at eight o'clock. A company of men was wanted to go and rescue them. Preparations were hurried . . . "[47]

Sixty Mormons volunteered and followed Joseph's commander, David Patten, to Crooked River, for the largest-scale, head-on clash yet between Mormon and Missourian.

Porter probably again rode at the front of the column towards the battle . . .

One posseman, Parley P. Pratt, records vividly, "This company was soon under way, having to ride through extensive prairies a distance of some twelve miles. The night was dark, the distant plains far and wide were illuminated by blazing fires: immense columns of smoke were seen rising in awful majesty, as if the world was on fire. This scene of grandeur can only be comprehended by those acquainted with scenes of prairie burning . . .

"The thousands of meteors, blazing in the distance like the camp-fires of some war host, threw a fitful gleam of light upon the distant sky, which many might have mistaken for the Aurora Borealis. This scene, added to the silence of midnight, the rumbling sound of the tramping steeds over the hard and dried surface of the plain, the clanking of swords in their scabbards, the occasional gleam of bright armor in the flickering firelight, the gloom of surrounding darkness, and the unknown destiny of the expedition, or even of the people who sent it forth; all combined to impress the mind with deep and solemn thoughts, and to throw a romantic vision over the imagination, which is not often experienced, except in the poet's dreams, or in the wild imagery of sleeping fancy.

"In this solemn procession we moved on for some two hours ... "[48]

Arriving an hour before dawn, the Mormon army entered the thick wilderness, and trod slowly towards Crooked River, where Reverend Bogart's army lay camped.

Suddenly the Mormons heard noises; they halted.

Waiting for the signal to attack, the Saints remained silent in the cold, greying mists. And then ... rifle-fire cracked the pre-dawn silence.

Lorenzo Dow Young claims one Mormon, "who was one step in front of me, fell."[49]

"Orders were issued to form in the brush, and under cover of the trees," reports Pratt. "The fire now became general on both sides, and the whole wilderness seemed one continued echo of the report of the deadly rifle."[50]

With one last assessment of enemy troop strength, commander Patten suddenly shouted the battle cry of Israel, "The sword of the Lord and of Gideon," then glanced quickly across his army and gave the final command ... to "Charge!"[51]

As he rose, he saw his entire force dive into the vortex of the battle ... with Porter probably still on the front line ...

clark Kelley Price
86

III

"As we rushed upon them the strife became deadly, and several fell on both sides," records Pratt.[1]

Rockwell, one may surmise, never flinched.

Lorenzo Dow Young continues the account, "A tall, powerful Missourian sprang from under the bank of the river and with a heavy sword in hand.

"... I succeeded in parrying the Missourian's blows until he backed me to the bank of the river. A perilous situation, for I could go no further without going off the perpendicular bank, eight or ten feet to the water. In a moment I realized my chances were desperate. At this juncture the Missourian raised his sword, apparently throwing all his strength and energy into the act, as if intending to crush me with one desperate blow.

"As his arm extended I saw a white hand pass down the back of his head and between his shoulders. For a moment his arm seemed paralyzed, giving me sufficient time to deal him a desperate blow with the breech of my gun, which parted at the handle, sending the butt some distance from me, and bending the barrel (as was afterward ascertained) ten inches. As my enemy fell his sword dropped from his grasp; I seized it and dealt him three desperate blows on the neck."[2]

Pratt summarizes, "At this instant a ball pierced the brave Colonel, David Patten, who was then at my side, and I saw him fall. Being on the eve of victory, I dared not stop to look after his fate, or that of others, but rushed into the enemy's camp. This was located on the immediate banks of Crooked River, which was here several rods wide, and not fordable. The enemy, being hard pushed, flung themselves into the stream, and struggled for the other shore. Those who reached it soon disappeared."[3]

The Mormons were victorious.

But the realities of the battle, rather than cheering the Saints, dispirited them. They saw their wounded apostle, David Patten, die in agony. And even though they had routed the Missourians, they had lost three men.

When Boggs heard Bogart's force had been routed, he was rabid. Especially as two Missouri settlers now added color to the tale: the two men, Joseph Dickson and Sashiel Woods of Carrollton, barged in breathless to see the governor; they claimed the Mormons were now moving on Richmond to lay it in ashes. "Our county is ruined — for God's sake give us assistance as quick as possible."[4]

Since Boggs already had the Mormon apostates' affidavits — those of Hyde and Marsh — and he also had the same report from "good, honest, Missouri folk" — he ordered 2,000 militiamen to the scene to oppose the maniacal, belligerent Latter-day Saints, who in fact were gloomily trudging back to Far West, the wounded receiving no medical attention until a relief column could meet them five miles from Far West.

The last straw for the governor's spine, however, was a filtered-down report originating from one of Reverend Bogart's men, who claimed ten of their force had been shot dead by the Mormons, with the remainder taken prisoners of war. By the time this one report reached the governor it was so blown out of proportion that he believed the Mormons had completely massacred the entire force at Crooked River, that all prisoners had been executed, and that the Saints were now marching on the whole of Missouri.

Boggs felt he had to retaliate. His next action was the now

famous "Exterminating Order." Issued to General John B. Clark October 27 Boggs states, "The Mormons must be treated as enemies, and must be exterminated or driven from the State if necessary for the public peace — their outrages are beyond all description . . . you will proceed immediately to Richmond and then operate against the Mormons."[5]

For safety, Mormons from outlying settlements abandoned their homes to flee into Far West. One stubborn proprietor of a mill could not leave his property in the hands of Missouri mobocrats. His settlement consisted of a blacksmith shop, a mill, and 30 families at Shoal Creek. But when he came to the city to confer with Joseph on the matter, the Prophet advised him to abandon the entire settlement.

Haun argued with the Prophet, claiming they could turn the mill into a fort and defend themselves if necessary. "Smith finally gave him permission to remain, saying they would consider him a tyrant if he forced them to leave and abandon their property and come to Far West."[7] This key statement was recorded in the *History of Caldwell and Livingston Counties* in 1886.

On October 30th, under a quiet autumn sky at Haun's settlement, thirty Mormon families were peaceably going about their chores, when over 200 Missouri militiamen thundered on the community and chased down unarmed farmers, blowing the brains out of one Mormon settler after another. As the Saints and their children scattered, the militiamen gave chase. A surviving woman reports, " . . . after our men were shot down by them, they went around and shot all the dead men over again, to make sure of their lives."[8] Another recalls, "I sat down to witness the dreadful scene. When they had done firing, they began to howl . . . They plundered the principal part of our goods, took our horses and wagons, and ran off, howling . . . "

"I came down to witness the . . . scene . . . My husband, and one son 10 years old, lifeless upon the ground, and one son 7 years old, wounded very bad; the ground covered with the dead . . . dogs [were also] howling . . . "[9]

Nathan Knight reports, "Sister Haun and my wife passed the

night in dressing the wounds and making comfortable, as far as possible, the wounded and dying. Their groans and shrieks made the night hideous and horrible beyond description . . . "[10] Joseph Young describes the aftermath: "When we arrived at the house of Mr. Haun, we found Mr. Merrick's body lying in the rear of the house, Mr. McBride's in front, literally mangled from head to foot . . . Mr. York's body we found in the house; and after viewing these corpses we immediately went to the black-smith's shop where we found nine of our friends, eight of whom were already dead, the other, Mr. Cox of Indiana, struggling in the agonies of death and soon expired."[11] Additionally, numerous others were dying.

David Lewis adds, " . . . the women were compelled to bury their husbands by throwing them into a well close to the black-smith shop."[12] (See Note 4 for details of the attack.)

The same day as the Haun's Mill massacre, Boggs' army arrived at Far West, camping outside the Mormon stronghold in preparation for a major offensive.

The next day, the dawn of another Halloween, the Missouri army met with a delegation of Mormons and negotiated with Colonel George M. Hinkle, a Mormon officer, for the surrender of Joseph Smith and other church leaders.

Colonel Hinkle agreed, and bargained away his prophet to avert war. (For details see Note 5.)

Joseph felt, naturally, he'd been betrayed. When his delegation came to inform him, he was probably too stunned to make an immediate decision of surrender, and ordered the Mormons to prepare for battle. Drums rolled and a trumpet sounded. The battle was ready. The Missourians marched forward. Porter Rockwell was among those implanted against the breastworks, and ready to fight for the Army of Israel. All along the line, Mormons clutched their rifles and aimed at the oncoming, marching Missouri militiamen.

But then Joseph surprised his own army. John D. Lee records, "Joseph Smith called all of his remaining troops together, and told them they were a good lot of fellows, but they were not perfect enough to withstand so large an army as the one now before them, that they had stood by him, and were willing to die for and with him, for the sake of the Kingdom of Heaven, that he wished them to be comforted, for God had accepted their offering, that he intended to, and was going to offer himself up as a sacrifice, to save their lives and to save the Church. He wished them all to be of good cheer, and pray for him, and to pray that he and the brethren that went with him might be delivered from their enemies. He then blessed his people in the name of the Lord. After this, he and the leading men, six in number went with him direct to the camp of the enemy [parting with his guard, Rockwell]. They were led by a Judas, Col. G. M. Hinkle. I stood upon the breastworks and watched them go into the camp of the enemy. I heard the yells of triumph of the troops, as Joseph Smith and his companions entered. It was with great difficulty that the officers could restrain the mob from shooting them down as they entered. A strong guard was then placed over them to protect them from mob violence."[13]

The participants at the earlier Battle of Crooked River, including Porter, now hid. Hiding, in fact, for a while, would becomes Porter's way of life.

Joseph and others were sentenced to be shot. The firing squad began practicing for the event, which was, according to Lee, "to take place at eight o'clock the next morning." When the sentence was announced, Mormon colonel Lyman Wight was defiant in the face of the mob: "Shoot and be damned."

Then a hero arose, at least in the Saints' eyes. General Alexander Doniphan, one of the Missouri militia commanders, defied Governor Boggs — he simply refused orders to execute the Prophet. "He said it was nothing more or less than cold blooded murder, and that every name signed to the decision was signed in blood, and he would withdraw his troops and have nothing to do in the matter, if the men were to be shot."[14]

Doniphan's stand gave the governor second thoughts.

Instead of being shot Joseph and other church leaders were now taken to Independence for a court trial.

The Mormon citizenry, meanwhile, was herded to the town square. The Missouri army watched as, under coercion, the Saints one by one sat at a desk under the Far West liberty pole and humiliatingly signed away their weapons and rights on a surrender document. Lee records, "We were to give a deed of all of our real estate, and to give a bill of sale of all our personal property, to pay the expenses of the war that had been inaugurated against us; that a committee of twelve [Missourians] should be appointed . . . who were to be the sole judges of what would be necessary to remove each family out of the State, and all of the Mormons were to leave Missouri by the first of April, A.D. 1839."[15]

A mock trial was then held for the Prophet. He and 45 other Mormons watched as one apostate after another was marched into a courtroom where each testified against Joseph. For obvious reasons of retaliation, and a desire "to save their own necks," Dr. Sampson Avard, John Corrill, Reed Peck, W. W. Phelps, Morris Phelps, and John Cleminson[16] testified against church leaders and further fed the myth of Danite attacks on innocents.

When Mormons at the trial attempted to counter these charges, they were, according to some sources, at gunpoint forced to silence. Nevertheless, the judge released 40 Mormons. Joseph and four others were then held for further trial, and eventually transported to Liberty Jail in Clay County.

There, Joseph and the four waited for their release. Week after week passed and most lost all hopes for freedom.

As the Saints struggled without Joseph to evacuate Missouri before April 1, they continued to be plundered. 240 Saints signed a pledge of rebellion against Boggs' Exterminating Order, including Brigham Young and Porter Rockwell.[17] But no significant action came of it.

Porter, meanwhile, faithfully supplied Joseph and other imprisoned officials with refreshments "many times."[18] Someone managed to smuggle shovels into the five at Liberty Jail, but just before their escape, the handles broke. When Joseph requested replacement handles, the jailor became suspicious of the "over-anxiety on the part of our friend," says Joseph,[19] and the plan was botched. Porter was likely that friend, whom Joseph leaves unnamed in an act of loyalty.

It was perhaps the first and last time Porter ever disappointed his Prophet.

Joseph then planned a second jailbreak. Alexander McRae, a fellow prisoner, reports Joseph had suggested they attempt the break one evening while they had an opportunity, but they disobeyed, procrastinating Joseph's suggestions until it was too late.[20] They did manage to grab the cell door — only to see it shut in their faces.

Just as the last week of October had often been the Saints' darkest hour, the first week in April was often their brightest. In early April, 1839, Joseph and the others were taken from Liberty Jail to Gallatin to appear before a Grand Jury, and were there found guilty of "murder, treason, burglary, arson, larceny, theft and stealing" (some dry observers have noted Missouri grand juries could not be accused of "piling it on") . . .

Three days later the court decided to send the church leaders to Boone County for sentencing. Their journey through lone Missouri woodland roads proved most interesting. Under the direction of Sheriff William Morgan, who either bungled the attempt, felt sorry for the Prophet, or was directed in his actions by a political superior, the law officers became drunk, and the five church leaders escaped into the woods.

Within hours the five Mormons galloped safely across the border back into Illinois.

Meanwhile, as the sheriff arrived at Gallatin, he was grabbed by angry locals and run out of town on a rail. The entire Missouri countryside then became a heated hornet's nest . . .

Their Number One Enemy had escaped . . . and they took it out on other Mormon settlers, a number of which, under defiance of Boggs' Exterminating Order, were still lingering in the state. Missourians swarmed over the countryside, completely destroying the last Mormon settlements, burning homes, shooting animals, and pillaging every Saint-looking thing in sight.

Thus the last remaining Mormons finally fled Missouri.

Again Joseph arrived to the arms of family and friends, who were establishing themselves in yet another land.

Illinois citizens had fumed at the Missourians' treatment of the Mormons, and Quincy township citizens quickly issued a formal invitation to the Saints.

After Joseph conferred with church leaders, however, he decided to purchase in Illinois what land he could afford — which amounted to two parcels of swampland at Commerce, Illinois.

Despite its malarial infestation, Joseph had high hopes. " . . . The place was literally a wilderness," he writes. "The land was mostly covered with trees and brushes, and much of it so wet that it was with the utmost difficulty a footman could get through, and totally impossible for teams. Commerce was so unhealthful, very few could live there; but believing that it might become a healthful place by the blessing of heaven to the Saints, and no more eligible place presenting itself, I considered it wisdom to make an attempt to build up a city."[21]

And build up a city he did. Joseph's people drained the swamp, cleared the land, constructed homes and stores, and within a year had 250 structures firmly planted in the new bastion. They renamed it "Nauvoo," meaning "the beautiful."

The city mushroomed. European converts swarmed their ranks by the thousands . . . and Nauvoo became the largest city in Illinois, dwarfing Chicago threefold in size.

But now the Saints struggled under a new burden.

Poverty. Most Mormons had been financially done in by the Missouri wars and were simply surviving from the surplus of more stable Saints. Their predicament reached such proportions that Joseph would embark on a new strategy: he would seek aid from Washington.

Rockwell, meanwhile, was facing his own problems. His first son was born October 26, 1839, and as a new father he struggled amidst general financial upheavals to merely stay alive. While thus treading, a church assignment came.

Two days before yet another Halloween, 1839, Porter was chosen to protect the Prophet.

Joseph, Porter, and three others set out for Washington, D.C. to seek redress. With his newborn son only two days old, Porter left Luana with faith that other Saints would succor them, and he rode away on a cold October morning in a two-horse carriage.[22]

Along the way they stopped to preach. Porter possibly preached, but probably didn't, as Joseph made no mention of it in his journal. For years now Rockwell had most likely been practicing his gunmanship, and more importantly had proven both his loyalty and his courage to church leaders during the Liberty Jail episode. It was no secret Joseph felt Porter had another mission in life — that of protector and church guardian — and the Saints were prepared to make full use of it. He would yet, however, engage in missionary activities as well.

On this journey, as on most previous ones, trouble wasn't long in coming, but this time it was of their own making. In Ohio Dr. R. D. Foster embarrassed the others by heavily flirting with women, caressing and speaking "lewdly" in public,[23] and thus hampering missionary intentions. Next, in Columbus, Ohio, Sidney Rigdon took ill; Rockwell and Foster remained behind with him. Meanwhile, Joseph and Elias Higbee transferred to a coach and set out for Washington, D.C. without Porter's protection.

But they never needed it.

What they needed was an appointment with President Martin Van Buren.

On reaching Washington, Joseph struggled to meet with Van Buren. He had prayed during the journey the President would even provide an audience, much less agree to their demands...and the President finally agreed to an appointment.

Van Buren listened respectfully. He thought for a moment about Joseph's request, and finally pronounced the decree that would be recorded in most every volume of Mormon history for a century:

"Gentlemen, your cause is just, but I can do nothing for you. If I take up for you I shall lose the vote of Missouri."[24]

Joseph walked away from the White House stunned. His assertive nature would not let him give up so quickly, however, and he took his cause to Congress.

There they asked for just one thing: evidence. Joseph would have to provide them with testimonies, so he sat down to write the Saints of Illinois.

While waiting for the church's High Council in Illinois to gather affidavits, Joseph journeyed to Philadelphia. Rockwell and Higbee would soon meet him there, but Rigdon would remain in Washington, still ill.

In early January, 1840, the documents arrived. Joseph finally had his evidence: 491 Saints had testified on paper of the injustices personally perpetrated on them, and to this stack, Porter and Joseph added their own. Claims totalled $1,381,044; Porter's was $2,000 and his father's $3,000.

Joseph took the stack to a congressional committee and waited their answer . . .

The committee replied with a resounding no.

Crestfallen and quiet, they returned home, having done their all.

On the journey home, Porter parted with them at Dayton, Ohio, where he likely visited his sister Caroline and her husband.

He eventually arrived at Nauvoo in March, to his five-month-old son Orrin DeWitt Rockwell (who, in admiration of his father, later changed his name to Orrin Porter Rockwell, Jr., much to the dismay of enemies who would label him a rouge even his children feared.)[25]

At about the time Porter was again building a new life in Nauvoo, an impressive new church convert arrived on the scene . . .

John C. Bennett came into the kingdom August, 1840. Smith quickly discovered in him a much-needed talent, and appointed him lobbyist to the Illinois assembly. Here Bennet proved a remarkable statesman. He pushed for passage of a bill to incorporate Nauvoo.[26] Largely through his efforts Nauvoo was authorized to organize a legion whose commander would be commissioned "lieutenant general," the highest-ranking military position in the land. According to research by S. Francis, editor of the *Sangamo Journal* in 1842, and the opinions of "experienced military men" with whom Francis conferred, if the militia were ever to be activated, a lieutenant general could assume complete command of all United States armies by nature of his rank. Even Brigham confessed later, " . . . If Joseph had lived when the [Mexican] war broke out, he would have become commander-in-chief of the United States armies."[27] This status was previously held only by George Washington.[28]

Joseph was appointed the rank, and Bennet, for his industriousness, was appointed mayor.

He was also to become the greatest thorn yet in the sides of Porter Rockwell and Joseph Smith.

But for now the city thrived. Joseph was especially pleased that

Bennett had managed to negotiate for the right to issue writs of habeas corpus, and to pass any ordinance not in conflict with state or federal constitutions.

Joseph's favorite hobby, meanwhile, was the Legion. He divided it into an infantry and cavalry, and the State of Illinois entrusted him with 250 rifles, 250 pistols, and three cannon.

Despite his growing power in the land, the Prophet was still both haunted and hunted by Missouri bounty-hunters, ever anxious to snare him and extradite him across the Mississippi.

Then one day it happened . . . he was ambushed. After completing a conference with the Illinois governor, he was captured by two Missouri deputies, who almost succeeded in dragging him across the river, but he received a writ of habeas corpus and placed the matter before Judge Steven A. Douglas of the Illinois Supreme Court. Douglas ordered Joseph released.

Porter, meanwhile, faced obstacles of his own. Luana was about to give birth to their fourth child, when she demanded to be with her parents. For Porter this was not a minor obstacle. Her parents lived in Independence, Missouri, the heart of his harshest enemies.

Porter no doubt argued vehemently. And, of course, the stronger-willed of the two won. Eight months pregnant, Luana, her children, and Porter set out across the Mississippi River. They probably left in the cover of darkness on a cold February of 1842, and stealthily made their way to her parents' home.

There, Rockwell tended a stallion for a Missourian named Ward,[29] and used an assumed name — of Brown.[30] The baby, Sarah Rockwell, was delivered March 25, but Porter stayed additional weeks caring for his family.

He eventually returned to Nauvoo alone, leaving Luana to return when she desired. One may surmise a rift was growing between them . . .

Rockwell was possibly present in Nauvoo May 15 when Joseph announced to a Sunday crowd that the recent governor of Missouri, Lilburn W. Boggs, had been shot.

Boggs did not die, but Joseph was implicated in the shooting by anti-Mormon newspapers. Joseph replied to one *Quincy Whig* editorial: " . . . you have done me manifest injustice in ascribing to me a prediction of the demise of Lilburn W. Boggs . . . Boggs was a candidate for the state senate, and, I presume, fell by the hand of a political opponent, with 'his [Boggs'] hands and face yet dripping with the blood of murder;' but he died not through my instrumentality . . . "

Joseph's defense was solid. Until once again the voice of an apostate rang through the air . . . this time it was that of his own master negotiator and Nauvoo's mayor, John C. Bennett.

Bennett had become quite a seducer of Mormon women, it seems, and when his activities came to light, he placed the blame on Joseph for granting him the privilege of holding "illicit intercouse with women." His excuse didn't hold water among the Saints, but he found willing and listening ears among the Illinoisans. Bennett was released as mayor and simultaneously excommunicated from the church.

And he decided to retaliate.

He published a series of claims for publication in the *Sangamo Journal*, indicting Rockwell as the man sent by Joseph to assassinate Boggs. Bennett writes, "Smith said to me, speaking of Governor Boggs, 'The Destroying Angel has done the work, as I predicted, but Rockwell as not the man who shot; the Angel did it.'"[31] Bennett perhaps twisted Joseph's words — if Joseph had ever even uttered them — and now claimed the angel was Porter Rockwell.

Thus with one fell stoke, Porter's new nickname, "The Destroying Angel," took shape. Anti-Mormon writers not only jumped on the Boggs bandwagon[32] but soon linked Porter to other crimes as well, including the murder of Mormon John Stephenson the same summer.[33]

Bennett claims the following scene took place between him and Rockwell as related by Justice Samuel Marshall:

"Rockwell said, 'Doctor, you do not know your friends; I am not your enemy, and I do not wish you to make use of my name in your publications.'

"Deponent [Bennett] replied, that he recognized Joe Smith and all his friends as personal enemies.

"To which Rockwell replied, 'I have been informed by Warner and Davis that you said Smith gave me fifty dollars and a wagon for shooting Boggs, and I can and will whip any man that will tell such a cursed lie; did you say so or not?'

"After looking at him for a moment or two, deponent [Bennett] said, 'I never said so, sir; but I did say, and I now say it to your face, that you left Nauvoo about two months before the attempted assassination of Ex-Governor Boggs, of Missouri, and returned the day before the report of his assassinaton reached there; and that two persons, in Nauvoo, told me that you told them that you had been over the upper part of Missouri, and in Boggs' neighborhood.'

"To which Rockwell replied, 'Well, I was there; and if I shot Boggs, they have got to prove it. I never did an act in my life that I was ashamed of, and I do not fear to go any where that I have never been, for I have done nothing criminal . . . If you say that Joe Smith gave me fifty dollars and a wagon to shoot Boggs, I can whip you, and will do it in any crowd.'

. . . "The conversation then ceased on that subject. Rockwell told deponent that he had been accused wrongfully of wishing to assassinate him, or of being ordered by Smith to do so; but deponent said, 'I believe that Joe ordered you to do it. I know that orders went from him to the Danites for that purpose.' Rockwell said that Smith had never given him any such orders, neither was it his intention; and further this deponent saith not."[34]

Despite their confrontation, the rumor escalated to the East Coast. The *New York Watchman* reports, "Since that [assassination attempt], the Prophet has presented said Rockwood [sic] with a carriage and horse, or horses, and he has suddenly become very flush of money, and lives in style."[35]

In later years, additional writers joined the chorus, including Wilhelm W. Wymetal and William Hall. Hall claimed he had heard Rockwell boast of the Boggs deed himself,[36] and Wymetal alleged that General Patrick E. Connor[37] and William Law[38] had claimed Joseph had sent Porter to perform the deed. Even apostate John Whitmer joined the song.[39] This one episode became a dividing line for decades between anti- and active Saints, with church enemies — some blatant, others subtle — claiming Rockwell had been hired by Joseph. If substantiated, the claim would indeed discredit a prophet's credibility. But the incident also gave birth to a label that would provoke Porter's enemies the remainder of his life; it was, in their eyes, the launching point for other "nefarious deeds," and he gained national prominence by it. The accusation would haunt the family name for generations.

Anti-Mormons even conjured up "witnesses" who claimed Porter confessed of the deed. The *Chicago Weekly Inter-Ocean,* for example, published the story of a Richmond local "who was himself a pretty rough character . . . " The man claimed he had heard Porter confess "to having shot the Governor . . . and that Rockwell asked him for $10 to enable him to leave the country . . . immediately after the shooting had been executed."[40] For this scenario one questions Porter's remarkably short foresight — taking off to another state with the intention of murder while lacking even the means for travel and survival. If his enemies were correct, certainly an official assassination would have been better funded by church hierarchists. That Porter would confess to such a deed as claimed by the "pretty rough character" is indeed unlikely, as even the most bitter anti-Mormon critics later admitted Porter's lips "could never be plied."[41]

Despite the clamor for Rockwell's head, Missourians conveniently overlooked their own first reports. Eight days after the assassination attempt a committee of prominent Missourians focused their suspicions on a non-Mormon. Among the committee was Samuel D. Lucas, a militia major-general in the Jackson County War against the Mormons. Lucas was also a political adviser and close friend to Boggs, and he was now one of the citizens' committee that advertised in the *Jeffersonian Republican*[42] a reward for $500 for the arrest of a "spare, well built man, about 5 feet 8 inches high, thin visage, pale complexion, regular features, keen, black eye, and remarkably long, slender hand . . . He landed at Owen's landing, Jackson county, off the steam boat *Rowlena,* on the 27th day of April, and departed on the same Boat, on the 29th of the same month, for Lexington, Mo., and on the evening of the assassination, was seen in the vicinity of Independence — which with many other corroborating circumstance, leaves no doubt of his guilt. When first in

Independence he called himself TOMPKINS, and professed to be a silver-smith by occupation. He is quite talkative, and has the appearance of an eastern man. He is about 38 or 40 years of age. [Signed at] Independence, May 9, 1842, Samuel D. Lucas, S. H. Woodson, Wilson Roberts, John King, Lewis Jones."

Whatever the "corroborating evidence" was it convinced prominent Missourians of Tompkins' guilt. Yet just one week later the *Jeffersonian Republican* reports him "fully acquitted and exculpated from all suspicion,"[43] and in the same issue reports a more popular suspect suddenly chosen: Porter Rockwell. In quoting apostates, the *Jeffersonian Republican* claims conveniently Joseph had made a prophecy about Boggs' death. Certainly Joseph denied ever making the "prophecy," and to his credit no evidence exists that he actually uttered it. Nonetheless, rumors from enemies floated about Nauvoo that he had, and they were careful to spread them to the Missourians.

Other circumstances push away the plausibility of Porter's guilt. A pistol was found just yards from Boggs' house after the assassination attempt, and it was traced to Uhlinger's Grocery.[44] Philip Uhlinger, age 40, was a baker.[45]

Motives of murder for Uhlinger or anyone else were abundant. Boggs had proved to be a highly unpopular governor, due to four primary reasons, any one of which provided reasons for an assassination attempt. While Boggs saved the State Bank during the "Panic of 1837" he made enemies of many St. Louis merchants with his tight money policy.[46] Any bankrupt businessman could blame the governor, and for a man to see his own family on the throes of starvation — which was not uncommon for the day — due in part to his governor's policies, inspires the obvious. Boggs' second reason for unpopularity was the new capitol building, a political boondoggle, where many jealous, competing contractors and angry budget-watchers were involved. The Legislature had appropriated $75,000 for the building,[47] but Boggs went on a spending spree — in 1837 he asked for $125,000 more and received it.[48] Assemblymen were infuriated when they later learned he had spent another $200,000 with the building nowhere near completion.[49]

After numerous inquiries, the Legislature cleared Boggs of any criminal activity.[50] Nonetheless the public was skeptical, and many were incensed. Boggs' third thorn that provoked the wrath of enemies was the Mormon issue. And while Jackson, Clay, and Caldwell counties supported him, the vast majority of Missouri exploded from his treatment of the Saints.[51] He was actually hated by some non-Mormons in certain quarters for the Mormon policy. Another of his enemy-producing activities was his recent campaign in the state senate. Although full copies of the *Western Monitor,* Independence's only newspaper, are no longer in existence and therefore cannot detail the extent of the bitterness of the campaign, the fact remains he did make enemies during it. The *Jeffersonian Republican,* for example, printed a premature obituary after the shooting, calling for political and personal ill-feelings to be buried with him.[52] The extent of his repertoire of personal enemies is today still unknown. But the *Republican* points out they included his former friends.[53]

Researchers have made a thorough search in Kansas City and in the attic of the old Independence Courthouse for court records, but none seem to exist before 1863, yet even a church enemy in 1873 supports Porter's alibi after he had proven he was several miles from the Boggs' home during the assassination attempt,[54] as legal entities also concurred.[55]

The obvious fact is that although much of history has pinned the shooting on Porter, not even Boggs knew who shot him. He may have suspected Porter,[56] but if he had known for a fact Porter was the shooter, too many questions rise to the surface. As a non-Mormon scholar later observes, why did Boggs wait two and a half months to swear out a warrant after the crime had been committed?[57] If he obtained information from other parties, why were their affidavits not included in the writ? As the *Lee County Democrat* reports after thoroughly investigating the crime, "the assassins escaped undetected."[58] (See Note 6 for more insights on the Boggs shooting.)

General Doniphan of the Missouri militia claimed no evidence was ever produced to connect Rockwell with the crime.[59]

In 1938 a researcher on Rockwell claims, "The Prophet once made the statement that the fact that Boggs was not assassinated is proof to him that Rockwell was not guilty. Porter would not have missed."[60]

After Rockwell's purported confrontation with Bennett, the former mayor next claimed Porter took up residence at the tavern of Amos Davis, and that "Smith told me that he furnished the carriage, horses, and gold sovereigns, to Rockwell. But said he, 'It is to enable him to convey passengers from the steamboats to the Temple and back again.' "[61]

With regard to the Boggs' shooting, Bennett's intentions were obvious — to slander, in any way possible, Joseph . . . But in the process he drew Porter into the scene . . .

Bennett next searched out Boggs at his Independence home and found him recuperating from wounds. There, Bennett "confided" in Boggs. Boggs then swore out an affidavit for the arrest of Porter and Joseph, and in the process petitioned the governor of Illinois.

Governor Carlin of Illinois complied with Boggs' request:[62] Porter and Joseph were arrested August 8th, 1842.

But Joseph and Porter out-foxed them. When two Illinois deputies were sent to haul them away, Joseph and Porter used the writ of habeas corpus once again,[63] and legally maneuvered out of their grasp.

The deputies, feeling, as it were, water running through their fingers, returned to Governor Carlin for further orders. Consequently they had left their two prisoners in the custody of the Nauvoo city marshal, who, of course, released the men when the deputies were out of sight.[64] (Legally the prisoners could only be held if the writ had stayed with the marshal, but the two deputies bungled their mission and took the writ with them. Thus Porter and Joseph were freed.)[65]

The deputies now received from Governor Carlin another warrant and returned to Nauvoo. "But neither Smith or Rockwell could be found. Their whereabouts was not known," reports the *Lee County Democrat.*[66]

The *Quincy Whig* adds with quiet indignation, "The Mormons treated the officers with every respect, and offered to assist them if necessary, in fulfilling their duty. The whole affair begins to look exceedingly like a farce."[67]

Porter and Joseph crossed the Mississippi River and went into hiding. The least likely place the deputies would search for them, they figured, would be on an island. And there Joseph made some of his first recorded plans to take the Saints to the Rocky Mountains.[68]

Also on that island Joseph called a council meeting. When other church leaders arrived, Porter reported to Joseph a false rumor that the governor of Iowa had issued a warrant for their arrest and extradition to Missouri. (The *Quincy Whig* had actually reported that a Missouri official had met with the Iowa governor[69] about the two men, but no warrant had ever been issued.) They nonetheless deemed it wisest that Joseph go into hiding in Iowa, and that Porter simply flee the state.[70]

The decision couldn't have hurt Porter more. He was seeking to heal domestic problems, and felt he needed to be with his children. Porter had found Luana increasingly disenchanted with him, it seems, probably for his child-like devotion to the Prophet — risking his life for the man and spending less and less hours with the family.

While his love for his children never waned, his love for Luana evidently took another route. His volatile nature had likely contributed to their split, but whatever the reasons, the "cause" now supplanted her as his first love.

Thus, Luana made a painful decision.

She left him. And took the children with her.

This was Porter's greatest trial. With his Prophet in hiding and his own life in jeopardy, he headed East, stopping in Indiana to search for employment, but could find none.

He next stopped in Ohio. Still nothing. The gloom he presented to prospective hirers further insured his lack of employment, and the cycle deepened.

Back home a reward of $1,300 was now placed on him, as well as on Joseph.[71] Not long afterwards, Porter's award alone would soar to $3,000, a hefty sum in its day for a skilled bounty-hunter.[72]

Joseph, meanwhile, tired of the island. Due in part to the persuasions of Wilson Law, Joseph returned to Nauvoo to hide among trusted Saints the evening of August 18th.

Bennett, of course, kept pressing for the arrest of Joseph, writing more Missourians, offering to enter further evidence if necessary . . . whatever it would take to nail the Prophet.

But Joseph remained secluded. In Nauvoo he took time to record in his journal comments about his most faithful friends, those who "have stood by me in every hour of peril, for these fifteen long years past," including Porter Rockwell: "who is now a fellow-wanderer with myself, an exile from his home, because of the murderous deeds, and infernal, fiendish dispositions of the indefatigable and unrelenting hand of the Missourians. He is an innocent and noble boy. May God Almighty deliver him from the hands of his pursuers. He was an innocent and noble child and my soul loves him."[73]

Porter trudged through Ohio, on to Pennsylvania, agonizing over his estranged children. Revealed turmoil surfaces in a letter Porter writes through a friend upon arriving at Philadelphia:

"Dear Brother Joseph Smith, I am requested by our friend Orrin Porter to drop a few lines informing you that he is in this place. His health is good, but his spirits are depressed, caused by his being unable to obtain employment of any kind. He has applied in different parts of the city and country, but all without success, as farmers can get persons to work from sunrise till dark for merely what they eat.

"He is most anxious to hear from you, and wishes you to see his mother and children and write all the particulars, how matters and things are, and what the prospects are. I pity him from the bottom of my heart. His lot in life seems marked with sorrow, bitterness, and care. He is a noble, generous friend. But you know his worth: Any comments from me would be superfluous. He will wait in this place till he hears from you. Please write immediately, as it will be a source of great comfort to him to hear.

"If Joseph is not at home, brother Whitney will be kind enough to write. He [Porter] says every other one [Mormon] he has come across [here] has been afraid of their shadows, but he watches them well. He comes to see me every other day, and I keep him . . . close!

"Answer this as soon as received. Yours truly, S. Armstrong for

Orrin Porter."[74]

Joseph felt for Porter, but could do nothing for him. Meanwhile, although Smith was practically imprisoned himself, he exulted in the election of a new Illinois governor, Thomas Ford, who had taken over a state almost in the throes of bankruptcy. Thus engaged in financial cares, Ford found himself too busy to meddle in religious problems, particularly in the private crusade of Lilburn W. Boggs against the Mormon Church.

But Boggs would not relinquish his obsession. He now petitioned Ford to hand over both Rockwell and Smith to the State of Missouri. Since Ford was too busy to concern himself with "such nonsense" he simply handed the Mormon matter over to the Circuit Court of Ilinois, mumbling to the magistrate his opinion that Boggs' request was illegal.

Judge Nathaniel Pope concurred. He declared Boggs' writ worthless. The language was nebulous, the logic unauthoritative, the evidence non-existent, and "his suspicions were light and unsatisfactory. The affidavit is insufficient, 1st, because it is not positive; 2nd, because it charges no crime; 3rd, because it charges no crime committed in the state of Missouri. Therefore, he [Joseph Smith] did not flee from the justice of the state of Missouri, nor has he taken refuge in the state of Illinois." Summarizing, Pope declares, " . . . The proceedings in this affair, from the affidavit to the arrest, afford a lesson to governors and judges whose action may hereafter be invoked in cases of this character . . . " And then he blasts Boggs' contentions as "mis-recitals and over-statements." He announces that Smith "must be discharged."[75]

But in Philadelphia Porter kept spiraling downward. With still no jobs available, and with his peculiar, natural intensity showing, his growing depression made his bearing more than somewhat foreboding.

He took his gloom to New Jersey. Searching up and down the state he again found no employment.

And at some point he finally broke.

Either through the pain of missing his children, or Luana, or his people . . . or through perhaps the sheer combined feeling of failure . . . he gave in. He turned West. And with his last remaining dollars he took passage on the Erie Canal.

On March 4, 1843 he stepped off the riverboat at St. Louis, ready to make the last leg of his journey into Nauvoo. Obviously he knew bounty-hunters could be anywhere, but he would take his chances and he went ashore. Only a hundred yards of water separated him from the Illinois shore from which his family and friends were waiting. And only a ferry could permit him to reach that much-longed-for shore, and only a gun stuck in his back, one held by a bounty-hunter, could actually keep him from boarding that ferry.

And that's exactly what happened . . .

IV

Porter's only detailed first-hand account from any episode in his life is the following remarkable story in the *Millennial Star* newspaper: [1]

"I, Orrin Porter Rockwell, was on my way from New Jersey to Nauvoo; and while at St. Louis, on the fourth of March 1843, was arrested by a Mr. Fox on the oath of Elias Parker, who swore I was the O. P. Rockwell advertized in the papers as having attempted to assassinate Lilburn W. Boggs, and was taken before a magistrate in St. Louis."

Porter had been travelling from the East with a Mr. Ivins, who quickly reported the arrest to Joseph. Meanwhile:

"I was then put into the St. Louis County Jail, and kept two days with a pair of iron hobbles on my ankles. About midnight, was taken into the stage coach, in charge of Fox and started for Jefferson City. There were nine passengers, two of them women. I sat on the middle seat. One of the men behind me commenced gouging me in the back. I spoke to him and told him that it was dark, and I could not see him, but that he was no gentleman. One of the ladies whispered to him and he ceased the operation.

"The next night, the driver, being drunk, ran against a tree, and broke the king bolt; and not knowing what to do, ironed as I was, I crawled into the boot, and found an extra bolt, and in the dark fixed the coach, got it off the tree, and we started on. Soon after ran against a mud bank, and could not move. I was asleep at the time, but the bustle woke me, then I told them if they would take off my irons I would get off and drive, as the driver was too drunk to manage the horses.

"They refused. I however got hold of the lines, and by the help of other passengers, lifted at the wheels, got it righted, and I drove to the next stand, near the Osage River. The roads were very bad, and the load heavy; so we got along slowly.

"There was an officer of the U.S. Army in the coach. We were two days and nights from St. Louis in reaching Jefferson City, where I was lodged in the jail two days and two nights. The U.S. officer went on.

"Started on for Independence, still in charge of Fox. At Boonville, overtook the U.S. Officer. We three were all that were in the coach all the way from Boonville to Independence. Sheriff Reynolds told me afterwards that when he looked into the stage he took me for the guard, and the officer for the prisoner, for he looked like the guilty one.

"Was about four days going to Independence; arrived there just at night. A large crowd gathered around making many remarks. Some were for hanging me at once.

"I was then placed in the jail."

Meanwhile, an interesting story comes from the *Lee County Democrat,* typical of accounts published: "We are also credibly informed that several hundred Mormons started off in wagons and on foot, to endeavor to rescue him from the officers."[2] Despite the report, no such attempt materialized. The Saints knew they were helpless to rescue him from the nest of their enemies.

Rockwell continues:

"In two or three days, [I] underwent a sham trial before a justice of the peace. The court house was crowded and the men were armed with hickory clubs. They set on boys from ten to twelve years of age to kick and punch me, which they did repeatedly, while in court. Fox was the main witness introduced and he swore falsely.

"Fox swore that I had stated to him that I had not been in the country for five years. I informed the court that Fox swore falsely, in proof thereof that the people of Independence knew that I had traveled through Independence several times during that time, for the people were all well aware of my having visited this place, which fact alone should satisfy them that Fox was swearing for money, which I afterwards learned that he obtained and divided with Parker.

"The magistrate committed me to prison for my safe preservation, as he was afraid the people would kill me; but he could find no crime against me. This I was told by the officer who conveyed me to prison.

"I was re-committed to jail, still wearing the iron hobbles, and was left in the upper part in the day time, and in the dungeon at night, with a little dirty straw for a bed without any bedding, no fire, and very cold weather.

"For eighteen days I was not free from shaking with cold. I then got permission to buy one and one-half bushels of charcoal, which when that was gone I could not obtain any more.

"After I was arrested at St. Louis, I was visited by Joseph Wood, an apostate 'Mormon,' who professes to be a lawyer. He was accompanied by Mr. B. Banerhasser, who told me that everything I had would be taken from me, and proposed to take charge, keep, and let him have a pair of pistols, a bowie knife and watch, which he never returned to me.

"After the weather got a little warmer, they furnished me with a few old newspapers to read.

"A family lived at the corner of the jail. The woman once in a while used to send out a little negro girl with a small basket of victuals. She handed up to the grate a big Mississippi whip-stock, with a piece of twine, which I tied to the pole, and drew up the basket, and let it down again.

"I made a pin-hook and tied it to the twine, and baited it with a chunk of corn-dodger hard enough to knock a negro down with, and stuck it out of the grated window and fished for pukes." [Illinoisians, without much affection for Missourians, commonly referred to them as "pukes."][3]

"When passersby came along they would stand and gawk at me

for awhile and pass on.

"A preacher who had a family of girls lived on the opposite side of the street. The girls would watch and laugh at me, and call out and ask me if I got any bites. I replied, 'No, but some glorious nibbles.'

"Numbers were put into the jail with me at different times, and taken out again. One of them who was charged with fraudulent issue of U.S. Treasury notes was allowed to have his saddle bags with him. They contained some fire-steels. He got the negro girl to get him a knife, and finished cutting the fetters with it. He would frequently call for a good supper and pay for it, which was allowed him but not allowed me," complains Porter. This aggravation lacks further details, yet did not seem to produce any particular resentment within Porter for his cellmate.

The prisoner was named Watson. He had been arrested at Sir William Drummond Stewart's Camp William before Stewart's planned expedition to the Rockies. Watson had been a member of the expedition and had been caught stealing;[4] he had also been arrested May 20th for "purloining, altering and passing treasury drafts,"[5] just two days before the expedition had been launched.

While Watson and Rockwell were in jail together, the assistant editor of the *Daily Picayune* and fellow member of the Stewart expedition, Matthew C. Field, decided to visit the prisoner. His report to the *Picayune* is revealing: "When in the town of Independence the other day we had sufficiently kind feelings for 'Watson,' as he called himself, to solicit permission to visit him, which was at once granted to us. In the evening, after tea, Gen. Owens took us to the jail, which is a building of massive brick work, with a strong upper apartment and a cell beneath . . . [The jail had been renovated 11 years previously[6] and was virtually indestructible and escape-proof.] We were conducted through strong doors and a guarded passage into the upper room, where an enormous trapdoor appeared in the floor, firmly secured with bars and padlocks. This was unfastened and raised by means of a crank and pulley, when the jailer lowered a ladder and the prisoner we sought was commanded to ascend. He [Watson] came up . . .

"Rockwell, the Mormon, upon whom rests the strong imputation of having attempted the assassination of ex-Gov. Boggs, was his only [fellow] prisoner and Gen. Owens called him up to satisfy our curiosity. He is a man of fair proportions and good looks, apparently about twenty-eight or thirty. His eye has in it something between cunning and insanity, but you look in vain for any indication of the desperate and determined villain. He was laughing joyously during the whole period of our visit and replied in a merry and nonsensical manner, which we were told had marked him ever since his arrest; whether assumed or not, it may, perhaps, be difficult to determine. One of our companions from St. Louis who was present on the occasion bears the precise cognoment of the Mormon Prophet, Joseph Smith, and we presented him before Rockwell as the 'Great Latter Day Saint,' junior, at which the Mormon prisoner laughed prodigiously; but his cunning, roving eye was scanning intently everybody present, and it seemed clear that there was no soul in the merriment he affected. He was heavily ironed and when we moved to go, he quietly descended to his cell with his only companion, Watson."[7]

As an interesting postscript, Field next observes, "We have had a whole week of storms since pitching our tents at this encampment, and some of them are of really terrific violence. The other night, a man was killed by lightning."

Some followers of Rockwell take note in the possibility the elements seemed displeased more than once when he or Joseph were imprisoned or in danger. But similar incidents have been considered by most Mormons as purely coincidental, and church officials have made no recorded assertions otherwise.

Porter resumed the account of his imprisonment, analyzing his new cellmate, Watson:

"He was very anxious to escape, and urged me to take it with him. He ordered a good supper and ate very heartily. I would not eat, telling him that he could not run if he ate so much.

"Nearly dusk, as the jailor came in to get the dishes, we sprang to the door and locked him in, and threw the key into the garden.

"In coming downstairs we met the jailor's wife. I told her that her husband was unharmed. I had only locked him up.

"We had a board fence over which [to climb and which] was about twelve feet high.

"I climbed it and ran about twenty rods, when he called me to come and help him over, which I did. If I had not I should have escaped. The pure air had so great an effect on me, that I gave out and slacked my pace.

"The populace of the place came up, and I told them to run [to catch Watson]; they would soon catch him; and that I had give out and could not run. They soon returned with him. I fell into the crowd and walked back to the jail yard.

"Sheriff J. H. Reynolds laid his hand upon my shoulder, he being the first to approach me. Asked where the key was. I told him in the garden.

"Smallwood Nowlin [Nowland] was the first to propose to hang me on the spot, when Reynolds gave me a push towards the crowd and said, 'There he is, damn him, do what you damn please with him.'

"Nowlin's son-in-law (by marrying one of his mulatto wenches), a Mexican, stepped up to me to lay hold of me, when I told him to stand off, or I would mash his face. He stepped back.

"I then walked upstairs into the jail. Was followed by Reynolds and others, until the room and stairs were full.

"Reynolds asked me what I had cut my irons off with. I went to the saddle bags and handed him the knife and fire-steel. While feeling for them I got hold of a piece of buckskin that had some three or four pounds of bullets tied up in it, which I intended to use in mashing in the head of anyone that should attempt to put a rope on my neck.

"A rope was passed along over the heads of the people into the room, and bowie knives were produced as if for a fight.

"In a few minutes the room was clear of all but three or four persons.

"I was then put into the dungeon, my feet ironed together, my right hand to my left foot so close that I could not half straighten myself. The irons, when put on my wrists, were so small, that they would hardly go on, and swelled them; but in eighteen days I could slip them up and turn them around my arm at the elbow.

"I was fed on cold corn-dodgers and meat of the poorest description; and if I did not eat it all up, it was returned the next time.

"About a month after the court sat, my irons were taken off, and

I was so weak that I had to be led to the courtroom by the officer.

"I was notified that a bill was found against me for breaking jail, and that the grand jury had failed to find a bill against me on the charge of shooting Boggs, as charged in the advertisement offering a reward for my apprehension.

"I was taken into the court, and was asked by the judge if I had any counsel.

"I told him that I had not.

"He asked me if I had any means to employ a counsel.

"I answered that I had none with me that I could control.

"He then said, 'Here are a number of counsellors.' If I was acquainted with any one of them I could take my choice.

"I told him that I would make choice of Mr. Doniphan, who arose and made a speech, saying that he was crowded with business, but that here was plenty of young lawyers who could plead for me as well as he could. The judge heard his plea, and then told me that he did not consider that a sufficient excuse, and could consider Mr. Doniphan my counsel.

"I was then ordered back to jail, and ironed again in the same way."

Porter was now about to be re-cycled: he was free of the first charge — the grand jury finding him innocent of the Boggs' shooting — only to be tried now for the attempted escape from jail, which, to Porter, must have seemed somewhat ironic, considering he should not have been jailed in the first place.

Doniphan was successful in changing venue to another county, one where he hoped less prejudice would exist.[8]

Porter resumes his account:

"When the officers came to Independence Jail for me to get ready in a hurry, as they feared the mob would kill me, I told them I wanted to put on a clean shirt, if it cost me my life, as I had not been permitted to enjoy the luxury of a change of linen since I had boarded at the expense of Jackson County. While I was changing my shirt, the officers told me several times to hurry, or the mob would be on me and kill me.

"When I got ready to start, the officers furnished me a very hard trotting horse, with a miserable poor saddle, tied my feet under the horse with ropes, and my hands behind my back, and started off at a good round trot, in charge of two officers.

"In a short time a strange gentleman fell into our company, who was also on horseback. It was six miles to the ferry where we could cross the Missouri River.

"When we got there we saw the boat land on the opposite side. Several men got off the boat [on the opposite shore], and took a course to the woods . . .

"The boat returned. This stranger asked, 'Where are those men going?' and was answered, 'They are going to the woods to hew timber.'

"We then crossed and took our way for Liberty. When we left the boat we saw no signs of people, nor heard any sounds of axes. After traveling some two or three miles, the woods became dense and brushy; we heard the crackling of brush, and the noise of men traveling through it. The officers and stranger appeared frightened, and urged speed, keeping close watch.

"We came to an opening in the woods, when the noise of crackling of brush ceased. We traveled safely to Liberty, where the stranger told his friends that he overheard several men in Independence planning to waylay me in the thick timber on the Missouri bottom, at the place where he heard the noises; but his being in company counteracted their plot.

"I was then lodged in Liberty Jail. In the few days afterward I learned that the men who went into the brush told it, that they went into the woods according to agreement to waylay me; but when they saw this stranger it frustrated their plans."

After all he had gone through, the new judge decided his papers had a discrepancy.[9]

"In about ten days, on pretext of informality in the papers, I was remanded back to Independence Jail."

Porter's consternation was obvious. "It was rumored that I was again going to be waylaid, when the two officers from Clay County took me by a different road, and so I escaped a second time.

"When I was put in Independence Jail, I was again ironed hand and foot, and put into the dungeon, in which condition I remained about two months. During this time Joseph H. Reynolds, the sheriff, told me he was going to arrest Joseph Smith, and they had received letters from Nauvoo which satisfied them that Joseph

Smith had unlimited confidence in me, that I was capable of tolling him in a carriage or on horseback anywhere that I pleased; and that if I would only tole him out by riding or any other way, so that they could apprehend him, I might please myself whether I stayed in Illinois or come back to Missouri, they would protect me and any pile that I would name the citizens of Jackson County would donate, club together, and raise, and that I should never suffer for want afterwards; 'You only deliver Joe Smith into our hands, and name your pile.' "

"I replied, 'I will see you all damned first and then I won't.' "

Joseph, meanwhile, was struggling to free Porter. His first and only opportunity came in the form of a fugitive, Joseph H. Jackson, who had appeared in Nauvoo and asked to see him. Jackson confessed to Joseph that he was a wanted man from Macon, Georgia, and had come to Nauvoo for protection, and then casually commented, "I can free Rockwell."

Joseph's hopes were high. Jackson claimed he had important friends in Missouri who could free Porter, and the plan was set.

But it was a trap. Smith soon learned Jackson was a spy, and that Harmon T. Wilson, a Carthage constable, had conspired with him to learn some of the Prophet's plans.[10] Adding to Joseph's frustration, he received a letter from Sheriff Reynolds:

"Sir, at the request of Orrin Porter Rockwell, who is now confined to our jail, I write you a few lines concerning his affairs ... My own opinion is, after conversing with several persons here, that it would not be safe for any of Mr. Rockwell's friends to come here ... neither do I think bail would be taken."[11]

While frustrated at his inability to free Porter, Joseph discovered his own impending danger ...

The same sheriff that had written Joseph was now determined to capture Joseph himself. From spies in Nauvoo, he learned the Prophet was to travel to Dixon, Illinois for a sermon.

As anticipated, when Joseph arrived June 23, he stayed at the home of his wife's nephew, Joseph D. Wasson.

"As the prophet visited friends in the backyard, two gentlemen arrived at the front door and told Mrs. Wasson they were Mormon elders and wished to see the Prophet." They walked to the backyard, strutted up to Joseph, and stuck two pistols in his chest. They were Sheriff Reynolds and Harmon T. Wilson themselves.[12]

The *Times and Seasons* reports, "The following is as near the conversation as we can gather ... Mr. Reynolds ... cried out, 'G-d you, if you stir I'll shoot. [Deletions as printed in original source.] G-d you, if you stir one inch I'll shoot you, G-d you. Be still or I'll shoot you by G-.'

" 'What is the meaning of this?' interrogated Mr. Smith.

" 'I'll show you the meaning by G-, and if you stir one inch I'll shoot you, G-d you.'

" 'I am not afraid of shooting,' answered Smith ...

"They then hurried him off to a carriage that they had."[13]

A Mormon, Stephen Markham, saw the incident, and dashed off for a writ of habeas corpus.

But Joseph never needed it. Through some experience in dealing with captors he had gained some skills of his own, so this time — with a few deft moves — he did more than just free himself from their grasp: he actually turned the tide against them. He issued a complaint to Dixon officials and the two lawmen surprisingly found themselves under arrest. The major reasons, as Joseph asserted, were that he had not only been, under legal terms, "kidnapped," but he'd actually been beaten, holed up in a cabin, and allowed no lawyers or visitors.[14]

Joseph was thus momentarily freed, but the two lawmen were not to be outdone. They obtained a writ of habeas corpus themselves, and, with their subsequent freedom, once again arrested Joseph ... this time successfully ... and now carted him off to Missouri.

Before reaching the Mississippi River, however, they were stopped by the townspeople of Pawpaw Grove, Illinois. Before the two lawmen could grasp what was happening, Joseph extended an invitation to himself to preach to the gathering. The folks were curious, and took him up on it. The two lawmen, before they could blurt out a word, found Joseph dismounting and preaching to the group.

The crowd listened patiently as Joseph preached on and on,

frustrating his captors, delaying their journey, while a friend of Joseph galloped off for another writ of habeas corpus. Meanwhile, Joseph was winning the congregation to his heart, pronouncing the joys of family life. Yet his delaying tactic was more than merely clever . . .

At one point Sheriff Reynolds rose to end the sermon: "I wish you to understand this man is my prisoner, and I want you to disperse—"[15] But a local citizen jumped in his face and shouted him down: "You damned infernal puke, we'll learn you to come here and interrupt gentlemen. Sit down there (pointing to a very low chair) and sit still. Don't open your head till General Smith gets through talking. If you never learned manners in Missouri, we'll teach you that gentlemen are not to be imposed upon . . . "[16]

Sheriff Reynolds sat down in silence.[17]

Joseph continued the filibuster. He spoke for an hour and a half further on the beauties of holy matrimony.[18]

Joseph's writ finally arrived, and the two disgruntled lawmen were forced to return Joseph to Dixon, Illinois.

Once in Dixon the two lawmen came upon a sight they had not reckoned: 100 of Joseph's most robust Nauvoo Legionnaires standing in the road, glaring at them. Casually Joseph commented to his two escorts, "Gentlemen, I think I will not go to Missouri this time . . . These are my boys."[19] The two lawmen looked into the faces of the cavalry and sheepishly nodded, then trotted along behind the Prophet back to Nauvoo.

"This took Joseph out of the power of his enemies once more to our great joy," records Wandle Mace in his journal. "News reached Nauvoo that Joseph was coming, and a multitude, with their band went out to meet him; as he entered the city the band played, Hail to the Chief who in Triumph advances, &c. Language fails me to describe my feelings upon this occasion, as Joseph with his wife by his side — each on horseback — rode in triumph among his friends, into his beloved city.

"Joseph looked upon the multitude of his friends whose every countenance beamed with joy inexpressible and said, 'I am out of the power of the Missourians again, Thank God! and I thank you all for your Kindness and love, I bless you all in the name of Jesus Christ. I will address you in the Grove near the Temple at four o'clock this afternoon.'

"A feast had been prepared for him, his lawyers and the company who came with him, many friends sat down to dinner with him, his captors also. Reynolds and Wilson, the kidnappers, were treated with all the kindness and courtesy of distinguished guests by Joseph and his wife, literally filling the words of the Savior, 'Love your enemies, bless them that curse you, do good to them that hate you, and pray for them that despitefully use you and persecute you.'

"At the meeting in the Grove, at 4 o.c. he rehearsed all the events as they had transpired, the treatment he had received, and how the Lord had raised up friends to defend and assist him, and had again delivered him out of the hands of his enemies."[20]

Joseph then appeared before the Municipal Court and was released. Sheriff Reynolds and Harmon Wilson, having failed, trotted away, this time threatening to return with the entire Illinois state militia.

At the office of Governor Ford they pled their case, but Ford denied their request.

Now boiling mad, the two men left, and Reynolds returned to Independence.

The following letter results from the pen of J. Hall of Independence to the entire town of Dixon, Illinois: "If the governor of Illinois is so imbecile as to allow his warrant to be disregarded by the Mormons, and permit the Prophet to go at large, then let him be impeached, and a new, honorable, energetic man will be placed in his stead. I have it from a high source that Missouri will hold the whole state responsible for the treatment of our messenger [Sheriff Reynolds], and for the delivery of the Prophet."[21] No love apparently was lost between the two states.

Joseph's concern now seemed to be his childhood friend, Porter Rockwell, who was still languishing in jail . . .

Rockwell continues:

"About the time that Joseph was arrested by Reynolds at Dixon, I knowing that they were after him, and no means under heaven of giving him [Joseph] any information, my anxiety became so intense upon the subject, knowing their determination to kill him, that my flesh twisted upon my bones. I could not help it; twitch it would.

While undergoing this sensation I heard a dove light on the window in the upper room of the jail, and commence cooing, and then went off. In a short time, he came back to the window, where a pane was broken; he crept through between the bars of iron, which were about two and a half inches apart. I saw it fly around the trap-door several times; it did not alight but continued cooing until it crept through the bars again, and flew out through the broken window.

"I related this as it was the only occurrence of the kind that happened during my long and weary imprisonment; but it proved a comfort to me; the twitching of my flesh ceased, and I was fully satisfied from that moment that they would not get Joseph Smith into Missouri, and that I should regain my freedom. From the best estimates that can be made, it was at the time when Joseph was in custody of Reynolds.

"In a few days afterwards, Sheriff Reynolds came into the jail and told me that he had made a failure in the arrest of Joseph.

"After the lawyers had been about two months in making out fresh papers, I was again conveyed to Liberty Jail on a miserable horse, with feet and hands tied as before, but a different road."

The same J. Hall who had accused the entire State of Illinois of imbecility now writes another letter, this one about Rockwell, claiming, "[It is] difficult to restrain the citizens from hanging him up without judge or jury. So far, however, we have succeeded in quelling it; but should he be discharged upon trial, the power of man cannot save him."[22]

While Saints were holding prayer circles for Porter in the Nauvoo Temple,[23] Mrs. Rockwell was obviously suffering over her son's imprisonment. She finally approached Joseph, requesting money for a lawyer.

Joseph was without means himself, but an idea struck. He rushed outside, mounted his horse, and sped off to the temple site, where, in his unique style, he grabbed everyone's attention: "Boys, has Bonaparte any friends in the French Army?" Wandle Mace picks up the account: "Of course we were all attention to know his meaning. He then told us he had learned from the mother of O. P. Rockwell, that for the sum of two hundred dollars, she could obtain Porter's release from prison. Joseph said he had not sufficient money himself, so he wanted the brethren to assist him; all present responded heartily. Some could give five dollars, others various amounts, those who had money with them gave it to him, some went to their homes for the money.

"While waiting for the brethren to return, Joseph dismounted from his horse and engaged in a friendly wrestle with some of the boys, as he called us. He often tried to get one to wrestle with him. I never could be induced to wrestle with him. I would not throw him down if I could; I was a strong man as well as he was, often when we met and shook hands he would pull me to him for a wrestle, and say slapping my shoulder with his hand — 'If you are not a strong man there is no use of putting up a fight.'

"Joseph obtained the necessary funds ... "[24]

Porter continues:

"In a few days afterwards my mother found where I was, and she came to see me and brought me one hundred dollars, whereby I was able to fee Mr. Doniphan for his services as counsel.

"The time of trial being continually delayed, I began to be uneasy. I was handcuffed in the dungeon, which is the basement story of the prison, and is about nine feet high. I took down the stove pipe, pushed my clothes up through the stove pipe hole, and then crawled through the hole in the floor, which was made of logs about fourteen inches thick, into the upper room. The hole was so small that it scratched my flesh, and made me bleed from my wounds. I then examined the inside door, and with the bail of the water pail I unbolted it; but finding I could not get through the outside door, I returned to my dungeon through the same narrow pass.

"The following night I made another attempt through the same way; but failing to get through the outside door, I lay down on the upper floor where the boys, who were bringing my meal the next morning, found me.

"They made an alarm, when five or six men came and again conveyed me to the dungeon. It caused quite an excitement.

"My mother learned that Doniphan had returned home. She sent to him and prevailed on him to come and speak to me at the dungeon grate.

"While he was talking to me, a little boy, the son of a poor widow, about five or six years old, who had previously been to see me, finding I had no fire, had run home and brought some fire and chips to the grate. Mr. Doniphan said, 'You little devil, what are you doing here with this fire?'

"He replied, 'I am going to give it to Mr. Rockwell, so that he can warm up.'

"Doniphan then said, 'You little devil, you take this fire and leave.'

"When the little urchin replied, looking him in the face, 'Mr. Doniphan, you go to hell; I am going to give Mr. Rockwell this fire, so that he can warm him[self].'

"And he pushed it through the grate, gave me the chips and continued to supply me daily with chips and fire while I continued in the dungeon.

"From Mr. Doniphan I learned that a special term of court was called, and my trial would come on in about fifteen days.

"The night following this visit some men came to the grates of my dungeon and asked if I wanted to get out.

"I told them no, as I had been informed that day that I should have a trial in a fortnight.

"They replied, 'Honor bright; if you wish to get out we'll let you out in a few minutes.'

"I replied that I would rather remain, as my trial would come on soon.

"Next morning one of the men came, put some money in a cleft on a stick, and put it through the hole to me. He refused to tell his name; but I knew by his voice that he was one of the men who came to me in the night.

"The trial came on according to my last notification. I was tried for breaking Independence Jail; and although the law of Missouri reads that in order to break jail a man must break a lock, a door, or a wall, still Judge King ruled that it was breaking jail to walk out when the door is open; and under this ruling the jury brought in a verdict of 'five minutes' imprisonment in the county jail; but I was kept there four or five hours, during which time several attempts were made to get up some other charge against me."

The attempts were made probably by Judge Austin A. King[25] and Sheriff Reynolds.

"About 8 p.m. on December 13, the General Doniphan took me out and told me I must trek across the country on foot, and not walk on any traveled road, unless it was during the night, as they would be apt to follow and again take me, as they did not care on what grounds, so they could make me trouble.

"Accordingly started, accompanied by my mother, and went to the house of a widow, where I obtained my first supper in freedom for more than nine months.

"I then took through the woods to the road, where I heard two men riding on horseback. I hid behind a shady tree, and overheard one of them say, 'He has not been gone many minutes; we shall soon overtake him.'

"I went round the houses and traveled in the fields by the side of the road. The moon was in its first quarter, and I traveled during the night about twenty-five miles.

"I carried a little food with me, and next day traveled on the road, and walked past Crooked River to a Mr. Taylor's, with all the skin off my feet. A neighbor offered to take me in for the night, if I would go back two miles.

"I did so. Found his wife very cross with her husband, who said, 'Stranger, you see my wife is very cross, I have got some whiskey; let's drink, my wife will soon have something to eat.'

"When supper was eaten she became good tempered. I stayed in peace through the night.

"Next morning I ate breakfast with them, and gave them fifty cents, when the man brought out a horse, and sent a little boy with me fourteen miles, which was a very great relief to my weary feet.

"Next night I stopped near where Haun's Mill Massacre took place.

"The third day I walked till noon, and then hired a man to carry me [on his horse] the remainder of the day for seventy five cents. Stayed at a house where I was well acquainted but the people did not recognize me, and I did not make myself known. Paid fifty cents for supper, lodging, breakfast, and being sent twelve miles on horseback next morning.

"I then continued my journey about thirty miles, where I rested three days to recruit my feet.

"I was then carried twenty-five miles, on horseback, and walked the same day twenty-five miles.

"The day following I walked forty miles, and then waited another day, and engaged a man to carry me to Montrose, to which place I was three days going.

"I immediately crossed the river to Nauvoo in a small boat, and came straight to the mansion."

Thus ends Porter's report.

Joseph continues the chronicle: On Christmas Eve "a large party supped at my house, and spent the evening in music, dancing, etc., in a most cheerful and friendly manner. During the festivities, a man with his hair long and falling over his shoulders, and apparently drunk, came in and acted like a Missourian. I requested the captain of the police to put him out of doors. A scuffle ensued, and I had an opportunity to look him full in the face, when to my great surprise and joy untold, I discovered it was my long-tried, warm, but cruelly persecuted friend, Orrin Porter Rockwell, just arrived from nearly a year's imprisonment, without conviction, in Missouri."[26]

Joseph's journal entry nine months earlier was now fulfilled, wherein he had heard of Porter's capture and prophesied, "in the name of the Lord Jesus Christ, that Orrin Porter Rockwell will get away honorably from the Missourians."[27]

At the party came another remarkable prophecy, one which would result in a lifelong trademark. James Jepson writes in his journal:[28] "The Prophet then told Porter not to cut his hair, but to wear it long, and to live faithful and that his enemies would have no power over him, that they would not be able to take his life." Jepson's parents attended the party and afterwards related the incident to their son. Jepson's is the only known first or second-hand recording of the incident of anyone present at the party.

Joseph now wished to aid his friend, and set Porter up in business.[29] But when Emma Smith returned home from a furniture-buying excursion in St. Louis, she was met with a scene she had not expected. Her son, Joseph III, describes the incident: "When she returned Mother found installed in the keeping-room of the hotel — that is to say, the main room where the guests assembled and where they were received upon arrival — a bar, with counter, shelves, bottles, glasses, and other paraphernalia customary for a fully equipped tavern bar, and Porter Rockwell in charge as tender.

"She was very much surprised and disturbed over this arrangement, but said nothing for a while. A few hours later, as I met her in the hall between the dining room and the front room, she asked me where Father was. I told her he was in the front room. She asked, 'Is anyone else there?' 'Yes,' I answered, 'quite a number.'

"Then she told me to go and tell him she wished to see him. I obeyed, and returned with him to the hall where Mother awaited him. 'Joseph,' she asked, 'what is the meaning of that bar in this house?'

"He told her of Porter's arrival and that a place was being prepared for him just across the street, where he would run a barber shop with a bar in connection, explaining that the bar in the hotel was only a temporary arrangement until the building referred to could be finished and ready for occupancy.

"There was no excitement or anger in Mother's voice nor in what she said as she replied, but there was a distinctness and earnestness I have never forgotten, and which had its effect upon Father as well.

" 'How does it look,' she asked, 'for the spiritual head of a religious body to be keeping a hotel in which is a room fitted out as a liquor-selling establishment?'

"He reminded her that all taverns had their bars at which liquor was sold or dispensed — which was true at that day — and again urged that it was only for a time and was being done for Porter's benefit, explaining that since Porter had been compelled to leave his own home and had, in a measure, been made a scapegoat for charges that had been made against the two of them, he felt obligated to help.

"Mother's reply came emphatically clear, though uttered quietly:

" 'Well, Joseph, the furniture and other goods I have purchased for the house will come, and you can have some other person look after things here. As for me, I will take my children and go across to the old house and stay there, for I will not have them raised up under such conditions as this arrangement imposes upon us, nor have them mingle with the kind of men who frequent such a place. You are at liberty to make your choice; either that bar goes out of the house, or we will!'

"It did not take Father long to make the choice, for he replied immediately, 'Very well, Emma; I will have it removed at once' — and he did. Whether it was established anywhere else or not, I do not know, but the building which was begun for Rockwell across the street was not finished."[30]

Parenthetically their son adds a revealing insight on his parents' personalities: "The disagreement mentioned above is the only one I ever heard, or heard of, as occurring between my father and my mother. It has been charged by certain ones ... that she was a thorn in his side, opposing his policies, and leading him an ill life. This is absolutely not true. I was old enough at the time to know what was going on around me, and was closely associated with both my parents. The sleeping room I shared with my brothers was never more than a door away from where Father and Mother slept. Because of the great love and concern Mother had for her children she never wanted us far from her, in order that she might be on hand to take care of us herself in case of necessity. So, I am sure that if there ever were angry words between my parents I should have known it, and I can truthfully state that nothing of the kind ever occurred. Father was a kindly man, and emphatically a home-loving one, whose wife and children were very dear to him and who was, in turn, loved and respected by them.

"Hence it came about that the bar which was so distasteful to Mother was promptly removed from the Nauvoo Mansion, and she became its first landlady."[31]

This was nine years after Joseph had received a heavenly revelation advising against the use of alcoholic drinks,[32] but since it did not become an actual commandment to the Saints until years later, Joseph evidently found the tavern idea permissible. After Emma's confrontation, however, Joseph changed Porter's duties to that of personal bodyguard.

From the bar at the Mansion House comes another description, perhaps the most succinct and revealing of its kind from the pen of a fellow Mormon, and more significantly, one active in the faith, as it reveals the same charisma which drew Porter and thousands of others to the man: " . . . after a short conversation with the bartender [in the Mansion House], who I afterwards learned was Oren Porter Rockwell . . . [and] After greeting my old friends heartily, I was introduced to the Prophet, whose mild and penetrating glance denoted great depth of tough and extensive forethought. While standing before his penetrating gaze, he seemed to read the very recesses of my heart. A thousand thoughts passed through my mind. I had been permitted by the great author of my being to behold with my natural eyes, a prophet of the living God when millions had died without that privilege, and to grasp his hand in mine, was a privilege that in early days, I did not expect to enjoy. I seemed to be transfigured before him. I gazed with wonder at his person and listened with delight to the sound of his voice. I had this privilege both in public and private at that time and afterwards. Though, in after years, I may become a castaway, the impression made upon my mind at this introduction can never be erased. The feeling which passed over me at this time is impressed upon me as indelibly and lasting as though it were written with an iron pen upon the tablets of my heart . . . I loved his company, the sound of his voice was music to my ears. His counsels were good and his acts were exemplary and worthy of imitation . . . In his domestic circle, he was mild and forebearing, but resolute, and determined in the accomplishment of God's work. Although opposed by the combined powers of earth, He gathered his thousands around him and planted a great city which was to be the foundation of a mighty empire and consecrated it to God as the land of Zion. At the same time, he endured the most unparalleled persecution of any man in the history of our country."[33]

Meanwhile, Porter was pleased to see his parents progress in the kingdom: his father had received his "patriarchal blessing" — a prophetic personal pronouncement given to faithful Latter-day Saints — from Joseph's father January 20, 1839,[34] but to Porter's grief the senior Rockwell passed away eight months later, September 22.[35] Porter's mother, now a faithful widow, set a record in Nauvoo, being "baptized for the dead" by proxy for 45 of her own and her husband's ancestors.[36] She would later receive her own patriarchal blessing July 2, 1845.[37]

Whether such events brought unity between Rockwell and his mother is not recorded, but one may surmise they had such an effect.

Porter was then presented property directly across the street from the Prophet's home. Joseph began construction there of a house for Porter, but due to coming problems the building was never completed . . .

The Prophet found certain Saints wishing to wage war on their enemies. He counseled against it; even so, he recognized the need for the city's self-defense, and appointed 40 policemen December 29, 1843. He counseled them, "We will be in peace with all men, so long as they will mind their own business and let us alone. Even 'Peace with Missouri' shall be the motto of the Church of Jesus Christ of Latter-day Saints, from this time forth, if they will stop their persecution and oppressive warfare against us."

He further instructed, "Let us keep cool as a cucumber on a frosty morning. Do not be excited. Say nothing about Missouri's oppression. 'A soft answer turns away wrath but grievous words stir up anger' . . . There are speculators in this State who are wanting to sell revolving pistols to us, in order to fight the Missourians, and at the same time inciting the Missourians to fight us. Don't buy: it would be better to buy ploughshares and raise corn with them."

But other concerns arose, those which caused the Mormon gun-buying problem to pale by comparison:

Porter reported to Joseph a major conspiracy. Porter had learned of it while languishing in jail, and now, upon his informing the Prophet, Joseph exploded, "My life is more in danger from some little dough-head of a fool in this city than from all my numerous and inveterate enemies abroad."[38] In his journal Joseph elaborates: "I am exposed to far greater danger from traitors among ourselves than from enemies without, although my life has been sought for many years by the civil and military authorities, priests and people of Missouri; and if I can escape from the ungrateful treachery of assassins, I can live as Caesar might have lived, were it not for a right-hand Brutus. I have had pretended friends betray me. All the enemies upon the face of the earth may roar and exert all their power to bring about my death, but they can accomplish nothing, unless some who are among us and enjoy our society, have been with us in our councils, participated in our confidence, taken us by the hand, called us brother, saluted us with a kiss, join with our enemies, turn our virtues into faults, and, by falsehood and deceit, stir up their wrath and indignation against us, and bring their united vengeance upon our heads."

Joseph later confesses, "The reason why I made the remarks I did [above] was on account of the reports brought from [the] Missouri jail by O. P. Rockwell, that my enemies were determined to get me into their power and take my life, and thereby thought they would accomplish the overthrow of 'Mormonism.' And to enable them to effect this, they had secured the services of some of my most confidential friends, whom I did not suspect, and who were living in Nauvoo, to deliver me into their hands . . ."[39] Rockwell was thus the first to warn Joseph of turncoats in their midst.

Immediately, William Law and William Marks, church leaders, made a public outcry that they had been singled out.[40] Astonished, Joseph confides, "What can be the matter with these men? Is it that the wicked flee when no man pursueth, that hit pigeons always flutter, that drowning men catch at straws, or that Presidents Law and Marks are absolutely traitors to the church, that my remarks should produce such an excitement in their minds. Can it be possible that the traitor whom Porter Rockwell reports to me as being in correspondence with my Missouri enemies, is one of my quorum?"[41]

With such concerns also in Porter's mind, Joseph nevertheless continued with new plans to expand the influence of the church: He announced he would run for the Presidency of the United States. Obviously as an educational maneuver, or as an opportunity to spread the name and mission of the church throughout the land, his chances at winning were infinitesimal at best. While Joseph concerned himself with this new mission, he learned of an assassination plot against him. Historian B. H. Roberts summarizes, "The Prophet was apprised by two young men, Dennison L. Harris and Robert Scott, the latter living in the family of William Law, of a secret movement then on foot to take his life, and the lives of several other leading men in the Church, among them the Prophet's brother, Hyrum. These young men were invited to the secret meetings by the conspirators, but before going conferred with the Prophet, who told them to go, but to take no part in the proceedings of these wicked men against himself. They carried out his instructions, and at the risk of their lives attended the secret meetings three times, and brought to President Smith a report of what they had witnessed."[42]

The conspirators included the Laws and four others.[43]

Porter would soon learn the actual blueprint of the conspiracy, but meanwhile guarded his friend with increasing intensity.

V

With Porter at his side and the scenario now in hand, Joseph launched a major battle upon the apostates. These enemies of the church would remember Porter for it, and he would pay. Presently, however, Joseph learned from informers that the conspirators were planning a major slander campaign against him. On March 24, 1844, Joseph publicly indicted C. L. Higbee as one of the enemy in their midst.

Robert D. Foster was arrested for gambling, and Joseph was finally able to bring a charge against him April 13 for slander and conspiring against his life.[1] Three other conspirators, William and Jane Law, and a brother, Wilson Law, were excommunicated.[2] Joseph then ordered the arrest of Augustine Spencer, and from this event alone came virtually a full-fledged war . . .

Spencer had assaulted his brother, Orson, and because of it, at 10 A.M. the same day, Marshal Greene had gone to arrest him. Spencer resisted arrest, so the marshal requested help from three nearby locals. The three happened to be Higbee and the two Foster brothers. "They swore they would not, and said they would see the mayor and the city d-d, and then they would not," reports the *Nauvoo Neighbor*.[3] So Marshal Greene grabbed Spencer and dragged him to Joseph's office single-handedly. Spencer's three friends followed.

Continuing the account, Joseph reports, "Charles Foster drew a pistol pointed towards me, and threatened to shoot while standing on the steps of my office. I ordered him to be arrested and the pistol taken from him when a struggle ensued."[4]

The marshal adds the weapon was "wrested from him [Foster]," and the three men "breathed out many hard threatenings" against Joseph.[5] The apostates were arrested and fined.

The case was appealed. Joseph quickly requested Robert Foster to drop his public denunciations. Foster rebelled, claiming Joseph was a false prophet, an adulterer, and that he had revived the Danites. Later Foster wished to publicly debate Joseph, but Joseph preferred they simply print a mutually agreeable statement of their positions in the *Nauvoo Neighbor.* Foster refused, and Joseph cursed him in the name of the Lord: "I have made the last overtures of peace to you and deliver you into the hands of God."

The court transferred the case to an alderman's court, and there Foster's case was dismissed.

While smoke billowed on the horizon, Joseph and Porter sought the escapism of, surprisingly enough, live theatre. Thomas A. Lyne came to Nauvoo from New York with the stage play, *Pizarro,* and the man chosen to play the part of Davilla was none other than Porter Rockwell. A church newspaper account several years later details, "This was the first play ever performed among the Latter-day Saints, and the brethren named sustained their parts at the request of the Prophet Joseph Smith, who attended every night the piece was performed."[6] No existing records report Porter's competency as an actor, but he probably performed the roll adequately, as he was asked to do so again years later.

The conspirators, meanwhile, began their own church with William Law as prophet.

On May 7, 1844, events in Porter's life began pouring like lava. The printing press for the *Nauvoo Expositor* arrived, and the conspirators began writing their first, soon-to-be released issue.[7] Simultaneously, William Law swore before a grand jury that Joseph was an adulterer. Law further claimed Joseph had illegally filed a complaint against another man.

The Carthage jury supported William Law.

Joseph H. Jackson and Robert Foster joined the accusations. Francis Higbee joined in but his testimony was dismissed for lacking credibility after a courtroom tirade against Joseph, claiming the Prophet had received stolen property.

When Joseph learned of the witnesses, he sent Porter to Carthage to declare them all liars. Porter mounted up and galloped off to Carthage, but by the time he arrived, the court had adjourned. So Porter returned to Nauvoo.

Still wishing to clear his name, Joseph decided to take Porter and several others to personally face the court at Carthage.

The court was in session when Joseph and his group arrived. Porter stood at Joseph's side as the Prophet faced the magistrate and demanded the court investigate the charges. The court informed them it would delay action on the case until the following term, so Joseph, Porter, and their associates returned to Nauvoo.

The following Sunday the Prophet unveiled his feelings about one of the conspirators: "Jackson has committed murder, robbery, and perjury, and I can prove it by half-a-dozen witnesses."[8] In 1890 historian Thomas Gregg summarizes: "If half of Jackson's statements were true, the prophet and some of his abettors should have been hung; if not true, Jackson himself should have been hung."[9]

Meanwhile, Porter proved unequivocally his loyalty to the Prophet. Joseph records in his journal, "While at Hamilton's [the tavern/hotel at Carthage where Joseph's group stayed during the court proceedings] Chauncey L. Higbee offered some insulting language concerning me to Orrin P. Rockwell, who resented it nobly as a friend ought to do. Hamilton [the owner], seeing it, turned Rockwell out of doors."[10] One can assume Porter punched the fellow's face.

Further evidence of Joseph's reliance upon Porter comes from Joseph's journal entries, which consistently indicate vast amounts of time spent together. On May 21, 1844, for example, Joseph writes, "A very pleasant morning. I rode out on horseback to the prairie, with Porter Rockwell . . . "[11] At times, of course, they separated: "June 1 . . . At one p.m., I rode out with Dr. Richards and Orrin P. Rockwell . . . Called on William Clayton's, while Dr. Richards and Orrin P. Rockwell called at the doctor's new house."[12]

Then came the first in a series of volcanic eruptions . . . the first edition of the *Nauvoo Expositor* hit the streets. The Prophet was, he felt, thoroughly slandered.

Three days later, June 10, Joseph made a decision that would rock western history to its bootstraps. In retaliation to the *Expositor* article he supported an ordinance outlawing libel.[13] As a self-proclaimed proponent of Constitutional privileges Joseph now declared he had weighed the balance between First Amendment rights and slander, and immediately called several witnesses to testify on the character of the *Expositor's* publishers. Porter was among those to issue a testimony: He claimed Foster had come to visit the Prophet at the Mansion House. Foster had asked Joseph to take a walk with him. Joseph refused, then discovered a gun beneath Foster's vest. Joseph put his finger on it and said, "What is that?"

Foster replied, "It's my pistol."

Porter said Foster "immediately took out the pistol, and showed it openly, and wanted the Mayor [Joseph] to go with him alone."[14] But Joseph would not leave the house with Foster.

Continuing with their deliberation George W. Harris records the turning point of the city council meeting: " . . . Councilor Taylor said no city on earth would bear such slander, and he would not bear it, and [was] decidedly in favor of active measures . . . He then read from the Constitution of the United States on the freedom of the press, and said, 'We are willing they should publish the truth; but it is unlawful to publish libels. The *Expositor* is a nuisance, and stinks in the nose of every honest man' . . ." (See Note 7 for additional details on this meeting.)

More statements were issued, and the City Council of Nauvoo officially resolved the matter with an order to Joseph to "cause said printing establishment and papers to be removed without delay."

What happened next set the stage for a war.

Nauvoo's marshal and posse rode to the *Expositor* office. There, Marshal Greene demanded the keys of the building.

Higbee refused.

Greene ordered the door forced open. The posse did so, then entered.[15] They broke up the press and pulled part of it into the street.

James Jackson, present at the scene, swore out an affidavit: "Most of the confusion ... was Higbee and his company throwing blackguard language to the posse, which they did not regard ... all was done in order. Higbee's blackguard language was not answered to at all by the ranks ... " Jackson also "heard some one damn the city authorities ... "[16]

Theodore Turley, also present, claims "that the order of the Marshal was executed quietly and peaceably. There was no riot or disturbance, no noise, no exultation; the Marshal endeavored to keep peace and silence, and the officers did also."[17] The posse was then marched back in front of the Mansion, and was dismissed.[18] Numerous others testified likewise. Only church enemies claimed Joseph personally rode to the press. The same enemies claim Joseph ordered Porter to "crash" the door down, and that Porter maniacally, single-handedly took on the press, gleefully smashing it to bits, and starting a riot.

In retaliation, the conspirators swarmed like hornets. They swore out complaints against city leaders, charging them with committing a riot. Both Porter and Joseph were listed as principals.

Joseph, of course, sought a habeas corpus hearing, in which the following was summarized:

"Court decided that Joseph Smith had acted under proper authority in destroying the establishment of the *Nauvoo Expositor* [and that the accusations of him leading a riot against the press] was a malicious prosecution on the part of Francis M. Higbee; and that said Higbee pay the costs of suit, and that Joseph Smith be honorably discharged from the accusations and of the writ, and go hence without delay."[19] (For more details of Porter's involvement in the press' destruction see Note 8.)

Losing to the Prophet was painful enough, but having to pay the court costs caused Higbee to broil. What happened next unravels like a bizarre adventure tale:

The conspirators ran to neighboring towns and blurted out their account. Infuriated by what they heard, crowds of Warsaw and Carthage citizens gathered for a mass meeting.

The *Warsaw Signal* immediately published their intentions: to "put an immediate stop to the career of the mad prophet and his demoniac coadjutors. We must not only defend ourselves from danger, but we must resolutely carry the War into the enemy's Camp . . . to exterminate, utterly exterminate, the wicked and abominable Mormon leaders, the authors of our troubles . . ."[20]

Blaming strangers for one's own problems was human nature, but Porter and Joseph were shocked by the proportions it soon took: They learned their enemies were not only stirring the Illinois populace to arms but that an entirely new offensive was about to be waged . . . on the legal battlefield.

The "legalists" sought Joseph's arrest. Although he had already been dismissed via the habeas corpus hearing, his own legal advisors invented a new strategy: Joseph would deliver himself to the court, submit himself to arrest, and be brought to trial before an objective, non-Mormon magistrate. The advice was intelligent. Joseph was cleared. And, although a free man again, the Prophet's problems were just beginning . . .

He received word[21] a lynch mob was gathering to move on Nauvoo. For protection he called out the Nauvoo Legion and issued an appeal to the neighboring public. In a *Nauvoo Neighbor Extra* he explained the Saints' position for destroying the *Expositor*.

Meanwhile, the conspirators moved on him from within and without. Joseph learned "that William and Wilson Law have laid a plan to burn the printing office of the *Nauvoo Neighbor* this night." In response, Joseph published: "I therefore stationed a strong police round the premises and throughout the city."[22]

Though thwarted once again — this time by Joseph's police — the earth beneath the conspirators' feet had not yet begun to rumble. They designed a letter which implicated Joseph in plans to kill Foster, and released the letter to the public to enrage them even further.

And it succeeded.

The next day Joseph proclaimed the city under martial law. In his journal he states: "About 2 p.m. the Legion was drawn up in the street close by the Mansion. I stood in full uniform on the top of the frame of a building."[23] From there he presented an emotional appeal to the Legionnaires — and it had a stunning impact. George A. Smith records the speech:

"I call God, angels and all men to witness that we are innocent of the charges which are heralded forth through the public prints against us by our enemies; and while they assemble together in unlawful mobs to take away our rights and destroy our lives, they think to shield themselves under the refuge of lies which they have thus wickedly fabricated."

He continued for ninety minutes, and at one point declared, "Will you all stand by me to the death, and sustain at the peril of your lives, the laws of our country, and the liberties and privileges which our fathers have transmitted unto us, sealed with their sacred blood?"

The crowd reported with a loud, "Aye!"

Drawing his sword and presenting it to the heavens, he declared, "I call God and angels to witness that I have unsheathed my sword with a firm and unalterable determination that this people shall have their legal rights, and be protected from mob violence, or my blood shall be spilt upon the ground like water, and my body consigned to the silent tomb ... "

His words were prophetic, particularly in light of what he then declared: "I call upon all friends of truth and liberty to come to our assistance; and by the thunders of the Almighty and the forked lightenings of heaven and pestilence ... war and bloodshed [shall] come down on those ungodly men who seek to destroy my life and the lives of this innocent people."[24]

(Details of this prophecy, the Saints point out, were made 12 years earlier.[25] In that declaration he stated, "Verily thus saith the Lord corcerning the wars that will shortly come to pass, beginning at the rebellion of South Carolina, which will eventually terminate in the death and misery of many souls; ... For behold, the Southern States shall be divided against the Northern States, and the Southern States will call on other nations, even the nation of Great Britain ... That the cry of the saints, and of the blood of the saints, shall cease to come up into the ears of the Lord of Sabaoth, from the earth, to be avenged of their enemies." The prophecy was recorded December 25, 1836[26], twenty-five years before the Civil War.)

Another notable prophecy regards Steven A. Douglas, front-runner in the presidential campaign of 1860 against Abraham Lincoln. Eighteen years before the campaign Douglas dined with Joseph, who prophesied, "Judge, you will aspire to the Presidency of the United States; and if ever you turn your hand against me or the Latter-day Saints, you will feel the weight of the hand of the Almighty upon you; and you will live to see and know that I have testified the truth to you; for the conversation of this day will stick to you through life."[27] Douglas did indeed turn against the Saints 14 years later,[28] and surprisingly he lost the presidential bid by a landslide, receiving all of one electoral vote. (He had earlier defeated Lincoln handily in a state election.) Oliver Boardman Huntington collected a three-piece suit from a bet on the election. "I have watched Joseph Smith's prophecies and never seen one fail," reported Huntington after the election to an astonished group of miners.[29]

Meanwhile, events snowballed in Illinois: In farms surrounding Nauvoo, mobbers threatened to kill the Saints unless they would turn against Joseph. Allen T. Wait reports a mob leader warned him, "... If the people would not give Smith up, they [the mobbers] would lay the whole city in ashes ..."[30]

One local citizen, James Guyman, claims he heard if the governor ordered his militia to stop the mobbers, "they would take the governor's head from his shoulders ..."[31]

Non-Mormon Guyman then said he asked the mob captain "if it was law to go and drive those innocent Mormons who were living in the neighborhood, or tyrannically compel them to do things not agreeable to their will?" The captain replied that "in this case it was."

Guyman asked the captain what he was going to do with the old settlers who would not fight against the Mormons. The captain replied, "They must fight either for one side or the other, or they must share the same fate as the Mormons."[32]

The threats turned to abuse as rural Saints were forced from their farms during a storm.[33] As these Saints gathered to Nauvoo, the mobs developed into a virtual army. An additional force of possibly 2,000 armed recruits[34] soon came with cannon from Missouri.[35]

By contrast Joseph, armed only with affidavits, sent a delegation to the governor at Springfield.

On the morning of June 21, 1844, as Joseph reviewed his Legionnaires on Main Street, two men rode up and handed Joseph a letter. It was signed by Governor Ford, who was now in Carthage. Ford had missed Joseph's peace delegation at Springfield, and now requested Mormon representatives to come to Carthage to declare their side of the story.[36]

Joseph fired off a letter and other affidavits within two hours. His delegation was still across the state but he felt "substitute" papers sent to Ford would suffice for now, until the delegaton could reach Ford the next day.

But the next day Almon W. Babbitt, Joseph's assistant, arrived from Carthage and advised Joseph not to send the delegation to the governor . . . Mobocrats were threatening death on sight to any Mormon approaching the city.

Joseph then received perhaps the most eventful letter of his life. At 10 P. M. on June 22nd, he opened the letter and read Ford's handwriting: it was a warrant for Joseph's arrest. The mobs had finally, fully swayed the chief executive.

In the letter Ford explained his primary concern: the *Expositor's* destruction. "In no other state, county, city, town or territory in the United States has ever such a thing been thought of before. Such an act at this day would not be tolerated even in England. Just such another act in 1830 hurled the king of France from his throne, and caused the imprisonment of four of his principal ministers for life. No civilized country can tolerate such conduct, much less can it be tolerated in this free country of the United States . . . "

Joseph was frustrated. He had more of the story to tell but from Babbitt's advice still feared to send his delegation — much less to meet with the governor himself.

And Ford's mind seemed set. Nevertheless, Joseph sat down to compile his most significant letter to date, addressed to Governor Ford:

"You have intimated that no press has been abated as a nuisance in the United States. We refer your Excellency to Humphrey versus Press in Ohio, who abated the press by his own arm for libel, and the courts [upheld him] . . . And we do know that it is common for police in Boston, New York, etc., to destroy scurrilous prints: and we think the loss of character by libel and the loss of life by mobocratic prints to be a greater loss than a little property, all of which, life alone excepted, we have sustained . . . The press was declared a nuisance under the authority of the charter as written in 7th section of Addenda, the same as in the Springfield [state] charter, so that if the act declaring the press a nuisance was unconstitutional, we cannot see how it is that the charter itself is not unconstitutional: and if we have erred in judgement, it is an official act, and belongs to the Supreme Court to correct it." (See Note 9 for more details of Ford's assertions and Joseph's defense.)

And then in his boldest measure yet, Joseph simply refused the governor's arrest:

"Sir, we dare not come, for our lives would be in danger, and we are guilty of no crime."[37]

VI

Joseph sent his letter with yet a third delegation. When the governor received it he had it read aloud.

John Taylor, present at the scene, claims the reading of Joseph's letter was shouted down by Ford's aides.[1] Nevertheless, Joseph's delegation argued forcefully in the Prophet's behalf. (See Note 10 for details.) After hearing their case, Ford gave his decision — one which surprised the Mormons:

"The people should be satisfied."

Joseph's delegation rode back to Nauvoo with heads bowed and a letter for the Prophet. After reviewing the letter, Joseph called a special consultation with other church leaders. One of those present in this milestone meeting, Abraham C. Hodge, records Joseph's reaction to the letter:

" 'Brethren, here is a letter from the Governor which I wish to have read.'

"After it was read through Joseph remarked, 'There is no mercy — no mercy here.'

"Hyrum said, 'No; just as sure as we fall into their hands we are dead men.'

"Joseph replied, 'Yes; what shall we do, Brother Hyrum?'

"He replied, 'I don't know.'

"All at once Joseph's countenance brightened up and he said, 'The way is open. It is clear to my mind what to do. All they want is Hyrum and myself; then tell everybody to go about their business, and not to collect in groups, but to scatter about. There is no doubt they will come here and search for us. Let them search; they will not harm you in person or property, and not even a hair of your head. We will cross the river tonight, and go away in the West.' "[2]

Joseph then records the final journal entry of his life — and in it he mentions Porter: "At sundown I asked O. P. Rockwell if he would go with me a short journey, and he replied he would. I told Stephen Markham that if I and Hyrum were ever taken again we should be massacred, or I was not a prophet of God."[3] Joseph concluded the entry with a comment about Hyrum — to the effect that his brother was determined not to leave him.

Joseph then visited his wife and children. Dispirited at the prospect of leaving, he knew this would be their longest parting yet. Emerging from his house he was seen visibly crying. "He held a handkerchief to his face," reports George A. Smith, "and followed after Brother Hyrum without uttering a word."[4]

They made their way to the river and waited an hour for a boat to take them across. Others of Joseph's closest associates, Willard Richards and William W. Phelps, soon joined Joseph and Hyrum. After consulting with them, Joseph sent Phelps back to all their families with a message: the families would be taken to Cincinnati.

At midnight the three church leaders left the river shore and visited Porter at his lodgings. Porter agreed to help them. With sleep in his eyes he emerged from his cabin and snuck with them back to the river at 2 A.M.

He rowed them across the Mississippi River in a leaky boat belonging to Aaron Johnson. George A. Smith records, " . . . it kept Joseph, Hyrum and the doctor busy baling out the water with their boots and shoes to prevent it from sinking."[5]

Finally, at dawn they arrived on the Iowa side of the river. Despite Porter's exhaustion Joseph asked him to return immediately to Nauvoo and return the next night with horses. His assignment would include crossing the river "in the night secretly, and be ready to start for the Great Basin in the Rocky Mountains."[6] Porter agreed without a moment's hesitation.

Later that morning a posse arrived in Nauvoo to arrest Joseph ... but the Prophet had disappeared.

When Rockwell arrived in Nauvoo he went directly to Emma. All she desired of Porter was Joseph's return. To effect this she insisted Reynolds Cahoon accompany Porter across the river to persuade Joseph to return.

Porter crossed the river again, taking Cahoon and two others. After his party arrived on the Iowa shore, Porter searched for and found Joseph, Hyrum, and Willard in a cabin. Wandle Mace records in his journal: " ... O. P. Rockwell ... said [to me, later], 'Cahoon brought a letter to Joseph from his wife, he [Joseph] opened and read the letter then handed it to his brother Hyrum [and] said, "I know my own business." ' "

Cahoon then replied to Joseph, "You always said if the church would stick to you, you would stick to the church, now trouble comes [and] you are the first to run!"

Mace adds, "Joseph made him no reply. He would not talk to him."[7]

Cahoon next told Joseph if the Saints were to follow him West, "their property would be destroyed, and they left without house or home. Like the fable, when the wolves came the shepherd ran from the flock, and left the sheep to be devoured."

To which Joseph replied, "If my life is of no value to my friends it is of none to myself."[8] Joseph then turned to Porter and asked, "What shall I do?"

Porter replied, "You are the oldest and ought to know best." Porter obviously looked upon him as not only his Prophet but as his older brother, as he had since childhood, and their roles were still intact. Porter pledged his support to stay with Joseph, whatever the decision.

Hyrum was the eldest. In need of his brother's advice, Joseph turned to him and asked the same question: "What shall we do?"

Hyrum replied, "The Lord is in it. If we live or have to die, we will be reconciled to our fate." Hyrum then suggested they return. In his journal Wandle Mace says Porter told him, "Hyrum read the letter [of Emma's] and thought 'we had better go back and if we die, we will die like men.' "[9]

After a pause, Joseph told Cahoon to prepare the boat.

While walking towards the river, Joseph fell behind with Porter and spoke with him privately. The others urged the Prophet to hurry, but he reminded them there was no reason. He then confided his wish for Porter to gather the Saints so he could speak that evening.

Porter said he would obey his wish, and would await Joseph's word.[10]

But it never came. When they crossed the river, Joseph walked hesitantly to the Mansion House. On the porch his family came out and surrounded him; he looked them over carefully, then went inside with them and stayed the night. He abandoned the idea of preaching to the Saints by starlight.

The next morning Joseph's posse arrived to escort him to Carthage. He emerged from the house and mounted his horse. As they began riding downstreet, Porter rode up; Joseph allowed his companionship only a few minutes, then gave Porter a final order: he discerned Rockwell's volatile nature, and sent him across town to a visiting businessman. Porter rode away as instructed.

As Joseph passed the Temple he paused. A witness wrote that he gazed "with admiration first on that, and then on the city, and remarked, 'This is the loveliest place and the best people under the heavens. Little do they know what trials await them.' " They continued riding towards Carthage.

Four miles from Carthage Joseph's entourage was met by 60 Illinois militia. Captain Dunn ordered Joseph to halt and surrender arms, then requested him to return to Nauvoo and aid the militia in disarming all the Nauvoo Legion. At this Joseph inquired if he were under arrest. "No" was the reply, but then Joseph muttered his immortal phrase, "I am going like a lamb to the slaughter, but I am calm as a summer's morning. I have a conscience void of offense toward God and toward all men."[11]

Joseph returned with the militia to Nauvoo, and within four hours the arms were collected. He made two additional visits with his family — both short — and on the final visit he could not seem to tear himself away. Just after 6 P.M., the Illinois militia knocked at his door; Joseph bid farewell to his wife and children, then trudged out to his horse and slowly mounted it. Riding towards Carthage the militia trotted beside him. One witness states, "When they passed his farm he took a good look at it, and after they had passed it, he turned round several times to look again."[12] Another says he appeared "solemn and thoughtful."[13] Townspeople watched as Joseph rode away, and he soon disappeared down the road to Carthage.

Just before midnight he arrived at Carthage. While passing the public square, the Carthage Greys saw him arriving with Captain Dunn's militia. One audible voice was heard and recorded amidst the cacaphony: "Clear the way and let us have a view of Joe Smith, the prophet of God."[14]

Joseph and party arrived at Hamilton's tavern. Ironically, the Laws, Higbees, and Fosters were quartered in the same building, and spent the night. The next morning Joseph surrendered himself to the constable.

He was now officially arrested.

The Illinois State militia exulted. Ford then spoke to the troops formed in the public square,[15] and afterwards, he entered Joseph's room and invited him "to walk with him through the troops." Joseph "solicited a few moments' private conversation with him, which the Governor refused."[16] Joseph was paraded through the troops. Afterwards, he found himself alone again with the governor and finally persuaded Ford to converse with him.

After a ten minute conference, Ford "pledged the faith of the state that he and his friends should be protected from violence."[17]

Rockwell in Nauvoo, meanwhile, happened to run across Francis Higbee. Porter accused him of plotting against Joseph's life, and Higbee swore at him. The two men went at each others' throats and found themselves in a bloody brawl.[18] From what happened next, Porter's greatest benefit to the Saints thus far occurred: Porter fisted Higbee again, and Higbee dropped a letter from his hat. He retreated from Porter's blows, and left the letter lying in the dust.

Not able to read, Porter took the letter to another Saint, who, upon deciphering it, discovered that a mob of 70 Illinoisians were planning to attack Nauvoo that very evening — and were in fact now in Iowa awaiting the signal.

Porter raced through town like Paul Revere to warn the Saints, and soon they rushed to the outskirts of Nauvoo to form lines of defense.

The Illinoisians marched forward, preparing to attack the city . . . and were taken by surprise. Upon approaching they saw the Mormons waiting for them — and they cancelled the attack.

In a revealing display of his heart's fondest friendship, Joseph, in his room at Carthage, now wrote only two people: his wife Emma, and Porter Rockwell. Joseph counseled Porter to not come to Carthage, "but to stay in Nauvoo, and not to suffer himself to be delivered into the hands of his enemies, or to be taken a prisoner by anyone."[19]

Upon finishing his letters, Joseph was visited by several militia officers "curious to see the Prophet."[20] Joseph asked them if there were anything in his appearance indicating he was the rogue they had expected.

The purported reply was, "No, sir, your appearance would indicate the very contrary, General Smith; but we cannot see what is in your heart, neither can we tell what are your intentions."[21]

Joseph snapped back, "Very true, gentlemen, you cannot see what is in my heart, and you are therefore unable to judge me or my intentions; but I can see what is in your hearts, and will tell you what I see. I can see that you thirst for blood . . . inasmuch as you and the people thirst for blood, I prophesy, in the name of the Lord, that you shall witness scenes of blood and sorrow to your entire satisfaction. Your souls shall be perfectly satiated with blood, and many of you who are now present shall have an opportunity to face the cannon's mouth from sources you think not of; and those people that desire this great evil upon me and my brethren, shall be filled with regret and sorrow because of the scenes of desolation and distress that await them. They shall seek for peace, and shall not be able to find it. Gentlemen, you will find what I have told you to be true."[22] Again, a reference to the Civil War, now 17 years away, sounded mysterious to the locals.

They left, and Joseph received another report about the apostates: the Laws, Fosters, and Higbees were now publicly preaching that although Joseph and Hyrum could probably not be reached by the law, "they should not go out of Carthage alive."[23]

Finally, Joseph's party was called to appear before a judge. There, 17 Mormon leaders were released on bail, all except Joseph and Hyrum. And then the only magistrate who could grant subpoenas for witnesses suddenly disappeared. The man apparently desired to prevent Joseph's witnesses from appearing.[24] Joseph was then told he would be imprisoned. The Saints pointed out the action was illegal, as he was not allowed an examination before a justice of the peace . . . nevertheless, he was told he would be taken to the jail — *if* he could reach the building safely.

Taylor reports, "At the same time, a great rabble was gathered in the streets and around the door, and from the rowdyism manifested, I was afraid there was a design to murder the prisoners on the way to the jail." As the two Smith brothers were anxious to get away safely, Taylor persuaded one of the guards to recruit other guards for an armed escort.

As they passed through the mob, two of the prisoners whacked several drunks. "Markham had a very large hickory cane, which he called 'the rascal-beater,' " reports Taylor. "Dan Jones had a smaller walking-stick, and they walked on either side of Joseph and Hyrum, beating off the drunken rabble, who several times broke through the ranks."[25]

Joseph's party finally made it safely to their cells.

A Nauvoo Legionnaire, Allen Joseph Stout, records a mysterious betrayal: " . . . while they were in jail Brother Joseph wrote an official order to Jonathon Dunham to bring the Legion and reserve him from being killed, but Dunham did not let a single man or mortal know that he had received such orders, and we were kept in the city [Nauvoo] under arms knowing but all was well [at Carthage] . . . "[26]

T. B. H. Stenhouse adds in 1904: " . . . This military commander [Dunham] put the Prophet's communication into his pocket and gave no heed to the call for help. No one was acquainted with the contents of the paper, and the officer was, therefore, he presumed, safe in disregarding [it].

"After the Prophet's death, by some accident or other, this communication was lost and was picked up on the street and read. The intelligence that Joseph had called for aid and none had been rendered him was soon bruited among the Saints, and excited their deepest indignation, as they were not only ready to march at a moment's notice, but were eager for the opportunity."[27]

Meanwhile, Joseph and Hyrum implored Governor Ford's aid.

As a former associate-justice of the State Supreme Court, Ford knew the illegalities of the proceedings, but still refused to intervene.

So the two prisoners appealed to the local magistrate, Captain Smith.

Captain Smith asked for advice from Ford.

The governor's only answer was, "You have the Carthage Greys at your command." (See details in Note 11.)

The next morning the jailor informed Joseph the mob had planned an attack on Nauvoo the night before with an expected turnout of 9,000 Illinoisians. But only 200 had showed.

The remainder of the morning was spent by Dan Jones and Stephen Markham "in hewing with a pen knife a warped door to get it on the latch, thus preparing to fortify the place against any attack."[29]

Joseph's group took turns preaching to the guards, several of whom left their posts early, according to historian George A. Smith (in his writings of 1854-1875), "because they admitted they were convinced of the innocence of the prisoners."[30]

Later, Richards wrote dictations by the Prophet, and Taylor sang. Joseph then related a dream about William and Wilson Law, and of a spiritual concern he had for them, but, to him, saving them was — like the dream — "trying to save a steamboat in a storm."[31]

The prosecution sought to lure Joseph away from jail, but Joseph suspected their motives and refused to leave the cell. He waited patiently for his promised, escorted journey with the governor back to Nauvoo.

A final move was made by mob leaders to move Joseph away from the safety of the jail, but the jailor refused, protecting Joseph by risking his own life.

Joseph then saw the mob foaming outside, and he feared they would stampede the cell. He knew he had to get to the courtroom.

Then he thought of a plan. He brisked outside into their midst, "politely locked arms with the worst mobocrat he could see, and Hyrum locked arms with Joseph."[32] Thus they strode through the street to the courtroom in relative safety.

At the court Joseph's lawyers called for witnesses, but since they would have to be brought from Nauvoo, the court was again adjourned. (See Note 12 for Joseph's reaction.)

Back to the cell they were again escorted. That night, despite an ominous tension in the air, they finally fell asleep.

Suddenly a gunshot awoke them. No more movement was heard, and they fell back to sleep. While drifting off, Joseph confided to his fellows a desire to see Emma again and to speak to the Saints.

Next morning, June 27, 1844, Joseph arose at 5:30 and asked Dan Jones to inquire about the gunshot the night before.

Jones left to investigate, and soon learned of additional threats to kill Joseph. Armed with evidence he rushed to the governor, but Ford dismissed the threats. (See Note 13 for details.)

When Cyrus H. Wheelock, one of Joseph's friends, learned of the plan, he protested boldly to Ford. He reports what the governor confided: "I was never in such a dilemma in my life." After his candid confession, Ford then made an unexpectedly curious decision: he would go to Nauvoo, leaving Joseph in jail.

Additionally, he would take Joseph's only true protecting force, the Illinois State militia under Captain Dunn, leaving the Prophet under protection of the Carthage Greys, the Mormon's worst enemies.

When Cyrus Wheelock left Ford he visited his friend Joseph in jail, sneaking through a pistol in his sidecoat.

Joseph ordered Wheelock back to Nauvoo to keep the Legion from retaliating, and "to use all the influence he possessed to have the brethren and friends . . . remain perfectly calm and quiet."[33]

When Ford left for Nauvoo, Joseph felt, obviously, he had been betrayed.

The *Randolph* (Co., Illinois) *Record* reports,"the Mormons had done every thing required of them by the existing laws of the State."[34]

Although his associates were giving up, Joseph was not finished fighting. He wrote a letter to another attorney, O H. Browning, requesting legal services, and he handed it to Dan Jones for delivery.

When Jones came outside with the letter, a guard shouted to the mob that the letter was destined to the Nauvoo Legion ordering a rescue. The mob charged him, but Jones outran them.

All his escape managed, however, was to galvanize the mob.[35] They wanted to kill Joseph "before the Mormon army would arrive," not knowing that the letter was merely meant for a lawyer. Whether Joseph had actually expected the Legion to arrive is speculative, and rests primarily on the above related (p. 103), somewhat questionable sources, which were based probably on rumor.

In jail Willard Richards took ill. Joseph sent Stephen Markham out for medicine, but when Markham returned, the mob forced him out of town at the point of bayonet.[36]

In the depths of gloom, Joseph sat in his cell. He spoke to the guard about the Nauvoo conspirators and the trumped-up charges. Andrew Jenson reports, "In the afternoon Elder John Taylor sang the hymn, 'A poor wayfaring man of grief,' etc., which pleased Joseph so much that he requested him to sing it again, which he did. Hyrum afterwards read extracts from *Josephus*.

"At 4 o'clock the guard was again changed, only eight men being stationed at the jail, while the main body of the Carthage Greys were in camp about a quarter of a mile distant on the public square.

" . . . As the guard turned to go out, somebody called him two or three times, and he went down.

"Immediately there was a little rustling at the outer door of the jail, and a cry of 'Surrender,' and instantly the discharge of four or five firearms followed. As Doctor Richards glanced an eye by the curtain of the window he saw about one hundred armed men around the door."[37]

The mob had arrived.

The guards fired their guns in mock resistance — and the mob stormed the building.[38] One anonymous member of the mob reports he saw "six flashes streaming toward the crowd, but nobody fell . . . .Most of them [the guards] were easy to handle; but one, who did not know that ball cartridges had been replaced with blanks in their guns . . . thought he had fired to kill, and was all in earnest throughout . . . [and, in fighting the mobbers who grabbed him,] made it rough for those who held him."[39] Thus, one of the guards actually proved a desire to protect the Prophet and take on the mob — a fact often ignored by Mormon historians.

Inside the cell, hearing the outside noises, Joseph sprang to his coat for a revolver, Hyrum for his single barrel, John Taylor for a hickory cane, and Willard Richards for his cane. "All sprang against the door, the balls whistled up the stairway, and in an instant one came through the door."[40] Taylor and Richards attempted knocking away the gun barrels shoved through the door, when Hyrum was shot in the face, the breast, side, and leg. After embracing Hyrum, Joseph exclaimed, "Oh my dear brother Hyrum." He jumped to the door and fired his revolver into the opening.

Taylor attempted jumping from the window, but he was shot back into the room. He rolled under the bed, nursing his wounds, when the mob aimed at him from the doorway and sent another flurry of shots into him. One passed through his body and smashed his watch, stopping the time at 5:16. "Large quantities of blood were scattered around the wall and floor," records Andrew Jenson.[41]

Willard Richards stood in the cell throughout, unscathed, fulfilling another of Joseph's prophecies from a year earlier: "the time would come that the balls would fly around him like hail, and he should see his friends fall on the right and on the left, but that there should not be a hole in his garment."[42]

"Joseph," continues Jenson, "seeing there was no safety in the room, turned calmly from the door, dropped his pistol on the floor and sprang into the same window from which Elder Taylor had attempted to leap, when two balls pierced him from the door, and one entered his right breast from without, and he fell outward, exclaiming, 'O Lord, my God!' "[43]

Richards records, "As his [Joseph's] feet went out of the window my head went in [from looking outside], the balls whistling all around. He fell on his left side a dead man."[44]

Lying two stories below the cell window, under overcast skies, Joseph lay still.

The mob gathered around him. One mobber reports, "It seems

to me — twenty rods distant, but in full sight — that he for a moment partly raised himself to a sitting posture against a well-curb beside which he fell."[45] At least two others claim that in the quiet, late afternoon stillness, a barefoot man made his way through the crowd with a sword, and walked up to Joseph. He raised his sword high, ready to decapitate him. Suddenly the sun burst through the clouds, onto the dead Prophet,[46] startling the man to the point of dropping his sword.

The mob stared in awe.

Two witnesses at the scene claim to have seen the small miracle; one of them, William Daniels, adds, "They all stood like marble statues not having the power to move a single limb of their bodies. By this time most of the men had fled in great disorder. I never saw so frightened a set of men before . . . This light, in its appearance and potency, baffles all powers of description."[47]

Daniels had his account published by John Taylor, who must have given credence to Daniels' version, but official church historian B. H. Roberts in 1930 discounts the report. Nevertheless, Littlefield published a letter from one William Webb in his book, *The Martyrs,* corroborating Daniels' story.[48] Webb claims to be the man who attempted to decapitate the Prophet when the pillar of light burst upon him.[49] Andrew Jenson also supports Daniels' account.

Another man named Brackenbury also claimed to have seen the miracle,[50] according to the *Atlantic Monthly* in 1869.

Meanwhile, in Nauvoo Porter witnessed the following scene: he returned to the Mansion House to retrieve a hat he'd left at an earlier conference when suddenly he walked in on Governor Ford holding a secret meeting. An Illinoisian was speaking to the governor's party: "The deed is done before this time." Suddenly they all caught sight of Porter and stopped their conversation cold. Porter did not know the meaning of the words, and simply picked up his hat and left.[51]

Presently, Ford left the Mansion House and began addressing the Saints at Nauvoo: "The city may be reduced to ashes, and extermination would inevitably follow. And it gives me great pain to think that there is danger of so many innocent women and children being exterminated. If anything of a serious character should befall the lives or property of the persons who are prosecuting your leaders, you will be held responsible."[52]

Ford then left Nauvoo, and while barely out of town received confirmation of Joseph's death.

The governor and his party immediately galloped to Carthage. There, they gathered all the inhabitants at the public square and advised them to leave town. Ford expected the Mormons would be fired with vengeance and soon be laying the torch to Carthage. Upon hearing this, the citizens of Carthage fled in all directions.[53]

Porter, meanwhile, headed for Carthage to visit Joseph. Gilbert Belnap joined him and the two men crossed paths with one George D. Grant.

Grant was being chased from Carthage by mounted horsemen, and as he stormed past Porter he blurted out the news of Joseph's death. Rockwell and Belnap dismounted and took cover. The mob, still charging full gallop, opened fire. The two Mormons returned the gunfire, and one by one Porter picked off the horsemen. The remaining mobocrats, seeing Porter's shocking accuracy, pivoted back in retreat.

Rockwell and Belnap re-mounted their horses and galloped full speed to Nauvoo. Anson Call journals, "On Thursday night I was one of the Temple guard. On Friday morning I met O. P. Rockwell coming with his horse upon the run through the City hallaing Joseph is killed! Joseph is Killed! They have killed him. They have killed him. God damn them, they have killed him."[54]

Porter's only childhood friend, his companion and prophet, was dead.

Wandle Mace records in his journal: " . . . the news did not reach us until early morning, we learned that Joseph and Hyrum was dead . . . The sad news spread from mouth to mouth instantaneously, almost paralyzing every one . . .

"Who can describe the scene, What pen, the sorrow and mourning manifested by all. Strong men wept like children, women moaned and they gathered their little children around . . . Who can describe this anguish . . . ?"[55]

Although they were crushed, the Mormons did not, as expected, retaliate. As instructed by Willard Richards they stayed home, and the next morning Richards brought to town the bodies of Joseph and Hyrum.

A throng of 10,000 crowded the roads and stared at the bodies in horror; among them, doubtless, was Porter.

The leaderless Saints were now in a quandary. The church's governing Twelve Apostles were all out of state, most on foreign missions, and the only surviving First Presidency member, Sidney Rigdon, was in Pittsburgh. Richards and Taylor rose to the task of maintaining the peace. Then, one by one, the Twelve Apostles returned.

Rigdon arrived before all the quorum had a chance to meet, however, and attempted a coup to take over leadership. Though Joseph had tried to "shake him off my shoulders," the general church membership had continued sustaining Rigdon as Joseph's counselor, and now because of it the future of the church was at stake. Rigdon made his case before the entire Nauvoo congregation, several thousand strong, bidding his final move.

But then Brigham Young came on the scene. On August 6, 1844, he returned to the city, and two days afterwards delivered a most unusual sermon to the Saints. From this meeting a number present, among whom was Anson Call, observed: "Before he had spoken many sentences I discovered that it was the voice of Joseph and had I have been where my eyes could not have beheld him I should have believed that Joseph had been speaking. It was Joseph's voice and Joseph's gestures through the entire discourse."[56] Witnesses even claimed Brigham took on the facial appearance of Joseph. "The whole assembly heard, as they thought, the voice, saw the form and felt the spirit and influence of the Prophet Joseph. And even non-members of the Church were startled, and expected to see the presence as well as hear the voice of the departed Seer," reports Andrew Jenson.[57] The apparent miracle was enough for the leaderless Saints: The Lord was endowing the "mantle of Joseph" on Brigham Young.[58] (See Note 14 for George Q. Cannon's description of the scene.)

But reports soon reached the Saints of yet another plan against them: "Wolf-hunts" were in the making, mob parties to burn them out.

Brigham reacted by calling the Nauvoo Legion for drills.

Reports of his action were trumpeted and twisted, and rumors reached neighboring counties. Since the locals already feared a reaction to Joseph's death, they were especially afraid of "The Lion of God" now in command of the Saints.

Anti-Mormons recruited militiamen from surrounding counties, even Missouri and Iowa, and word passed through ranks that Brigham-the-Lion was raising a formidable army. The only chance the Illinoisians had, they were told, was to attack the Mormons before the Mormons attacked them.

Plans were soon under way for a full-scale war on the Saints. Anti-Mormon forces gathered and waited the signal.

But then a sympathizer to the Saints stepped in: Brigadier General J. J. Hardin recruited 500 armed non-Mormon allies, and just as the mobbers were ready to attack, Hardin's army drove them off.

Leaders of the anti-Mormons fled to Missouri,[59] where, in reaction, they would formulate yet another plan of destruction . . . this one more subtle . . . via that double-edged organ . . . the press.

Their scapegoat, interestingly enough, would be not so much The Lion, but The Exterminator ... the Mad Demon ... the Royal Executioner ... the Destroying Angel: Porter Rockwell!

The local papers had "informants" from Nauvoo, and they seemed anxious to print most anything handed them. The *Sangamo Journal,* for example, published in October, 1844 a fascinating little incident; whether true or not is another matter: "O. P. Rockwell and a Mr. Kimball had a regular set to, at 'fisticuffs.' Rockwell got his shirt torn off, but he whipped Kimball, and gave him a regular chase through the streets. The Mormons are very much afraid of Rockwell and his overbearing spirit is making him exceedingly troublesome to them."[60]

In the following months, Porter became the subject of almost every newspaper article imaginable. The *Burlington Hawkeye* and

Iowa Patriot claimed Porter was a burglar,[61] while the *Warsaw Signal,* the *Alton Telegraph,* and the *Quincy Whig* claimed he was far worse, as they escalated their attacks on the Saints in general and Porter in particular.

Thievery had become an important topic in recent months, as Brigham felt non-Mormons were invading the territory and increasing the crime rate. Many low-lifes felt they could get away with —literally — murder, while church members would be blamed by the outside press. Indeed, small groups of Mormons formed to retaliate against the Gentiles by robbing them, but church leaders quickly called a halt to the measures, and in stern fashion came down with harsh disciplinary action of excommunication and disfellowship. Yet the work of robbing and murdering by infiltrating outsiders continued, and neighboring communities blamed the Saints. Brigham saw a wave of outside mob spiritism foaming higher, and reacted by calling a police force of 500[62] to squash the thieving and to prevent street murders. He also sent out 50 delegates to neighboring communities "to prevent stealing and secure peace."[63] (See Note 15 for details on Mormon reaction to thievery in Nauvoo, and exploitation by church enemies.)

But the State of Illinois feared Brigham's call for 500 police, and they rescinded the city charter. No longer could the Nauvoo Municipal Court issue writs of habeas corpus. No longer were church leaders immune from legal warrants of neighboring sheriffs.

So Brigham countered their move: he called these church leaders on missions. Ironically, he knew this resistance would play directly into enemies' hands, as he so confessed in his journal: "the policy of commencing a mob persecution has always been to get out vexatious writs [against the Saints] in order to provoke resistance [on the part of the Saints] to the form of legal authority and thereby produce a collision between us and the state."[64] He found himself in a no-win situation, and chose the immediate advantage of sending away those in danger.

As expected, this enraged the local populace even further.

Meanwhile, a court considered prosecuting Joseph's murderers, until two months later when they were released.[65]

While church members bemoaned their treatment at the hands

of the law, their enemies remounted an entirely new offensive: they ceased issuing warrants which Brigham could screen, and began arresting Saints openly.

Brigham records June 23rd, "The sheriff came in with writs for a number of brethren and succeeded in arresting O. P. Rockwell and J. P. Harmon, but Rockwell got away from him."[66]

Porter's escape made the Illinoisians angrier than hornets. For the next few weeks he secreted himself about Nauvoo, yet participated in Brigham's Council decisions. As a member of the church's Council of Fifty — an organization of Elders and non-Mormon allies to recommend policy to church leaders — Porter tried to help determine their next course of action.

But then another explosive series of events was launched . . .

At Green Plains, Illinois, an anti-Mormon meeting was disrupted by gunshots fired into the group. No one was hit, but Brigham's reaction to the episode surprised his enemies: Brigham claimed the affair had been staged by anti-Mormon strategists — *agent provocateurs,* as it were — in an attempt to further provoke the Illinoisians against the Saints.

But his excuse failed to convince the mobs. The thundering earth now cracked open with fire, and Latter-day Saint communities in Lima, Morley, and Yelrome, Illinois, were reduced to ashes: anti-Mormon militia leader Levi Williams galloped his army through the countryside, leading night-riding locals with painted faces, burning everything Mormon-owned in sight.

Sheriff Backenstos from Carthage went to Warsaw and attempted to raise a posse to stop the burning, but he failed — the citizens simply refused to support him.

"Forty-four buildings have been burned by the mob," notes Brigham.[67]

As the lava poured, the mob spirit turned on even their own law enforcement officials.[68] After failing to raise a posse, Sheriff Backenstos rode to Nauvoo. He "arrived in great haste and somewhat excited, [and] said that the mob had driven him from his house in Carthage yesterday, and he went to Warsaw and stayed overnight. He soon ascertained that the people were so enraged at him for trying to stop the house-burning that there was little probability of getting away alive, but finally prevailed on an influential mobocrat to escort him out of Warsaw this morning, who came with him about three and a half miles and on leaving cautioned him that ... there were deep plans laid to kill him. Soon after he was pursued by a party of the mob on horseback, three of whom took the lead ... [one] of the three had a swifter horse and gained a hundred yards in advance of his party [but] in a short time ... his horse stumbled and threw his rider. Backenstos maintained his speed, driving as fast as his horse could go.

"The mob took the nearest road to cross his track and on his arrival at the old railroad crossing, the mob were within about 200 yards, they being on horseback and he in a buggy, [as] they had gained on him considerably.

"Orrin P. Rockwell and John Redding were refreshing themselves near the crossing as they had been out to bring in some of the burnt-out families who were sick, and on looking up saw Backenstos coming down the hill at full speed, and asked what was the matter. Backenstos replied the mob were after [him] and determined to kill him and commanded them in the name of the people of the state to protect him. Rockwell replied, fear not, we have 50 rounds." Porter had with him two fifteen-shooter rifles besides revolvers.[69]

Jesse W. Crosby describes the small mob in his journal as "four or five ruffians on horseback."[70]

Sheriff Backenstos "then turned to the mob and commanded them to stop, and as they continued to advance raising their guns, he ordered Rockwell to fire; he did so aiming at the clasp of the belt on one of the mob, which proved to be Frank Worrell, who fell from his horse and the rest turned back and soon brought up a wagon and put his body into it."[71]

While Porter had at least wounded — and likely killed — enemy horsemen the day after Joseph's death, this was his first actual *recorded* killing. His victim was an officer of the Carthage Greys, and a "leading hand at Joseph's murder."[72] One witness at the scene, Peter Wilson Conover, records, "Rockwell fired and the man jumped four feet in the air and rolled away from his horse dead."[73]

Jacob Baum, a farmer living near the road, reports Porter "rushed up to their gate, threw his bridle rein over the post and hurriedly rushed into the road and fired his rifle, and said, with great satisfaction: 'I got him.'

" 'Got who?'

" 'Worrell,' he said. I was afraid my rifle couldn't reach him, but it did, thank God. Come, Jacob, get your rifle. Let's see if any more mob demons hid in your straw stack!' "[74]

The anti-Mormon press literally exploded. They not only accused the sheriff and Porter of murder, of course, but they reported the Mormons had gone wild, laying waste to the entire Illinois countryside, burning out innocent Illinoisians and sending them fleeing for safety into Missouri and Iowa.[75] They even reported two Mormon dissidents had been liquidated by Brigham in Nauvoo for opposing him.[76] Brigham commented two weeks later, "I went with the Twelve to Elder Taylor's and saw Judge [Steven A.] Douglas and Sheriff Backenstos. They said it was hard to make the people on the other side of the Illinois river believe that it was not the Mormons that were burning houses in Hancock county." Although beginning to vacillate, Steven A. Douglas was still somewhat on the Saints' side for another nine years, until political expediency would force him to cross the threshhold of Joseph's warning.

Since Backenstos had sought to raise a posse among the Illinoisians and had failed, he now tried among the Mormons. He succeeded and they dispersed the rioters.[77]

In this venture Porter was acting as messenger between Brigham and the sheriff,[78] but the press claimed "the Notorious O. P. Rockwell" and Backenstos were sweeping the countryside, leading an army of 300 men — on one occasion intimidating a small party of Illinoisians.[79]

Governor Ford also heard the tales and now reacted by sending out a regiment of 400 Illinoisians to quell the Mormon uprising. All they found, however, were Mormons peaceably meandering about the streets of Nauvoo.

Reports Brigham, "I went onto the hill and met General Hardin and staff surrounded by his troops, four hundred in number. He read us his orders from the governor to come here and keep the peace if he had to keep the county under martial law; said he wished to search for the bodies of two dead men who were last seen in Nauvoo and it was supposed they had been murdered."

Brigham smiled. "I told him he was welcome to search for dead bodies or anything else he pleased. He inquired if I knew anything about them or of crimes having been committed in Nauvoo. I replied I knew nothing of the kind, but that I had reliable information that some hundred houses had been burned in the south part of the county [by Illinoisians] and probably if he would go there, he would find the persons who had done it."[80]

Brigham shook his head as they poked with pitchforks in the mud of the Mansion House stable, searching for the murder victims.[81]

Then the *Warsaw Signal* decided the war was not escalating fast enough. To speed things up, they called on the locals to arm themselves, and to seek revenge for Worrell's death.

Such was the charged atmosphere when Brigham announced to the Army his wish to appear before them and speak. Before the uniformed masses, he told them what the Council had decided: The Saints had had enough.

They were going West.

He notes in his journal, "Resolved that a company of 1500 men be selected to go to Great Salt Lake valley and that a committee of five be appointed to gather information relative to emigration."[82] As a member of the Council, Porter had participated in the decision.

The Prophet then met in council with state and military officials, including General Hardin and Steven A. Douglas.[83]

The army left, but for some reason the press would not cease its clamor. Casting aside the perhaps obvious motive of self-defense, the *Warsaw Signal* called for the arrest of Sheriff Backenstos and Rockwell for murdering Frank Worrell.

Soon a mob formed just for that purpose. And Porter was becoming more infamous by the minute.

The mob then turned on General Hardin — it simply wanted results. He assured them he would go to Nauvoo with his troops and either arrest Rockwell or "unroof every house in Nauvoo."[84] Three hundred mobbers volunteered to join him.[85]

They marched on Nauvoo and searched for Porter but could not find him. Whom they found was Backenstos, whom they grabbed and took into custody. Porter, meanwhile, remained in hiding. His intentions were to wait out the storm until interest in his case died.

But his strategy backfired. Frustrated by their inability to snare him, the anti-Mormon press unleashed a new series of attacks on him. They sought to rile up the locals even further against the Saints and used Porter as a scapegoat. Porter was still waging a war on "unarmed and unresisting" citizens, they claimed, and to further reveal his sordid character they claimed he stole the wife of another Mormon.[86] With this new story, apostate Mormons also jumped on the bandwagon, and successfully added fuel to the fire by claiming Brigham had given the woman to Porter after taking her away from her rightful husband.[87]

Governor Ford believed the rumors, and later records in his memoirs — although never seeing Porter and his alleged mistress first-hand — that Rockwell had courted her openly in Nauvoo society where they were "freely admitted to the best society in the place, to all the gay assemblies, where she and her husband frequently met in the same dance."[88] The rumors grew fast and furious. Before long they included a story that the Saints had even placed blame on the woman's husband, Amos Davis, rather than on Rockwell for the death of Frank Worrell, "for the purpose of running Davis out of the City, he being in the way of the Mormon pet, Rockwell."[89]

The *Warsaw Signal* further states, "We learn that one day last week, O. P. Rockwell and his new wife ... went together to the house of said Davis. Rockwell stood at the door, with pistol in hand, while his delectable partner entered the house and took from it such furniture as she desired. This was in open day light and in the face of the whole City; yet no one was shocked or astonished."[90] The absurdity of the comment lies in contrast to the remarkably consistent Victorian morals upheld by most townspeople, as evidenced by the dozens of active Saints' diaries of the period. Had the reports been accurate, Porter would have been run out of town on a rail. Eventually the rumor held that Rockwell and his mistress would walk arm and arm into her husband's tavern, where he "did not dare refuse to deal or he would have been assassinated ... "[91]

But the rumor didn't stop there. The *St. Louis Daily New Era* picked it up and added more color — that Porter was stabbed by her husband![92]

Although church enemies had spread the stories, suspicion rests on a solid possibility that Amos Davis himself had instigated the rumors. Three years earlier, Joseph had recorded in his diary certain information about "the City of Nauvoo versus Amos Davis, for indecent and abusive language about me while at Mr. Davis' the day previous." It had been the first of several cases in which Davis apparently went for the Prophet's throat (see Note 16 for details), but Davis never succeeded. Mad as a wounded bee, he apparently concocted the retaliatory tale to attack Joseph's loyal surviving compatriot.

Amidst the clamor fabricated by both apostates and the press, Porter kept a low profile. He did, however, continue serving in various church capacities. Contrary to reports of an adulterous escapade, Rockwell received his temple endowments January 5, 1846, and possibly participated in the temple ceremony itself.[93]

Meanwhile, Backenstos requested a non-partisan trial, and received a change of venue to Peoria, where he was acquitted.

About the same time, Brigham and several others of the Twelve were sought by federal and state authorities ... this time for counterfeiting U.S. coin.

Brigham thought the assertion so absurd that he all but ignored it. But when federal officers, accompanied by state troops, rode into Nauvoo one afternoon to arrest him, he saw they were indeed serious. With his inimitable style, feeling that a confrontation was beneath him, he decided to give them their money's worth:

He sent his coachman to the door of the Temple, who announced to the waiting troops that Brigham Young would soon appear. Another Mormon, William Miller, donned Brigham's cap and another's cloak and "went downstairs, meeting the marshal and his assistants at the door." They thought this was Brigham Young, and as he climbed into Brigham's carriage they arrested him. "Miller told him there must be some mistake about it, as he was not guilty of anything of the kind, but the marshal insisted it was right."

Miller requested to go to the Mansion house to seek legal counsel, and subsequently led the authorities on a wild goose chase through the streets of Nauvoo. The U.S. marshal finally became impatient, and insisted they head off for their own destination. Miller again protested, claiming "he certainly was not guilty of any such things as were charged in the writ."

The authorities, still believing him to be Brigham, dragged him off to trial. Miller reports, "On the way to Carthage the marshal was very social, and remarked [to me] that the people had got quite a joke upon him for letting Turley [another Mormon who had likewise tricked the marshal] give him the dodge."

As they arrived in Carthage, "the troops began to whoop and holloa and went into town in high glee." They thought they had snared their Prophet.

At Hamilton's tavern the marshal pulled in for the evening, and there his prisoner, Miller, was recognized by the county commissioner's clerk. Miller was taken to a private room and the marshal came in to confront him: "I am informed you are not Mr. Young."

"Ah, then if I should prove not to be Mr. Young, it would be a worse joke on you than the Turley affair."

The marshal, realizing the gravity of the situation, sent for two others to come double-check the prisoner. When the two witnesses arrived at the tavern they walked into "Brigham's" room, took one glance at him, and informed the marshal he had arrested the wrong man.

The marshal left the room, anguished. He soon returned with Miller's attorney, "who was laughing heartily at him." The lawyer, Edmonds, finally asked the marshal, "Have you anything more to do with 'Mr. Young?' "

The next day came a report, "William Miller remained last night at Carthage . . . Miller said he could not sleep being interrupted by Edmonds' continued roars of laughter . . . "[94]

Meanwhile, except for his temple work, Porter remained in hiding.

The Saints worked feverishly to evacuate. They converted homes into construction shops where 12,000 wagons would be built by spring. Farms and livestock were forced into auction. Illinois speculators paid the Mormons pennies for property. It was a buyer's market and the Saints had no choice but to sell, and — in most cases —practically give it away.

John D. Lee, for example, had built a 27-room house for $8,000. "In Salt Lake City it would have been worth $50,000," he claims. But it was sold for $12.50.[95]

Porter, meanwhile, had his own problems. His ex-wife, Luana Beebe Rockwell, married Alpheus Cutler on January 14. Cutler was president of the High Council, and although Porter may have been pleased — for his children's sake — to find Luana still active in the church, he nonetheless suffered seeing his children sealed away to Cutler. "Sealing" was the Mormons' temple ordinance of uniting children to their parents, and parents to each other, for eternity. (Their sealing to Cutler was later "nullified," however, as described later.)

Throughout the winter the Saints migrated across Iowa, calling themselves the Camp of Israel.

Porter marched with them as they forged on in freezing weather, with little food.

Soon Brigham gave him the assignment as messenger between Nauvoo headquarters and the wagon train.[96] Through two months of spring, March 14th to May 8th, 1846, he carried dispatches across the state five times.

Whether or not he actually believed it himself, Editor Thomas Sharp of the *Warsaw Signal* claimed Rockwell was planning to return "to take his [Sharp's] life, and the lives of some others. Yet there are some," says Sharp, "who say that the Mormons are a 'peaceable and honest people,' who would harm no one . . ."[97]

On Rockwell's last trip an event occurred which sent the anti-Mormons celebrating . . .

Porter was caught — and arrested — for the murder of Frank Worrell. The capture occurred because of his own indiscretions, claims the *Quincy Whig.* The paper further reports Chauncey Higbee had been in town on business, and Sheriff Backenstos had promised him protection. When Rockwell discovered the apostate Higbee, he terrorized him, following him about, "threatening his life, firing pistols over his head, etc." The militia were sent for, and Porter was arrested.[98] It was a somewhat amusing incident perhaps to Porter, and possibly true, but likely spiced.

At the time of his arrest the *Daily Missouri Republican* reports Porter possessed enough guns to fire 71 rounds without reloading, plus knives,[99] but he made not even "the slightest resistance," according to the *St. Louis American* [100] and the *People's Daily Organ*.[101] *The Lee County Democrat* adds Porter "was amusing the citizens with some of his characteristic antics."[102]

News of the incident reached Major Warren at Carthage, who sent six riflemen to the scene to arrest Rockwell. Sheriff Backenstos told them where he was. Then, with the sheriff accompanying them, "they surrounded the house in which he was lodging." In a dramatic confrontation, former ally Backenstos, whose life had once been saved by Rockwell, "compelled him, though reluctantly," to march towards the jail.[103]

Unfortunately for the mobbers, the cheers rising from Illinois taverns ended at the ceiling. Porter, it seems, had purposely allowed himself to be arrested.

Although the *Burlington Hawkeye* editorializes, "This is a new move which we do not understand,"[104] the reason was obvious: He did it to clear himself. Apostates, of course, spread a new wave of rumors, one claiming Rockwell had plotted with Backenstos to split the reward money of $2,000 offered for Porter's arrest.[105] Rockwell probably had safer means of earning money, but what he and church leaders likely concerned themselves with was his reputation. Perhaps it was beyond repair in the eyes of the populace, but on the legal books he could set himself straight. In the process he could buy time for the Saints, diverting press attention from driving away the remaining Saints to a new cover story: the capture of Mormondom's most colorful desperado.

The *Quincy Whig* reports, "The excitement when the fact was made known that Rockwell was actually in the city, was sufficient to draw a large crowd in the vicinity of the jail [The *Republican* at St. Louis describes it as "an immense crowd"[106]], and he was almost instantly put under lock and key."[107]

With characteristic "objectivity," and even before his trial, the *Whig* reports, "Rockwell has become a perfect desperado — reckless and ruffianly to the last extreme."[108]

Porter probably felt if he could receive an impartial trial he would be acquitted. Under these circumstances he more than likely agreed to face a first-degree murder charge if the court could be held outside Hancock County,[109] a move his lawyer anxiously sought.

But his enemies refused to lose him. They piled on other charges ... counterfeiting and passing bogus currency[110] ... but to no avail. His trial was transferred to Daviess County, 150 miles north.[111]

The *Quincy Whig* reports, "He appears to be in good spirits, and has very little to say in regard to the critical position in which he is placed."[112]

The jury at Galena indicted Porter and ordered him to appear before the court in July.[113]

There, Porter languished another four months in an enemy prison.

Backenstos was finally subpoenaed as a witness, and Porter was acquitted of all charges.[114]

To the nearly deserted streets of Nauvoo,[115] Porter finally returned. While walking down a lonely road he quietly reminisced on his former friendship with the Prophet, and chanced to come upon his son, Joseph Smith, III, a 13- year-old lad.

Young Joseph mentions in his memoirs, "I saw him coming down the street, and I ran across our yard, climbed the fence, and jumped down on the other side close by him, greeting him and extending my hand. He shook it warmly, put an arm affectionately across my shoulders, and said, with much emotion, 'Oh, Joseph, Joseph! they have killed the only friend I have ever had!'

"He wept like a boy. We spoke but little, for even then an air of suspicion had crept abroad in the city and whoever was friendly to my mother or her family was under surveillance. I tried to comfort him, but to my astonishment he said, 'Joseph, you had best go back. I am glad you came to meet me, but it is best that you are not seen with me. It can do me no good and it may bring harm to you.'

"It was with my heart in my throat and my eyes dim with tears — as they are now as I recall the incident after all the years that have passed — that I climbed back over the fence, to wonder, in my boyish way, how it was possible for men to be so wicked and cruel to good men. I write this with no shame or any consciousness of unfitness in thus expressing my friendship for the man ... .Going back to the house I told my mother whom I had seen, what he had said, and how he had cried." In a parting comment, the younger Joseph adds, "He was absolutely fearless, and cared little about the amenities of society."[116]

As Porter and young Smith parted, it was the last time they ever saw one another. (For another anecdote on Rockwell by the Prophet's son, see Note. 17.)

Porter gathered his last belongings in the warm summer moonlight and struck off for the east banks of the Mississippi River.

There, some of the last Saints were waiting to cross the wide, turbulent waters of the Mississippi.

Weeks later, Porter arrived at Council Bluffs, Iowa, where church leaders were about to administer a priesthood blessing to William Clayton, camp clerk. Notes Clayton, "When they had been in a few moments President Young called O. P. Rockwell into the tent and the feelings we had on seeing him cannot be described. He has been in prison some time . . . The brethren all laid hands on me and rebuked my disease in the name of the Lord, President Young being mouth. I immediately felt better and slept well all night being the first sleep I had had of any account for three days and nights."[117] Porter was undoubtedly still faithful to church precepts, as it was common for only straight-line Mormons to participate in such ordinances, considered sacred in Mormon theology.

When he had a free moment, Porter reported details of his arrest to church leaders.[118] Brigham soon met with him alone, and assigned him to transport messages among the eight wagon-train camps stretched throughout Iowa. But then Brigham told him about a new setback: 500 of the best Mormon men had been picked by the United States Army to assist in the war with Mexico. Brigham had complied with what seemed to many an unreasonably request, a request by the government to press into service the very people its citizens had been oppressing. As if Porter were obligated to such service, two Missouri newspapers actually criticized him[119] for not having gone on the expedition . . . despite the fact he had been sitting in a Missouri prison during the recruiting. The resulting short-handed pioneer effort, Brigham explained, would require Porter to perform double duty.

"The Mormon Battalion," according to Army sources at the time, went on to complete the longest military march in recorded world history. But the immediate effect of their loss to the wagon train was staggering.

Brigham then called a camp meeting that stunned the Saints: He announced what he had just learned from a messenger — that Missourians were planning to imprison all church leaders. William Clayton writes in his journal, "He advised the brethren to have their arms clean and their ammunition ready at a moment's warning, to pray with their families ... etc."[120]

That night, Brigham took the six Apostles from camp and fled across the river into Indian territory, awaiting the attack of the huge Missouri militia. And for his bodyguard he took Orrin Porter Rockwell.[121]

Once across the river Porter had a chance to visit with Brigham more intimately. He told the Prophet details of his arrest, and in a gesture of friendship, Brigham sent a messenger to Illinois to retrieve Porter's gold watch which Rockwell had used as payment for Babbitt, the church's lawyer at Galena. The church — not Porter — would pay for Porter's court expenses, insisted Brigham.[122]

The Prophet and his fellow fugitives soon learned the Missouri attack had fizzled — or had simply been a rumor — and they returned to Council Bluffs, Iowa.

There the Saints continued preparing for the exodus, spending their majority of time building barges to cross the river, but progress was slow. The major challenge — survival. Malarial fever from river bottom pools swept through camp, killing eventually over 600. Brigham's immediate challenge was to move the Saints out — quickly. But then another problem plagued them ... starvation.

In desperation Brigham met with Omaha tribal chiefs and the U.S. Indian agent. Brigham negotiated for the Saints to stay two years, with rights to timber and firewood, while the Indians in return could borrow Mormon teams for plowing.

On December 29th, 1846, a council meeting determined to send an advance party to the Rocky Mountains.[123] Porter was among the 15 attending,[124] and it was here that he was chosen as scout and chief hunter, while Brigham was chosen to lead the 147-member party. Porter was also assigned to the tenth section of ten, with Appleton Milo Harmon his captain. After the meeting, "Pres. Young spoke in tongues and conversed with Elder Kimball in an unknown tongue,"[125] records George A. Smith in the church's official Journal History.

Porter's party, however, would not leave until spring.

Meanwhile, Rockwell maintained a busy schedule as guide to two church leaders, Erastus Snow and Ezra Taft Benson. Porter led the two leaders to the camp at the Niobrara River "to organize the Saints . . . and teach them their duty."[126] Erastus Snow records in his journal, "We started February 1st 1847 the weather more intensely cold and considerable snow. We were accompanied by O. P. Rockwell . . ."[127] Porter's mission with the two Apostles lasted until mid-February.

Unceasing in their attacks, the "anti" press took one parting potshot at Porter: the *Warsaw Signal* claimed in March that Porter had a prostitute for a "spiritual" wife, or at least the sister of a prostitute, but the inference was clear. Porter at this point was not married in any form.

Then, on April 14, 1847, Porter's advance party began moving out. He accompanied the party 35 miles, when Brigham sent him and Jesse C. Little back to Winter Quarters for one final delivery of mail.

Five days later the two men returned to Brigham "laden with letters,"[128] plus two more men . . . and a surprise for Willard Richards: his lost horse. Porter had discovered the animal and chased it down near the Elk Horn River. William Clayton adds, "I received by Porter, some few fish hooks and lines, a ball of fish line and three pencils . . ."[129]

Amasa Lyman records in his journal for the day: "Took a glass of brandy with the 12 & a few others, at the invitation of O. P. Rockwell which he received as a present from Thomas L. Kane."[130]

Howard Egan's diary, meanwhile, records the routine of wagon train camp life: up at five with a bugle call, moving by seven, half-circling the wagons at sunset, bed call by bugle at eight-thirty, prayer, and campfire lights out by nine.[131] Additionally, Egan reported Brigham's mandate: "Every man is to put as much interest in taking care of his brother's cattle, in preserving them, as he would his own, and no man will be indulged in idleness. Every man is to have his gun and pistol in perfect order."[132]

On April 26, two weeks into their journey, the Mormons were moved on by Indians. At 3:30 A.M. a half-dozen Braves were seen crawling toward camp, presumably to steal horses, when the guards drove them off with rifle fire.[133]

A short time after this, Porter faced his own troubles with the Indians. Willard Richards' horse had run off again and Porter now led three other Saints to track it down. Clayton records the event:

"Looking off towards the river they saw something move in the grass at the foot of a high mole. They proceeded towards it thinking it was a wolf, when within about twelve or fourteen rods Porter stopped to shoot at the supposed wolf. The moment he elevated his rifle, fifteen Indians sprang to their feet, all naked except the breech cloth, and armed with rifles and bows and arrows. Each man having a rifle slung on his back, and his bow strung tight in his hand and about twenty arrows."[134]

It was Porter's first confrontation with Indians . . . and in the tense moment that followed, several of the whites — including Porter — probably pondered if it would not be their last . . .

VII

"The Indians advanced towards them but the brethren motioned and told them to stop and held their rifles and pistols ready to meet them," records Howard Egan.

"When the Indians saw this they began to holler 'bacco! bacco!' The brethren told them they had not tobacco. One of the Indians came close beside J. Matthew's horse to shake hands with Mathews but kept his eye on the horse's bridle. When nearly within reach of the bridle, Brown cocked his pistol and pointed at the Indian shouting if he did not leave he would kill him.

"At which, the Indian seeing the pistol ready to fire, retreated.

"The Indians made signs to get the brethren lower down the river, but the brethren turned their horses to come to camp, thinking it unsafe to go near to the timber where they expected more Indians lay in ambush.

"When the brethren turned to come back the Indians fired six shots at them with their rifles and the brethren immediately faced about at which the Indians fled towards the timber below. The brethren did not shoot at the Indians, even when the Indians shot at them."[1]

Porter and the others galloped back to camp.

In the New Land Porter and his fellow Easterners faced challenges they'd never imagined.

Within two weeks they crossed the Wood River, and, hungering for fresh meat, they came upon their first buffalo herd. Clayton describes the scene:

"A feeling of exciting interest appeared to prevail throughout the camp, they having heard and read so much of the mad ferocity of buffalo when hotly pursued, and knowing that all the hunters were inexperienced in regard to hunting the wild buffalo . . .

"Soon as the herd commenced galloping off, the hunters followed in pursuit at full gallop and soon closed in with them. At this time I got my glass and rested it on Brother Aaron Farr's shoulder, determined to see as much of the chase as possible. I soon discovered O. P. Rockwell ride into the midst of the herd which then appeared to number over 200 . . . Porter was soon enveloped in the cloud of dust caused by the heavy tramp of the buffalo on the dry sandy ground, but in a very short time the herd began to separate and scatter in every direction . . . The hunters closed in on the first party and commenced their fire, especially at one cow which they finally succeeded in separating from all the rest, and determined to keep to her until they killed her, except Porter, who as soon as he had wounded her, left her with the hunters and pursued some of the rest."[2]

Porter was having a field day. The New West was his element indeed.

But his courage — or perhaps his curiosity — almost proved his undoing . . .

"O. P. Rockwell said he had heard it said that a buffalo could not be hurt with a ball shot at his head," continues Clayton. " . . . he determined to satisfy himself . . . The hunters made choice of a large and very furious bull . . . [Porter,] gaining a little in advance came right in front within about a rod of him and discharged his rifle pistol which struck the center of his head, but with no other effect than to make it smoke a little, some dust fly and the raving animal shake savagely."

Needless to say, Porter's curiosity was satisfied. Out of

ammunition and with the buffalo almost down his throat, Porter spurred his horse.

Soon he realized the buffalo had quit chasing him, and decided to return and kill the beast, but he was too late. "The brethren. . . succeeded in dropping him and laid him dead at their feet."[3] Porter resumed his hunting, and sustained the camp with buffalo steaks.

Reports of Indians again reached Brigham, and the Saints stepped up defense drills. Then Brigham, "while chasing the cows from the buffalo herd . . . " lost his spyglass.[4] Egan's diary reports Brigham returned to search for it, but could not find it. Because it was an invaluable instrument, the Prophet was worried. He realized it could have been dropped any number of miles back. Egan's diary details the outcome: "May 7th . . . O. P. Rockwell went back this morning to hunt President Young's spy glass . . .   About 4 p.m. Porter returned. He found the spyglass."[5] Clayton adds, " . . . which was a source of joy to all the brethren."[6]

As the expedition continued, Appleton Milo Harmon records a typical journal entry about the buffalo: "The plain was perfectly black with them . . . O. P. Rockwell killed a two-year-old heifer which was good."[7]

On this same day, May 8th, Amasa Lyman records, "the line of buffalo reaching from the river to the bluffs looked like a solid dark wall." He then adds simply, "O. P. Rockwell killed a cow."[8]

William Clayton also says of Porter's kill: "the meat looks nice."[9]

Lorenzo Dow Young writes for the day: "the dry excrement of the buffalo was used for camp fires."[10]

On the same day Howard Egan adds: "The prairie on both sides of the river is literally covered with buffalo."[11]

While these diarists detailed life on the journey this day with richness, Brigham was more to the point: "Traveled 12 miles." His only three words for the day.[12]

Two days later Amasa Lyman records, "Rockwell and T. Brown chased a wild horse . . . O. P. Rockwell shot a bull . . . "[13] Same for a week later: "O. P. Rockwell shot a bull."[14]

After five weeks the party had driven 400 miles. Near Scotts

Bluff they ate antelope, provided by Porter, and enjoyed themselves with mock courts, in parody of their Missouri and Illinois persecutors. One note penned to Porter reads, "Pioneer Camp, Wednesday, May 26, 1847. To Marshall O. P. Rockwell: Sir — You are hereby commanded to bring, wherever found, the body of Col. George Mills, before the Right Reverend Bishop Whipple, at his Quarters, there to answer to the following charge, viz.: — That of emitting in meeting on Sunday last, a sound . . . diverting their minds from the discourse of the speaker."[15]

William Clayton records, "We have many such [mock] trials in the camp which are amusing enough and tend among other things to pass away the time cheerfully during leisure moments."[16]

Within a few days a number of church leaders, the Twelve and nine others, retired to a bluff away from the wagon train, and "stationed O. P. Rockwell and A. Carrington on the look out, while the rest . . . prayed," Brigham "being mouth."[17] Porter's duty was simply to prevent interruptions, which he probably performed quite well.

On the journey West, Clayton describes the romantic imagery of the new world. He chronicles Porter's exploits, detailing his duties as scout and chief hunter. Both Clayton and Rockwell were apparently enthralled by the whole adventure. Following are most of Clayton's excerpts on the man who quietly kept them alive:

April 24th, 1847: " . . . The bluffs on the other side look beautiful from here, and the Indian graves show very plain . . . Soon as we arrived Porter Rockwell discovered that there were many sun fish in the lake. I took a couple of hooks and lines, handed some to him, and went to fishing myself with the others and we had some fine sport."

May 5th: " . . . O. P. Rockwell and John S. Higbee chased the one [buffalo calf which had been] brought in alive until a dog seized it and Porter left his horse and caught it without shooting at it and led it to camp." An interesting sight this was to the group: Porter leading a wild buffalo into camp on a leash, with an envious dog following.

May 6th: " . . . Porter has shot one about two years old, the meat looks nice."

May 9th: " . . . They saw multitudes of buffalo coming to water.

Porter and Phineas Young went within six or eight rods of them to try to get one, but in the whole herd, they could not find one fit to kill." Porter held to a code of not killing big game for sport. Orson Pratt adds, "We have killed no more of them than what the present necessities of the camp require."[18]

May 15th: " ... Late at night Porter Rockwell came in and reported that he killed a buffalo. The cutter was sent for it to bring it to camp."

May 16th: "The wagons halted at a quarter to four ... [The cutter] immediately returned to fetch the other buffalo which was killed by Porter Rockwell."

May 22nd: " ... A while after we halted, Porter Rockwell came in and said he had been on the high bluff about a mile northwest of us and had seen the rock called Chimney Rock which appeared a long distance off ... I turned to gaze on the romantic scenery above ... I have noticed a variety of shrubs, plants and flowers ... the air appears impregnated with the rich odors."

May 24th: "The chief and his squaw ... signified a wish to abide with our camp tonight. The brethren fixed up a tent for them to sleep under; Porter Rockwell made them some coffee, and they were furnished with some victuals. The old chief amused himself very much by looking at the moon through a telescope for as much as twenty minutes." Porter was amazed at the childlike curiosity of the Indians, and this information would be useful. Lorenzo Dow Young also records this day, "Porter Rockwell killed 2 antelope."[19]

May 25th: " ... The buffalo appear to have left this region ... The evening was very pleasant and the brethren passed away their time till after nine o'clock dancing. Porter Rockwell shot the two antelope spoken of above. He also shot two wolves."

May 26th: " ... Porter Rockwell has killed two antelope and John Brown one which were brought into camp and are being divided amongst the companies as usual."

May 27th: "The morning very fine. We have seen a number of romantic spots on our journey, but I consider our view this morning more sublime than any other ... To the southwest, Scott's Bluffs look majestic ... The prairie over which our route lies is very level and green as far as we can see ... The scenery is truly delightful beyond imagination. Porter Rockwell has killed two

antelope and Amasa Lyman one, which were brought to the wagons and distributed."

But on May 28th an incident occurred which spun the Saints in a new spiritual direction. Brigham Young became fed up with their "bickering and small-mindedness," and gathered the entire camp together for a general dressing-down.[20] (See Note 18 for details.) Most of the pioneers re-committed themselves spiritually and the attitude change was remarkable.

On June 1, 1847, they arrived at Fort Laramie, the first white outpost from civilization. "The trader opened his store and Brigham Young entered into conversation with him," records Clayton.

Appleton Milo Harmon adds in his journal the following day: "We obtained a flatboat from Mr. [James] Bordeaux to ferry our teams across the North Fork for which we had to pay $15 . . .

"He said that there were buffalo two days' drive ahead and some grizzly bears. [For details on the fort see Note 19.]

". . . June 4 . . . O. P. Rockwell traded a horse to Mr. Bordeaux for two cows and calves, one heifer, two pair of moccasin shoes, and two lariats."[21]

The next day the Mormons struck out across the North Platte at the rate of one wagon every fifteen minutes.

Within several days the Saints found themselves facing the same river — the North Platte snaked around to face them again — this time a hundred yards across and 15 feet deep in a raging spring run-off.

Much to their surprise, a Missouri wagon-train arrived on the scene, and sought the Mormons' help in ferrying across the river. Despite the irony of the situation, Brigham was quick to come to their aid, and both parties profited:

"We made $34 in provisions, which is a great blessing to the camp inasmuch as a number of the brethren have had no bread stuff for some days,"[22] records Clayton. (See Note 20 for details of the trade.) "One of the men of the Missourian company undertook to swim across the river with his clothes on. When he reached the current he became frightened and began to moan. Some of our men went to him with the cutter and arrived in time to save his life."

The Saints left their rafts and nine men until the next wagon-train of Mormons would arrive. In the meantime they would earn money from other westbound non-Mormon trains, and further financially aid the Kingdom.

Meanwhile, a year earlier, Governor Boggs of Missouri had passed through the same territory.[23] Porter found this information useful, as his problems with Boggs were far from over.

Of singular interest was the newspaper account published by the *Weekly Reville* at St. Louis a year earlier. The article had claimed "a collision had taken place between the party of Mormons now emigrating to California, and Gov. Boggs's party journeying to the same destination. In the encounter, Boggs and several of his company were killed."[24]

The *Missouri Republican* was quick to call the story "a hoax."[25] Unfortunately for the Mormons, few newspapers would ever label such stories with such accuracy.

Clayton continues:

June 8th: " . . . Porter Rockwell has killed a deer and someone else an antelope. Porter says he has been on the Platte which is about four miles from here following the La Bonte."

June 19th: " . . . The mosquitoes are very bad indeed at this place which adds to the loathsome, solitary scenery around. Porter Rockwell returned from hunting soon after we had camped and reported that he had killed a fat buffalo about two miles off. A team was sent to fetch in the meat which they did not return till long after dark."

At Pacific Springs they chanced upon mountain man Moses Harris, who knew the Salt Lake area well. Clayton adds, "From his description, which is very discouraging, we have little chance to hope for even a moderately good country anywhere in those regions. He speaks of the whole region as being sandy and destitute of timber and vegetation except the wild sage."

On June 28th, 1847, they came upon three other trappers, including the famed Jim Bridger. Clayton states, "The twelve and several others" sought Bridger's report. At a campfire near the Little Sandy River he detailed to the Mormon leaders what he knew of the valley. In contrast to Moses Harris' report, Bridger's report was optimistic: "There is one mountain in that region and the country adjoining in which he considers if ever there was a promised land, that must be it."

Bridger parted company with the Saints the next day. The day following, after trudging through a prairie, the Saints found themselves stranded at Green River. Spring run-off swelled the banks, causing them to build more ferries.

Then a new enemy struck: mountain fever. Extreme stomach sickness and fever gripped several, while the healthier souls worked to cross the river. At these banks Brigham had a visitor he would not soon forget ... nor would Porter:

Sam Brannan. Leader of 250 Saints on the chartered ship *Brooklyn,* he had taken charge of the voyage since its departure at New York City and had seen the Saints through a number of trials. The ship had sailed around Cape Horn and arrived at California, and now Brannan had a thriving settlement at Yerba Buena, the present-day San Francisco.

Sam was a natural leader. In California he had already become the publisher of a newspaper, and had now come to greet Brigham and persuade him to keep going West — even until they should hit the Pacific. The Great Basin was not the promised land, he asserted, California was. But he found it difficult to persuade a Prophet, whose vision of the Promised Land was clear, that he had the wrong vision.

Brannan remained through the journey westward, remonstrating, cajoling, and pestering the Prophet all the way.

On July 5th the Mormons came in sight of the Uinta Mountains. Here they followed a stream for two days, finally arriving at Fort Bridger.

Clayton describes the fort as "composed of two double log houses about forty feet long each and joined by a pen for horses about ten feet high constructed by placing poles upright in the ground close together, which is all the appearance of a fort in sight. There are several Indian lodges close by and a full crop of young children playing around the door ... The country all around looks bleak and cold."[26] After bartering and repairing wagon wheels, the Saints moved on. One day's journey later they found an oil spring a mile from camp, and used it to lubricate their shoes and guns.

On July 10 they came across Miles Goodyear, who gave the Saints a more favorable image of Salt Lake Valley. But Clayton describes Goodyear as "anxious to have us make a road to his place through selfish motives."[27]

Nonetheless, Porter and several others followed Goodyear along his suggested route. After exploring it carefully Porter returned to Brigham and reported the trail was too rough and would take them off course. But Goodyear did an effective sales job on the Saints, and they decided to take the route.[28]

July 11th: "There are some in camp who are getting discouraged about the looks of the country but thinking minds are not much disappointed, and we have no doubt of finding a place where the Saints can live which is all we ought to ask or expect. It is evident the country grows better as we proceed west, and vegetation is more plentiful and looks richer. After dark, a meeting was called to decide which of the two roads we shall take from here. It was voted to take the right hand or northern road, but the private feelings of all the twelve [based on Porter's recommendation] were that the other would be better. But such matters are left to the choice of the camp so that none may have room to murmur at the twelve hereafter."[29]

Brigham then came down with mountain fever — with such fury that he ordered the Saints to move on without him — and on July 12 he was left behind with several wagons.

The same evening, a cave was discovered by a Mormon named Redden. There, an advance party was organized to find a pass to the Great Salt Lake Valley. Rockwell was chosen as the scout, Orson Pratt as the leader.

They searched for the route utilized by the disaster-ridden Donner-Reed party the year before, and, not finding it, they nearly met disaster themselves: Rockslides, ravines, and rattlesnakes blocked the journey. Eventually they managed to dig out a passageway, and soon discovered the Donner-Reed trail.

Porter galloped back to the main camp with the news.

On July 16th "O. P. came to us, reported,"[30] says Amasa Lyman. He then rode further back, to Brigham himself, and reported both the discovery and the wagon train's progress.

The Pratt party, meanwhile, forged on, over the crest of Big

Mountain, Little Mountain, and, finally descending the last steep mountainside with wheels double-locked, it arrived in Immigration Canyon on July 21, 1847.

Rockwell left Brigham and rode towards the canyon. He arrived at Pratt's expedition and told Pratt of both Brigham's improving condition and of instructions to plant seeds in the new valley to test the soil. Pratt then chose six men to accompany him into the new valley, and one was Porter.

Although Orson Pratt and Erastus Snow first rode into the valley on July 21, Porter was likely the third Mormon to enter Salt Lake Valley. He did so July 22, as scout for the seven-man "seed-planting mission."

Pratt describes the experience: " . . . a broad open valley . . . lay stretched out before us . . . the Great Salt Lake glistened in the sunbeams, containing high mountainous islands . . .

"After issuing from the mountains among which we had been shut up for many days, and beholding in a moment such an extensive scenery open before us, we could not refrain from a shout of joy — which almost involuntarily escaped from our lips the moment this grand and lovely scenery was within our view."[31]

Erastus Snow describes, "we simultaneously swung our hats and shouted 'Hosannah,' for the Spirit witnessed that here the Saints should find rest."[32]

Two men returned to Brigham July 23rd to announce the arrival. Meanwhile, most of the wagon train poured into the valley.

The next day Brigham led the remaining wagons down Immigration Canyon into Salt Lake Valley. Upon arrival, Brigham scanned the valley and uttered his immortal phrase, "This is the right place." He then considered the formidable task before them: providing enough food for themselves and for two thousand additional Saints expected within the year.

But when the first plow literally broke on the crusty soil, they knew they were in for problems.

Brigham claimed irrigation was their only hope. And he assigned Porter to explore the surrounding mountains and survey irrigation possibilities.

After Porter made his recommendations to Brigham, he was

assigned to organize hunting and tree hauling.

In the next week the Saints received another wave of migrants: a party of Mississippi Mormons, plus those relieved for illness from the Mormon Battalion in California.

Because three Batallion members and Ezra T. Benson of the Twelve needed his services, Porter was sent back to the plains.

Two weeks later at Deer Creek, Wyoming, Porter's party met scouts coming from another Mormon migration, and then Porter's entourage came upon the wagon train itself.

Meanwhile, in the desert valley Sam Brannan continued prevailing upon Brigham to leave for the California paradise, but Brigham adamantly refused. Porter would see the man again, but under almost startling circumstances.

President Young soon realized he was needed personally at the main migration, and saddled up to head eastward. Four days later he came across Ezra T. Benson returning from the oncoming wagon train.

Porter was still several hours behind Benson, scouting. Brigham wanted to see Porter, so Brigham and Benson decided to ride ahead and hope to cross paths with Porter.

George A. Smith records in his daily log what had occurred hours previously at the main migration: "In company with Orrin P. Rockwell he [Benson] had left the foremost company [among nine companies, consisting of over 1300 Saints] on Sweetwater, where they had lost a great many cattle through sickness, besides quite a number of horses and cattle which had strayed away and had been taken by the Crow Indians ..." Porter had at that time parted from Benson to scout the terrain.

Brigham Young and Benson continued riding eastward, still hoping to find Porter. Smith continues, " After proceeding a short distance, they met Orrin P. Rockwell on horseback."³³

Howard Egan adds, "Porter took supper with Brother Kimball ... "³⁴ and presumably with Brigham and Benson.

Immediately, Brigham requested Porter to accompany him eastward again, to the main migration. This unusual concern for Rockwell's whereabouts and desire for his aid and companionship was rare in the Prophet's life.

Once again, as he always had and forever would, Porter complied with Brigham's requests. After riding with Brigham awhile, he again provided the company with food, despite heavy rain, snow, and cold. And when provisions ran out, Porter's rifle alone kept them alive.

And he worked while others slept. One night Porter forged on to Fort Bridger and returned to the Mormon camp before dawn without sleep, then led them all the next day.[35]

But another night, as the Saints slept, Indians attacked. While the braves drove off over forty saddle horses, "a number of our men, well armed, started after them."[36] And Porter was among the pursuers.

While the group returned with only seven or eight horses, Porter kept searching. Amasa Lyman records September 10th: "O. P. Rockwell & others came in early & reported the trail [still] scattered."[37] Finding the remaining horses was hopeless.

A few weeks later 200 Sioux Braves attacked the wagon train, and attempted to stampede the horses, but the Mormons drove them off with Porter at the forefront.

At Sweetwater, Brigham released Porter from his scouting assignment, finally freeing him to return to the Valley.

At Great Salt Lake City — so named by the Saints August 22 — Porter found a growing, almost reverential respect for him among the Saints . . .

Additionally, the High Council determined September 9, "that Orrin P. Rockwell, in consideration of services rendered, be rewarded equally with those who worked on the wall of the fort . . ."[38]

A week later the Council announced only three men could trade with the Indians in behalf of the Saints — and two of them only temporarily. But "Orrin P. Rockwell is permitted to trade with the Indians at his pleasure."[39]

In October a captain of the Mormon Battalion, Jefferson Hunt, returned from duty in California and offered to lead a company of hand-picked men back to California to make necessary purchases for the Valley Saints' survival. The High Council adopted his proposal, and, of course, Porter was one of those picked.

On November 15, Porter struck out on the first Utah journey to California, with 17 others, armed with an epistle to Mormon Battalion members. The U. S. Army had apparently been pleased with the Battalion's service at San Diego — so much so that they requested another battalion of Mormons for Los Angeles. (The Mormon Battalion at San Diego had engrained themselves in the citizens' hearts, it seems, by rebuilding the city, planting gardens and even constructing buildings at no pay.)

The church Council's letter to the Mormon Battalion would answer the Army's request: "You will be advised and counseled by our confidential brothers, Asahel A. Lathrop, Orrin P. Rockwell, and Elijah K. Fuller, whom we hereby authorize and fully empower as our representatives to trade and make all contracts in our behalf, and in behalf of this people for our mutual benefit and prosperity . . . We counsel all of you not to re-enlist as soldiers . . . But as fast as you are liberated from your previous engagements, and as your circumstances will permit repair to this place [Salt Lake Valley, and] bring with you all you can of things that will be of value."[40]

On this expedition Porter was also the man entrusted with the mail.

But the trip to California was not as easy as he had thought. During the first month of the journey things went smoothly . . . until, as John Hunt records:

"We found the directions of Weber very hard to follow and lost the trail so often, and spent so much time hunting it again, that we finally ran out of provisions before we had reached the vicinity of Las Vegas. We then did what I think no other party of 'Mormon' emigrants ever had to do — we killed and ate our horses. Three horses in all were consumed."[41]

Two members of the expedition struck out for California alone in hopes of returning with food, but, upon arriving at civilization, the two men "sent a Mexican to us with beef and fresh mounts, and we moved on again . . . " No records here mention Porter's activities during the journey, nor does Hunt provide any more details except, "We were exhausted when we reached the Chino ranch, but Col. Williams was very generous in his treatment of us." At the ranch, Porter lived on "wild cows which we milked after strapping them down, and plenty of flour from which to make our bread." The Mormons had become so drained by the journey that, "We remained there five or six weeks, resting up and preparing for the return trip."

The Chino Ranch was one of two which figured prominently in the Mormon settlement of Southern California. Chino was later taken over by Mormons and leased. The other settlement was the San Bernardino ranch which church settlers bought in 1851.[42]

At Chino, rancher Isaac Williams sold them what they had come for: 200 cows at $6 each, plus mares and mules, and he gave them forty free bulls. The group started back February 15 for Great Salt Lake City.

But Porter refused to make the return trip. Undoubtedly, he felt taking the southern route again was suicide. He may have also wished to remain because his group still had unfinished business with the Mormon Battalion. In any case, the party struck on without him, and subsequently lost all but one of their 40 bulls and "about 100" of their 200 cows. "Occasionally the Indians would sneak up close enough to kill one of them, but otherwise they did not bother us,"[43] reports Hunt of the return trip.

Remaining in California, Porter negotiated to deliver mail to Great Salt Lake City. Lieutenant William Tecumseh Sherman answered Rockwell's request: "In relation to trusting a mail to Mr. Rockwell for the United States," writes Sherman to Colonel Stevenson at Los Angeles, "I am directed to say that at this time there is not sufficient necessity . . . I send, however, one package addressed to the Adjutant General of the Army, Washington, D.C., which Col. Mason directs be entrusted to Mr. Rockwell."[44] Porter obviously had the confidence of the Army to carry such a package, but the Army changed its general policy and decided to transport that package itself.

Rockwell now sought out the Mormon Battalion. He and James Shaw rode to San Diego and rounded up 25 discharged veterans who needed to return to the Valley as quickly as possible. Porter led them on the southern route, and this time also transported a wagon, the first vehicle in American history to make the passage north.[45]

Seven weeks later they arrived, and on June 5, 1848 delivered all 135 mules to Great Salt Lake City without a single animal's death, and in one-half the time of Hunt's disastrous trek.

Porter's reputation as a scout was soaring. Meanwhile, freedom from supervisors — Porter's making more and more decisions — enhanced an apparently growing independence, and Brigham could see the obvious sketchings on the wall.

Meanwhile, at the American River in California a Mormon by the name of James S. Brown was among the first crew to spot gold, but the real turning point to American history came when Sam Brannan publicized it in San Francisco, "holding up a bottle of dust in one hand, and swinging his hat with the other, [he] passed along a street shouting, 'Gold! Gold! Gold from the American River!' "[46] (For details on Mormons and the gold discovery, and for amusing incidents, see Note 21.)

Upon Porter's arrival in Great Salt Lake City he was asked to answer charges of deserting John Hunt's party. Porter plead his case before the High Council on June 11 and they dismissed it.[47]

Church leaders at headquarters now penned a message to Brigham, who was still leading the main migratory wave towards the valley: " . . . the brethren [here in the valley] are in pretty good spirits. As it always has been, some few are disaffected and have got what we call the California fever . . . Orrin P. Rockwell has just arrived from California, in company with Capt. Davis [of the Battalion], and after he rests a few days intends to go to meet you . . . "[48]

Porter went eastward again and met Brigham at the rear of the wagon train. Brigham immediately told Porter that a First Presidency had been reestablished seven months earlier in Iowa, and that, although Brigham had been reigning over the church before, he at that time had been officially sustained as President.

Rockwell and two of his companions now stayed with President Young as bodyguards and to keep an eye on prairie savages, as two Mormons had recently been wounded by Indians.[49]

While not enough animals survived to pull the wagons, the Saints nonetheless pushed and grunted onward. Precious but heavy possessions ditched along the trail became a common sight.

Porter, meanwhile, discovered the easiest possible ford across the Platte River.

He soon rode ahead and found a relief party coming from the

valley. He briefed them on the approaching wagon train and its position, then rode back and found it bogged down at the Sweetwater with disease, thirst, dying animals, and horrendous weather.

Finally the relief train came, complete with extra oxen, and Brigham oversaw distribution.[50]

During this time Porter made a lasting friend. He presented a Mrs. Catherine Wooley with buffalo meat and developed a kinship of sorts with her family.[51]

As the expedition resumed, some felt they could travel no further, but Brigham drove them on.[52]

Porter stayed with Brigham's company,[53] and on September 20 the main migration finally arrived at Immigration Canyon where the Saints in the valley greeted them with cheers.

It was apparently time for Porter, finally, to settle down.

Rockwell evidently wished so strongly to homestead away from the city that he even refused an "inheritance lot" — free lots of land given the Saints.[54] From this, Brigham doubtless assumed Porter was not one to be reigned in with the rules and mores of civilization. Yet Porter still had his gregarious moments. He dined regularly, for example, at the home of Mrs. Wooley's family[55] until he was assigned to the roundup of stray cattle in the valley.

This roundup was the first cause of minor conflict in the Kingdom. A number of cattle had strayed because of their owners' neglect, yet owners became irrate when Porter and his four comrades herded them to the city fort: Ranchers were now bothered with having to reclaim them. From the verbal abuse they took, Porter and his group felt like resigning, but Brigham sustained them, chastising the ranchers: " ... Natural feelings would say let them and their catle go to Hell, But duty says if they do not take care of their cattle, we must do it for them ... Then don't be bluffed off by insults or abuse.[56]

But then came another problem: Predators began killing their animals. The Council of Fifty decided to destroy the pests, and Porter found himself on a gigantic predator hunt as one of ninety-four hunters. By the end of their hunt in March, they had killed 15,000 predators.

In January, meanwhile, Porter took a break from the hunt . . . he led nine others 50 miles south to Utah Valley and scouted there the feasibility of sending cattle to graze. Eight inches of snow had covered Salt Lake Valley,[57] and cattle were dropping hard from hunger and cold.[58] When Porter and his group returned to Salt Lake Valley they reported to the Council of Fifty, " . . . the Snow was almost as deep in the Eutauh Valley as it was here & almost impassible for weak catle to get there on account of the Snow drifts."[59]

Meanwhile, Rockwell was mentioned in late November for another assignment to California,[60] but it never materialized.

In early March he was assigned to the Platte ferry for the expected wave of spring immigrants,[61] but that assignment never developed either . . .

What did develop was his most significant assignment yet. On March 12, 1849, in the first public election of the valley, he was appointed deputy marshal.[62] Just several days earlier the Nauvoo Legion had been reorganized, and Rockwell had been assigned as an officer.[63]

He then received his first Indian assignment. Brigham sent 30 Saints to settle Utah Valley — who were now being harassed by Timpanogos Utes. Porter and an 18-year-old lad, George W. Bean, were sent to pacify the tribe.

Bean would not carry a weapon to negotiate with the Utes, but Porter's methods differed. Bean describes his companion: "Orrin Porter Rockwell, as I knew him, was a diamond in the rough. It was great to know his inner self. His honest loyalty to church, country and friends was deep and lasting. He abhorred deceit and intrigue as did I. He knew the need and power of prayer, as did I. He was above average height, quick in movement, with strong arms and chest, and gray eyes — cool and searching. He was always well armed since his Nauvoo experiences . . . "[64]

Porter thus rode into Ute country like a walking arsenal, loaded with rifle, two revolvers, and a bowie knife. A half mile from the Ute village the two men stopped their horses.[65] "We both began to say, 'If we both go on horseback, we'll be killed.'

"After a bit of discussion, Porter said, 'George, you go to the Camp alone. You know the language and maybe some of the Indians. Your personality is better than mine, too. I'll hide in these willows, ready to run to you when you give the signal.'

"And I added, 'And Brother Brigham sent us with a message of Peace, and a "God Bless You." ' So I went forward without fear. As I neared the camp, I saw them dancing about a bonfire, with their pants and feathers, and squaws beating tomtoms.

"When they saw a man coming, they feared, and three 'bucks' came out to meet me, tied my hands behind me and took me to their camp (one on each side of me and one walking behind me), and stood me on a buffalo robe and there I stood for two hours. I was not permitted to say a word until after they related all their bad feelings; boasted over their depredations and successful battles with other tribes, too numerous to mention; and told what they expected to do with the 'Whites' now stealing their hunting grounds, and how the crows would pick our bones, etc.

"Being over six feet tall, much taller than any of them, and stretching up still taller as they talked, calm . . . I stood for two long hours. When they saw I was not afraid but friendly, one war-horse Indian after another slunk away saying: 'OAH'OAH" with appropriate gesture, meaning 'all right.' The 'Gift of Interpretation' was given to me, as I called it, for I understood every word they said, even to each other. The tomtoms tapered down and the Chief said: 'Now you talk.'

" . . . I delivered the message of friendship from the 'White Chief' Brigham Young, who represented the 'Great Spirit' in his feelings toward the Indians and all mankind, a brotherly feeling that must last forever, etc.

"The dancers stopped and listened, for they were as tired as I, perhaps, and their rituals were over, and Chiefs Walker, Sow-i-ette and a Sub-Chief accompanied me to where Porter Rockwell held our horses.

"As I had given no signal, he thought I had been killed, and I feared for him, but not myself. Porter also delivered the word from Brigham, the 'White Chief.'

" . . . When friendship was agreed, we mounted our horses and rode away."[66]

Brigham was so pleased with Porter's and young George's success that he authorized them to speak in the future on his behalf to any Indian tribe, at any time they deemed necessary.[67]

Bean further describes his association with Rockwell: " ... on many occasions when he stayed over night with me, my wife Elizabeth would plait or brain his hair and Porter would comb it into a flair next morning, which emphasized his high forehead, and his aristocratic air. He raised thoroughbred horses and drove a fine team on his favorite vehicle, the buckboard, and his riding horses were the *best ever*, we thought. His mouth was expressive of his moods, whether jovial, reckless, worried, or pleasant ... He was demanding [as an employer of ranch-hands]. His humor made his stories click. In our missionary work, he was humble and earnest. We spent many years of dangerous and worthwhile service together in teaching the Red Men the Gospel of Jesus Christ and of their origin and duties, and in aiding the officials of Government to subdue and punish outlaws. Anyone who really does things worthy of attention, is often misunderstood and misrepresented."[68] (Emphasis his.)

On April 11 the First Presidency and Council of Twelve Apostles met, and Rockwell became the subject of yet another mission: "The subject of a Mail to be sent through to the Pacific Coast was talked of & finally decided that Amasa and O. P. Rockwell be del[e]gated to select a company of 30 men and Go through with the Mail, teaching the Brethren what to do and read the Epistle to them [a special letter to the Mormon Battalion still in California]; and gather up Tithing."[69]

Meanwhile, church leaders tried to build a peaceful community, free from the counterfeiters and thieves which had somewhat plagued them in Nauvoo. Consequently, the *Scientific American* reports of the Saints in 1849, "They are very strict in the administration. One of their number stole a pair of boots from an [non-Mormon] emigrant, he was sentenced to pay four times their value, fined $50, and was compelled to work fifty days on the public roads."[70]

Nor would church leaders tolerate disrespect from enemies. "When they arrived they were very much troubled by some Indians," reports the *Scientific American*, "who killed their cattle and stole from them. They sent to remonstrate with them, and the Indians replied that their president was an old woman, and they would not mind him. They [the Mormons] then sent out a company of soldiers and [upon facing the Indians, who tested them in fighting] killed a few, since which time they have not been annoyed."[71]

Porter then faced another personal trial . . . his 16-year-old daughter, Emily Amanda Rockwell, was "kidnapped." Apparently she had either eloped with one Hiram Gates or had simply chosen to leave with him and his friend . . . or she had indeed been kidnapped. In any case church leaders "deliberated on the abduction of Orrin P. Rockwell's daughter by Hiram Gates and Levi Fifield,"[72] according to the church's Journal History, and shortly afterwards church leaders sent him to California — possibly in search of her — possibly for other reasons. Nevertheless, she later married Gates,[73] in California, but was widowed by his death sixteen months afterwards. (See Note 22 for details.)

How close Porter was to his children at this point is purely speculative. His former wife, Luana, meanwhile, had found her new marriage a disaster. Her husband, Alpheus Cutler, had apostatized from her church. Shortly after Joseph Smith's death, Cutler had announced he would someday start the "true church." Nine years later he decided it was time, and in 1853 led 40 families into his fold at Winter Quarters, convincing them not to make the journey West. Whether Luana had joined him doctrinally at any point is questionable. They remained in Fisher Grove, Iowa, and 11 years later he died. Fourteen years after his death in 1878, Luana Beebe came to Utah and lived in Juab County with one of Porter's sons. She died March 6, 1897 and was buried in Provo City Cemetery. The capstone above her grave boasts, "Luana Hart Beebe, Wife of O. P. Rockwell."

Whether or not church leaders and Rockwell actually knew his daughter was in California is also speculative, as the only information recorded is another reason for which he was sent . . .

He and Apostle Lyman confronted Sam Brannan in his elegant San Francisco home[74] and presented to him a letter.[75] Written by Brigham personally, the letter urged Brannan to pay the two church representatives tithing money owed to Great Salt Lake City headquarters. But Brannan had adopted a bold scheme. He had apostatized from the church upon leaving Utah, yet had continued collecting tithing money from the Saints in California. Thus, his palatial home. Brigham had apparently not known of the man's spiritual condition because in a letter to Brannan he not only requested a minimum of $10,000 — which he figured the California Saints owed the Kingdom in tithes — but he also pled with Brannan to donate an additional $40,000 to aid the struggling Utah Saints.

Brannan simply laughed. He told Lyman and Rockwell, as a miner reports, that he "would surrender it upon the Lord's proper written order; otherwise not."[76]

Apostle Lyman later reported to Brigham: "Bro. Sammuel Brannan has disclaimed all connexion with the church ... "[77] He was summarily excommunicated.[78] Parley P. Pratt mentions in his journal another reason why: " ... for combining with lawless assemblies to commit murder and other crimes."[79] Brannan had been the foremost organizer and first president of the Vigilance Committee of 1851,[80] and although that in itself may not have been grounds for excommunication, certain activities associated with the group had caused the action.

But the journey to California had begun with high hopes. On April 13[81] Porter and Apostle Lyman had left Great Salt Lake City, crossed thick snow and raging icy rivers in sub-zero weather, and had struggled four agonizing days over the snowy summit of the Sierra to arrive at Sutter's fort May 25th.[82]

While Lyman had collected tithes from the now-money-oriented Saints digging for gold in California — to the sum of $4,000 (doubtless a paltry sum in Brigham's eyes compared to what Lyman should have collected) — he also performed missionary work.

Porter, meanwhile, panned for gold. And shortly thereafter with his success opened a saloon in California at Murderer's Bar, a traveler's inn at Buckeye Flat, and another inn near Mormon Island on the American River.[83] Not one for tedious labor, Porter enjoyed the challenge of proprietorship and the opportunities inn-keeping provided: one side of him which intermittently emerged was a hopelessly gregarious social animal. His tavern was known as Round Tent Saloon.

Several months later, shortly after Christmas, Porter rendezvoused with Lyman and visited Brannan — with the aforementioned lack of success — and then Porter returned to his taverns.

Since abstinence was not yet a church commandment — Brigham would not decree it so for another several years[84] — Porter could enjoy his business in good conscience. When he hauled whiskey from Sacramento by mule train he would arrive at a hilltop above town and blare his bugle. His partner at the tavern would fire a shot in the air. Gold-panners along the river knew it was time to celebrate.[85]

Lyman saw Brannan once more,[86] giving him another opportunity to return the tithes, but Brannan was obstinate. Lyman wrote May 31, "Traveled to Mormon tavern, there met with Capt. Hunt and O.P."[87] Lyman continued his missionary labors, as did possibly Porter. Whether or not Rockwell lived true to his First Presidency blessing during this stay in California — to serve as a part-time missionary — is not recorded. What is recorded is that he used an alias: Louisa Barnes Pratt writes of it in her journal, "July 16th [1850] — Camped in an oak grove near Brown's, a fictitious name for Porter Rockwell,"[88] the same alias possibly used in Missouri.[89] Rockwell used the alias for a reason . . . John Letts records in his memoirs. "At the time of which I am writing, Gov. B [Boggs] and two sons, were in California. They had heard of Porter's rendezvous, and were supposed to be in search of him." As a result, Porter "went armed with a brace of revolvers, and one of duelling pistols; he had a dog that was constantly with him, sleeping with him at night to give the alarm in case of danger. He declared his determination to sell his life dearly if attacked."[90]

Thus he hoped to decoy Boggs, now living in Sonoma, and his best friend apparently now in fact became his dog. The animal was small and white, and generally rode on the rump of his horse, frequently perching its paws on Porter's shoulder, searching the road ahead. The dog was also trained to lick Rockwell's face — rather than bark — to sound an alarm after dark.[91] Porter's pistols, meanwhile, were constantly loaded with buckshot.[92]

Porter's need for an alias was obvious, beyond the fact Boggs' sons were "out to get him:" Missourians and Illinoisians comprised a goodly number of the gold-panners, and, no doubt, he often sat in his saloon hearing patrons tell "Porter Rockwell stories" without their even knowing who he was. It was an interesting community of miners, as many Mormons were in their midst. Non-Mormon John Letts mined alongside the Saints: "Those were a *good* set of fellows [his emphasis], somewhat reckless, fine horsemen, fond of sprees, and an occasional fight. They were all hard workers . . . "[93] He particularly describes Porter as "a reckless, daring fellow."[94]

But Porter knew he lived on touchy ground. One Mormon, Thomas J. Orr, Jr., left Provo for the gold of California. "A man was keeping a trading post there and father had known him in Illinois and at Salt Lake. Father recognized him and called him by name, Porter Rockwell. He [Porter] was alarmed and told father to call him Brown in the future." Rockwell was concerned, continues Orr, that "his life wouldn't be worth much if people discovered his real identity."[95]

Nevertheless, Rockwell appreciated California. Orr continues, "Father asked Brown where he thought the best place to settle and was told it was no use going further and that place was as good as any to locate."

Porter was also helpful to travelling missionaries. Jonathon Crosby and his wife Caroline, on their way to the Sandwich Islands in the Pacific, stopped at Rockwell's inn and found him a gregarious fellow as he tended the tavern while selling to miners.[96] The Crosbys also found him especially helpful to missionaries: " . . . we camped a day & sold our teems and waggons to P. Rockwell . . . but we had the use of them to take us to Sacramento & Porter send a man along to take the teems back."[97]

Rockwell may next have helped guide Apostles Lyman and Rich part way to Great Salt Lake City. Joseph Cain records, "We left the Mormon Tavern the 17th of August,"[98] then details in his journal that non-Mormon immigrants were beginning to pour into California, and had been arriving *en masse* for a month. His missionary group passed non-Mormon immigrants "at an average, one thousand per day" for fifteen days. "Most of them were in a state of starvation." On the desert, "we found an awful destruction of property. Wagons, carriages, harness, etc., were strewed from one end of the desert to the other; and so wilful were the owners that, lest these articles should be of any use to any other person they have cut and destroyed them in a way not to mistake their meaning. On this desert, the dead animals were so numerous, that the stench was almost intolerable; one of our company, whilst riding along, counted fourteen hundred head by the road-side, beside hundreds more [which] were scattered over the plain . . .

"The Indians are very troublesome and hostile, many of the emigrants having been shot while on guard. These Indians have become so bold, that they will attack a small party; rob, and often kill the men, and drive away their animals into the mountains, although our company had no trouble with them."[99]

The Mormon party arrived at Great Salt Lake City six weeks later. Porter possibly never made the trip; if he did he probably went only as far as the Humboldt Valley, and returned.

In any case, he was now at work in California. One early writer states Porter "settled . . . between Sacramento and Mormon Island, and kept, for several years, the 'Halfway House.' Here he practiced rifle shooting, and made a great deal of money at matches."[100]

Another account, whether true or not, makes a good story: "In 1850 a match was made at the Halfway House for shooting."[101] The gold-miners were starved for entertainment, so it was only natural that when Boyd Stewart challenged Porter Rockwell to a rifle match, word spread like wildfire. Hundreds of men swarmed on Porter's Half-Way House to witness the event. Stewart put up a good challenge but Rockwell took him handily. When Porter won the $1,000 gold prize the town went wild; it was another excuse to party. Porter had been the most popular man in town anyway, but now he was idolized.

The jealous, defeated Stewart then lit a fuse . . . he announced to the mob who Brown really was . . . and, because of the number of soused Missourians and Illinoisians in the mob, "that night Brown (Rockwell) mounted his fleetest horse and vanished, leaving his business just as it stood at the time. The citizens imagined, naturally enough, that he had been assassinated."[102]

The above account comes from one Samuel D. Sirrine, that almost-anonymous soul calling himself Achilles and penning *The Destroying Angels of Mormondom*. The *Salt Lake Herald* reports

Sirrine as "a person whose name has figured in rather disgraceful connection in this territory during late years. The book seems to be regarded in its true light, that is, as a fraud, hence it finds little sale."[103]

Because of the volatile nature of fleeting popularity, Porter was, as it were, chased out of town with a hangman's noose.[104]

He left his business permanently September 5, 1850 and led 50 Mormon missionaries to Great Salt Lake City. Whether under mob pressure, as "Achilles" asserts, or simply because Rockwell merely sold his business, is not actually known. What is known, according to a November *Deseret News,* is that under Porter's guiding hand, the Mormon party "lost not a man on the route . . . though the Indians followed them in large numbers on Mary's River [in California], and for nearly 400 miles."[105] The missionaries he was leading had labored in California and the Pacific Isles, and had rendezvoused when Rockwell decided to leave.

On this journey comes another revealing journal entry: "After we crossed the Sierra Nevada Mountains we camped a few days and the Indians stole some of our horses and some of them belonged to Porter Rockwell which made him feel out of patience with the red men. In crossing the 40 mile desert, there arose a terrible wind storm called a hurricane. We had to stop on the middle of the desert and during the night a great many of our animals went off with the storm and never could be found. Porter Rockwell and two other of the boys took off [for] the Indians. They took ten head [of the Indians' horses] to make up for a number that was driven off by the Indians in Carson Valley."[106]

One evening an Indian came into camp attempting to trick them. Porter wasn't fooled. The Indian took out running. " . . . At this said Rockwell fired 2 shots with his dragoon pistol. In the morning we found the intruder about 300 yards from camp lying dead on his face."[107] Reporting this incident was Goudy E. Hogan, a young Mormon adventurer who had panned for gold and was returning to Utah. "We thought Bro. Porter Rockwell a well known brave man."

Within six weeks Rockwell led the missionary party into Great Salt Lake City.

Here, life, as Porter found it, was booming. The Mormons were now publishing their own newspaper, the *Deseret News*, and operating five flour mills around-the-clock. The flour was merchandised to gold-rushing prospectors coming from the East, and trading flourished.[108] The valley indeed was "blossoming as a rose," as Brigham had prophesied of the once hopeless desert. Brigham's people in fact were now successfully irrigating the mountains, due to Porter's earlier scouting recommendations, and Mormon crops were bountiful.

At this point, the *Saint Louis Daily Journal* produced an article of surprising counterpoint to the nation's one-sided anti-Mormon press: In its description of Utah the *Journal* summarizes, "The present population of Deseret [the first name for Utah] is estimated at 20,000, but the emmigration of the present year, it is expected, will swell the amount to 40,000. Last year [1850] they adopted a constitution, admirably consistent with the constitution of the United States, and as thoroughly republican as the constitution of any state in the union. They have not legislated on the subject of slavery, but they express their conviction that slavery can have no legal existence where it has never been recognized. They are devotedly attached to the American Union, and say that it has the best government the world has ever produced or will ever produce until Christ shall come and reign over the earth.

"The Mormons live harmoniously together, are industrious and frugal, and are described as very hospitable. It is but three years since they settled in the valley of the Great Salt Lake, and in that time they have opened good farms, built houses and barns, erected mills of various kinds, made bridges across the river, built school-houses and established schools, built a State House, chartered a University, and, in fact, they have done more to advance the real prosperity of the State, than some of the original Thirteen. They have raised funds to assist their brethren in Europe to emigrate. Last year they sent out 6000 dollars, and this year their subscriptions amount to 500,000 dollars. Their chief crop is wheat, for which both climate and soil are well adapted. Fifty bushels per acre is about an average crop. Corn is an unproductive crop with them; other grains generally produce very well. Stock of all kinds do well ... The valley of the Great Salt Lake is described as peculiarly healthy; agues and bilious fevers are entirely unknown, and the boys and girls look as fair and fresh as the flowers in May."[109]

Despite this good press for the Saints, Porter was suffering from the aftereffects of scuttlebutt and slander. And although his critical stock was on the rise, his good name was constantly debased by gossip. Certain non-Mormons and apostates congregated in masses and passed stories among themselves that Rockwell was an incurable murderer, and that he had been since Illinois. Because of the velocity with which gossip spread from tavern to tavern, he found himself the focal point of every floating rumor both sides of the Rockies. "Mention of the name of Porter Rockwell had sent a chill to every heart," claims William P. Bennet, one Nineteenth Century writer.[110] Everywhere Porter rode, every tavern into which he entered, he found himself the center of controversy and outlandish tales, rivaling as it were — as unbelievable as it may seem — the exploits of Ulysses and Robin Hood combined. His killings would come, but to label them under murder would be, indeed, stretching it.

Even in California he had been accused of murder. One J. M. Flake had died[110] from falling off his mule,[111] but rumor had accused Rockwell of murdering him.[112] Now in Utah anti-Mormon writers heaped on additional bellicose rhetoric.

Writer Nelson Slater, in his unintentionally amusing *Fruits of Mormonism,* details one Rockwell manhunt: "The emigrant [a non-Mormon] saw his pursuers [Porter and the sheriff] coming after him, and ran his horse, being aware of their intention. Discovering that he was likely to be overtaken, he turned off from the road to get among willow bushes. The mormons came up to him, and without trial, judge, or jury, they cut off his head."[113]

It was marvelously detailed reporting from a writer not even witness to the event . . . nor, evidently, had anyone been. Equally impressive was Slater's research . . . except for one slight flaw: Porter was not in Utah when the alleged incident occurred, he was in California. (Nor had non-Mormon immigrants arrived in Utah until June, 1849, two months *after* Porter had left with Lyman to California.)

Even so, when Slater arrived in Coloma, California with fellow immigrants, he published his book, detailing Porter's crime to the world. Rockwell was still obviously a scapegoat to church enemies and at this point in his life was able to take it in stride.

His next assignment was to serve in the Nauvoo Legion — now reorganized in Great Salt Lake City — by tracking down thieves from non-Mormon wagon trains.[114] This service lasted February 19 to February 27, 1851 and Porter's success in the venture is unknown.

His next call came as an Indian fighter. The Utes had recently attacked Fort Utah on the Provo River in an all-out battle — but the Mormons had routed them. In retaliation the Indians attacked a white settlement of non-Mormon immigrants in Tooele, west of Great Salt Lake City, by galloping through and stealing horses.

Naturally enough, Porter was called to the scene. Despite his recent bout with Indian thieves in California he seemed determined to treat them in such a manner that would bolster the Indians' trust in the Saints.

Riding into Tooele, Porter recruited Lorenzo D. Custer of Akron, Ohio and other immigrants. As a substantially powerful posse they headed after the Indian thieves.[115] First they tracked down the Indians at a small village by Rush Lake, but when they confronted the savages Porter realized he could not differentiate the guilty from the innocent. So he took 30 Indians prisoner, and marched them back to Tooele for questioning.[116]

His own possemen were now critical of Porter. Understanding neither Brigham's decree nor Rockwell's intentions to use the peace pipe where possible, the non-Mormons felt Porter was unwisely treating the braves with kid gloves.

And they were right. Porter allowed the Indians to pack their own guns,[117] feeling the majority would check any violence. All went well until sunset, when the Indians began to get uneasy.

And suddenly they scattered.[118]

The posse rounded them up until, about 9 P.M. under the moonlight, the Indians tried running off again.[119] At this point they were only a quarter mile from the approaching white settlement.

Lorenzo Custer spurred his horse to get around the braves and herd them into a cluster, when he made the mistake of pulling his revolver: He aimed at one Indian and shot ... but missed.[120] The same Brave wheeled around and killed Custer cold.

One of the possemen, W. R. Dickinson, records, "I shot the ingine that shot Custer we then laid Custer on the horse and wente to the settlement Brought Him to town today and burid Him and quit."[121] The simple yet remarkable prose nutshells the story.

Porter continues the account in a dictated letter: "The Indians then made their escape with the exception of four who are now with us as prisoners, whom I intend to take along with us as guides."[122] In this letter to Brigham, Porter requested more possemen for help. Tullidge records later in 1889, "He considered it best to make another effort to obtain the stolen horses. He took a party of men, and with them the four Indian prisoners, and went through the mountains west of Grantsville into Skull valley. The prisoners were evidently in sympathy with their thieving brethren and professed to know nothing of those who had stolen the horses. Their assertions received no credit from the whites. The party formed camp, went hunting, and left Harrison Severe to guard the Indians for some twenty-four hours — rather a precarious business for one man under the circumstances. Rockwell and his men not finding any trace of the stolen horses, deemed it unwise to turn the thieves in their power loose to commit more depredations, and they were sacrificed to the natural instincts of self-defence."[123]

Typical of attacks on Rockwell, enemies of the church now claimed Custer, the dead immigrant, had worked on a sawmill for Apostle E. T. Benson but had not been paid.[124] The rumor continues that Rockwell was rushed to the scene to kill Custer, who was complaining about the wages.[125] To support that tale, critics Hoffman and Birney later claimed Rockwell refused to kill the Tooele Indians in order to keep peace with their fellow tribesmen at his Skull Valley Ranch.[126] However, Porter did not establish the ranch until the early 60's, at least ten years *after* the Custer affair. On Porter it was another typical hatchet-job.

Brigham's trust in Rockwell remained untainted. Several weeks later on June 3 Brigham called him into his office:[127] The Prophet likely updated Porter on Indian affairs and gave him a new assignment. Although the specifics of that meeting are not recorded, Rockwell was probably assigned to additional missionary activity with George W. Bean among the tribes,[128] where he spent the next several months.

And then Cupid struck. Rockwell became involved in a real estate transaction, and through a joint partnership with John Neff — in which the two purchased "the first canyon south of Mill Creek"[129] near Great Salt Lake City — the 38-year-old Porter Rockwell naturally met the 22-year-old daughter of John Neff.

And her name was Mary Ann . . .

VIII

While his romance blossomed, Porter set aside certain hours for church activities. Still close to the Kingdom he officiated January 3, 1852 in the Temple Ceremonies of the Endowment House.[1] While engaging in business activities, church responsibilities, and missionary work among the Indians, the new year of 1853 dawned, and Porter found himself feeling a wisp of déjà vu. In the new Social Hall the city's second-ever theatrical production opened January 19. As in Nauvoo Porter now found himself not only in the play, *Pizarro,* but playing the part of Davilla, the Spanish soldier. Yet this time he would have problems — perhaps because his true-love was watching. O. F. Whitney records the performance: "His speech, addressed to the old Peruvian, 'Another word, grey-headed ruffian, and I strike,' being uttered, Porter, turning nervously toward the prompter, asked in a loud whisper, "Shall I stick him?'"[2] The theatre rocked with laughter. Whitney concludes: ". . . Porter convulsed his audience . . ." Evidently time — or romance — had taken its toll on his Thespian abilities.

In March he and Franklin Neff, undoubtedly a relative to John Neff, were granted rights to the canyon just south of Mill Creek;

they were authorized to charge for loads of firewood and fence poles taken from the canyon — but with one catch: They had to first build a road to the canyon.[3]

Whether Rockwell himself worked on the road or simply hired others is not known, but several weeks later at the first signs of spring he made preparations for a journey to California. On the trip he probably herded horses to Carson Valley; the *Daily Alta California* reports he rode with "Cogswell's Train of 20 wagons."[4]

On returning to Salt Lake Valley Porter participated on a committee to find the best location for a penitentiary. After two weeks of searching throughout both Salt Lake and Utah valleys, he and several others chose a site four and a half miles east of the city's then existing city limits, near the mountains.[5]

Porter, meanwhile, continued courting Mary Ann, visiting her between journeys and assignments. Mary Ann obviously possessed the patience for such a courtship, as the relationship continued to solidify. She waited patiently as he galloped off again, now to play a key role in his most important assignment yet . . .

Brigham's people were now on thin ice — their thinnest ice ever — because of an explosive incident that had occurred with the Indians . . .

The scene was described by George McKenzie, friend to several of the principals involved:

"Walker, the war chief of the Ute nation, with his braves and their families were camped on Spring creek about one mile north of the present town of Springville, (Utah Co., Utah) all at peace with the white settlers, spending their time fishing and hunting, and trading and begging from the people. James Ivie at that time had built a cabin, and was living in it with his wife and one child about half a mile north and west of where the Indians were camped. In the forenoon of July 17, 1853, an Indian and squaw came into Ivie's cabin.

"The squaw had three large trout which she wanted to trade to Mrs. Ivie for some flour. Flour being very scarce at that time, Mrs. Ivie called her husband in to get his views on the trade of that kind, he being at work digging a well. When he saw the trout, he said, 'They look mighty good to me,' and suggested that Mrs. Ivie might give three pints of flour for them, if the squaw would trade that way.

"He then went out of the cabin to resume his work. Just after Ivie left two more Indians came into the cabin, one of whom seemed to be the husband or had some kind of claim on the squaw who had closed the trade with Mrs. Ivie. When this Indian saw the three trout, and the small amount of flour received in exchange, he became enraged and began beating the squaw, knocking her down, kicking and stamping her in a brutal manner.

"While this assault was being committed, Mrs. Ivie ran and called her husband. Mr. Ivie came to the cabin, and while the Indian was still beating the squaw he took hold of the Indian and pulled him away, the squaw lying prostrate on the floor. Ivie tried to push the Indian out of the cabin. When the Indian came, he left his gun standing by the door, and as Ivie pushed him out he grabbed his gun and tryed to get in position to shoot Ivie. Ivie got hold of the muzzle of the gun, and in the struggle the gun was broken. The Indian retaining the stock and Ivie the barrel.

"When the gun broke, Ivie dealt the Indian a hard blow on the head with the barrel of the gun. The Indian fell to the ground, apparently dead, but did not expire until some hours later.

"The other Indian who came to the cabin the same time as his companion drew his bow and arrow and shot Ivie, the arrow passing through the shoulder of Ivie's buckskin hunting shirt.

"At this Ivie struck the Indian a violent blow and he fell unconscious by the side of the prostrate body of the other Indian. Just as Ivie got through with this second Indian, the squaw that he had been trying to protect came out of the cabin door with a stick of wood in her hand which she had picked up by the side of the fire in the cabin. With it she stuck Ivie a blow in the face cutting a deep gash in his upper lip, and the scar showed plainly from that time until his death.

"Ivie again used the gun barrel to defend himself and struck the squaw. She fell unconscious by the side of the prostrate bodies of the two Indians. At this stage in the drama Joseph Kelly, one of the foremost settlers of Springville, came upon the scene, and while looking at the three Indians lying apparently dead he was told by Ivie what had taken place.

"Kelly took a bucket of water that stood in the cabin and poured it on the Indians, trying to restore them. He then sent the

Indian who first came to the cabin with the squaw for another bucket of water to try to restore the Indians to life, this Indian having taken no part in the trouble.

"Kelly told Ivie to take his wife and child and go into town before the Indian camp was notified of the trouble, which he did.

"The Indian that Kelly sent after the water went to the Indian camp and told of what had taken place at the Ivie cabin. The news of the trouble soon spread through the camp and the settlement of whites. Intense excitement reigned, both in the Indian camp and the settlement."[6]

The enraged Indians then swept down on Mormon settlements, killing whatever whites they could find. George W. Bean continues his report:

"This outbreak, called the Walker War, caused much suffering and loss of life . . . Many small settlements were broken up and farmers living outside of towns were obliged to move in and suffer great loss of improvements, our family among the rest.

"People traveling had to go in armed parties for several months . . .

"It was in April word came from Parowan, Iron County, that the great Chief Walker had appeared there apparently friendly and desired to hear from President Young, so the President forthwith sent O. Porter Rockwell, John R. Murdock, myself and others to meet Walker and make such proposals as would bring about a good lasting peace. We departed with a letter and some presents and met the Old Chief and party at Beaver."[7]

The peace mission's activities were reported by Thomas D. Brown, member of the mission:

"Porter Rockwell, Bean . . . met Walker and the train on the Beaver . . . to induce Walker to accompany them to Gt. Salt Lake City to have an interview with Govr. Young. Walker declined, urging as an excuse, that he wished to remain at home till his wheat was sown."[8]

Bean relates his chronicle of the all-important meeting: "The Beaver Chief, 'Beaver-ads,' was present and Walker was disposed to show off his importance . . . in illustrating how he would treat all his enemies, he struck the Beaver Chief in the face with his pen-knife opened, and made the blood fly profusely, and there came near being a scene as Old Beaverads jumped and caught up his gun to shoot Walker. We disarmed him, but his wrath was not appeased until Walker gave him some presents we had just handed him.

"The result of the visit with Walker was a tentative arrangement to meet him in company with President Young at upper Chicken Creek in fifteen days and, if plenty of beef cattle, flour and Indian goods were brought, then all might be well, otherwise not. This was afterwards all fulfilled.

"President Young had called Orrin Porter Rockwell and myself to the task of keeping Chief Walker in hand and peaceable for a year if it cost the Church $10,000, and to labor and teach and trade among the Utah Indians and try to heal up the feelings made by the occurrences of last Summer.

"When we met Walker at Beaver he was coming north, full of complaints, so we travelled with him several days and showed him much attention, and succeeded, to some extent, in softening his warlike spirit. We left him encamped at Chicken Creek, while we went on to make up a trading outfit for the season."[9]

During this break in the action Rockwell returned to Mary Ann, and either from a long, planned engagement, or as one of those spur-of-the moment decisions for which he was known, he married her May 3, 1854, and the marriage was performed by Brigham Young.[10]

The very next day Porter left her . . . on another journey south with Brigham and company. This was Brigham's annual trip for warmer climes, specifically St. George, and his train included 101 souls and 34 wagons. Rockwell, Bean, and Amos Neff rode in the 25th wagon.[11]

Bean resumes his chronicle, with a report on a plan of Porter's that backfired:

"President Young . . . got the Old Chief to accompany him . . . O. P. Rockwell and myself preceeded the President's party a few minutes, just long enough for Porter to slip a bottle of whiskey into the Old Chief's hands, about half of which went down his throat instanter, as it were, and when President Young arrived, Walker was half drunk and sulky." Rockwell walked away, head bowed, while Brigham looked on, shaking his head. Bean continues:

" . . . The President intended to go on farther that night, but Walker forbade it, [saying] that he [Brigham] was not to move before the next morning, giving some superstitious reasons therefore.

" . . . after much pleading and finding the Old Chief immovable because he had a very sick child, the President decided to stay rather than cause a rupture between parties, as about eighty Lodges of Indians were encamped.

"The Elders administered to the child and it got better, so that Walker decided to go with us next morning as far south as Harmony, Iron Co., which took fifteen days or more. Being in good company had a good effect on him . . .

"As we returned from the south, President Young promised Walker that he would send Porter Rockwell and myself and others with goods to trade and supply his needs without his going to the City. The President privately told us to keep peace with the Indians at all costs this season, as the people had suffered so much the last year by the Walker War that this year they must raise their crops. He gave us that mission to keep peace with the Indians."

An artist named S. N. Carvalho had accompanied the Mormons on the journey. Carvalho had been with John C. Fremont's final expedition when exhaustion and frost-bite had overtaken him and forced him to reside temporarily with the Mormons. To his private journal he records that Brigham Young "has appointed the following gentlemen to take up a permanent residence with Walkara's band of Utahs, viz.: Porter Rockwell, James A. Bean, interpreter; John Murdoch, and John Lott. These persons will follow them in their wanderings, and will, most probably, prevent many depredations and murders."[12]

Bean continues:

"President Young [then] promised Walker that goods would be furnished him through Porter Rockwell and myself . . . "[13]

Brigham wished to add frosting to the cake by trading blankets for horses. The horses under consideration had been stolen from the Mormons — and Brigham knew he was trading for what belonged to the Saints anyway — but the transaction won Walker's heart.[14]

Brigham then returned to Great Salt Lake Valley. Despite all the Prophet's efforts, Walker seemed to possess a certain inconsistency, based perhaps on deep, underlying resentments and jealousy. Andrew Love, a settler in Nephi, confides in his journal, "He [Walker] feels to trample under foot the authority of Brigham."[15]

After parting from the old chief, another problem quickly arose:

"While in the city after goods," writes Bean, "word came to President Young that Walker had come to Nephi and found the people all busily engaged in building an earthen wall around their settlement, which exasperated him [Walker] very much[16], and he forbade any further work thereon, saying it was an evidence [that] they intended to keep the Indians away, and was therefore an unfriendly act, for after the wall was done, [Walker feared that] when he came to visit them and get something to eat, they would let him stand outside and possibly toss a biscuit out to him over the wall like he was a dog or a slave. He reminded them that he had given Brigham and the Mormons the privileges of settling on these lands and jointly occupying them with the Indians, using land, water, grass, timber together as brothers, but if 'Whites' separated and fenced off their settlements, they would have to stay inside and Indians outside — no more getting wood and grass for the 'Whites' if they continued the wall business.

"To avoid trouble the people stopped work until word came from President Young. He was much disturbed by this new move of the wiley old Chief, and he immediately wrote a strong letter to Walker and gave it to me to carry forthwith to the Indian Camp and interpret the same to them. This I did, with O. Porter Rockwell, Amos Neff and 'Squash,' as he was commonly called, 'Washear' being his Indian name. We found 80 Lodges (tents) of Indians camped one mile above Nephi. We were a little over time with our goods for Walker and he had become very impatient waiting for us.

"We drove into camp with a four-horse team and immediately I gave Walker the letter or read it to him and translated it, in which President Young expressed his surprise that Walker had so soon forgotten the good time they had in travelling together and that he was acting foolishly in opposing the building of walls around the settlements. He warned Walker that this was the Lord's work, and His people, and for him to mind his own business, and the people would do the same; and that if he troubled the Lords' people any more, he would likely suffer for it.

"At this point Walker snatched the letter from my hand in the greatest rage and trampled it under his feet, and then struck into a boastful tirade, saying that he would let Brigham Young know that he had lived before he came here and he had fought the Sioux, the Snakes, the Arapahoes, and Cheyennes, and the Crow Indian tribes — that his scars were all in front, and not on his back, and if he said so War would comence this very day, and finally ordered his Camps to move instantly. At this there was a great scattering of the crowd around us, and a howl of grief from the squaws, and a pulling down of lodges. The boys and young 'Bucks' gathered in the ponies and packed the tents, etc. This was hastily carried on for thirty minutes, and the ground was clear and the whole cavalcade moved toward Salt Creek Canyon.

"About fifty warriors remained, however, surrounding us, including all the old Sub-Chiefs, as Battiese, tintick, Bear-Scratch and others who each in turn took great pleasure in boasting to me and Porter of their brave and bloody deeds during the War the year before . . . and in fact all the chief exploits of the Walker War were shown up and their present willingness to do lots more of it was plainly manifest, and the snapping of caps, swaying of bow strings was not very pleasant music to us.

"However, I picked up the letter of President Young's from under Walker's feet and told him I would return to Salt Lake and tell Brigham how his words of counsel had been treated by him.

"At this he got into a rage and said: 'No, you won't go and get all the Mormons after us again.' Walker asked what we were going to do with our guns and other trade that we had in the wagon.

"I told him we would take them back.

"He said: 'No you won't. We have waited till I'm sore for those goods and must have them.'

"Amos Neff was holding the reigns of the four-horse team nearby, ready to move at any moment.

"At this point, Washear, or Squash, spoke up and said: 'Walker you talk like a fool. I was with George when Brigham gave him the letter and Brigham was not mad, but he talked straight and he wants you to do right and not act foolish. "Poorets" (as they called me, meaning one arm man), is only talking for Brigham, and he wants you to listen and do right and all will be well.'

"Washear grew very earnest and Walker talked loud, too, and the Braves all began to talk and [in the apparent heated argument among the Indians, it] gave us a chance to slip away, get on our wagon and quietly drive down to Nephi settlement, one mile distant, unmolested.

"We forthwith got up an armed escort to guard us back to Payson. Just before we started off, we looked across the plain just above the town and saw old Chief Walker coming toward the town on foot, leading his little son, and Washear leading his horse. We forthwith interpreted this action to mean his repentance, and a peaceful conclusion of the morning's trouble. I met him a short distance out, and met them with this remark from Walker: 'I'm not angry now. "Shenentz," my relative, has convinced me I was wrong in my suspicions of Brigham and his Mormons and I'm sorry for all the trouble.'

"He begged us to overlook everything and go right along with them over to Sanpete Valley, near Fort Ephraim, to do our trading just as if nothing had happened. After some consultation we decided to do so, but took the old Chief Walker and his son into our wagon with us, so that if any treachery was attempted, we could have some show to keep even. We arrived at Fort Ephraim that night and stayed five days to trade with the Indians gathered there. We had several rather stormy bouts with Walker's impudent greed, and were obliged to take eight little Indians (Slaves), rather than have them butchered by the cruel Utes, they having lost their New Mexico Spaniards' trade by purchase."

Bean's last comment refers to the fact Mexicans had arrived in the territory to trade horses for Indian slaves, which trading was approved by the superintendent of Indian Affairs in New Mexico, James Calhoun. Brigham countered the bureaucrat's actions, and labeled any such trading illegal.[17]

Thus ends the chronicle of the Walker War.

An interesting aside, revealing the core of Bean's faith and philosophy in dealing with the Indians — as well as, perhaps, the same philosophy incorporated by his cohort, Rockwell — can be summarized by his next statement in his autobiography:

"We found there was plenty need of praying under all conditions, and not always on our knees. These hair-raising experiences gave evidence that the Lord can raise up a protective power from a source the least expected when it becomes necessary, as in the case of Washear taking the trouble off us at the critical moment. This happened in or about October, 1854. Washear, or Squash, was one of my truest friends. He came to me in 1849 at intervals during my desperate illness, after the cannon explosion when I lost my left hand. He taught me the Indian language, as I taught him our language."

Unlike their problems with Indians, the Mormons' problems with the press seemed interminable. Newspapers and books continued to twist facts about the Saints at every turn. For example, two Pahvant Braves were slain by a company of Missouri immigrants. In retaliation Indians killed eight Pacific Railraod surveyors. It seems the leader of the railroad surveying crew had written a book, *History of the Mormons,* somewhat critical of the church. Anti-Mormon writers were now quick to assume "that Captain Gunnison and his party were murdered by the 'Danites,' disguised as Indians, by, and with the knowledge and 'counsel' of the Prophet."[18] And of course Rockwell was again implicated. Years later, in a truly remarkable piece of propaganda entitled *Holy Murder, the Story of Porter Rockwell*, writers Hoffman Birney and Charles Kelly assert that the above atrocity "was charged to the Indians — Goshutes of the band headed by Kanosh — but to this day gossip in Utah alleges that Rockwell and the Danites participated in the slaughter."[19] "Gossip in Utah" is perhaps as authentic a source as they cite in the entire volume.

Critics went so far as to report in 1860 that the Danites had assassinated Jim Bridger[20] because he was selling weapons to the Indians. To their dismay he died 21 years later in Missouri of natural causes.

Porter, meanwhile, returned home, but his days with Mary Ann were again brief, as he soon undertook yet another assignment: He now teamed with James S. Brown, one of the Mormons who had discovered gold at Sutter's Mill five years previously.[21] (Six, possibly seven of the original nine white male workers in the Sutter's Mill crew were Mormons, members of the discharged Mormon Battalion, when the crew discovered gold.)[22] Brown describes the mission: "I began a journey back to Green River, but met Porter Rockwell at Fort Bridger. He had a license from Governor Brigham Young for me to trade with the Indians; also some two or three thousand dollars' worth of Indian goods for me to market. At that time there was no opportunity to trade, as the Indians had disposed of their robes, pelts and furs for the season, so we sent the goods to Fort Supply and had them stored there.

"I accompanied Rockwell to Salt Lake City, arriving there on July 19 [1853]. We reported conditions to the governor, who received us very kindly ... "[23]

Porter next became involved in the outcome of a major confrontation between Brigham Young and the United States Government. The government wished to replace Brigham as governor of the territory, but Brigham had other plans. He told a congregation, "We have got a Territorial Government, and I am and will be Governor, and no power can hinder it, until the Lord Almighty says, 'Brigham, you need not be Governor any longer' ... "[24]

So when Lieutenant Colonel Edward Jenner Steptoe rode into Great Salt Lake City with 300 U. S. troops to put him in power, the Mormons all but laughed. They were not to be intimidated in their own country. This was not Missouri.

But U. S. President Franklin Pierce demanded Steptoe to be governor ... and the makings of a major war were at hand.

Steptoe, however, four months after dwelling with the Saints, realized he knew a better leader for the people when he saw one, and declined Pierce's appointment.

This provided more fertilizer for anti-Mormon writers, already of fertile imagination. They claimed Steptoe was coerced by Brigham in his decision.[25] (The likelihood that a seasoned military commander would knuckle under the demands of a religious leader were far-fetched at best; Steptoe, had he wished for a power struggle, could have called upon a sizeable United States infantry to come to his aid. Instead, he actually signed a petition, along with other influential Utahns, to the President of the United States, requesting Brigham to be reappointed as governor.)

Brigham now seemed willing to abide by Pierce's decision either way, as he remarked, "If the gallant gentleman [Steptoe] who is now in our midst had received the commission of governor of this territory, as was reported, and had accepted it, I would have taken off my hat and honored the appointment," thus mollifying his previous position.

And, rather than mistrusting the Mormons, Steptoe's next action was to seek Brigham's help: He wished to find the eight Pahvant warriors responsible for the murders of the eight railroad surveyors; specifically, he sought from Brigham men who could move among the Pahvants and boldly confront tribal chieftains.

Brigham offered him Porter Rockwell and George Bean.

Steptoe simultaneously requested help in locating a shorter route to Carson Valley, California, and for this Brigham offered him another scout.

While Steptoe remained at the Army garrison in Great Salt Lake City, Porter and George Bean rode off to the Pahvant chieftains with a Frenchman named Nicholas Janise. All three were hired by Steptoe at $5 per day,[26] and were given an escort of 20 troops to fulfill their assignment. Their task was to arrest the eight Indian murderers from the chiefs and hopefully in a single day.

But George Bean claims the wiley Chief Kanosh outsmarted the Army: "It is laughable to think of our first trip in a Government outfit Ambulance and four good mules, expecting to bring the criminals back with us. It required many trips, and finally, Kanosh, Parashont and all the Chiefs agreed to give up the number. Eight Indians were surrendered on certain conditions, just after New Year, 1855 ... Kanosh and his friends had the number on hand — but such a turn-out of 'murderers' was never before seen: one squaw, for the Mormon killed; one old blind fellow, one foolish chap, one outsider, that had no friends, another old sick fellow, and three little boys, ten to thirteen years old, made up the number ... This group shocked us all. Kanosh said it was the best he could do without a fight [among the Braves], as the Indians were determined to shield the Chief Braves who participated,[27] as they felt justified pretty much in the killing because of the treatment some of them had received from [Eastern] Emigrants going to California ...

"So the Soldiers took charge of the Prisoners ...

"We made the journey back to Salt Lake City and the prisoners were guarded by the soldiers until court time."

Bean smiled at the fiasco, as no doubt did Porter.

At the trial of the eight "murderers," the government officials and army personnel did not particularly enhance public relations with the Mormons, as the federáles now became sexually involved with local squaws,[28] while Steptoe and another judge showed up drunk in court.[29] The Army, admirably, did not execute the eight misfits.

With the Indian wars over, Porter returned to Mary Ann and soon found other problems on the homefront. He ran the following advertisement in the *Deseret News,* October 26: "$15.00 Reward ... STOLEN (Supposed by the Indians) about the middle of August last, from John Neff's Mill, on Mill Creek, a dark bay or light brown French Mare, six years old ... "[30]

Steptoe's concerns, however, were on a larger scale. Of Steptoe's two major projects in which he had sought help from Brigham, the first — securing the eight murderers was now "resolved." The second — finding a better route to California[31] — was still in question. Although he had hired a scout based on Brigham's suggestions, Steptoe was not pleased with the scout's efforts and fired the man.[32] He again turned to Porter, now assigning him to find the best possible route to Carson Valley.

And again Porter left his bride ...

Rockwell's trip was bizarre. He, George Bean, and three others trudged across a salt swamp, fighting frigid temperatures in the arctic-like desert, only to come upon an Indian graveyard: at several large springs they gazed underwater and found "six Indian bodies standing bolt upright and crusted over with the salty deposit in this, giving them the appearance of mummies."[33] Heavy stones had probably been tied to the corpses' ankles to keep them vertically positioned underwater. Rockwell and Bean thought they also saw other corpses buried still deeper in the water.

Porter scouted ahead alone and found the salt swamps unnavigable. The marshes eastward and southward were also impossible to traverse. Rockwell returned to his four companions and reported. Then, together, the party struck back for Great Salt Lake City.

With salt-mud clinging to boots they made their way towards civilization, finally arriving at Steptoe's office.

The following letter came from Steptoe's quartermaster to the Army's Quartermaster General: "As a matter of security, another party [after the first scout was released] was organized under 'Porter Rockwell,' a Mormon, but a man of strong mind and independent spirit, a capital guide and fearless prairie-man."[34] (For more of the letter see Note 23.)

With Steptoe's projects finally concluded, Porter was free to return to his family . . . where Mary Ann gave birth March 11, 1855 at her parents' home in Mill Creek Canyon to a child they named Mary Amanda Rockwell.[35]

After mulling over his reports, Steptoe decided to take his men on Rockwell's recommended route to California. And then the obvious dawned on him — he should actually take Rockwell also. Once again Porter left wife and family, and trudged westward, leading the U. S. Cavalry. As their guide,[36] he again received $5 per day.

Once in California, Rockwell visited Joseph L. Heywood in San Francisco. Heywood had been the first in Utah to name Porter as a deputy in the territory. Now in California Heywood writes a friend, "O. P. Rockwell calls upon me occasionally."[37]

Porter then had an experience that would change his life permanently . . .

Despite Joseph Smith's warning, blessing, and promise for protection, Porter cut his hair. Although he had probably never conceived of disobeying his childhood Prophet, his weakness, like Samson of old, was a woman . . . but, unlike Delilah, his temptation was far from sexual; nonetheless, it produced problems which haunted him for a lifetime . . .

IX

In California Porter visited the widow of the late Don Carlos Smith.[1] A friend details, "When he saw [Agnes], she was just recovering from typhoid fever, the consequence of which her hair had all fallen off. Porter wore his hair long, as he said the Prophet had told him that if he wore his hair long his enemies should not have the power over him neither should he be overcome by evil. When he met Sister Smith he had no gold dust or money to give her, so he had his hair cut to make her a wig and from that time he said that he could not control the desire for strong drink, nor the habit of swearing."[2]

But Porter's visit to California was short-lived. He soon heard about an Indian attack on two foreigners, and sought to organize a posse of revenge. Whether he was successful is unknown.

He then met a returning missionary from Calcutta, and together they rode with several others eastward, back to Great Salt Lake City. Porter's wilderness savvy was by now incomparable, as on this journey the party left Carson Valley September 22 and arrived in Great Salt Lake City in less than two weeks.[3]

Porter again returned to Mary Ann. His home was now south of

the city near the entrance to Neff's Canyon — he had moved there
in 1850 from Porter's Spring — now Perry, Utah — north of the big
city.[4] Evidently Mary Ann had wished to live closer to her parents,
not unlike his first wife, Luana.

Soon, Porter was visited by John Bennion, who requested
permission to graze cattle in Rush Valley, to which Porter
consented.[5]

Two visiting Frenchmen then stirred the interest of city
hierarchists: Jules Remy and Julius Brenchly were travelling
through America to report their adventures in a book; the two
daring Frenchmen had been wounded by Shoshone Indians in
Carson Valley, and now sought refuge in Mormon country to both
recover from wounds and to explore[6] and report on the culture
and terrain of this strange land and people.

After meeting with Brigham they found themselves the center of
attention. On their way out of town October 20 they camped in Big
Cottonwood Canyon. Remy chronicles the event: "Scarcely had we
got all things in order when we saw two smart carriages
approaching at a gallop, which suddenly drew up. They contained
our friends of Salt Lake City, who had come to take a final leave of
us at our first encampment. Others soon afterwards arrived on
horseback. In this agreeable surprise we saw a proof that our
feelings at parting were shared by others, and we were very
pleasurably affected by it. Amongst others there were ... Mr. O.
P. Rockwell, the celebrated friend of Joseph Smith ...

"We passed the night very jollily under the clear sky, around
our fire, some playing, some singing, others chatting, all making
numerous libations. Victor fried pancakes and sang
madrigals ... Never did a night-bivouac pass more gaily. Old
General Burr seemed to have grown young again, and one would
have supposed he felt himself all the more obliged to be in good
humour because he had married a French-woman, and for this
reason looked upon me as a quasi-fellow-countryman ... A little
before daybreak, our amiable visitors took their way back to the
city, with the exception of Mr. Rockwell, who desired to stay with
us until we broke up our camp." Remy singled him out from the
crowd to study more intently:

"Rockwell is a person sufficiently well known in the history of the Mormons for us to bestow a word on him. He is a man without much education, and of very ordinary intelligence, but at the same time extremely amiable and polite, with exceedingly distinguished and graceful manners. He has an imposing look, with a dash of the aristocratic in it . . .

"He has been accused, on no evidence — and many still persist in accusing him — of having, in May, 1842, fired a pistol at Governor L. W. Boggs, of Missouri.

" . . . What appears clear to us is, that Rockwell is incapable of doing wrong [unless] under the impression that he is doing right; so persuaded are we of this, that we would trust him with life and property without any hesitation. He is a lion in a lamb's skin, that we admit; but a brave and generous lion, full of heart and greatness, capable of the grandest devotedness, ready to sacrifice himself in behalf of any one who has gained his esteem, without exception of sect or person, whether Jews, Pagans, Mussulmans, or Mormons. He is of the stuff from which heroes are wrought, and if the blood of heroes can be inferred from the expression of the face, or the qualities of the heart, one would swear there were traces of a lofty origin in him. It is he who is ever at hand where there is a perilous service to be accomplished, a crime to be avenged, a sacrifice to be made which can be of advantage to the oppressed.

"He it was who at Carson Valley wished to put himself at the head of a company of volunteers for the purpose of avenging our reported death; and yet we were entire strangers to him then; but our boldness, our rashness possibly, in exposing ourselves alone in the desert, had touched him, and won for us a place in his affection.

"He [now] proposed to escort us as far as California, and had we accepted his offer, he would have accompanied us happy and content, without the remotest thought of any advantage to himself, proud of being able to give us this proof of his sincere regard . . .

" . . . we harnessed four fresh animals to our wagon, and set off, after receiving Rockwell's good wishes and farewell."[7]

Regarding the accusation for shooting Boggs one report claims a stranger asked Porter if he shot him. Denying the accusation, Porter simply looked at the man, then mumbled, "He's still alive, ain't he?"

Porter, for awhile, again remained with Mary Ann ... until Brigham found him yet another assignment.

The church president had become disgruntled with the non-Mormon operated mail service between Great Salt Lake City and Independence, Missouri, and now sought to win his own contract with the government. The service of Magraw and Hockaday was so inept that not only had mail been frequently lost but it had in its illustrious history arrived on schedule a grand total of three times.[8]

In his campaign to win the mail contract, Brigham now sought Porter's help as a public speaker. On January 9, 1856, Porter took the stand with several influential locals to address the Legislative Assembly at Fillmore,[9] seeking to rouse their aid and interest in maintaining the proposed mail system — if the government would comply. Then, on January 26 and February 2, Porter accompanied Brigham to the Old Tabernacle in Great Salt Lake City and again spoke. But it was Brigham who held the audience in the palm of his hand, arousing them to a standing ovation.[10]

The motion was carried, the locals were excited, and, acting on faith that the government would approve it, the Brigham Young Express and Carrying Company was launched. Two months later at General Conference, 19 church brethren were sustained as missionaries to specially build the supply cabins on the mail route East.

In Washington, of course, lay the final decision. Government officials debated amongst themselves, but the bottom line, as they realized, was the competency, or lack of it, of the existing mail company, and they conceded finally that Brigham should be given a chance.

Porter, meanwhile, actively pursued church responsibilites. Committed to missionary work and all it entailed, he accompanied Joseph Young in March "to Ogden City for to ordain Seventys," according to the journal of Edwin Ward Smout.[11] The Seventy was an advanced position in the Melchizedek Priesthood for Mormons pertaining primarily to missionary work, which meant that Rockwell actually had to hold the office before he could participate in ordaining others.

Rockwell was then given an assignment that would change the

course of western history. Innocently enough, he was asked to guide a party of prominent Utahns from Great Salt Lake City back to the United States. A. O. Smoot would lead the party while Porter would act as scout and hunter. Among the party would be several missionaries en route to Europe, as well as several territorial officials traveling to Washington,[12] including Almon W. Babbitt, whose involvement with Rockwell would eventually so enrage Washington that President Buchanan would actually declare war on Utah, and send a major invasion force of the United States Army . . .

The party of 38 Mormons launched their journey April 22, 1856 from Immigration Canyon. Within days they lost several horses necessary to survival, and Porter galloped off to find them. On April 29, he emerged from the mountains with the horses and was greeted with hurrahs from his brethren.[13]

Little did they know, but they were traipsing through territory under patrol by disgruntled Indians, who were at that moment on the verge of an all-out plains war.

This situation had begun, surprisingly enough, because of a cow. The animal had wandered from a Danish Mormon wagon train; a Miniconjou Brave had discovered the beast and butchered it for food. The Mormons later reported the incident to the Army at Fort Laramie only as a matter of record. But an intense young army officer, John L. Gratten, took it further. He saddled up a platoon of 29 cavalrymen and galloped off with two howitzers to arrest the culprit.

The Indian refused the arrest. The scene became heated and soon the soldiers found themselves in a fight for survival with frenzied Brule Sioux warriors. Despite their howitzers and firepower, the soldiers were all massacred.[14]

In retaliation Brigadier General William S. Harney returned to the Sioux camp and slaughtered 80 Indians — men, women, and children — and achieved the distinctive title "Squaw-killing Harney."[15] Harney then forced the plains tribes into a shaky truce at Fort Pierre, Nebraska in March, 1856, a matter of days before Porter's party arrived. Such was the tension when the 38 Mormons passed through Indian territory, heading eastward. Additionally, they were struck by yet another enemy they had evidently not considered . . .

Snowblindness. May 4th had begun with a blizzard[16] which paralyzed the camp 56 hours, causing them to blanket horses and spend two sleepless nights in the shivering cold. Through it all, Porter's paramount concern was the safety of the horses. He succeeded in leading the animals to a grove of trees three miles from camp for feeding.[17] There, two horses died, but when the storm let up the company moved on, unaware of the dangers the sun would pose in such circumstances. The company kept going, disregarding the blinding glare reflecting off the snow.

That night Orson Pratt was the first struck with pain.[18] And then one by one, others were hit . . . each with the torturous sensation of salt being poured in their eyes. They spent a nightmarish day and a half in camp. Despite the agony, they gathered about a campfire the evening of May 7th and listened, as best they could, to Porter as he related anecdotes of Joseph Smith's early days at the Hill Cumorah in New York.[19]

It wasn't long after the company resumed marching that they were met by another severe storm. This time at Greasewood Creek. Then on May 12 came yet another in a series of tribulations: Their horses ran off. Porter and a scout headed into the mountains to search them out. They returned with six.

On May 16 a heavy rain descended. Rockwell compensated for the inclement weather by hosting a large antelope feast.

After having been alone for weeks, George A. Smith writes in his journal May 29th: " . . . have passed trains almost hourly . . . May 30 — We have found the road to-day literally filled with emigrant trains . . . The rumor is that the Mormon emigration is tremendous; 5,000 are said to be fitting up at Omaha city, and as many more in other points."[20]

These foreign emigrants heading westward — mostly the harvest of overseas Mormon missionaries — were hauling their meager belongings in handcarts, the first such mode of cross-country transportation seen in America; and the reason was obvious: They couldn't afford wagons. The sight stunned non-Mormons, who mused on both the motivations and the pragmatism of such travel.

On June 8th, Porter guided his company beyond the Big Blue, near Atchison, 10 days ahead of schedule, despite the storms and setbacks, and without losing a life. From this accomplishment alone, Porter's name was becoming legendary. For efficiency in other matters, however, his name was spreading with equal velocity throughout non-Mormon circles . . . and soon that legend would reach Washington.

Almon W. Babbitt journeyed straight to the Capitol. In parting with Porter and the other Mormons, he had set out to accomplish his singular mission: obtaining goods and gold from the government to line his own pockets and to adorn the territorial government in Utah. Babbitt was an excommunicated Mormon.[21] Church court action had been taken in Kanesville for his purported immorality, yet despite Babbitt's standing in the church Brigham had appointed him Secretary of Utah Territory.

Then, two months after his excommunication, Babbitt had distributed congressional funds ineffectively.

Brigham suspected Babbitt had also become involved with Territorial Secretary Broughton D. Harris to sneak $24,000 of government funds out of the territory. This money had been distributed by Congress for Utah Territorial Government use, but Harris — and possibly Babbitt — sought to keep it away from Brigham in order, supposedly, to return it to Washington. Babbitt had been halted outside town, but did not have the money. Harris had it. Brigham learned of Harris' possession, yet was apparently of such a surprisingly mellow disposition toward apostates — contrary to anti- Mormon newspaper accounts — that he allowed Harris to leave Utah with the money and return it illegally to Washington.[22]

To his glee Babbitt finally arrived in Washington, where he now had a heyday. He purchased left and right, and two months later began his return trip to Utah in a small buggy. His purchased goods were in several huge wagons pulled by oxen he had procured in Washington, and the train was moving west ahead of him. Accompanying his wagons were four teamsters and a Mrs. Wilson and her child.

Meanwhile, on the plains ahead, a group of Cheyennes had skirmished with a mail driver. In retaliation the Army had ridden forth to punish the Cheyennes,[23] and the result of the battle was an all-out plains war, a war into which Babbitt's wagon train was directly riding.

Behind the supply train, Babbitt's buggy sped sprightly along. He soon came upon a Mormon handcart company at Cutler's Park, Nebraska, where one Mormon emigrant records, "He seemed in high glee, his spirits seemed very elastic, almost mercurial . . . He was very confident that he should be in Salt Lake within fifteen days."[24]

Meanwhile, on the trail ahead, cavalrymen battled with Cheyenne warriors, killing ten.[25] In revenge, a number of warriors sighted Babbitt's supply train and decided to attack it.

On August 30, Babbitt rode heedlessly along the trail in his buggy when he suddenly came upon ruins of his wagon train. One of his teamsters had been killed, another wounded; the child had been butchered, and the mother dragged away,[26] only to be killed later the same day.[27]

Babbitt made his way to Fort Kearny a day later and found Porter Rockwell. He hired the scout "during the last days of August (precise date not remembered)," 1856[28] and agreed to pay him $790.02 to carry 33 cases of books, two crates of window blinds and fixtures, four cases of ink, a case of stationery, and two rolls of carpeting for the Utah statehouse[29] which had been left by the Indians at the supply train.

Babbitt led Rockwell back to the ruins on September 4, and there found the Willie handcart company. Members of the company had already arrived and buried Babbitt's dead teamsters.[30] Babbitt complained to James G. Willie, handcart captain, of the Indian attack, and then took Porter back to the fort.

At Fort Kearney Babbitt prepared to leave for Great Salt Lake City. The U. S. Army commander at the fort attempted to dissuade him, as did several Mormons, but Babbitt was stubborn.[31] Captain H. W. Wharton even offered Babbitt an armed escort if he would wait until a returning patrol could arrive, but Babbitt was adamant, feeling the cavalry would only slow his journey.[32]

Before leaving for Utah, Babbitt confessed to the Mormons at the fort that he might be killed, but nevertheless felt he had to leave immediately.[33] It was Porter who attempted to dissuade him one final time.[34]

Babbitt sought recruits to join him; all except one guard and a driver possessed enough sanity to refuse his offer. The three men moved out September 6, 1856,[35] straight into the warpath.

The next day "they stopped at 2 o'clock when . . . a band of twelve mounted Cheyennes . . . bore down upon them with a wild shout and a hideous yell. Mr. S[utherland] [Babbitt's driver] was away from the wagon a short distance. Mr. R[owland] [Babbitt's guard] stood nearby, apparently petrified, and was shot down by a score of well aimed arrows. Mr. B[abbitt], after hailing the Indians, fired first his rifle, then his revolving pistols at them, but being still hard-pressed, clubbed his rifle and backing toward his carriage fought desperately and effectually, and Indians crept behind the . . . uncovered wagon and [one Indian] with his tomahawk felled him to the earth.

"Mr. S[utherland] endeavored to save himself by flight but was also overtaken and killed."[36]

The above details of the ambush came from the Cheyennes themselves, who later went to the fort and reported the story.[37]

Despite all the details, witnesses, and confessions (see Note 24) Porter was somehow dragged into the fury. He'd no sooner arrived at Fort Laramie — with Babbitt's supply train of five wagons and eleven yokes of oxen — than gossip began. By the time he passed through the fort, stories were rampant among non-Mormons, perpetrated by certain anti-Mormons in their midst, that Brigham had hired Porter to assassinate Babbitt.[38] This story would make its way to Washington, where, in reaction, President Buchanan would send a major retaliatory force against the Mormons; the accusation against Porter being one of the prime reasons for the war.[39]

Porter, meanwhile, wisely remained at Fort Laramie for the season. Several Mormon handcart companies proceeded to Utah and were caught in blizzards. Hundreds were killed. Porter waited till the worst weather passed, then began his own journey and soon arrived at Fort Bridger. There, Oliver Boardman Huntington records in his journal that Porter had his oxen shod.[40] Porter resumed his journey, arriving at Great Salt Lake City November 4, 1856.[41]

Mary Ann had given birth to Sarah Rockwell three months previously, August 5. Since Porter had been gone seven months, he was anxious to see the new child.[42]

Back in Zion, his first opportunity for employment came from Hiram Kimball, the man Brigham had chosen to run the Mormon mail service.[43] Kimball's bid to the U. S. government of $23,000 easily iced the contract.[44] (The inept Magraw-Hockaday company had added additional mud to its face by overpricing their bid at $39,000.)

Kimball, in turn, chose the two toughest men he could find — men who would be the forerunners to the Pony Express: Porter Rockwell for the first leg of the journey — between Great Salt Lake City and Fort Laramie — and John Murdock for the second half — between Fort Laramie and Independence, Missouri.[45]

Interestingly, personality conflicts may have existed between Rockwell and Kimball: Thirteen years earlier they had reportedly had their fist-fight.[46]

(Years after this epistology enterprise, Bill Hickman, claiming to be in charge of the second leg of the journey, wrote a book, confessing his killings for Brigham Young. The record was, by his own admission, a "lie from beginning to end."[47] He became disaffected from Brigham and the church before writing the book, but at least one reason exists to question the following chronicle of his mail trip eastward, years before his excommunication: "Several of these nights I thought I would freeze to death, but stood it better than any of the others . . . We finally got to Independence, men and animals tired out, having been two months and three days making the trip."[48] Obviously, this gasconading wasn't Hickman's only personal weakness; other sources say John Murdock was the conductor from Laramie eastward — yet Hickman took the credit.)

Porter, meanwhile, slugged his wagon team eastward through the snow. He headed out three weeks after Murdock — or Hickman — on March 1, 1857, and dropped off supplies at Devil's Gate station along the way.[49]

Porter possibly traveled as far as Independence, Missouri. Another doubtful source, John I. Ginn, claims Porter chanced upon the Pacific Wagon Road Survey campsite and asked the company captain about lost mules from a Mormon mail station. The captain just happened to be William M. F. Magraw, of the Magraw-Hockaday mail service team, whose bid had been lost to the Mormons.[50] Ginn claims Magraw led his men to lynch Porter, but Ginn interfered — yelling at Magraw to not harm Porter — and in that moment Porter was able to draw his weapons and back out of the camp unharmed.[51] (Why Porter was searching for lost mules in the middle of Independence — especially since Hickman or Murdock had been assigned the second half of the mail route — Ginn does not say. Furthermore, the plausibility of Porter meeting Magraw personally is slim at best, much less the lynching aspect of the story.)

In any case, because of Porter's assignment to cover the Fort Laramie-to-Great Salt Lake City leg of the express, he found himself at Fort Laramie. Within days the first delivery came from the East: 24 sacks of mail. Porter took the sacks and, on the first pre-Pony Express ride in history, galloped the long leg into Great Salt Lake City. Not having received mail for nearly half a year, the *Deseret News* rejoices: " ... much credit is due ... to Mr. O. P. Rockwell, conductor from that point [Fort Laramie] to this city, for the perseverance, prudence and energy displayed in the transportation of so large a mail in such good time and condition ... "[52]

But what the mail contained shocked the Saints ... a damning exposé of Mormon society had been splashed all over the eastern papers and, although that was nothing new, this one was different — it was more convincing than any the public had yet seen.

However, the story, unknown to the eastern public, went deeper:

The former Associate Justice of the territory, W. W. Drummond, had lived "in sin" in Utah. The story goes that his woman friend had actually sat in court with him. The public outcry, of both Mormons and non-Mormons,[53] had become so vehement[54] — especially after a letter his wife had written against him appeared in the local press[55] — and more especially after his public confession, "Money is my God"[56] — that he had decided his only recourse was to "flee Zion."

Amusingly, Bill Hickman, an erstwhile lawyer at the time, stated that if he had to appear in court before Drummond and if he found "that woman on the bench, I would kick them both out of the house."[57] Drummond heard about the remark, and issued a bench warrant for his arrest for contempt of court. Hickman laughed, "I heard of it when I got in town, and said if he served a writ on me I would horsewhip him. It was not served."[58]

When Drummond arrived East he publicly resigned his position as Associate Justice of Utah Territory. In that one simple letter to the Attorney General — which the newspapers then trumpeted before the public — he did more damage to the Saints than all the anti-Mormon books and news articles had yet combined.

Several factors had contributed to the Saints' recent notoriety, particularly four: first, the outcry of Magraw from losing his mail contract; second, bitter federal officials in Utah who had clashed with Brigham when they could not overpower him; third, Indian agents who had disagreed with Brigham's non-reactionary dealings with Indians; and fourth, the press' vitriolic outcry against polygamy. (Despite the sensational stories of women being dragged to Utah to become slaves and polygamist wives, the system of polygamy thrived, with wives sharing not only household duties and a husband, but for the most part — though certainly with some exceptions — a sense of sisterhood as well, as revealed by numerous pioneer journals.)

Despite such propagandizing against the Saints, according to non-Mormon Jules Remy[59] who investigated the incidents first-hand, none of these factors had much effect until Judge Drummond's letter of resignation was published. And this one letter now sent the entire nation buzzing:

" . . . no law of Congress is by them considered binding in any manner . . . I know that there is a secret oath-bound organization among all the male members of the church to resist the laws of the country, and to acknowledge no law save the law of the 'Holy Priesthood,' which comes to the people through Brigham Young direct from God; he, Young, being the viceregent of God and Prophet, viz.: successor of Joseph Smith, who was the founder of this blind and treasonable organization . . . the records, papers, &c., of the Supreme Court have been destroyed by order of the Church, with the direct knowledge and approbation of Governor B. Young . . . the federal officers are daily compelled to hear the form of the American government traduced, the chief executives of the nation, both living and dead, slandered and abused from the masses, as well as from all the leading members of the Church, in the most vulgar, loathsome, and wicked manner that the evil passions of men can possibly conceive ... that my illustrious and distinguished predecessor, Hon. Leonidas Shaver, came to his death by drinking poisoned liquors given to him under the order of the leading men of the Mormon Church in Great Salt Lake City; that the late Secretary of the Territory, A. W. Babbitt, was murdered on the plains by a band of Mormon marauders, under the particular and special order of Brigham Young ... "[60]

After Drummond's letter of resignation was published, national newspapers took up the hue and cry, and with evangelical zeal called for the Mormon "uprising" against federal authority to be crushed.[61]

In reaction, on May 20, 1857, President Buchanan issued his exterminating order, and the U. S. Army was sent to Utah to rid the territory of Brigham Young and Porter Rockwell.[62] The man Buchanan chose to lead the expedition was "Squaw-killing Harney," the general that had escalated the prairie war. Harney received his orders directly from the President:

"The community and, in part, the civil government of Utah Territory are in a state of substantial rebellion against the laws and authority of the United States," writes the President. "A new civil governor is about to be designated, and to be charged with the establishment and maintenance of law and order.

"The principles by which you should be guided have been already indicated in a somewhat similar case, and are here substantially repeated."[63] Some observers wondered if this order were not an open invitation to repeat the Brule-Sioux incident ...

Further in his orders Harney was advised by the President: " ... You are warned not to be betrayed into premature security or over confidence." Perhaps no more deeply ironic words were ever uttered by a Commander-in-Chief to his commanding general.

In regards to Drummond's charges, one non-Mormon merchant, William Bell of the company Livingston and Bell, who had lived with the Mormons seven years and had since returned to New York, was interviewed in the February 23, 1858 issue of the *New York Herald,* and denounced Drummond's charges. In summarizing his views on Babbitt's murder — by Cheyennes and not Mormons

— he concludes, "There is no room for doubt." Bell had also served on the coroner's jury that had investigated Judge Shaver's death. "There were no grounds for the insinuation of the Judge being poisoned by the Mormons."[64]

Meanwhile, Babbitt's wife issued a statement, also to the *New York Herald,* July 25, 1857, refuting Drummond's charges:

"I have not a shadow of suspicion that white men were in anyway concerned in his death. The newspaper story that he was killed by 'Mormons' to the contrary notwithstanding."[65]

Her brother, who was the editor of the *Crescent City Oracle* in Iowa, had thoroughly investigated Babbitt's murder and also denounced Drummond's charges: " . . . he there, [Drummond] among other very grave charges, asserts that the Hon. A. W. Babbitt was murdered by white men disguised as Indians, by order of the authorities of Utah. In justice to the parties thus maligned, we will state that we have taken much pains to gather all the information possible . . . and we have not a shadow of doubt but that Indians of the Cheyenne nation murdered him for revenge and plunder . . . "[66]

With regards to Drummond's charges that Utah Supreme Court documents had been seized by the church, Curtis E. Bolton, Deputy Clerk of the Supreme Court of Utah reports, "I do solemnly declare this assertion is without the slightest foundation in truth." He adds that the documents "are all *safe* and *complete* in my custody, and not one of them missing, nor have they ever been disturbed by any person." (Emphasis his)[67]

As to Drummond's charge of federal officers' mistreatment, the editor of *The Contributor,* writing under the pen-name of "Vaux," reports, "Chief Justice L. H. Reed, and his successor J. T. Kinney, both testified in the highest terms of praise to the cordial reception they met, and kind treatment received among the 'Mormon' people. Many officers since . . . bear witness to this."[68] (See Note 25 for a related analysis.)

Nevertheless, General Harney's forces gathered at Fort Leavenworth, Kansas,[69] and as they prepared to march to war on the Mormons, the *New York Times* published:

"Today it seems well understood that Judge Drummond will be tendered the office of Governor of Utah . . . and I have it from the judge himself that he will accept upon condition that General Harney is sent into the country with force sufficient to enable the officers to enforce the law. In case General Harney and Judge Drummond go to Utah backed by the government, the Mormons will yield or be compelled to find refuge in another country."[70]

Junius Wells reports, "These various officers started upon the overland journey with flying colors, buoyant spirits and sanguine expectations."[71]

Meanwhile, contention reigned in Utah. Brigham's enemies took up the torch and carried the story of "white Indians" — Mormons painted up — suddenly becoming responsible for every problem conceivable.[72]

Throughout the escalating smear campaign in the press, Brigham remained calm. Other church leaders, however, contended with the attackers: "If they want to send troops here let them come to those who have imported filth and whores . . . If we were to establish a whorehouse on every corner of our streets, as in nearly all other cities outside of Utah, either by law or otherwise, we should doubtless then be considered good fellows," preached Brigham's counselor, Jedediah M. Grant, at the Salt Lake Tabernacle.[73] This lecture was prophetic in the sense that he referred to troops coming to Utah — particularly since the lecture was delivered 15 months earlier.

So now the Army was coming — as another incursion on their society — and it was an invasion of which the Saints weren't yet even aware.

Porter, meanwhile, rode eastward with the mail, straight towards the on-coming Army . . .

Clark Kelley Price
86 ©

X

600 miles east of home, Porter spotted two men in the distance, and soon came upon them: Abraham O. Smoot, mayor of Great Salt Lake City, and Judson Stoddard, taking mail company stock west. The news they bore shook Porter to the core.

Mayor Smoot had been refused mail at Independence — of all days on July 4[1] — and had learned that the Army was on its way west to suppress the "Mormon rebellion." He had also learned that another governor with legions of federal officials were coming to oust Brigham Young, and that the government no longer recognized the Mormon mail company. Congress, they were told, had annulled the contract — with the excuse that Brigham's company had begun shipping too late. (The contracted date for service had been set to begin December 1, 1856, but the Mormons had not learned they had been awarded the contract until January 1857; their enemies later admitted to the discrepancy, and thus invented a new reason for the government rescinding the contract: they claimed the Mormons had tampered with the mail).[2] Actually two other Utahns, Feremoeze Little and Ephraim Hanks, had heard rumors of a movement against Utah five months previously but had dismissed the reports.

At Fort Laramie Porter and the two Mormons left their stock and immediately rigged up a fast wagon. They headed out toward Great Salt Lake City at record-breaking speed. Porter drove the wagon, and within five days arrived at the city of the Saints.

There, Brigham was nowhere to be found.[3] In fact, the entire city was deserted.

When Rockwell and the two men reined in at the postmaster's office they learned the Saints were celebrating their ten-year anniversary 25 miles east, up Big Cottonwood Canyon. Ironically, Brigham was staging a military show, complete with light artillery, a company of infantry, a platoon of swordsmen, and six brass bands. "The stars and stripes were unfurled on two of the highest peaks in sight of the camp, and on the tops of two of the tallest trees," reports one pioneer at the scene.[4] At the sight of shimmering Silver Lake, under the umbrella of the high Wasatch Mountains, 2,600 citizens were gathered.

Porter and his two companions, plus the postmaster for Great Salt Lake City, galloped up the canyon and arrived at the Mormon leader's tent by noon. Here, Porter briefed Brigham on the impending attack.

The venerable church president gathered other hierarchists in for a short meeting. The Lion then came forth to address the crowd.

Repeating to them his words of a decade earlier, "Give us ten years of peace, and we will ask no odds of Uncle Sam or the Devil," he now proclaimed, "God is with us and the devil has taken me at my word."[5]

He then told his Saints of the invasion. A local reporter notes, "Though at the conclusion of his speech the cry was, 'On with the dance, let joy be unconfined' ... intense feeling existed in the breasts of all at the insult we had received, [yet] the philosophic faith of the people enabled them to throw off any apprehension of danger that otherwise would have rested upon them ... So far from succumbing to the promptings of fear, the liveliest spirit of indifference prevailed. The extreme folly of sending an army to subdue a people guilty of no crime, was so apparent ... [that] relief from such feelings was found in the dance, the singing and rhyming, the patriotic toasts, and in the general sport liberally provided.

"The following extract from lines and chorus hastily composed and sung by Brother Poulter, were taken up and sung by the multitude, to the tune of 'Camptown Races,' and for years after were a favorite among camp-fire rhymes:

> *'Squaw-killer Harney's on the way, Doo-da, doo-da,*
> *'The Mormon people for to slay, Doo-da, doo-da day.*
> *'Then let us be on hand,*
> *'By Brigham Young to stand,*
> *'And if our enemies do appear,*
> *'We'll sweep them from the land.'* "[6]

Additional lyrics have appeared from various sources:

> *There's seven hundred wagons on the way, Doo-da, doo-da.*
> *Their cattle are numerous so they say, Doo-da, doo-da day.*
> *To let them perish would be sin, Doo-da, doo-da.*
> *So we'll take all they've got for bringing them in, Doo-da doo-da day.*

(Chorus, then:)

> *Old Sam has sent, I understand, Doo-da, doo-da.*
> *A Missouri ass to rule our land, Doo-da, doo-da day.*
> *But if he comes we'll have some fun, Doo-da, doo-da.*
> *To see him and his jurors run, Doo-day, doo-day day.*

(Chorus, then:)

> *Now if he comes, the truth I'll tell Doo-day, doo-dah.*
> *Our boys will drive him down to hell. Doo-dah doo-da day.*
> *Then let us be on hand,*
> *By Brigham Young to stand,*
> *And if our enemies do appear,*
> *We'll sweep them from the land.*[7]

Underlying it all, the Saints found little humor in their predicament. The next day they evacuated the canyon and returned to their homes.

The following days were hectic. Brigham organized field operations with Lieutenant General Daniel H. Wells as commander, then assigned a special force to harass the invading army. Leading this guerrilla operation would be Porter Rockwell and Bill Hickman,[8] who would not only captain companies of 100 men each but would deal directly with Brigham himself.[9] All other troops would deal through the chain-of-command to General Wells.

Two other detachments were assigned to watch the enemy, one of which went immediately to spy out the Army and the other a month later to survey the northern route in case the Army changed directions. Still another detachment was sent to scout mountain passes near Ogden Canyon to find points of retreat for the Saints.[10]

"A distinguishing feature of this military organization," writes a reporter at the scene, "was the uniform cordiality between officers and men. Anything in the shape of dress parade demeanor on the part of petty officers was promptly frowned down by their superiors, and very soon after entering upon active service, everything in the nature of invidious distinctions disappeared. Discipline was preserved more by the good sense and good feeling of the men than by the rigid enforcement of military law ... The nature of the campaign was such that individuals were selected for certain service without regard to their official station; thus officers of the highest rank were found performing the duties of company captains, or sharing the labors of men of the line."[11]

Meanwhile, the more the Saints on the homefront thought about the invasion, the more they steamed. Brigham's counselor, Heber C. Kimball, proclaimed to a large crowd gathered at the Bowery: " ... I have been driven five times, been broken up and my goods robbed from me, and I have been afflicted almost to death ... Send 2,500 men here, our brethren, to make a desolation of this people? God almighty helping me, I will fight until there is not a drop of blood in my veins. Good God! ... "[12]

And then Brigham topped it off: " . . . I guess that James Buchanan has ordered this Expedition to appease the wrath of the angry hounds who are howling around him . . . But woe, woe to that man who comes here unlawfully to interfere with my affairs. Woe, woe to those men who come here to unlawfully meddle with me and this people . . . "[13]

General Wells further pronounced, "If an exterminating war be purposed against them [the Saints], and blood alone can cleanse pollution from the Nation's bulwarks, to the God of our fathers let the appeal be made."[14]

The passion of the Saints climaxed as Brigham issued a proclamation of war:

"Citizens of Utah . . . We are invaded by a hostile force who are evidently assailing us to accomplish our overthrow and destruction." Brigham then cited twenty-five years of disappointment, wherein they had "trusted officials of the government, from constables and justices to Judges, Governors, and Presidents, only to be scorned, held in derision, insulted and betrayed.

"We have had no privilege, no opportunity of defending ourselves from the false, foul and unjust aspersions against us before the nation. The government has not condescended to cause an investigating committee or other persons to be sent to inquire and ascertain the truth, as is customary in such cases.

"We know those aspersions to be false, but that avails us nothing.

"We are condemned unheard, and forced to an issue with an armed mercenary mob which has been sent against us at the instigation of anonymous letter writers ashamed [to admit their identities] . . . , slanderous falsehoods which they have given to the public, of corrupt officials [who once served in Utah] which have brought false accusations against us to screen themselves in their own infamy, and of hireling priests and howling editors who prostitute the truth for filthy lucre's sake." As usual, Brigham pulled no punches.

"The issue which has been thus forced upon us compels us to resort to the great first law of self preservation and stand in our own defense . . .

"Therefore I, Brigham Young . . . Forbid all armed forces, of every description, from coming into this Territory under any pretense whatever . . . "

He then proclaimed, "Martial Law is hereby declared to exist in this Territory . . . "[15]

Meanwhile, the U. S. Army moved westward, including a rather formidable armada: the Fifth Infantry and eight companies of the Tenth Infantry, supported by 12 artillery pieces.

And then occurred perhaps the most amusing military blunder of the 19th Century. The United States War Department sent the assistant quartermaster of the U. S. Army, Captain Stewart Van Vliet, ahead to Great Salt Lake City to learn what fuel and forage the Army could acquire from the Mormons upon its arrival.[16] Van Vliet was also ordered to scout out a fort location near the city, from which they could subdue the Mormons. When Van Vliet entered the city, he was taken to Brigham Young, who respectfully told him they considered the advancing force nothing less than an invading army, and that not only would the Mormons not sell fuel to the Army, but they would not allow them to enter the valley.[17] As simple as that.

Van Vliet was then presented by Brigham a letter to deliver to his superiors, written by Mormon Adjutant General James Ferguson. In this letter Ferguson, with his tongue firmly in cheek, requested from his enemies manuals on infantry tactics, cavalry tactics, fortifications, "and others as you may judge useful to us." The Mormon officer mentioned they have only a few on hand "which will answer our present needs in that line." He concludes with, "The difficulty in procuring such works so far from the seat of Government furnishes my apology for thus troubling you.

"Wishing you all success . . . and rapid promotion . . . " And then he signed it.[18]

As Van Vliet rode eastward, returning to his Army, Porter and two other Saints accompanied him[19] for 143 miles,[20] and then Rockwell returned home within six days.[21] But the Mormons kept Van Vliet under surveillance on his entire journey eastward to headquarters without his slightest knowledge — so thoroughly in fact that General Wells later reports, "I had him followed almost to the Missouri River by day and night, and when he made his report I had men in his camp watching him there."[22]

At headquarters Van Vliet reported[23] the efforts he had made among the Mormons:

"I told them [The Saints] that they might prevent the small military force now approaching Utah from getting through the narrow defiles and rugged passes of the mountains this year, but that next season the United States government would send troops sufficient to overcome all opposition . . . [24]

"I attended their service on Sunday, and, in course of a sermon delivered by Elder Taylor, he referred to the approach of the troops and declared they should not enter the Territory. He [Taylor] then referred to the probability of an overpowering force being sent against them, and desired all present, who would apply the torch to their own buildings, cut down their trees, and lay waste their fields, to hold up their hands. Every hand, in an audience numbering over four thousand persons, was raised at the same moment."

Van Vliet sat in the Tabernacle, mesmerized by the scene. He continues, "During my stay in the city I visited several families, and all with whom I was thrown looked upon the present movement of the troops towards their Territory as the commencement of another religious persecution, and expressed a fixed determination to sustain Governor Young in any measures he might adopt."[25]

The Saints, in fact, had won an ally in Van Vliet, who now at headquarters boldly protested against the impending war, but failed to convince his commanding officers.[26] After his report, Van Vliet learned that a new leader had been assigned to the Army replacing "Squaw-killer Harney:" Colonel Albert Sidney Johnston. For the Mormons this could be worse: Johnston, a Southerner, was steeped in an intense hatred for Brigham Young and the abolitionist Mormons. (The southern viewpoint about Mormons had been adequately summarized by *The Savannah News:* "It [the *News*] can see no reason why they should not prevent the insane

Mormons of Europe from converting Utah into a social and political hell. Mormonism is in opposition to all laws, human and divine. Slavery is in accordance with both. Mormonism is a curse to the country and to its deluded victims, while slavery is a blessing to the African, to the white race, and to the State.")[27]

Accompanying Johnston to Utah was the new governor-appointee to replace Brigham Young: Alfred Cumming, the former mayor of Atlanta, with a coterie of federal appointees. Drummond, alas, had fallen by the wayside: expecting to become the new governor-appointee after his famous letter against the Mormons had catapulted him to national prominence, Drummond's hopes were dashed when his reputation suddenly caught up to officials in Washington. And then his life seemed to plummet. (Seven years later he was divorced as an adulterer and convicted on two counts of fraud.[28] Fifteen years afterwards he was discovered by a reporter in St. Louis and described as a "seedy" sewing machine salesman.[29] Five years later he was arrested in Chicago and sentenced to a house of corrections for stealing postage stamps, and three years afterwards died in a Chicago asylum.)

As Johnston's army marched forward, the Nauvoo Legion patrolled up and down the Rockies. They finally spotted the Army September 22nd, two months after its start from Fort Leavenworth.

The Legionnaires reported the citing to Commanding General Wells, headquartered at Cache Cave, just outside Salt Lake Valley. Junius Wells records, "There was no movement of the enemy . . . that our officers were not speedily apprized of. Scouts and spies were with them continually . . . "[30]

As the troops marched westward, a war of words preceded the impending battle. Brigham's reputation as "the lion" was graphically portrayed. The commander of the infantry, Edmund B. Alexander, arrived at the far west supply trains, set up camp, and now awaited the arrival of the cavalry as well as the commanding general, Johnston, before issuing his attack.

Brigham wrote a strange letter to Alexander:

"By virtue of the authority thus vested in me, I have issued, and forward you a copy of, my proclamation forbidding the entrance of armed forces into this Territory. This you have disregarded. I now further direct that you retire forthwith from the Territory, by the same route you entered. Should you deem this impracticable, and prefer to remain until spring in the vicinity of your present encampment, Black's fork, or Green river, you can do so in peace and unmolested, on condition that you deposit your arms and ammunition with Lewis Robison, quartermaster-general of the Territory . . . [signed] Brigham Young."

The reception to Brigham's invitation was met with incredulity. After Alexander read Brigham's letter he quickly replied that he, Alexander, was subject only to the direction of "competent military authority," and that "it becomes you to look to the consequences, for you must be aware that so unequal a contest can never be successfully sustained by the people you govern."

Brigham was incensed, and shot back a reply to Colonel Alexander that this time minced no intentions. It was possibly the most aggressive, gritty, plucky piece of postage ever pony-expressed to a United States military commander in the 19th Century:

" . . . we shall treat you as though you were open enemies . . . If you came here for peaceful purposes, you have no use for weapons of war. We wish, and ever have wished for peace, and have ever sued for it all the day long, as our bitterest enemies know full well. In the name of Israel's God we will have peace, even though we be compelled by our enemies to fight for it.

"We have, as yet, studiously avoided the shedding of blood . . . you can easily perceive that you and your troops are now at the mercy of the elements, and that we live in the mountains, and our men are all mountaineers. This the government should know, and also give us our rights and then let us alone.

" . . . both we and the Kingdom of God will be free from all hellish oppressors, the Lord being our helper. Threatenings to waste and exterminate this people have been sounded in our ears for more than a score of years, and we yet live. The Zion of the Lord is here, and wicked men and devils cannot destroy it!

"If you persist in your attempt to permanently locate an army in this Territory, contrary to the wishes and constitutional rights of the people therein, and with a view to aid the administration in their unhallowed efforts to palm their corrupt officials upon us, and to protect them and blacklegs, black-hearted scoundrels, whore-masters and murderers, as was the sole intention in sending you and your troops here, you will have to meet a mode of warfare *against which your tactics furnish you no information.*"

At this point Brigham becomes — if it were possible — even bolder: "In regard to myself and certain others having placed ourselves 'in a position of rebellion and hostility to the general government of the United States,' [as asserted by Col. Alexander] I am perfectly aware that we understand our true and most loyal position far better than our enemies can inform us . . . if George Washington was now living, and at the helm of our government, he would hang the administration as high as he did Andre . . . the administration and the troops they have ordered to Utah are, in fact, themselves the rebels . . .

" . . . we look for the United States to endeavor to swallow us up, and we are prepared for the contest, if they wish to forego the Constitution in their insane efforts to crush all . . . human rights . . .

"If God is for us we will prosper; but if He is for you and against us you will prosper, and we will say amen . . ."

Brigham then challenges the colonel personally:

"As to your obeying 'orders,' my official counsel to you would be for you to stop and reflect until you know wherein are the just and the right . . . "

Brigham then actually challenges his competency:

"Inasmuch as you consider your force amply sufficient to enable you to come to this city, why have you so unwisely dallied so long on Ham's Fork at this late season of the year?" . . . and then he seeks to intimidate him: "Now we, for the first time, *possess the power to have a voice in the treatment that we will receive.*"

Brigham explains his confidence: " . . . True, in struggling to sustain the Constitution and constitutional rights belonging to every citizen of our republic, we have no arm nor power to trust in but that of Jehovah and the strength and ability that He gives us.

"Were you and your fellow soldiers as well acquainted with your soldiers as I am with mine, and did they understand the work they are now engaged in as well as you may understand it, you must know that many of them would immediately revolt from all connexion with so ungodly, illegal, unconstitutional and hellish a crusade against an innocent people, and if their blood is shed *it shall rest upon the heads of their commanders.*

"With us it is the kingdom of God or nothing.

"[Signed] ... Brigham Young."[31] (Emphasis ours)

But the infantry kept coming, not knowing the power which lay in Brigham's hands ... nor of his secret weapon: the likes of Porter Rockwell ...

XI

The Mormon soldiers, outnumbered ten to one, were confident. Church leader Wilford Woodruff journals: "[Johnston's Army] will be at Pacific Springs tonight and our brethren will commence operation upon them."[1]

The man chosen to lead the operation was Porter Rockwell, who handpicked five men. His objective: to raid the camp and — rather than killing soldiers — to run off the mules. This in fact became the unmistakable mandate from Brigham: "Defeat the U.S. Army, but do not shed blood."[2] Writer Junius Wells adds, "How to do it successfully was the question . . . the advancing troops [were] well supplied with food and ammunition, and eager to try their strength with their Mormon foes."[3] The word "eager" crops up elsewhere: an Army officer confesses in a letter to his wife, "Every person in the expedition is 'eager for the fray' . . . "[4]

At 2 A.M. Porter's six-man army came into sight of the enemy camp, an isolated supply train. Porter and his men snuck closer, slowly at first on horseback, then they charged into the campsite. Galloping between rows of tents so the infantrymen could not fire for fear of shooting each other, Porter's men broke into a terrifying ruckus — clanging bells, screaming, and firing weapons.

Jesse W. Crosby records, "They rode through and through the camp before any one could be aroused."[5] Whether the infantrymen simply enjoyed their sleep or were too frightened to come out has never been defined. In any case Porter and his men found the mission frustrating ... charging through camp "again and again" with no soldiers even willing to emerge from their tents.

Crosby continues, "The bugles at length made a faint noise, and the men began to turn out."

Army Captain Jesse A. Gove reports, " ... several shots were fired immediately behind my tent, and immediately the whole herd of mules stampeded with a terrific rush ... The Herders commenced the halloo and cry, 'Soldiers turn out, we are attacked.' It was an hour when everybody was sound asleep."[6]

The Mormons jarred the infantry so thoroughly that "One man in H. Co., Capt. Tracy's, died of fright," reports one angry infantry officer. "He had the heart disease, hence the sudden fright killed him."[7]

But in their mule-stealing mission, Hosea Stout records in his journal, " ... the attempt of our troops to stampede our enemies animals had proved a failure the animals being tied down or Hobbled with iron hobbles."[8] Captain Gove further explains: " ... the bell mule by the merest accident got caught by the picket rope in a wild sage bush, stopping him, and with him most of the herd stopped. They were brought in at once ... "[9] Crosby summarizes, "It was at night and the horses and mules seemed inclined to run to the tents and wagons instead of running away; and the plan of stampeding was therefore abandoned."

After Pacific Springs, Porter and other patrols of Saints attempted additional raids, and now succeeded in accomplishing more than killing army officers with heart attacks ... [10]

Commander Wells soon learned Johnston's Army would attack the valley through Echo Canyon. This was the same trail through which the Saints had entered the valley 11 years previously, and by now they presumably knew the canyon well enough to fortify themselves against any invading army.

Mormon soldiers dug trenches above the canyon. Then they built breastworks, rolling huge boulders to the precipice of mountain tops; these elevated areas were accessible only by a few hidden trails, known only to the Mormons.

The canyon road passed directly beneath the cliffs. To force the Army to stay on this road, the river was dammed. The depth of the water would not hamper the army so much as the quicksand made active by soaking. Jesse W. Crosby adds, "Here the enemy could be raked from all our positions, and immense rocks were pried up and fixed in readiness to roll down some hundreds of feet at a given signal; here the main body of our men took up their quarters; but the horse companies formed themselves into scouting parties and proceeded near the enemies camp."[11]

Porter next decided to focus on Army supply trains . . .

One company — Russel, Majors and Waddell — had dispatched to Utah twelve wagon trains of their own plus others under sub-contractors. Each train consisted of 26 wagons filled with supplies, and they had preceded the Army by several months. The trains were now camped in Utah on the Big Sandy, the Green River, and at Ham's Fork, ahead of the infantry.

Alexander's infantry marched speedily ahead and caught up to all three supply trains. He then gathered two of the trains and resumed marching towards Zion.

Little did he realize they were hours away from the turning point of the war . . .

What happened next was reported by a civilian who later claimed to have participated as one of Alexander's teamsters: "Soon after we passed through it [collecting the supply trains] a force of Mormon cavalry under Bill Hickman descended upon it, set fire to the wagons and consumed them and their contents . . . The same night or early next morning Hickman's and other Mormon cavalry burned up the two large supply trains [collected from] Green river and Big Sandy — thus depriving the army of about 500,000 pounds of provisions intended for its maintenance during the long and severe winter then settling in . . . "[12]

Among the Army's civilian supply teamsters were 11-year-old "Buffalo Bill" William F. Cody and "Wild Bill" James B. Hickok, who witnessed the wrath of the Mormons.[13]

As the battlelines were drawn, U. S. Captain Jesse A. Gove was not pleased with his superior officer, Colonel Alexander: "He is . . . frightened to death."[14] One cannot help but wonder if Brigham's letters were not haunting the intrepid colonel.

Seeking to thoroughly demoralize the enemy now, Wells pressed the advantage.

Porter's men galloped towards Fort Bridger. Mormon leaders knew that if the enemy reached the fort, they could lodge safely in for the winter. So at Fort Bridger the Mormons had but one alternative.

To burn it.

After torches were set to the wood, the sky of the entire valley was lit like a display of meteoric showers, and Porter watched in awe at what he had done.[15]

He and the Mormon guerrillas next galloped to Fort Supply,[16] where, "We took out our wagons, horses, etc.," reports one Mormon officer at the scene, "and at 12 o'clock set fire to the buildings at once, consisting of 100 or more good hewed log houses, one saw-mill, one grist mill, one thrashing machine, and after going out of the Fort, we did set fire to the Stockade and grain sacks, etc. After looking a few minutes at the bonfire we had made, thence on by the light thereof."[17]

Portraying the passion they felt for the cause and the intense determination to never again be driven by enemies, Crosby reports, "Owners of property in several cases begged the privilege of setting fire to their own, which they freely did, thus destroying at once what they had labored for years to build, and that without a word."[18]

Then they galloped on to City Supply, where they took "10 or 15 buildings perhaps, and warmed ourselves by the flames."[19]

A month later the U. S. Army came upon Fort Bridger, expecting to find their refuge in the wilderness. But all they found was a huge pile of ashes.

Jim Bridger took one look at his fort and exploded. Acting now as Alexander's guide, Bridger flew into a verbal tirade against the Mormons, claiming they had stolen his fort and destroyed it, screaming they were thieves, and effectually instigating the infantrymen to even greater determination to conquer the Mormons. (Interestingly, Salt Lake County mortgage records of 1855[20] and 1858[21] proved Bridger had sold the fort to the

Mormons, with even his own mark attached.[22] Additionally, Bill Hickman — who years later would have no reason to defend the church — admitted he had been "one of the carriers of the heavy load of gold it took to purchase said place [Bridger's fort] with the stock and goods thereon.")[23]

Porter next met with General Wells, who ordered him to recruit 40 men from Major McAllister's company in order to carry out more extensive guerrilla activities.[24] As a died-in-the-wool guerrilla fighter now, Porter undoubtedly enjoyed what happened next — as recorded in the journal of Henry Ballard, one of the Mormon recruits: "We started again for the Soldiers camp 40 of us led by Orin Porter Rockwell our plan was to drive off their cattle so as to cripple them in their movements."[25]

But all they found was sharp thinking by the Army. Officers had wisely positioned the cattle behind the infantry to protect them from Mormon invaders. So Rockwell devised another plan,[26] as Ballard reports, wherein they "commenced burning grass only a half mile from their camp. O. P. Rockwell posted himself so he could watch the camp and give us Signal they [the Army] started after us about noon and we retreated into the Mountains till toward evening when we come back got supper and commenced fireing the grass again ... "

The Army turned their cannon upon them. Porter and his men fled, after having destroyed their feed.

Meanwhile, over the hill, Lot Smith intercepted a government supply train, and provided history with perhaps the liveliest journaled account of the war:

" ... October 3rd ... We rode nearly all night, and early the next morning came in sight of an ox train headed westward ...

"On calling for the captain, a large fine-looking man stepped forward and gave his name as Rankin. I informed him that we wanted him to turn his train and go the other way, until he reached the States. He wanted to know by what authority I presumed to issue such orders. I replied, pointing to my men, that there was part of it, and the remainder was a little further on concealed in the brush. He swore pretty strongly ... however, he faced about and started to go east ...

"After traveling fourteen miles, we came up to the train, but discovered that the teamsters were drunk, and knowing that drunken men were easily excited and always ready to fight, and remembering my positive orders not to hurt anyone except in self-defense, we remained in ambush until after midnight."

Later the Mormon guerrillas decided to advance, but as they entered the Army's camp they discovered — to their surprise — they were vastly outnumbered. And it was too late to turn back. But then, as they approached the Army's campfire, Smith realized in the light "that we had the advantage, for looking back into the darkness, I could not see where my line of troops ended, and could imagine my twenty followers stringing out to a hundred or more as well as not. I inquired for the captain of the train. Mr. Dawson stepped out and said he was the man. I told him that I had a little business with him. He inquired the nature of it, and I replied by requesting him to get all of his men and their private property as quickly as possible out of the wagons for I meant to put a little fire into them. He exclaimed: 'For God's sake, don't burn the trains.' I said it was for His sake that I was going to burn them, and pointed out a place for his men to stack their arms . . .

"Captain Dawson [wagon train captain] and I shortly after went up to the second train. Dawson, shaking the wagon in which the wagon-master slept, called loudly for [the wagon-master whose name was] Bill. 'Bill' seemed considerably dazed and grumbled at being called up so early. Dawson exclaimed with peculiar emphasis, 'Damn it man, get up, or you'll be burned to a cinder in five minutes!' Bill suddenly displayed remarkable activity."

Lot Smith seemed to enjoy the war:

"One old man, shaking with St. Anthony's dance or something . . . tremblingly said he thought we would have come sooner and not waited until they were in bed and some of them liable to be burned up. My big Irishman [assistant] told him we were so busy that we nearly left him without calling him up at all, at all.

"When all was ready, I made a torch . . . At this stage of our proceedings an Indian came from the Mountaineer Fork and seeing how the thing was going asked for some presents. He wanted two wagon covers for a lodge, some flour and soap. I filled his order and he went away much elated.

"While riding from wagon to wagon, with torch in hand and the wind blowing, the covers seemed to me to catch very slowly. I so stated it to James. He replied, swinging his long torch over his head, 'By St. Patrick, ain't it beautiful! I never saw anything go better in all my life.'

"About this time I had Dawson send in his men to the wagons, not yet fired, to get us some provisions, enough to thoroughly furnish us, telling him [Dawson] to get plenty of sugar and coffee for though I never used the latter myself, some of my men below, intimating that I had a force down there [though it was non-existent], were fond of it.

"On completing this task I told him that we were going just a little way off and that if he or his men molested the trains or undertook to put the fire out, they would be instantly killed. We rode away leaving the wagons all ablaze.[27]

"On the morning following we met another train ... we disarmed the teamsters, and I rode out and met him [the captain] about half a mile away. I told him that I came on business. He inquired the nature of it when I demanded his pistols. He replied: 'By G-d, sir, no man ever took them yet, and if you think you can, without killing me, try it.' We were all the time riding towards the train, with our noses about as close together as two Scotch terriers would have held theirs — his eyes flashing fire; I couldn't see mine — I told him that I admired a brave man, but that I didn't like blood — you insist on my killing you, which will only take a minute, but I don't want to do it. We had by this time reached the train," where the Mormons disarmed him and the others. Smith continues:

" ... I told them to hurry up and get their things out, and take their two wagons for we wanted to go on. Simpson [of the infantry] begged me not to burn the train while he was in sight, and said that it would ruin his reputation as a wagon master. I told him not to be so squeamish, that the trains burned very nicely, I had seen them before, and that we hadn't time to be ceremonious. We then supplied ourselves with provisions, set the wagons afire and rode on ... "[28]

Thus Lot Smith raided three government supply trains and captured and burned 75 wagons, all near Green River.[29] *U. S. House Executive Document No. 71* for 1858 adds they were "supply teams . . . Nos. 5, 9, and 10 . . . "[30]

Porter now wanted to press the advantage. But a new challenge struck him face-on: low rations for his men. While some of his men sunk to despair, others waited patiently, and eventually a rescue team brought relief.[31]

Then news came for which Porter was itching. Bill Hickman reigned in and announced to Porter they were near the government cattle camp at Ham's Fork . . . and that the Army camp was momentarily unguarded . . .

Porter and his men launched out with fire in their eyes.

When they arrived, they discovered an altogether unexpected obstacle . . . in the form of the old codger . . . Lot Smith. Lot was Porter's ancient rival; both had become hardened, seasoned, mountain scouts and their ways of working often clashed.[32] So when Porter almost literally stumbled across him one morning on a hillside just five miles from the Army, he saw no other use for the old character but to use him. To their mutual surprise, Porter found the war had united them — to the point they could agree on a strategy . . .

They gathered 100 Mormon guerrillas from three nearby detachments. Smith describes what next happened, with first a brief introduction of Porter:

"Rockwell and I were good friends, on the following basis: I did as I pleased and he, regularly, damned me for it. When we arrived within sight of the camp, I discovered a herd of cattle numbering about fourteen hundred head on the bottom lands below. We were on the bluff. I told Porter we would take those cattle. He said that was just like me. The stock was left there as a trap laid on purpose to catch me. The troops had found out what a damphool I was, and that I didn't know any better than to put my foot into that kind of a trap. The willows were full of artillary, and the minute I exposed myself among the stock they would blow me and my command higher than Gilderoy's kite.

"I told him to sit down and I would go and take the cattle myself. He replied very roughly that he would see me in 'limbo' first, and said that he had waited forty years for such a chance, and now I wanted to spoil it.

"While he stopped to survey the situation with his glass, I

started down the bluff, only about one-third of the men being able to keep up as we rushed down the steep descent.

"Porter came on in a terrible rage, swearing at me for going so fast, and at the men for being so slow. He wanted me to wait for them all to catch up.

"There was, however, no time to wait. We had to run about two miles to reach the cattle, and by the time we got to them the guards had yoked up teams . . . We intercepted them, unyoked the cattle and turned their heads the other way . . . The [Mormon] boys then gave a shout . . .

"The [Army] guards were frightened as badly as the cattle and looked as pale as death. They came to me and asked me if we were going to take the stock. I replied that it looked a little as if we would. Captain Roupe, the head wagon master [who had sworn the teamsters should have no pay because they would not fight when the trains were burned] was with this company of guards and appeared to be as badly scared as any of them. When he recovered a little from his fright, he asked me to let him have enough cattle with which to take his wagons to camp.

" . . . I gave him about twenty head, and when we returned to where his men were, they made what appeared to me at the time a most singular request. They wanted to know if I would give them their arms back. As we hadn't seen their arms, this request led to an inquiry, when we found that on seeing us coming down the bluff, so much like a lot of wild men, they threw their guns away, some one saying if we found them unarmed we would spare their lives. I told the men they could go and get their guns as we had all we wanted."[33]

Regarding this same incident, George Albert Smith records the official Church Historians Record Book entry for this day: "Mr. Romp was spoken to by O. P. Rockwell, who told him to *tell the troops they could not come in* [to Salt Lake Valley]."[34] (Our emphasis) The simplicity of Porter's statement to Mr. Romp is a classic.

Lot Smith resumes his narrative:

" . . . about fifteen of our men [Mormon guerrillas] came back over the bluff where they were following the cattle . . . thinking that Porter and I had got into a fight. When they found us all right, they returned . . . [to camp]. Rockwell told Roupe [a teamster] to tell the Colonel when he got to [the government soldiers'] camp that we had commenced in earnest, and would kill every man of them if he didn't liberate his prisoners, there being three of our men in his custody at that time. The guards then started for camp. They were the worst frightened men I ever saw. They ran the three teams until some of the cattle dropped dead, but they never stopped until they got within the lines.

"We rode on and soon overtook our men with the stock. We divided the cattle into suitable herds and drove all night, Porter and I piloting the way. As we rode along in the darkness together, he thoroughly enjoyed reflecting upon the events of the day. He would repeat what he had said to the guards and chuckle to himself over their discomfiture until his sides ached.

" . . . Rockwell went in with the cattle, very much to my regret. I never found many men like him. I think our officers were afraid that he and I could not get along together. But we could."[35]

Porter cantered his horse ahead to Fort Bridger[36] and possibly saw General Wells, and then drove 624 steers and four mules into Great Salt Lake City,[37] leaving hundreds of other steers for Mormon patrols to eat in the mountains. Lot Smith leaves this narrative of his final weeks in the war:

" . . . General Wells had told us that our numbers would be magnified in the eyes of the enemy, and it proved to be so. We passed [in the eyes of the Army] . . . for from five hundred to a thousand men, while in fact the whole number never exceeded at any time one hundred, and generally was not half that many.

" . . . President Young said it was providential for all parties [of Smith and Rockwell not finding other Army supply trains], for if we had burned another train we would have been compelled before the end of winter to feed the enemy to keep them from starving.[38]

" . . . Having Rockwell's men left with me, I felt that my command was pretty strong, and began maneuvering accordingly. We soon struck the trail of a detachment of troops and following it found ourselves unexpectedly in close quarters with quite a large force . . . We halted about forty yards from them and I advanced and met Captain Marcy about twenty paces from his line of battle. He introduced himself, saying he supposed I was Captain Smith. I replied in the affirmative. He then said that the soldiers he commanded were United States troops, and asked me what armed force it was I had. I told him they were from Utah.

" 'What is your business out here?' he inquired.

" 'Watching you. What's your business?' I asked.

"He said they were looking out a way into Utah.

" 'Nonsense,' said I . . . "[39] Smith then truthfully told the Army they were off course, but while they were talking, Smith's Mormon guerrillas " . . . were nearly surrounded by Marcy's command, the troops forming a long line below us. There was no apparent way of escape but up a steep mountain or to cut through the line . . . Matters then looked pretty blue for a few moments, as we could hear the troops thundering on as they drew in their circle around us. I ran [to escape] up the river some distance, and found the bank cut by a ravine." But the Mormons escaped through the ravine and up a hill, continues Smith, while the Army's "main body gave up chase, as we leisurely rode up the hill. I sat down on the hillside, and looking across the river at them, imagined how chagrined they must feel, having let us slip through their fingers after having their hands fairly upon us."[40]

Smith was of course confident they had escaped the infantry, but: "I had just started down the hill . . . when [Mormon] Lieutenant Abbot came riding down . . . exclaiming, 'The troops are upon us!' I could not believe it . . . They [the enemy] jumped off their horses, took good aim, and sent forty shots . . . Luckily for us they were in short range and over shot the mark — except Mark Hall of Ogden, who got a bullet through his hat. Two horses were shot; a grey one falling near me. The troops thought I had fallen and shouted exultingly. I felt happy to know that they were mistaken.

" . . . We fell back on Fort Supply, eating the beef we had borrowed and sampling some half-cooked government beans. This experiment developed, as never before conceived in my imagination, the enormous pressure the human stomach is capable of sustaining without damage, and came very near developing the necessity for some one else to write this . . .

"I was again ordered to the front. I started with twenty-six men and one baggage wagon on the coldest day that I ever experienced. While making up the detachment, a number of young men volunteered and insisted on going with us." Lot Smith was impressed with these Mormon strapplings: "The General thought them too young to take so severe a trip, and it was decided that Joseph Rich and Howard Spencer [two lads in question] remain in camp. The latter had a fever sore on his leg, and to show his indifference to a little hardship and express his disgust at being kept in camp, he remarked to his comrades: 'Boys, if you want to get out of doing anything, just scratch your leg a little.' He then rolled up his pants and filled the gaping wound with hot embers. I thought him then the right kind of stuff to make a soldier."

" . . . My horse proved himself a . . . man's best friend. I shall never forget how he plowed his way through the drifts, breaking the track and leading the company safely to camp. When we arrived, John Woolley said my nose was frozen. I told him I didn't think it possible, for it was so short.

" . . . We took our stand, receiving deserters from the enemy daily, and sending them to the Valley.

"When General Johnston turned towards Salt Lake, after going up Ham's Fork, one would have thought that he would go right through in a few days, but the General began to see how far off Salt Lake really was.

"Our duty was to watch the troops as they slowly came up to the ruins of Bridger and went into winter quarters. I suppose that it was this position, which the *London Punch* so graphically pictured in a cartoon in which the flower of the American army is being herded by ten Mormons.

"It soon became evident that the army would settle for the winter. The snow fell and covered the ground a great depth, but it was not so deep as our chaplain prayed for. He asked for twenty feet.

" . . . The word came to us to leave ten men on the Yellow Creek Mountains to guard the army.

"The detail of this illustrious little band was made, and the rest of us turned towards home. When crossing the two mountain ranges, I felt satisfied that Uncle Sam would not attempt to follow.

"I shall never forget my feelings on that homeward march; I had been 'keyed up' to a higher tension for ten weeks than I ever thought a human frame could stand. I could ride night and day for weeks and not feel fatigued, but now when turning my back upon the scenes of such absorbing interest, the weariness of months seemed to overpower me, and I was as weak as a child.

" . . . we reached President Young's office. He came out to the steps and spoke about ten words; I did not remember one of them, but they had the effect to dispel every sense of weakness or weariness. I was ready that moment to return to the mountains. I would like to know the words he uttered, though it was not the words but the spirit which dictated them that touched the key note of my heart. I don't know how many men could have done it; he could."[41]

The hit and run tactics of the Mormons had proved indefensible.

General Wells later admitted why he had resorted to burning government supply wagons: "I had a company of men in the rear of their teams which would arrest a certain number of teamsters every day, and often leaving them sufficient stores to regain their base of supplies, they were turned to the right about. But we found that they would merely go back until we ceased to watch them, and then return. So it became necessary to burn their teams and incapacitate them for a campaign . . . Every night [that] those troops encamped I had men among them. Their conduct showed significantly what they meant to do to us. They had doggerel songs, copies of which were captured, announcing their intention to make a barrack of Brigham Young's house, and enjoy his family. These songs inflamed our people, and united us as one man in the defence of our settlements."[42]

By October U. S. Army Colonel Alexander saw the futility: " . . . We are powerless . . . to effect any chastizement of the marauding bands that are constantly hovering about us."[43]

Mormon soldier Jesse W. Crosby records, "All were determined to stop them, and firm in the faith that we could do it and not half try."[44] He recalls their overall defensive position of the war: "the Troops [had] fired at our men several times, but the fire was not

returned, strict orders having been given to that effect."[45]
Porter and his men had simply held the Army.

Colonel Johnston sent a report of their situation: "Headquarters
Army of Utah ... November 30, 1857 ... Major: Since my last
report the troops and all the supply trains have arrived at this
place, and will remain here, or in this district, during the winter."[46]
The Army was thus holed up in a burned-out fort.

Anti-Mormon writer John I. Ginn, in an attack on the Saints,
portrayed the following events in a revealing light:

" ... on the 5th of November Colonel Johnston reported to
headquarters in the east that in his opinion the time for further
argument was past and that the time for prompt and vigorous
action had arrived, as the Mormons had, with premeditation,
'placed themselves in rebellion against the Union, and entertain
the insane design of establishing a form of government thoroughly
despotic and utterly repugnant to our institution.' He [Johnston]
had therefore ordered that wherever they were met in arms that
they be treated as enemies ... "

While Mormons claimed "the Lord was on our side," Ginn took
into account the Mormon claims:

"November 6, 1857, Colonel Johnston commenced his march
from the camp ... to Camp Scott (Fort Bridger), a distance of
thirty-five miles, but so heavy was the snow, so intense the cold
and tremendous the loss of battery horses, draught mules, and
oxen of the contractors that it required fifteen days to cover this
distance ...

" ... Lieutenant Colonel Philip St. George Cooke ...
encountered heavy rain on the fifth day out ... rain poured
continuously, increasing the pull on his team mules and at the
same time steadily diminishing their strength.

"At Bitter Creek November 8th, after a three days' tramp
through deep snow and a freezing, blinding fog, twenty-three mules
gave out and five wagons and their harnesses abandoned.

"On the night of the 9th fifteen animals froze to death, and on
account of the bitter cold wind facing them ... three fourths of
these remaining perished from the cold ...

"On the night of the 10th the mercury went 25 degrees below zero, and on the morning of the 11th . . . three wagons were abandoned . . . two of them empty and the other hidden in the brush and filled with 74 extra saddles and bridles and some sabres."

The troops obviously thought things could not get worse, but they did. "On the 11th . . . the mules were tied to the wagons, where nine of them perished, while the others gnawed and destroyed four wagon tongues, a number of wagon covers, ate their ropes, and, getting loose, ate the sage brush fuel collected at the tents, and *attacked the tents*. [Our emphasis]

"From the loss of horses more than half of the men were now dismounted, and on the morning of November 12th a number were frost-bitten . . .

"November 15th Green River was reached and crossed on the ice, and on the 16th nine wagons and forty-two mules were left there.

"On reaching Johnston's headquarters Lieutenant Colonel Cooke made a report of his journey:

" 'I have 144 horses and have lost 134. Most of the loss has occurred, much this side of south Pass, in comparatively moderate weather. It has been of starvation. The earth has a no more lifeless, treeless, grassless desert; it contains scarcely a wolf to glut itself on the hundreds of dead and frozen animals, which for thirty miles nearly block the road, with abandoned and shattered property. They mark, perhaps beyond example in history, the steps of an advancing army, with the horrors of a disastrous retreat.' "

Ginn angrily concludes his summary:

"As might have been expected, when the rigourous weather . . . began to cast the shadow of death . . . , the Mormons . . . [with] recalcitrant fanaticism . . . retired into the warm valleys behind their formidable fortifications in Echo Canyon, leaving only a few squads to watch the mountain passes and the movement (if any) of the army . . .

"The winter of 1857-8 was an unusually severe one, even for that region of severe winters, and the snow fall was uncommonly heavy. Of course in the deep, warm valley of Salt Lake City there was little if any snow, the precipitation being in the form of gentle showers of rain . . . the Mormon apostles and elders, preaching in the Tabernacle every Sunday would 'point with pride' to the eastern mountains and call the attention of the people to the 'fact' that the Lord was punishing the 'Gentile army' with heavy snows and blockading the mountains against their approach, while at the same time He was sending to the Saints warm, gentle rains to fructify their soil."[47]

Ginn was furious, and all the more so since the Saints had built an interesting case: After all, seldom in warfare do an army's pack animals attack its own army. Ginn continues, "No Mormon seemed to question that this simple occurance was anything short of a direct, visable and tangible interference in their favor on the part of Heaven so simple and credulous were these ignorant zealots."

Nevertheless, Ginn finally confesses General Johnston's letter to General Garland had termed the month previous as "unprecedented cold weather."[48]

While Johnston's Army was camped in for the winter, Mormon soldier Jesse W. Crosby records, "President Young sent them a load of salt on hearing they were out but they would not receive it, and our men scattered it in the snow outside their guards, and returned home."[49] To supply the Army its salt, "Buffalo" Bill Cody reports, " . . . the officers mess was soon after supplied by the Indians at the rate of five dollars a pound!"[50]

Many of the soldiers and officers, embarrassed at the fact they'd been effectively harassed by mere religionists, soon came down with acute cases of selective perception. Sour grapes, as it were. Army Captain Albert Tracy, for example, passed through the canyon and reported the Saints could not have actually held off the Army, stating that the Army's artillery could have knocked the Mormons' boulders "about their ears," where guerrillas were located atop the canyons.[51]

Van Vliet, however, the designated scouting officer for the Army, contradicts him: "There is but one road running into the valley on the side which our troops are approaching, and for over fifty miles it passes through narrow canyons and over rugged mountains which a small force could hold against great odds."[52]

Reporter Junius Wells at the scene also disagrees with Captain Tracy, stating the positions occupied by the Mormons in Echo Canyon "would have enabled them to successfully defeat an army of a thousand times their force."[53]

And Ebenezer Crouch, although admiring the Army's pomp, "with all their fine display," could see problems with them even several years later. "No doubt they would have been alright fighting in open field, but seemed to be too stiff and precise for mountain service. The cavalry men would sit so stiff in the saddle with the tips of their toes just touching the stirrups that they looked more like statues than living men . . . In fancy I see the cowboy . . . sizing one up and I see the grin on his face."[54]

The Saints again took up singing, this time with a ballad that swept the mountain community:

> *As we were going up the Platte singing many a lusty ditty, Saying 'we'll do this and we'll do that when we get to Salt Lake City,'*
> *And sure enough when they got there, they made the Mormons stir, Sir;*
> *That is, I mean they would have done, but oh, they didn't get there.*

> *Then they returned with awful tales, saying "The Mormons beat the devil:*
> *"They ride up hill, and over rocks as fast as on the level;*
> *"And if perchance you shoot one down, and surely think he's dead, Sir,*
> *"The first you know he's on his horse and pushing on ahead, Sir!"*

> *Then on 'Ham's Fork' they camped awhile saying, "We'll wait a little longer,*
> *"Till Johnston and his crew come up, and make us a little stronger.*

"Then we'll go on, take Brigham Young, and Porter, his companion;"
        That is, I mean they would have done, but were afraid of Echo Canyon.

Now Uncle Sam, take my advice; you'd better stay at home, Sir!
        You need your money and your men to defend your rights at home, Sir!
        But if, perchance, you need some help, the Mormons will be kind, Sir.
        They've helped you once, and will again, that is, if you've a mind, Sir!

The last reference was to the Mexican War and the Mormon Battalion...

For now the war was stalemated until spring. Porter, meanwhile, returned to Great Salt Lake City.

According to a highly questionable source for a number of reports (see Note 26 for details) — John I. Ginn was captured by Mormon guerrillas after having deserted the Army's wagon trains. He then claimed to have been walking down a road, ahead of his captors, when, "I came upon Porter Rockwell ... standing in the road with his arms and chin resting on the saddle of his favorite little mule.

"The recognition was mutual and instantaneous — for I had seen Rockwell early in the spring of that year [1857] when he came into Magraw's Camp, near Independence, to enquire about some missing mules belonging to the Salt Lake mail line in which he was interested prior to its withdrawal, and he recognized me as 'the boy who had promptly protested against it,' when Magraw ordered the men to hang him.

"After a few inquiries and answers, Rockwell remarked that the ford at Bear River was rough, the current strong and the water cold, and then asked me to mount his mule and ride across to his camp on the opposite bank, remarking that he could jump on behind one of the boys driving the cattle and ride across himself.

After Rockwell gave him his own mule and rode across on the rear of another, "I rode across the river and up to the campfire where Mormons were cooking supper for this whole command. Recognizing the mule and seeing it in possession of a stranger and a hated Gentile at that, they did not know what to make of it. They were dumfounded, but looked daggers at me, and while I was hitching the mule one of them picked up his gun, brought it to a ready and demanded sharply, 'Where did you get that mule?' I told him, when he put down his gun and went on with his cooking. When Porter Rockwell arrived in camp he introduced me to the principal men of his command and after that I was treated with the greatest respect. After supper Rockwell took myself and Franks [Ginn's fellow prisoner] to one side and told us they desired to push the cattle a few miles further over that night to Yellow Creek to the camp of General Wells, the Commander in chief of the Mormon army, and promised us a good supper there if we would assist by following behind in the road and pushing up the laggards, while the mounted men would do the flanking and keep the cattle in the road. We did so and got the supper.

"We reached the camp of General Wells about midnight, and while Rockwell entered the General's tent Joe Franks and myself walked up to a large campfire to warm ourselves.

"While standing there one surly Mormon began abusing Gentiles in general and us in particular, when a South Carolina Mormon . . . struck the fellow across the head with a rifle, knocking him into the fire across a large bed of live coals.

"Others sprang to the rescue and jerked the man from the fire, and just then Porter Rockwell ran out to see what the commotion was about and was closely followed by General Wells. The man with the gun [the South Carolina Mormon defending the prisoners] explained that his comrade had insulted and started in to abuse the prisoners when he [the South Carolina Mormon] knocked him down, whereupon General Wells ordered the wounded man [the surly Mormon] to the guard house and invited Joe Franks and myself to his own tent to spend the night.

"The next day we moved on with the cattle, Rockwell proffering Franks and myself the finest dinner that could be gotten up in the city if we would help drive the cattle in. We gladly accepted the offer as we had to follow Uncle Sam's cattle in anyway.

"At Cache Cave, at the head of Echo Canyon, we met a Mormon train going out with supplies for the [Mormon] army. Porter Rockwell overhauled it and distributed necessities and luxuries to his own command, giving Franks and myself an equal share with his own men. Passing down Echo Canyon, with its bristling fortifications and great excavations made to flood the road and render it impassable, we reached its mouth . . . Here we rested one day and then proceeded over the Big and Little Mountains, reaching Salt Lake City about noon.

"Rockwell gave us the promised dinner, and then we were released or allowed the freedom of the city . . .

"Porter Rockwell, who conceived a genuine friendship for me . . . directed me to the home of 'Mother Taylor,' the mother of John Taylor of the Twelve Apostles, and afterward Brigham Young's successor as President of the Church. There I procured a comfortable room and good board at the family table, and there I remained until I left for California.

"Old Mother Taylor was a kindly and rather intelligent old lady for a woman steeped to the eyes in Mormonism . . . "

Ginn concludes his "first-hand" account, claiming Porter was "Chief of the Destroying Angels and Brigham Young's confidential and most trusted lieutenant."[55]

When Rockwell returned to Great Salt Lake City, he was assigned to escort six prisoners from town. This incident later became one of the hottest newspaper controversies of the West, known as the Aiken case, and Porter was a principal in the story. The six strangers had originally come from California "with the intention of starting a gambling hall and house of prostitution among the Mormons."[56] They were also suspected by some Saints as "robbers from the mountains,"[57] or as "spies for the enemy."[58] In any case, these six men were taken because of the existing martial law: They had entered without passports and were prevented from continuing eastward toward Johnston's Army, where they could possibly report Mormon fortifications and troop strengths. The six men had been apprehended at Box Elder,[59] and brought into the city[60] where they were imprisoned a short time at the Townsend House[61] where Hosea Stout and others helped guard them.[62] After the authorities released the men, two were allowed to remain in the territory "at large,"[63] but, as Stout expands, "O. P. Rockwell with 3 or four others started with 4 of the prisoners, which we have been guarding for some days, south to escort them through the settlements to California."[64]

All six men eventually disappeared. The *New York Times* the following March printed a report from the Placerville, California *Index* which assumed the prisoners had been assassinated by the Mormons. The article said the men were John and Thomas Aikens and two others (four men, not six) and that they had, during their brief confinement, written someone in Mariposa County, California detailing the fact they had been imprisoned. The *Index* claims the four men had never returned home, having mysteriously disappeared on the return journey west.[65] The *Index,* of course, may have jumped to some fairly speculative conclusions, as robbers or even Indians could have massacred the men on the way home, or they may have simply died in the desert. In any case it was convenient stuff with which to fuel the flames of prejudice against the Mormons, and the national press now had a field day. Frontier newspapers especially were notorious for reporting — even inventing — the wildest of rumors, many of which were unabashedly anti-Mormon; additionally, newspaper competition was fierce and any good story would sell papers. (See note 27 for further details on the Aiken case, and why the court later declared Rockwell innocent.)

After having escorted the prisoners away from jail, which is all that has been reliably documented, Porter remained among the Saints for most of the winter. In addition to the Aiken case another affair called the Mountain Meadows Massacre brought shame to the Saints. One hundred and thirty-six Missouri and Arkansas emigrants were slain by Indians and a coterie of willful Mormons, all acting independent of — indeed contrary to — church authority and counsel. The most celebrated figure of this ignominious episode was John D. Lee, who purportedly helped lead the massacre and who turned against Brigham Young, his adopted father, eventually even laying blame for the massacre on him. William F. "Buffalo Bill" Cody and analyst/historian Henry Inman disagree: " . . . it was proved that the Mormon Church had nothing

to do with the massacre; that Lee, in fact, had acted in direct
opposition to the officers of the Church."[66] Lee was later
excommunicated by the church and executed by civil authorities.
While church enemies claimed the act was also perpetrated out of
vengeance against Missourians, some active church members felt
otherwise: One diarist, Murray Averett, records, "After moving to
Washington, Utah[,] Ma became acquainted with some of the
wives of men that was in that affair and she thinks, or did think, it
was done for robbery. John D. Lee's wives and those of Hate and
Higbee had silk dresses and fine carpets and bedding for years
after the crime was done."[67] But the church was blamed, despite
the robbers' intentions.

Rockwell, meanwhile, continued activity in his church. On
January 28, 1858, a pioneer in Provo named William Marsden
journals, " . . . Whent to Meeting at Night when Porter Rockwell
preached."[68]

Meanwhile, in the wilderness, the infantry was suffering.
Johnston gave up on the burned-out ruins of Fort Bridger and
decided instead to settle at nearby Black's Fork. Here they
conducted an interesting court, indicting over one thousand
Mormons for "wickedly and maliciously" conducting war on the
United States. Rockwell had the honor of being the seventh name
listed.[69] An embittered federal grand jury convened in the
wilderness and handed down the indictment December 30, 1857.

In desperate need for supplies Johnston then sent for a rescue
party to New Mexico. Led by Captain Randolph B. Marcy, it was
perhaps the high point of gallantry for the Army in the entire
campaign.[70] They braved the worst storms of the 19th century and
plowed through blizzards into New Mexico, where they purchased
replacement mules, horses, and supplies for Johnston's withering
army, then began their march northward again in the spring of
1858.

Back in Utah, meanwhile, Johnston's army all but froze.[71]
Nearby, of course, the Mormons waited.

Apparently in January Porter took a jaunt into the mountains to
spy them out. The *New York Herald* reports, "The redoubtable

Porter Rockwell told Mr. Bell [the *Herald* reporter] that he and his company stood on the mountains by the side of which Colonel Alexander was marching his command . . . and so near that they could have thrown rocks upon the troops passing."[72]

While the weather tormented the Army, it came to the rescue of Mormon spies: Army Captain J. A. Gove reports, "Last week the picket guard stationed about one mile west of the fort fired upon a man who, I feel assured, was Louis Robinson, the former proprietor of this place. A slight snow fall during the night obliterated all traces of his whereabouts in the morning. That a man of his high standing among the Mormons should be prowling about camp during this inclement weather is most strange."[73]

Aside from the fact his footprints disappeared in a timely snowfall, Army officers were baffled by the Mormon army philosophy of rank possessing no privileges.

Then Colonel Johnston received a visitor . . . Colonel Thomas L. Kane, eastern ally and friend of the Saints.[74] When Kane rode into camp his anxiousness surprised the general,[75] according to an artillery officer who witnessed the meeting, but Kane's sincerity convinced Governor Cumming that the Mormons may in fact be more harmless than the press had led them all to believe. Within three weeks — it took Kane that long to convince him — Cumming acceded to Kane's wishes, and agreed to meet for himself this master of men, this modern Moses, Brigham Young. On April 5th, Governor Cumming set out on his journey with Kane and no armed escort.

"They travelled about fifteen miles, upset one of the carriages in the snow, and there [were] stuck for the night," writes John Kay in a letter. "It so happened that W. H. Kimball, E. Hanks, O.P. Rockwell, Howard Egan, and myself, with a few other good boys, were out scouting in that vicinity; and on the morning of the 6th April, we took the Governor and his small party under our protection."[76]

Army Captain Jesse Gove elaborates that the Mormons were "under the command of the villain, Porter Rockwell. For shame, that he [Governor Cumming] should have put himself in a position to be so far humiliated by being escorted, more like a prisoner than the chief executive of this territory, by a band of lawless men,

led by a notorious murderer and rebel!"[77] Despite his
not-so-subtle aspersions, the statement possesses a certain
melodramatic Nineteenth Century charm, portraying typical
prejudice nurtured by Eastern City newspapers.

As Cumming and Colonel Kane were escorted deeper down
Echo Canyon, they were halted numerous times by bands of
Mormon guerrillas. Campfires burned all night along canyon walls,
so when Cumming reached the mouth of the canyon, he estimated
he had seen between 2,000 and 3,000 Mormon guerrillas![78]

Little did he know he'd been the target of an elaborate hoax.
Rockwell and his cohorts had staged the entire episode, complete
with phony, unmanned campfires. The numerous bands of
Mormon guerrillas had simply been the same single band circling
back over and over to re-dramatize the same scene: stopping the
governor's buggy, interrogating him, and letting him pass.
Governor Cumming was now convinced Johnston's army hadn't a
prayer ... even with reinforcements. So when he arrived into the
valley of the Saints, he was prepared to negotiate peace at any
cost.

Yet he now found Great Salt Lake City ... surprisingly, eerily,
all-but-deserted. He nevertheless soon found the Prophet ... and
he was stunned. Brigham proposed that he turn his entire
gubernatorial powers over to Cumming!

Needless to say, Cumming was elated.

Brigham, hoping among other things to avoid bloodshed, had a
few other tricks up his sleeve. He knew if he could negotiate at the
bargaining table, he could outsmart these Easterners.

Meanwhile, in Washington President Buchanan, this same week,
had launched a peace commission towards Utah to release the
Mormons from all indictments of treason. (Jesse W. Crosby later
analyzes the peace commission's arrival from the Mormon
viewpoint: "Proclamation consisted of a routine of slanders and
abuses, and finally granting us a full and free pardon — unasked
for on our part. The object of this seemed to be to justify the
administration in their blunder and to make the world believe they
had committed no blunder. Yet, it was easy to see they felt
whipped and anxious to get out of the scrape.")[79] President
Buchanan had signed the proclamation April 6th,[80] ever an eventful
date for Mormons.

Cumming's curious arrival in the city — of finding few inhabitants — was the result of a recent directive Brigham had issued the Saints. It was another psychological trick and it worked on the new governor. In obedience to Brigham, the Mormons had exodused 50 miles south to Provo. If the U. S. troops were to attempt taking over Great Salt Lake City, Cumming learned, the Saints would simply leave Provo to some designated spot south, perhaps Mexico.[81] And if the Army did march on Great Salt Lake City, a number of Brigham's police would simply lay it to ashes.[82] Cumming was impressed, of course, with what he felt was the military manpower of the Saints in the mountains and with the deserted civilian populace who were so willing to leave this contingent of federal officials high and dry in a burned-out city — with no one, in effect, to govern. He also "looked over the Records of the Supreme Court and also the Library, found all correct . . . [which] will contradict the reports which have gone abroad," he said.[83] He then wrote to the U. S. Secretary of State, "I shall restrain all operations of the military for the present . . . "

On May 3rd Porter began escorting Cumming back to Johnston's Army where he arrived a week later. After depositing the governor at his burned-out fort, Porter returned to the city.

Three weeks afterwards, Buchanan's peace commission[84] arrived, and after hearing Cumming's comments, the commission decided Cumming had been too soft on the Mormons. The peace commission still felt the Mormons needed to be whipped into line. True, they bore news of Buchanan's amnesty, but as *bona fide* government officials now, they would see to it no one would defy their power. The Mormons would submit, period. And if anyone could see to it — they would. On June 1 the peace commission wrote to the U. S. Secretary of State: "this deluded people [shall] submit quietly and peacefully to the civil authorities."[85] The commission consisted of 13 men, including Senator Lazarus W. Powell of Kentucky and Major Ben McCullough of Texas.

The "peace" commission now rode forth to Great Salt Lake City, where they were surprised by sudden movements in the dark. Mormon scout Joseph Fielding Smith chronicles, "I was on picket guard, with a party of men under O. P. Rockwell, when

Commissioners Powell and M'Cullough met us near the Weber River . . . "[86]

After giving them a little start — a foretaste of coming events — Porter and his men finally made themselves known and escorted the commission into the city.[87]

On June 11th the commissioners arrived and met with Young and other leading Mormons in the Council House. After the commissioners presented their case before the Council, Brigham presented[88] the Mormons' case. Historian Tullidge reports in 1886: "The aspect of affairs was favorable. Presently, however a well-known character, O. P. Rockwell, was seen to enter, approach the ex-Governor and whisper to him. He was from the Mormon army. There was at once a sensation, for it was appreciated that he brought some unexpected and important news. Brigham arose; his manner self-possessed, but severe. " 'Governor Powell, are you aware, sir, that those troops are on the move towards the city?'

" 'It cannot be!' exclaimed Powell, surprised . . . 'we were promised by the General that they should not move till after this meeting.'

" 'I have received a dispatch that they are on the march for this city. My messenger would not deceive me.'

" . . . the Peace Commission," says Tullidge, "could offer no explanation."[89]

Brigham, in response, made a tactically brilliant move. As a master of psychological interplay he suddenly called for — of all things — the singing of a hymn. Upon hearing the lyrics the peace commissioners understood the point, loud and clear:

> *O ye mountains high, where the clear blue sky*
> *Arches over the vales of the free;*
> *Where the pure breezes blow,*
> *And the clear streamlets flow,*
> *How I've longed to your bosom to flee,*
> *O Zion! dear Zion! land of the free,*
> *My own mountain home, now to thee I have come,*
> *All my fond hopes are centered in thee.*

Here our voices we'll raise, and we'll sing to thy
praise,
    Sacred home of the prophets of God;
    Thy deliverance is nigh,
    Thy oppressors shall die,
    And the gentiles shall bow 'neath thy rod.
    O Zion! dear Zion! home of the free;
    In thy temples we'll bend, all thy rights we'll defend,
    And our home shall be ever with thee.

"The action of Brigham had been very simple in the case," explains Tullidge, "but there was a world of meaning in it ... There have been times when the singing of that hymn by the thousands of saints has been almost as potent as that revolutionary hymn of France — the *Marseillaise.* Such was such a time."[90]

Two of the peace commissioners, McCullough and Governor Cumming, were apparently overheard talking as they left the meeting for a walk: McCullough desired to let the army march on the Saints and fight them. Cumming's reasoning was more realistic: "Fight them? ... You might fight them but you would never whip them ... Did you notice the snap in those men's eyes ... No, sir; they would never know when they were whipped!"[91]

The next day before a congregation of elders and government representatives, "the Peace Commissioners heard more from Brigham," and, as Tullidge describes, it was "the roar of the 'lion of the Lord.' "[92]

"President Young arose. He said, 'I have listened very attentively to the commissioners, and will say, as far as I am concerned, I thank President Buchanan for forgiving me, but I really cannot tell what I have done ...

" 'We have always been loyal, and expect to so continue; but, hands off! Do not send your armed mobs into our midst. If you do, we will fight you, as the Lord lives! Do not threaten us with what the United States can do, for we ask no odds of them or their troops. We have the God of Israel — the God of battles — on our side; and let me tell you, gentlemen, we fear not your armies. I can take a few of the boys here and, with the help of the Lord, can whip the whole of the United States.' "

Brigham then introduced his next move, from a very deep bag of marvelously-mixed tricks:

" . . . Now let me say to you Peace Commissioners, we are willing those troops should come into our country, but not to stay in our city. They may pass through it, if needs be, but must not quarter less than forty miles from us."

Evidently of great surprise to both the commissioners and the Saints, Brigham now allowed for the Army to actually enter their sacred valley, but, he cautioned, "If you bring your troops here to disturb this people, you have got a bigger job than you or President Buchanan have any idea of.

" . . . Our wives and children will go to the canyons, and take shelter in the mountains; while their husbands and sons will fight you; and, as God lives, we will hunt you by night and by day, until your armies are wasted away. No mob can live in the homes we have built in these mountains. That's the programme, gentlemen, whether you like it or not. If you want war you can have it."[93] .

The peace commissioners could see the next move was clearly theirs. They gazed at the stern thousands and their Prophet, and, wherein they had earlier informed President Buchanan they would make the Saints say uncle, they now visualized an unexpectedly bizarre scenario unfolding; and, that without some rather quick negotiating with General Johnston, they could visualize the Army marching into the eerily deserted territory, only to be bombarded by a full-scale, bloody guerrilla war, complete with fully mobilized hit-and-run attacks which could, over the months, completely annihilate them. The one hope the peace commissioners had, they felt, was Brigham's closing remarks: "but, if you wish peace, peace it is; we shall be glad of it."[94]

The one chance the commissioners had now was to stop General Johnston before he entered the valley and opened fire . . .

XII

General Albert Sidney Johnston, recently promoted from colonel, had in Governor Cumming's eyes committed two mortal sins: He'd been hasty in issuing his marching orders and he had broken his agreement with Cumming and the peace commissioners. Cumming, in fact, felt Johnston's action now jeopardized the peace conference and tipped the scales against them in bargaining with Brigham.[1]

The general had received supplies from New Mexico and Fort Leavenworth, and with his new promotion freshly under his belt, was anxious to march on the Mormons.

Meanwhile, the press clamored — worldwide editorials in fact screamed — *against* the government's actions.

Tullidge records, "Deep sympathy, blended with a mighty admiration, was felt for a people who could at once dare a war with the United States, in defence of their religious cause ..."[2]

The *New York Times* published a gigantic question mark on society's outlook of the affair: " ... [If we have] been the means of driving away 50,000 of our fellow-citizens from fields which their labor had reclaimed and cultivated, and around which their affections were clustered, we have something serious to answer for ... .Was it right to send troops composed of the wildest and most rebellious men of the community, commanded by men like Harney and Johnston, to deal out fire and sword upon people whose faults were the result of honest religious convictions? Was it right to allow Johnston to address letters to Brigham Young, and through him to his people, couched in the tone of an implacable conqueror towards ruthless savages? ... Posterity must not have to acknowledge with shame that our indiscretion, or ignorance, or intolerance drove the population of a whole State from house and home, to seek religious liberty and immunity from the presence of mercenary troops."[3]

The *London Times* editorialized, "Does it not seem incredible that, at the very moment when the marine of Great Britain and the United States are jointly engaged in the grandest scientific experiments that the world has yet seen, 30,000 or 40,000 natives of these countries, many of them of industrious and temperate habits, should be the victims of such arrant imposition?"[4] (For other notable editorials see Note 28.)

While the press was conducting an "about-face," the peace commissioners were trying desperately to stop the on-coming army of General Johnston.

The commissioners caught Johnston before his entrance to the valley and prevented the guns and torches from laying waste to the deserted homes. From their meetings with church leaders, the government officials had come to the conclusion they had no alternative now but to comply with Brigham's master-plan.

However, the troops resumed marching ... but now with guns unloaded ... into Great Salt Lake City.

Tullidge comments, "They were merely permitted to pass through the streets of Salt Lake City on their way to a location in the Territory well removed from the Mormon people ... If faith was not kept with them they [the civilians] did not intend to return, and war would have been re-opened in deadly earnest."[5]

Brigham had made a bold move at the negotiating table ... he had demanded the peace commission to "not quarter [the Army] less than forty miles from us."[6] One wonders if he had not foreseen the aftermath of his proclaimed "bloodless war" all along, and had not perhaps planned on the resulting economic harvest.

The soon-to-come economic windfall boon to the Saints, in fact, would be unprecedented.

After Johnston's Army arrived in Salt Lake Valley, Tullidge reports, "It was one of the most extraordinary scenes that have occurred in American history. All day long, from dawn until after sunset, the troops and trains poured through the city, the utter silence of the streets being broken only by the music of the military bands, the monotonous tramp of the regiments, and the rattle of the baggage wagons ... The stillness was so profound that during the intervals between the passage of the columns, the monotonous gurgle of the City Creek struck on every ear ... Some of the officers were deeply moved by the scene and the circumstances. Lieutenant Colonel Philip St. George Cooke, who had commanded the Mormon battalion in the Mexican war, rode through the city with uncovered head, leading the troops, but forgetting not his respect."[7]

African explorer Captain Richard Burton of the British Army investigated the matter firsthand and capsulized the entire affair: "Such is His Excellency, President Brigham Young ... who, governing as well as reigning, long stood up to fight with the sword of the Lord, and with his few hundred guerrillas, against the then mighty power of the United States; who has outwitted all diplomacy opposed to him; and, finally, who made a treaty of peace with the President of the great Republic, as though he had wielded the combined power of France, Russia, and England."[8]

Tullidge summarizes, "General Johnston and his army came not as conquerers into Zion. The entire chain of circumstances ... had been but a series of disasters and failures."[9]

The Army marched toward their assigned spot. "Cedar Valley," writes Tullidge, "forty miles west of the city, was chosen as their permanent camping place, which was named Camp Floyd, in honor of the then Secretary of War."[10]

"Buffalo" Bill Cody, a civilian teamster at the scene, finalizes his own summary: "The army was powerless before the people they had come to punish. All that remained to do was to forgive the Mormons and let them go."[11]

A final fitting tribute to the war comes from Wells: "It is here proper to remark that the cattle, horses, and other stock taken

during the campaign were, on the conclusion of peace, returned to
the officers . . . for which act neither thanks nor compensation was
ever rendered. Among the animals that fell into our hands was a
pet mule, owned by Col. Alexander; an old, white, gentle creature,
the pride of the Colonel's household. Governor Young was
particularly requested to take charge of this distinguished favorite,
and accordingly had it sought out from the herd, stabled in a
reserved stall of his barn and fed on the fat of the land. The
attention bestowed upon it became the subject of diplomatic
correspondence between the commandants of the opposing forces;
yet, notwithstanding the enduring fame thus achieved and the
tenderest care of experienced hostlers and veterinary surgeons,
the poor prisoner succumbed to age and aggravated grief, at being
ruthlessly torn from its associates and friends, and during the
winter died, lamented by two armies."[12]

Thus ended the Utah War.

On July 5th, the day before Johnston's Army had arrived at
camp, the Saints began their march northward again and now *en
masse* re-filled Salt Lake Valley.

Porter, meanwhile, returned to the homefront. He joined Mary
Ann and their two children at his in-laws' ranch, then left the Neff
property altogether to move his family to his new property near
Lehi, not far from the Army at Camp Floyd.

In addition to his 42 acres near Provo,[13] on July 29 he
purchased sixteen additional acres near Point of the Mountain, half
way between Provo and Great Salt Lake City.[14] Here he
constructed a tavern/hotel, where he would work the horses and
stable, hiring out others to tend the hotel. The bar was later added
January, 1861,[15] but by August, 1860 the premises had been titled
"Hot Spring Brewery Hotel."[16] Of Porter's two original partners,
Charles Mogo and David H. Burr, the *Valley Tan* — a Camp
Floyd-oriented paper often critical of the Mormons[17] — reports,
"We understand that our friend Hereford has purchased Dave
Burr's interest in the lager beer manufactory. Bob is just the man
for a brewer."[18] But then came problems with Porter's partners:
Hereford and Mogo sought to sell the establishment without

Porter's consent — apparently to pay off debts. They advertised for a public auction in the *Mountaineer* paper: " . . . Hogs, sows, shoats, mules, oxen, wagons, harness, household furniture, etc., and everything necessary for carrying on a large and extensive brewery. The property consists of a large and commodious Hotel, situated half way between Camp Floyd and Great Salt Lake City; a Brewery capable of making 500 gallons of beer per day, a stable and Corral and all necessary outhouses."[19] But Porter refused to sell. Advertising in the same paper as his partners — in the same issue in fact — he warned the public that he was "the rightful owner and possessor of the undivided one-third of said premises, and the sale is without my consent. All persons are hereby warned not to purchase, or in anyway interfere with, said premises, unless they wish to involve themselves in a troublesome and expensive lawsuit, as I am determined to maintain my rights therein."[20]

The inn had obviously not fared as well as Porter's partners had hoped, so they now further advertised, "All indebtedness of the concern will be taken in payment for purchases at the sale."[21] His partners were obviously anxious to bail out of the enterprise, but their plan to railroad the sale past Porter fell flat on its face.

Rockwell, however, soon worked out a solution. He maintained ownership of the inn and hired Hereford as manager.

By October, 1860, George A. Smith visited the inn and jotted in his journal that Porter had hired a bartender, "Miner Frisby, a man lately joined the church,"[22] likely a civilian teamster for the Army. Not mentioned is the possibility Porter had converted the man. Porter was still a church Seventy, a special Mormon priesthood office for part-time missionary labor.

Running a tavern while remaining a "good" Mormon was an apparent contradiction, one resolved by the fact that although Brigham had in recent years declared Joseph Smith's Word of Wisdom no longer "by way of suggestion," but as a commandment, many Saints, including Porter, looked upon abstinence as a minor rule compared to the Saints of later years. It took time for the rule to take effect.

On October 20, George A. Smith elucidated on his night's sleep at the "hot Spring brewery which O. P. Rockwell owns: . . . I remained over night, dreamed I was dead and was so heavy they could not carry me, the coffin dropped on the floor and broke to pieces, I thought Uncle John Young had made it. I saw my body much mutilated, and wondered why they did not apply to Col. Little and get a coffin in which to lay me, as it should have been. Upon waking I accounted for the dream in this wise, I thought there had been so much wickedness committed in that house, while the Gentiles occupied it, that foul spirits haunted my sleep."

Smith continues, "Sunday Oct 21, 1860 . . . examined O. P. Rockwell's brewery, a round sum has been expended there to establish a good brewery. Porter sent his team with G. A. [George Albert Smith, himself] to Lehi where he preached twice morning and afternoon.

"We spent the evening with O.P.R. and slept on a wool bed."[23]

Two days later Porter's son, John Orrin Rockwell, was born.[24]

Porter actually lived near Crystal Springs, and from this location he dictated another business proposition, sent to Colonel Kane, now back in Philadelphia: "Mr. J. C. Naile, a friend of mine forwards by today's mail, four several [different] bids for carrying the Mails of the United States on Routes in this Territory, in which I am interested. Should they reach Washington in time to be considered, and you can render me any service in making these bids successful, it will be a favor that I shall appreciate and remember with gratitude. My health is good and that of my family and of your friends generally in this Territory so far as my knowledge extends.

"I remain your faithful and undeviating friend.

"O. P. Rockwell."[25]

Utah's new federal marshal, P. K. Dotson, meanwhile, had problems with Porter. And Porter had problems with the law.

As Dotson explained to anti-Mormon Judge John Cradlebaugh — who issued a warrant for Porter's arrest — Dotson was finding difficulty in making the arrest "against Porter Rockwell, [and] John A. Wolf, president of the Seventies . . . for the murder of the Aiken Brothers and two others." He explains why: " . . . such [is] the feeling of the Mormon Church, and the community in their favor, that I cannot rely on a civil posse to aid me in arresting them . . . I called on Governor Cumming to make a requisition on the commanding general of this Department for a small number of troops to assist me as a posse." Marshal Dotson then complains of his own "utter inability to execute the warrants without such military aid." And then adds, "His excellency [Governor Cumming], after considering the matter, finally refused to make the requisition. I therefore do not feel warranted in again troubling His Excellency with another application."[26] Why Governor Cumming was coming to Porter's aid is not clear — it may be he saw the source of the commotion — the church critics — and simply passed off the matter. Cumming could easily have called for a posse of troops to arrest Porter at his hotel had he desired.

Porter, meanwhile, was serving warrants of his own. He was still recognized as the true enforcer of the law — certainly more so than the federal marshal, since to the Saints the anti-Mormon federal officials and judges were just so many buzzing, obnoxious wasps — so the very next month after his own warrant was dropped, Porter served one against Charlie Clark,[27] nicknamed "the horsestealer."[28]

Clark had apparently stolen a mule belonging to Daniel Spencer, and, needless to say, where the federal marshal had failed, Porter got his man.

This was the first recorded action Porter had made against the lawless white community as deputy, and it was his first in an incredible string of successes. It was also the beginning of a new phase of the Rockwell legend . . . the category for which his name would become immortalized: his incomparable tracking ability.

Two months later Clark was sentenced to three years at hard labor.[29]

Meanwhile, Rockwell's inn was mushrooming in clientele, although it was likely still under additional construction.

Porter apparently still had a happy marriage, and the Saints in general were prospering. But they would soon begin to face new problems — from both the Army and the press:

Jesse W. Crosby explains. "Our enemies are not satisfied but still seek to stir up new subjects of strife and fill the papers with lying slanderous abuses to excite people. Some excitement continued at Camp Scott supposing the Mormons might suddenly attack and destroy them. But on our part all have attended to their own business, except a few who have partaken of the spirit of the Army and its followers and are converted to the habit of swearing, drinking, stealing, etc."[30]

New York Tribune editor, Horace Greeley, father of the phrase, "Go West, Young Man," took his own advice that same summer of 1859.[31] From his visit to Denver the *Leavenworth Daily Times* reports, "Horace Greeley confirms the richness of the new country. He made a speech to the miners, at which some 4,000 were present." Greeley's fame was remarkable, even in Mormon Utah, and when he visited Brigham's backyard he was treated with more than a little cordiality. Of the Saints he observes, "Formerly they drank little or no liquor; but, since the army came in last year, money and whiskey have both been more abundant . . . "[32]

Although not a Mormon concern, Brigham was informed about the heyday rustlers and outlaws were having with Army stock: Over 80 mules per day were being stolen at the fort.[33]

The city's newspaper, the *Deseret News,* reports more murders had been committed in the first eight months of the Army's arrival than in the entire previous decade.

Although of questionable accuracy, excommunicated Mormon writer T. B. H. Stenhouse reports, "The programme of the police authorities seemed to be to give the desperadoes the largest liberty, so that they might, in their drunken carousals, 'kill off each other' . . . "[34]

To the contrary, George Morris records in his autobiography: "I spent 3 months day and night on the regular police.

" . . . On the 22nd of November I had a very narrow escape from being shot. A big crowd of rowdies had collected in front of Goldberg's Drug Store with drawn pistols and knives, hooting, yelling [and] thinking that the police would interfere with them from breaking the peace. The principal part of the police had taken refuge in that building . . . But seeing [another, larger crowd of] the police it looked as though they were going to come in full force[;] the rowdies drew away and scattered. There was a great deal of drunkenness and fighting on the streets continually. We frequently had to arrest as many as half a dozen in the 24 hours. There was a good deal of shooting and stabbing done and quite a number killed at one time or another. If it had not been for this large police organization in all probability many good men would have lost their lives. A constant guard was kept around the houses of the leading men of the church towards against whom the army followers was particularly directed at first, but afterwards against the police who were too strong for them to cope with."[35]

The second of the Saints' two-fanged problem, the press, is touched on by Jesse W. Crosby: "The Eastern papers team with reports from lying scribblers at Camp Floyd. The sutlers and other Gentile merchants fanned the flame to keep up the excitement and cause more and more money to be expanded here." But Crosby feels the presses' attacks backfired: . . . "the administration [later] determined to remove the troops as it threw money into the Mormon's hands and done no good as nothing was accomplished."[36]

The temporary presence of the Army seemed to some Mormons a blessing in disguise. Crosby adds, " . . . the faithful Saints have been able to see most clearly the hand of a kind and merciful God in turning the evil designs of our enemies into good insomuch as they have supplied us to overflowing with good mules, oxen, wagons, and iron in abundance, and money to purchase them with . . . Money which was very scarce when the Army came in was soon so plenty that any men with industry could fill his pockets with gold."[37]

He summarizes, "The great Mormon War . . . now seems to be winding up it is said, at a cost of $20,000,000."[38] A report elsewhere lays the figure at $40,000,000.[39]

Crosby capsulized the outcome of the war with evangelical zeal, yet he may have been more accurate than his enemies cared to admit:

" . . . the Nation was impoverished and the administration disgraced, while the Mormons were made rich by this useless outlay of money-millions . . . "[40]

Porter, meanwhile, continued his duties as deputy marshal. His enemies, however, would blame him for most every mysterious occurrence that would yet befall Zion . . .

XIII

One mysterious such occurrence was the suicide of John Gheen, as reported by the *Mountaineer* October 8, 1859: "It is suspected that he fell by the hands of another than himself."[1]

Three weeks earlier Hosea Stout had recorded in his journal that a non-Mormon, Frank McNeill, was fined $10 plus court costs for threatening Gheen's life.[2] Despite the fact McNeill was the only man on record with a motive to kill Gheen, the acrimonious Achilles asserts, "Porter Rockwell killed this man at the orders of Brigham Young ... "[3] Typically, Achilles offers no evidence. Others' wild assertions stem from the fact Gheen was possibly suicidal, having killed a man ten years previously[4] and now with a supposedly seared conscience had asked someone to kill him. Rockwell, others asserted, was that man. (See Note 29 for the *Mountaineer*'s complete article.)

Rockwell then hunted a gang of cattle thieves. He first led one Sheriff Razer and a small company to Las Vegas. John D. Lee records in his diary: "The thieves were off their guard and entirely unprepared for resistence. [Joachim, but actually named H. Keitt] Johnson [Johnston] said to Porter Rockwell, I did not think that your People would have followed me for Stealing from your enemies. Government officers Robed and broke up my Establishment at camp floyd & I am determined to be avenged of them. They [the thieves] however gave up [to Rockwell] the animals, but requested the prevelege to go on to California. Rockwell gave him 2 mules & let him go, as he had bought the animals from others ... "[5] Porter was actually bargaining with the irate rustler: He talked Johnston into letting him take Johnston's four comrades back to court to testify against the other men Johnston had hired to steal the cattle, the professionals who had been plaguing the community.[6] Rockwell was thus trading one set of thieves for a harsher set of thieves.

The next known recorded incident in Porter's history occurred two and one half months later, as reported by the *Deseret News* February 1, 1860:

"On Thursday last, late in the afternoon, a man named Martin Oats, who came to this Territory in the fall of 1858 as a teamster in one of the Government supply trains, called at the Hot Spring Brewery Hotel, near the point of the mountain, on his way to Camp Floyd."

Porter's proprietor, Bob Hereford, apparently lacked the tact necessary for frontier survival and told the man point blank he was a thief. In reaction, Martin Oats "drew a knife and flourished it about, declaring that he would cut out the heart of any man that accused him of stealing.

"After abusing Mr. Hereford, he turned to Mr. O. P. Rockwell, who was present — having heard his name called by some one — and accused him [Rockwell] of stealing cattle from him or something of the kind; continuing to brandish his knife and to make threats of violence; to which Rockwell paid but little attention, merely saying that he had no acquaintance with the fellow, did not even know his name and did not wish to have any altercation with him.

"Hereford having no weapons with which to defend himself against an attack that might be made upon him by the boasting and threatening desperado, went for his pistols and on his return found Oats and Rockwell clinched, the former, knife in hand, having the latter by his beard and Rockwell holding Oats off by the hair of his head.

"On appearance of Hereford, Rockwell requested him

[Hereford] to take away the madman, as he did not wish to hurt him . . .

"Some time after Oats had thus been started off and the two men who escorted him had returned to the hotel, Rockwell mounted his steed and started for Lehi, his place of residence."[7]

The *Mountaineer* continues the story:

" . . . the muss was considered over; but as Mr. Rockwell was returning home, Oats was standing on the road, evidently awaiting his approach. On Mr. R. trying to pass him, Oats sprung out and seized the bridle of the mule, and renewed his knife threats. Finding remonstrance and warning of no avail and his life jeopardized, Mr. R. drew his revolver, and as Oats thrust at him he fired and killed him."[8]

The *Deseret News* details further: "Mr. Rockwell returned to the hotel and informed Mr. Hereford of what he had done, requested him to send out some men and take care of the body and of the dead man's team, and then went to Lehi and gave himself up to the civil authorities."[9]

The *Mountaineer* concludes:

"The body of Oats was taken back there, and an inquest held over it next morning. At the investigation, Mr. Rockwell was acquitted — the jury were unanimous in the verdict of 'justifiable homicide.' "[10]

Porter soon became the father of David Porter Rockwell, born February 19, 1860.[11]

Three weeks afterwards he rode south with a Lehi resident to gather mules he'd taken from the Johnston gang three months earlier. John D. Lee, a fugitive from the government for his part in the Mountain Meadows Massacre and still years away from his capture, records the following episode in his diary: "Mond., March 12th, 1860. About 7 we all startd for Harmony . . . I met an Indian (Wah patch) by Name with an express, stating that Gen. Johnson [Albert Sidney Johnston] was on the road with 50 men enrout for Washington city by way of California . . . & [for Lee] to look out & not be caught naping. From this caution I took due Notice & governed myself accordingly."

Of singular interest is the Indians' siding with Saints over the government soldiers. Lee continues: " . . . a small Ravine close by concealed me while they [the Army, who was on the look-out for

Lee] passed. After talking with Rockwell near the grapevine springs, I conceald my Self near the Road and Saw the Train pass, near which quite a No. of Indians had collectd to defend Me provided I Should have fallen into Searious difficulties.

"Both parties [the Army and the Indians, which apparently crossed paths] cocked their guns on each other. In the Mean time the Indians saw me and Made for me, & I luckily was in time to squash the rowe." Thus Lee prevented the Indians from ambushing the cavalrymen.

But Lee adds an interesting postscript to the account: The Indians now asked Rockwell and his companion —a fellow named Hollingshead — who they were. Hollingshead in jest answered the Indians that he was a U. S. soldier — a "Mericat." "At this the Indian cocked his rifle. Rockwell Seeing his intention, shoutd out, Kotch [Not] Mericat [but] Mormon, which to geather with my Name being Mentiond that I was close by, was all that Saved them."[12]

Porter then presumably found the grazing mules and returned them north to the valley.

By September he was leading a train of over 30 supply wagons to Pike's Peak.[13]

Meanwhile, a cattle rustler named Alfred Higgens was captured. Higgens had allegedly stolen fourteen government cattle on the Provo road. Under safeguard in prison he soon proved the facility was weak, and adroitly escaped. He again rode through Provo and this time proclaimed he would have his revenge on Rockwell: He shouted on the street that Porter was the "informer" that had gotten him captured.[14] Higgens was caught again, but later escaped, was again caught, and again escaped, this time for good.[15]

Porter soon met the famed British world traveler, adventurer, army officer, author, and master of a dozen languages, Sir Richard Francis Burton, who, because of prior contact with church enemies, upon meeting Porter, envisioned him as "a leader of the Danites." Nevertheless, Burton painted the following fascinating and most revealing portrait:

"He had the manner of a jovial, reckless, devil-may-care English ruffian.

"The [Army] officers called him Porter, and preferred him to the 'slimy villains' who will drink with a man and then murder him. After a little preliminary business about a stolen horse, all conducted on the amiable, he pulled out a dollar, and sent to the neighboring distillery for a bottle of Valley Tan. The *aguardiente* was smuggled in under a cloth, as though we had been respectables in a Moslem country [evidently Brigham's new proclamation of abstinence from alcohol was taking hold on some Saints, though certainly not all], and we were asked to join him in a 'squar' drink, which means spirits without water.

"The mode of drinking was peculiar. Porter, after the preliminary sputation, raised the glass with a cocked little finger to his lips, with the twinkle of the eye ejaculated 'Wheat!' that is to say 'good,' and drained the tumbler to the bottom: we acknowledged his civility with a 'here's how,' and drank Kentucky-fashion, which in English is midshipman's grog.

"Of these 'squar' drinks' we had at least four, which, however, did not shake Mr. Rockwell's nerve, and then he sent out for more. Meanwhile he told us his last adventure, how when ascending the kanyon he suddenly found himself covered by two long rifles; how he had thrown himself from his horse, drawn his revolver and crept behind a bush, and how he had dared the enemy to come out and fight like men. He spoke of one Obry, a Frenchman, lately killed in a street quarrel, who rode on business from Santa Fe to Independence, about 600 miles in 110 hours. Porter offered, for the fun of the thing, to excel him by getting over 900 in 144.

"When he heard that I was preparing for California he gave me abundant good advice — to carry a double-barrelled gun loaded with buckshot; to 'keep my eyes skinned,' especially in kanyons and ravines; to make at times a dark camp . . . and never to trust to appearances in an Indian country . . .

"I observed that, when thus speaking, Porter's eyes assumed the expression of an old mountaineer's, ever rolling as if set in quicksilver. For the purpose of avoiding 'White Indians,' the worst of their kind, he advised me to shun the direct route, which he represented to be about as fit for travelling as h-ll for a powder magazine [Burton's deletion], and to journey via Fillmore and the wonder-bearing White Mountains; finally, he comforted me with an assurance that either the Indians would not attempt to attack us and our stock — ever a sore temptation to them — or that they would assault us in force and 'wipe us out.'

"When the drinking was finished we exchanged a cordial *poignée de main* with Porter our hospitable host, who appeared to be the *crème de la crème* of Utah county, and soon found ourselves again without the limits of Camp Floyd."[16]

Anti-Mormons of course labeled "White Indians" as Mormons in disguise. Rockwell, speaking to Burton freely — and ever a defender of the church — had evidently referred to the "White Indians" as mere bands of land pirates and certain outlaw gangs who raided innocents while so disguised.

Burton interviewed hundreds of souls among Mormon society — both inactive and active Saints, as well as Gentiles — and left the City of the Saints to write his book by that title, a comparative best-seller of the day.

Upon returning to England Burton shipped a bottle of brandy to Rockwell for his kindness. (See Note 30 for additional details on Burton's description of Porter.) Burton also seemed quite taken with Brigham Young. (See Note 31 for his sketch.) Additionally, Burton's insights into the Mormon practice of plural marriage were interesting. Devoid of the traditional perceptions typically associated with Eastern writers, Burton had acquired a unique perspective by having lived among polygamist societies in the Near East and Asia. His comments, though critical of certain aspects of Mormonism, were surprisingly supportive of the Saints on this controversial subject. (Note 32 contains Burton's analysis of polygamy, with Note 33 containing additional comments on the practice by other non-Mormon analysts — Fitz-Hugh Ludlow, William Chandless, and Jules Remy.) Burton was also impressed with the entire migratory aspect. (See Note 34.)

Months passed before Rockwell is again mentioned in history. In 1861 Captain Albert Tracy traveled eastward from Camp Floyd and stopped at Porter's inn, where he took " . . . dinner at a kind of half-way house across the Jordan — and relish[ed] the same, with the appetite of the wayfarer."[17]

Porter's inn was the stop-off point for other wayfarers, and business was booming. Yet problems concerned him on the homefront; while accusers ever claimed he "lived above the law," Porter took a rustling incident involving his neighbor, Israel Evans, before a church court. Diarist George Laub records, "January 26, 1861 this day I met at the Seventys Counsil Hall to which the Trial of Br. O Porter Rockwell and Israel Evens of Lehi was in Question."[18] Evans had evidently stolen one of Rockwell's cattle, and was soon disfellowshiped from the church by Brigham Young and Heber C. Kimball.

While Rockwell struggled with ranch problems, he and the Saints in general dealt with the increasingly difficult problem of restless Army personnel. Ebenezer Crouch, an acquaintance of Porter's, recalls: "The part of Camp Floyd where the citizens lived and where the business houses were was called Dobe Town and was divided from the soldier's barracks by a small Creek. The business part of Dobe Town was made up of saloons, gambling houses and every kind of business that goes to make up a rough place. There were always Indians camped close around and what with Indians and soldiers there was always something rough going on. The Indians would get crazy drunk and go riding through the town on their ponies whooping and yelling until they came in contact with drunken soldiers and then there would be some gun play. Every store used to sell liquor and the one Father kept was no exception. Across one end of the store was a row of forty gallon barrels containing liquor of different kinds. The store was often filled with soldiers buying and drinking liquor. They were the worst lot of petty thieves I ever saw. They would steal anything in the store they could lay their hands on and then turn around and trade it to Father for drink as he would be so busy serving them he could not watch them all. He used to stand me upon the counter where I could see them all and I would give him the alarm if they stole anything. I often thought of those rough times and wondered how Father escaped bodily injury but he seemed to have a way with him that commanded their respect and he would calm them down when it seemed they were about to tare him to pieces.

" . . . I remember one day scores of them came into Dobe Town, commenced drinking and then proceeded to clean out the town. They destroyed property and threatened the lives of the people. Some of the citizens were wounded and some of the soldiers. I think one was shot to death. Every business and dwelling house was closed and doors bared to keep out the mob [of soldiers]. Two young men that happened to be out on the street were chased by the mob and had to run for their lives. They made for the hills and with drawn revolvers kept the mob back until two men from town rode out on horse back, took them up behind and rode to the hills and escaped.

"Porter Rockwell often came to town and then there was generally something doing. One day a house of ill fame was set on fire and burnt to the ground. The provost guard — army police — blamed Port for it and threatened to arrest him but Porter dared them to do it and promised them that the army would not get around the point of the mountain on their way east with a wheel on their wagons if they laid a hand on him."

Incredibly, " . . . they seemed to think it best to let him alone."[19]

Colonel Johnston soon left the fort to join the ranks of the Confederacy. 1500 of his troops would leave Camp Floyd in the following weeks to reinforce the Union Army. In a panic, the government put up four million dollars of goods for auction, which Utahns purchased at 2.5% the original value. The soldiers, as Crouch explains, were enraged. Retaliating, certain numbers burned buildings bought by Mormons. Because of this Porter complained to Brigham.[20] In addition to seeing buildings destroyed, Ebenezer Crouch recalls watching the soldiers at work:

"The army had thousands of fire arms and many tons of ammunition in their arsenal that they would not sell to the Mormons, fearing it might be used against them. I saw hundreds of new muskets destroyed. They would pack them out of the arsenal by the arm full, smash each one on a rock to render the lock useless and beyond repair, then throw them in a large pile and burn them. The ammunition they hauled out on the bench and dumped it in piles then touched a match to it. When they had reduced the amount of ammunition in the arsenal to make it safe they touched a match to that. They had two large guns called mortars. They [the mortars] threw a shell weighing forty six pounds. These shells were filled with powdered lead and grape-shot. They had tons and tons of these shells which they wasted after dark in the evenings. These mortars are used for dropping shells into a city or fortification and are made to explode when they strike some object. The gun is set at a high elevation and sends a ball of fire through the sky which makes a grand sight.

It took several nights to dispose of all their shells. They throw them out [through the air] on the bench about a mile or so from town and left cast iron scattered all over the bench. After the army left we used to pick it up and sell it. One old lady, Mrs. Panrod, used to go out with a hand cart and she and her little grand daughter picked up tons and sold it.

" . . . Some of the shells would miss exploding. Two young men named Albert Jones and Robert Pettit, found one of these and tried to cut the plug out with a cold chisel and hammer; there was an explosion and those poor boys were mangled frightfully. Jones was hurt the worst and oh how he did plead for some one to shoot him and end his misery. He lived about an hour. Pettit was put into a wagon and started for Salt Lake to get surgical aid but died on the way."[21]

Meanwhile, the burning of Mormon-bought buildings continued, and it raised Rockwell's ire to such an extent that — according to neighbor Orson Twelves — Porter galloped off to Camp Floyd and shouted to the soldiers. Neighbor Orson says of Porter's warning: "If they burned anymore barns they would never leave Utah alive."[22]

No more burnings occurred.

One infantryman, Charles A. Scott, records in his diary, "The Mormons seem wrathy at the munitions being destroyed and make threats that we will never reach Fort Leavenworth; there is certainly a crowd of desperadoes in this vicinity at present, headed by the notorious Porter Rockwell."[23]

Bill Hickman, in a rare display of accuracy, sums up the Army's relationship with Utah:

"They had come here, spent a great quantity of money, and went away without hurting anybody — a victory, of course,"[24] he notes sarcastically.

He also summarizes the 1861 Saints' feelings accurately: "There was rejoicing when the troops left the Territory."

After General Albert Sidney Johnston left the territory he was killed one year later, April 6, 1862,[25] and he died still a critic to the Saints. The Civil War itself had begun April 6, 1861.

Porter then launched his own crusade: a campaign against outlaws and desperadoes unlike any in history. His enemies would continue blaming him for every conceivable non-outlaw killing, even those in which he would be hundreds of miles from the scene. (See Note 35 for details.) But it was at this point his legend as a lawman took on staggering dimensions.

Both Porter's prowess as a marshal and his long hair now seemed to attract outlaws like flies from across the continent, and many wished to take him on. Stories were passed from tavern to tavern and bets were placed. Eventually, of course, someone would have to kill him.

Certain records have been kept of his accomplishments, and legends throughout his most-frequented town of Lehi, Utah, still circulate. For example, he evidently sustained a dry well on his property in which he stuffed dozens of outlaws. Judges and juries apparently had their place to Porter's way of thinking, but he did not always take time to report his gunfights, nor the attempted ambushes and distant desert trackings. He was often seen riding through Lehi with a lifeless outlaw draped across the saddle of his second horse, or on the back of his buckboard.

Examples of unsubstantiated but fascinating "Porter Rockwell stories" are exemplified by the following incident, reported in the journal of Austin Gudmundsen of Lehi, Utah:

"I remember my father relating to us many times the period in his life when he was sixteen years old and working for Porter Rockwell, who was then the 'law' in the state ... Father (Abraham Gudmunsen) worked in Skull Valley taking care of Porter's horses. It was a small cabin of [a] home, with lantern for light. One evening father was expecting Porter and heard horses coming. He opened the door of the cabin and called out. Immediately a bullet whizzed past his head. He quickly shut the door and blew out the light. It was a group of men after Porter's horses. They took them from the corral and rode away. Porter came an hour or so later. When father told him what had happened, he said, 'You little fool you shoot first then call out.' It was only seconds before Porter was after the men. About midnight he came back, with his string of horses, plus two or 3 more. When father asked where the thieves were, he replied, 'Oh the last time I saw them, they were face down in a wash, with bullet holes through them.' "[26]

Some of these legends are today told by direct descendants of Rockwell's contemporaries, others would more comfortably fit the folklorian category. One such example is that told of Porter riding at dusk past an obscure farmhouse, stopping for a chicken crossing the road before him, pulling out his revolver, and blowing the bird away. Then, smiling, he turns to a seven-year old boy: "Tell your mama Porter Rockwell's here for supper."

Verbal stories of his killings would fill volumes. Because of the rampage of killing he now launched, estimates of earned notches on his pistols have soared past two hundred — some estimates have been less, some more — but certainly more than the killings of all the best-known lawmen of the Old West combined.

Those who knew him claimed his personality was paradoxical, yet for the most part they admired him; inactive Mormons and non-Mormons thought him "a good ole boy," ever willing to give them a hand and sit down for a drink or just good knee-slapping conversation, while active Saints — almost without exception — admired his rock-like loyalty to the Prophet to the point of placing him on a pedestal, despite his indulgence in whiskey and harsh language. Israel Bennion asserts, "As a neighbor ranchman, I have partaken of his hospitality, have ridden with him on the range, have noted the sagacity and skill with which he directed the breeding and feeding of his herds. I have been edified by accounts of my father of his neighborly relations with this old friend, from before my time. And so I bear my testimony to the honorable character of Orrin Porter Rockwell."[27] Bennion also tagged a reason to Rockwell's prowess: He "studied the art of woodcraft, emulating and far out-distancing the Indians in reading sign, tracking with most unbelievable skill, [discerning even] a slight break or crack in a horse's hoof." He could even follow tracks as he "would gallop along without the least uncertainty."[28] Truly the stuff from which legends were wrought, despite the varying degrees of accuracy.

In many cases Porter simply conducted manhunts without utilizing his revolver. The next recorded occurrence of his chronological history reveals such an incident, and also reveals the almost instantaneous rapport he could develop with strangers; as he was now beginning to age, some seemingly looked upon him as some sort of old relative, even on first acquaintance. In the *Salt Lake Herald* appears an article July 30, 1885, twenty-one years after such an incident. Reporter "Gax" pens his article from Pueblo, Colorado, and the editor headlines it, "After The Horse Thieves: A Pueblo Man who Found 'Port' Anything but a Destroying Angel."

The reporter prefaces his article with details of a wagon trip through the Pueblo countryside with, among others of the wagon party, a Pueblo resident named Frank Karrick, "a typical westerner and cattle rancher, rough, hearty, big-hearted," who had frequently traveled Utah in earlier days. Non-Mormon Karrick had known Rockwell personally.

" . . . The conversation diverged naturally to the Pioneers, then to President Young, and passing to the inevitable topic of the 'Destroying Angels,' brought up finally at Porter Rockwell. Two eastern men who were of the party, Messrs. Bullis and Ramsdell, were at once alive with interest to learn what they could of the noted character, and Mr. Karrick, it appears, was in a considerably better position for enlightening them than I was, so that I listened with as much interest as the others manifested, while he told the following narrative: 'They may say what they like about old Uncle Port's being a "Destroying Angel," ' said Mr. Karrick, 'but I can tell you that it was a very different kind of an angel that I found in him. It was a good many years ago — I can't give the precise dates, but you can about locate the time because it was just when they were stringing their first telegraph wires over in Utah [1861], and I was freighting wire from Sacramento to Salt Lake with my big mule train. I had unloaded in Salt Lake, had got my money, and sent the teams on back south intending to join them on horseback somewhere about where Tintic is; in those days, a freighter's riches consisted mainly of his outfit, and my 15 or 20 mule teams, I can tell you, represented a good deal of money to me; the mules I had, I reckon, would have cost $400 or $500 each. Well, I rode into camp late one night — it was about 70 miles south or southwest of Salt Lake — and the first thing that struck me was that there was something wrong among the herd of mules. I woke the teamsters up and said, "Boys, there's something the matter here;" they were all sleepy and insisted that everything was all right. I routed them out, however, and we counted up the herd and found eight mules and one big grey horse missing. It was easy to see from the tracks that they had been driven off, but in the road the marks of the high calks in their shoes disappeared. I couldn't make this out till next morning, when I saw that the thieves had cut some sage brush thereabouts, and dragged it after them to cover up the tracks. I was in something of a sore stress, I can tell you, and like a d—d fool [verbatim as printed] I jumped on my horse and followed the road for forty miles till I came to where the tracks separated, a band of horses going one way, and my mules taking the other direction. I saw then that I could do little alone, and I made up my mind to camp, and in the middle of the night, when everyone was asleep, I dug a hole under the hind wheel of my wagon and buried there all the money I had in the world — $15,000 — in coin. There was no one with me I could trust, you see, and I considered that was the safest way.

" 'I then jumped on my horse, and never stopped till I was in Salt Lake City. I went at once to Brigham Young, and laid my troubles before him. He thought a little while, and then said he was sorry for me, and asked whether I was sure the animals were stolen. I told him my reasons for thinking so, and he said: "I only know one way by which you can get your mules back, and that is by getting the help of Porter Rockwell. I don't know whether he will go with you, but if he will you are all right."

" 'I thanked him, and at once went in search of Uncle Porter, whom I knew from some previous transactions. When I told him what I wanted, he said at once in his usual peculiar, but hearty voice, "I'll go with you, my boy, and I'll get your mules back." That was all I wanted, and we lost no time in starting. There was no delay, I can tell you, till we covered the road back to where I had seen the mules tracks separate and take another direction. We rode along all day and suddenly came to a point where the mule tracks disappeared. It was as if they had taken suddenly to the air. "Never mind," said Porter, "they've only taken their shoes off, we'll keep this road."

" ' "Uncle Port," said I, "if they take the shoes off the big grey horse, we've got them. His feet are so tender he can't travel fast." We went on and before long Porter uttered one of his peculiar hollers. "They're ours," he said; "they've taken off the big horse's

shoes. You'll have your mules back now before long." I felt entire
confidence in him and we galloped along, stopping neither day nor
night. On the third day at sunset we came on top of a hill and I saw
a dust a long way ahead. Porter uttered a yell, and seized his glass.

" ' "Two men with some horses and mules," he cried, "come
on!"

" 'We dashed over the ground and before long came up to a
couple of hard looking roughs camped innocently beside a stream;
on the opposite side to my great joy, were my eight mules and the
old grey horse, but a swift deep stream was running between them
and me, the cunning rogues had seen our dust in the distance and
had swam them across you see, and now disclaimed all knowledge
of them.

" ' "My name's Porter Rockwell," said Uncle Port riding up to
them, "throw up your hands."

" 'Both men threw up their hands with the greatest promptness.

" ' "Now whose animals are those across there?"

" 'Both men swore they didn't know; they said they rather
thought they belonged to some men who were concealed over
there.

" ' "They're yours, my boy," he [Porter] said to me. "Go across
and take them."

" 'I told him frankly that I couldn't swim a lick.

" ' "Very well, my boy," he said, "then I'll have these men get
them for you. Here you!" turning to one of the rascals. "Strip and
swim across there to those mules."

" 'The fellow said he couldn't swim. "That's a lie and you know
it," said Port with one of his characteristic yells. He pulled his gun,
leveled it on the man and again ordered him to strip.

" 'The fellow slowly complied, entered the water and swam
easily across; once there he again hesitated.

" ' "Turn them animals into the stream and swim them across,"
yelled Porter again, pulling his gun.

" 'The man did as he was ordered, and within a very few
minutes, all my animals were safe at my side.' "

Part of Porter's reputation was his thoroughness — his
obsessive nature to "follow through:"

" ' "Now, my boy," said Porter, "you ride on about ten miles, and camp near an old hut you will find there. I am going on across the river to see if there are any traces of any more of them. I will come to you in the middle of the night and whistle, so that you will know it's all right."

" 'About midnight I heard his whistle, and went out to him. He had seen nothing of any more men, he said, and was pretty tired; so I let him lay down and kept watch over him till the morning. We then rode back to where my train was camped, and the first thing I did was to dig up my sack of coin under the hind wheel of my wagon. It was just as I had left it, and I took out $500 in shiny coin, and tendered it to him. "Oh, no, my boy," he said laughing, "Keep your money, I have got more of it than you have, I guess." But I insisted, and he finally put it into his pocket, bade me goodbye, and left me, saying if I ever lost any more animals to be sure and let him know.

" 'When I got to California one of the first things I did was to buy a fine $100 nickel plated saddle and a gallon demijohn of the best whiskey I could find in the State. I sent them both to Uncle Porter with my compliments, and I afterwards heard that he was vastly more tickled with the whiskey than with the saddle, and that he had expressed the extremest gratification that "the boy had not forgotten their little old ride together." ' "[29]

Porter's next known recorded incident occurs with the Lot Huntington gang. The outlaws had terrorized and beaten Governor John W. Dawson — which in itself was a bizarre story. Dawson had swept into Zion, replacing Cumming, and three weeks later had swept out. Having been imported from Indiana, Dawson had immediately found himiself over his head in trouble, making "indecent proposals" to a Mormon widow of unquestionable reputation.[30] Anti-Mormon writers, of course, claimed Dawson had been "set-up" by church officials.[31] Others, however, claimed he had been set up by non-Mormon government officials to — for some undefined reason — get rid of him.[32] Still others claimed nobody had set him up: He had simply bungled his entrance into Zion by propositioning the first woman he had met. In any case, he then found himself on New Year's Eve, 1861, at a stagecoach station waiting for the next stage East. And, although he was leaving "dishonorably," he claimed he was leaving "feeling that I had no enemy to any one there."[33] Yet he was well aware that, even in Zion — though his moral conduct was shunned and his career there now useless — his life was certainly in no danger because of it. But he did mention, "Ephraim Hanks rode up and said that there were some desperate men in the city who it was possible might follow me . . . "[33] One of the ruffians happened to be related to the widow,[35] but the outlaws seemed to simply target him for robbery.

At the station, while waiting for his stage, he was robbed and beaten. Law officers searched for the outlaws without success. The same outlaws then committed another robbery. The *Deseret News* continues the chronicle: " . . . a writ was issued by the Probate Judge of the county for the arrest of the said Lot Huntington and John P. Smith."[36]

What happened next was reported years later, in 1924, by Glynn Bennion of the *Salt Lake Tribune:* Lot Huntington stole a horse from Sam Bennion at a church New Year's Eve "tithing settlement" party — a religious and social yearly event where Saints met for a dance, party, and private interview with their bishop.

"Deep snow covered the ground, but the many people gathering toward the West Jordan meeting house had beaten smooth the highways from the surrounding settlements.

"When he [Sam Bennion] came out to return home, his mare was gone. Heartbroken at the thought of losing the animal, the youth hastily began to hunt for her tracks. But the futility of trying to trace anything in the mass of tracks of the much traveled thoroughfares in the nighttime was quickly borne in on his excited throughts and he gave up on the attempt.

"In those days when any of the country folk felt the need of help in such exigencies, his thoughts turned invariably to the noted scout, Orrin Porter Rockwell, who was always ready to take hold of anything that promised excitement of pursuit.

"So, in his dismay, young Sam's thoughts soon turned to the wizard of tracks — the man who could track anything anywhere. Striking out afoot to the family home distant several miles, the youth procured another horse and rode to Rockwell's home in the suburbs of Salt Lake City, arriving there in the small hours of the night.

"Luckily finding the old frontiersman at home, young Sam wakened him and told his story. The freezing cold of a midwinter night was no deterrent to 'Old Port' when such game was afoot. With characteristic disregard for physical vicissitudes, Rockwell pulled on his fighting clothes and hitching a team to the inevitable buckboard, set out with young Sam toward West Jordan."

After securing the aid of two others, "the start was made and Rockwell began to apply his uncanny genius to the enigma of tracks. In spite of the travel over the network of roads and trails of the district since the horse had been stolen, Rockwell professed to see signs at intervals, as trail after trail was searchingly examined, that corresponded with the peculiar structures of the lost mare's feet.

"If all the tracks ascribed to Brown Sal had really been made by her then evidently the mare had been led about by a very circuitous route in order to fail any attempts to follow her. But whoever had stolen the mare had reckoned without Rockwell. For hours the old scout studied carefully, intently, minutely the thousands of tiny marks left in the beaten snow of the roads of the district by the hundreds of traces superimposed upon each other. And he finally led the party along a road ... toward the town of Harriman in the southeastern part of the valley.

"At Fort Harriman another delay was encountered in the maze of tracks in the village roads. No information could be secured from the townspeople [there] regarding Brown Sal, causing some to fear that the trip out to Fort Harriman was a wild goose chase. But Rockwell was in no way disturbed by such doubts ... The fact that no one had seen the horse only proved to him that she had been brought there in the night ...

"Night came on, but the party of pursuit did not stop. Young Sam had now been two days and a night without sleep and Rockwell had had little more.

"Following the trail in Cedar valley, the pursuers were dismayed to find that ... the tracks had [now] been covered by a herd of cattle driving westward along the road."

While the others probably wished to give up, Porter's dogged determination pushed them on to the next town. "Rockwell led the party through the settlement to see if the outlaws had gone beyond it. Sure enough, at the southern outskirts of the town, a light struck in the road showed the tracks, not yet obliterated of Brown Sal and the two footmen.

"Going over the whole circumstance now with the idea of determining from computation of time and rate of travel" Rockwell figured the thieves were at Faust Station, 25 miles westward. He pushed his men on again, all night long. Upon arriving before dawn, "Rockwell placed his men at once in strategic positions surrounding the buildings ... about the haystacks, corrals and sheds for observation and shelter from the bitter chill of the night wind.

"Gradually a faint bloom of light appeared in the east, and presently a man emerged from the house. As he approached the stable Rockwell recognized him as H. J. Faust, the stationkeeper, from whom the station received its name. 'Doc' Faust, as he was familiarly known, was an ex-pony express rider and one of Utah's noted frontiersmen.

"Signalling from his place of concealment, Rockwell motioned Faust to him and made inquiry as to the men who came there with Brown Sal. Faust told him that the three men were at that moment eating breakfast in the house. One of them, he said, was Lot Huntington, who had said they were on their way to California. Rockwell asked Faust to go back to the house and tell them to come out and surrender. The fact that Lot Huntington was one of the men in the house in no way caused Rockwell to relax his watchful caution. He knew Huntington to be one of the most fearless and dangerous outlaws in the country.

"Rockwell was not surprised that after Faust returned to the house no one came out for some time. Finally, Lot Huntington himself stepped out of the house. Carrying a big cap-and-ball pistol in his hand, and with eyes searching shrewdly and swiftly every detail of the corrals and outbuildings for sign of his foes, Hungington made directly toward the stable where the mare was tied. As the desperado was about to enter the building, Rockwell called to him from concealment to surrender. Huntington's only answer was to laugh tauntingly and enter the stable.

"In a moment he reappeared, leading the mare.

"Cleverly keeping the mare between himself and the possible points of concealment of his enemies, he maneuvered out toward the bars of the corral surrounding the doorway of the stable. At the gateway he carefully held the mare behind him while he drew out the boards. Every man in the party knew that if the young desperado got safely on the mare's back and out of gunshot [range] no horse available could catch him. All this time a quiet, formal conversation was being carried on between Rockwell and Huntington. From behind a pile of cedar posts Rockwell kept repeating to the youthful outlaw that he would be shot if he tried to get outside the corral, and Huntington from behind Brown Sal just as quietly told Rockwell where he would send the old scout or anyone else that dared so much as show his face; and Hungtington's reputation for skill with a pistol was such that every face was kept out of sight. It seemed as though no one would dispute the outlaw's exit from the corral.

"But at the moment Huntington was pulling out the last bar from the gateway his iron nerve overdid the thing just a trifle, and he jerked out the pole a trifle too vigorously. The end of it rebounded and struck the mare in the flank. Plunging away from it, she momentarily exposed the outlaw to someone's hiding place [Porter's]. In that instant the bad man got a half-dozen buckshot in the chest. He fell dead across the slanting bars."[37]

The church's Journal History reports a more grizly account: "Huntington drew his revolver where upon he was shot in the belly with 8 slugs cutting the arteries to pieces. Huntington fell with part of his body in the corral and one leg outside of the corral. He bled to death in four minutes.

"Moroni Clawson and John Smith surrendered without any more difficulty."[38]

Porter's men placed the corpse in the buckboard, then headed back towards Great Salt Lake City with their two prisoners. On the trail, they came across Howard Egan, who records that Porter said to him, " 'Hello kids, all right?'

" 'Yes, all right so far,' replied Egan.

" 'Good! Your Father told me to tell you . . . to be very careful and keep a good watch on the cattle and guard them well.'[39]

Rockwell rode on, without even mentioning the killing. When

sober, Rockwell was apparently somewhat modest.

Egan further mentions he later learned Rockwell had the dead Huntington even as they spoke, and Egan never knew it. Huntington had actually joined Egan for dinner just two nights previously, and had told Egan he might join him on a cattle drive later — presumably to steal Egan's cattle. "If there was a plot laid for me, old Porter burst the bubble and I got through safe."

The *Deseret News* continues the chronicle:

" . . . At about five o'clock on Friday morning, being very much fatigued, Rockwell delivered the prisoners to three or four policemen, who were at hand, to take to the county prison . . . The prisoners, supposing probably that the policemen were unarmed, started to run, and were shot at and both killed before getting far away."[40]

In conclusion, the *News* editorializes, "The thanks of the community are most certainly due Mr. Rockwell and those who were with him and assisted in making the arrests . . . "[41]

Yet church critics saw foul play. Stenhouse notes, "Resistance to an officer, or the slightest attempt to escape from custody, was eagerly seized, when wanted, as the justification of closing a disreputable career . . . "[42] In a footnote Stenhouse elaborates: "After they reached Salt Lake City, the police, in taking them to the calaboose, said that the prisoners tried to escape, and they shot them down. *It was believed* that the prisoners were walking in front of the officers when the latter quietly put their revolvers to the back of their heads and 'stopped them.'" (Our emphasis; "it was believed," was a standard phrase used by critics.)

Rockwell now returned home and won a lucrative mail contract. The Government awarded him $2,100 per year for five local mail routes in and near the valley.[43]

Meanwhile, the Saints prospered. *The Chicago Tribune* in June 1862 reports, "Utah now has a population of 100,000 . . . "[44]

But their peace was quickly evaporating. Mail drivers were being killed and the mail burned by Indians with increasing frequency.

Soon, because of the Indians' terrorism, Brigham was forced to act. He sent a message to Washington that "the militia of Utah are ready and able . . . to take care of all the Indians, and . . . protect the mail line."[45]

President Lincoln replied by authorizing Brigham to raise a company of cavalry for three months. For his commander, Young chose Lot Smith,[46] who now, ironically, was authorized to fight *for* the Government. During this campaign Daniel H. Wells congratulates Rockwell with a letter on "your kind offer of animals,"[47] then requests him "to have so many as you can spare fit for service in the city Tomorrow Evening or as much sooner as possible."

Since the mail trains would now be protected by armed Mormons, the Indians decided to instead turn their marauding to farmers and travelers.

But the Army decided it all had to come to a stop.

As the Saints' three-month assignment to protect the mail came to an end, Colonel Patrick Edward Connor began marching a regiment of 300 California volunteers toward Great Salt Lake City.

Even knowing the Army was coming, Indians kept raiding the whites, both Mormons and Gentiles. Horses were stolen in northern Utah,[48] six emigrants were massacred near City of Rocks,[49] and 23 other emigrants were killed farther west on the Humboldt River.[50] Finally, after another Indian attack, the *Deseret News* summarizes, "This is reported to have been the fifth or sixth company of emigrants, some of them large and having a great amount of stock which has been attacked and used up in that vicinity within the last six or eight weeks . . . "[51]

As the Army regiment arrived in Great Salt Lake City October 20, 1862, the Saints took heart. Although a reversal of earlier days, one Mormon comments in the Logan Branch records, "We, the people of Cache Valley, looked upon the movement of Colonel Connor as an intervention of the Almighty, as the Indians had been a source of great annoyance to us for a long time, causing us to stand guard over our stock and other property the most of the time since our first settlement."[52] This attitude was verified by Lieutenant William D. Ustick, Acting Assistant Adjutant General, in his orders from Colonel Connor which were read to the troops, describing the local Indians who had "for the last fifteen years been the terror of the emigrants, men, women and children and citizens of those valleys, murdering and robbing them without fear of punishment."[53] Further evidence of the Saints' supportive attitude toward the Army's effort is a report from Colonel Martineau: "Indian outrages against settlers and travelers had grown more and more frequent and audacious, until they became unbearable, and Colonel Connor determined to put an end to them."[54] Yet Brigham's critics, such as Stenhouse, claimed the Army's action infuriated Brigham, and that he only looked upon them as his enemies. Other sources — directly from the Saints and Army personnel present — indicate otherwise, although, obviously, not all Mormon opinion was polarized. In the process, Colonel Connor created Camp Douglas on the east bench of Great Salt Lake City near the very canyon through which the Mormons had entered fifteen years previously.

Yet despite the sizeable force of soldiers present, the Indians did not slow their marauding. At Bear River, emigrants now had their stock stolen, and from it, events began to snowball. In retaliation a detachment of Colonel Connor's men were sent to the spot where they captured four Shoshone Braves. A fifth Brave was sent back to the tribe to inform tribal chiefs that unless the stock were released, the four captives would be executed. The chiefs ignored the mandate. The four Braves were tied up before a firing squad and fired upon 51 times until dead, "and then the cords by which they were fastened were cut and the bodies tumbled into the river."[55]

Needless to say, local tribesmen were infuriated. Nearby, Mormons heard that the whites would "pay."[56]

Soon a party of miners at Bear River were attacked. The whites attempted to cross the river on a barge, and Indians fired upon them like sitting ducks. One white miner was killed and several were wounded.

Shortly thereafter two mail carriers were reported missing; according to other Indians near the Portneuf River the whites had been ambushed by Shoshones. But the final straw was a report to the city marshal from miner William Bevins: his mining partner John Smith had been killed by Shoshones near Bear River, and "another party of ten miners en route to Salt Lake City had been assaulted and murdered by the same Indians."[57]

Marshal Isaac L. Gibbs marched over to Colonel Connor's tent and requested aid to arrest the tribal chieftains. That was all the excuse needed by the colonel to send his own force *en masse* against the hostiles.[58]

But, surprisingly, the Indians were *waiting* for a showdown with the Army. Shoshone and Bannock warriors had even fortified themselves in a most unusual manner at the Bear River.

The inevitable battle, Connor felt, would allow him to punish the pesky warriors with such intensity that they would think twice before plundering white men again. Connor actually now confessed a cold plan — he told Marshal Gibbs he would take no prisoners.[59]

Three hundred soldiers moved out January 22, 1863.[60]

Porter Rockwell was hired as guide — and possibly as a fighter — in what was to become the greatest Indian massacre ever recorded on the American continent.[61] Rockwell's specific mandate was to not only lead them into battle, but to protect as many infantrymen as possible . . .

clark Kelley Price
85

XIV

Marching forward with Rockwell, Captain Charles H. Hempstead describes the "fearful night march:"

"Clear and brilliant shone the stars upon the dreary earth mantled with deep snow, but bitter and intense was the cold . . .

"Motion only made it possible for them to endure the biting freezing blast. All that long night the men rode on, facing the wintry wind . . . Hour after hour passed on, dragging its slow length along, with not a word save that of command at intervals to break upon the monotonous clamp, clamp of the steeds and the clatter of sabres as they rattled in their gleaming sheaths."[1]

Upon arriving at the Shoshone fortress January 29th[2] the U. S. soldiers were shocked to find their enemy now invincibly fortified: "The position of the savages was one of great natural strength, and they had improved it with considerable ingenuity," reports Whitney in 1893. "A narrow, dry ravine with steep, rocky sides, sheltered them from the fire of the soldiers . . . "[3] The *Deseret News* reports: "Anticipating an attack, they had cut steps in the east side of the banks of the ravine, from which they could conveniently fire without exposure, and descend again for perfect security."[4] The Indians were, in fact, fortified as they never had been in U. S. history.

Standing across an icy river, the soldiers were shocked. But what stunned them even more now was *hearing* the savages: they were being cursed in English. "They [also] waved the scalps of white women," according to commander Connor,[5] "and challenged the troops to battle . . . "

The correspondent for the *Deseret News* adds: "As the troops formed in line of battle, the Indians seemed to look upon the coming struggle with particularly good humor. While one of the chiefs rode up and down in front of the ravine, brandishing his spear in the face of the volunteers, the warriors in front sung out: 'Fours right, fours left; come on, you California sons of b—hs!' [expletive as published] [6] Where the Indians had learned the rhyme was to the soldiers a mystery. Obviously one of the Indians was fluent with white slang, or had been taught by a white renegade.

The *Deseret News* reports the start of the battle: "The first companies galloped up to the base of a range of hills to the east and formed in line of battle; but before all the men had dismounted, the Indians sent a shower of lead among them, wounding one of the volunteers."[7]

Then, according to Harmon Zufelt, a witness at the scene: "as one of the cooks went down for a bucket of water, the Indians shot him in the right temple and the bullet came out of his right eye. Then the soldiers opened fire upon them, but the willows were so thick that they could not do much good . . . The battle then commenced, which was pretty hot shooting. The Indians were getting the best of the fight . . . "[8]

The cavalrymen crossed the freezing waters, dodging sheets of ice,[9] egged on by taunts from the mocking Indians. "This was too much for the soldiers," records Ebenezer Crouch. "They would wait no longer but plunged into the river and waded across. The weather was extremely cold and some got their feet and legs frozen . . . "[10] Water gushed over the saddles, horses lost their footing, and numerous riders were swept downstream.[11]

The Army's position looked bleak indeed. The *Alta Californian* claims, "The Volunteers now say that with the same number of troops as Indians in such a position, they could have held at bay

2,000 soldiers."[12]

Colonel Connor adds: "Up to this time, in consequence of being exposed on a level and open plain, while the Indians were under cover, they had the advantage of us, fighting with the ferocity of demons."[13]

In summarizing the first phase of the battle, The *Deseret News* reports: "The Indians in the opening of the fight had the best of it, and the volunteers 'fell like the leaves in autumn.' But then something happened — that indescribable emotion that sweeps across a regiment of troops like a wave and can turn the course of events. And the tide of fortune changed."

A California correspondent of the appellative "Verite" describes the wave: "Skirmishing as they went northward, the detachment outflanked the Indians on the left, while the other cavalry engaged them in front. Hearing the firing, while yet at a distance, the infantry hastened up to the river, and in their eagerness for a share of the fight attempted to ford the river on foot, but finding it impossible . . . fell back. The cavalry horses were sent over to them, and dripping wet, on a severe cold morning, our . . . volunteers mounted, crossed the river, and galloped up to the battle."[14]

Officers left and right were killed[15] and wounded.[16] Colonel Connor continues, "My men fell thick and fast around me, but after flanking them we had the advantage and made good use of it.

Verite reports the infantry "kept up their fire directly in the rear of the Indians . . . forming, with the cavalry in front, about three-quarters of a circle. By this enfilading fire from three points, the Indians were gradually driven to the centre and southward."[17]

As the Indians were forced out of their fortress into the ravine, "I had a company stationed who shot them as they ran out," reports Conner.[18] "I also ordered a detachment of cavalry across the ravine to cut off the retreat . . . "

The *Deseret News* continues, "The Indians being thus encircled and brought to bay, an almost hand-to-hand conflict ensued all along the river bank."[19]

Reporter Verite adds: "The Indians fought bravely; but now, away from their lodges and places of natural and artificial defence . . . The Indians there fell in heaps . . . Other Indians sought refuge in thick willows of the ravine, and on the border of the river; but ... one after one was dislodged ... "[20]

The *News* describes the pitiful ending: " ... Soon the Indians were completely broken and in full retreat; but very few of them escaped."[21]

Colonel Connor adds: "The most of those who did escape from the ravine were afterward shot in attempting to swim the river."[22]

The battle had ended in a massacre. Whitney elaborates, "At a single spot forty-eight corpses were afterwards counted. By 10 o'clock the savages were completely routed and the slaughter was ended ... Among them were the chiefs Bear Hunter ... and Lehi, the first, it is said, falling into the fire at which he was moulding bullets, and being literally roasted."[23]

In summarizing the battle, Connor reports, "We found 224 bodies in the field ... I captured 175 horses, some arms, destroyed over seventy lodges ... I left a supply of provisions for the sustenance of 160 captive squaws and children who were released by me on the field."[24]

But Colonel James H. Martineau details a more gruesome account: " ... the Indians, whose dead, as counted by an eye-witness from Franklin, amounted to 368, besides many wounded, who afterwards died."[25] And then he quotes the astonishing report: "About ninety of the slain were women and children."[26]

Army Corporal Hiram S. Tuttle records in his journal that his fellow soldiers slaughtered "nearly 400 warriors, say nothing about squaws and young bucks that got in the way."[27]

Martineau adds, " ... Several squaws were killed because they would not submit quietly to be ravished. Other squaws were ravished in the agonies of death."[28]

Harmon Zufelt, a resident of the nearest town to the battle, claimed the troops were under orders to kill every Indian in sight.[29] But the report was probably exaggerated, as 160 squaws and children were indeed released by Connor.[30] Nonetheless, with 90 squaws and children killed, one suspects the percentage somewhat high for a group of innocents who merely "got in the way." In speculation, Connor's alleged policy to not massacre the women and children may have been negated by some troops. On the other hand, as reported by others, Connor may indeed have ordered to spare no one, which means his troops may have violated his "take no prisoners" orders by sparing the 160. The *Army and Navy Journal* of 1866 adds further light: "As soon as the squaws and children saw that the soldiers did not desire to kill them, they came out of the ravine and walked to the rear"[31] of the troops. Soon they sat in the snow "like a lot of sage hens,"[32] claims John Kelly in the Blackfoot, Idaho *Daily Bulletin.*

As to the raping and massacring of squaws, certain numbers of soldiers had undoubtedly indulged — but perhaps few in number; likewise relatively few Indian tribes had been marauding and killing white emigrants and Mormons. The Saints, at least, were on good terms with numerous tribes. Possibly a minority of Indians and whites had given both races a bad name to each others' perspective.

The *Deseret News* summarizes the Bear River massacre as "a larger amount of Indian killing than ever fell to the lot of any single expedition of which we have any knowledge."[33]

At the commander's office, General H. W. Halleck reports the following remarkable fact about the Army: "Our loss in the battle was fourteen killed and forty-nine wounded."[34]

Porter's participation in the battle was significant. Whitney describes: "Colonel Connor employed as his guide on this expedition the experienced mountaineer, O. P. Rockwell, who rendered the command very efficient service, without which, it is believed, many more of the soldiers would have perished by being frozen. This fact accounts for the friendly feeling that Connor always entertained [afterwards] toward Rockwell."[35]

After the battle, the *Alta Californian* reports, "A drove of about a hundred head of Indian horses entering the camp was the first announcement of the returning of the men. Then rode up the Colonel in a 'buggy,' with the renowned Porter Rockwell, of great Mormon notoriety, who had been his guide . . . "[36]

Rockwell worked tirelessly to save the wounded. During the night, "Porter was sent to Franklin to engage ten teams to haul the wounded to Camp Douglas . . . Three wounded were placed in each sled, which was then pulled to the top of the hill by baggage mules. The dead were carried in baggage wagons."[37]

In summary, of the 300 troops under Connor's command, only 200 participated — a hundred others being disabled from cold and illness, 79 from "frosted feet" alone.[38]

Of the battle's aftereffects Whitney took a hard-nosed stand: "If the battle in its latest stage had possessed less the elements of a massacre, Colonel Connor and his command would have been more generally praised by some people; but perhaps it would not then have proved a lesson so well remembered by the savages."[39]

Perhaps it was because of this stand the Saints provided moral support for the troops. Colonel Martineau reflects the citizens' participation: "On their return the troops remained all night in Logan, the citizens furnishing them supper and breakfast, [with] some parties . . . entertaining ten or fifteen each. The [Mormon] settlers furnished teams and sleighs to assist them . . . Bishop W. H. Maughan gathered all the men and teams in the place and assisted the troops through the pass to Salt Lake Valley."[40]

Eb Crouch furnishes another first-hand account of the returning parade: "When the troops were returning after the fight, Colonel Conner and his staff came into Salt Lake in advance of the main body. They went into the store of Thomas Box on Main Street. I followed them in and saw the spear and scalp used by Chief Bear Hunter and other trophies of victory. The Colonel had on a high crowned military hat with a bullet hole through the top part. As a result of this battle the Indians behaved themselves pretty well for awhile."[41]

Until later months when he became personally acquainted with the Saints, Colonel Connor was under the assumption that Mormons had abetted the enemy. After the battle he claimed, "no assistance was rendered [to the Army] by the Mormons, who seemed indisposed to divulge any information regarding the Indians." He also reported his men had destroyed "a large quantity of wheat and other provisions which had been furnished them by the Mormons."[42] The colonel had approached the land of Mormons from the land of rumors; wheat and other provisions, rather than having been supplied by Mormons, had simply been stolen by Shoshones from passing immigrant trains. Even his own soldiers had told reporters, after inspecting the Indian fortress at Bear River, that there were "numerous evidences of emigrant plunder, such as modern cooking utensils, looking glasses, combs, brushes, fine rifles and pistols, and such things as the Indians were likely to consider worthy of preservation, when they had attacked and robbed the emigrants. Wagon covers, with the names of their unfortunate owners, were also lying around and patching up the wick-i-ups."[43]

As reports of the battle's aftermath trickled in, the settlers learned a report which probably baffled the colonel, contradicting his earlier assumptions: One of the three chiefs, Sagwitch, had escaped the massacre, but "was shot through the hand, and was very angry at the Mormons because they helped the soldiers fight."[44] (See Note 36 regarding the Saints' support of the Army.)

With the battle over and Porter back on the homefront, the war-weary pioneer now sought to finally settle down. But his plans were once again thwarted, as he heard upsetting news: His close friend, Prophet, Seer, Revelator, and companion — Brigham Young — was arrested.

And Porter would just have to do something about it.

XV

Church officials had been developing an increasing distaste for federal bureaucrats. They had recently petitioned President Lincoln with 2,000 signatures to remove the governor, Stephen S. Harding, as well as associate justices Charles B. Waite and Thomas J. Drake.

But military officers counterpetitioned Lincoln. At Camp Douglas they drew up papers to support the federal officials, so the rift began again between Brigham and the military.

And then the news hit the streets.

Eb Crouch, a child at the time, reports, "One day while school was in session as usual there was a knock at the door. Mr. Mously went to the door and we heard him talking with a man. In a minute he came back, dismissed the school, went into his house and came out with a gun on his shoulder and started up town as fast as he could walk. All the boys were following him and as we went along we could see men coming from all directions with their guns on their shoulders and all making for up town. When we got up to where the Brigham Monument now stands we soon learned what was the matter. It seemed that the military authorities at Fort Douglas had trumped up some charge against President Young and were threatening to arrest him and take him to Fort Douglas. The Mormon people were preparing to resist them.

"At that time there was a stone wall about ten feet high extending about one half block north of the corner where now stands the Hotel Utah and east along South Temple to a little beyond the Eagle Gate. Behind this wall they were erecting a scaffold just high enough for a man to stand and shoot over the top. Soon all was ready for an attack. A large detachment of cavalry rode out of the Fort and came charging down the hill towards the city and it looked as though there was surely going to be a fight. They rode down to the edge of the hill where it drops down to the level of the city and there they halted and stood for a long time as if in consultation, then turned and rode slowly back to the Fort. This action on the part of the soldiers took the strain off of the minds of the people to some extent but for several days and nights a heavy guard was kept around the residence of President Young and horsemen were out patrolling the city."[1]

Tensions continued growing between troops and citizens, and when U. S. Marshal Isaac L. Gibbs finally approached Brigham with a warrant March 9th, 1863 — for violating the anti-polygamy bill of 1862[2] — Brigham could have given the signal that would have poured more blood in the streets than either side had ever imagined . . . but, upon looking across the battle-lines, he merely shook his head and decided to cooperate. He walked up the street unarmed and appeared before Chief Justice J. T. Kinney. Kinney demanded $2,000 bail if the Prophet desired freedom until the upcoming Third District Court convened. Immediately, four of his friends stepped forward to issue the bail money, including Porter Rockwell.[3] All four testified a total net worth of $20,000,[4] and signed bonds totaling $5,500 to make the bail.[5]

As Connor now dipped his hands into Utah's civilian matters — with particular interests in mining — he possibly involved himself in other matters, such as the arrest of Brigham. But because of either his friendship with Porter or his realization that he had a tiger by the tail — Connor never made the arrest. Some claimed he never even received such orders.[6]

In any case, it was Marshal Gibbs who did the dirty work and arrested Brigham, but the Prophet was soon acquitted by a grand jury.

Porter came to the city again and, as Amasa Lyman records March 28, 1863, "Taried in town and during the day met with O. P. Rockwell who was in town buying horses for the Mail Service."[7] Rockwell apparently had the reputation for possessing the best eye for horses in the Kingdom — and possibly the West.

While in town he stopped at the courthouse and witnessed the trial of a civilian accused of purchasing a soldier's gun. The *Deseret News* reports, "The jury retired in charge of Bailiff J. D. Ross. O. P. Rockwell was sworn in as a bailiff."[8] Although nothing significant came from the day in court, an interesting note surfaces: Rockwell's reputation at this point was still reputable enough for both civic and church service.

Yet he still possessed another side to his character. Ebenezer Crouch witnessed it in the spring of 1863: "Porter Rockwell could be seen any day on the street. He was usually horseback with his dog sitting behind him on the rump of the horse. One day Port, drunk as usual, rode back and forth on the porch in front of the Salt Lake Hotel and into the store of Gilbert Girish. The police threatened to arrest him but decided not to. Port seemed to be a privileged character."[9]

Meanwhile, on the hill above, Camp Douglas was ripe for a celebration. That party came when its commander, Colonel Connor, was promoted to brigadier general.[10] So absorbed by their exuberancy were they, in fact, that the soldiers set off several cannon.[11] The Saints also applauded the promotion: "We congratulate him upon his promotion and wish him all the good fortune that an honorable soldier can desire; and if he keeps clear of politicians and wire-workers, we have no doubt that his own 'back bone' will carry him where the country can appreciate him."[12]

Conflicting feelings existed towards Conner, as the Mormons in general were impatient with his soldiers. Crouch reports, "The coming of the army brought quite a rough element into Salt Lake City. Drunken soldiers could be seen on the streets every day. They would go about with a canteen strapped over their soldier filled with Valley Tan whiskey. Every little while they would retire into some back yard and take a good big swig then come out on the street filled with patriotism and a desire to lick some disloyal Mormon. As a consequence there were many street brawls . . . and there was some bad feelings between the soldiers and citizens."[13]

But others saw things differently: The Army proved a continuing ally to the Saints, and many were grateful.

Then, once again, the Army proved why the Saints should have been. Indians attacked the Saints near Spanish Fork Canyon and Cedar Valley . . . and because of it the Army came to the rescue. They engaged 50 Indians, killing one[14] and wounding several.

In a counter-retaliation the Indians ambushed an Army detachment near Pleasant Grove,[15] where soldiers were chased into a house. As Indians continued firing upon them, the soldiers escaped penetrating bullets through cabin walls by hiding under floorboards. Having dragged a howitzer into the house, the soldiers then shot their own horses outside, purposely, so Indians could not steal them, but the braves managed to steal several,[16] and galloped away.

As a consequence, General Connor cantered off to Pleasant Grove personally to investigate the Indian attacks.[17] One Mormon, William H. Seemiller, found Porter in Pleasant Grove with the general. Exactly why Porter was among the troops is unclear. Perhaps he merely wished to lend a hand, as he was no longer needed as a guide; certainly the troops by now knew the geography of surrounding townships.

Afterwards, Seemiller rode into Great Salt Lake City for an appointment with Brigham Young, and there again saw Porter. He provides history with another revealing portrait: "While I was conversing with the President, Orrin Porter Rockwell called and gave President Young an account of the affair with the Indians at Pleasant Grove. I listened very attentively to his recital of the matter, and he freely told the above as I understood it.

"O. Porter Rockwell while at Pleasant Grove was taken to be slightly intoxicated. He was active in moving among the crowd at the soldiers' camp; this all seems very distinct even now. I thought him almost silly with drink and had little respect for him, until this interview with President Young. On that occasion he was well dressed in a black broadcloth suit, wore neatly polished shoes and a black silk hat; his language was free and grammatical. I concluded then that Rockwell lived a double life in the interest of his friends and God's cause on the earth. I will ever remember him with esteem."[18]

On April 15th in Spanish Fork Canyon the Army engaged the Indians again. They killed over 30 Braves, then, in an adrenal climax, scalped the warriors and took home 27 hair-pieces.[19] In the process they re-captured stolen Army horses.[20]

Nevertheless, one more Indian attack occurred . . . and one that affected Porter personally . . .

Rockwell's life had evidently been running smoothly: Mary Ann had delivered their fifth child, Letitia,[21] and Porter was held in esteem by both non-Mormon stage drivers at his tavern and by living prophets who also visited the station. In fact, Brigham Young stopped to spend the evening May 19th,[22] 1863 as he had twice previously in September.[23]

But in June an incident occurred which turned Porter's stomach. He sent a young stage driver under his employ to the next station twelve miles southwest. Before leaving the valley, his driver, Frederick Scarlett, was warned by a Mrs. William Ball that on the next day the Indians "were going to kill the [next passing] mail driver and 'Blue coats.' "[24] Mrs. Ball had inside information because her family was "extremely friendly with the Indians."

But Scarlett drove ahead anyway.

And nothing happened. As he rode out the next day, however, he overheard gunshots. A northbound stage had driven past him and was now being attacked. The *Deseret News* reports, "It is supposed that the man [Porter's driver, Scarlett] gave but little heed to the monition [from Mrs. Ball], and whether or not he [had] related what he was thus told [to the other stage driver when he had an opportunity to at Fort Crittenden] . . . has not transpired."[25] In any case he "was not more than three or four miles behind the stage when it was attacked by the savages."[26]

The incident was reported in 1913 by Hamilton Gardner in *History of Lehi*. Also down the road was George Kirkham, "then a boy of twelve, [who] was herding cattle west of the Jordan, about one mile north-west of the Cold Springs. Seeing the mail coach come flying in the distance, his curiosity was aroused, and he followed its course closely. In a short time he could discern a number of horsemen following the vehicle and then he could see they were Indians firing at it. Ever faster they came . . . The driver's name was Wood Reynolds."[27]

The *Deseret News* continues the story: "When within a mile or two of the place where the attack and murder was consummated he [Scarlett] heard the report of a gun some distance off. He soon after saw some blood in the road which increased in quantity as he advanced. The coach was next discovered about a quarter of a mile from the road, to which he immediately proceeded, supposing that the team had run away; but on arriving at the wreck he was horrified at the sight presented; for there lay the bodies of the two murdered men — one on each side of the coach — stripped naked and mutilated in a most horrid manner, pierced with balls, arrows and spears, cut with knives and scalped in an unusual way, as the hairy part of their heads had been literally flayed. Two of the horses were also lying dead, another incurably wounded, and the fourth was missing. The coach was completely dismantled, and riddled with balls. The mail sacks were missing, having been ripped open and emptied of their contents . . . "

Scarlett then "put the dead bodies into the coach, together with all mail matter they could find, hitched on the animals Scarlett was bringing back, and started for Rockwell's station. A few miles out from the station they met Mr. Rockwell,"[28] who had learned of the massacre, and was now taking command. Porter put the mutilated corpses in his coach and brought them into the city, delivering them to the agent of the Overland Mail Company.[29]

Ebenezer Crouch adds, "I looked at the bodies, they were frightfully mutilated. Both were scalped and one's ears were torn off with the scalp. Their hearts were cut out and no doubt eaten by the Indians as they admired a brave man . . . "[30]

Gardner summarizes, "The next morning William Ball, who was returning from Goshen, met this band of assassins, glorying in their scalps and proudly displaying the bugle and other property of the unfortunate men. Although a squad of soldiers was dispatched from Fort Douglas in search of the murderers, they were never apprehended."[31] The *Deseret News* adds, "The Indians are reported to have fled Southward from whence they came, by way of the mountains West of Utah Lake . . . "[32]

Possibly because of the massacre, possibly for other reasons, Rockwell moved his family into Great Salt Lake City.

Not long afterwards he teamed with four other Mormons to scout for suitable ranch property in Skull Valley,[33] southwest of the valley, but he would never move his family out of the city again. Within six days he and the others found their ranch lands. Rockwell filed for the area entitled "Government Creek," west of the Sheeprock Mountains near the Juab-Tooele line (where, eleven years later, he would receive a land patent).[34]

In commenting on his choice Rockwell told the son of one of his four fellow purchasers, John Bennion, his trick for choosing prime land: "John, for a cattle ranch, you want a place where you can track 'em out."[35]

His ranch would become the next project in a mushrooming private enterprise, and would garner him quite an estate as one of the territory's largest. Everything he now touched, in fact, seemed to turn to gold.

Meanwhile, everything back East written about him also turned to gold. "Porter Rockwell" was becoming more than just another saleable name. *Anything* written about him — especially to satisfy the public's insatiable appetite for sensationalism — sold copies.

Because of this a writer for the *Atlantic Monthly* rode into town to explore the Mormons. Fitz Hugh Ludlow possessed an unusual curiosity about the people, and eventually managed to meet Rockwell: "He has a face full of bull-dog courage, but vastly good-natured, and without a bad trait in it. I went out riding with him on the Fourth of July, and enjoyed his society greatly, though I knew that at a word from Brigham he would cut my throat in as matter-of-fact style as if I had been a calf instead of an author. But he would have felt no unkindness toward me on that account. I understood his anomaly perfectly, and found him one of the pleasantest murderers I ever met."[36]

Ludlow was convinced Rockwell was the mythical "Destroying Angel," and, among other things, he confused facts on Porter's home life. "He has two very comely and pleasant wives," writes Ludlow. (One cannot help but imagine the basis for such a statement, unless perhaps Ludlow had chanced upon Mary Ann visiting a neighbor woman, and, with preconceived ideas that all

Mormons practice polygamy, had labeled Porter a polygamist.)

But for a non-Mormon coming to Utah with certain prejudices, his portrait of Porter is admirably accurate. Upon completion of the *Atlantic Monthly* piece he then set out to write a book, describing in more detail his visit: "During our stay at Townsend's, we were one morning sitting on the veranda, when our landlord, a portly, kindly man, brought up a friend of his to introduce to us. It was Porter Rockwell, the Destroying Angel and chief of the Danites. Apart from his cause, I felt an abstract interest in this old fighter, and was glad to become acquainted with him. He welcomed us very cordially to Utah, and told us we ought to stay: our only bad taste was exhibited in merely going through. We could not avoid telling him, with a smile, that Utah had a reputation for stopping people who showed such taste, to take a permanent residence. He answered good-humoredly that he had heard the rumor, and intended so far to verify it that he should halt us on our way past his door, when we started to cross the desert, put our horses in his own stable, carry us to his table, and inflict on us the penalty of a real Mormon dinner — after which (if our horses had got through their feed) we should be let off with an admonition never to try to pass his door if we came that way again. 'Bless yer soul, but we're savage!' said Porter Rockwell.

" 'Once drew a sassige on a Yankee Gentile myself — crammed it right down his throat with scalding hot gravy and pancakes. We Mormons torture 'em awful. The Gentile I drew the sassige on bore it like a man, and is livin' yet. Well, I'll soon see ye agin.' So he shook hands with us, jumped on his mustang, and ambled away as gently as if, instead of being a destroying angel, he were a colporteur of peace tracts, or a peddler of Winslow's Soothing Syrup.

"He kept his word to us, seeing us soon and frequently. Next to Brigham Young, he was the most interesting man and problem that I encountered in Utah. His personal appearance in itself was very striking. His figure was of the middle height, and very strongly made; broad across the shoulders, and set squarely on the legs. His arm was of large girth, his chest round as a barrel, and his hand looked as powerful as a grizzly bear's. His face was of the mastiff type, and its expression, fidelity, fearlessness, ferocity.

"A man with his massive lower jaw, firm mouth, and good-humored but steady and searching eyes of steel-blue, if his fanaticism takes the Mormon form, must infallibly become like Porter Rockwell.

"Organization and circumstances combine to make any such man a destroying angel.

"Having always felt the most vivid interest in supernatural characters of that species, I was familiar with most of them from the biblical examples of those who smote Egypt, Sodom, and Sennacherib, to the more modern Arab, Azrael, and that famous one who descended, all white-bearded and in shining raiment from Judges' Cave, to lead the van of Quinnipiack's forlorn hope and smite the red-skinned Philistines.

"Out of this mass of conflicting and particular angels I had abstracted an ideal and a general angel; but when I suddenly came on a real one, in Porter Rockwell, I was surprised at his unlikeness to my thought.

"His hair, black and iron-gray in streaks, was gathered into a cue, just behind the apex of the skull, and twisted into a hard round bunch, confined with a comb — in nearly the same fashion as was everywhere prevalent among Eastern ladies twenty years ago.

"He was very obliging in his manners, placable, jocose, never extravagant when he conversed, save in burlesque. If he had been converted to Methodism in its early times, instead of Mormonism, he might have been a second Peter Cartwright, preaching and pummeling his enemies into the Kingdom instead of shooting them to Kingdom Come.

"No one ignorant of his career would take him on sight for a man of bad disposition in any sense ... In his build he was a gladiator; in his humor a Yankee lumberman; in his memory, a Bourbon; in his vengeance, an Indian. A strange mixture, only to be found on the American Continent."

Ludlow next reports on his journey to the north end of the city. His pen could not doff the subject of Rockwell.

"In the forenoon of the Fourth of July, Porter called at our hotel to invite us to take a drive with him. His carriage was a large coach of the most ancient Overland fashion, with a boot; room for nine inside ... He had bought this vehicle at the auction of a deceased stage company's effects. It used to run from Salt Lake City to Nephi, or some other Mormon settlement, and upon its emancipation from these diurnal labors struck the eye of the angel [Rockwell], he told me, as the fair thing to air the angelic 'ole wimmen' [his "wives"] and the little destroying angels [his children] in. It still bore its original coat of flaming vermilion, and the name of the company, if I recollect, which used to employ its services.

"Porter, in his desire to do the hospitalities of the occasion in the most graceful manner, proposed to mount the box, and take the reins himself. But we represented, as was true, that we should feel much more pleased and honored if he gave us his company inside the stage. We wished to converse with and see this interesting man, not to ride behind him, and so persuaded him to let a stable-boy drive for us ... "[37]

After next describing the mountain formations in view, Ludlow comments, "Porter showed us from the window of the coach the superannuated remains of ... a bath house. The Springs we sought were reached by a ride of about three miles from Townsend's ... "[38] Porter's coach stopped at the perennial 128 degree hot springs, which Ludlow inspected; the author took samples of the colorful algae, which fascinated him, and he even gauged the springs' temperature before returning to Porter's coach.

On their return trip to the hotel, "Porter Rockwell studiously avoided referring to Mormonism seriously, though he seemed willing enough to talk about it in a playful manner if any one else broached the subject. [In the coach with them were three other Easterners]. He was rough, but kind and conciliatory, in everything he said, and sometimes very amusing. A description he gave, accompanied by pantomime, of the way in which he had seen a Goshoot family sitting in a circle on their haunches when the grasshoppers were plenty, using their palms as scoops and 'paying' the insects into their mouths with a windless motion as fast as their hands could fly, was irresistibly laughable.

"It seemed strange to be riding in the carriage and by the side of a man, who, if universal report among the Gentiles were correct, would not hesitate to cut my throat ... It was like an Assyrian taking an airing in the chariot of the Angel of Death . . . I felt pretty tranquil upon the subject of any change in Porter Rockwell from his present agreeable relation of entertainer to the less pleasant one of executioner, though an hour's study of him enabled me to say that though, if he had it to perform, less heart might be in his execution of the latter than of the former function, there would be at any rate no less efficiency and sureness. He had the reputation of having killed many men . . . "[39]

Ludlow then recounts an incident in which Rockwell was allegedly insulted by a non-Mormon who had retired from Great Salt Lake City to Camp Floyd "for self-protection." The man was later found "with a revolver hole from temple to temple . . . Of whose pistol killed him, there is no eye-witness, and as little doubt."[40] Ludlow had picked up the tale, without a particle of evidence, from a personal enemy of Porter's.

Mr. Ludlow the same evening attended the July 4th ball.[41] (For perhaps the most incisive portrait ever penned on Brigham Young from a non-Mormon viewpoint, despite certain inaccuracies, see Ludlow's detailed account at Note 37.)

Ludlow then rode on to California and sailed to New York. Nine months later his first account appeared in the *Atlantic Monthly*, and six years afterwards in his book *The Heart of the Continent*. In the *Atlantic Monthly* article was a succinct description of the physical appearance of Porter's kingdom: "Salt Lake City, Brigham told me, he believed to contain sixteen thousand inhabitants. [Additional dozens of thousands had scattered to other settlements in later Idaho, Utah, California, Nevada, Arizona, and old Mexico.] Its houses are built generally of adobe or wood, a few of stone, and though none of them are architecturally ambitious, almost all have delightful gardens. Both fruit and shade trees are plenty and thrifty. Indeed, from the roof of the Opera House the city looks fairly embowered in green. It lies very picturesquely on a plain quite embasined among mountains, and the beauty of its appearance is much heightened by the streams which run on both sides of all the broad streets, brought down from the snow-peaks for purposes of irrigation."[42]

The following summer, 1864, a year after Ludlow's visit, Rockwell's increasing wealth was made manifest by the arrival of a custom-made coach he had ordered from General B. M. Hughes of

Atchison, Kansas, a carriage-maker. Its description in Porter's words is: "One Concord Buggy — Leather top (which can be taken off ...)"[43] Thus, for frontier Utah, he was now living fairly high on the hog.

And of hogs he also took active interest: By Christmas a $500 monstrous hog of his was hanging from a hook at Jennings' Meat Market on Main Street, for Christmas shoppers to covet.[44]

He probably prided himself in the following *Deseret News* article: "On Saturday, 24th, preparatory for Christmas sales, the meat market presented a display that, in quantity, variety and general tastefulness of arrangement, would gratify the most fastidious ... .Paul & Co. gratified the public with a sight of the huge hog fed by Mr. O. P. Rockwell ... "[45]

Meanwhile, as he raised such illustrious livestock he coined some rather interesting logo for his brands. Cattle-markings were the pride of prairie-men and mountain-ranchers alike, so when Rockwell decided the art-work of his cattle would bear an "OP," three inches high on the right hip, and that his horses would have a Cedar Tree brand on the right thigh,[46] he was undoubtedly proud of his designs.

Then came to Zion an interesting party of dignitaries. In 1865, four Eastern and Midwestern analysts arrived and began studying his people. Consisting of two journalists and two politicians, all four gentlemen developed their own opinions of Rockwell. The party consisted of Lieutenant Governor William Bross of Illinois, Speaker of the U. S. House of Representatives Schuyler Colfax, Albert D. Richardson of the *New York Tribune*, and Samuel Bowles, editor of the *Springfield Republican* in Massachusetts. Bowles interviewed Rockwell at length during their eight-day visit and as a result refused to believe the slanders targeted him by earlier reporters: "One of the characters of Mormondom is Porter Rockwell, the accredited leader of the Danites or 'Avenging Angels' of the church. We were presented to him, and were invited to eat strawberries and cream at his 'ranch,' but our engagements did not permit our accepting and partaking. Though given to heavy whiskey drinking of late years, he is as mild a mannered man as ever scuttled ship or murdered crews; and I really do not think that any anxiety for our lives entered into our declination of his hospitality, inexplicable as it may seem that for any less reason we should have omitted any opportunity at strawberries. There is a difference of opinion, even among the 'Gentiles,' as to his real share in the mysterious and terrible takings-off of parties in bad odor with the saints of the church; though unlettered, he is strong-minded and strong-hearted, and, unless under the influence of a shocking fanaticism, I can hardly believe, from his appearance and manners, he could be guilty of such crimes as are laid at his door by the more implacable and suspicious of the 'Gentile' residents. I should not be willing, however, to see Mr. Fitz-hugh Ludlow fall in his way again; there might not be murder, but the author of the largely imaginative articles in the *Atlantic Monthly* on this western journey would certainly feel the sharp vengence of the injured and irate 'Avenger.' Mr. Ludlow tells the worst stories about Rockwell, such as that he had committed about fifty murders for the church and as many more on private account, as if accepted, proved facts; at the same time that he acknowledges being his guest, and availing himself of his courtesies to see the country. Porter shuts his teeth hard when the subject is now mentioned, and mutters that he supposes 'it is all wheat,' this being Utah idiom for all right. Which means, of course, that he don't suppose any such thing."[47] Such were Bowles' impressions as published in *Across the Continent.*

In a letter published by the *Utica Morning Herald* and *Daily Gazette* Bowles adds, "Mr. Ludlow has not left a very savory reputation in all this country — he not only has drawn a very long bow in his published sketches, but he has been careless and wanton in his treatment of individuals and important interests."[48]

Bowles finally describes Rockwell in the *Springfield Republican* as "one of the institutions of Mormondom."[49]

Accompanying Editor Bowles was the future vice-president of the United States, Schuyler Colfax, who would return with Bowles in four years and form his own opinion of Rockwell ...

After the four "Eastern" gentlemen journeyed to California, Albert D. Richardson of the *New York Tribune* returned to Great Salt Lake City while the other three sailed home. "During this visit in September and October, I found a good deal of bitterness toward me existing among zealous Mormons, caused by the return of my *Tribune* letters. I had written frankly, but in no unkindly spirit. I could say nothing except ill of polygamy; and that excited their indignation . . . Porter H. Rockwell [reporters shunned with derision the Saints' criticalness of their off-the-mark details, but Porter "H?"] reputed one of the leading Danites or destroying angels of the church, also confused me in his mind with Fitz Hugh Ludlow, who had passed through two years before, and given an unflattering description of him for the *Atlantic Monthly.* Some one told Porter, or he dreamed it, that I had characterized him as the murderer of one hundred and fifty men; and he significantly remarked, that if I had said it he believed he would make it one hundred and fifty-one! He finally concluded it a mistake, and contented himself with complaining to me that he had been cruelly slandered by Ludlow, and afterward while in his cups, assuring me that he would kill any journalist who should publish falsehoods about him. He is a man of medium size, noticeable for his long black hair, which he wears parted in the middle and hanging upon the shoulders. In general he is said to be hospitable and kind; and his manners mild and courteous."[50] Rockwell *was* probably responsible for the number of killings reported by Ludlow and Richardson; it was the label "murder" which struck his indignant streak.

The following spring Rockwell became implicated by enemies in the killing of one Brassfield. "A sly wink from Brigham Young to Porter," satirized one Mormon analyst, "and another soul would be 'used up.' A beautiful theme for ten cent fiction."[51]

Brassfield, a Nevadan, had talked a polygamist wife into running off with him when her husband was away on a church mission. Brassfield boasted it was "the entering wedge to burst up polygamy."[52]

She didn't bother seeking a divorce, but simply married him March 20, 1866.

Twelve days later Brassfield was dead. The killer went undetected.

Outlaws and personal enemies of victims apparently found this the golden age of throat-cutting: The church officially would be accused of all crimes, and such was the case with Brassfield.

Although logic leads one to believe an angry family member committed the crime — since in-laws had indeed resisted his taking the children — none but Rockwell would receive the blame . . . and then only years afterwards by writers Kelly and Hoffman. For their facts they would again resort to quoting a personal enemy of Porter's.[53]

Because of high-pitched railings and rampant rumors, certain non-Mormons in the city felt forced to send a telegram to General Sherman, explaining, "Life in Utah is as secure as anywhere else."[54]

Then Porter met a personal tragedy. Mary Ann Neff Rockwell, his second wife — and as stated by family tradition[55] the love of his life — died from childbirth complications September 28, 1866. (Family tradition also has it that his next wife, Christina Olsen, sensed Porter's undying love for Mary Ann, and one day in a rage of jealousy took the scissors to all of Mary Ann's photographs.)[56]

Meanwhile, on her deathbed Mary Ann had given birth to a son five weeks earlier, August 24. Joseph Neff Rockwell lived only seven weeks.

Recuperating from the greatest emotional trauma of his life, Rockwell would receive blame for a case occurring two months later, that of Dr. John King Robinson. Robinson, who had his private practice in Great Salt Lake City, was a former Army doctor under Connor and had married a Mormon girl.[57] He had since built a shanty on city land, which the city claimed by legal title. In the ensuing litigation Chief Justice Titus, a non-Mormon and not regarded by church officers as friendly, rendered the decision in favor of the church-dominated city corporation. Three days afterwards, late in the evening, Robinson was returning home from work and was gunned down. Six or seven men were seen making an escape but none were recognized. As a non-apologist for the church, T. B. H. Stenhouse advances a plausible theory: He felt the attackers had planned to give the doctor a thrashing —certainly for any number of reasons — but their victim was strong and in the scuffle he recognized several. To cover their identities they shot him. "If they had intended to murder him certainly not six or seven were needed."[58]

Obvious suspicion surrounded the murder and church enemies made the most of it. Although a city official may have held Porter under suspicion, the chief of police replied to questioning about Rockwell's whereabouts at the time of the murder, and Porter was not further mentioned.[59] Church enemies were obviously anxious to snare any shadowy possibilities connected with the case, despite the fact Robinson was killed *after* the court decision and not before. (Five years later crusaders revived the case: Two men, Charles Baker and Thomas Butterwood, claimed a sudden recall of memory, but after several Saints were tried, the two accusers were dismissed by the court as perjurors.) Nonetheless, enemies of Rockwell years later decided to lay the blame solely on him.[60]

Whoever the murderers were, they escaped.

On December 11, the body of one Thomas Colbourn was found east of the city.[61] Known also as Thomas Coleman,[62] the black Mormon[63] was found with his throat cut, and of course the blame fell from church enemies to Porter[64] without grounds. (Others, however, possessed motives for killing him: In April, 1859 he had committed manslaughter[65] while fighting with another black over two black women,[66] and had made other enemies throughout his life . . . but, of course, only Rockwell received the blame.)[67]

Of these enemies an Englishman and travelling author who studied in Utah for several months assessed: "I was walking one day up the City Creek, when I became aware of an aged man seated on a stone by the roadside. His trousers were turned up to his knees, and he was nursing one of his legs as if he felt a great pity for it. As I approached I perceived that he was in trouble — (I perceived this by his oaths) — and getting still nearer I ventured to inquire what annoyed him . . . But there was no response, at least not worth mentioning. He only bent further over his leg, and I noticed that his coat had split down the back seam. His cursing accounted for that. And then his hat fell off his head into the dust . . . At this he swore again horribly. By this time I had guessed that he had been bitten by red ants.

" . . . so I said, 'bitten by red ants, eh?' "

" . . . 'Red ants!' said he. 'Red Indians, red devils, red hell!' And then relapsing into the vernacular, he became unintelligibly profane, but ended up with 'this damned Mormon city.'

"Now here was a man . . . cursing the Mormons because he had been bitten by red ants. Of his own stupidity he had gone and stood upon an ants nest.

" . . . That man went back to his hotel (for he was evidently a visitor) a confirmed anti-Mormon . . . He saw at a glance that all he had ever heard about 'the Danites' was quite true, and much more too that he had never heard but could now easily invent for himself. There was no need for anyone to tell him, after the way he had been treated within a mile of the Tabernacle . . .

"Here in Salt Lake City there is the most extraordinary ignorance of Mormonism that can be imagined. I have actually been assured by 'gentiles' that the Saints do not believe in the God of the Bible — that adultery among them is winked at by husbands under a tacit understanding of reciprocity — that the Mormons as a class are profane and drunken and so forth. Now, if they knew anything whatever of the Mormons, such statements would be impossible (unless of course made in wilful malice) . . .

"But it is a fact, and cannot be challenged, that the only people in all Utah who libel these Mormons are either those who are ignorant of them, those who have apostatized (frequently under compulsion) from the Church, or those, the official clique and their sycophants, who have been charged with looking foward to a share of the plunder of the Territorial treasury. On the other hand, I know many Gentiles who, though like myself they consider polygamy itself detestable, speak of these people as patterns to themselves in commercial honesty, religious earnestness, and social charity."[68]

The above observer, Phil Robinson, offered an additional insight: "Whence have the public derived their opinions about Mormonism? From anti-Mormons only. I have ransacked the literature of the subject, and yet I really could not tell anyone where to go for an impartial book about Mormonism later in date than Burton's 'City of the Saints,' published in 1862 [although it too has many inaccuracies] . . . But put Burton on one side, and I think I can defy anyone to name another book about the Mormons worthy of honest respect. From that truly awful book, 'The History of the Saints,' published by one Bennett — even an anti-Mormon has styled him 'the greatest rascal that ever came to the West' — in 1842, down to Stenhouse's in 1873, there is not, to my knowledge, a single Gentile work before the public that is not utterly unreliable from its distortion of facts. Yet it is from these books — for there are no others — that the American public has acquired nearly all its ideas about the people of Utah."[69]

One of the most notable of such works, *Holy Murder, The Story of Porter Rockwell,* by Hoffman and Birney, was reviewed by the *New Republic* in 1934: "This is the kind of book that has been written about the Mormons almost since their organization. The authors are inspired by unintelligent hatred of everything Mormon . . .

"Except for a few pages of quotations from hitherto unpublished manuscripts, the book is content to quote with authoritative assurance the unsubstantiated rumors of the huge body of anti-Mormon literature."[70]

Another critic of the Hoffman and Birney volume analyzes in 1938: "As a justification for most of these murder charges [against Rockwell] they cannot even resort to legend, and where they do resort to legend these writers seem to be the only ones that are aware of their existence."[71]

The literature thus piled up, but the Saints peacefully went about their lives. Among them, of course, remained Porter, whose life was not so peaceful. Neighbors, strangers, law officers — anyone with a problem — seemed to come knocking at his door. If a horse were stolen or a man murdered, Rockwell was sent to the scene.

He soon opened a downtown Salt Lake City mail station. The word "Great" was now being dropped from Great Salt Lake City for convenience. Downtown was Porter's new business address; he paid Wells Fargo and Co. $7,500 for 1 1/4 acres two blocks east and one and a half blocks south of the Temple,[72] and closed the transaction December 19, 1866. Although he had moved into the city, he kept his Point of the Mountain enterprise — or at least part of it — through March of 1867.[73]

In March his friend Alexander Toponce, a non-Mormon who had come with Johnston's Army in 1857 and had remained in Utah as a freighter, reported how he had sold his produce and wagon at Helena, Montana, then: "I went back to Salt Lake on the stage . . . One of the noted characters . . . in Utah was Porter Rockwell. I knew him very well. For some reason he took quite a fancy to me. He was reputed to be a friend and confederate of William Hickman, one of the so-called 'Danites' or 'Destroying Angels.'

"There were wild stories whispered around . . .

"However, I knew Porter Rockwell quite intimately. He wore a full beard and long hair like an Indian. Sometimes he let his hair hang loose, but generally had it done up in two braids, which hung down his back.

"Naturally he was a figure that attracted a good deal of attention as he passed along the streets.

"I had a room at the old Salt Lake house and Rockwell liked to come up there and sit and smoke [Toponce's facts may have been confused in some areas: for example, Porter didn't smoke] and talk over the news of the mining camps, and we got along fine together. I would also invite him to go down to the dining room with me.

"Once I had started my wagon to Montana and the driver of the stage from Ogden handed me a letter . . . stating that . . . eighteen head of oxen had strayed, or been stolen, from the camp during the night . . .

"Porter was in my room at the time the letter was given to me. After I read it, I had 'a hunch' and threw it across the table to Rockwell.

"After he read it [Rockwell couldn't read either; Toponce's memory had obviously faded] I said, 'Porter, do you think you could find those cattle for me?'

"He laughed, 'Old wheat in the mill,' he said. That was his favorite expression, 'Old wheat in the mill.' 'They will be at your train tomorrow night.'

"He put his hat on and went out at once. I did not see him again for some days, but I got a letter from the wagon boss, dated two days later telling me that, while camped on the sand ridge west of Ogden, the missing cattle had come back to the herd. He found them all present at roll call that morning. When I tried to talk to Porter about it and thank him he just laughed."

Toponce relates one more incident: "I missed some yoke-oxen while camped near Salt Lake and was riding around looking for them." He came upon the church's cattle Tithing Yards "located where the Hotel Utah now stands." He confronted the ornery old yard keeper Barnum Stringham. "I spoke to Stringham and told him that I was certain some of those cattle were mine ... " Stringham had probably heard the story from strangers often. Many believed they could obtain free cattle from the church herd just by verbal claim. Additionally, Toponce's arrival did look suspicious: "Just as I got there a big bunch of stray cattle was driven up." Toponce could have seen various brands on the church cattle before making his claim, and Stringham knew it.

"I knew better than to make any trouble so I rode away and almost the first one I met was Porter Rockwell. He had just ridden in from his ranch at the Point of the Mountain, and about twenty miles south of Salt Lake and had just hitched his horse in front of the Salt Lake House.

"I told him my story and he got on his horse and we rode back up to the Tithing Yard. He called Stringham to the gate and said, 'Barnum, you bring out Alex Toponce's cattle.'

"Stringham commenced to argue.

" 'Never mind, now,' said Porter, 'you heard what I said ... ' "

Toponce claims Rockwell then threatened the church herdsman: "Porter put his hands to his pistol belt [Rockwell rarely wore pistol belts — he kept pistols in his coat pockets, and certainly in March he would be wearing a coat]."

Toponce continues, "I suggested that I would help Stringham cut them out, but Porter said, 'No, let the ornery cuss do his own work.'

"In a few minutes Stringham drove out all my missing cattle, five in number. 'There's 50 cents a head stray pound charges on those cattle,' he [Stringham] said.

"I reached for my pocketbook, but Porter said, 'Don't you pay him a cent,' and then he told Stringham, 'Any time that Alex claims any cattle in this yard, you let him have them, and don't ask any questions.'

"And after that I never had any further trouble of that sort."[74]

An interesting anecdote to Toponce's record is the notation in his Introduction: He had been a freighter for the famed Russell, Majors and Waddell line, had driven a stage line on the Santa Fe Trail, had ridden the Pony Express, had become enamored by

Mexican girls, and had been the assistant wagon boss for General Johnston during the Utah War. He praised Brigham Young as "the squarest man to do business with in Utah, barring none."[75] As for certain questionable details in the narrative, his editor claims "those who knew the innate honesty of the man will say 'he tells the truth as he saw and remembered it.' "[76]

In his 1899 edition of *The History of Wyoming,* C. G. Coutant reports a remarkable incident involving Rockwell: " . . . during 1865 Tom Ryan, a soldier in the Nevada volunteers . . . made a discovery of fine gold quartz on the Carissa, but not having an opportunity to develop the property he afterwards reported the find in Salt Lake. Being known as a reliable man, his disclosures created no little excitement in the Mormon city, and the result was a considerable company organized there in the winter of 1866 and 1867 . . .

"Early in the spring a number of men started out with the avowed purpose of finding the place where Ryan had uncovered the rich gold quartz. In this party were . . . Bill Hickman (a noted Mormon), Porter Rockwell . . . and a large number of others . . . [See Note 38 for related details of the discovery.]

"Through the early spring of 1867 there were constant arrivals at South Pass, and as soon as the snow left the tops of the hills the prospectors spread themselves over the country. On June 8th . . . [several] succeeded in finding the Carissa lode, which Tom Ryan had told about. The rock was rich beyond anything that any of the party had before seen; the walls were well defined, and there was every probability that a great producer had been discovered. The news spread like a great conflagration all over the camp; nor did it stop here.

"Prospectors hastily sent word in all directions to their friends at home, and then commenced the rush to the new mining camp. New York, San Francisco, and all intermediate points in a few weeks were well informed of the great strike at the Carissa. The little army of pioneer miners in the camp dreamed of wealth even beyond that which falls to the lot of men the most fortunate, but this happiness and exultation was of but short duration, for in July a war party of the Sioux tribe of Indians made an attack on the men engaged in sinking a shaft on the Carissa."[77]

Porter possibly suspected the coming attack. After scouting

and seeing suspicious behavior among several Indians, Bill Hickman reports, "I told at camp what I had seen, and that there would be trouble, but could get few to believe it. I then told them I had only a day or two longer to stay, and if they did not go to work and organize [for defense], I would start home the next day . . . .The next morning I, in company with ten others, left for Salt Lake. The next morning the Indians made a raid on their camp . . . ."[78]

Rockwell probably stayed with the camp. Coutant continues, "The excitement of the discovery had driven the fear of Indians from the minds of the white men, and consequently they were unprepared to meet the wild charge of the painted savages. Capt. Lawrence rallied the miners and attempted to hold the position, but his men were without arms and practically defenseless. Their only weapons at hand were picks and drills, but with these they made a bold stand until Capt. Lawrence fell mortally wounded. His followers, realizing that they would all be killed if they remained in the mine, rushed out and down the hill toward Willow creek, which they crossed in mad haste. Keeping on, they finally reached the Sweetwater, the red devils close at their heels. Here Tony Shields, another of their number, was killed. At this point the Indians turned back."[79]

Porter likely swung his pick with the other miners, defending the hill, then he scampered with the survivors down to safety.

Immediately they evacuated camp but later returned . . . and in larger numbers than ever.

No known records for Rockwell exist the following year, and it's possible he was not even present during the Indian attack at Carissa. (150 miners were at the mines with Hickman, and many had come from Salt Lake; only ten had returned with Hickman to Salt Lake before the attack — so chances are Rockwell was one of the 140 who had remained at the mines.)

Rockwell's phrase, "Wheat" or "All wheat" took on increasing significance. In his next recorded incident, the phrase saved his life — or at least his allies — when his group came upon two other bands of lawmen. Both other groups of lawmen thought Rockwell's band was the band of thieves. The journal of Volney King reports the incident: "The officer in charge of the S L Party [Rockwell's] . . . called out All Wheat All Wheat & O P Rockwell's

slang word was too well known by all through the country not to
know who used it. & the excitement soon subsided & all three
parties then joined & finally the outlaws were captured, & their
band completely broken up ... "[80]

Army officer William Elkanah Waters, after meeting Rockwell,
reports in 1868 a revealing description: "He does not look like a
murderer, and it is my impression that the Danite Band has been a
good deal of a bugbear. Gentiles feared the Destroying Angels as
negroes in our Southern cities fear the doctors after dark.

" ... Porter Rockwell has become exceedingly fond of whiskey
in these latter days, and but seldom visits the city without getting
drunk. On such occasions he manifests none of that violence
which one might suppose would then almost certainly exhibit itself
in one so desperate as he is represented to be. When drunk he is
perfectly harmless, and the exuberance of vitality on such
occasions is relieved by loud shouts, which may be heard for
squares. He is otherwise orderly and well-behaved, even when
drunk."[81]

When Herman Francis Reinhart discovered in early 1868 that
his fourteen horses had been stolen near Stockton, a federal judge
told him he had, "better get a good hunter or mountaineer who
understood the country."[82] Reinhart went to Brigham Young for a
lead. The man Brigham recommended of course "was the famous,
or infamous, Porter C. Rockwell." (Why writers had such problems
with his middle initial is yet a mystery.)

Reinhart was disgusted with the thought of working with a
murderous heathen, but swallowed his pride and went to find the
Mormon. He was apparently more than a little surprised to find
Rockwell not only easy to work with, but engagingly "square."
Records Reinhart: "He made me a fair offer, better than any
Gentile or white man in Salt Lake City. He said he would take one
of his horses, let me have one, and we could put a pack of blankets
and provisions on the third, and he would go with me to his place
at [his ranch], 180 miles, and hunt all the way there, and then get
his herders to start from there to hunt my horses. He would be to
all expense and if we got the horses I was to let him have a choice
of two horses for his trouble. He seemed to act perfectly square
and like a liberal gentleman, if he was a Mormon. I was to let him

know in a few days if I should conclude to take his offer so as to prepare him for our trip."[83] But Reinhart received a message from Fillmore that his animals had been found with two horsethieves, so Rockwell's services were not needed. Reinhart was nonetheless somewhat surprised by his encounter.

Rockwell's next known recorded account, described by Hamilton Gardner in 1913, came in 1868: "During the close of the year 1868, Lehi was witness to one of the most diabolical crimes ever committed within her boundaries. On account of the White Pine mining boom, west of the city, considerable freighting was carried on with Lehi as the starting point. Among the miners who passed through were Harlem P. Swett and a man named Mayfield, together with a teamster whom they had hired in Salt Lake, Chauncy W. Millard. It later developed that Millard was a street Arab of New York, who, after a short service as a Union soldier, had drifted west in search of adventure. Passing south along the west side of the lake, the three men camped December 11 at the Stone House. Here Millard attempted to put into execution a fiendish scheme, which he had no doubt planned since joining his companions."[84]

The *Deseret News* of December 12 describes the incident as occurring "at about 1 p.m., not far from Lehi, on the west side of Jordan River."[85]

Gardner continues, "Securing possession of Mayfield's revolver, the depraved youth [Millard]   he was only 18 — cowardly shot Swett in the back as he sat unsuspectingly before the fire, killing him instantly. Turning his attention next to Mayfield, who was in the wagon just then searching for his revolver, Millard [the outlaw] fired point blank at him, but in some way barely missed his aim. Mayfield [the wagon owner] jumped from the wagon and fled for the lake, followed by Millard who emptied his revolver [at Mayfield] as he ran. One shot took effect in Mayfield's hand."[86]

The *Deseret News* reports, "The murderer . . . started off in the direction of Cedar Valley."[87]

Gardner continues, "Crossing the lake on the ice, the wounded man gained the present site of Murdock's resort, and from there managed to reach Lehi."[88]

The *News* elaborates that Millard, the killer, five days later on

December 17th, " . . . and about dark, reached the place of John Irvin, herder, near the Big Cedar Patch, about a mile and a half south of the road, going from Lehi to Fairfield. Upon arriving there he said he wanted a place to stop at for the winter; and as nothing was known of the murder at Irvin's he was permitted to remain. He stayed there till near sundown on Tuesday evening last, when he departed taking with him a horse, blanket, big coat, double-barreled shot gun and some ammunition, a spy glass and a loaf of bread, the property of Bro. Irvin, and rode off into the hills east, towards Utah Lake. In about half an hour, Bro. Irvin returned home from Fairfield, and learning of the departure of the stranger, he went in pursuit and tracked him as long as he could see. He then went to Lehi, where he obtained a fresh horse, fire arms, and three men to aid him in the pursuit of the fugitive . . . probability is, that by this time, he is captured."[89]

Millard's account is picked up the next day by the *News*. He was reported to have been seen "early on Wednesday morning . . . by a teamster from American Fork."[90]

Gardner continues, "Orrin Porter Rockwell, who was living in Lehi at this time, then took up the search. Rockwell was one of the most famous frontiersmen of his time and soon located Millard at a sheep ranch in Rush Valley. Upon being brought back to Lehi, the murderer freely confessed his crime and did not seem to feel at all sorry about it. Later he was taken to Provo and executed, while his victim, Swett, was buried in the Lehi cemetary. This crime, one of the worst ever committed in Lehi, aroused no little excitement.

"The execution proved what a human fiend Millard was. Selling his body to Doctor Roberts of Provo for a pound of candy, he calmly ate the sweets while sitting in the executioner's chair awaiting the fatal shot."[91]

At the execution the *Deseret News* January 29 concludes, "Four hundred persons were present, and order was observed."[92]

The following July Rockwell aided a Mr. Nelson from Hamilton, Nevada. Ten of Nelson's horses had been rustled by two hired hands. In desperation Nelson telegraphed ahead to Salt Lake City for assistance. Days later he "suddenly came upon them, and with the assistance of Porter Rockwell, succeeded in catching them."[93] Through the *Hamilton Empire,* Nelson congratulated "the Sheriff, police and citizens of this city generally for the efficient aid they rendered him in securing his property and the capture of the criminals."[94] Some if not most of that praise was directed towards Rockwell.

Three months later, October 4, 1869, Rockwell won an award. At the ninth annual Deseret Agricultural and Manufacturing Society exhibition in Salt Lake City he received $10 for the best one-year-old mule colt and $5 for the best four-year-old filly.[95]

A reason Rockwell possessed such superior stock was his attachment to the Wells Fargo Express Company. Along with other duties, he aided the company by protecting their stage line from Salt Lake City westward, and this connection offered him a source for prime horses. After a prize horse would become crippled, Porter would buy it for a small sum, then at his Skull Valley ranch would breed it, thus producing a remarkable strain of colts. Parenthetically, one of Porter's stallions was burned in a fire at Lehi in 1859, one of the first fires in the city.[96]

Through his adventures Rockwell possessed one attribute which won incalculable respect: He almost always managed to put aside his own plans to help others — even strangers — and in this regard he was showered with accolades.

He was also tenacious, as indicated by the next known recorded event in his life:

"The Overland Stage," reports the *Salt Lake Tribune*, "was . . . held up somewhere near Riverbed, on the western desert, and robbed of $40,000 in gold bullion from California."[97]

Rich and lively details of the incident come from an old man on the Faust Ranch, years later, who claims to have known Rockwell: "Port was sort of a special agent for the Overland Stage Company. It was in the summer of the sixties, which one I don't remember, that a telegram came along saying a large shipment of gold was coming through on a certain stage and the company wanted a special guard — they called them 'Bullion Guards' — to follow the shipment through. They notified Port he was to guard it from here . . .

"Port was a-waiting here when he saw the stage coming down from Lookout like a house afire, so he called to the holster and the driver to get ready. He strapped on an extra pistol, grabbed a rifle, and waited. The stage came right up to him and stopped all of a sudden and the driver called out, 'We been robbed.'

" 'Where?' Port asked.

" 'Back on River-bed flat.'

" 'How come? Ain't a place for a jack rabbit to hide there.' "

The driver of the stage then explained his story to Rockwell:

" 'When we came down off Dugway mountain we saw a lone horse standing out in the flat. When we got closer we saw a man laying in the dust along side the road. I stopped and called to him but got no answer, so called again but the man never moved; so I told Sam to get down and see if the man was dead. Well, when he turned the man over he came to life and had Sam covered with his revolver. Made Sam drop his guns and me throw mine down and then told me to toss the express box off to him. He shot the lock off, looked inside, smiled, and told me to drive on.'

"The stage went on east, but Port kept asking the remaining driver about the robber, his horse, his clothes and about a thousand other things. Port went to the house, took off his extra gun, mounted a horse, and rode west. Near sundown he got to Simpson, where he fed and watered his horse and got a bite to eat. Then he took a few biscuits to put in his saddle bags, filled his canteen with water, and rode on.

"Arriving at the place of the robbery about midnight he found the safe and the shooting irons. The stars were a-shining, but he had to wait till the moon got up to pick up the horse tracks. He had a habit of talking to himself or his horse when worried, so was a-saying, 'Now, Nig, if an' you and me had a-robbed that stage just where would we go to hide out?' "

Rockwell tracked the man down, then held him under surveillance for days, waiting for the outlaw to uncover his hidden gold. " . . . He knew the thief would have it buried some distance away just in case some one happened along." So Rockwell dared not charge the outlaw. He waited till the man uncovered his gold.

"Evening came and when the man went to bed Porter sneaked down the canyon . . . He staked his horse and walked down the canyon to wait. Morning came, and then he heard a horse coming up the trail.

"Well, he got the jump on that man and made him drop his gun. Then he took the bridle reins and tied the horse to a small tree, all the while keeping the thief covered with his gun and making him hold his hands high in the air."

As Porter tied him to the horse, "the thief kicked at him. Port let his gun fall on that shin bone, accidently on purpose, and as he raised up said, 'If an' you want to ride out of this canyon sitting up, best you be careful.' His hat had fallen off when he dodged that foot and his long hair fell down over his shoulders.

" 'Port Rockwell!' was all the surprised thief could say, and Port answered with, 'Who else did you think would come after you, some school marm?'

"Well, Port tied that man's feet together under the horse's belly, led the animal up to where his was, took a long stake rope, tied it to the horse and the other end to his saddle horn, and with the prisoner leading the way, they started out for Port's ranch on Government Creek.

"When they got there Port's hired man helped get the thief loose, remove the saddles, and then Port had him place the man's horse in the stable while his own was put in the pasture . . . They took the saddles in the house and started supper. When it was ready those two men ate like hungry coyotes.

"Supper over, Port dragged the man's saddle from under his bed, opened the saddlebags, and there was the gold still in the sacks with the seals not broken. He put these sacks and all the guns, except the one he carried, under a quilt on his bunk. Then he tied the prisoner's hands together behind his back, and removed the man's boots, tossed them under his bed with the saddles, motioned the prisoner to a bunk in the corner and told him to make himself comfortable.

"He took his hired man outside and told him he was very tired and asked if the man could watch the prisoner during the night. The man said he could, so Porter got a four-year-old club, put a chair just inside the door and told this man if the prisoner made any move, to wear the club out on him. Then Port flopped down on top of the bed, on top of the gold and the guns, and went to sleep. He woke once, but the prisoner was sleeping and the guard was awake, so he turned over and was dead to the world.

"Slowly he came to realize a horse was running somewhere. He jumped up. The prisoner was gone. The guard was asleep in his chair. Out to the pasture he went, caught his horse, saddled it up, got the gold, which he put in his saddlebags, and rode away while the guard still snored like a hog in its wallow."[98]

Another story indicates this robber was later seen wounded by a gunshot;[99] perhaps it was from Rockwell's firearm when the robber had fled.

The old man continues, "Up Rocky-ridge he [Rockwell] went and over the mountains . . . he slowed up not to leave a string of dust the prisoner could see. Into Vernon he rode . . . No one had seen a man fleeing with no boots on his feet and a quilt for a saddle. He lost a lot of time but picked up the tracks of the horse about a mile above town and followed them . . . towards Fairfield. It was getting dark, so he rode to the town. No one had seen the much-wanted man, and though the town was searched, they never found a thing.

"Port got a fresh horse and rode on to Salt Lake. He turned in the gold, and the officials wanted him to give up the chase, for all they cared for was the gold, but Port said he would 'never let no man' get away from him. He got another fresh horse and rode all over the valley but couldn't find anyone who had seen the prisoner.

"Two days later a message came for Port. It was one of those not sent from any station but what they call a 'jump message' sent from somewhere along the line. Don't know how it was done, but it came through and came from east of Salt Lake but west of Bridger. It bothered Port, for it kidded him about not being able to catch a man who had no boots and only a quilt for a saddle.

"Port insisted on going east, but the officials would not give him permission. So he took a month's layoff and went out between here and Bridger. Some days later another message came for Port — another 'jump message,' but this one came from east of Bridger. It told him he was a failure and bid him goodbye.

"Then one of those officials remembered a man who had worked for the company some months previous and how he was always experimenting with a homemade instrument. They were satisfied he was the man.

"Port never again heard from that man and returned home a disheartened, discouraged man, but he never gave up the chase, for wherever he went he was looking for the only man who ever got away from him."[100]

The old man then concludes that Rockwell never got it off his mind, and that it bothered him till his last day.[101]

Another account, describing probably the same outlaw, states that a man "came to our place riding a horse. He had a quilt for a saddle and never had no shoes nor hat, besides had a bullet wound in his leg [possibly from Rockwell] . . . Dad looked at his leg and wanted to get a doctor from Bridger, but he said he knew more than any doctor and would not let him get one.

"He stayed in the bunkhouse and got me to get him two pieces of wire about ten feet long. Then he took some kind of a thing from his pocket, fastened it to them wires, went to a telegraph pole, hooked the wires over the ones on the pole, and, durned if that thing didn't start perking. He listened some time, and when we went back to the cabin, he told Dad a lot of things; and Dad asked how he knew and he said he had been tapping the wires.

"You know he took that dingus and tried to teach me how to learn the alphabet by dots and dashes. Too much for me. Well, next day we went back to them wires and listened, and when the ticking stopped, he took hold of that thing and began to work it, smiling all the time. Said he was sending a message [presumably to Rockwell].

"Two or three days later, he got on his horse about sunset and rode away. I followed, for I wanted to see where he went. He rode beyond Bridger, set his contraption up, tapped a while, and came back to the ranch. That ride was too much for him. Next day Dad went to Bridger and got the doctor, but it was too late. Blood poison was all through his system. He talked a long time with Dad, and next morning he died . . . We buried him right alongside of them poles as carried the wires. Dad said he wanted it that way." Ironically, Rockwell never learned that his bullet had taken effect, and that in actuallity he did get his man.[102]

Another source claims the telegraphman never died, but that he telegraphed his sardonic message from Fort Bridger itself. When Rockwell learned of it he sped off to the fort, picked up the robber's trail, and followed him to Butte, Montana where he "got his man."[103]

Despite all the details, since the first two accounts come from the same writer, the entire episode may have been fictionalized.

The Vice-President of the United States, Schuyler Colfax, now visited Utah four years after his original visit. On October 3, 1869 he spoke to a crowd at West Temple Street. Seventeen years later his biographer reports the event: "[Colfax] expressed in plain language the American people's condemnation of the practice of polygamy, and of the generally exclusive non-American policy of the Mormon leaders ... The meeting was disturbed by Port Rockwell, a Mormon ruffian in liquor, who shouted occasionally: 'I never killed any one who didn't need killing.' "[104]

Five months later Porter found himself in one of several posses searching for Albert H. Haws, the murderer of Marshal William R. Storey.[105] The *Deseret News* reports, "We understand that O. Porter Rockwell was also out with a party of men in the direction of Simpson's Springs, it being thought that Haws might have gone in that direction."[106] A posse found the desperado; Haws refused arrest and found himself caught in a shoot-out; he killed two citizens and wounded another, then was himself shot and killed.

Porter returned to the ranch. His business interests, meanwhile, continued with mining. He laid a claim in August, 1870 to a 3,000-foot piece of property in the Ophir Mining District, and although it was in conjunction with several friends, it was titled the Rockwell Lode of the Rockwell Mining Company.[107] His friends apparently appreciated the prestige of co-ownership under his name.

Two months later in the *Salt Lake Herald* appears this tasty historical tidbit: "O. P. Rockwell was brought before Justice Clinton yesterday morning on a charge of drunkenness and disturbing the peace by an assault on the bar-keeper of the Salt Lake House on Friday evening. He was bound over in $500 to keep the peace."[108] What instigated the assault is a mystery, but one may assume a reference was made to his "murders."

Finding moments to pursue his other interests, Rockwell began courting a woman twenty-five years his junior. In 1871 — or possibly 1870 — he married the thirty-four-year-old Christine Olsen, his house-keeper.

Then, the following spring, came the launch of an all new anti-Mormon movement. Brigham Young was again arrested . . . this time for "lewd" conduct.

The puritanical church leader — who in fact had initially found problems facing the prospects of practicing polygamy years earlier — was now labeled a law-breaker for participating in such lewdness.

Famed eastern reporter George Alfred Townsend of the pen name "Gath," having gained pre-eminence as a nationally-noted Civil War correspondent, came to Utah to investigate the church and society. Because of fellow newspapermen's reports, Townsend expected to find a wild, weird, sectarian world, with civilization all but vanished amongst a dark, evil district of dangerous, religious fanatics, but in his investigations he surprisingly discovered, "Human life in Utah is safer than probably anywhere in civilization. The motives and causes of murder exist in a less degree — as avarice, liquor, gambling, quarrelsomeness and prostitution. The industrious political vagabonds who write letters from Utah to the East have created the band of 'Danites' and other hob-goblins out of air and foolscap.

"I talked to Porter Rockwell, the alleged leader of the 'Danites,' a fat, curly-haired, good-natured chap, fond of a drink, a talk, and a wild venture. The United States authorities have several times used him to make arrests of lawless characters."[109] Townsend's report was dated October 27, 1871 to the *Cincinnati Commercial.*

Townsend was also amused by the federal officials infesting the territory. Among them, for example, was J. H. Taggart, United States Assessor: "a person who was bitten by a dog some time ago, and charged the bite to Mormon assassins."[110] Another of Townsend's victims for barbs was O.J. Hollister, United States Collector: "Hollister deluges Eastern press, from Chicago to New York, with letters of locums picked up at hearsay, and hardly reliable enough for a comic paper."[111] He also adroitly analyzed Associate Justice S. C. M. Hawley, who "bores people on the streets by reading his long opinions to them. He nearly made O. P. Morton a polygamist lately by reading to him opinions the other way."[112] Not last on his list was Hawley, Jr., the "son of the aforesaid, a weakish, flop-whiskered, insubstantial young man who ... was arrested by the city police and confined two hours; he now has a suit against the [city] corporation for twenty-five thousand dollars damages, and one of the usual packed juries may award it." (See Note 39 for further details on the federáles' treatment of Mormons, and for additional trenchant Townsend commentary.)

But at his trial, Brigham was released.

Then a new surge of anti-Mormonism was launched. After several weeks on the manhunt, Marshal Sam Gilson finally snared Bill Hickman at a cabin west of Nephi. All Gilson desired actually was a statement from Hickman implicating Mormon Church leaders to his murders, and for this cooperation Gilson would wield necessary influence to aid Hickman in the outcome of his trial. Gilson's strategy was to use one main crime of Hickman's on which to pin the Prophet ... the murder of Richard Yates during Johnston's War.[113]

After the deal was struck, Gilson took Hickman before a judge, then transported him to Camp Douglas.

In his first two weeks in jail Hickman wrote the "confession." A grand jury was assembled at the camp, and the confession was laid before anxious eyes. Two weeks later Mayor Daniel H. Wells of Salt Lake City and attorney Hosea Stout were arrested. William H. Kimball was also arrested for an alleged involvement in the Aiken case.[114] Brigham Young was jointly indicted with Kimball,[115] but was out of town on an annual journey to Southern Utah. The Prophet's case would be reviewed upon his return in March.

Wells was freed on $50,000 bail, but Stout and Kimball were denied bail and imprisoned at Camp Douglas with Hickman.

George Bean and Porter Rockwell saw the inevitable, and volunteered for service as official church guardians to protect church leaders from the witch hunt, which, as Bean describes, was "under the old Sectarian 'Bigot' Judge James B. McKean ... from Vermont. He had been fed on the vicious falsehoods concerning the Mormons and was here to 'clean the platter' and establish a new form of government as to his liking. It fired some of us to action when he permitted falsehoods to bring fine men and even Brigham Young to trial. It kept some of us busy at times to keep the brethren out of the clutches of his merciless Myrmidons. Many of the brethren had to be guarded safely through and between settlements and again O. P. Rockwell and George W. Bean [referring to himself] were on duty. Many other brethren offered and quietly guarded our innocent leaders."[116]

Bill Hickman's charges against Brigham were countered by Daniel W. Jones. During the Utah War, Hickman had presumably murdered Yates, then ridden into Jones' camp. "Hickman killed Yates for his money and horse the same as any other thief and murderer would have done, and then excused himself by telling he was counseled to do these things. I know positively that Governor Young's orders were to avoid bloodshed in every possible way."[117]

Newspaperman Alfred Townsend formulated his own ideas about Hickman: " ... a Judas ... a Missouri border ruffian ... a human hyena,"[118] whose reports could not be trusted.

Meanwhile, prosecutor R. N. Baskin pushed for Brigham's earlier trial to be convened, and he demanded Brigham to appear in court immediately or lose $5,000 bond, a substantial sum even for Brigham's kingdom. Immediately, Rockwell galloped south and scoured the countryside for the Prophet.

On December 20th Rockwell found him at Cedar City. In a race against time they launched north towards Salt Lake City the same day. Brigham had only until January 9th to return or lose the $5,000.

On the trip north they came across General Connor, who again proved to be an ally to the Saints. This claim came from a member of Brigham's party, contrary to widely-held views Connor frightened Brigham and that Brigham wished for the man's "assassination," as purported by Hickman in his "confessions" book. In fact, Connor now offered at least $100,000 additional bail for Brigham, if needed, according to Brigham's Manuscript History.[119] Also, according to A. M. Musser, a witness at the scene, Connor even agreed to not mention seeing Brigham on his journey so the judge could not construe any possibility Connor coerced Brigham to appear in court. Connor knew it would help the Prophet's case if he would appear solely on his own accord.[120]

When the church president was led by Rockwell into Salt Lake City, "Naturally," reports the *Salt Lake Herald,* "they took a good look at his countenance." They could not believe it was actually Brigham Young, returned so soon from southern Utah. According to Whitney, he "had come through tempests and torrents and snow-slides, a distance of nearly four hundred miles, to show the little terriers who had been barking at him, that . . . he had faith in the ultimate verdict of the people . . . "[121]

And his faith proved remarkable. Three months later, in a landmark decision, the U. S. Supreme Court nullified all indictments handed down the previous year and a half against over 135 Saints, freeing Brigham Young, Wells, Kimball, and Stout. Unfortunately for the Saints, Bill Hickman's slate was also wiped clean, and whether or not he continued murdering at random is not recorded, but what is known is the pathetic, self-induced paranoia of which he now seemed possessed. Traveling author John Codman reports in 1879 an eyewitness account: "As we drove out of the town [Camp Floyd] the driver pointed to a seedy-looking vagabond, apparently sixty years of age, who was walking slowly along, smoking his morning pipe. The expression of his countenance was truly diabolical, and betokened a scoundrel whose society one would instinctively avoid. This was the notorious Bill Hickman, whose residence is in the neighborhood.

"Why the fiend is permitted to live is a mystery. His confessions of bloody deeds, if true, should expose him to the vengeance of Gentiles whose friends he has slain; if false, the wonder is that he is not riddled by Mormon bullets [Codman, an Easterner, was still under the popular assumption that the church officially disposed of its enemies]. It is a mark of the astonishing forbearance of this people that, believing him to be a malignant liar, they allow him to go about the country unmolested, and the only accountable reason for his safety from the wrath of the Gentiles is, that they hope at some future day to use him as a witness to prove the murders committed by him at the bidding of the church. But the troubled conscience of the desperado is never at ease. He must have revelations, and terrible ones too; he must have angel visits at night, for the angels of darkness must hover around his unquiet bed, and hell must yawn at its side. He walks the streets by day armed with two revolvers and a belt of cartridges, looking furtively about him to see if some avenger is not nigh. He steeps his damning memory in rum, yet dares not drink himself totally insensible, lest, if found dead drunk away from home, he should never wake again. So fearful is he of a surprise that he never enters a bar-room where other men are present without standing with his back to the bar when the liquor is poured out for him. And thus he lives in a continual hell."[122]

That hell continued another eleven years, until Hickman died of natural causes August 21, 1883 at Lander City, Wyoming.

After seeing Hickman, Codman continues, "Happily he soon passed out of our minds, as after a short drive across the plains we came to a slight elevation, from which, in the distance, we could see the pretty town of Lehi, not far from the northern bank of Utah Lake."

Rockwell claimed Lehi as his own, enjoying both the beauty and the quaintness of the small Mormon town, and from both there and Salt Lake City he continued his gunslinging. Because of his ever-growing legend, a song was written by an anonymous lyricist, to the tune of *Solomon Levi*:

Have you heard of Porter Rockwell?
He's the Mormon triggerite.
They say he hunts for horse thieves
When the moon is shining bright.
So I'll tell you what to do,
Get the drop on Porter Rockwell,
Or he'll get the drop on you.

They say that Porter Rockwell
Is a scout for Brigham Young—
He's hunting up the unsuspects
That haven't yet been hung.
So if you steal one Mormon girl
I'll tell you what to do,
Get the drop on Porter Rockwell
Or he'll get the drop on you.[123]

Another anonymously-written song also emerged:

> *Old Porter Rockwell has work to do,*
> *So he saddles his sorrel and rides away;*
> *And those who are watching wonder who*
> *Will be a widow at break of day.*
> *The waiting wife in the candle light,*
> *Starts up as she hears a wild hoof-beat,*
> *Then shrinks in terror as down the night*
> *Comes the wailing of Port's dread war cry, 'Wheat!'*

> *Wheat!*
> *She looks at her babes and tries to pray,*
> *For she knows she's a widow and orphans are they.*

> *Old Port Rockwell looks like a man,*
> *With a beard on his face and his hair in a braid,*
> *But there's none in the West but Brigham who can*
> *Look in his eyes and not be afraid.*
> *For Port is a devil in human shape,*
> *Though he calls himself 'Angel,' says vengeance is sweet;*
> *But he's black, bitter death, and there's no escape*
> *When he wails through the night his dread war cry,*
> *'Wheat!'*

> *Wheat!*
> *Somewhere a wife with her babes kneels to pray,*
> *For she knows she's a widow and orphans are they.*[124]

Backing up the ballads were myriads of legends. In one account an ex-miner simply refers to a gory gun battle in which the victim recovered sufficiently to spend his remaining days mining diamonds. W. G. Tittsworth left history with merely a brief report of the miner: "Hank Langford, from Park City, Utah, who was in camp, hale and hearty, after being disemboweled on the streets of Salt Lake City by Porter Rockwell, one of Brigham Young's notorious destroying angels, also found a few, smaller, inferior stones."[125] No elaboration by Tittsworth.

In an 1878 issue of the *Salt Lake Tribune* comes another fascinating report of Rockwell: " . . . on the road to Camp Floyd, there is a deep well, where there was, in early days, a stage station. This place he firmly believed to be haunted by evil spirits, who delighted in bringing trouble upon him or his horses every time he passed . . . As an explanation of all this, Porter told his hired men that in the old well five or six men had been buried years ago . . . [presumably placed there by Rockwell himself, after gunning them down]."[126]

In his autobiography, James T. Harwood reports a new angle of stories, the fibre from which Rockwell's legend now took on almost biblical proportions:

"The year that the railroad reached Lehi, and when I was twelve years old, Porter Rockwell met a man whom he had quarreled with in a saloon near my father's harness shop. This man emptied every chamber of his six-shooter at Porter, and the balls splattered all around him, but not one touched him."[127]

This launched a whole new category of legends — those involving the supernatural. In these stories Rockwell receives a shining distinction, setting him apart from other renowned gunfighters: Wyatt Earp, Bat Masterson, and Doc Holladay never had the spice of *divine intervention* laced with their legends.

Rockwell's were not only divine, they were numerous. Like other aspects of his life, however, the accounts actually recorded were scarce. While such stories still slosh about verbal swap meets among old-timers in Utah, the only known newspaper-written inference of his Samson-like qualities comes years later by a reporter in a 1924 *Salt Lake Tribune* article: "All were intrigued by the matter of the long hair and the reputed supernatural immunity from bullets."[128]

One actual story comes from John Everett, an old friend of Rockwell's interviewed in 1934: "A man named Dave Debble pulled a six-shooter on Porter and at close range emptied his gun with intent to kill. Debble was known to be a good shot, but Porter was unscratched. The incident so upset Debble that he fled from the saloon. He warned his friends later to never attempt to shoot Rockwell for he could not be hit."[129]

Another journal story claims the immunity came as a result of the promise of Joseph Smith. The incident occurred "one evening about dusk in his 'Buck Board Wagon.' He used this kind of travel often. As they came to 7 miles pass, Porter left father with the outfit while he went inside the way station on an errand. Father heard loud noises —the door burst open and out came Porter with his hands raised yelling to the top of his voice. He was backing out of the small store or bar. Someone was shooting at Porter. Father could see the stabs of fire going right past Porter's body. Some of them went through the spokes of the buggy or 'Buck Board.' Porter came to the buggy and took out his rifle. (He seldom carried his firearms.) Porter had gone in to see if anyone had seen this man he was after. It was the Very man, an outlaw, he was seeking. Strangely enough, he shot at the man going up the hill as he ran away. Porter killed the man instantly, but not one bullet struck Porter."[130]

Still another tale has Rockwell facing a gang of ambushing outlaws, who, upon seeing their weapons were useless against him, galloped off in fright. Afterwards, when Porter shook his coat, bullets dropped onto the ground like a grundle of dead lice. Witnesses spread the story with relish, but even before the story could travel far, he would emerge from still other miraculous gun battles; and thus the stories swept Zion.

One account displaying his ingenuity more than his miraculous protection occurred at the Point of the Mountain. A *Tribune* reporter interviewed several old-timers who knew of the incident:

" . . . at a certain gathering of rough characters in one of the little towns on the southern [Mexican] border . . . a wager was laid touching hair and invulnerability. The idea challenged the assemblage . . . A pistol notched for Rockwell would be . . . highly prized . . .

"A certain ambitious daredevil . . . set forth on the long trail from the southland to Utah to interview the famous Rockwell and find out by direct methods the truth regarding the long hair.

"As Rockwell was one day riding out from Salt Lake City toward his Skull valley ranch, he was accosted . . .

" 'Are you Mr. Rockwell?'

"The stranger leaned forward gracefully on the horn of his saddle upon hearing the affirmative answer.

" 'Thought so,' he said easily. 'Say, I've heard tell that as long as you don't cut your hair no bullet can touch you. Is that true?'

"Rockwell answered with a bewildered grunt.

"At that instant the stranger jerked out a .45 Colt's cap and ball pistol from its holster and pointed it at Rockwell. The surprised old man was taken completely off his guard. The stranger's face had suddenly grown hard.

" 'Well,' he said grimly. 'I've come clear from California t' kill you.'

"[For Rockwell] to draw now was suicide. He had been covered before the idea of danger entered his head. The average man, paralyzed with fright and surprise, would simply have shuddered and taken what was coming to him. But, quick as Rockwell's hands were, his wits were quicker.

" 'You wouldn't try to shoot a man without a cap on your pistol, would you?'

" . . . the killer grimaced at his gun, held out to kill, to see if all caps were in place.

"Just the briefest hesitation.

"But in that split second Rockwell's hand . . . flashed to his own weapon . . . The would-be murderer suddenly jerked tense, a surprised expression over-spreading his face. The heavy revolver slipped out of his nerveless grasp, and he presently slumped gently down out of his saddle to the ground."[131]

Susan Trane of Lehi, Utah relates to her grandson a first-hand incident with the lawman:

"One night there was a knock come on the door and this man hurried in and it was Porter Rockwell. Somebody was chasing him. Remember that Joseph Smith gave him a blessing that as long as he kept his hair long nothing would bother him. So these men were chasing him — I think it was three or four white people — to cut his hair. So he rode his horse into my grandmother's father's

place. And you know they used to wear those long dresses — so
they [the women of the home] let Porter in and they dressed him
up as a woman and these three women went out to the well to get
some water and then they went and poured some for the horses,
and they had [with them] Porter dressed in one of these dresses, so
then they give him a fresh horse and put him out the other way
and he left and those people [the white pursuers] stayed there
pretty near all night waiting for him to come out of the house."[132]

Glen Trane of Lehi relates a fascinating account from his
grandmother: "The Indians respected him because they couldn't
kill him. Indians tried to shoot at him but they couldn't hit him
because he was promised in that blessing that a bullet would never
strike him . . . So the Indians tried to shoot him but they couldn't
do it and he'd shoot those Indians. And then [eventually] when the
Indians would see that Porter was driving stage they left him
alone."[133]

Rockwell was also reputed with "a sharpening of the senses
until they were the equal of any Indian's."[134] And he was described
as having "passed through dangers, unscathed, as numerous as
those recorded in the most lurid fiction. He had a natural and
uncanny instinct in following the trails of law breakers. Where
other men could hardly see a trail with the horses at a walk, Porter
could follow at a gallop."[135]

In another analysis: "His senses and instincts were sharpened
so that he could see signs which did not exist to others."[136]

One revealing portrait — although inaccurate to an extent —
was a *Tribune* report: "Among other eccentricities, he had a habit
of whispering when talking with close friends. Except when in his
cups with some crony, he seldom spoke to anyone [by contrast,
most reports indicate him extroverted and notoriously gregarious],
and then his voice was high-pitched, reaching a squeak in
moments of intense excitement. The startling quality of his hoarse,
shrill tones had the invariable effect of unnerving an opponent in a
showdown. This quality together with his incomparable ability to
read tracks, his shrewd strategy, his faculty for noticing everything,
his tireless persistence, and the painstaking care with which he
built up his infallible calculations [in which he] prepared against
every possible contingency, made his success as a hunter of

outlaws proverbial."[137]

Such is Rockwell, the legend.

Among fellow townspeople, some watched him with a raised eyebrow. Reports one, "Old Port was a good neighbor, a picturesque, stately rider. Having heard stories my home folk were a little leery of our neighbor, but for me, I thought he was just fine.

"Despite his long hair neatly done up at the back, and . . . aside from his fondness for whiskey, I was glad to hear my conservative father's comment: 'After all, Old Port is, was, and will be always loyal to the kingdom.' "[138]

Pioneer researcher on Rockwell, Nicholas Van Alfen, after interviewing numerous old-timers, records in 1938: "His circle of friends is large and includes both gentile and Mormon. Some of his neighboring ranchers at Skull Valley were gentiles . . . but Porter received their hearty support."[139] Van Alfen further defends Rockwell as "taking the part of the people in this grim struggle of society vs. chaotic banditry. The same struggle that was being carried on in every other frontier community of the West. Porter carried it on with no more nor less callousness and hardness than was necessary in any other region . . .

"William Slade began his career in Montana by tying his victim to a corral post and between every swallow of whiskey would send a slug through one of the legs . . . Either before or after the man was dead Slade cut his ears off and carried them the rest of his life in his vest pockets as a souvineer. After a long career of crime the vigilantes made him a guest at one of their frequent entertainments [by hanging him] . . .

"[But] Salt Lake City never had organized vigilante groups. Regular judicial proceedings were followed here sooner . . . And as Porter viewed the situation, it is evident that he believed it needed more the flavor of vigilante tactics. However, in a modified form, he would bring his victim back to be legally tried — if he offered no resistence. In the case of resistence he seemed to have neither the patience nor would he take the chance, so he brought these in with their toes turned up."[140]

After analyzing Rockwell's life he concludes: " . . . these cases were always in the performance of his duty as an officer of the law. Notwithstanding the many attempts of Rockwell's critics to slander him, there is not a single proof of him ever having taken a life wantonly."[141]

From early Twentieth Century interviews Rockwell is further described as "hated and feared by the criminals, because he could shoot faster, ride faster, fight better and track them to the remotest corners of the deserts . . . "[142]

Additionally, he "never used a rope."[143] Not surprisingly, " . . . these murder accusations did not find their origin in the citizens who continually depended on Porter to return their stolen stock and rid them of the scourges of outlawry."[144]

(Other anecdotes and comments about Rockwell are in Note 40.)

From his third wife, Rockwell now fathered their first child, Irene (apparently named after his grandmother), born July 27, 1872. But the child died the same day.[145]

Displaying the complexities of human relationships, Brigham's brotherhood with Rockwell remained boundless. In his family journal Murray Averett reports on Brigham's annual trip to Southern Utah: "Porter Rockwell was along for a bodyguard to Brigham, and while at Pipe on the way back Port got rather drunk, and as they left Pipe Brigham and the driver of the team were sitting in the front seat looking solemly ahead and Port was shouting and waving his hat . . . "[146]

Despite his inadequacies, Brigham found the man a reliable church emissary. After the above incident in the summer of 1873, " . . . the First Presidency called us [George W. Bean and Porter] to proceed as soon as possible into Grass Valley and gather up and colonize the straggling bands of natives in that vicinity. The Presidency advised us to teach them honesty, industry, morality, and religion so far as they can understand . . . "

Meanwhile, about the time their church call came, Rockwell's next child was born, June 3, 1873, and she was named Elizabeth Christine.[147]

Before launching his church-assigned journey, the rugged missionary/mountaineer found himself battling with the federal government — or more specificallly — the Treasury Department. They owed him $1,310.63 for his services, he claimed, and through his attorney, J. D. T. McAllister, he authorized bankers in

Washington to collect the money. Rockwell's letter of authorization was dated June 22, 1873, and with the help of associates in Washington, the bankers acted and the Treasury Department complied.[148]

By August Porter's preliminary affairs were settled and he found himself journeying south on his mission with George W. Bean. One who knew the missionaries personally, Peter Gottfredson, records, "these men with some of their sons and some others including the noted Porter Rockwell commenced operations in Grass Valley."[149] Bean contributes more details: "By August 1st we began the move south, with our boys, teams, tools and accompanied by Orrin Porter Rockwell and son and a gentile named Clark."[150] After establishing a settlement at Cedar Grove in Grass Valley, complete with a sawmill and hay-producing facilities, "We had visitors from various places," reports Bean, "as the fame of Grass Valley was spreading abroad,"[151] due, no doubt in no small measure, to the efforts of Rockwell.

Porter probably spent several months in Ceder Grove — until a certain incident occurred. When four Indians attempted stealing horses, two white farm boys killed three Braves and wounded the fourth.[152] Repercussions were expected and Rockwell left.

"All the whites left Grass Valley,"[153] according to Gottfredson, except four men and some family. Rockwell was not listed among those remaining. Nor does Bean's journal mention him again. After all their efforts on the assignment, Bean returned to Provo within only three months. By early 1874 Bean learned he was not allowed to return to Grass Valley, "owing to the killing of some Navajo Indians down on Otter Creek."[154]

For the next four years, Rockwell's life is a mystery. While Bean continued his missionary labors — where he and an associate "devoted ourselves to serving the Indians in assisting to open their farm at Greenwich"[155] — Rockwell likely continued sporadic missionary efforts elsewhere under Brigham's direction, but for the most part probably pursued mining and ranching concerns, interspersed with law enforcement opportunities.

During this period, two other recorded Rockwell killing-incidents occurred. Of one incident the report simply states, "He brought back two bad men, they were brothers. He delivered them home to their mother. They were both dead in his buckboard."[156]

The other account states that four men held up and beat a baggage man. Rockwell was hired by Union Pacific to track them down. Riding out alone, he returned with all four desperadoes, one of them badly wounded and the other three "pale with death."[157]

History's next known record of Rockwell is in 1877, during a speech of Brigham Young's regarding Rockwell's love for mining. Delivered June 17 at Farmington, Utah, the Prophet teasingly chides his old comrade: "Porter, as we generally call him, came to me one day, saying, 'They have struck within four inches of my lode, what shall I do?' He was carried away with the idea that he must do something [to protect his gold discovery from being taken away]. I therefore told him to go with the other brethren interested, and make his claim. When he got through talking, I said to him, 'Porter you ought to know better; you have seen and heard things which I have not [referring to mutual dealings with Joseph Smith, of supernatural experiences they had mutually witnessed], and are a man of long experience in this church. I want to tell you one thing; they may strike within four inches of that lode as many times as they have a mind to, and they will not find it.' They hunted and hunted, hundreds of them did; and I had the pleasure of laughing at him a little, for when he went there again, he could not find it himself."[158]

Five weeks later, on July 24, 1877, the 28th anniversary of the Saints' arrival in the valley, Rockwell bought mining property from Henry J. Faust,[159] and three weeks later from Seth Fletcher, for a total of $8,000.[160]

As he was getting along in years, an eccentric streak began making its way into Rockwell's psyche: The aging gunfighter for some reason purportedly bought two giant red stagecoaches.[161]

Also due to his age, not many of Porter's old cronies still kicked about, so when Brigham took ill with cholera, Rockwell saw the inevitable handwriting on the wall: On August 29, 1877, the old Prophet passed away.

Rockwell then saw other old friends coming back into the limelight. John D. Lee had recently been found guilty by an all-Mormon jury for his participation in the Mountain Meadows

Massacre 19 years earlier, and was now executed by firing squad March 23, 1877. And then Rockwell found enemies targeting in on yet other old friends ... those not so guilty:

Church enemies weaved together a remarkably bold grand jury which cooperated with almost every indictment its perpetrators sought; they dug up old crimes from bar-room story-tellers and even pulled aging Mormons out of retirement for trial. Despite the lack of witnesses and passage of time, they manufactured some fairly interesting cases: Old Jeter Clinton, for example, a staunch, old Mormon and former justice of the peace, was the first to be arrested. He was now accused of murder from 25 years earlier! Two years passed with his prosecutors struggling to nail him, when U. S. Attorney Philip T. Van Zile finally conceded there was insufficient evidence, and his case was dismissed.

And then Porter was arrested ...

XVI

Porter Rockwell was officially accused of murdering John Aiken in the alleged disappearance of Aiken and party 19 years earlier.[1] (See Note 27 for details.)

Included in the indictment was Sylvanus Collett, Porter's "co-partner" in crime. The day after Porter's arrest, his self-defined nemesis, the *Salt Lake Tribune*, reports September 20, 1877: "Thus another one of the red-handed many of the Mormon Church stands a show of being dealt with according to law, twenty years after the commission of the crime of which he is accused. And this gives the Mormon dress another chance to howl at the Government officers for meddling with 'one of our best society . . . '"[2]

The *Tribune* further reports he was "sent to the penitentiary for safe keeping." Six days later Porter received restricted freedom. The October 6 *Tribune* reports: "Judge Emerson admitted O. Porter Rockwell to bail yesterday, fixing his bonds at $15,000. The surities are Sam McIntyre, J. A. Cunningham, and Orin Dix."[3] The *Tribune* later reports, " . . . his attorneys, Messrs. Tilford and Hagan, never could draw out of Rockwell so much as an intimation of his true relations to the crime, or a hint as to who took part in it. All he would say was, 'Wheat! Wheat!' And therefore [the *Tribune* felt Rockwell was covering up facts] it was a characteristic of his that he was true to his friends."[4]

The *Tribune* in still a different issue reports Rockwell "was to be tried at the next September term of Judge Emerson's court,"[5] but adds, " . . . it is extremely doubtful whether a jury could have been empaneled that would convict him on proof of the crime charged."[6]

On October 13, 1877, Porter found himself in court with his brother, Horace, over an entangled series of trades involving steers, saddles, manual labor, and promissory notes. In the settlement the court declared Porter owing Horace $1,270.57.[7]

Then, in January, three months after his arrest, at the age of 65, Rockwell conceived his twelfth and last child, Ida May, who would be born October 4, 1878.[8]

During this period Rockwell "was a large owner of horses and horned stock, owned three ranches, two in Rush and one in Skull Valley, and was worth from $25,000 to $30,000," according to the *Tribune*.[9] An interesting side note is the report that he now "usually dressed in Brigham's homespun, and wore a faded felt hat turned up at both sides."[10]

For the sake of convenience, according to the *Deseret News,* he was living in his [downtown Salt Lake City] Colorado Stable "which he had been using for some time past, while selling stock."[11]

Then shocking news finally hit the streets — and with an impact that stunned Zion — but it was the news for which his enemies had been drooling for decades . . . the news that would spread throughout the territory like wildfire . . .

On June eleventh, 1878, the following article appears in the *Salt Lake Tribune*: "Rockwell was at the theatre on Saturday evening in a state of intoxication" [being an evening of culture, it's likely Porter was in fact perfectly sober — he generally drank only among fellow drinkers, and "society" in this era — those who attended cultural events — were predominately active Mormon]. The *Tribune* further claims — possibly with accuracy, possibly not — that, "When the play was over he spent several hours about town and in the saloons." And then comes his enemies' long-awaited report: "the hostler in charge of the Colorado says it was between 12 and 1 o'clock that night before Porter came in and got to bed. On Sunday morning he complained of being cold, and soon afterwards was seized with a fit of vomiting. He kept his bed all day and talked quite freely, though never intimated that he thought his time had come. About 5 p.m., he was seized with another fit of nausea and chill, and . . . he insisted on getting up. He sat on the side of his bunk and put on his shoes; then he fell back and almost instantly expired . . .

"On Sunday evening the news spread rapidly among the citizens that Porter Rockwell had died suddenly at 6 o'clock p.m. in the Colorado stables on First East street in this city. Immediately a large crowd of people went to the place designated, and sure enough, there, in a little dark room, on a couch of blankets, [he] lay . . .

"Dr. Douglas and others had been making an effort to resusitate [him] . . . but it was no use.[12]

The *Deseret News* reports at this point in the evening, "We understand that his family, who reside on the Rockwell ranche, in Rush Valley, were at once sent for."[13]

The *Salt Lake Herald* adds, "His funeral will take place on Wednesday afternoon at 2 o'clock, from the 14th ward assembly rooms, his remains in the meantime being taken care of by Sexton Taylor."[14]

Because of Rockwell's notoriety, the *Tribune* adds, "A post mortem examination was made . . . and it was found that he died from natural causes."[15] Presenting more details than the *Tribune* version is the *Herald's* account: "At the request of the relatives of Porter Rockwell, a post mortem examination was held on his body last evening, conducted by Drs. Benedict and Williamson, in the presence of Drs. Douglass and Thompson. The result of the examination shows that Mr. Rockwell 'came to his death by a failure of the heart's action, caused by a suspension of the nervous power. There were no evidences of injury, nor any symptoms of poisoning.'

"Immediately after the result had been ascertained Coroner Taylor impanneled a jury to hold an inquest over the deceased. The jurors were Hamilton G. Park, John W. Snell and B. H. Young, who rendered a verdict in accordance with the facts as brought forth at the examination."[16]

The day after the autopsy, Orrin Porter Rockwell was buried.

The *Herald* editorializes, "He is said to have been the oldest member of the church up to the time of his death; and has ever figured prominently in the trials and hardships endured by the early members of the church ... he was the worst enemy that cattle thieves have ever had in Utah, and that had it not been for the fear they entertained for him the number of their depredations would have been much greater. He had many personal friends, to whom it was a characteristic of his to remain true and firm. His history is prominently associated with the early history of the west."[17]

The *Tribune* publishes a different epitaph: "Brutal in his instincts, lawless in his habits, and a fanatical devotee of the Prophet, the commands of this gloomy despot he received as the will of the Lord, and with the ferocity born of mistaken zeal, he grew to believe that the most acceptable service he could render the Almighty, was, as Lear expressed it, to 'kill, kill, kill, kill, kill!'

" ... Death steps in to save these destroyers of their race from the penalty they so richly deserve, but their evil deeds live after them, and of this aged criminal it can be truly said:

" 'He left a name at which the world grows pale,
" 'To paint a moral and adorn a tale.' "

The *Tribune* finally notes, "The funeral of Porter Rockwell was numerously attended, yesterday ... [June 12, 1878]"[18]

But then came a speech that shattered the still air. One of the church's Twelve Apostles, Joseph F. Smith, son of Hyrum and destined to become the future Prophet and President of the church, spoke at the funeral service, and what he proclaimed stunned those present. While angering church enemies, his words simultaneously provided a certain degree of, perhaps a surprising amount of, relief to those who knew and admired the lawman. In the sermon Smith proverbially pounded his fist to the pulpit: "They say he was a murderer; if he was, he was the friend of Joseph Smith and Brigham Young, and he was faithful to them, and to his covenants, and he has gone to heaven and Apostates will go to hell."

The Smith proclamation, of course, rose the hackles on a few hundred necks. The Saints no doubt smiled. Some amused, some for joy. In the sermon Smith summarizes, "He led a useful life, and take him all in all, he was an ornament to the Church."[19]

In reaction, the *Tribune* labeled the Apostle's sermon "a fitting tribute of one outlaw to the memory of another."[20]

Five days later the *Tribune* was still bitter over the funeral address, charging Elder Smith's discourse "entirely unprogressive and behind the times."[21]

The *Tribune* eventually published more of the Apostle's sermon, with more details of the text, including the most revealing semi-official church statement yet on Rockwell, as the deceased bodyguard to Joseph Smith and Brigham Young was now "eulogized as a true Latter-day Saint, who had kept his covenants faithfully and earned the reward of eternal life. The only fault which could be charged against the . . . deceased, was that he had a weakness for [whiskey], while his virtues were a life of devotion to the interests of the kingdom of God and earth . . .

"Porter Rockwell was yesterday afternoon ushered into heaven clothed with immortality and eternal life, and crowned with all the glory which belongs to a departed Saint. 'He had his little faults,' said Joe [Joseph F. Smith], 'but Porter's life on earth, taken altogether, was one worthy of example, and reflected honor upon the church. Through all his trials he had never once forgotten his obligations to his brethren and his God.' "[22]

And thus with a sermon ends the saga of one of the guttiest gunmen in American history, and with it an era of controversy, the taming of a frontier, a barrel of gunpowder, and a few roses.

Notes

Note 1

[From page 5]

Family Branches

From the *Deseret News,* August 31, 1935:

"In the Church Genealogical archive is being deposited a pedigree of fifteen pages containing the names of 180 of his progeniters. A glance over this shows him to be a close relative of many leading families of the Church. His father was Orin Rockwell . . . the son of James Rockwell, one of the well-known Rockwell family of Windsor, Connecticut, descended from Deacon William Rockwell of Dorchester, England, the emigrant to America. Through the Norton line he is connected with President Wilford Woodruff, and through the Wells with President Daniel H. Wells. On the Alford line he becomes a distant relative of President

Rudger Clawson, and through the Lathrap with the Prophet Joseph, Wilford Woodruff, and many others.

"His father's mother was Irene Porter ... She was descended from John Porter, and Ann White, progenitors of the prophet; Thomas Stanley, ancestor of President Woodruff; and from the Babcock, Curtis, Gay, Richards, Raymond, Ladd, Knowlton, Harris and Abbott lines. As you read this, many of you will find your ancestors are also those of Porter Rockwell. He was a distant cousin of Abraham Lincoln through the Gillman line which they had in common; with President U. S. Grant and Grover Cleveland through the Porter line; Senator William H. King and Porter Rockwell are both descended from good old Deacon Edmund Rice and Thomas King. The prophet, Brigham Young, and he were all descended from the selfsame Merriam line.

"The mother of Porter Rockwell was Sarah Witt ... She was born Sept. 9, 1781 at Belchertown, Hampshire county, Massachusetts, the daughter of Ivory Witt and Abigail Montague. Ivory Witt was descended from four generations of John Witts. His mother was Sarah Ivory, whose pedigree is probably traced seven generations back to about the year 1476 in Offley, Hertfordshire, England. An excellent record of the Montague family has been searched out and printed. Abigail Montague, wife of Ivory Witt and grandmother of Orrin Porter Rockwell, was the daughter of Josiah Montague and Abigail Montague, both descended from John Montague, and his wife, Hannah Smith. Other families on the line are the Church, Churchill, Cowles, and Dickinson lines."

Note 2

[From page 12]

Governor Dunklin Creates a Snowball

The governor advised the Saints to try the law against those who would threaten their lives, and if the law were resisted Dunklin personally guaranteed it would be enforced. He also advised them to sue for damages.

They took him at his word and scraped together $1,000 for four local attorneys to prepare a lawsuit against the mobbers.

In retrospect, some Mormon historians feel the Saints were possibly "set up" by the governor.

Note 3

[From page 29]

Here a Danite, There a Danite, Everywhere A . . . .

Joseph Smith records in his journal:

"Saturday, 27 [October, 1838] . . .

"And here I would state, that while the evil spirits were raging up and down in the state to raise mobs against the 'Mormons,' Satan himself was no less busy in striving to stir up mischief in the camp of the Saints: and among the most conspicuous of his willing devotees was one Doctor Sampson Avard, who had been in the Church but a short time, and who, although he had generally behaved with a tolerable degree of external decorum, was secretly aspiring to be the greatest of the great, and become the leader of the people. This was his pride and folly, but as he had no hopes of accomplishing it by gaining the hearts of the people openly he watched his opportunity with the brethren — at a time when mobs oppressed, robbed, whipped, burned, plundered and slew, till forebearance seemed no longer a virtue, and nothing but the grace of God without measure could support men under such trials — to form a secret combination by which he might rise a mighty conqueror, at the *expense and the overthrow of the Church* [his emphasis]. This he tried to accomplish by his smooth, flattering, and winning speeches, which he frequently made to his associates, while his room was well guarded by some of his followers, ready to give him the signal on the approach of anyone who would not approve of his measures.

"In these proceedings he stated that he had the sanction of the heads of the Church for what he was about to do; and by his smiles and flattery, persuaded them to believe it, and proceeded to administer the few under his control, an oath, binding them to everlasting secrecy to everything which should be communicated to them by himself. Thus Avard initiated members into his band, firmly binding them, by all that was sacred, in the protecting of each other in all things that were lawful; and was careful to picture out a great glory that was then hovering over the Church, and would soon burst upon the Saints as a cloud by day, and a pillar of fire by night, and would soon unveil the slumbering mysteries of heaven, which would gladden the hearts and arouse the stupid spirits of the Saints of the latter-day, and fill their hearts with that love which is unspeakable and full of glory, and arm them with power, that the gates of hell could not prevail against them; and would often affirm to his company that the principal men of the Church had put him forward as a spokesman, and a leader of this band, which he named Danites.

"Thus he duped many, which gave him the opportunity of figuring [himself] as a person of importance. He held his meetings daily, and carried on his crafty work in great haste, to prevent mature reflection upon the matter by his followers, until he had them bound under the penalties of death to keep the secrets and certain signs of the organization by which they were to know each other by day or night.

"After those performances, he held meetings to organize his men into companies of tens and fifties, appointing a captain over each company. After completing this organization, he went on to teach the members of it their duty under the orders of their captains; he then called his captains together and taught them in a secluded place, as follows:

"Avard's Instructions to His Captains

" 'My brethren, as you have been chosen to be our leading men, our captains to rule over this last kingdom of Jesus Christ — and you have been organized after the ancient order — I have called upon you here today to teach you, and instruct you in the things that pertain to your duty, and to show you what your privileges are, and what they soon will be. Know ye not, brethren, that it soon will be your privilege to take your respective companies and go out on a scout on the borders of the settlements, and take to yourselves spoils of the goods of the ungodly Gentiles? for it is written, the riches of the Gentiles shall be consecrated to my people, the house of Israel; and thus you will waste away the Gentiles by robbing and plundering them of their property; and in this way we will build up the Kingdom of God, and roll forth the little stone that Daniel saw cut out of the mountain without hands, and roll forth until it filled the whole earth. For this is the very way that God destines to build up His kingdom in the last days. If any of us should be recognized, who can harm us? for we will stand by each other and defend one another in all things. If our enemies swear against us, we can swear also. (The captains were confounded at this, but Avard continued). Why do you startle at this, brethren? As the Lord liveth, I would swear to a lie to clear any of you; and if this would not do, I would put them or him under the sand as Moses did the Egyptian; and in this way we will consecrate much unto the Lord, and build up His kingdom; and who can stand against us? And if any of us transgress, we will deal with him amongst ourselves. And if any one of this Danite society reveals any of these things, I will put him where the dogs cannot bite him.'

[Joseph resumes:]

"At this lecture all of the officers revolted, and said it would not do, they would not go into any such measures, and it would not do to name any such thing; 'such proceedings would be in open violation of the laws of our country, would be robbing our fellow citizens of their rights, and are not according to the language and doctrine of Christ, or of the Church of Latter-day Saints.'

"Avard replied, and said there was no laws that were executed in justice, and he cared not for them, this being a different dispensation, and dispensation of the fullness of times; in this dispensation he learned from the Scriptures that the kingdom of God was to put down all other kingdoms, and the Lord Himself was to reign, and His laws alone were the laws that would exist.

"Avard's teachings were still manfully rejected by all. Avard then said that they had better drop the subject, although he had received his authority from Sidney Rigdon the evening before. The meeting then broke up; the eyes of those present were opened, Avard's craft was no longer in the dark, and but very little confidence was placed in him, even by the warmest of the members of his Danite scheme.

"When a knowledge of Avard's rascality came to the Presidency of the Church, he was cut off from the Church, and every means proper used to destroy his influence, at which he was highly incensed, and went about whispering his evil insinuations, but finding every effort unavailing, he again turned conspirator, and sought to make friends with the mob.

"And here let it be distinctly understood, that these companies of tens and fifties got up by Avard, were altogether separate and distinct from those companies of tens and fifties organized by the brethren for self defense, in case of an attack from the mob. This latter organization was called into existence more particularly that in this time of alarm no family or person might be neglected; therefore, one company would be engaged in drawing wood, another in cutting it, another in gathering corn, another in grinding, another in butchering, another in distributing meat, etc., etc., so that all should be employed in turn, and no one lack the necessaries of life. Therefore, let no one hereafter, by mistake or design, confound this organization of the church for good and righteous purposes, with the organization of the 'Danites,' of the apostate Avard, which died almost before it had existed."[1]

Some observers have mistakenly claimed the 83 signers of Rigdon's manifesto were members of the Danites, but the allegation is groundless. Equally speculative are claims the Danite organization followed the same listing as contained in the Elders' Journal of the Church of Latter Day Saints (Far West, Missouri), Vol. I for the July Fourth parade. Despite Smith's clarification, some critics have confused the church's organization's band of self defense with Avard's "Danites." When the Saints at times did band together for defense, the Missourians claimed those fighting were the "Danites."[2]

In an act of retaliatory bitterness, Oliver Cowdery denounced certain aspects of the church (possibly also tying Smith to the Danites, although that specific charge was attributed to Cowdery in a document that was probably forged, and first published by anti-Mormon evangelist R. B. Neal in 1905)[3] before Cowdery's return to the church in 1848, with his subsequent retraction of earlier claims.

In the 1906 forgery Cowdery purportedly claims that Rigdon influenced Smith into forming the Danites, which committed "depredations upon Gentiles and the actual assassination of apostates from the church."

Other apostate Mormons, John Corrill, John Cleminson, and Reed Peck, in an attempt to rile up the locals against the Saints, claimed they heard Joseph address the Danite band and approve of Avard's teachings.[4] And, of course, Avard himself testified to the court that Joseph was "the organizer."[5]

William Swartzell also lashed out against his former Prophet by claiming Joseph preached to the Danites.[6] As did John Whitmer, who claimed Joseph ordered the band to drive the dissenters from town, even tying Joseph into the responsibility for Rigdon's damaging "salt sermon."[7]

Fairly detailed sketches of the Danites have appeared, including those who unwittingly partook of their covenants before learning of the group's "apostate" nature.[8] The Danites did adopt signs and secret pass words, and, before its exposure, some Mormons had actually thought it indeed was for "the protection of our families, property and religion."[9]

The Danites possibly went so far as to draft a constitution,[10] and even an oath for members.[11] The same sources also claim the Danite rank and file became quickly disenchanted, when, for example, Avard ousted even "Captain General" Jared Carter for complaining.[12]

Note 4

[From page 42]

Churning the Mill at Haun's

Perhaps the most objective account comes from a non-Mormon scource in 1886, *History of Caldwell and Livingston Counties.* The author claims the Saints at Haun's settlement brought on their own problems, beginning with Haun's confrontation with the Prophet. Joseph counseled Haun, "Move in, by all means, if you wish to save your lives." Haun replied if the settlers left their homes all their property would be lost and the Gentiles would burn their houses and barns. Smith said, "You had better lose your property than your lives, but there is no danger of

losing either if you will do as you are commanded." Haun thought
he and his neighbors could protect and defend themselves, and
Smith finally gave them permission, saying they would consider
him a tyrant if he forced them to leave and abandon their property
and come to Far West.[1]

Haun galloped back to the settlement, where his cohorts also
wished to stay. " . . . Some of the women, too, urged the men to
stand firm, and offered to mould bullets and prepare patching for
the rifles if necessary."[2]

"The 30th of October," writes B. H. Roberts, "is said by some
[who witnessed the event] . . . to have been a most beautiful one
— one of those days in mid-Autumn when smoky mists hang about
the horizon . . . when the gentle breezes rustle through the ripened
corn and softly stirs the leaves of the forests that have been kissed
by the early frosts and autumn sun to purple and gold . . . "[3]

The ambience of the community was laughter of playing
children mingled with snatches of song from mothers working in
the settlement.[4]

"All told there were perhaps thirty families of the Saints located
around the mill," reports Andrew Jenson in 1889, "several of which
had just recently arrived from the Eastern States, and were camped
in their wagons and tents behind the blacksmith shop adjacent to
the mill."[5]

Most of the men were in the fields, gathering crops, when
Joseph Young witnessed the following scene:

"It was about 4 o'clock, while sitting in my cabin, with my babe
in my arms, and my wife standing by my side; the door being open,
I cast my eyes on the opposite bank of Shoal Creek, and saw a
large company of armed men on horses, directing their course
towards the mills, with all possible speed. As they advanced
through the scattering trees that stood on the edge of the prairie,
they seemed to form themselves into a three square position,
forming a van guard in front. At this moment David Evans, seeing
the superiority of their numbers (there being two hundred and
forty of them, according to their own account) swung his hat and
cried for peace. This not being heeded, they continued to advance,
and their leader Mr. Cornstock, fired a gun, which was followed by
a solemn pause of ten, or twelve seconds, when, all at once they
discharged about one hundred rifles, aiming at a black smith's

shop, into which our friends had fled for safety: and [charged]up to the shop, the cracks of which, between the logs, were sufficiently large to enable them to aim directly at the bodies of those who had there fled for refuge from the fire of their murderers ... "[6]

Meanwhile, another witness at the scene, David Lewis, reports, "When men ran out and called for peace they were shot down; when they held up their hats and handkerchiefs and crying for mercy, they were shot down; when they attempted to run, they were cut down by the fire of guns; and when they stood still, they were shot down by putting their guns through the cracks of the building."[7]

Joseph Young adds, "There were several families, tented in rear of the shop, whose lives were exposed, and amidst a shower of bullets, fled to the woods in different directions."[8]

David Lewis continues, "One woman by the name of Mary Steadwell was shot though the hand while holding it up in the attitude of defence. As she ran from the mob, others pierced her clothes; after running as far as she could, she threw herself behind a log, whilst a volley of balls poured after her, filling the log where she lay ... One small boy was killed, having his brains blown out ... begging for his life, ... and during the affray, two other boys, belonging to Warren Smith (who was also killed at the time) hid themselves under the bellows, and ... lay concealed from their view by being covered with blood and dead bodies of the slain. The elder of the boys, crying for mercy from his hiding place, was immediately put to death by putting the muzzle of a gun to the lad's ear and blowing off the top of his head," and, by another report, "leaving the skull empty and dry, while the brains and hair of the murdered boy were scattered around and on the walls of the building."[9]

Resumes Lewis, "The other lad was supposed to have been killed, but they did not quite accomplish their object, the younger receiving a wound in his hip which carried off his hip bone — While the mob were in the shop, if they perceived life remaining in any of the wounded, while struggling in the agonies of death, they were immediately dispatched, at the same time plundering the pockets of the dead, stripping off their boots, shoes, and clothing."[10]

Smith's journal adds, "The little fellow himself states that seeing his father and brother killed, he thought they would shoot him again if he stirred, and so feigned himself dead, and lay perfectly still, till he heard his mother call him after dark."[11]

The boy's mother meanwhile relates her account: "Our men took off their hats and swung them, and cried 'quarter' until they were shot. The mob paid no attention to their cries nor their entreaties, but fired incessantly.

"I took my little girls — my boys I could not find — and started for the woods. The mob encircled us on all sides but the brook. I ran down the bank, across the mill pond on a plank, up the hill into the bushes. The bullets whistled all the way like hail, and cut down the bushes on all sides of us."[12]

David Lewis continues: "Among those who attempted to escape, was a man by the name of Thomas McBride, a soldier and Patriot of the revolution . . . while making the best use of his totering limbs . . . For his escape, he was met in his retreat by a young man from Daviess county by the name of Jacob Rogers, who immediately demanded the old man's gun, which was delivered up, and was then shot down by said Rogers. This not killing the old man, he lifted his hands in the attitude of supplication and begged for mercy . . . .But the young man . . . seizing an old corn cutter or piece of a sythe, commenced first to hew off the old man's fingers while holding them up for mercy, and next cutting his hands from his arms, and then severing his arms from his body, and last of all, laying open the skull and beheading the body."[13] Another detail was added by another: " . . . his brains oozing from his cracked skull, and his white hairs crimson with his gore."[14]

As a witness to the scene, Lewis adds, "Cows, hogs, and horses were driven off in droves. They robbed the families of all their beds and bedding, and . . . took the widow's cloaks . . .

"They burned all the books that they could find, they shot the hogs and cattle . . . "[15]

Joseph Young concludes his report: "According to their [the Missourians'] own account, they fired . . . upwards of fifteen hundred shots at a little company of men of about thirty in number!"[16]

With certainly no motives for boasting of Mormon blessings, John D. Lee later admits after his own "apostasy" a remarkable incident: "Isaac Laney was shot seven times, leaving thirteen ball holes in his person; five of the shots were nearly in the centre of the chest; one entered under the right arm, passed through the body and came out under the left arm ...

"The mob left, and in about two hours Laney was taken from under the cabin floor nearly lifeless. He was then washed, anointed with oil, the elders praying for his recovery, according to the order of the Holy Priesthood, and he was promised, through prayer and faith in God, speedy restoration. The pain at once left him ... I heard Laney declare this to be a fact, and he bore his testimony in the presence of many of the Saints. I saw him four weeks after the massacre and examined his person. I saw the wounds, then healed. I felt of them with my own hands, and I saw the shirt and examined it, that he had on when he was shot, and it was cut in shreds. Many balls had cut his clothing, that had not touched his person."[17]

After the battle, the Missourians proudly surveyed the scene ... 18 Mormon corpses lay strewn across the woodland floor.[18] Another 15 were wounded severely.

Wilford Woodruff, later to become President of the church, also records in his journal about Isaac Laney, who "showed me 11 bullet holes in his body. There were 27 in his shirt, seven in his pantaloons, and his coat was literally cut to pieces. One ball entered one arm-pit and came out at the other. Another entered his back and came out at the breast. A ball passed through each hip, each leg and each arm. All these shots were received while he was running for life, and, strange as it may appear, though he had also one of his ribs broken, he was able to outrun his enemies, and his life was saved."[19]

Amanda Smith, another eye-witness, states, " ... after our men were shot down by them, they went around and shot all the dead men over again, to make sure of their lives."[20]

Nathan Kinsman Knight details for the *History of Caldwell and Livingston Counties:* "Two men had Bro. Warren Smith stripped of his coat, hat, and boots, and were dragging him around after he was dead and kicking him."

When Knight saw the mob approaching, he "caught his gun and hung his powder-horn over his neck, when the buckskin string was cut by a ball fired by one of the mob leaders, which also passed through his vest pocket, taking out his pocket knife."[21]

"The first wound I received was in the finger of my right hand. The next in my left leg and the next in my body, the ball entering just above the small of my back and lodging just below the pit of my stomach. The last shot brought me to my hands and knees. I recovered myself and tried to escape. I made out to get three-quarters of a mile farther through timber and brush, and secreted myself in some fallen tree tops. I remained about three quarters of an hour. A little after sunset I saw Sister Polly Wood (formerly Polly Merrill). I motioned for her to come to me. I could not call her, neither could I stand up. She came and tried to lead me back, but I was too weak. She then kneeled down and placed her hands on my wounds and prayed the Lord to strengthen and heal me. I never heard a more powerful prayer. The Lord answered her prayer, and I received strength and walked back to Haun's house by resting three or four times.

" . . . I had nothing left but a small trunk; the contents were gone excepting a bottle of consecrated oil, which they had left on the ground . . .

"A few days after the massacre the mob returned to the mill, and ground up all the brethren's grain in that region of country. They numbered about 100, and remained about a month, killing hogs, robbing bee stands and hen houses. I and my family suffered much for food. At the end of six weeks I began to get around a little, and was again fired upon by a mob of 14. I escaped into the woods unhurt."[22]

Andrew Jenson records: "Elder Walker stopped under some lumber leaning against the bank, which, however, afforded him but little protection; but in answer to his earnest prayer, the eyes of the mobbers were blinded, and although they looked directly at him, they apparently did not see him . . .

"William Yokum was shot in the leg, which was subsequently amputated in consequence of the wounds received at the massacre. He was also shot through the head, the ball entering near the eye and coming out of the back part of the head. Another ball wounded him in the arm . . .

"Some of the dead were dragged out of the shop into the yard, in order to give the mobbers a better chance and more room to strip them of their clothing. All who had on good coats and boots were rifled of these articles ...

"Brother Austin Hammer, who was mortally wounded — seven balls were shot into his body, breaking both thigh bones — had on a new pair of boots that fitted him tightly, and in the efforts to get them off he was dragged and pulled out of the shop and about the yard in a barbarous manner. In his mangled condition this cruel treatment must have caused him the most excruciating pain ... he died twelve o'clock the following night. Two men also stripped Warren Smith of his coat, hat, and boots, and dragged him around before he was dead and kicked him.

" ... Afterwards this William Mann showed the boots on his own feet, in Far West, saying, 'Here is a pair of boots that I pulled off before the d—d Mormon was done kicking.' [Deletion as in original]

" ... Brother Nathan K. Knight states that they took everything that belonged to him, except a small trunk, the contents of which were carried off. All they left was a bottle of consecrated oil, which they had thrown on the ground.

" ... The children were crying loudly ... at the loss of fathers ...

" ... In places, where there were small hollows in the soil, the blood stood in pools from two to three inches deep.

" ... Margaret Foutz, a survivor of the massacre, who is yet alive and resides at Pleasant Grove, Utah County, Utah, says ... 'As we were returning I saw a brother, Myers, who had been shot through his body. In that dreadful state he crawled on his hands and knees, about two miles, to his home ... One [other Mormon] in particular asked me to give him relief by taking a hammer and knock his brains out, so great was his agony. And we knew not what moment our enemies would be upon us again.'

" ... One [Missourian] carried away an empty 10-gallon keg, which he carried before him on his saddle and beat as a drum. Another had a woman's bonnet, which he said was for his sweetheart."[23]

One Livingston County man, William Reynolds, killed a ten year old boy and afterwards boasted of it to another Missourian, Charles R. Ross, who described with "glee" how "the boy struggled in his dying agony."[24]

Jenson further certifies, "While in camp at the mill, according to the statements to the writer of two members of the company (Robert White and James Trosper), the militia lived off the country, and 'lived fat, too.' The Mormon cattle and hogs had been turned into the fields and were fat and fine, the mill furnished plenty of breadstuffs, and there were other articles of provisions to be had for the taking. The company remained at the mill until peace was entirely restored."[25] Meanwhile, the remaining Mormons practically starved. The Missourians would not feed the women.

According to the *Missouri Historical Review:* "Perhaps the best account of this massacre ever written came from the pen of Major Reburn S. Holcombe, one of the most prolific of Missouri historical writers, and the author of the best of Missouri county histories ... He wrote over the name of 'Burr Joyce,' and his account of the massacre appeared in the *St. Louis Globe-Democrat* for October 6, 1887, as follows:

" ' ... The Gentiles advanced, and began to use their rough, home-made swords, or corn knives, with which some of them were armed ...

" 'Charley Merrick, another little boy only nine years old, had hid under the bellows. He ran out but did not get very far until he received a load of buckshot ... He did not die, however, for nearly five weeks.

" ' ... the Gentiles began to loot the place. Considerable property was taken ... At least three wagons and perhaps ten horses were taken ... .Two of the survivors have stated to me that the place was pretty well cleaned out ...

" 'Timidly and warily came forth the widows and orphans from their hiding places, and as they recognized one a husband and one a father, another a son, and another a brother among the slain, the wailings of grief and terror were most pitiful. All that night were they alone with their dead and wounded. There were no physicians, but if there had been, many of the wounded were past all surgery. [There were] dreadful sights in the moonlight, and dreadful sounds on the night winds.

" 'By and by, when the wounded had been made as comfortable as possible, the few men who had returned gathered the women and children together, and all sought consolation in prayer. Then they sang from the Mormon hymn book a selection entitled "Moroni's Lamentation" . . . And so in prayer and song and ministration the remainder of the night was passed.

" 'Herewith I give an extract from an affidavit made by Mrs. Amanda Smith, whose husband and little son were killed in the massacre . . .

" ' "The next day the mob came back. They told us we must leave the state forthwith or be killed. It was bad weather, and they had taken our teams and clothes; our men were all dead or wounded . . . We had little prayer meetings; they said if we did not stop them they would kill every man, woman, and child. We had spelling schools for our little children; they pretended they were 'Mormon Meetings' and said if we did not stop them they would kill every man, woman, and child. I started the 1st of February, very cold weather, for Illinois, with five small children and no money. It was mob all the way. I drove the team, and we slept out of doors. We suffered greatly from hunger, cold and fatigue; and for what? For our religion . . ." ' "[26]

Thus ended the "Haun's Mill" episode.

Note 5

[From page 42]

Uniforms, Waistcoats and Turncoats

While Rockwell was at Smith's side, John D. Lee details the event: "Col. George M. Hinkle had command of the troops at Far West, under Joseph Smith. He was from Kentucky, and was considered a fair weather Saint. When danger came he was certain to be on the strong side. He was a fine speaker, and had great influence with the Saints.

"Previous to the attack on Far West, Col. Hinkle had come to an understanding with the Gentile commanders that in case the danger grew great, they could depend on him as a friend and one through whom they could negotiate and learn the situation of affairs in the camp of the Saints.

"When our scouts were first driven in, Col. Hinkle was out with them, and when they were closely pursued he turned his coat wrong side out and wore it so. This was a peculiar move, but at the time it did not cause much comment among his men, but they reported it to the Prophet, and he at once became suspicious of the Colonel. The Prophet, being a man of thought and cool reflection, kept this information within a small circle, as that was a bad time to ventilate an act of that kind. The Prophet concluded to make use of the knowledge he had gained of Hinkle's character, and use him to negotiate between the two parties. I do not believe that Joseph Smith had the least idea that he, with his little handful of men, could stand off that army that had come up against him . . . Joseph wished to use Hinkle to learn the destiny of the Gentiles, so that he could prepare for the worst. Col. Hinkle was sent out by Joseph to have an interview with the Gentiles.

"The Colonel returned and reported to Joseph Smith the terms proposed by the Gentile officers. The terms offered were as follows: Joseph Smith and the leading men of the Church, Rigdon, Lyman White, P. P. Pratt, Phelps and others, were to give themselves up without delay, the balance of the men to surrender themselves and their arms by ten o'clock the following day, the understanding being that all would be tried for treason against the Government, and for other offences. The Prophet took advantage of this information, and had every man that was in imminent danger, leave the camp for a place of safety. The most of those in danger went to Illinois. They left at once, and were safe from all pursuit before the surrender took place, as they traveled north and avoided all settlements."

Note 6

[From page 54]

Assassinations and Understatements

Perhaps the most incisive anaylsis of the Rockwell-Boggs affair comes from Monte B. McClaws, writing under a research grant for the *Missouri Historical Review.* McClaws, certainly no proponent of Mormonism (describing it as "a rather peculiar religious sect") summarizes: " . . . there are inconsistencies and unanswered questions that cast a definite shadow of doubt on Rockwell's supposed guilt. Any one of hundreds of people could have shot the ex-Governor. Independence was filled with wild and reckless people, and killing was not unusual to many of them. The assailant could have been a despondent debtor of the Boggs' store or an offended customer fitting out a wagon train or stocking up for a trapping expedition. Why did not people suspect Uhlinger? After all, it was his gun they found outside Boggs' window, and he was a commercial competitor. Any one of a number of brooding political enemies could have performed the deed. No evidence seems to exist to affix guilt on anyone so described, but in reality neither does there exist anything but circumstantial evidence to condemn Rockwell, and much of this can be explained away.

"John C. Bennett's affidavit against Rockwell admits his conclusions were based on circumstances, circumstances insufficient to warrant an indictment by the Grand Jury. Had there been any concrete evidence of guilt, citizens of Independence or former enemies of the Mormons would probably have gone the extra mile to convict Rockwell. To their credit, they did not.

"As the chief advocate of Rockwell's guilt, and the source of most of the assumptions, Bennett himself leads one to suspect the weight of his statements. Overlooking his natural bias, he being an excommunicate of the Mormon Church, his own statements reveal weaknesses. In reporting a conversation with Rockwell he made the following statement, which is typical of his whole book. ' . . . And two persons in Nauvoo told me that you told them that you had been over the upper part of Missouri . . . I know nothing of what happened, as I was not there. I draw my own inferences . . . I believe that Joe ordered you to do it . . . ' He admits that he only believed, and that his own belief was based on heresay.

" . . . Moreover, if Rockwell was Smith's bodyguard and, as was shown later, had two pistols of his own, why would he need to steal a gun from Uhlinger's store? If he did it to throw suspicion on someone else, why did he take the risk of stealing it a week before he shot Boggs? Would not this place him in risk of apprehension even before he carried out his planned deed? And just how was it the citizens of Independence were so positive the criminal was the silversmith, Tompkins; then, after his vindication, became equally convinced it was Rockwell? Possibly their certainty of Rockwell's guilt was as ill-founded as their suspicions of Tompkins. Did someone see the criminal leave Boggs' house after the shooting? If so, descriptions of Tompkins and Rockwell clearly show the impossibility of confusing the two.

" . . . Few have attempted to explore Boggs' political career in search for the would-be assassin and, except for the newspaper, none seemingly have even mentioned the silversmith Tompkins. Without some rather startling discovery of new and conclusive evidence, the attempted murderer will undoubtedly remain unknown."

Even "conclusive" evidence would be difficult to ascertain, as Nineteenth Century forgeries were not only commonplace but prolific. And Twentieth Century inventions of alleged "original documents" is equally difficult — if not impossible — to determine. (See December 1985 issue of *Utah Holiday* magazine, pp. 84-88, "The Chameleon & The Salamander," by Paul Larsen, for an excellent treatment of counterfeit documents — how both ink and paper can be artificially aged, as admitted by forensic document examiners at crime laboratories, leaving even the so-called "document experts" easily fooled.)

Note 7

[From page 88]

Exposing the *Expositor*

George W. Harris continues his report of this landmark meeting: "Mayor read from Illinois Constitution, Article 8, Section 12, touching the responsibility of the press for its constitutional liberty.

"Councilor Stiles said . . . 'If we can prevent the issuing of any more slanderous communications, he would go in for it. It is a right for this community to show a proper resentment; and he would go in for suppressing all further publications of the kind.' . . .

"Alderman Orson Spencer accorded with the views expressed, that the *Nauvoo Expositor* is a nuisance. Did not consider it wise to give them time to trumpet a thousand lies. 'Their property could not pay for it. If we pass only a fine or imprisonment, have we any confidence that they will desist? None at all. We have found these men covenant-breakers with God, with their wives, etc. Have we any hope of their doing better? Their characters have gone before them. Shall they be suffered to go on, and bring a mob upon us, and murder our women and children, and burn our beautiful city? No! I had rather my blood would be spilled at once, and would like to have the press removed as soon as the ordinance would allow; and wish the matter might be put into the hands of the Mayor, and everybody stand by him in the execution of his duties, and hush every murmur.' ...

"Councilor Levi Richards ... considered the doings of the Council this day of immense moment ... [he] would go in to put a stop to the thing at once. 'Let it be thrown out of the city, and the responsibility of countenancing such a press be taken off our shoulders and fall on the State, if corrupt enough to sustain it.' ...

"Councilor Phineas Richards said that he had not forgotten the transaction at Haun's Mill, and that he recollected that his son George Spencer then lay in the well referred to on the day previous, without a winding-sheet, shroud, or coffin. He said he could not sit still when he saw the same spirit raging in this place. He considered the publication of the *Expositor* as much murderous at heart as David was before the death of Uriah; [and that he] was prepared to take [a] stand; by the Mayor, and whatever he proposes; [and that he] would stand by him to the last. The quicker it is stopped the better."

Note 8

[From page 89]

He Goats, She Goats, and Scapegoats

At Joseph's trial, more facts were released pertaining to the destruction of the *Expositor* newspaper press. Minutes of the court report Rockwell had been implicated in the "riot" which had purportedly occurred at the destruction of the press: "E. Wingott, of Boston . . . was by the door when it was opened, and knew that nothing more than a knee was put against it. All was done quietly." When Wingott was cross-examined, he swore he "did not know the name of the man who opened the door," but that he did know Porter Rockwell.[1]

Rockwell had obviously been implicated by the prosecution as the first man to "burst" inside. His reputation as scapegoat was mushrooming. After reviewing additional evidence, "the court discharged the prisoners."[2]

Information from the habeas corpus hearing before the trial reveals additional background on the destruction of the *Expositor:*

"Orrin P. Rockwell sworn. Some three or four weeks ago said Francis M. Higbee said he would go [to] his death against Joseph and Hyrum Smith. Francis said, 'I know my course is wrong; but if I stop I shall get hell, and if I go on I shall only get hell,' . . . and would destroy the General if possible . . .

. . . "John Hughes said, Higbee said, 'By God, all I want to live for is to see this city sunk down to the lowest hell, and by God it shall!'

. . . "Joseph Dalton: Higbee said, if they laid their hands on the press from that hour they might date their downfall; that ten suns should not roll over their heads till the city was destroyed."[3]

Note 9

[From page 94]

Getting Ford's Goat

Joseph Smith continues his defense from another accusation in Ford's letter: "Our 'insisting to be accountable only before our own Municipal Court,' is totally incorrect. We plead a habeas corpus as a last resort to save us from being thrown into the power of the mobocrats, who were then threatening us with death, and it was with great reluctance we went before the Municipal Court, on account of the prejudice which might arise in the minds of the unbiased; and we did not petition for a habeas corpus until we had told the constable that on our lives we dare not go to Carthage for trial, and plead with him to go before any county magistrate he pleased in our vicinity (which occurrence is common in legal proceedings), and not a member of our society, so that our lives might be saved from the threats thus already issued against us."

Ford's letter had also asserted, "It has also been reported to me that martial law has been declared in Nauvoo; that persons and property have been and are now forcibly imprisoned and detained there, and that the Legion has been ordered under arms to resist any attempt to arrest the persons accused. I have not particularly inquired into the truth of these latter reports."

Joseph replies: "As to martial law, we truly say that we were obliged to call out the forces to protect our lives; and the Constitution guarantees to every man that privilege; and our measures were active and efficient, as the necessity of the case required; but the city is and has been continually under the special direction of the marshal all the time."

When Ford asserted the rumor that non-Nauvoo citizens were "left and right" being arrested in Nauvoo, Joseph answers: "No person, to our knowledge, has been arrested [except] only for violation of the peace, and those some of our own citizens [not outsiders], all of whom we believe are now discharged."

Joseph was also concerned about the entire affair for one basic reason. He informs Ford of it in his letter: "How it could be possible for us now to be tried constitutionally by the same magistrate who first issued the writ at Carthage we cannot see, for the Constitution expressly says no man shall twice be put in jeopardy of life and limb for the same offense ... "

Note 10

[From page 97]

On Deaf Ears

John Taylor writes, "We were frequently rudely and impudently contradicted by the fellows he [Governor Ford] had around him, and of whom he seemed to take no notice. He opened and read a number of the documents himself, and as he proceeded he was frequently interrupted by, 'That's a lie! That's a G-d—d lie!'[1] [Deletions as published]

The delegation countered: "We represented to him [Ford] the course we had taken in relation to this matter, our willingness to go before another magistrate other than the Municipal Court [Nauvoo's own], the illegal refusal by the constable of our request, our dismissal by the Municipal Court [which is] a legally constituted tribunal, our subsequent trial before Esq. Wells [a non-Mormon at the time] at the instance of Judge Thomas [the circuit judge], and our dismissal of Judge Thomas [the circuit judge], and our dismissal by him; that we had fulfilled the law in every particular; that it was our enemies who were breaking the law, and, having murderous designs, were only making use of this as a pretext to get us into their power."

Note 11

[From page 104]

Promises, Promises . . .

The Saints later point out the magistrate was acting as both military enforcer and judge, which in itself was unconstitutional.

John Taylor writes, "As I was informed of this illegal proceeding, I went immediately to the Governor and informed him of it."[1]

George A. Smith adds, "The Governor replied that he was very sorry that the thing had occurred; that he did not believe the charges."[2]

According to various eye-witness accounts given George A. Smith, "the prisoners and their friends had amusing conversations on various interesting subjects, which engaged them till late,"[3] then they sprawled out on the floor to sleep.

The next day Joseph was visited by messengers from the Governor, who apologized for not meeting him at Joseph's request the previous evening. Finally, the Governor personally appeared, and Joseph again explained his case.

Forty-five minutes later, "The Governor left after saying that the prisoners were under his protection, and again pledging himself that they should be protected from violence, and telling them that if the troops marched the next morning to Nauvoo, as he then expected, they [Joseph and Hyrum] should probably be taken along, in order to insure their personal safety."[4]

A messenger then arrived from Nauvoo, but the guard refused to let him see Joseph.

A gloom cast itself upon Joseph, who sat in silence and meditated. Finally, he remarked to the others, "I have had a good deal of anxiety about my safety since I left Nauvoo, which I never had before when I was under arrest. I could not help those feelings, and they have depressed me."[5]

Note 12

[From page 105]

Chasing Wild Geese

Smith now sent a messenger to find Almon W. Babbitt, another attorney. He then sought a messenger to gallop to Nauvoo to obtain documents for the trial.

But to his consternation, the court justice altered the return of subpoenas for an additional two days, without consulting either prisoners or counsel, apparently insuring another delay in the trial. This meant Smith would be held in Carthage even longer, while the Carthage Greys roamed about the jail.

When Smith's messenger arrived at Babbitt, the lawyer replied, "You are too late, I am already engaged ... "

Note 13

[From page 105]

The Carthage Merry-go-Round

Frank Worrell, one of the Carthage Greys and officer of the guard, faced Dan Jones privately and warned him to leave while he still could.

Jones went to inform the governor of the threat. On the way to the governor's office Jones heard another threat on Smith's life.

Returning from the governor, Jones attempted to see Joseph but the guard refused. Ex-Mormon Chauncey L. Higbee sidled up to Jones and informed him they would soon kill the Prophet.

Again Jones called to see the Governor, and by now the threats along the streets were cacophonous —even those coming from the jail guards. "But the Governor took no notice of them although it was impossible for him to avoid hearing them."

Note 14

[From page 110]

A Mantle Above The Fire

Edward E. Tullidge reports:

"Apostle Cannon, describing the circumstance, says: 'It was the first sound of his voice which the people had heard since he had gone east on his mission, and the effect upon them was most wonderful. Who that was present on that occasion can ever forget the impression it made upon them? If Joseph had risen from the dead, and again spoken in their hearing, the effect could not have been more startling than it was to many present at that meeting; it was the voice of Joseph himself; and not only was it the voice of Joseph which was heard, but it seemed in the eyes of the people as though it was the very person of Joseph which stood before them.

" 'A more wonderful and miraculous event than was wrought that day in the presence of that congregation we never heard of. The Lord gave his people a testimony that left no room for doubt, as to who was the man he had chosen to lead them. They both saw and heard with their natural eyes and ears; and then the words which were uttered came, accompanied by the convincing power of God to their hearts, and they were filled with the Spirit and with great joy.

" 'There had been gloom and, in some hearts probably, doubt and uncertainty; but now it was plain to all that here was the man upon whom the Lord had bestowed the necessary authority to act in their midst in Joseph's stead.' "

Note 15

[From page 112]

It Takes A Thief

Hyrum Smith lectured March 25, 1843: "I have had an interview with a man who formerly belonged to the church, and he revealed to me that there is a band of men, and some who pretend to be strong in the faith of the doctrine of the Latter Day Saints, but they are hypocrites, and some who do not belong to the church, who are bound together by secret oaths, and obligations and penalties, to keep the secret; and they hold that it is right to steal from any one who does not belong to the church provided they consecrate two-thirds of it to the building of the Temple. They are also making bogus money.

"This man says he has become convinced of the error of his ways, and has come away from them to escape their fury. I wish to warn you all not to be duped by such men, for they are the Gadianters of the last days . . . I tell you to-day, the man that steals shall not long after be brought to the Penitentiary. They will soon be brought to condign punishment. I demand in the presence of God that you will exert your wit and your power to bring such characters to justice, if you do not the curse of God will rest upon you, such things would ruin any people. Should I catch a latter day saint stealing, he is the last man to whom I would shew mercy."

Joseph Smith adds, "I think it best to continue this subject. I want the elders to make honorable proclamation abroad concerning what the feelings of the first presidency is, for stealing has never been tolerated by them. I despise a thief above ground. He would betray me if he could get the opportunity. I would know that he would be a detriment to my cause."[1]

Later, in the December 1, 1841 issue of *Times and Seasons,* the editor writes, "We are highly pleased to see the very energetic measures taken by our citizens to suppress thieving. It has been a source of grief unto us that there were any in our midst, who would wilfully take property from any person which did not belong to them; knowing that if any person, who does, or ever did belong to this church, should steal, the whole church would have to bear the stigma, and the sound goes abroad, that the Mormons are a set of thieves and robbers, a charge which we unequivocally deny, and pronounce a falsehood of the basest kind. That there are some amongst us base enough to commit such acts we do not pretend to deny, but whether they are all members of this church or not, we do not know; but some who are, have been caught in their iniquity . . .

"We are informed that some of those characters have said that such things are sanctioned by the authorities of the church; this is the most base of all lies."[2]

In the same issue is an extract from "Proceedings of a meeting of the Church of Jesus Christ of Latter Day Saints, held at Ramuz, Nov. 18th, 1841," and signed by Brigham Young, president of the Twelve, with the signatures of the eleven other quorum members:

"We have been informed that some of them have been talking of moving into this place; but we would here inform them, that persons whose conduct has exposed them to the just censure of an indignant public, can have no fellowship amongst us, as we cannot, and will not, countenance rogues, thieves, and scoundrels, knowingly; and we hereby warn them that the law will be as rigorously enforced against them in this place as in any other, as we consider such characters as a curse to society.

"We have been told that some individual or individuals, have, under false pretenses, been wishing to palm their wicked and devilish principles upon the authorities of the church, stating that it was part and parcel of the gospel which God had revealed, and that is one of the mysteries which the initiated only are acquainted with. We know not how to express our abhorrence at such an idea, and can only say that it is engendered in hell, founded in falsehood, and is the offspring of the devil; that it is at variance with every principle of righteousness, and truth; and will damn all that are connected with it; for all mysteries are only such to the ignorant, and vanish as soon as men have sufficient intelligence to comprehend them, and there are no mysteries connected with godliness, and our holy religion, but what are pure, innocent, virtuous, just and righteous; if this is a mystery, it is the 'mystery of iniquity' ... such men are either avowed apostates, or on the eve of apostacy, or have only taken the name of religion to cloak their hypocracy; we fear the latter, in some instances, is the case, and that Mississippi scoundrels palm themselves upon us to cover their guilt. We further call upon the church to bring all such characters before the authorities, that they may be tried, and dealt with according to the law of God, and delivered up unto the laws of the land.

" ... should any, who call themselves Latter Day Saints, be found in their midst, they will be cut off from the church ...

"We hope that what we have written may suffice, and take this opportunity of expressing our decided and unqualified disapprobation of any thing like theft, in all its bearings, as being calculated to destroy the peace of society, to injure the Church of Jesus Christ, to wound the character of the people of God, and to stamp with eternal infamy all who follow such diabolical practices."[3]

Joseph Smith issued an affidavit eleven days later, November 29, 1841: " ... It has been proclaimed upon the house-top and in the secret chamber, in the public walks and private circle, throughout the length and breadth of this vast continent, that stealing by the Latter Day Saints has received my approval; nay, that I have taught the doctrine, encouraged them in plunder, and led on the van — than which nothing is more foreign from my heart. I disfellowship the perpetrators of all such abominations — that are devils and not saints, totally unfit for the society of Christians, or men. It is true that some professing to be Latter Day Saints have taught such vile heresies, but all are not Israel that are of Israel." [4]

Church leaders cut two Nauvoo Legion officers from the ranks in consequence of stealing.[5]

In the "Proceedings of the City Council Preamble" of Nauvoo Willard Richards writes the words of Mayor Spencer: "We learn that the inhabitants of various parts of this state are seeking to accumulate all the real and supposed crimes of the whole community for the secret or ostensible purpose of raising a tide of influence against the Mormon community that shall sweep them into irrecoverable ruin. This course of conduct, originating with our moral enemies and gathering in its wake other men that would revolt at the idea of lending a hand to oppress a long abused people that are struggling against foes within and foes without, is at the present almost insupportable to our feelings."

The Nauvoo Council was also concerned with "those who are stealing from quiet citizens of the State and palming upon them a spurious and false currency, and charging to the Mormons their own crimes.

"Resolved, 'That we defy the world to substantiate a single instance, where we have concealed criminals . . . ' "[6]

Then, at another "large meeting of the citizens of Nauvoo," the Committee "retired and in a short time, returned the following, which were adopted unanimously:

"Whereas . . . enemies to the common welfare of the people of this State, are attempting to get up an extensive popular excitement, prejudicial to this people and the country at large . . .

"And whereas, the *Warsaw Signal,* the *Alton Telegraph,* and the *Quincy Whig* have been, as we believe, industriously engaged in circulating falsehood; disseminating discord, and the principles of mobocracy . . .

"And whereas bee yards have been robbed, the hives left at the Mormons doors, to palm the theft upon us, when the honey has been found in the houses of our enemies, and whereas an innumerable number of such infamous tricks have been played upon us, by our enemies, as we believe, for the purpose of blackening our character in the eyes of honest men.

"And whereas, the Chief Magistrate of this State, after a second and protracted visit to this city, and much pains taken to investigate the charge of promiscuous stealing, reports to the Legislature as follows:

" 'Justice, however, requires me here to say, " ' "that I have investigated the charge of promiscuous stealing, and find it to be greatly exaggerated. I could not ascertain that there were a greater proportion of thieves in that community, than in any other of the same number of inhabitants; and perhaps if the city of Nauvoo, were compared with St. Louis, or any other western city, the proportion would not be so great." ' "

"And whereas, The printing office of our open and avowed enemy, Dr. Foster, was set on fire, in this city by himself, or by his instruction as we believe, to fan the flame of mobocracy, which fire was only prevented by our vigilant police . . .

"Resolved, unanimously, That 50 delegates be sent to the surrounding country to inform the people of the designs of our enemies now concocting in their secret and public meetings, so that the honest part of the community may unite with us, to prevent stealing and secure peace."[7]

Then the non-Mormon deputy sheriff of Hancock County came to the Saints' defense: "There seems to be a connection of these friends thirty or forty miles back into the country on this side of the river, who, with five or six in this city, seem to have a line for running stolen property through Nauvoo to the Territory of Iowa; and I have good reason to believe that those in the country on this side of the river, those in the city, and those in the Territory, are one clan, but they are not Mormons; nor have the Mormons any fellowship with them.

"I have taken pains to go with a person from the country, with a writ, and have searched every house suspected, till the person was satisfied, and till I was satisfied myself that no such property, as claimed, was in the city.

"I have good reason to believe that scoundrels stay in Nauvoo, and when stolen property comes into the city, they are ready to pass it on to the Territory, and screen themselves under the cloak of Mormonism, in order that the Mormons may bear the blame. If people will satisfy themselves as I have done, they may find a 'Depot' in the regions of Iowa, containing the greater part of the property charged to the Mormons.

"I would state further, that the Mormons had no agency in the searches I made, but that I made them, at the instance of men from the country . . .

"Joseph A. Kelting,

"Dep. Sheriff of Hancock Co."[8]

Note 16

[From page 118]

Hounded

Amos Davis was unrelenting. He apparently proved to the Prophet an inexorable pest. In his first court fight with Joseph, "The charges were clearly substantiated by the testimony of Dr. Foster, Mr. and Mrs. Hibbard, and others. Mr. Davis was found guilty by the jury, and by the municipal court, bound over to keep the peace six months, under $100,000 bond . . . "[1]

Eight months later Joseph brought suit against him again for "ridiculous and abusive language . . . depreciating Deponents' [Smith's] moral and religious character."[2]

According to the clerk's recordings at the District Court, despite the fact Joseph produced four witnesses and Davis none, Davis' lawyer, Higbee, found Davis technically had not broken the law. "Mr. Higbee alleged that evidence had not been produced to support a breach of the ordinance."[3] Joseph's version gives more detail, however, as he asserts, " . . . in consequence of the informality of the writ drawn by Squire Daniel H. Wells, I was non-suited."[4]

On the following day Joseph brought another suit against Davis, and Davis was fined $50 (actually $66.81 and 1/4 cent, when court fees were added).[5]

On December 3rd, Joseph was again in court with the man.[6]

Three days later Davis came against the Prophet in still another trial. The court clerk records in Joseph's favor: "the judgement of the Court is, that the fine [including court costs of the previous trial] stand affirmed with full costs of this Trial."[7] The added costs of this trial sent Davis somersaulting with anger.

With bulldog tenacity he brought further suit against the Prophet and also against J. P. Green for trespassing, during the *Expositor* affair, in June 1844.[8] Davis lost again.

Despite enemies' claims of Joseph's tyrannical exercise of power, Davis was, on June 25th, 1844 issued a Nauvoo Mercantile License for one year.[9] Later, in September, 1846, during a battle with anti-Mormons, Davis "ran away from fight."[10]

Thus ends all known information on Davis vs. the Prophet.

Note 17

[From page 123]

A Dauntless Doniphan

Joseph Smith III, not a Mormon himself, records in his autobiography: "In 1884, when in the city of Richmond, Missouri, on a matter of church business, I learned that General A. W. Doniphan was living there. In company with my brother, Alexander, after obtaining permission to do so, I called upon him at the hotel where he was boarding. We told him we were the sons of Joseph Smith, the Prophet, and had come to pay our respects to one who had befriended our father. The distinguished gentleman was at that time, I think, over seventy years of age — a tall, handsome, and splendidly built man.

"We had quite a long visit with him, in the course of which I asked him if he had been pretty well acquainted with the Saints during their occupation in Jackson, Daviess, and Caldwell Counties. He said he had been, and that to his knowledge not a member of that church had ever been arrested for crime or prosecuted for misdemeanor during his stay in those counties, with the exception of the false charges made against Porter

Rockwell. Coming from a man who had been a lawyer and very active in his profession throughout that region, this statement seemed a fair tribute to the uprightness and good citizenship of the Saints living there.

"Asked about Porter Rockwell, he smiled and said he had known him quite well, for the young man had lived in the same town with him. He said he had been employed as an attorney for Rockwell when the latter was tried for the alleged attempted assassination of ex-Governor Boggs, and went on to relate some of the incidents connected with the case. When asked if he thought Rockwell guilty of the crime as charged, he answered, emphatically.

" 'No, indeed! There was not one scintilla of evidence to connect him with it in any way, or to prove he ever had knowledge of it. The only thing they had against him was that he was a member of the Latter Day Saints Church, or, as stated by the prosecution, "a Mormon." He was honorably acquitted, and I took him home with me for supper. Afterward we had a talk, and I advised him to leave the state at once and to get to his friends in Illinois as soon as he could, for feelings there still ran high.

" 'At first he objected to this procedure, saying he had done no wrong, had been raised in the town, it was his home, he belonged there, and saw no reason why he should leave. But I counseled him to go. I told him that Mr. Smith, the President of his church, had sent word to me to see that he had a fair trial, which I had done, and now he was fully acquitted, and I thought it best for him to leave and that at once, not staying even another night, for I felt if he did he would surely be killed, for his enemies would not let him alone.

" 'So he agreed to go, and did. I gave him a ten-dollar gold piece as we parted, to help him bear his expenses in getting to his friends.' "

Note 18

[From page 138]

Prairie Fire: A Promethean Prophet

William Clayton records in his *Journal*:

"Saturday, 29th [May, 1847] . . . About ten o'clock, the weather looked a little better and at half past ten the bugle sounded as a signal for the teams to be got together. After the teams were harnessed, the brethren were called together to the boat in the circle. President Young taking his station in the boat, ordered each captain of ten to lead out his respective company and get all his men together. He then called on the clerk to call over the names of the camp to see if all were present . . . President Young then addressed the meeting in substance as follows:

" 'I remarked last Sunday that I had not felt much like preaching to the brethren on this mission. This morning I feel like preaching a little, and shall take for my text, "That as to pursuing our journey with this company with the spirit they possess, I am about to revolt against it." This is the text I feel like preaching on this morning, consequently I am in no hurry.

" 'In the first place, before we left Winter Quarters, it was told to the brethren and many knew it by experience, that we had to leave our homes, our houses, our land and our all because we believed in the Gospel as revealed to the Saints in these last days. The rise of the persecutions against the Church was in consequence of the doctrines of eternal truth taught by Joseph. Many knew this by experience. Some lost their husbands, some lost their wives, and some their children through persecution, and yet we have not been disposed to forsake the truth and turn and mingle with the gentiles, except a few who have turned aside and gone away from us, and we have learned in a measure, the difference between a professor of religion and a possessor of religion.

" 'Before we left Winter Quarters it was told to the brethren that we were going to look out a home for the Saints where they would be free from persecution by the gentiles, where we could dwell in peace and serve God according to the Holy Priesthood, where we could build up the kingdom so that the nations would begin to flock to our standard.

" 'I have said many things to the brethren about the strictness of their walk and conduct when we left the gentiles, and told them that we would have to walk upright or the law would be put in force, etc. Many have left and turned aside through fear, but no good upright, honest man will fear. The Gospel does not bind a good man down and deprive him of his rights and privileges. It does not prevent him from enjoying the fruits of his labors. It does not rob him of blessings. It does not stop his increase. It does not diminish his kingdom, but it is calculated to enlarge his kingdom, as well as to enlarge his heart. It is calculated to give him privileges and power, and honor, and exaltation and everything which his heart can desire in righteousness all the days of his life, and then, when he gets exalted into the eternal world he can still turn around and say it hath not entered into the heart of man to conceive the glory and honor and blessings which God hath in store for those that love and serve Him.

" 'I want the brethren to understand and comprehend the principles of eternal life, and to watch the spirit, be wide awake and not be overcome by the adversary.

" 'You can see the fruits of the spirit, but you cannot see the spirit itself with the natural eye, you behold it not. You can see the result of yielding to the evil spirit and what it will lead you to, but you do not see the spirit itself nor its operations, only by the spirit that's in you.

" 'Nobody has told me what has been going on in the camp, but I have known it all the while. I have been watching its movements, its influence, its effects, and I know the result if it is not put a stop to. I want you to understand that inasmuch as we are beyond the power of the gentiles where the devil has tabernacles in the priests and the people, we are beyond their reach, we are beyond their power, we are beyond their grasp, and what has the devil not to work upon? Upon the spirits of men in this camp, and if you do not open your hearts so that the Spirit of God can enter your hearts and teach you the right way, I know that you are a ruined people and will be destroyed and that without remedy, and unless there is a change and a different course of conduct, a different spirit to what is now in this camp, I go no farther. I am in no hurry.

" 'Give me the man of prayers, give me the man of faith, give me the man of meditation, a sober-minded man, and I would far rather go amongst the savages with six or eight such men than to trust myself with the whole of this camp with the spirit they now possess. Here is an opportunity for every man to prove himself, to know whether he will pray and remember his God without being asked to do it every day; to know whether he will have confidence enough to ask of God that he may receive without my telling him to do it. If this camp was composed of men who had newly received the Gospel, men who had not received the priesthood, men who had not been through the ordinances in the temple and who had not had years of experience, enough to have learned the influence of the spirits and the difference between a good and an evil spirit, I should feel like preaching to them and watching over them and telling them all the time, day by day. But here are the Elders of Israel, men who have had years of experience, men who have had the priesthood for years, and have they got faith enough to rise up and stop a mean, low, groveling, covetous, quarrelsome spirit? No, they have not, nor would they try to stop it, unless I rise up in the power of God and put it down. I do not mean to bow down to the spirit that is in this camp, and which is rankling in the bosoms of the brethren, and which will lead to knock downs and perhaps to the use of the knife to cut each other's throats if it is not put a stop to. I do not mean to bow down to the spirit which causes brethren to quarrel. When I wake up in the morning, the first thing I hear is some of the brethren jawing each other and quarreling because a horse has got loose in the night.

" 'I have let the brethren dance and fiddle and act the nigger night after night to see what they will do, and what extremes they would go to, if suffered to go as far as they would. I do not love to see it. The brethren say they want a little exercise to pass away time in the evenings, but if you can't tire yourselves bad enough with a day's journey without dancing every night, carry your guns on your shoulders and walk, carry your wood to camp instead of lounging and lying asleep in your wagons, increasing the load until your teams are tired to death and ready to drop to the earth. Help your teams over mud holes and bad places instead of lounging in your wagons and that will give you exercise enough without dancing. Well, they will play cards, they will play checkers, they will play dominoes, and if they had the privilege and were where they could get whiskey, they would be drunk half their time, and in one week they would quarrel, get to high words and draw their knives to kill each other. This is what such a course of things would lead to. Don't you know it? Yes. Well, then, why don't you try to put it down? I have played cards once in my life since I became a Mormon to see what kind of spirit would attend it, and I was so well satisfied, that I would rather see in your hands the dirtiest thing you could find on the earth, than a pack of cards. You never read of gambling, playing cards, checkers, dominoes, etc., in the scriptures, but you do read of men praising the Lord in the dance, but who ever read of praising the Lord in a game at cards? If any man had sense enough to play a game at cards, or dance a little without wanting to keep it up all the time, but exercise a little and then quit it and think no more of it, it would do well enough, but you want to keep it up till midnight and every night, and all the time. You don't know how to control your senses. Last winter when we had our seasons of recreation in the council house, I went forth in the dance frequently, but did my mind run on it? No! To be sure, when I was dancing, my mind was on the dance, but the moment I stopped in the middle or the end of a tune, my mind was engaged in prayer and praise to my Heavenly Father and whatever I engage in, my mind is on it while engaged in it, but the moment I am done with it, my mind is drawn up to my God. The devils which inhabit the gentiles' priests are here. The tabernacles are not here, we are out of their power, we are beyond their grasp, we are beyond the reach of their persecutions, but the devils are here, and the first thing you'll know if you don't open your eyes and your hearts, they will cause divisions in our camp and perhaps war, as they did with the Lamanites as you read in the Book of Mormon.

    " 'Do we suppose that we are going to look out a home for the Saints, a resting place, a place of peace where they can build up the kingdom and bid the nations welcome, with a low, mean, dirty, trifling, covetous, wicked spirit dwelling in our bosoms? It is vain! vain! Some of you are very fond of passing jokes, and will carry your jokes very far. But will you take a joke? If you do not want to take a joke, don't give a joke to your brethren. Joking, nonsense, profane language, trifling conversation and loud laughter do not belong to us. Suppose the angels were witnessing the hoe down the other evening, and listening to the haw haws the other evening, would they not be ashamed of it? I am ashamed of it. I have not given a [sarcastic] joke to any man on this journey nor felt like it; neither have I insulted any man's feelings but I have hollowed pretty loud and spoken sharply to the brethren when I have seen their awkwardness at coming to camp. The revelations in the Bible, in the Book of Mormon, and Doctrine and Covenants, teach us to be sober; and let me ask you elders that have been through the ordinances in the temple, what were your covenants there? I saw you should remember them. When I laugh [too long] I see my folly and nothingness and weakness and am ashamed of myself. I think meaner and worse of myself than any man can think of me; but I delight in God, and in His commandments and delight to meditate on Him and to serve Him and I mean that everything in me shall be subjected to Him. Now let every man repent of his weakness, of his follies, of his meanness, and every kind of wickedness, and stop your swearing and profane language, for it is in this camp and I know it, and have known it. I have said nothing about it, but I now tell you, if you don't stop it you shall be cursed by the Almighty and shall dwindle away and be damned. Such things shall not be suffered in this camp. You shall honor God, and confess His name or else you shall suffer the [spiritual] penalty. Most of this camp belong to the Church, nearly all; and I would say to you brethren, and to the Elders of Israel, if you are faithful, you will yet be sent to preach this Gospel to the nations of the earth and bid all welcome whether they believe the Gospel or not, and this kingdom [in the distant future, after the Second Coming of Christ, according to Mormon theology] will reign over many who do not belong to the Church, over thousands who do not believe in the Gospel. Bye and bye every knee shall bow and every tongue confess and acknowledge and reverence and honor the name of God and His priesthood and observe the laws of the kingdom whether they belong to the Church and obey the Gospel or not, and I mean that every man in this camp shall do it. That is what the scripture means by every knee shall bow, etc., and you cannot make anything else out of it.

" 'I understand there are several in this camp who do not belong to the Church. I am the man who will stand up for them and protect them in all their rights. And they shall not trample on our rights nor on the priesthood. They shall reverence and acknowledge the name of God and His priesthood, and if they set up their heads and seek to introduce iniquity into this camp and to trample on the priesthood, I swear to them, they shall never go back to tell the tale. I will leave them [here in the wilderness] where they will be safe. If they want to retreat they can now have the privilege, and any man who chooses to go back rather than abide the law of God can now have the privilege of doing so before we go any farther. Here are the Elders of Israel who have the priesthood, who have got to preach the Gospel, who have to gather the nations of the earth, who have to build up the kingdom so that the nations can come to it, they will stop to dance as niggers. I don't mean this as debasing the negroes by any means; they will hoe down all, turn summersets, dance on their knees, and haw, haw, out loud; they will play cards, they will play checkers and dominoes, they will use profane language, they will swear!

    " 'Suppose when you go to preach, the people should ask you what you did when you went on this mission to seek out a home for the whole Church, what was your course of conduct? Did you dance? Yes. Did you hoe down all? Yes. Did you play cards? Yes. Did you play checkers? Yes. Did you use profane language? Yes. Did you swear? Yes. Did you quarrel with each other and threaten each other? Why yes. How would you feel? What would you say for yourselves? Would you not want to go and hide up? Your mouths would be stopped and you would want to creep away in disgrace. I am one of the last to ask my brethen to enter into solemn covenants, but if they will not enter into a covenant to put away their iniquity and turn to the Lord and serve Him and acknowledge and honor His name, I want them to take their wagons and retreat back, for I shall go no farther under such a state of things. If we don't repent and quit our wickedness we will have more hinderances than we have had, and worse storms to encounter. I want the brethren to be ready for meeting tomorrow at the time appointed, instead of rambling off, and hiding in their wagons to play cards, etc. I think it will be good for us to have a fast meeting tomorrow and a prayer meeting to humble ourselves and turn to the Lord and he will forgive us.' "

Clayton continues:

"He then called upon all the High Priests to step forth in a line in front of the wagon and then the bishops to step in front of the High Priests, which being done, he counted them and found their number to be four bishops and fifteen high priests. He then called upon all the seventies to form a line in the rear of the high priests. On being counted, they were ascertained to number seventy-eight. Next he called on the elders to form a line in the rear of the wagon. They were eight in number. There were also eight of the quorum of the twelve. He then asked the brethren of the quorum of the twleve if they were willing to covenant, to turn to the Lord with all their hearts, to repent of all their follies, to cease from all their evils and serve God according to His laws. If they were willing, to manifest it by holding up their right hand. Every man held up his hand in token that he covenanted. He then put the same question to the high priests and bishops; next to the seventies, and then to the elders, and lastly to the other brethren. All covenanted with uplifted hands without a dissenting voice. He then addressed those who are not members of the Church and told them they should be protected in their rights and privileges while they would conduct themselves well and not seek to trample on the priesthood nor blaspheme the name of God, etc.

"He then referred to the conduct of Benjamin Rolfe's two younger brothers, in joining with the Higbees and John C. Bennet in sowing discord and strife among the Saints in Nauvoo and remarked that there will be no more Bennet scrapes suffered here. He spoke highly of Benjamin Rolfe's conduct, although not a member of the Church and also referred to the esteem in which his father and mother were held by the Saints generally. He then very tenderly blessed the brethren and prayed that God would enable them to fulfill their covenants and then withdrew to give opportunity for others to speak if they felt like it.

"Elder Kimball arose to say that he agreed with all that President Young had said. He receives it as the word of the Lord to him and it is the word of the Lord to this camp if they will receive it. He has been watching the motion of things and the conduct of the brethren for some time and has seen what it would lead to. He has said little but thought a great deal. It has made him shudder when he has seen the Elders of Israel descend to the lowest, dirtiest things imaginable, the tail end of everything, but what has passed this morning will make it an ever lasting blessing to the brethren, if they will repent and be faithful and keep their covenant. He never can rest satisfied until his family is liberated from the gentiles and their company and established in a land where they can plant and reap the fruits of their labors, but he has never had the privilege of eating the fruits of his labors yet, neither has his family, but when this is done he can sleep in peace if necessary but not till then. 'If we will serve the Lord, remember His name to call upon Him, and be faithful, we shall not one of us be left under the sod, but shall be permitted to return and meet our families in peace and enjoy their society again; but if this camp continues the course of conduct it has done, the judgement of God will overtake us.' He hopes the brethren will take heed to what President Young has said and let it sink deep in their hearts.

"Elder Pratt wanted to add a word to what has been said. 'Much good advice has been given to teach us how we may spend our time profitably by prayer, and meditation, etc.' But there is another idea which he wants to add:

" 'There are many books in the camp and worlds of knowledge before us which we have not obtained, and if the brethren would devote all their leisure time to seeking after knowledge, they would never need to say they had nothing with which to pass away their time. If we could spend 23 hours out of the 24 in gaining knowledge and only sleep one hour of the 24 all the days of our life, there would still be worlds of knowledge in store for us yet to learn. He knows it is difficult to bring our minds to diligent and constant studies, in pursuit of knowledge all at once, but by steady practice and perseverance we shall become habituated to it, and it will become a pleasure to us. He would recommend to the brethren, besides prayer, and obedience, to seek after knowledge continually. And it will help us to overcome our follies and nonsense; we shall have no time for it.'

"Elder Woodruff said he remembered the time when the camp went up to Missouri to redeem Zion, when Brother Joseph stood up on a wagon wheel and told the brethren that the decree had passed and could not be revoked, and the destroying angel would visit the camp and we should die like sheep with the rot. He had repeatedly warned the brethren of their evil conduct and what it would lead to, but they still continued in their course. It was not long before the destroying angel did visit the camp and the brethren began to fall as Brother Joseph had said. We buried eighteen in a short time and a more sorrowful time I never saw. There are nine here who were in that camp and they all recollect the circumstance well and will never forget it. He [Woodruff] has been thinking while the President was speaking, that if he was one who had played checkers or cards, he would take every pack of cards and every checker board and burn them up so that they would no longer be in the way to tempt us.

"Colonel Markham acknowledged that he had done wrong in many things. He had always indulged himself, before he came into the Church, with everything he desired and he knows he has done wrong on this journey, he knows his mind has become darkened since he left Winter Quarters. He hopes the brethren will forgive him and he will pray to be forgiven and try to do better. While he was speaking he was very much affected indeed and wept like a child. Many of the brethren felt much affected and all seemed to realize for the first time, the excess to which they had yielded and the awful consequence of such things if persisted in. Many were in tears and felt humbled.

"President Young returned to the boat [atop the wagon to speak] as Brother Markham closed his remarks and said in reply, that he knew the brethren would forgive him, and the Lord will forgive us all if we turn to Him with all our hearts and cease to do evil.

"The meeting was then dismissed, each man retiring to his wagon. And being half past one o'clock we again pursued our journey in peace, all reflecting on what has passed today, and many expressing their gratitude for what has transpired. It seemed as though we were just commencing on this important mission, and all realizing the responsibility resting upon us to conduct ourselves in such a manner that the journey may be an everlasting blessing to us, instead of an everlasting disgrace. No loud laughter was heard, no swearing, no quarreling, no profane language, no hard speeches to man or beast, and it truly seemed as though the cloud had burst and we had emerged into a new element, a new atmosphere, and a new society."

Note 19

[From page 138]

Oasis Warning

William Clayton describes the trading post at Fort Laramie: "A pair of moccasins are worth a dollar, a lariat a dollar, a pound of tobacco a dollar and a half, and a gallon of whiskey $32.00 ... The blacksmith shop lies on the south side of the western entrance. There are dwellings inside the fort beside that of Mr. Bordeau's. The south end is divided off and occupied for stables, etc ... "[1]

Appleton Milo Harmon records: "Mr. Bordeau said that he had bought out Fort Platte some years ago. There were thirty-eight men employed by the American Fur Company to manage the fort. Twenty of them were now absent on business for the company. They had just sent off six hundred packs of robes to Fort Pierre on the Missouri River, the distance nearly three hundred miles. They said that some traders were there yesterday who said that six days' drive ahead [west] the snow was middle deep ten days ago and that it would be difficult to find feed for our teams."[2]

Note 20

[From page 138]

Turning Tables

Clayton details the Saints' expenses with the Missouri wagon train: "The Missourian company offered to pay them well if they would carry their company over in the boat and a contract was made to do so for $1.50 per load, the brethren to receive their pay in flour at $2.50 per hundred. They commenced soon after and this evening finished their work, and received the pay mostly in flour, a little meal and some bacon."

Note 21

[From page 147]

The Rush Is On ...

In 1888 Hubert Howe Bancroft analyzes, "The conversion of San Francisco was complete. Those who had hitherto denied a lurking faith now unblushingly proclaimed it; and others, who had refused to believe even in gold specimens exhibited before their eyes, hesitated no longer in accepting any reports ... "[1]

One Gillespie reports he had "a whole quinine bottle full, which set all the people wild."[2]

Another, Carson, was finally convinced: "I looked on for a moment; a frenzy seized my soul; unbidden, my legs performed some entirely new movements of polka steps — I took several. Houses were too small for me to stay in; I was soon in the street in search of necesary outfits; piles of Gold rose up before me at every step; castles of marble, dazzling the eye with their rich appliances; thousands of slaves bowing to my beck and call; myriads of fair virgins contending with each other for my love — were among the fancies of my fevered imagination. The Rothschilds, Girards, and Astors appeared to me but poor people; in short, I had a very violent attack of the gold fever."[3]

And, thanks to Brannan, San Francisco became all but a ghost town. "Men hastened to arrange their affairs, dissolving partnerships, disposing of real estate, and converting other effects into ready means for departure."[4] The *California Star* reports, "Stores are closed and places of business vacated, a large number of houses tenantless ... everything wears a desolate and sombre look, everywhere all is dull, monotonous, dead." [5]

Henry Bigler records in his diary, "The inhabitants of the place seemed to be panic-struck and so excited and in such a hurry to be off, that some of the mechanics left their work, not taking time even to take off their aprons."[6]

Brooks likewise records in his diary May 10th, 1848: "Nothing has been talked of but the new gold placer, as people call it. Several parties, we hear, are already made up to visit the diggings." May 13th: "The gold excitement increases daily, as several fresh arrivals from the mines have been reported [here] at San Francisco." May 20th: "Several hundred people must have left here during the last few days."[7]

Because of the gold panic, servants, sailors, and day-laborers fled civilization. "Labor rose tenfold in price."[8]

Brooks records, May 17th: "Work-people have struck. Walking through the town to-day I observed that laborers were employed only upon half a dozen of the fifty new buildings which were in the course of being run up." May 20th ... "Sweating tells me that his negro waiter has demanded and receives ten dollars a day."[9]

Larkin reports June 1st: "Mechanics and teamsters, earning the year past $5 to $8 per day, have struck and gone ... A merchant lately from China has even lost his Chinese servant."[10]

Soon, according to Bancroft, "a Peruvian brig entered the bay, the first within three weeks. The houses were there, but no one came out to welcome it. At length, hailing a Mexican who was passing, the captain learned that everybody had gone northward, where the valleys and mountains were of gold. On the instant the crew were off."[11]

"One commander," continues Bancroft, "on observing the drift of affairs, gave promptly the order to put to sea. The crew refused to work, and that night gagged the watch, lowered the boat, and rowed away."[12]

Another vessel to be deserted was a ship of the Hudson Bay Company lying at anchor in the bay. The sailors departed and the captain followed them, leaving the vessel in charge of his wife and daughter.[13]

Every ship lost most of her crew within 48 hours after arrival.[14]

The first steamship, the *California,* arrived February 28, 1849 and was immediately deserted by her crew. Captain Forbes of the vessel asked Jones of the U. S. squadron for men to take charge of the ship, "but the poor commodore had none."[15]

Some Mexicans arrived in the deserted town and "broke into vacant houses and took what they would."[16]

Bancroft reports, "May had not wholly passed when at San Jose the merchant closed his store, or if the stock was perishable left open the doors that people might help themselves . . .

"So the judge abandoned his bench and the doctor his patients . . .

"Soldiers fled from their posts; others were sent for them, and none returned.

"All along the coast from Monterey to Santa Barbara, Los Angeles, and San Diego, it was the same.

"The alguacil, Henry Bee, had ten Indian prisoners under his charge in the lock-up, two of them charged with murder. These he would have turned over to the alcalde, but that functionary had already taken his departure. Bee was puzzled how to dispose of his wards, for though he was determined to go to the mines, it would never do to let them loose upon a community of women and children. Finally he took all the prisoners with him to the digging, where they worked contentedly for him until other miners, jealous of Bee's success, incited them to revolt. By that time, however, the alguacil had made his fortune."[17]

C. L. Ross records in his manuscript, "Experiences from 1847:" "I found John M. Horner, of the mission of San Jose, who told me he had left about 500 acres of splendid wheat for the cattle to roam over at will, he and his family having deserted their place entirely, and started off for the mines."[18]

J. Belden writes from San Jose, "A man just from there told me he saw the *governor* and Squire Colton there, in rusty rig, scratching gravel for gold."[19] (Our emphasis)

Bancroft adds, "As the officers who remained could no longer afford to live in their accustomed way, a cook's wages being $300 a month, they were allowed to draw rations in kind, which they exchanged for board in private families. But even then they grew restless, and soon disappeared, as Commodore Jones asserts in his report to the secretary of the navy the 25th of October.

"Nov. 2d he again writes: 'For the present, and I fear for years to come, it will be impossible for the United States to maintain any naval or military establishment in California; as at the present no hope of reward nor fear of punishment is sufficient to make binding any contract between man and man upon the soil of California. To send troops out here would be needless, for they would immediately desert ... Among the deserters from the squadron are some of the best petty officers and seamen, having but few months to serve, and large balances due them, amounting in the aggregate to over $10,000.' "[20]

Writes J. D. Borthwick in *Three Years in California:* "General Mason, Lieutenant Lanman, and myself form a mess ... This morning for the fortieth time we had to take to the kitchen and cook our own breakfast. A general of the U. S. army, the commander of a man-of-war, and the alcalde of Monterey, in a smoking kitchen grinding coffee, toasting a herring, and peeling onions!"[21]

General Vallejo claims Governor Boggs, then alcalde of Sonoma, "started at once for Sacramento to test the truth of the [gold] report."

Note 22

[From page 152]

After the Fox

In California Emily Amanda Rockwell was left alone to raise Hyram Gates' two sons from his previous marriage, but the two lads were soon killed by Indians; Emily Rockwell Gates then married a Mormon Battalion veteran, Henry W. Brizzee, and after he died she married David Tyrrell. She died April 9, 1909 and was buried near Grouse Creek, Utah.[1]

Meanwhile, "Judge Heber C. Kimball issued his first warrant to the marshal [Horace Eldredge], for the arrest of those two men, upon taking her to California, on charges of kidnapping, and signed the document on his knee."[2]

Note 23

[From page 178]

A Guiding Star

The Army quartermaster reports on their intrepid guide:
"He went out as far as the great desert tracts lying southwest of the lake, and very nearly on a level with it, and found that at that season they could not be passed over, 'unless with wings,' and returned ... [Porter's report was in contrast to the first scout's report — which claimed the trail could easily be followed and save the army between 150-200 miles] ... Rockwell and others are of the opinion that by going on a line some thirty miles farther south, along the foot of mountains seen in that direction, a fine road can be laid out, avoiding in a great degree, the desert.
"I believe such to be the case myself ... "

Note 24

[From page 191]

Killing the Bear

Captain W. J. Hawley received the detailed account of Ammon W. Babbitt's death from Twiss, the Indian agent. Hawley had interviewed Twiss several days, and reported the results to the *Council Bluffs Bugle.*[1] Hawley's report concludes: "The Indians said the Colonel fought like a grizzly bear."
The *Crescent City Oracle* adds: "They had ... lay in wait; when he [Babbitt] passed, they followed him a short distance until he had stopped, the second day in the afternoon. Then they rode down upon him, yelling and screaming. Mr. Babbitt shouted at them and motioned them to stop and pointed his pistol at them; but they passed on and he fired at them ... The Colonel [Babbitt] ... fought the whole twelve savages, disputing every inch, as he slowly backed up to his carriage for protection behind.

He had seriously wounded several, when one . . . jumped up into the wagon, and, with the tomahawk, killed [him] . . ."[2]

In a final gesture of fury they scalped him,[3] then burned the buggy.[4]

According to the *Oracle*, "Some weeks later, an Indian came in to a French trader's station with a gold watch, which bore the initials of Mr. Babbitt's name, and soon another came with a massive ring, which was also marked as a seal ring . . . together with some articles of minor value . . .

"The Indians then being charged with the murder acknowledged they had done it."[5]

A wagon train owner, Auguste Archambeau, recovered Babbitt's bank drafts for $13,000 on the prairie,[6] and returned them to Captain Wharton. Among his effects were some gold coin.[7]

Edward Martin's handcart company then came upon the site September 23rd, finding only "a little harness, two wheels and the springs of a burnt carriage or buggy . . ."[8] Martin had been informed of the attack by Archambeau's train four days previously.[9]

Babbit's effects were taken to the fort by Archambeau, where Babbitt's widow would later claim them.[10] The scene was finally scoured by the cavalry, where "nothing of the unfortunate victim" was found "but a few bones."[11]

The facts were clear Porter had attempted changing Babbitt's mind about leaving. Pioneer Franklin D. Richards records the day Babbitt left: "Babbitt felt a foreboding of this mischief [from Cheyennes;] he wanted Ferguson and some others to leave me and come with him. Porter tryed to stop him, but he would not listen."[12]

(Brigham's complicity in "Porter's hired gun for the assassination of Babbitt" defies logic: Brigham even sent Babbitt's wife and brother-in-law on a fact-finding mission to Fort Kearney, as Babbitt's brother-in-law reports in his journal.[13] If Brigham had sought the $24,000 under Babbitt's possession he would likely have "taken care of" Babbitt and company while they were still in Utah; an "accidental death" might just as easily be arranged at home as away among potentially suspicious non-Mormon emigrants and cavalrymen.)

The two commanding officers at Fort Kearney, Captain H. W. Wharton and Captain William Hoffman, knew Babbitt was slain by Cheyennes and so reported to Babbitt's wife when she visited the fort the following year.[14]

Even more ironic is the fact that Twiss, the Indian Agent, was not at Fort Laramie to inform the story-mongers of Babbitt's actual murderers. Twiss was off negotiating for peace with Cheyenne chiefs, who were at that moment admitting to him their having killed Babbitt.[15] To Twiss, the murder had been just another Indian attack; his submission of the affair to Washington had been so routine that one can hardly blame Buchanan for not knowing of the report's existence. Other historians argue the Chief Executive could easily have investigated the matter more thoroughly by going directly to army personnel and Indian agents in the region of Babbitt's murder ... rather than prematurely declaring war on Utah.

Note 25

[From page 196]

A Scapegoat the Size of Utah

Junius Wells, a Mormon correspondent during the war, put the entire affair in perspective: "There were other influences brought to bear [for the reason why war was declared on Utah] upon the cabinet of President Buchanan at this time. The question of southern disaffection might be avoided, if the indignation of the people could be wrought up and directed away from Washington. There being no foreign foe to answer for this purpose, the nearest thing to it was made to appear by clothing 'the phantom of the mountains' in the garb of an adversary — at whatever the gaze of the nation — and directing the gaze of the nation there." This succinct statement was perhaps more accurate than most Nineteenth Century historians cared to admit.

Note 26

[From page 230]

Suspicions, Suspicions, and More John Ginn

In analyzing "Mormon and Indian Wars: The Mountain Meadows Massacre, And Other Tragedies And Transactions Incident to the Mormon Rebellion Of 1857. Together With The Personal Recollection Of A Civilian Who Witnessed Many Of the Thrilling Scenes Described," a reviewing librarian writes the following forward to John I. Ginn's imaginative manuscript: "It was apparently written to be published in a book but the author, who purports to be an experienced newspaperman, tells many personal experiences which are highly implausible. He does not, as a journalist should, cite names for the mistreated Mormons, the Editor of the *Deseret News,* and others. When he cites names it is for such prominent men as President Young, Porter Rockwell, General Wells and the like. From about page 30 the author turns from personal experience to a bigoted Mormon-hater, so prejudiced that no publisher of this century would expect it to sell under the adverse criticism which reviewers would give to it.

"The author also claims to be a 'Captain,' but is not listed in known army lists, such as the Civil War, although the material here was apparently written during the present century. Nor is he mentioned in known diaries of the 1857 period, although he purports to have spent considerable time in Salt Lake City, associated with such prominent people as Porter Rockwell, General Wells, John Taylor's mother, Albert Carrington (editor of the *Deseret News*) and the like ... N. I. Butt, February 6, 1952."[1]

In his report of the Utah War, Ginn exaggerates statistics, contrives scenes of Mormons farcically bungling the Pacific Springs incident and others, and generally seeks to discredit Wells' army; additionally, he contradicts himself: on page seven he claims 2,000 army mules were at stake which the Mormons had attempted stealing, on page 77 he claims 48 mules, the correct number.

Ginn advanced to a not-so-illustrious editing career at six Nevada papers, lasting at each: one issue, five months, two months, four months, two years, and seven months, respectively.[2]

In his preface to *1858-1958 The Newspapers of Nevada; A History and Bibliography,* Richard E. Lingenfelter issues a timely warning: "Some editors were subject to human frailties, including dishonesty, and historians should be alert ... "[3]

Note 27

[From page 233]

An Aching Case for the Saints: The Aiken Case

The same *Index* article claims the Californians "were much respected ... and were useful and worthy members of society." This account conflicts sharply with the (St. George) *Union,*[1] which reports the Californians had in their possession "24 revolvers, four thousand dollars in gold and ... gambling apparatuses."

John I. Ginn claims to have spoken with the prisoners,[2] and asserts the church planned to plunder the men for their $8,000.[3] Ginn's story mushrooms, however, as he later claims the men possessed $18,000.[4] Bill Hickman's anti-Mormon editor, J. H. Beadle (and possibly the "idea man" behind much of Hickman's confessions book) makes the story even better, stating the men had $25,000.[5] Ginn then depicts a conversation somewhat lacking in credibility as he claims a Mormon had told him the church would murder the prisoners before they'd arrive in California, in order to plunder their gold.[6] With rumors rampant, other anti-Mormons took up the crusade, including Nevada House Representative John Cradlebaugh[7], Anthony Metcalf[8], Ann Eliza Young[9], R. N. Baskin[10], and Reverend T. DeWitt Talmage[11].

After his death, Rockwell was again implicated in the murder. A bizarre court case occurred, wherein the prosecution, specifically Thomas Singleton,[12] Richard Ivie,[13] and Joseph Skeen,[14] claimed Rockwell, Sylvanus Collett, and two others had accompanied four of the prisoners from Lehi, Utah.[15] After spending the night in Nephi, the four Mormons with their four prisoners rode out of town. Two of the prisoners were purportedly never seen again.

Two witnesses at the hotel, Guy Foote and Reuben Down, claimed two of the prisoners returned, bleeding, first one in the morning, the other the same afternoon.[16] Guy Foote claimed his mother repaired one of the men's moneybelts, which was laden with gold.

Two other men, Joseph Skeen and his son, William, testified Collett had confessed to them that Rockwell and Collett had been ordered to murder the prisoners,[17] and had succeeded in killing two, but that the other two had escaped, wounded.

The two wounded prisoners reportedly recovered and set out for Salt Lake City. Guy Foote of the hotel claimed the two men paid their hotel bill with their only weapon, a revolver.[18]

Reuben Down claimed the two Californians set out north, then he saw Rockwell and several others begin their ride north.[19]

William Skeen added Collett later confessed to him personally that Collett had — on this journey northward — murdered the two Californians at Willow Creek, eight miles above Nephi, and then weighted the corpses with rocks and tossed them into the springs. B. H. Johnson testified he had followed tracks to the springs, where he had seen bubbles emanating from the waters the next morning. Timothy B. Foote claimed that a year after the incident he helped hook out the two bodies.

The next day, a third prisoner's jacket was claimed to have been discovered by Guy Foote, riddled with bullet holes and blood stains. This was the testimony of both Reuben Down and Guy Foote. Foote further claimed he had seen friends with the dead prisoner's (Aiken's) coat and saddles.

Bill Hickman later claimed Rockwell and his men had come upon the fifth prisoner further north, at Point of the Mountain. They had attempted to murder him, but he had escaped. Hickman bragged that he eventually killed the man.[20]

The prosecution seemed to have a fairly solid case. Myriads of witnesses seemed to support each other, and were it not for some fairly healthy cross-examination, Rockwell would have appeared guilty. A careful scrutiny of the case, however, reveals interesting information, generally overlooked in Twentieth Century reports. The total story is contained in indictment papers and collateral material from the court,[1] daily reports in the *Salt Lake Tribune, Salt Lake Daily Herald,* and *Deseret News* of October 10, 11, and 12, 1878, and the trial's synopsis as contained in the 1893 edition of

Whitney's *History of Utah*.[22] Reviewing this material, one sees the prosecution actually failed to prove any murders ever even occurred. Absolutely no evidence exists of any deaths. Secondly, the defense proved the witnesses had motives which rendered their testimonies worthless, and were of such a character that they could not be trusted. Thirdly, their account of the alleged murders were carefully picked apart point by point.

For example, Mrs. Martha J. Coray stated that she lived 40 rods from the springs described by B. H. Johnson and that she would have seen him wandering about the springs. Alonzo W. Rhodes testified the springs were practically hidden by grass and tules so the water could not readily be seen. Even so, fish from the water would occasionally bubble from the bottom — not necessarily bodies.

Dr. J. M. Benedict[23], Dr. W. H. Leach[24], and Dr. Walter R. Pike[25] testified that the bodies thrown into the springs would have deteriorated by the time Timothy B. Foote claimed to have hooked them out — a *year* later — and that only scattered bones would have existed.

James Pexton, a blacksmith, denied ever having made a grappling hook for Timothy B. Foote to use for the bodies.

And Timothy B. Foote seemed to possess a remarkable memory for so many details of the alleged murders and alleged conversations surrounding them, but could not for some reason manage to remember who helped him fish out the bodies, where the springs were located, or where he afterwards buried the bodies.

Timothy B. Foote was then proven to have suffered "crazy spells," and confessed to having suffered and having been diagnosed for bouts of insanity previously, lasting for up to three days at a time. The defense was prepared to prove he had also attempted suicide the previous year, but the judge sustained an objection.

A major obstacle to the witnesses' story came from a woman: Guy Foote's mother contradicted her son's testimony and testified she had not repaired the prisoner's moneybelt, nor had she even seen the belt with its supposed gold coins.[26]

Other inconsistencies also occurred, revealing the difficulty of the prosecution to keep their stories straight. For example, Reuben Down claimed the prisoners paid for their stay at Foote's hotel with a watch, before Guy Foote persuaded them to instead pay with a gun. But Guy Foote contradicted Down's story (the contradiction was over the prisoner ever commenting about losing his only weapon).[27]

The main defendant, Sylvanus Collett, was supported by witnesses that he was away from the scene of the alleged murder, carrying express between Great Salt Lake City and Tooele for Bryant Stringham.

Five witnesses then testified that Guy Foote's reputation as a liar among his neighbors was incomparable west of the Mississippi. They included Richard Peay, James Pexton, Charles Sperry, Henry Goldsborough, and Matthew Douglas.

The principal witness against Rockwell and Collett was William Skeen. Five other men testified William Skeen's word was thoroughly unreliable; they included L. W. Shurtliff, William Geddes, John Spiers, John Draney, and Charles Neal. Additionally, Skeen had been convicted of grand larceny April 22, 1869.

The motive behind Skeen's slam against Rockwell and Collett was obvious. Skeen's brother, David, had been killed in 1862 by Sheriff Ricks, and Skeen suspected Collett had taken part. Skeen had afterwards sought conviction of Ricks on the death of his brother, but had failed, and now, 20 years later, had apparently decided to take it out on Collett and Rockwell.

On October 16, 1878, the jury handed down their verdict: Not guilty.

Rockwell's name was cleared. Collett was freed.

Perhaps the most amusing version of the stories comes from a San Francisco newspaper, the *Daily Alta Californian* January 25, 1858. The story reads that two of the Aiken prisoners had been killed by Indians and that two others, riding back into town, had begged the Mormons for protection, but were instead "shot down in the streets in daylight by the people."[28]

In more recent years, an equally amusing article appeared in a western tabloid (published in 1976) fictionalizing the above testimony of Skeen and presenting it as fact. The absurdity of the article is iced off with photographs of an iron ball found near the "death springs." The article claims the ball was used to weigh down a body, but the assertion crumbles under logic: Foote would not have neglected to include mentioning the iron ball, nor could he physically have hauled up the bodies and the connected ball with merely a grappling hook without the year-old decomposed bodies falling apart. Yet he claimed to have pulled up both the bodies and the "weights."

Capping off the incredulity of the article is a photograph: The iron ball is perfectly black and round, without a speck of rust, after sitting underwater for a year, then presumably at the pond's side for another 117 years. A second photograph reveals a rim of the buggy supposedly sent with the bodies into the pond, with the rim now in the mud near the spring — still silvery, shining, and bright.

Apparently, both Nineteenth and Twentieth Century writers have heaped on a one-sided argument against Rockwell and Brigham, using the Aiken Case, and, to construct it, they have swallowed a number of assertions which, at best, are palpably absurd.

Note 28

[From page 244]

The World Press Presses the U. S.

The *London Times* further suggests, "Does it not seem impossible that men and women, brought up under British and American civilization, can abandon it for the wilderness and Mormonism? They step into the waves of the great basin with as much reliance on their leaders as the descendants of Jacob felt when they stepped between the walls of water in the Red Sea. [They are comparable to] the ancient world and individual Curiatti, Horatii, and other examples of herosim, ready to sacrifice everything . . . "[1]

Reynolds' Newspaper, representing the British Republicans, comments: "After we have . . . proved his [Joseph Smith] followers to be a mixed multitude of the gravest knaves [a reference to polygamy] . . . that ever walked the earth, Mormonism still remains a great human fact — perhaps the greatest — certainly the most wonderful fact of this nineteenth century. As such, it is entitled to our earnest and respectful consideration.

"There can be no doubt that, in one thing at least, Mormonism has been eminently successful. It has, in the great majority of instances, really improved the earthly condition of those who have embraced it.

" . . . the Mormons, not as fanatics or sectaries, but as heavily-oppressed, long-suffering, and earnestly struggling men, are entitled to the sympathy of the enslaved classes throughout the world.

"But they have a claim to something more than sympathy. Their heroic endurance and marvellous achievements entitle them to the respect and admiration of their fellow-creatures.

" . . . and how many thousands of the down-trodden and penury-stricken victims of European tyranny were leaving the land of their birth, in order to find in the Mormon territory, that hope and encouragement denied to them in their native countries; how all this has been accomplished by the reviled followers of Joseph Smith, all Europe and America have heard, and, though hating, admired."[2]

The *New York Times* adds, "Whatever our opinions may be of Mormon morals and Mormon manners, there can be no question that this voluntary abandonment by 40,000 people of homes created by wonderful industry, in the midst of trackless wastes, after years of hardships and persecution, is something from which no one who has a particle of sympathy [for] . . . pluck, fortitude and constancy can withhold his admiration . . . we think it would be most unwise to treat Mormonism as a nuisance to be abated by a *posse commitatus.* It is no longer a social excresence to be cut off by the sword . . . When people abandon their homes to plunge with women and children into a wilderness, to seek new settlements, they know not where, they give a higher proof of courage than if they fought for them . . . "[3]

Note 29

[From page 255]

The Questionable Corpse of John Gheen

"Another victim fell, last week, by violence. No doubt the jury has done its best duty, on examination of the facts, in returning a verdict of *felo de se*. But doubts exist in the minds of many, of the practicability of any right-handed man shooting himself from the left side of the skull, the bullet passing through the head in a nearly horizontal line; and the pistol found under him in or near his right hand. The arrival of a certain party from the West [the article is not implying Rockwell, who was already in the valley], who felt aggrieved with John Gheen, who had also been threatened by the former, is likewise a matter of grave suspicion. I would not, by any means, cast willfully an imputation on any man, yet it is the gossip of the city, and we have a right to weigh every circumstance that affects the public security."

- *The Mountaineer,* October 8, 1859

Note 30

[From page 260]

"Introducing Mr. Rockwell On Our Left"

Sir Richard Francis Burton:

"Porter Rockwell was a man about fifty [actually forty- seven], tall and strong, with ample leather leggings overhanging his huge spurs, and the saw-handles of two revolvers peeping from his blouse [which further reveals the possibility Rockwell didn't wear holsters]. His forehead was already a little bald, and he wore his long grizzly locks after the ancient fashion of the U.S., plaited and gathered up at the nape of the neck; his brow puckered with frowning wrinkles contrasted curiously with his cool determined grey eye, jolly red face, well touched up with 'paint,' and his laughing good-humored mouth."

Note 31

[From page 260]

"And Mr. Young On Our Right"

Sir Richard Francis Burton:

"Shortly after arriving, I had mentioned to Governor Cumming my desire to call upon Mr., or rather, as his official title is, President Brigham Young, and he honored me by inquiring what time would be most convenient to him . . .

"After a slight scrutiny we passed the guard — which is dressed in plain clothes, and to the eye unarmed — and walking down the veranda, entered the Prophet's private office. Several people who were sitting there rose at Mr. Cumming's entrance. At a few words of introduction, Mr. Brigham Young advanced, shook hands with complete simplicity of manner, asked me to be seated on a sofa at one side of the room, and presented me to those present.

"Under ordinary circumstances it would be unfair in a visitor to draw [describe] the portrait of one visited. But this is no common case. I have violated no rites of hospitality. Mr. Brigham Young is a 'seer, revelator, and prophet, having all the gifts of God which He bestows upon the Head of the Church:' his memoirs, lithographs, photographs, and portraits have been published again and again; I add but one more likeness; and, finally, I have nothing to say except in his favor.

"The Prophet was born at Whittingham, Vermont, on the 1st of June, 1801; he was consequently, in 1860, fifty-nine years of age; he looks about forty-five. *La célébrité vieillit* – I had expected to see a venerable-looking old man. Scarcely a gray thread appears in his hair, which is parted on the side, light colored, rather thick, and reaches below the ears with a half curl. He formerly wore it long, after the Western style; now it is cut level with the ear-lobes. The forehead is somewhat narrow, the eyebrows are thin, the eyes between gray and blue, with a calm, composed, and somewhat reserved expression: a slight droop in the left lid made me think that he had suffered from paralysis; I afterward heard that the ptosis is the result of a neuralgia which has long tormented him.

For this reason he usually covers his head, except in his own house or in the Tabernacle. Mrs. Ward, who is followed by the *'Revue des Deux-Mondes,'* therefore errs again in asserting that 'his Mormon majesty never removes his hat in public.' ... The hands are well made, and not disfigured by rings. The figure is somewhat large, broad-shouldered, and stooping a little when standing.

"The Prophet's dress was neat and plain as a Quaker's, all gray homespun except the cravat and waistcoat ...

"Altogether the Prophet's appearance was that of a gentleman farmer in New England — in fact, such as he is: his father was an agriculturalist and revolutionary soldier, who settled 'down East.' He is a well-preserved man; a fact which some attribute to his habit of sleeping, as the Citizen [Pierre Joseph] Proudhon so strongly advises, in solitude.

"His manner is at once affable and impressive, simple and courteous: his want of pretension contrasts favorably with certain psuedo-prophets that I have seen, each and every one of whom holds himself to be a 'Logos' without other claim save a semi-maniacal self-esteem. He shows no signs of dogmatism, bigotry, or fanaticism, and never once entered — with me at least — upon the subject of religion. He impresses a stranger with a certain sense of power; his followers are, of course, wholly fascinated by his superior strength of brain. It is commonly said there is only one chief in Great Salt Lake City, and that is 'Brigham.' His temper is even and placid; his manner is cold — in fact, like his face, somewhat bloodless; but he is neither morose nor methodistic, and, where ocasion requires, he can use all the weapons of ridicule to direful effect, and 'speak a bit of his mind' in a style which no one forgets. He often reproves his erring followers in purposely violent language, making the terrors of a scolding the punishment in lieu of hanging for a stolen horse or cow.

"His powers of observation are intuitively strong, and his friends declare him to be gifted with an excellent memory and a perfect judgement of character. If he dislikes a stranger at the first interview, he never sees him again.

"Of his temperance and sobriety there is but one opinion. His life is ascetic: his favorite food is baked potatoes with a little buttermilk, and his drink water: he disapproves, as do all strict Mormons, of spirituous liquors, and never touches any thing stronger than a glass of thin Lagier-bier; moreover, he abstains from tobacco. Mr. Hyde has accused him of habitual intemperance: he is, as his appearance shows, rather disposed to abstinence than to the reverse.

"Of his education I can not speak: 'men, not books — deeds, not words,' has ever been his motto; he probably has, as Mr. Randolph said of Mr. Johnston, 'a mind uncorrupted by books.' In the only discourse which I heard him deliver, he pronounced impetus, impētus. Yet he converses with ease and correctness, has neither snuffle nor pompousness, and speaks as an authority upon certain subjects, such as agriculture and stock-breeding.

"He assumes no airs of extra sanctimoniousness, and has the plain, simple manners of honesty. His followers deem him an angel of light, his foes a goblin damned . . . He has been called hypocrite, swindler, forger, murderer. No one looks it less . . . He is the St. Paul of the New Dispensation: true and sincere . . . and if he has not been able to create, he has shown himself great in controlling circumstances.

"Finally, there is a total absense of pretension in his manner, and he has been so long used to power that he cares nothing for its display. The arts by which he rules the heterogeneous mass of conflicting elements are indomitable will, profound secrecy, and uncommon astuteness.

"Such is His Excellency President Brigham Young, 'painter and glazier' — his earliest craft — prophet, revelator, translator, and seer; the man who is revered as king or kaiser, pope or pontiff never was; who, like the Old Man of the Mountain, by holding up his hand could cause the death of any one within his reach; who, governing as well as reigning, long stood up to fight with the sword of the Lord, and with his few hundred guerillas, outwitted all diplomacy opposed to him . . .

"The Prophet received us in his private office, where he transacts the greater part of his business, corrects his sermons, and conducts his correspondence. It is a plain, neat room, with the usual conveniences, a large writing-desk and money-safe, table, sofas, and chairs, all made by the able mechanics of the settlement. I remarked a pistol and a rifle hung within ready reach on the right-hand wall; one of these is, I was told, a newly-invented twelve-shooter. There was a look of order, which suited the character of the man: it is said that a door badly hinged, or a curtain hung awry, 'puts his [Brigham's] eye out.' His style of doing business at the desk or in the field — for the Prophet does not disdain handiwork — is to issue distinct, copious, and intelligible directions to his employees, after which he dislikes referring to the subject. It is typical of his mode of acting, slow, deliberate, and conclusive. He has the reputation of being wealthy. He rose to power a poor man. The Gentiles naturally declare that he enriched himself by the tithes and plunder of his followers, and especially by preying upon and robbing the Gentiles. I believe, however, that no one pays Church-dues and alms with more punctuality than the Prophet, and that he has far too many opportunities of coining money, safely and honestly, to be guilty, like some desperate destitute, of the short-sighted folly of fraud.

"In 1859 he owned, it is said, to being possessed of $250,000, equal to 50,000 pounds, which makes a millionaire in these mountains — it is too large a sum to jeopardize. His fortunes were principally made in business: like the late Imaum of Muscat, he is the chief merchant as well as the high priest. He sends long trains of wagons freighted with various goods to the Eastern States, and supplies caravans and settlements with grain and provisions. From the lumber which he sold to the federal troops for hutting themselves at Camp Floyd, he is supposed to have netted not less than $200,000. This is one of the sorest points with the army: all declare that the Mormons would have been in rags or sackcloth if soldiers had not been sent; and they naturally grudge discomfort, hardship, and expatriation, whose only effect has been to benefit their enemies.

"After the few first words of greeting, I interpreted the Prophet's look to mean that he would not dislike to know my object in the City of the Saints. I told him that, having read and heard much about Utah as it is said to be, I was anxious to see Utah as it is. He then entered briefly upon the subjects of stock and agriculture, and described the several varieties of soil . . .

"The humanity of the Prophet's followers to the Lamanite [American Indian, as described in the *Book of Mormon*] has been distorted by Gentiles into a deep and dangerous project for 'training the Indians' to assassinate individul enemies, and, if necessary, to act as guerillas against the Eastern invaders. That the Yutas — they divide the white world into two great classes, Mormon and Shwop, or American generally — would, in case of war, 'stand by' their patrons [the Mormons], I do not doubt; but this would only be the effect of kindness, which it is unfair to attribute to no worthier cause.

" ... When conversation began to flag, we rose up, shook hands, as is the custom here, all round, and took leave. The first impression left upon my mind by this short seance, and it was subsequently confirmed, was, that the Prophet is no common man, and that he has none of the weakness and vanity which characterize the common uncommon man.

"A desultory conversation can not be expected to draw out a master spirit, but a truly distinguished character exercises most often an instinctive — some would call it a mesmeric — effect upon those who come in contact with it; and as we hate or despise at first sight, and love or like at first sight, so Nature teaches us at first sight what to respect ... I also remarked an instance of the veneration shown by his followers, whose affection for him is equaled only by the confidence with which they intrust to him their dearest interests in this world and in the next. After my visit many congratulated me, as would the followers of the Tien Wong, or heavenly King, upon having at last seen what they consider 'a per se' the most remarkable man in the world."

Note 32

[From page 260]

"And Mrs. Young, and Mrs. Young, and Mrs. Young ... "

Sir Richard Francis Burton's notes on polygamy are scattered throughout his book, *City of the Saints*. In prefacing his analysis on the subject, he regards the Mormon city by the giant salt lake as "this lovely panorama of green and azure and gold ... this land, fresh as it were from the hands of God."

Although generally critical of the Saints and skeptical of their leaders' claims to divine authority, he admires aspects of the Saints' practical application of their religion, including, surprisingly, polygamy:

"In quality [role] of doctor I have seen a little . . . There is in Mormondom, as in all other exclusive faiths . . . an inner life into which I cannot flatter myself or deceive the reader with the idea of my having penetrated."

In contesting the blatant anti-Mormons' assertions that Momon women are ugly, badly dressed, and depressed, he observes they are "exceedingly pretty and attractive. I looked in vain for the outhouse-harems in which certain romancers concerning things Mormon had informed me that wives are kept, like any other stock. I presently found this but one of a multitude of delusions." He further compares American women generally to Mormon women as "a sex which is early taught and soon learns to consider itself creation's cream, enhanced and improved among the Mormons."

While federal census takers in 1850 and 1860 claimed more males than females existed in Utah, thus disclaiming the Mormons' argument for the need of polygamy, Burton sagely discerned that the federal officials were hostile towards the Mormons — and thus he doubted their figures. He believed from what he saw that approximately 2,000 more females lived in Utah than males.

Unlike some polygamist populations of the world, he felt the Mormons shunned immorality like Puritans. "A suspicion of immorality is more hateful than the reputation of bloodshed," he inaccurately notes, yet he correctly ascribes the Mormon view of chastity as high on the commandment list. "In point of mere morality the Mormon community is perhaps purer than any other of equal numbers."

Burton comments on the deterioration of U. S. Government relations with Indians, stating that only the Mormons' relationship with the Indians remained good. "The Mormons treat their step-brethren with far more humanity than other western men . . . they feed, clothe, and lodge them, and attach them by good works to their interests."

Before commenting in detail on polygamy, Burton quotes

official church statements of the 1860's:

" 'The one-wife system is confined principally to a few small nations inhabiting Europe, and to those who are of European origin inhabiting America. It is estimated by the most able historians of our day, that about four-fifths of the population of the globe believe and practice, according to their respective laws, the doctrine of a Plurality of Wives. If the popularity of a doctrine is in proportion to the numbers who believe in it, then it follows that the Plurality system is four times more popular among the inhabitants of the earth than the one-wife system.

" 'Those nations who practise the Plurality doctrine consider it as virtuous and as right for one man to have many wives as to have one only. Therefore, they have enacted laws, not only giving this right to their citizens, but also protecting them in it.

" 'The posterity raised up unto the husband through each of his wives are all considered to be legitimate, and provisions are made in their laws for those children, the same as if they were the children of one wife ... Indeed, Plurality among them is considered not only virtuous and right, but a great check or preventative against adulteries and unlawful connections, which are among the greatest evils with which nations are cursed, producing a vast amount of suffering and misery, devastation and death; undermining the very foundations of happiness, and destroying the frame-work of society, and the peace of the domestic circle.

" 'Some of the nations of Europe who believe in the one-wife system, have actually forbidden a plurality of wives by their laws; and the consequences are that the whole country among them is overrun with the most abominable practices; adulteries and unlawful connections prevail through all their villages, towns, cities, and country places, to a most fearful extent. And among some of these nations, sinks of wickedness, wretchedness, and misery are licensed by law; while their piety would be wonderfully shocked to authorise by law the Plurality system, as adopted by many neighboring nations.

" 'The Constitution and laws of the United States, being founded upon the principles of freedom, do not interfere with marriage relations, but leave the nation free to believe in and practice the doctrine of a Plurality of wives, or to confine themselves to the one-wife system, just as they choose. This is as it should be: it leaves the conscience of man untrammelled, and so long as he injures no person, and does not infringe upon the rights of others, he is free by the Constitution to marry one wife, or many, or none at all, and becomes accountable to God for the righteousness or unrighteousness of his domestic relations.

" ' . . . In one of the revelations through him [Joseph Smith], we read that God raised up wise men and inspired them to write the Constitution of our country, that the freedom of the people might be maintained, according to the free agency which He had given to them; that every man might be accountable to God and not to man, so far as religious doctrines and conscience are concerned. And the more we examine that sacred document, framed by the wisdom of our illustrious fathers, the more we are compelled to believe that an invisible power controlled, dictated, and guided them in laying the foundation of liberty and freedom upon this great Western Hemisphere. To this land . . . [foreignors] can emigrate, and each bring with him his . . . wives and his . . . children, and the glorious Constitution of our country will not interfere with his domestic relations. Under the broad banner of the Constitution, he is protected in all his family associations; none have a right to tear any of his wives or his children from him. So, likewise, under the broad folds of the Constitution, the Legislative Assembly of the Territory of Utah have the right to pass laws regulating their matrimonial relations and protecting each of their citizens in the right of marrying one or many wives, as the case may be. If Congress should repeal those laws, they could not do so on the ground of their being unconstitutional.

" ' . . . Tradition and custom have great influence over nations. Long established customs, whether right or wrong, become sacred in the estimation of Mankind. Those nations who have been accustomed from time immemorial to the practice of what is called Polygamy, would consider a law abolishing it as the very height of injustice and oppression; the very idea of being limited to the one-wife system would be considered not only oppressive and unjust, but absolutely absurd and ridiculous; it would be considered an innovation upon the long established usages, customs, and laws of numerous and powerful nations; an innovation of the most dangerous character, calculated to destroy the most sacred rights and privileges of family associations to upset the very foundations of individual rights, rendered dear and sacred by being handed down to them from the most remote ages of antiquity.

" 'On the other hand, the European nations who have been for centuries restricted by law to the one-wife theory, would consider it a shocking innovation upon the customs of their fathers to abolish their restrictive laws, and to give freedom and liberty, according to the plurality system. It is custom, then, in a great degree, that forms the conscience of nations and individuals in regard to the marriage relationships. Custom causes four-fifths of the population of the globe to decide that Polygamy, as it is called, is a good, and not an evil practice; custom causes the balance, or the remaining fifth, to decide in opposition . . .

" 'Those who are completely divested from the influence of national customs, and who judge concerning this matter by the word of God, are compelled to believe that the Plurality of Wives was once sanctioned, for many ages, by the Almighty; and by a still further research of the Divine oracles, they find no intimations that this Divine institution was ever repealed.

" 'It was an institution, not originated under the law of Moses, but it was of a far more ancient date; and instead of being abolished by that law, it was sanctioned and perpetuated: and when Christ came to fulfil that law, and to do it away by the introduction of a better covenant, He did not abolish the plurality system: not being originated under that law, it was not made null and void when that law was done away. Indeed there were many things in connection with the law that were not abolished when the law was fulfilled; as, for instance, the ten commandments which the people under the Gospel covenant were still obliged to obey . . .

" 'If the people of this country have generally formed different conclusions from us upon this subject; and if they have embraced religions which are more congenial to their minds than the religion of the Saints, we say to them that they are welcome to their own religious views; the laws should not interfere with the exercise of their religious rights.' "

Burton then begins his own analysis of the system:

"They ... [assert] that the liberty which man claims by the dignity of his nature, permits him to choose the tie, whether polyandric, monogamic, or polygamic."

Burton then quotes Mormon Parley P. Pratt, from *Marriage and Morals in Utah,* p. 3: " ' ... If such institutions are older than Moses and are found perpetuated and unimpaired by Moses, and the Prophets, Jesus and the Apostles, then it will appear evident that no merely human legislation or authority, whether proceeding from emperor, king, or people, has a right to change, alter, or pervert them.' " While Pratt says, "no merely human legislation" can change ancient institutions, Latter-day Saints believe their modern Prophets — all since 1890 — have been instructed by God to repeal polygamy.

" 'There is a prevailing idea,' continues Pratt, 'especially in England, and even the educated are labouring under it, that the Mormons are Communists or Socialists of Plato's, Cicero's, Mr. Owen's and M. Cabet's school.' " [Owen began a society at New Harmony, Indiana in 1825 while Etienne Cabet, from France, established one at Nauvoo, Illinois in 1846 after the Saints fled the city, thus causing perhaps some of the confusion.] The Saints did in fact attempt a "United Order" on an experimental basis in various western communities, with varying degrees of success, but claimed theirs was different than "man-made" communal systems, as it was "inspired by God," with voluntary involvement and no freedoms detached, in contrast to the more typical forms of socialism and communism.

Burton continues:

"[Some Englishmen also believe of the Mormons] that wives are in public, and that a woman can have as many husbands as the husband can have wives — in fact, to speak colloquially, that they 'all pig together.' The contrary is notably the case.

" ... They adopt every method of preventing what they consider a tremendous evil, viz. the violation of God's temple in their own bodies.

"The marriage ceremony is performed in the temple, or, that being impossible, in Mr. Brigham Young's office, properly speaking by the Prophet, who can, however, depute any follower, as Mr. Heber Kimball, a simple apostle, or even an elder, to act for him.

When mutual consent is given, the parties are pronounced man and wife, in the name of Jesus Christ; prayers follow, and there is a patriarchal feast of joy in the evening.

"The first wife, as among polygamists generally, is the wife, and assumes the husband's name and title. Her 'plurality'-partners are called sisters — such as sister Anne or sister Blanche — and are the aunts of her children. The first wife is married for time, the others are sealed for eternity [actually the first is married for both time and eternity]. Hence, according to the Mormons, arose the Gentiles calumny concerning spiritual wifedom, which they distinctly deny. Girls rarely remain single past sixteen — in England the average marrying age is thirty — and they would be the pity of the community, if they were doomed to a waste of youth so unnatural.

"Divorce is rarely obtained by the man who is ashamed to own [up to the fact] that he cannot keep his house in order; some, such as the President, would grant it only in case of adultery; wives, however, are allowed to claim it for cruelty, desertion, or neglect.

" . . . The literalism with which the Mormons have interpreted Scripture has led them directly to polygamy. The texts promising to Abraham a progeny numerous as the stars above or the sands below, and that 'in his seed (a polygamist) all the families of the earth shall be blessed,' induce them, his descendents, to seek a similar blessing . . . Baptism for the dead — an old rite, revived and founded upon the writings of St. Paul quoted in the last chapter — has been made a part of [their] practice, [just as] vicarious marriage for the departed also enters into the Mormon scheme.

" . . . The Mormons, with Bossuet and others, see in the New Testament no order against plurality; and in the Old dispensation they find the practice sanctioned in a family, ever the friends of God, and out of which the Redeemer sprang . . .

"The 'chaste and plural marriage' being once legalized, finds a multitude of supporters. The anti-Mormons declare that it is at once fornication and adultery — a sin which absorbs all others. The Mormons point triumphantly to the austere morals of their community, their superior freedom from maladive influences, and the absence of that uncleanness and licentiousness which distinguish the cities of the civilised world. They boast that if it be an evil they have at least chosen the lesser evil, that they practise openly as a virtue what others do secretly as a sin — how full is society of these latent Mormons! — that their plurality has abolished the necessity of concubinage, crytogamy, contubernium, celibacy, *mariages du treizieme arrondissement,* with their terrible consequences, infanticide, and so forth; that they have removed their ways from those 'whose end is bitter as wormwood, and sharp as a two-edged sword' . . .

"There are rules and regulations of Mormonism — I cannot say whether they date before or after the heavenly command to pluralise — which disprove the popular statement that such marriages are made to gratify licentiousness, and which render polygamy a positive necessity. All sensuality in the married state is strictly forbidden beyond the requisite for ensuring progeny — the practice, in fact, of Adam and Abraham. During the gestation and nursing of children, the strictest continence on the part of the mother is required — rather for a hygenic than for a religious reason. The same custom is practised in part by the Jews, and in whole by some of the noblest tribes of savages; the splendid physical development of the Kaffir race in South Africa is attributed by some authors to a rule of continence like that of the Mormons, and to a lactation prolonged for two years. The anomaly of such a practice in the midst of civilisation is worthy of a place in De Balzac's great repertory of morbid anatomy; it is only to be equalled by the exceptional nature of the Mormon's position, his [a Mormon's] past fate and his future prospects. Spartan-like Faith wants a race of warriors, and it adopts the best means to obtain them.

"Besides religious and physiological, there are social motives for the plurality. As in the days of Abraham, the lands about New Jordan are broad and the people few. Of the three forms that unite the sexes, polygamy increases, whilst monogamy balances, and polyandry diminishes progeny. The former, as Montesquieu acutely suggested, acts inversely to the latter, by causing a preponderance of female over male births . . .

"The anti-Mormons are fond of quoting Paley: 'It is not the question whether one man will have more children by five wives,

but whether these five women [would] not have had more children
if they had each a husband.' The Mormons reply that — setting
aside the altered rule of production — their colony, unlike all
others, numbers more female than male immigrants; consequently
that, without polygamy, part of the social field would remain
untilled.

"To the unprejudiced traveller it appears that polygamy is the
rule where population is required . . . in Arabia and in the wilds of
the Rocky Mountains it maintains a strong hold upon the affections
of mankind . . .

"The other motive for polygamy in Utah is economy. Servants
are rare and costly; it is cheaper and more comfortable to marry
them. Many converts are attracted by the prospect of becoming
wives, especially from places where, like Clifton, there are
sixty-four females to thirty-six males. The old maid is, as she
ought to be, an unknown entity. Life in the wilds of Western
America is a course of severe toil: a single woman cannot perform
the manifold duties of housekeeping, cooking, scrubbing, washing,
darning, child-bearing, and nursing a family. A division of labour is
necessary, and she finds it by acquiring a sisterhood . . .

"The moral influence diffused over social relations by the
presence of polygamy will be intelligble only to those who have
studied the workings of the system in lands where seclusion is
practised in its modified form, as amongst the Syrian
Christians . . .

"[Among the Mormons] . . . the consent of the first wife to a
rival is seldom refused . . . there is household comfort, affection,
circumspect friendship, and domestic discipline. Womanhood is
not petted and spoiled as in the Eastern States . . .

"It will be asked what view does the softer sex take of
polygamy? . . .

"For the attachment of the women of the Saints to the doctrine
of plurality there are many reasons. The Mormon prophets have
expended all their arts upon this end, well knowing that without
the hearty co-operation of mothers and wives, sisters and
daughters, no institution can live long . . . a modified reaction
respecting the community of Saints has set in throughout the
States; people no longer wonder that their missionaries do not

show horns and cloven feet, and the Federal officer, the itinerant politician, the platform orator, and the place-seeking demagogue, can no longer make political capital by bullying, oppressing, and abusing them. The tide has turned, and will turn yet more. But the individual still suffers: the apostate Mormon is looked upon by other people as a scamp or a knave, and the [apostate] woman worse than a prostitute. Again, all the fervour of a new faith burns in their bosoms, with a heat which we can little appreciate, and the revelation of Mr. Joseph Smith is considered on this point as superior to the Christian as the latter is in others to the Mosaic Dispensation. Polygamy is a positive command from heaven . . .

"I have heard . . . a well-educated Mormon woman who, in the presence of a Gentile sister, urged her husband to take unto himself a second wife. The Mormon household has been described by its enemies as a hell of envy, hatred, and malice — a den of murder and suicide. The same has been said of the Moslem harem. Both, I believe, suffer from the assertions of prejudice or ignorance. The temper of the new is so far superior to that of the old country, that, incredible as the statement may appear, rival wives do dwell together in amity; and do quote the proverb 'the more the merrier.' Moreover, they look with horror at the position of the 'slavey' of a pauper mechanic, at being required to 'nigger it' upon love and starvation, and at the necessity of a numerous family. They know that nine-tenths of the miseries of the poor in large cities arise from early imprudent marriages, and they would rather be the fiftieth 'sealing' of Dives than the toilsome single wife of Lazarus. The French saying concerning motherhood — '*le premier embellit, le second détruit, le troisième gâte trout,*' is true in the Western World. The first child is welcomed, the second is tolerated, the third is the cause of tears and reproaches, and the fourth, if not prevented by gold pills, or some similar monstrosity, causes temper, spleen, and melancholy, with disgust and hatred of the cause. What the Napoleonic abolition of the law of primogeniture, combined with centralisation of the peasant class in towns and cities, has effected on this side of the Channel, the terrors of maternity, aggravated by a highly nervous temperament . . . have brought to pass in the older parts of the Union.

"Another curious effect of fervent belief may be noticed in the married state. When a man has four or five wives with reasonable families by each, he is fixed for life: his interests, if not his affections, bind him irrevocably to his New Faith . . .

"I am conscious that my narrative savours of incredibility: the fault is in the subject, not in the narrator. *Exoneravi animam meam.* The best proof that my opinions are correct will be the following quotation. It is a letter addressed to a sister in New Hampshire by a Mrs. Belinda M. Pratt, the wife of the celebrated apostle . . . Most readers, feminine and monogamic, will remark that the lady shows little heart, or natural affection; [but] the severe calm of her judgement and reasoning faculties and the soundness of her physiology cannot be doubted.

" 'Great Salt Lake City, Jan. 12, 1854

" 'Dear Sister,

" 'Your letter of Oct. 2 was received on yesterday. My joy on its reception was more than I can express . . .

" 'We are all here, and are prosperous and happy in our family circle. Health, peace, and prosperity have attended us all the day long . . .

" 'It seems, my dear sister, that we are no nearer together in our religious views than formerly. Why is this? Are we not all bound to leave this world, with all we possess therein, and reap the reward of our doings here in a never- ending hereafter? If so, do we not desire to be undeceived, and to know and to do the truth? Do we not all wish in our very hearts to be sincere with ourselves, and to be honest and frank with each other?

" 'If so, you will bear with me patiently, while I give a few of my reasons for embracing, and holding sacred, that particular point in the doctrine of the Church of the Saints to which you, my dear sister, together with a large majority of christendom, so decidedly object. I mean, a "plurality of wives."

" 'I have a Bible, which I have been taught from my infancy to hold sacred. In this Bible, I read of a holy man named Abraham, who is represented as the friend of God, a faithful man in all things, a man who kept the commandments of God, and who is called, in the New Testament, "the father of the faithful." See James ii.23; Rom. iv. 16; Gal. iii.8,9,16,29.

" 'I find this man had a plurality of wives, some of which were called concubines. See Book of Genesis; and for his concubines, see xxv.6.

" 'I also find this grandson Jacob possessed of four wives, twelve sons, and a daughter. These wives are spoken very highly of, by the sacred writers, as honourable and virtuous women. "These," say the Scriptures, "did build the house of Israel."

" 'Jacob himself was also a man of God, and the Lord blessed him and his house, and commanded him to be fruitful and multiply. See Gen. xxxv. and particularly xxxv.10,11.

" 'I find also that the twelve sons of Jacob, by these four wives, became princes, heads of tribes, patriarchs, whose names are had in everlasting remembrance to all generations.

" 'Now God talked with Abraham, Isaac, and Jacob frequently; and His angels also visited and talked with them, and blessed them and their wives and children. He also reproved the sins of some of the sons of Jacob, for hating and selling their brother, and for adultery. But in all His communications with them, He never condemned their family organisation; but, on the contrary, always approved of it, and blessed them in this respect. He even told Abraham that He would make him the father of many nations, and that in him and his seed all the nations and kindreds of the earth should be blessed. See Genesis xviii.17-19; also xii.1-3. In later years I find the plurality of wives perpetuated, sanctioned, and provided for in the law of Moses.

" 'David the Psalmist not only had a plurality of wives, but the Lord Himself spoke by the mouth of Nathan the Prophet, and told David that He (the Lord) had given his master's wives into his bosom; but because he had committed adultery with the wife of Uriah, and had caused his murder, He would take his wives and give them to a neighbor of his, &c. See 2 Samuel xii.7-11.

" 'Here, then, we have the word of the Lord, not only sanctioning polygamy, but actually giving to king David the wives of his master (Saul), and afterward taking the wives of David from him, and giving them to another man. Here we have a sample of severe reproof and punishment for adultery and murder, while polygamy is authorised and approved by the word of God.

" 'But to come to the New Testament. I find Jesus Christ speaks very highly of Abraham and his family. He says, "Many shall come from the east, and from the west, and from the north, and from the south, and shall sit down with Abraham, Isaac, and Jacob, in the kingdom of God." Luke xii.28,29

" 'Again he said, "If ye were Abraham's seed, ye would do the works of Abraham."

" 'Paul the Apostle wrote to the saints of his day, and informed them as follows: "As many of you as have been baptized into Christ have put on Christ; and if ye are Christ's, then are ye Abraham's seed, and heirs according to the promise."

" 'He also sets forth Abraham and Sarah as patterns of faith and good works, and as the father and mother of faithful Christians, who should, by faith and good works, aspire to be counted the sons of Abraham and daughters of Sarah.

" ' . . . She is so highly commended by the Apostles, and by them held up as a pattern for Christian ladies to imitate.

" 'Again, John the Revelator describes the Holy City of the heavenly Jerusalem, with the names of the twelve sons of Jacob inscribed on the gates. Rev.xxi.12.

" 'To sum up the whole, then, I find that polygamists were the friends of God; that the family and lineage of a polygamist were selected, in which all nations should be blessed; that a polygamist is named in the New Testament as the father of the faithful Christians of after ages, and cited as a pattern for all generations; that the wife of a polygamist, who encouraged her husband in the practice of the same, and even urged him into it, and officiated in giving him another wife, is named as an honourable and virtuous woman, a pattern for Christian ladies, and the very mother of all holy women in the Christian Church, whose aspiration it should be to be called her daughters; that Jesus Christ has declared that the great fathers of the polygamic family stand at the head in the kingdom of God; in short, that all the saved of after generations should be saved by becoming members of a polygamic family [Abraham's]; that all those who do not become members of it are strangers and aliens to the covenant of promise, the commonwealth of Israel, and not heirs according to the promise made to Abraham; that all people from the east, west, north, or south, who enter into the kingdom, enter into the society of polygamists, and under their patriarchal rule and government; indeed, no one can even approach the gates of heaven without beholding the names of twelve polygamists (the sons of four different women by one man) engraven in everlasting glory upon the pearly gates.

" 'My dear sister, with the Scriptures before me, I could never find it in my heart to reject the heavenly vision which has restored to man the fulness of the Gospel, or the Latter Day Prophets and Apostles, merely because in this restoration is included the ancient law of matrimony and of family organisation and government, preparatory to the restoration of all Israel.

" 'But, leaving all Scripture, history, or precedent out of the question, let us come to nature's law. What, then, appears to be the great object of the marriage relations? I answer, the multiplying of our species, the rearing and training of children.

" 'To accomplish this object, natural law would dictate that a husband should remain apart from his wife at certain seasons, which, in the very constitution of the female, are untimely; or, in other words, indulgence should be not merely for pleasure or wanton desires, but mainly for the purpose of procreation.

" 'The mortality of nature would teach a mother, that, during nature's process in the formation and growth of embryo man, her heart should be pure, her thoughts and affections chaste, her mind calm, her passions without excitement, while her body should be invigorated with every exercise conducive to health and vigour, but by no means subjected to anything calculated to disturb, irritate, weary, or exhaust any of its functions.

" 'And while a kind husband should nourish, sustain, and comfort the wife of his bosom by every kindness and attention consistent with her situation, and with his most tender affection; still he should refrain from all those untimely associations [during pregnancy] which are forbidden in the great constitutional laws of female nature; which laws we see carried out in almost the entire animal economy, human animals excepted.

" 'Polygamy, then, as practised under the Patriarchal law of God, tends directly to the chastity of women, and to sound health and morals in the constitutions of their offspring.

" 'You can read, in the law of God, in your Bible, the times and circumstances under which a woman should remain apart from her husband, during which times she is considered unclean ...

" 'The polygamic law of God opens to all vigorous, healthy, and virtuous females a door by which they may become honourable wives of virtuous men, and mothers of faithful, virtuous, healthy, and vigorous children.

" 'Dear sister, in your thoughtlessness, you inquire, "Why not a plurality of husbands as well as a plurality of wives?" To which I reply: ... God has never commanded or sanctioned a plurality of husbands ... Such an order of things would work death and not life, or, in plain language, it would multiply disease instead of children. In fact, the experiment of a plurality of husbands, or rather of one woman for many men, is in active operation, and has been, for centuries, in all the principal towns and cities of "Christendom!" It is the genius of "Christian institutions," falsely so called. It is the result of "Mystery Babylon, the great whore of all the earth." Or in other words, it is the result of making void the holy ordinances of God in relation to matrimony, and introducing the laws of Rome, in which the clergy and nuns are forbidden to marry, and other members only permitted to have one wife. This law leaves females exposed to a life of single "blessedness," without husband, child, or friend to provide for or comfort them; or to a life of poverty and loneliness, exposed to temptation, to perverted affections, to unlawful means to gratify them, or to the necessity of selling themselves for lucre. While the man who has abundance of means is tempted to spend it on a mistress in secret, and in a lawless way, the law of God would have given her to him as an honourable wife. These circumstances give rise to murder, infanticide, suicide, disease, remorse, despair, wretchedness, poverty, untimely death, with all the attendant train of jealousies, heartrending miseries, want of confidence in families, contaminating disease, &c.; and finally, to the horrible license system, in which governments, called Christian, license their fair daughters, I will not say to play the beast, but to a degradation far beneath them ...

" ' ... A noble man of God, who is full of the Spirit of the Most High, and is counted worthy to converse with Jehovah, or with the Son of God; and to associate with angels, and the spirits of just men made perfect; one who will teach his children, and bring them up in the light of unadulterated and eternal truth; is more worthy of a hundred wives and children, than the ignorant slave of passion, or of vice and folly, is to have one wife and child. Indeed the God of Abraham is so much better pleased with one than with the other, that he would even take away the one talent, which is habitually abused, neglected, or put to an improper use, and give it to him who has ten talents.

" ' . . . He also has a head, to whom he is responsible. He must keep the commandments of God, and observe His laws. He must not take a wife unless she is given to him by the law and authority of God. He must not commit adultery, nor take liberties with any woman except his own, who are secured to him by the holy ordinances of matrimony.

" ' . . . Hence a nation organised under the law of the Gospel, or in other words, the law of Abraham and the Patriarchs, would have no institutions tending to licentiousness; no adulteries, fornications, &c., would be tolerated. No houses or institutions would exist for traffic in shame, or in the life-blood of our fair daughters. Wealthy men would have no inducement to keep a mistress in secret, or unlawfully . . . the poor would be open for every virtuous female to form the honourable and endearing relationships of wife and mother, in some virtuous family, where love, and peace, and plenty would crown her days, and truth and the practice of virtue qualify her to be transplanted with her family circle in that eternal soil, where they might multiply their children, without pain, or sorrow, or death; and go on increasing in numbers, in wealth, in greatness, in glory, might, majesty, power, and dominion, in worlds without end.

" 'O my dear sister! could the dark veil of tradition be rent from your mind! could you gaze for a moment on the resurrection of the just! could you behold Abraham, Isaac, and Jacob, and their wives and children, clad in the bloom, freshness, and beauty of immortal flesh and bones; clothed in robes of fine white linen, bedecked with precious stones and gold; and surrounded with an offspring of immortals as countless as the stars of the firmament, or as the grains of sand upon the sea shore; over which they reign as kings and queens for ever and ever! you would then know something of the weight of those words of the sacred writer which are recorded in relation to the four wives of Jacob, the mothers of the twelve Patriarchs, namely: "These did build the house of Israel."

" 'O that my dear kindred could but realise that they have need to repent of the sins, ignorance, and traditions of those perverted systems which are misnamed "Christianity," and be baptized — buried in the water, in the likeness of the death and burial of Jesus Christ, and rise to newness of life in the likeness of his resurrection; receive his Spirit by the laying on of the hands of an Apostle, according to promise, and forsake the world and the pride thereof. Thus they would be adopted into the family of Abraham, become his sons and daughters, see and enjoy for themselves the visions of the Spirit of eternal truth, which bear witness of the family order of heaven, and the beauties and glories of eternal kindred ties; for my pen can never describe them.

" 'Dear, dear kindred ... You say you believe polygamy is "licentiousness;" that it is "abominable," "beastly," &c.; "the practice only of the most barbarous nations, or of the dark ages, or of some great or good men who were left to commit gross sins." Yet you say you are anxious for me to be converted to your faith; and that we may see each other in this life, and be associated in one great family in that life which has no end.

" 'Now in order to comply with your wishes, I must renounce the Old and New Testaments; must count Abraham, Isaac, and Jacob, and their families, as licentious, wicked, beastly, abominable characters; Moses, Nathan, David, and the Prophets, no better. I must look upon the God of Israel as partaker in all these abominatons, by holding them in fellowship; and evcn as a minister of such iniquity ... I must consider Jesus Christ, and Paul, and John, as either living in a dark age, as full of the darkness and ignorance of barbarous climes, or else wilfully abominable and wicked, in fellowshipping polygamists, and representing them as fathers of the faithful, and rulers in heaven ...

" 'I feel as though the Gospel had introduced me into the right family, into the right lineage, and into good company. And besides all these considerations, should I ever become so beclouded with unbelief of the Scriptures and heavenly institutions, as to agree with my kindred in New Hampshire, in theory, still my practical circumstances are different ...

" 'For instance, I have (as you see, in all good conscience, founded on the word of God) formed family and kindred ties, which are inexpressibly dear to me, and which I can never bring my feelings to consent to dissolve. I have a good and virtuous husband whom I love. We have four little children which are mutually and inexpressably dear to us. And besides this my husband has seven other living wives, and one who has departed to a better world. He has in all upwards of twenty-five children. All these mothers and children are endeared to me by kindred ties, by mutual affection, by acquaintance and association; and the mothers in particular, by mutual and long-continued exercises of toil, patience, long-suffering, and sisterly kindness. We all have our imperfections in this life; but I know that these are good and worthy women, and that my husband is a good and worthy man; one who keeps the commandments of Jesus Christ, and presides in his family like an Abraham. He seeks to provide for them with all diligence; he loves them all, and seeks to comfort them and make them happy. He teaches them the commandments of Jesus Christ, and gathers them about him in the family circle to call upon his God, both morning and evening. He and his family have the confidence, esteem, good-will, and fellowship of this entire territory, and of a wide circle of acquaintances in Europe and America. He is a practical teacher of morals and religion, a promoter of general education, and at present occupies an honourable seat in the Legislative Council of this territory.

" ' ... You mention, in your letter, that Paul, the Apostle, recommended that Bishops be the husband of one wife. Why this was the case, I do not know, unless it was, as he says, that while he was among Romans he did as Romans did. Rome, at that time, governed the world, as it were; and although gross idolaters, they held to the one wife system. Under these circumstances, no doubt, the Apostle Paul, seeing a great many polygamists in the Church, recommended that they had better choose for this particular temporal office, men of small families, who would not be in disrepute with the government. This is precisely our course in those countries where Roman institutions still bear sway. Our Elders there have but one wife, in order to conform to the laws of men.

" ' ... Dear sister, do not let your prejudices and traditions keep you from believing the Bible . . .

" 'With sentiments of the deepest affection and kindred feeling, I remain, dear sister, your affectionate sister,

" 'Belinda Marden Pratt.' "

As stated, church leaders rescinded the practice of polygamy among the Saints in 1890, declaring that its time had come. Those who practice it today are promptly and without exception excommunicated from the church.

Note 33

[From page 200]

Desert Surprises

Another noted visitor to the Saints was British author William Chandless, who discounts Eastern reports of licentiousness among the Saints. In observing their practice of polygamy, he states in 1857:

"They are not a specially sensual people . . . the wretchedness of wives in Utah has been greatly exaggerated."[1]

Jules Remy adds in his *Journey to Great Salt Lake City:* "The Mormons appeared to us less licentious than we were naturally inclined to suppose."[2]

Fitz Hugh Ludlow, at the Fourth of July Ball of 1863, continues his commentary after reporting on Brigham Young (as contained in Note 37):

"I excused myself from numerous kind invitations by the ball-room committee to be introduced to a partner and join in the dances, because (though I did not give my reason then) I wished to make a circuit of the ball-room for the purpose of thorough physiognomical study of Utah good society."

Despite criticisms, he produces some favorable commentary:

" . . . Where saintly gentlemen came with several wives, the oldest generally seemed the most elaborately dressed, and acted much like an Eastern chaperon toward her younger sisters. (Wives of the same man habitually be-sister each other in Utah. This is what Heber Kimball would call another 'triumph of grace.') Among the men, I saw some very strong, capable faces ... To my surprise, I found among the women no really degraded faces ... I saw multitudes of kindly, good-tempered countenances."[3]

Note 34

[From page 260]

Migrating Flocks: Birds Flying West

Although Sir Richard Francis Burton was skeptical of church doctrine, he seemed to incorporate the *London Times'* philosophy of regarding the Mormon Church as "the most singular phenomenon of modern times."[1] He was further, no doubt, amazed — as most of Britain's analysts apparently were — that from 30,000 to 40,000 Mormon converts had flocked to Utah from Great Britain within two decades.[2] Burton's perceptions of these British Saints — all, as he felt, immigrating for inner, religious convictions — contrasted that view held by Charles Dickens, who felt at least the "single women of from thirty to forty [were] ... going out in quest of husbands."[3]

Note 35

[From page 264]

Piling It On

"Achilles," for example, claims: "About twelve miles east of Salt Lake city ... [Kenneth and Alexander McRae] were found, placed under arrest and were disarmed. On the return to Salt Lake city, in a lonely spot in Emmigration Canyon, they were shot by Rockwell and the officer, double-barrelled shot-guns being the weapons used. The bodies were placed in a wagon, and taken to the house of their father and mother. They were here taken out and laid in the yard.

"The horror-stricken mother came out, and in her anguish

denounced Rockwell as a murderer and a villain. He retorted upon her by saying, that if she had done her duty, her sons would have been good Saints ... "[1] Despite Achilles' claim, Rockwell is not mentioned in records associated with this killing. Both Judge Smith's journal[2] and other records and journals[3] state that the two brothers were simply "killed after they were arrested in an attempt to escape,"[4] by deputies, Porter not even being present, and that "they attempted to run away and were killed while fleeing."[5]

Other, similar tales of sensational murders laid to Rockwell's blame were exemplified by headline-seeking anti-Mormon crusader Judge John Cradlebaugh. Cradlebhaugh claimed, for example, that John Tobin, a former Army sergeant,[6] had been converted to the church,[7] then "put out of the way" by Brigham Young[8] for his relationship with Brigham's daughter, Alice.[9] Assassins or robbers had tried killing him en route to California,[10] but he had survived.[11] In later years he sold his business to fulfill a church mission to Scotland, but was eventually excommunicated for adultery.[12] As an apostate Mormon Tobin now lashed out in typical fashion against the church, and laid blame for his near-death 22 years earlier upon the Mormons, conveniently waiting for a bandwagon of anti-Mormon press before surfacing with his own story.[13]

But it was Rockwell's first actual biography, resplendent with slander, that specifically laid blame of Tobin's attempted murder 22 years earlier directly on the redoubtable Rockwell.[14] Unfortunately for the author, that interesting soul calling himself Achilles, the book's credibility took a nose dive when facts later revealed Rockwell was hundreds of miles from the scene in February 1857, at the time of the alleged murder attempt, on the mid-western plains, with Brigham's mail company.

Also laid to Rockwell's blame was the murder of Henry Jones and his mother, with whom Jones was allegedly involved in an incestuous relationship.[15] Achilles claims Porter had found Jones in a saloon, had taken him outside, and castrated him. Then, the next day with several others, found Jones and his mother traveling through Payson, Utah. They attacked the bizarre couple, but the lad allegedly escaped. Porter and his gang nonetheless cut Mrs. Jones' throat, then chased down Henry and shot him.

Despite Achilles' wishful thinking, again no evidence exists of Rockwell's involvement. That a Henry Jones was murdered by assailants is almost certain, but other contemporary accounts conflict.[16] One, for example, states several unnamed persons — ruffians disguised as Indians — had "dragged him out of bed with a whore and castrated him . . . "[17] But only Achilles drags Porter into the account.

Hoffman and Birney claim Rockwell urged one Milo Andrus to cut his wife's throat for infidelity. But Andrus' son, another personal acquaintance of Rockwell, countered the charges: "My father's wife, who it is stated in this scandalous article [Hoffman and Birney's *Reader's Digest* book abridgement in 1934] was murdered by my father at the command of Porter Rockwell, was not murdered by my father or anyone else . . . "[18]

A witness to the woman's death wrote a letter to Andrus, which is on file at the Church Historians Office, swearing the woman was killed from the effects of a buggy accident October 20, 1890, and not by Andrus' knife in Porter's presence, as Hoffman and Birney assert. In fact, the alleged victim out-lived Porter by *12 years.*[19]

Andrus continues his affidavit: "When [she] died, my father was in Idaho in very feeble health so that he could not attend the funeral . . . "[20] Much less kill her.

Andrus continues, "I was well acquainted with President Brigham Young and very well acquainted with Orrin Porter Rockwell. He often came to our house and we often visited with him and his family. I have delivered hay and other farm products to his ranch which was at the point of the mountain and have eaten at his table and partaken of the hospitality of his family. From personal contact with Porter Rockwell, I know the charges made against him are not true but have been circulated by his enemies."[21]

Two men, Joachim Johnston and Myron Brewer, an apostate Mormon,[22] were caught in the act of counterfeiting. They claimed Brigham had put them up to it. Governor Cumming, sensing the fatuousness of their tirade, dismissed the allegation.[23]

In May the two counterfeiters were still at liberty, when the *Deseret News* reports Joachim Johnston, "a prominent member of one of the [outlaw] bands, and a well known government horse and mule thief, and one of the party who lately killed the Indians on the

Sevier ... was swaggering about the streets and shops, and without reserve told his business ... that he would follow a company that had gone east and steal their mules; but before leaving he intended to take a few scalps ... "[24] That same evening Johnston and Brewer were ambushed and shot.[25] The city marshal and the police chief reported the two criminals had quarrelled and killed each other. Excommunicated Mormon writer T. B. H. Stenhouse, however, ever anxious to grind his historical ax, claims the law enforcement officers' story was "feeble."[26] Later, other anti-Mormon writers, Charles Kelly and Hoffman Birney, insinuated the killing was an unfair ambush, and laid the blame directly on Porter, with no supporting evidence offered.[27]

Note 36

[From page 287]

Stars, Stripes And Mormon Flags

That church enemies claimed the Mormons were allied with Indians in attitude as well as materiel support can further be discounted by the following summary from Colonel Martineau:

"The victory was of immense value to the settlers of Cache County and all the surrounding country. It broke the spirit and power of the Indians and enabled the settlers to occupy new and choice localities hitherto unsafe. Peter Maughan, the presiding bishop of the County, pronounced it an interposition of Providence in behalf of the settlers; the soldiers having done what otherwise the colonists would have had to accomplish with pecuniary loss and sacrifice of lives illy spared in the weak state of the settlements. This was the universal sentiment of the County. It made the flocks and herds and lives of the people comparatively safe; for though the [Indian] survivors were enraged against the people of the County, whom they regarded as in a manner aiding and abetting the troops, they [the Indians] felt themselves too weak to forcibly seek revenge."

The Saints seemed to be stronger allies to the Army than some historians have painted.

Note 37

[From page 301]

Fitz-Hugh Ludlow on Brigham Young

"Before our ride with Rockwell, we received notes of invitation to certain festivities in the Mormon Academy of Music, intended for the commemoration of our national independence.

"These festivities took the form of a ball, and afforded such an opportunity for studying Mormon sociology as three months' ordinary stay in Salt Lake might not have given me.

" . . . On entering the theatre, we were surprised to see how remarkably it had been improved since we stood on the stage in daylight, listening to Heber Kimball, and seeing the women busy in the preparation of the festive trimmings. Fragrant ropes of evergreen hung in symmetrical festoons from the cornice and the edge of the galleries; others wound spirally about the pillars, and wreathed the capitals. A great central chandelier was similarly ornamented, while interspersed among the pine and cedar were immense garlands and bunches of natural flowers, native and exotic . . .

"We sought out our entertainer, Brigham Young, to thank him for the flattering exception made in our Gentile favor. He was standing in the dress-circle of the theatre, looking down on the dancers with an air of mingled hearty kindness and feudal ownership . . . Like any Eastern party-goer, he was habited in the 'customary suit of solemn black,' and looked very distinguished in this dress, though his daily homespun detracts nothing from the feeling, when in his presence, that you are beholding a most remarkable man. He is nearly seventy years old, but appears very little over forty. His height is about 'five feet ten, The height of Lord Chesterfield's gentlemen;' his figure very well made, and slightly inclining to portliness. His hair is a rich curly chestnut, formerly worn long, in supposed imitation of the apostolic *coiffure,* but now cut in our practical Eastern fashion, as accords with the man of business whose metier he has added to apostleship, with the growing temporal prosperity of Zion. Indeed, he is the greatest business man on the Continent, the head and cashier of a firm of one hundred thousand silent partners, and the only auditor of that cashier besides. Brigham Young's eyes are a clear blue-gray, frank and straightforward in their look; his nose a finely chiseled aquiline; his mouth exceedingly firm . . . and he wears a narrow ribbon of brown whiskers meeting on the throat. But for his chin, he would greatly resemble the best portraits of Sidney Smith, the humorist.

" . . . Brigham's manners astonish any one who knows that his only education was a few quarters of such common-school education as could be had in Ontario County, Central New York, during the early part of the century. There are few courtlier men living. His address is a fine combination of dignity with the desire to confer happiness, of perfect deference to the feelings of others with absolute certainty of himself and his own opinions. He is a remarkable example of the educating influence of tactful perception wedded to entire singleness of aim, without regard to its moral character. His early life was passed among the uncouth and illiterate; any tow-headed boy coming into the Clifton Water-cure to sell Ontario County maple-sugar has, to all external appearance, a better chance of reaching supreme command than Brigham had in his childhood; his daily associations since he embraced Mormonism have been with the least cultivated grades of human society, a heterogenous horde, looking to him for its erection into a nation; yet he has so clearly seen what is requisite in the man who would be respected in the Presidency, and has so unreservedly devoted his life to its attainment, that in protracted conversation with him, I heard only a single solecism ('ain't you' for 'aren't you'), and saw not one instance of breeding which would be inconsistent with noble lineage.

"I say this good of him frankly, disregarding any slur which may be cast on me as his defender by those broad-effect artists who always paint the Devil Black . . . " [Here, Ludlow nevertheless labels Brigham an "enemy" to society, and though Ludlow is remarkably observant of the man he is nonetheless highly critical of his faith.]

"Brigham began our conversation at the theatre by telling me I was late — it was after 9 o'clock. I replied that this was the time we usually set about dressing for an evening party in Boston or New York.

" 'Yes,' said he, 'you find us an old-fashioned people; we are trying to return to the healthy habits of the patriarchal age.'

" 'Need you go back so far as that for your parallel?' suggested I. 'It strikes me that we might have found four-o'clock balls among the early Christians.'

"He smiled, without that offensive affectation of some great men, the air of taking another's joke under their gracious patronage, and went on to remark that there were, unfortunately, multitudinous differences between the Mormons and Americans at the East besides the hours they kept.

" 'You find us,' said he, 'trying to live peaceably. A sojourn with people thus minded must be a great relief to you, who come from a land where brother hath lifted hand against brother, and you hear the confused noise of the warrior perpetually ringing in your ears.'

"Despite the courtly deference and scriptural dignity of this speech, I detected in it a latent crow over that 'perished Union,' which, up to the time of Lee's surrender was the favorite theme of every Saint one met in Utah, and hastened to assure the President that I had no desire for relief from sympathy with my country's struggle for honor and existence.

"The Opera-house was a subject which Brigham and I could agree upon. I was greatly astonished to find in the desert heart of the Continent a place of public amusement which, regarding comfort, capacity, and beauty, has but two or three superiors in the United States. It is internally constructed somewhat like the New York Academy of Music, seats twenty-five hundred, and commodiously receives five hundred more when, as in the present instance, the stage is thrown into the paraquet. My greatest surprise was excited by the remarkable artistic beauty of the salt gilt and painted decorations on the great arch over the stage, the cornices, and the moulding about the proscenium boxes. President Young, with a proper pride, assured me that every particle of the ornamental work was by indigenous and Saintly hands.

" 'But you don't know yet,' he added, 'how independent we are of you at the East. Where do you think we got that central chandelier, and what d'ye suppose we paid for it?'

"It was a piece of work which would have been creditable to any New York firm, apparently a richly carven circle, twined with gilt vines, leaves, and tendrils, blossoming all over with flaming wax-lights, and suspended by a massive chain of golden lustre. So I replied that he probably paid a thousand dollars for it in New York.

" 'Capital!' exclaimed Brigham; 'I made it myself! That circle is a cart-wheel of one of our common Utah ox-carts. I had it washed, and gilded it with my own hands. It hangs by a pair of ox-chains, which I also gilded; and the gilt ornaments of the candlesticks were all cut after my patterns out of sheet tin!'

"This is but one among a thousand illustrations of the versatility which characterizes this truly remarkable man. They are familiar to every Mormon; you can go nowhere in the Territory without hearing them admiringly recounted by the people. As I have said, in the society sense of the word, Brigham is far from being an educated man. He knows neither Latin, Greek, nor, so far as I am aware, any modern foreign language, unless, perhaps, like several prominent men among his subordinates, he has acquired sufficient acquaintance with the dialects of Shoshone, Ute, and other neighboring Indian tribes, to help in their reduction to the condition of tools and emissaries of the Church. I am not at all sure that he possesses even this slight lingual accomplishment, for, as I may hereafter show; the division of labor has been so clearly systematized, that even the business of learning Indian is apportioned chiefly to a class of Mormons . . . [with] the use of those incoherent grunts which constitute its language.

"Brigham's knowledge of mathematics stops at a moderate practical acquaintance with surveying, and the ability to keep books with a particularly cheerful credit side. Every deficiency in the matter of polite education which his enemies can lay to his charge, Brigham acknowledges with a simple-hearted frankness and an evident appreciation of the advantages denied his youth, challenging the admiration of all fair minds far more than any mere accomplishment could.

"In hearing him, one naturally feels that Brigham must possess some compensatory gifts and acquirements, in whose presence ordinary attainments become a matter of trifling moment, and that the man able to confess his weak places with such modest dignity has elements of strength within him sufficient to brace them, even in the most trying exigencies of his life.

"Among such elements, his versatility is by no means the least. The great American talent of un-cornerableness; the habit of always striking on one's feet; that Promethean faculty which in the grand passage where Zeus sends his blacksmiths to rivet the titan down on Caucasus, Aeschylus through the mouth of Force calls the ability to break away — 'out of unengineerable evils,'— this, Brigham Young enjoys to a degree which I have never seen surpassed in any great man of any nation. He cannot be put into a position where he is at the end of his resources; earthly circumstances never take to him the form of a *cul de sac.* He has been at a college whose president is Multiform Experience, whose matron is Inexorable Necessity. If he were obliged to support himself by farming, he understands soils, stock, tools, rotation, irrigation, manures, and all the agricultural economies so well that he would speedily have the best crops within a hundred miles' radius. With his own hands he would put the best house in the settlement over the heads of himself and his family, while other Desert Islanders in a ship-load of Crusoes were bewailing the loss of their carpenter.

"On Sundays he can preach sermons cogent and full of common sense, if not elegant or always free from indelicacy. On week-days he sits in the Church office, managing a whole nation's temporalities with secular astuteness that Talleyrand or Richelieu would find him a match should the morning's game be diplomatic, and the Rothschild family could not get ahead of him if the stake were a financial advantage. On the perilous and untried road to Utah, he was faith, wisdom, energy, patience, expedience, courage, enthusiasm, veritable life and soul to all the fainting Saints; they never would have reached the Rocky Mountain watershed, much less the Great Salt Basin, without him; he was the grand incarnate will and purpose of the Mormons' fiercely tried fanaticism; and though he naively said to me, in speaking of the height of Ensign Peak, 'I got Brother Pratt, who had the book-learning, take the observations, not knowing enough about such things to do it myself,' there was not a 'slewed' ox-cart on the way to that peak's base, at whose wheel his was not the first and sturdiest shoulder; and after wrestling with angels or remaining instant in prayer all night, he could yoke up his team, and trudge along by its travel-chafed necks, urging it on with ge-haws as cheerful and getting out of his black-snake cracks as resonant as the lightest-hearted bumpkin in a smock frock. In a new country and an infant civilization, specific gravities take care of such a man's position; he infallibly determines to the top of things ... He must govern, because he is the only one of his lot who is necessary to everybody; he is not elected, but he is; not because he is fortunate, an heir of the past, but because among men he is the manliest, and thus what Homer meant, not the king of lands and coffers, but — the king of men! I believe that Brigham Young was brought out by Mormonism; but I believe that if any other cause with which he might have identified himself had taken as strong possession of his nature, it would have developed him as fully, and that with the usual Christian creed and training, he would have made another Beecher in the pulpit, another Webster in the Senate, and a Sherman in the army unsurpassed by Tecumseh."

Note 38

[From page 311]

Rushing For Yellow At Carissa

Tom Ryan went with his command through the South Pass country. A miner himself, he was particularly interested when he heard reports of gold in the area. Gold had been discovered in 1842 by a fur company staffer, with other mining having been engaged in and publicized in 1855, 1858, and in the early 60's, but now Ryan learned more about it than anyone else — and exactly where it was located. Yet his knowledge was useless to him. He was now a soldier.

According to Coutant's *The History of Wyoming,* Ryan, "not having an opportunity to develop the property ... afterwards reported the find in Salt Lake ...

"Through the early spring of 1867 there were constant arrivals at South Pass [mostly from Salt Lake City], and as soon as the snow left the tops of the hills the prospectors spread themselves over the country. On June 8th ... [several] succeeded in finding the Carissa lode, which Tom Ryan had told about."

Note 39

[From page 324]

A Reporter's Reporter Reports

Prize-winning Civil War correspondent George Alfred Townsend displayed true-to-form investigative reporting abilities with a series of letters to the *Cincinnati Commercial.*

One letter, dated October 23, 1871, treats the claim-jumping federal judges and their associates, including their conspiratorial ring, the "Jumpers Club" — officially titled the "Wasatch Club" ...

While gathering his notes, Townsend heard from Daniel H. Wells: "We are nearly, or quite twenty thousand people; our city is as old as many great towns in the Mississippi Valley; but here men are allowed to pre-empt farms right in the midst of us as if they meant to plow us under."

Wells was referring to "the ring," which even duped Ulysses S. Grant, President of the United States. According to the *Pittsburgh Leader,* Grant's favorite pastor, Reverend J. P. Newman, preached, "The Mormons should be rooted out by all means."[2]

Seven months later, in October 1875, Grant and his wife visited Salt Lake City and, before leaving, confessed, "I have been deceived."[3]

Meanwhile, Judge Hayden of the Gentile League of Utah claimed the streets of Salt Lake City would run with blood.[4]

On August 3, 1872 an outdoor mass meeting was called to ratify the nomination of the GLU's liberal candidate. Two months later, Edward Tullidge, a *Salt Lake Tribune* reporter, attended a meeting, having been tipped that armed members of the league were awaiting the chairman's signal to attack Mormons in the crowd. District Attorney Baskin had prophesied before the meeting, "We'll have a hundred coffins at our next meeting."

But Associate Justice Strickland exposed their plan accidentally when at the first sound of an opposing Mormon in their midst he arose: "The first man who interrupts this meeting I will order shot!"[5]

Tribune reporter Tullidge claims Gentile League Union members were disappointed, groaning that Strickland should have waited, "instead of [giving] this timely warning."[6]

For further details of the ring, as well as other colorful insights into Mormon society — including an interview with the aging Daniel H. Wells and personal observations of Brigham Young and the changing empire — the following abridgement of Townsend's complete series of articles is presented. Townsend paints a perceptive picture of not only the federal judicial system within Nineteenth Century Utah, but a flavorful, witty, rustic, portrait of old Salt Lake City:

"The march of the children of Israel from Egypt around the corner of the Mediterranean was a little affair compared to the Mormon migration . . . And yet we, who are preached at from childhood out of the old books of Exodus and Deuteronomy, refuse to see any equities, wonders, or heroisms in the history and condition of a native church, whose legends are no less miraculous. I cannot confess to a deep interest in these ecclesiastical subjects . . . But I do take pride in the material achievements of the United States, however brought about. Religous movements, however motely, have been the making of us. Amongst the names of John Robinson, Roger Williams, William Penn, George Whitefield, Count Zinzendorf, and Lord Baltimore, founders of American communities, the name of Brigham Young will unquestionably stand. He has made the boldest, most rapid, and most remarkable colonization we have had; in a political point of view it has been fortunate to us all.

" . . . As to the camp-meeting jurists and their camp-followers out there, I am indifferent to their abuse and proud of their disapproval . . . Be rid of polygamy; cast out by this course the Federal officials who prey upon you, and become an American State in good faith, represented amongst us, and blessed by neighborhood rule.

"THE MORMON CITY AND CHIEF
"Salt Lake, October 20. [1871]

" . . . We enter the environs of Salt Lake . . . the lean and often low, sun-dried houses, of a bluish-white color; and wide, straight streets, down whose lazy declivities the snow-water gurgles, passing at every other gate into the vegetable patches and the lawns of wheat and wild oats.

" . . . Then we are set down at the 'Townsend House,' a long, low, sprawling hotel, with a comfortabe piazza and shade trees . . . We feed well at the Townsend House at $4 a day, and sleep in the delicious dry air of this Wahsatch Valley; and next day we take a warm sulphur plunge bath in the environs of the town, the hot water pouring from the mountain side into a pool, and a cold shower bath standing convenient, like an ice-cream at the end of a warm dinner. I observed in this bath-house and its dressing-rooms what was altogether exceptional in American outhouses — no vulgar writings on the wall . . .

"The valley and city of Salt Lake are marvels of patient, unskilled labor, directed by a few powerful native minds. The spirit of John Smith and the hands of the Puritan English meet in this mid-world colony — the brawn all peasant, the pluck all Yankee. Maine, Vermont, and New York were the fathers of this frontier, and folks out of the northwestern races of Europe . . .

"The morning after my arrival I found everybody going up to see Brigham Young, some accompanied by an introducer, others falling in as interlopers. My chaperon was a bright young Mormon editor, as rosy as the sun on the mountains, who conducts a live salt newspaper, possesses a singular family, in that it is limited, and has built the first house with a Mansard roof in the heart of the continent . . .

"Passing under the small shade trees, across the flowing rills, past Godbe's flaming drug store, past Hon. Thomas Fitch's new law office, where he sits arranging his books with his cultivated wife; past the market where lake trout as big as young pigs lie speckled and fresh; past Delegate Hooper's bank, whence he looks out like one of Velasquez's Spanish gentlemen . . . past the theatre, and up a gentle hill among the painted adobe houses . . . we see the sun shine hotly along the long, tall wall which encloses Brigham's palace. An eagle over a sunny gateway, a plaster or wooden bee-hive, and a lion above the roof, denote the clump of dwellings and offices just behind the wall, and seen through the gateway gap in it, where 'President' Young keeps state. The scene is like pictures of scenery in Tunis or Morocco ...

"Their humble apostles have passed the barriers of language, and the crude Danes and Swedes are pouring into Utah as well as the English-speaking nations. Compact, disciplined, devout, no cowards, at times desperate men, yet soft and diplomatic, so that they have pacified hostile Indians and checkmated the United States, they illustrate the nobility of delusion when attended with labor, fired with purpose, and properly organized. [Townsend, unlike other Easterners, was critical of the Saints' religion — primarily polygamy.]

"Brigham Young soothes mankind with seignoral hospitality. We are all introduced.

"We see he is more perfectly at home than anybody in the crowded room ... [He is possessed] of self-pride, cool self-management, and self-will ... "

Reflecting a cool opinion of federal officials, Townsend's next letter unleases his caustic wit:

"THE FIRST CONVICTION FOR POLYGAMY
"Salt Lake, October 24, 1871
"Today Thomas Hawkins, English, from Birmingham, better known around Salt Lake as "Tummus Awkeens," is to be sentenced in the best elocution of which Judge McKean is capable, to the Territorial Penitentiary for a term of years.

"The offense of Thomas was somewhat uncommon ... committing adultery with his wife, Elizabeth Mears, on complaint of his wife Harriet Hawkins ...

"No witnesses were adduced as to the criminal act, owing to the fact that ... [only] his third wife was quartered in the upper part of the house, and there was no way to observe what happened there, except by looking down the chimney.

" ... [Meanwhile] the Marshal, M. T. Patrick, had gone to Southern Utah to shoot snipe ... and arrest a Mormon Bishop.

"The Marshal stood behind a remnant of dry-goods box in one corner, and the jury sat upon two broken settees under a hot stove-pipe and behind the stove. They were intelligent, as usual with juries, and resembled a parcel of baggage smashers warming themselves in a railroad depot between trains. The bar consisted of what appeared to be a large keno party keeping tally on a long pine table.

"When some law books were brought in after a while, the bar wore that unrecognizable look of religious services about to be performed before the opening of the game. The audience sat upon six rows of damaged settees, and a standing party formed the background, over whose heads was seen a great barren, barn-like area of room in the rear, filled with the debris of some former fair . . . .

"The entire furniture of the place might have cost eleven dollars at an auction where the bidding was high. The room itself was the second story of a livery stable, and a [Mormon-owned] jackass and several [Indian] mules in the stalls beneath occasionally interrupted the Judge with a bray of delight. The audience was composed entirely of men, perfectly orderly and tolerably ragged, and spitting surprisingly little tobacco juice; almost all of them Mormons, with a stray miner here and there mingled in, wearing a revolver on his hip and a paper collar under his long beard.

"At the bar table, on one side sat Baskins and Maxwell, the prosecutors, the former frowsy, cool, and red headed, the latter looking as if he had overslept himself for a week, and got up mad.

"On the opposite side sat Tom Fitch, late member of Congress from Nevada, a rotund . . . young man, with . . . great quantities of forensic eloquence wrapped away under his mustache.

"The Court is the victim of Baskins, the Prosecuting Attorney *pro tem.* Baskins comes from Ohio, and gets his red hot temper from his hair. He is related to have shot somebody in Ohio . . .

"About six months ago . . . the [Utah] Judge, by an order, came between Baskins and a fee. Baskins threw the paper on the floor, and ground it with his boot-heel into an inoffensive tobacco quid. The Judge, who is slender, conscious, and respects himself and his rulings, told Mr. Baskins he would fine him.

" 'Go ahead with your fine!' said Baskins, 'you're of no account.'

"The Judge fined Baskins one hundred dollars, and sent him to Camp Douglas for ten days. Baskins twitched the order out of the Judge's hands and said that being an 'old granny' the Judge should forthwith be kicked down the stairs. At this Baskins threw open the door to expedite the descent of the venerable man, and rushed upon him, like Damon upon Lucullus. The Marshal interposed to save [the judge] . . . and Baskins went to the Camp in custody. But as this notable Bench in Utah never consult together, . . . Judge McKean [another judge] let Baskins out on *habeas corpus* in four days, and Baskins disdained to pay his fine. It is Baskins, therefore, who insists, as Prosecuting Attorney, that the laws of the United States and the Courts thereof must be respected in Utah.

"As for McKean's two Associate Judges, they are off holding District Court at Provo and Beaver, Hawley harassing some rural justice of the peace with his last printed opinion, and Strickland playing billiards for drinks, between sessions, with Bill Nye. But Judge McKean himself does not use tobacco nor a billiard cue in any form; his sole recreation is to practice elocution and parlor suavity in anticipation of his appearance in the United States Senate from the State of New York. A trim, apprehensive, not unsagacious man, with a great, burning mission to exalt the horn of his favorite denomination upon the ruins of the Mormon Bishopric, McKean is resolved in advance that everybody is guilty . . .

"There stand the guilty fold, without the bar of the court — most of them look as if they wanted a new razor and a square meal — the Mormon rank and file. Grave and listening, and so respectful as to irritate the prosecuting attorneys very much (so that they would like to make premeditated good behavior a conspiracy punishable at law) . . . .

"[They are] docile people, as well, though not without the courage of the poor, so that when on the late occasion of the great Methodist camp meeting, Brigham said to them in the Tabernacle: 'I want you all to go to this camp meeting, and listen to what is said!' They filled it to over-flowing every day . . . And when, on one occasion only, at some harangue upon polygamy, a mutter arose over that great congregation, Brigham, himself present, stood up and waved his finger, and the complaint hushed to utter peace. [This] people also dance and waltz between religious benedictions, and yet can listen four hours in ardent delight to dry dissertations and discussions in their Tabernacle, which might make nature snore in her processes. How infinite are the possibilities or our nature when we reflect that these grave, unrebellious people, the waifs and findings of all lands, many of them dignified in apparel and culture, and steadily ascending in the scale of comfort and possessions, hold still with the tenacity of a moral purpose to the loose and spreading life of polygamy.

" ... From the windows of the court, the rolling or serrated line of mountains, enfolding a valley like the lawn of Paradise, suggested far different men and women ... Mrs. Hawkins is accompanied by her daughter, Lizzie Hawkins, a timid, embarrassed girl of about sixteen years, and while the mother is a prompt and rather bright witness, the daughter is measurably dumb.

"Thomas Hawkins looks like one who might enjoy married life, and yet be a rather mean husband ... A light-blue, animal eye, which would pick out a woman quickest in a landscape ... such is the meager hero of three marriages, brought up seven years after date to answer the charge of adultery. I have understood that Hawkins stands in doubtful odor among his church people for not equalizing himself more among his families, both socially and financially. The common expression among the Mormon is —

" 'There's wrong on both sides in that family;' but the inevitable addenda is — 'just as in plenty of monogamous families.'

" ... There seemed to be no feeling in the town except regret at the wife's suit for divorce, but a notion that the prosecution for adultery was malicious, and set on by the court and its favorite lawyers.

"The oratory was mixed in the case. Maxwell, who was admitted at his own solicitation to assist Baskins in the prosecution, making the point against Mormons that in twenty-two years their Legislature had never made a statute validating polygamy even by inference.

"To this, Muller, the Mormon lawyer, replied that marriage was not a civil, but an ecclesiastical rite in Utah, that polygamy was established prior to the formation of any American government here, and relied upon a clause of the treaty of Guadaloupe Hidalgo, whereby the newly annexed inhabitants were guaranteed against interference with their religion. The speeches of Maxwell and Baskins [the anti-Mormons] were bold and acrid, but the large Mormon audience listened without a murmur.

"To carry out its relentless purposes, this court — which had announced itself as a United States Court, ... punishes polygamy with the penalty of adultery. Mr. Fitch's argument [for the Mormon defense] was that ... the command, 'Thou shalt not commit adultery,' was delivered to a polygamous people, and engraven upon stone by the husband of three wives ....The rulings of the courts in Utah, both probate and district, for twenty years, had been in accordance with this theory of marriage.

"Judge McKean delivered a harangue to the jury answering every point made by the defense. It was a speech of three quarters of an hour, and amounted to an exhortation to convict.

"The Mormon paper, the *Herald,* rendered Judge McKean's charge and conduct of the trial as follows, on the following morning:

" 'You have your duties, gentlemen, and I have mine. My duty is to pick you out and pack you in; to fix the trial at such a time as will be least convenient to the defendant; to exclude all evidence that may help him, and to admit all evidence that may hurt him; to rule all points of law against him; to pick out from acts of Congress and acts of the Utah Assembly those laws which, combined, may convict him ... to dramatize the case, and elocutionize my opinions; to follow my instructions from Rev. Dr. Newman, and avenge his defeat at the Tabernacle; in short, gentlemen, my duty is to secure a conviction.'

"Directed by this peremptory charge, the jury found a verdict of guilty in one hour, and it was heard by the large audience, standing with breathless eagerness and silence. As this case came up on complaint of a wife, and the testimony as to the second cohabitation was clear, it was thought to be the easiest case to obtain a conviction, and made comparatively little excitement. The streets of Salt Lake were quiet, as usual, and no knots of people discussed the affair unless in privacy ...

"About the close of the trial, the only disturbance occurred between the reporter for the anti-Mormon organ and a deputy marshal. It was on the supposed occasion of the administration of sentence, and, either to express sympathy with the prisoner or to find out what might be the penalty of such wedlock, the room was filled with Mormon women. Suddenly a man came up the stairs from the livery stable, and said that the floor showed signs of coming down. At this, the court was profoundly exercised. The deputy marshal, under pretence of regulation admissions, got near the door, and just at this juncture, the Gentile reporter strutted in . . .

"The marshal [decided to] pitch him down stairs . . . [and the courtroom went wild]. Quantities of lead pencils and free tickets to the theater strewed the courtroom . . .

"The reporter . . . struck the marshal, and they clinched and fell down [the] stairs. The marshal [landed] on top [and took him off to the police]. The reporter . . . was discharged that afternoon by a Mormon judge.

"THE FEDERAL ENEMIES OF THE SAINTS.
"Salt Lake City, October 23.

"There are now two places in Salt Lake City of . . . superstitious consequence . . . These are the Wahsatch Club — the headquarters of the anti-Mormon 'Ring' — and the United States District Court room, over a livery stable.

" . . . Except for the good counsel prevailing among the Mormons, and the powerful control [of] Brigham Young, . . . the homesteads of one hundred and thirty thousand people might today have been ashes and desert.

" . . . On the occasion of my last visit here, four months ago, I wrote probably as severe strictures upon the essence of this civilization [as have been written] . . . As any tourist, I have found the Mormons anxious to encourage the slightest disposition to represent them to the Eastern people, and without resentment for expressions of opinion.

"Near the Townsend House, the principal hotel of Salt Lake, and a Mormon's property, in a pleasant two story adobe house of a gray color, is a lounging place and a mess-room called the Wahsatch Club, denominated here by three-fourths of the Gentiles as the 'Jumpers' Club,' in allusion to the tendency of the judicial judges and their satellites to 'jump' or possess without right and by force the neighboring valuable mining claims.

"In this club meet by accident or design the members of the Federal Administration who are moving on the Mormon works, and at the same time upon the substantial interests of Utah. As they have written themselves up copiously for the Eastern press, they may not object to taking this current and third-party opinion of their qualifications. I give them in the order of brains and consequence:

"1. Chief Justice of Utah, J. B. McKean, of New York State; and officer in the volunteer army during the war, and a prominent Methodist, formerly, it is said, a preacher. McKean came here upon a crusade against polygamy, and his fair abilities and great vanity have carried him through it thus far with about equal flourish and fearlessness. He is a wiry, medium-sized man, with a tall baldish head, gray side-locks, and very black, sallow eyes, at time resinous in color, like tar-water. He looks, however, to be in the prime of strength and will; has never communicated with Brigham Young personally since he arrived, and is absorbed in the purpose of intimidating the Mormon Church or breaking it up. His behavior on the bench has been despotic and extra-judicial to the last degree, and he has also been unfortunate enough to compromise his reputation by mining speculations which have come before his court, and received influential consideration there.

"2. R. N. Baskins, the author of what is called in Congress the 'Cullom Bill,' and at present temporary Prosecuting Attorney before McKean's Court; a lean, lank, rather dirty and frowsy, red-headed young man, but a lawyer of shrewdness and coolness, and inflamed against Mormonism . . .

"3. George R. Maxwell, an ex-officer from Michigan, with a game leg, a strong dissipated face, and Register of the Land Office here; an indomitable man, but accused of corruption, and a chronic runner for Congress against [Mormon] delegate W. H. Hooper; thinks Congress is a vile body because it will not put Hooper out of Congress for his creed as promptly as Judge McKean would put him off a jury.

"4. J. H. Taggart . . . imperfect, indeed doubtful record in the army as surgeon, and chiefly potential as a gadder and street gossip against the Saints.

"5. O. J. Hollister, United States Collector; uninteresting man, who married the half sister of the Vice- President, and, although a determined anti-Mormon, does not agree with several of the Ring; the same is the case with several others; all want to be boss . . .

"6. Dennis T. Toohy, editor and late partner with Hollister in the *Corinne Reporter;* an Irishman, witty and abusive, and incapable of working in harness. The Ring tactics have generally been to combine the Godbyites and the Gentiles in a 'Liberal' or anti-Brigham party . . .

"7. Frank Kenyon, proprietor of the *Review,* a paper which has superseded the *Salt Lake Tribune* in irritating the Mormons; a Montana man and with . . . little fortitude . . .

"9. George A. Black, Secretary of the Territory, author of the proclamation against the Fourth of July here.

"10. George L. Woods, of Oregon, the Governor; a red-headed, gristly, large man, of little mental 'heft.' Woods refused to let the Mormon militia celebrate the Fourth of July last year, and ordered, through Black, General De Trobriand to turn out his regular army garrison and fire on the Nauvoo Legion if they disobeyed. De Trobriand, who has a contempt for the Gentile Ring, like all the regular army officers, . . . told Woods to go to the devil, and said it was an outrage, anyway, to forbid the Mormons to celebrate the Fourth, as they had been doing for twenty years. De Trobriand was removed as soon as Dr. Newman, the Methodist preacher, could see [President] Grant, and General Morrow was ordered here.

"These people represent the average character of Territorial officers; political adventurers, for the most part, paid the low stipends allowed in the wisdom of the Federal Government, and possessing in common only an intense feeling, begotten of conviction and interest, against every feature of the Mormon Church . . . .

"Utah, although the richest and most populous Territory in the Union, really affords less political pap than any other. But the mining enthusiasm, the large trade of Salt Lake, the elasticity of real estate here, and the large acquisitions of Brigham Young and others in the church, give lawyers in favor with the United States Courts unusual chances to thrive, and the anti-Mormon lawyers and the Court make a close society . . .

" . . . In criminal cases affecting Mormons the Saints say that their only chance is to fee the Ring lawyers . . . .The Court has given moral support to unlicensed liquor dealers and encouraged them to resist paying the hitherto almost prohibitory rates of license . . .

"W.S. Godby, leader of the Godbyites, [an anti-Mormon "fundamentalist" group] but a liquor dealer and a polygamist . . . applied to Judge McKean for an injunction to restrain the city from suing him for violating the license law. When McKean was applied to for a dissolution of the injunction, he put it in his pocket, saying he would hold it under advisement, while meantime Godby goes on selling liquor.

"Prostitution, taking encouragement from these cases, has quadrupled in Salt Lake, every bagnio being composed of Gentile women. A day or two ago a streetwalker was arrested from drunkenness and swearing, but some of her friends, the poker players at the Wahsatch Club, prompted her to sue the city for ten thousand dollars.

"In short, the Officeholders' Ring, led by the United States Court, and supported by the liquor and lewd interests, and all who want to throw off city taxation, is engaged in an unequal grapple with the [Mormon-run] municipal corporation. The East is liberally supplied with inflammatory correspondence, charging mutiny upon the Mormons, in despite of the fact that Brigham Young has submitted to arrest and appeared, unattended, in court. The garrison has been increased to about 1,200 men, unwilling allies of the Ring. A large amount of capital invested in the rich argentiferous galena mines has been diverted to Nevada, Idaho, and Montana; and other foreign capital, apprehensive of a war, has declined to come here. Brigham Young, with whom the United States has dealt upon terms of encouragement in a hundred ways while as much of a polygamist as now — using him to build telegraph and railways, to furnish supplies, to repress Indians, and carry mails — and which appointed him first Governor of Utah and continued him in the place for seven years — this old man, at seventy years of age, is suddenly admonished that he is a criminal, and put on trial for offenses committed twenty years ago.

" . . . To try the representatives of twenty-two thousand votes, a jury is picked by the United States Marshal from one-fourth of two thousand Gentiles; because less than one-fourth of the Gentiles living here indorse the action of the Court. No wife, neighbor or acquaintance of Brigham Young has made any [legal] complaint against him. The Court which is to try him packs a grand jury to do the work of inquisition, a petit jury to try him, and comes down itself amongst the lawyers to prosecute him. This is persecution, because there is no law for it. The Court enacts the Cullom Bill, which never passed Congress, and prosecutes under it by the very man who wrote it.

"The present movement against Brigham Young at one time comprised a large portion of the Gentile and apostate population here, but nearly all these have fallen away, and the Ring is left nearly alone, with scarcely enough citizen material to get sufficient juries from it.

"Bishop Tuttle, the Episcopal functionary here, to whom Brigham Young gave a liberal subscription for the Episcopal Chapel, as he gave $500 to the new Catholic Church, is said to deprecate the precipitate action of the Court, as does Father Welsh, the priest. Dr. Fuller, ex-Republican acting Governor here; ex-Secretary and Governor S. A. Mann; Major Hempstead, District Attorney here for eight years, and even General Connor . . . express contempt for these sensational court processes.

"Connor has just written a letter to Hempstead, saying that this action was altogether unfortunate as a repressory measure. The late Chief Justice, Charles C. Wilson, is even more pronounced in his condemnation of the Court. I.C. Bateman and D. E. Buell, as well as the Walkers, the latter the leading merchants of Salt Lake apostates, and the former two great mining capitalists, are said to be of the same mind. Joseph Gordon, late Secretary to Governor Latham, calls the Court hard names. The large law firms are nearly all in like attitude. Every Representative and Senator west of the Rocky Mountains, including Cole, Williams, Corbett, Nye, Stewart, Sargent, and other Republicans, stand opposed to any measure which shall sacrifice Utah to blind bigotry without statesmanship . . .

"The original movement against the Mormons, through which the *Salt Lake Tribune* was started — first paper here to attack the Church — began for quite a different interest. The valuable Emma Mine was then in litigation, and a decision of Judge McKean confirmed the Walker Brothers and others in the occupation and use of it, as against the claim of James E. Lyon, of Colorado.

"The Walkers occupied the mine jointly with W. M. Hussey,

President of the opposition bank of Salt Lake, the Sclovers, capitalists of New York, and Tranor W. Park, of Vermont, late financial agent of the John C. Fremont ring and a candidate for the United States Senate from California. None of these wished to consummate the arrest of Brigham Young, or provoke any collision or debate in Utah, but they were forced to support McKean because his decision confirmed them in the mine. Meantime, Lyon, [James E.] preferred charges against McKean, for his corrupt transaction in the Velocipede Mine, wishing to get him off the bench in the Emma Mine case. The Walkers and Hussey — to whom McKean was necessary — started the newpaper to sustain him [McKean] ...

"While the effort was being made to remove McKean, the Lyon interest called upon Brigham Young to give it aid through his [Brigham's] great, but silent, influence in Eastern circles.

" 'No,' replied Brigham; 'whoever will be sent here in his place will proceed to rob and plunder us in the same way. I have no choice between thieves, and can't help you.'

"When the Emma Mine litigation, the unconscious entering wedge to Mormonism, was pending, Tranor W. Park (who had lived in Nevada, and knew the desperate means often resorted to there to get antejudicial possession of a valuable mine) became apprehensive that Lyon and his lawyers would import roughs from Nevada and seize the mine by force. He cozzened Governor Woods for the sake of the military which Woods controlled, with the gift of the presidency of a tunnel company, and thus ... it happens that the Governor ... is now worth fifty thousand dollars ... —a large commercial increase in a short while.

"You can see from these data how much more than the Mormon question there is out here in Utah, and all the adventurers secrete themselves behind the halloo of 'polygamy.' No wonder the Mormons are afraid of our judicial morals more than our justice ...

"Young, Wells and Cannon are the vitality of the Mormon Church. Young is the organizer of the industry of Utah, and the ablest executive spirit west of the Rocky Mountains. His power is in his will, his Yankee materialism, and his position, now so long maintained as to be traditional with his people. They are proud of him, of his hale old age, fearlessness, sagacious enterprises, attention to their wants, and high rank amongst the great men of the time. He has brought the mass of them out of English, Danish and Swedish beggary, to a country of land, fruit and scenery.

"He can put ten thousand men to work any day on his three railways, for their daily board, paying them wages in stock, and he needs no land grant or bonded indorsement. His enterprises generally pay speedy dividends.

"His tithing system brings out immigrants, who in time return the passage-money to the Church, and it reappears in large systems of mechanism and traffic.

"He has built five hundred miles of the Deseret telegraph line, connecting all his settlements from St. George, where the Mormons cultivate cotton and mill it; past Provo, where a granite woolen mill, seven stories high, costing two hundred thousand dollars, and adapted to five hundred hands, is about to move its infinite spindles; up to Brigham city, where his narrow-gauge road is progressing toward Idaho.

"He has built sixty miles of cooperative railway in Utah, one hundred and fifty miles of the Union Pacific Railroad, and many hundred miles of the Western Union Telegraph.

"There is no ecclesiastic in the Methodist or any other American church, with a title of his versatile and vigorous administrative ability. Of his sixty odd children, many are married to Gentiles, and all are endowed never with money, but with occupation. Brigham Young is still a credulous sincere convert to the Mormon Church . . .

"The church has made him, as well as he has dignified it; for he was only a painter and carpenter, with a serious nature, and an inclination for the Methodist Church, when the gospel of Joseph Smith overtook him, and drew him in. The prophet himself predicted a career for Brigham, and sent him abroad on a mission. Given thus a consequence and experience which old and beaten faiths would not have proffered, Brigham Young was ten years a traveling preacher and agent, and the doctrine of polygamy was no part of his suggestion. He accepted it as he did every declaration of Joseph Smith . . .

"This man whose life in all but polygamy has been abstemious, ardent and powerful, and who, considering his want of education, is, perhaps, the greatest living instance of human development without advantages.

"Wells, the Mayor of Salt Lake, is a man of willing administration, entirely faithful to Young, in nothing else great, and he has a disagreeable cock-eye, but he is a diligent Mayor, and Salt Lake City is in much his creation.

"Geo. Q. Cannon is one of the most intelligent Mormons, an Englishman and a good writer; outside of his family he is a pure man.

"These three are selected for indictment upon the complaint of nobody but a grand jury picked especially with this object.

"Bearing in mind these natures, strong men but zealous of forty years' standing (for Brigham was converted in 1832), you may imagine the situation when the indictment was served upon them.

"There were gathered together in the Lion House Brigham's chief counselors: old John Taylor, who stood by Joe Smith when he was shot in Carthage jail and was himself wounded, and would rather take his chances in the open air than go to a Gentile jail again; a tall, good-looking, severe man with gray hair.

"There was George A. Smith, cousin to Joseph, and, next to Young, the highest man in the church, also a witness of the sack of Nauvoo . . .

"There was Orson Pratt, the chief theologian and expounder, whose brother, Parley Pratt, was shot dead by the Gentiles — a venerable-looking, Mosaic sort of man, with flaming beard, and large, introspective eyes, a Greek student, and a sort of Mormon Matthew Henry. The natty and flowery Dr. Newman of Washington, who came out here with six Hebrew roots carefully committed to memory, expecting to demolish Orson with them, found the old fellow capable of talking Hebrew with Moses or Daniel.

"There was Joseph Young, President of the Seventies, a lean face and low forehead, with a mouth like Abraham Lincoln's — elder brother of Brigham Young.

"These and others, baked dry in the furnace of old Mormon dangers which they now account their glory, gave counsel to Brigham Young as to his duty. Almost unanimously they urged that he must never give himself up: the people would rise if he were to be convicted, whether he forbade them or no. Their counsel was to cut the irrigation ditches, burn every Mormon settlement in the Territory, leave the valley of Salt Lake in desolation, and march across Arizona with their herds and portables to Mexican soil; these were their own, and they had a right to annihilate the property they had created.

"Brigham Young, himself in the condition of an old lion, not uncertain that his prowess was now a part of his nature and religion, urged that he was promised safe conduct and fair treatment.

"To this old John Taylor retorted:

" 'So was Joseph! I saw the safe treatment they gave him in jail!'

"There was a general exclamation of deep feeling and cry of perfidy at this — and I am writing no fancy sketch, but the statement of two attorneys who were present. Brigham himself was deeply moved. Perhaps the recollection of his more youthful Captaincy of the Mormon exodus across the alkali plains inspired him with enthusiasm. To this urgent statement of the Gentiles that he could not hold out a week against the United States, the old man retorted with a strange, almost childish confidence, that if he were disposed to resist, the ally of Moses, of Gideon, and of David, would appear upon his side.

"Then, after a minute, Brigham closed his great square mouth and jaw, and said calmly:

" 'God is in courts as well as in battles and marches. There will be no resistance. I shall obey the summons.'

"In due time he dismounted from his buggy before the little old squalid stone stable where the United States Court meets, climbed the creaky outside stairs, and at his colossal, venerable appearance, the whole Court unconsciously arose, bar and audience. He was the overshadowing presence there, and when he answered 'Not guilty,' Judge McKean's elocution flew out of his head and he forgot, temporarily, to be dramatic.

"INTERVIEW WITH THE MAYOR OF SALT LAKE
"Salt Lake City, October 25, 1871.

"Mr. Hiram B. Clawson, son-in-law of Brigham Young, and Superintendent of the great co-operative store at Salt Lake, said to me last night:

" 'D. H. Wells, a member of the first Presidency in our church, and the Mayor of Salt Lake City, wishes to state to you the distress under which we labor about our titles to property here. We have inhabited this place twenty-two years. Almost every other town in the territory has obtained its patents under the municipal town site act. But we, the oldest settlement in Utah ... are so bullied and injured by Maxwell, the Land Register here ... that we continue in only possessory rights, and we are annoyed by ... fraudulent claim.

" 'The Associated Press [newspaper wire service] Agent here, one Sawyer, is under the thumb of the ring, and we have no means to communicate with our fellow citizens in the East.'

" 'Do you suppose General Wells will talk upon other matters if I listen to him on this subject?' " said Townsend to Clawson.

" 'Yes. Anything legitimate. He is a bugbear to some people who don't know him, but you will find him, on contact, to be a simple, sincere, agreeable man, like any respectable American.'

"Soon afterward this celebrated Mormon warrior, the right-bower of Brigham Young, the Lieutenant General of the great Nauvoo Legion, numbering five thousand men, the commander of the Utah forces in the Sidney Johnston war, and the Fouchet of Salt Lake City, and terror of the criminals there, was ushered into my presence.

"I beheld a tall, long-nosed, sharp-browed man, with gray hair ... and a bent back, the result of age and unrelieved labor. He would have been several inches over six feet high had he not stooped, but eminent service in the Mormon Church is of almost monastic rigor upon one so distinguished, and this old man had a way of winking which suggested eyes and head worn out in the Secretaryship of that mighty energy, "Uncle Brigham," while his clothing was poor and worn, and he talked with gentleness, almost like meekness. The Mormons have admonished me that, although he is a natural fire-eater and a military commander by instinct, he has latterly been a uniform counselor for peace and submission, and has helped to sway Brigham Young to wise advices.

"As I never 'interview' people off their guard, I took up a quire of paper and a pen, and made notes as the answers came to my questions.

"The old man sat across the table, and his voice was seldom pitched higher than if he had talked to himself.

" 'My errand to you,' began this guarded old Mormon — who was reared in St. Lawrence County, New York, and is an American typically — 'My errand is to relate to you the embarrassing — the needlessly embarrassing condition of our titles here.

" 'I am the Mayor of Salt Lake, and, as this was the first town settled in the Territory, I had an ambition to see it entered first among the town sites, according to general law. I made application, even before there was a Land Office opened at Denver, according to the prescriptions of the law of 1867, and followed it up respectfully and solicitously, when, in July, 1869, the Land Office was opened at Salt Lake.

" 'It is no fault of the United States Government that we are not now peacefully possessing the titles to the ground we have redeemed, and which Congress wishes us to retain. It is the fault of the unrelenting Land Register here, Maxwell, who has entertained and abetted every petty and malicious claim contesting our right to the site, and who hinders the entry of our city apparently with the object of being bought off or of discouraging us, or even of robbing us of it.' "

[Specifics are found on pp. 27-28 of *The Mormon Trials*, by Townsend.]

" ' . . . a score of unlicensed liquor dealers seem emboldened to defy us. The liquor sellers have now, I am told, by the advice of the satellites of the Court, raised a fund to sue the city when we interfere with them. The prostitutes newly landed among us rise up in that Court to assail our ordinances. The Court entertains every complaint, and those too preposterous to treat with seriousness it puts in its pocket and staves off, while crime takes advantage of the interregnum.

" 'Our Aldermen's courts have been delegalized, and we are told by McKean that a Legislature has no right to bestow discretionary powers on a jury or a civic corporation. In short, Mr. Correspondent, there is an end in Utah to any equality before the law . . . Our Probate Courts are declared to have no power to grant divorces, and yet Mr. Baskins, the United States Prosecuting Attorney, is married to a woman divorced by a Probate Court.

" 'When Mr. Hawkins was sentenced for adultery, it is current that at least one man on the bench that sentenced him was guilty of that crime. But, then, we are Mormons! Finally, professional murderers like Bill Hickman are permitted to give themselves up by collusion with the Courts, and affect to turn State's evidence against us to prejudice us in the eyes of civilization.'

" 'Who is Bill Hickman?'

" 'He is a Missouri desperado, who attached himself to our Church many years ago, and was turned out of it several years since. We have had him twice in custody for murder, and once, at least, the United States military authorities have taken him out of our hands. By occupation he is a cattle-stealer. He is the terror of the territory . . . Yet his evidence is admitted to prejudice respectable men in the estimation of their countrymen.'

" 'Who arrested him?'

" 'One Gilson, one of the numerous deputy Marshals who have been sworn in from the lowest orders of society to overawe us. Gilson has been with Bill Hickman all summer, and there was probably an agreement between them.'

" 'What does Hickman look like?'

" 'He is a thick-set, burly, sandy man with dyed beard, unable to look you in the eye. We took him up for killing a Mexican who had married his [ex-]wife. He beat and deserted the woman, and she was divorced from him. He shot the Mexican dead in his doorway, and galloped off. Now, I am told, he is having his life written and embellished for sale. Since his incarceration he has taken to wearing broadcloth.'

" 'Who was Yates, the man he [Hickman] swears he killed at the suggestion of yourself and others?''

" 'Yates was a trader of some sort whom Hickman brought to my camp in the Mormon war with a shackle on his heel. I ordered him released, and he wanted to go to Salt Lake, which was accorded him. He disappeared with Hickman and was never seen again. Hickman now swears that I said he was a scoundrel, and ought to be dead. Also that Joseph Young said he deserved death. What evidence to indict men of our age and position! . . . They transpired fourteen years ago. Drown and Arnold were two other men whom Hickman confesses to have killed, and he implicates us there also' . . .

" 'General Wells, had you ever seen any military experience before you joined the Church?'

" 'No, except in the militia.'

" 'How did you fall in with the Mormons?'

" 'Why, I had lived about ten years at a little place called Commerce, Illinois, and was a young man, Justice of the Peace there, when (in 1839) the Mormons were driven out of Missouri and came across Iowa to find a site for a settlement. They struck Quincy first, and scouted up the river to pick a place. Our town of Commerce was a 'paper city' only; the land was cheap, and we were not altogether sorry that the Mormons took it up. There were along about one thousand of them at first, and a poor, sick lot they were for several seasons. Joseph Smith began very soon to get up a memorial to the Government on the subject of the plunder of his people in Missouri, and they came before me to make their affidavits. Joseph Smith in person took those affidavits and the memorial on to Washington to President Van Buren, and I often thought that the Mormon troubles began out of that errand of his.'

" 'How, sir?'

" 'You see, a good many of the leading Mormons had, while in their Gentile state, been Democrats, among others the Smiths and Brigham Young. Joseph Smith expected that Van Buren would recognize him to some degree because of their predilections for the same party, but when he presented his case Van Buren made this unsatisfactory reply: "Your cause is just, but I cannot help you. Address your story to the magnanimous State and people of Missouri." When Joseph Smith returned to Nauvoo he told his people to vote for Harrison in 1840, which they did solidly, and this irritated the Democrats, who counted upon the Mormon vote. Afterward, Joseph directed his people to vote for men friendly to them rather than for mere parties. The idea got abroad, after awhile, that the Mormons could not be counted upon politically by either side, and it got to be a notion among the Illinois vote-getters that they could intimidate these poor people against supporting the opposite side. The intimidation thus begun led to the mob spirit which sacrificed Joseph in 1844.

" 'I was a Whig, and I thought the Mormons were sometimes as far wrong as their enemies, but I could not shut my eyes to the fact that even my party did not treat them like human creatures. I remember well that reared young man, named Morrison. He said to me one day: "By God! we mean to make them vote our ticket this year. The Democrats forced them to support theirs last year, and we can do the same thing this time." '

" ' "How?" said I.

" ' "Well. We'll get a requisition from the Governor of Missouri for Joe Smith and we'll hold that requisition over his head and force him to give us the votes of all his crowd or serve it on him."

" 'This looked like a mean trick to me, and I found myself, perhaps out of natural combativeness, standing between the Mormons and their persecutors, and finally, after a good deal of consideration, I joined the Church, several years after my acquaintance with the leaders.'

" 'What was the origin of the word, Nauvoo?'

" 'They say it meant in Hebrew, "beautiful site" or "beautiful city." I know nothing of Hebrew and can't tell whether that is true or not.'

" 'General, what became of Sidney Rigdon, Joseph's early coadjutor?'

" 'Well, he is living now at Friendship, a town I think in Western New York, near Buffalo. He took it to heart that he was not promoted in the Church, and left us; at present he is a very old, pusillanimous man, who sometimes addresses us communications. He offered at one time to guarantee us the protection of Providence if we would make up one hundred thousand dollars for him, and still later we hear that he has predicted our early overthrow.'

" 'He has been supposed by some to have been Joseph's intellectual and executive superior, and to have given Mormonism its original impetus?' " asked Townsend.

" 'Oh, no. Joseph was the man. Oliver Cowdery, an educated person, was of more assistance to Joseph than Rigdon; for he wrote a good hand and acted as Joseph's Secretary, Smith himself being at first illiterate, unable to write, and obliged to confine his correspondence to dictation. However, Joseph burnished up greatly in the fourteen years of his Presidency; such trials as his would educate almost any man.'

" 'Is Cowdery living?'

" 'No. He left the Church while we were still at Nauvoo; then he repented and followed us across the plains, and was rebaptized and recieved into fellowship. Paying a visit or going upon a mission to Missouri, he was taken sick and died there.'

" 'What was the fate of Joseph's refractory wife, Emma Smith?'

" 'She, like Rigdon, was dissatisfied with the amount of consideration she received in the Church after Joseph's death, and would not come with us, but remained in Illinois, near Nauvoo, and I understand that she married another husband and is living there now.'

" 'Have you ever visited Nauvoo since the exodus in 1846?'

" 'No, sir; not since the destruction of the temple. President Young appointed me Adjutant to keep the emigrant and supply teams well up through Iowa, and afterward across the Plains. I remember that when we had crossed the Mississippi upon improvised rafts, floats and boats, the poorest and most despairing body of halt, lame, sick and uncertain people you ever saw in the world — that the military mob marched up in front of the temple, planted a cannon and fired across into our camps of sick, adding panic to wretchedness. All that is past and forgotten with us, but it is accurately set down in our church history, and we got converts all around the country, from among the witnesses of those scenes.'

" 'Where is Joseph's body buried?'

" 'At Nauvoo. It was buried secretly. He was shot in several places in the breast, if I remember well, and Hyrum Smith was shot in the face. I was not present at Carthage at the massacre, but around Nauvoo I saw many frightful scenes, which confirmed me in my already half-formed idea that these Mormons were a persecuted people and better Christians than my neighbors. The mob used to get in the bushes, for instance, on the out skirts of Nauvoo, set a man's barn or haystack a fire, and then by the light of the blaze shoot him as he ran away.'

" 'Are those good pictures of Joseph and Hyrum Smith at President Young's office?'

" 'Yes; good likenesses. Hyrum was the devoted brother of

Joseph, believed in him from the first, kept with him all the way down, and they died together, as I had seen them a many hundred times, walking fondly side by side. Brigham Young, also, was a bosom friend of Joseph Smith, and an eminent man in the Church at that early day. He was President of the Quorum of the Twelve Apostles.'

" 'Can you give me an idea of Joseph Smith, so that I can realize him?'

" 'He was a large man, weighing two hundred pounds, and about six feet high, with a countenance never sanctimonious, but always cheerful and bright; brown hair and light eyes, and I might call him a real jam-up free-and-easy good fellow. He used to play ball, run and wrestle with the people, and if a big man joined the Church, Joseph would pick him out and try him for a throw, for he had a conceit that he was a match for "most anybody." You can see that we keep up in the Church his example of liveliness in our theater and Social Hall.'

" 'Was it at Nauvoo that Joseph proclaimed the revelation of polygamy?'

" 'Oh, no. He had received it a long while before his death, and his counselors knew of it, but he was afraid to make it public.'

" ' . . . General Wells, I wish you would tell me what it was that began the Mormon war of 1857.'

" 'I can answer that in one word — Bill Drummond!'

" 'Who was he?'

" 'One of the United States Judges. He came here from Illinois and spent most of his time at the town of Fillmore. There were frequent rows at his Court, resembling McKean's wranglings with us at present, but we did not know that he was backed up by the Government, and we set his attitude down to general personal "cussedness." He wanted to be transferred to another Court, it seems, nearer the Pacific coast, and thought before leaving us that he would fire a parting shot. So after he slipped away, there appeared at Washington a report, signed by him, charging us with every sort of crime, and this was immediately followed by a general yell from the newspaper press.

" 'As we had only a monthly mail, we were for a long time perfectly unaware of this rising storm. But one of our friends in

Washington cut from the newspapers nearly a hundred denunciatory extracts of us and sent them out to us.

" 'They arrived here one Sunday in the month of May, 1857 . . .

" 'The next we knew, a mail contract that we had purchased and had fully stocked with teams, stations, horses, and every appurtenance, at a cost of $300,000 [to us] and which was subsidized with only $20,000 a year [from the government], was taken from us at Washington and given to other parties for $100,000 [per year — five times what the Mormons charged the government] . . .'

" 'What reasons are there for his [President Grant] taking up polygamy at this critical time in the period of mining and railway development here?'

" 'Well, sir, our offense is like that of the Caffirs against the Dutch. The Caffirs said: 'Our greatest crime is that we have received a beautiful country from the Almighty, and you want it.'

"SALT LAKE AND UTAH PICTURES.

"Salt Lake, October 27.

"So much attention has been paid to Salt Lake City by tourists and journalists that the Eastern public possess little or no idea of the other thriving towns and cities of Utah. From Brigham City to St. George, a distance of about three hundred and fifty miles, there is a chain of settlements reaching through Central Utah north and south, almost entirely . . .

" . . . Provo . . . is, next to Salt Lake and Ogden, the most important place in the Territory. Provo stands upon the Timponayos River, near Utah Lake, a clear, deep, fresh-water wheel, full of heavy trout, and it contains the best water power in the Territory. Here is Brigham's seven-story granite woolen mill . . . Fillmore, ninety-six miles from Salt Lake, [is] the real capital of the Territory . . . Before Fillmore, upon a 'divide,' is a telegraph operator, quartered in a stone fort to protect him from Indians, who are sometimes bad here. At Beaver, a town of two thousand one hundred people, forty miles south of Fillmore, one of the three United States District Courts is held. The next important place is Parowan, founded by Geo. A. Smith, in 1852, and then Cedar City, in a coal and iron region, with a deserted forge. Just south of this place we cross the rim of the great Salt Lake basin, and almost immediately the country turns red in color, and wears that wizard look as if scorched by fire. The first town beyond is Toquerville, founded in 1859; then the town of Washington, with six hundred inhabitants and Brigham's celebrated cotton mill. Finally, in the southwest corner of the Territory stands St. George, on the Rio Virgin, a town of tropical looking groves and neat cottages of wood, adobe and stone upon a plain between mountain 'benches' . . .

"Hundreds of miles of canals and dikes, a people distributed over all the reclaimable region of the Territory, co-operation reduced from a religious duty to a voluntary and profitable system and upon a relative scale larger than elsewhere in the world — these, no matter how they came about, are triumphs not to be gainsayed by the political economist and statesman, however the zealot and the prowling territorial politician may belittle them.

"Utah, agriculturally, as nobody else but the Mormons could have developed it, is a necessity to the mining, railroad, and military operations of the central continent; for these enterprises subsist upon the produce of these farms, and a large human settlement here is also a strategic experiment. The neighboring mines of Idaho, Nevada, Montana and Colorado draw much of their store supplies from the valley.

" 'It isn't like Nevada,' said a miner to me, yesterday; 'here you can just walk down the mountain, from the mine to the foot, and find eggs, butter, and milk in the Mormon settlement.'

"The army and the railroads . . . must also subsist upon Mormon agriculture. The time may come when the mines of the neighboring territories must be abandoned by reason of the cost of labor and living around them, but here agriculture and population had preceded mines and railways nearly a quarter of a century, and even under the present mining excitement mining labor costs only two dollars and a half a day, while in Nevada, barren of farms, it costs four dollars. It is largely Mormon labor which is completing the whole central railway system, striking out as boldly at present down the affluents of the Columbia and Colorado Rivers as it did upon the heavy work in Echo and Weber Canyons for the Union Pacific Railway.

"It is the opinion of many of the ablest men in the country that Utah will be the main manufacturing country for the Pacific Coast, like the Pittsburgh region of the East. Already the manufactures here embrace cotton and woolen mills, iron, leather, flour, gloves, and small wares. The system of farming by irrigation is readily adaptable to water power uses. Coal is found just east of Salt Lake, which is used along eight hundred miles of the Pacific Railway, and other facts indicate Salt Lake as the emporium of all the business between the Rocky Mountains and the Sierra Nevada.

"But what elements of population will take this soil and conduct agriculture here if the Mormons should abandon it? Gentiles tell me that between the drought, grasshoppers, alkali, the need of perpetual co-operation to regulate the ditches, and the primitive poverty of the ground, Mormon frugality and unity only can sustain the miracle of this garden in the desert. There are not five Gentile farmers in Utah. An exodus to Mexico, with their abundance of fine heads of cattle, sheep and horses, might give Mormonism a better empire, but what race would revive this one?

"The probability of emigration is a widespread theme already, in view of the harsh attitude of the Courts here. Mormonism has been a series of emigrations, from Kirtland to Missouri, eight hundred miles; thence to Nauvoo, four hundred miles; thence to Salt Lake, fifteen hundred miles; and each exodus has been an epoch and an advantage to the church.

"From St. George it is but four hundred miles across Arizona by a well defined and serviceable road to the Republic of Mexico, and there are settlements and military posts as far as Tucson and Tabae on the brink of Mexico. The Mexicans will welcome anywhere between Chihuahua and Sinaloa, these quiet settlers who can create a power on the Gulf of California, and curb the Apaches by either the Quaker or the Crook method.

"The remarkable man who presides over these people added to the many conquests of his life, the final victory over his absolute spirit when he put by the counsels of his elders and went into court upon an indictment which, in its language and tone, is at variance with whatever is known of his life by any third party.

Brigham Young is just as guilty of 'lewd and licentious conduct and cohabitation' as the Viceroy of Egypt, the Chief of the Cherokees, the Emperor of Japan, or the patriarch Moses, with their several wives. His children and wives are all acknowledged and provided for; of the latter he has sixteen, and of children sixty odd. His offense is polygamous marriages, practised for twenty years with the full knowledge of an unbroken series of United States officials, Judges and Presidents included, by all of whom he has been treated with equality, and by many with distinction.

"The statute under which he is indicted was passed by Mormons in their Territorial Legislature, and made punishable by from three to ten years' imprisonment, at the time of the formation of their code — that of Massachusetts, passed in 1790; and this, as construed, provides that the lewdness and lasciviousness must be public, and that secret cohabitation is not intended; in other words, the offense is against decency and not chastity. There has been no complaint of this nature ever made in the present instance, but the Judge and the Prosecuting Attorney, the *avant guard* of that supposititious distant sentiment, *packed* a grand jury — there is no other word applicable — to indict Young, and will pack a petit jury to convict him. In my opinion, and in the apprehension of every business man and military officer in Utah, if this is done, and Brigham Young be sent to jail, the Church authorities, including himself, will not be able to prevent an outbreak or an exodus . . . [His emphasis]

"Six months ago, before Judge McKean arrived here, like a Catholic Jesuit dropping down in the vale of the wilderness, the Mormons were thoroughly reconciled to the United States and anxious for its benefits. Their past persecutions were forgotten. It is we, or our inquisitorial Courts, who have recalled together our aggressions and the Mormons' excesses.

"Let us be cool-headed, and not jump behind our century!

"Co-operation, advocated by the press and reformers as a benefit everywhere else, had no sooner been adopted among the Mormons than there went up a howl of 'monopoly,' 'commercial restriction!'

"To get at the bottom of this matter, I went right to William Jennings, the richest Mormon, Brigham excepted, and who was alleged to have been compelled by Brigham to give his store to the enterprise. Mr. Jennings inhabits a large and beautiful house, which probably cost two hundred thousand dollars, and he dispenses cheer of a hearty and ninou quality. He has but one wife living, and his daughters expressed themselves indignantly that their deceased mother was to be declared impure and themselves illegitimate by a Court of Judges belonging to another religion.

"Mr. Jennings said that he lived in Missouri, at St. Joseph, and was not a member of the church, nor cognizant of its existence, when he left England. The plan of the co-operation store was Brigham Young's, and he proposed it as early as 1853, but Jennings, Lawrence, Walker Brothers and Godby, to whom it was suggested, did not think favorably of it. These merchants made large sums of money — sums out of proportion to the producer and consumer — in consideration of brotherly equity. Wheat was bought from the Mormon farmers at seventy-five cents a bushel, often paid for in merchandise, and then sold in the form of flour in the mining regions for twenty-five dollars gold per hundred weight, a profit of several hundred percent.

" 'Thus,' said Mr. Jennings, 'we all prospered inordinately, and I had meditated retiring from business in 1867, when again President Young revived his plan of a co-operation store. Those of us who intended to remain steadfast to the Church found it now imperative to agree [although some left the church, desiring to maintain their remarkable profit scale] . . . I at once rented my store for five years to the co-operation society . . . We made the thing democratic, so that five dollars would constitute a stockholder, and we tightened it only with regard to the transferral of shares; for if this Court up here could by any means entrap us into its precincts, we should have injunctions, receivers and mandamuses without stint.

" 'The capital is not far from half a million, and we pay [out] ten percent a month, so that our customers who are stockholders get their proportion in dividends. We have brought down prices to our poor people who are not stockholders, and Mr. Clawson, the manager, seeks to regulate profits down to ten percent upon articles of prime necessity.

" 'While the co-operative store has been a gratifying and

beneficent success, other merchants are doing a large, independent business. Mormons are free to buy anywhere, and their only incentive to go to the "co-op" is interest. We have only one branch which we directly control, at Ogden, but our plan is imitated in every ward of Salt Lake, and in every settlement of Utah.'

"Speaking of Godby, Mr. Jennings said that he was flighty and ambitious, and that he had done a mean thing in taking a fifth wife after apostatizing. 'No man has a right to be a polygamist,' said Mr. Jennings, 'unless he believes in it as a revelation.'

"Not only is monogamy the practice of the entire 'Josephite' or Young Smith school of the Mormon Church, but even at Salt Lake it has exemplars, such as Fermamorz Little and William Jennings, who are considered the richest men in the Territory next to Brigham Young. Jennings at one time had two wives, but since the death of the first he has never re-married. These men are probably worth one million dollars apiece, and worth half as much as W. H. Hooper, Mormon banker and Delegate in Congress, also a monogamist in practice and prejudice. Bolivar Roberts, who is very rich in real estate, and who is reputed to have received three hundred thousand dollars for his interest in the Sweetwater Mine, is likewise the Mormon husband of one wife. John T. Caine, editor of the *Salt Lake Herald,* the leading newspaper between Denver and Sacramento; D. E. Calder, Superintendent of the Utah Central Railroad; H. T. Fantz, and many others, find the cares of one family sufficient.

"Polygamy, however, is warmly defended, even by Mormon monogamists, as right . . .

"Brigham Young's most noted wife is called Amelia; she is a vivacious, spirited woman, about thirty-two years old, American born, and without children. Another of President's wives is Mrs. Decker, who retains indications of much former beauty, and her daughters are the handsomest of Brigham's children. The old gentleman looks out well for avocations for his sons-in-law, and it is said that in his will he has divided all his property into seven hundred shares, given the bulk of it to the church, and distributed the rest equally among his families.

"I saw Brigham at the Social Hall, on the occasion of my last visit here, bid four of his wives adieu. The old gentleman had been dancing, but had fatigued the legs of seventy years, and he approached the cluster of his helpmates, buttoned up in a blue overcoat with a white vest underneath, a red woolen comforter around his neck, and a worn silk hat in his hand. He looked very large, square, and bland, and he said with tenderness and dignity, shaking each by the hand:

" 'My dear, I bid you good night!'

"The wives crowding up, with apparent emulation, asked if it was his wish that they also should accompany him home.

" 'No,' said Brigham, 'stay as long as you please. I will have the carriage come back and wait for you at the door below. Good night!' ...

"INSIDE VIEWS OF UTAH SOCIETY

"Salt Lake, Oct 27.

"One day, as the period of the semi-annual Mormon conference approached, he [Mr. Kinzer, a Californian] met a very old woman driving a cart to which an ox was attached. The miner peeped into her cart and saw that it contained nothing to eat except a little salt meat and a bag of meal, with fodder for the ox. This was somewhere in Juab County.

" 'Old lady,' said the miner, 'where are you going?'

" 'Up to our conference, sir. I ha'n't been there now for two year, but I want to get my soul warmed up a little. It appeared as if I could not stay away any longer. I have been in church twenty-two years, and I always go to the conference when I can, but I live 'way down here on the Santa Clara River, and it takes me three weeks to go to Salt Lake.'

"This poor old zealot had actually been more than two weeks on the way to her church conference; she camped out every night, and was entirely alone and unbefriended. The miners gave her some cheese and bread and sent her on her way rejoicing.

"The Mormon confereces are fearfully apostolical. Twelve thousand people often attend them.

" ... Go into that vast enclosure, and you will see the Mormon Church conducting its business, the hands of its officials held up by the whole broad public sentiment. W. H. Hooper told me that for nearly twenty years he had attended these conferences, and he had never heard a half dozen nays voted against any measure propounded by the High Quorum."

Earlier, Wells had elaborated: "We have two annual conferences, one meeting on the 6th of April, the day our church was organized in the year 1830, and the other on the 6th of October. Each conference continues in session from four days to a week, and all the people of the Territory come up."

Townsend continues:

"He [Brigham] is only aware of the fearful mightiness of democratic sentiment in America from the few troops camped in his vicinity, from the miserable character of the Federal officials who go out there to blackmail him, and from the stream of respectful visitors, for whom he holds a levee every morning, and who butter him with praises, while perhaps the same people are indicting letters to the East raising a hue and cry against his Empire. He will leave behind him in that State a name never to be rivaled in the future prosperous history of Utah . . .

"I was talking one day with a distinguished apostle of the Mormon Church, and he used this curious illustration:

" 'Suppose, Mr. Townsend,' he said, 'that Joseph Smith had been born 3400 years ago, and Moses in the year 1800, A. D., thus reversing the order of their several revelations — which would be the harder to believe?'

"I replied: 'You ask me too much. I am not familiar with the story of Moses. My notion of Moses is obtained from one of Michael Angelo's statues; he always seemed to me to be a fair man.'

" 'Now,' said this apostle, 'the story of Joseph Smith is, that he discovered a set of golden plates, and he was divinely endowed to translate them. You ask where are those plates? We answer that Joseph Smith gave them back to the angel, who kept them. Moses on the other hand went up into Mount Sinai, taking no witnesses with him, and is alleged to have had a familiar talk with the Lord. The Lord gave him two tablets of stone on which the commandments are engraved; but Moses never showed the people those stone tablets, any more than Joseph Smith showed the golden plates. When Moses came down from Sinai with the tablets, he found the people worshipping a golden calf, and it says in the ninth chapter of Deuteronomy, that he cast down the tablets and broke them to pieces. Then he went up into the mountain again, as the tenth chapter of Deuteronomy discloses and was permitted by the Lord, to hew himself a new set of tablets, on which the commandments were engraved, these tablets were put into the ark, and they were everlastingly concealed from the public eye. Now had Moses been named Joseph Smith, the gentile world would have scoffed at this story, and would have said that the non-appearance of the stone tablets, the breaking of the original pair, and re-engraving of an imitation by the prophet himself, were all subterfuges such as those which accompanied the chiseling of the Cardiff giant. But you have had preached at you for eighteen hundred years, the legend of Moses, and you take it without question while you laugh at the altogether more consistent story of the translation of the golden plates. Both instances must be accepted by faith and not by reason. Our people out here believe equally in the tale of Moses, and in that of Joseph, and you who accept one half of the gospel, want to put us in jail and break us up for believing the other half. You came in here just like the Catholic priests got into the vales of the Waldenses. Failing to convert us or rather to unconvert us, you begin to persecute us. It is no fault of ours that we offend you; for we left civilization fifteen hundred miles behind us, in order not to irritate you. We think that our revelation treats of matters if possible more important to human nature than the Old Testament. It solves the problem of the past history of America. It has the only new gospel and indigenous prophet and seer on the hemisphere. It has grown more rapidly than the Jewish power, and if it were not for our notion on the subject of marriage, I believe we would have more converts in the United States, than any other sect.

" 'Mormon Utah is a congregation of all the good institutions which you separately maintain . . . ' Townsend concludes Wells' comments and continues with his own:

"This is a case arising under Judge McKean's system of ruling Mormons off a jury in civil as well as criminal trials affecting them in any way. Engelbrecht, a liquor seller, refused to take out a city license . . . and after being notified of the consequences by the Justice of the Peace in his ward, one Clinton, the liquors of Engelbrecht were poured into the street. He sued Clinton and the officers of the corporation for malicious destruction of his stock, under a territorial statute, making malicious damage punishable three times the value of the property destroyed. McKean ruled every Mormon off the jury on the ground of bias and incapability of giving a verdict according to the evidence. The liquor seller won the case by the packed jury, and for nineteen thousand dollars worth of liquors got an award of fifty-seven thousand dollars ... The Mormons [thus] ... regard the Supreme Court of Utah as a mixture of fanaticism, dullness and draw-poker ... '

"In Utah, as generally in the Territories, the Federal administration is loose, discordant and slip-shod. The late Prosecutor, Hempstead, was hated by McKean, for objecting to the jury-packing system, and the present Prosecutor is appointed by the Court only; the post military commanders are invariably friendly with the Mormons, because they perceive nothing admirable or lovable in the Federal officials. Judge Strickland frequently smokes cigars and whittles sticks while holding court.

"A vague impression, started by the preacher 'Doctor' Newman, [is] that [President] Grant wants a general movement made on polygamy ... [Newman is] an ambrosial notoriety seeker ... he devised a trip to Utah many months ago, and the Mormons, in Democratic fairness, threw open their tabernacle to him to let him say the worst against their theology. Imagine a Methodist Bishop giving up his pulpit to a Mormon in like circumstances. Newman now returns the courtesy of the Mormons by setting on foot, through the President, this whole precipitate assize against polygamy. Thus are schemes of statesmanship balked by theological pretenders, and shallow preachers are given the scope and influence of Cardinals like Richelieu and Antonelli ...

"There is no doubt that the successor of Brigham Young is already resolved upon by that old Moses himself, and that he is advised of his nomination. It is George A. Smith, cousin to Joseph Smith, and the Historian of the Church, and also at present one of the three members of the 'First Presidency.' [Townsend's speculation was amiss: John Taylor succeeded Young, but George A. Smith's portrait was pertinent, as indeed he was a pillar of the Prophet's empire.]

"A man more unlike Brigham Young it would be difficult to conceive. Brigham is the incarnation of will and purpose, a materialist, a Yankee Turk. George A. Smith is the spirit of reverence, gentleness and accord, and in his hands Mormonism will cease to offend its neighbors, and resolve to a quiet, docile, but still numerous and proselytizing body of worshipers. Smith is very little of a polygamist. He has none of Brigham's consideration for money and clearheadedness upon the great unit of the interest-bearing dollar. Smith is one of us literary folks, a man of the stamp of Thackeray, Peter Force and Washington Irving ... He has no avarice, no love of war, no vindictiveness, and he is yet a sincere, hale, immovable Mormon, believing in Joseph's revelations without question. I am told that there is no historical society in any county or State of the Union so perfectly complete in archives as that of the Mormons. The recording angel might have gone off on a holiday as far as they are concerned; for George A. Smith has kept the account for him.

"And yet, this lolling, easy Bohemian has energies of his own not to be despised, and Brigham Young is more frequently in his society than with any of the Madames Young. He has a wonderful memory, power of language and stump-speaking, and adroit political management. He loves politics and is not a bigot. The Mormons have a weakness for the Smith family ... and there never was any Smith with more sagacity and *bonhommie* than this one. He is a very large, heavy, and self-enjoying man in appearance — resembling ex- Senator Toombs, of Georgia, but without Toombs' opinionatedness or passion. He weighs as much as Brigham Young, wears a brownish auburn wig and spectacles, walks with a cane, and has a ready smile and a big mouth to spread it upon. Although having two or three wives, I dare believe that George Smith is at heart a chaste, tender, and religious husband, father, friend and gentleman ...

"Let a convention be called promptly, even at once, before Congress gets well under way with next session's business. Let this convention prepare a State constitution and concede polygamy in return for the right of local government, trial by jury, and a share in the benefits of representation in the nation."

Not understanding the Latter-day Saint belief that polygamy came by revelation and could only be revoked by revelation, Townsend's plea to church leaders was in vain. As it was, church leaders did announce 19 years later, in 1890, that the revelation had indeed come.

Polygamy was no longer a part of Mormonism.

Note 40

[From page 334]

More Rockwell Gems

John F. Everett, in an interview in 1938, claims Rockwell "did not bother with the courts." If a man stole a horse, "and he had to be chased a hundred miles, he used to say, 'he deserves to be killed.' "[1]

Everett adds:

"I knew Rockwell and talked to him many times. He was as fine a man as could be found to talk to . . . He always got his man . . . He always recovered what was stolen. Porter was just the man the people needed here. Every law abiding citizen respected him, but every criminal hated and feared him. He was a moderate drinker, but I have never seen him smoke. He thought enough of his Church not to profane or use vulgar language [although the consensus is that pedestrian, milder "swear words" were common in his vocabulary after he cut his hair for the widow Smith in California]. When in a saloon they all had to drink with him; if they wouldn't they had to leave, because then, 'it was no place for them,' he used to say.

"He never killed a man unless he deserved it for he was always protecting the rights and lives of good citizens. It is inconceivable for people today [1934] to understand the conditions of that day, prior to 1870. Outside of the towns one carried his life at his hip. Many people that came out west to Utah as well as to other states, were criminals . . .

"In mining towns like Bingham men were shot every day . . . No time was wasted on trials.

"I carried a sixshooter and a bowie knife all the time; everyone did. We had to in order to be safe. I was shot at once. So you see the conditions Rockwell had to combat, he had to use our law weapons and methods to fight them with."[2]

Everett further claims Rockwell used a particularly novel method to nab his victims:

"Sheriff Rockwell when in pursuit of a criminal used a buckboard, when he could, drawn by a pair of his fleet horses which were relayed about every twenty or twenty-five miles."[3] This means Rockwell may have had horses stationed at various ranches throughout the communities.

Another old-timer interviewed in 1938, Caroline Lamb Slack of Toquerville, Utah, reports, "Yes, I remember Porter Rockwell, he generally traveled around with President Young."[4]

James H. Jennings of Rockville, Utah, reports, "I saw Porter Rockwell many times . . . He was a very husky man, cheerful and liked by all."[5]

Glen Trane of Lehi, Utah states that his grandmother, who used to see Rockwell in town, told him: "Quite a number of white men tried to cut his hair to see if they could catch up with him."[6]

A. Ralph Curtis of Tucson, Arizona, writes, "My grandfather bought a span of mules from Port Rockwell. One named Port — one named Rock. They were the best from Port's Ramuda — Port raised good mules — my grandfather knew Port well."[7]

A resident of Sandy, Utah, whose great-grandfather was a witness to the scene, relates one day Porter was warned by two famous outlaw-gamblers to leave town by midnight. Since Porter refused, the two men decided to ambush him. They went searching for him at Brigham Young's stables and found him. A number of gun blasts were heard inside the barn. Witnesses waited outside while the door finally squeaked open. Porter emerged with a horse, and over it were draped two bloodied corpses.[8]

Zelma S. Thompson wrote a prize-winning short-story based on her grandmother's interaction with the marshal. The account exemplifies the folklorian hero-status of Rockwell. As one of several stories — but the only one about Rockwell — it is included in a forth-coming book, *Grandma's Pioneer Stories,* by Beverly B. Thompson of Draper, Utah. In the story, a child takes a kettle of stew to the pasture and leaves it, then returns for the empty pot on a regular basis, not knowing why or who it's for. The child one day recruits little brother and they follow their mother to the pasture. For a better view they climb a tree:

"From our perch there we could hear voices but could see nothing. So we crept a little further out on the limb. I had no idea what I was expecting to see . . . When I finally caught sight of Ma I would not have been more surprised if she had been talking to the

Angel Moroni, himself, for there she was brushing the long black
hair of a strange man. She would sprinkle a little corn meal on his
scalp then brush and brush and brush. Many a time I have
watched Ma card wool, but never have I seen it so soft and silky.
Then she reached in her pocket for a comb. Then she divided his
hair by making a straight line from the center of his forehead to the
nape of his neck and made two long braids, one on each side of his
head. She wrapped the braids around his head and fastened them
with two hairpins out of her own bob. Why they were the very
ones Pa and I had made for her. I had spent hours filing them and
making them smooth on the ends.

"When he turned around to thank her, I recognized him. It was
Porter Rockwell himself. I was so flabbergasted I forgot to hold on
to my limb . . .

"Years later whenever I heard stories about the wonderful
things Porter Rockwell did for Brigham Young, how he saved his
life at the risk of his own, I began to realize what a colorful
character he turned out to be. And my heart swells with pride
when I say, 'And Ma combed his hair.' " The reference to Rockwell
saving Young's life is another, but unknown tale.

Laurit Smith, who knew Rockwell, was the grandmother of
Zelma Thompson,[10] the author of the above story. In her "Notes"
following the short story she writes, "In the early days, Brigham
Young often travelled back and forth from Salt Lake City to Saint
George. At meal time he would often stop at the various homes of
the saints . . . On one of these occasions Brigham Young
complimented my grandmother on her excellent cooking. Then in
the same breath he commissioned her to provide food for Porter
Rockwell whenever he was in that area."[11]

Russell Stocking of Midvale, Utah wrote a manuscript history,
"Andrus Half Way House," in which he reports the daughter of
John Eddins, Harriet Susanah Eddins Smith, remembering people
stopping at the well at the Half Way House to refresh themselves
[at Dry Creek, later Crescent, and now Sandy City[12]]. "She
remembers very vividly Porter Rockwell being one of them as he
was a frequent visitor and that she often combed and braided his
long black hair."[13]

Harriet Susanna Eddins Smith related the story to her mother,
who related it to her son, Ty Harrison, with an additional detail: as

a child she would sit on Rockwell's lap while she combed his hair.[14]

The stories no doubt continue, and the author invites readers who know of Porter Rockwell stories — preferably written primary sources, but even handed-down verbal accounts — to contact the author by writing the publisher.

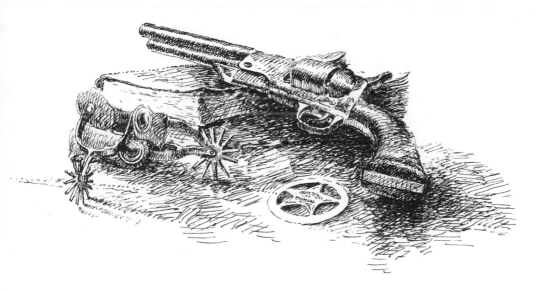

References

Chapter One

1. *Deseret News,* August 31, 1935

Biographical History of Northeastern Ohio, Embracing the Counties of Ashtabula, Geauga and Lake (Chicago, 1893), p. 684

"Records of Early Church Families," *Utah Genealogical and Historical Magazine* (Salt Lake City, 1935), Vol. XXVI, p. 154

2. Mrs. M. C. R. Smith article, *Naked Truths About Mormonism* (Oakland, California), Vol. I, No. 2 (April 1888)

3. Elizabeth D. E. Roundy, "Porter Rockwell" letter, Jenson's Biographical Manuscripts, Church Historical Department (hereafter cited as "CHD"), Salt Lake City, unpublished

Deseret News, August 31, 1935

4. Parley Parker Pratt, "Discourse by Parley P. Pratt" (of September 7, 1856), *Deseret News,* December 24, 1856

5. Joseph Smith, Jr., *History of the Church of Jesus Christ of Latter-day Saints. Period I. History of Joseph Smith, the Prophet, by Himself* (Salt Lake City, 1902-1912), Vol. I, p. 79 (six volumes, hereafter cited as DHC, for "Documentary History of the Church")

6. C. M. Stafford article, *Naked Truths About Mormonism.* Vol. I, No. 2 (April 1888)

7. DHC, Vol. I, p. 86

8. Mrs. M. C. R. Smith article, *Naked Truths About Mormonism,* Vol. I, No. 2 (April 1888)

9. *Doctrine and Covenants of the Church of the Latter Day Saints, Carefully Selected From the Revelations of God, and Compiled by Joseph Smith, Jr., Oliver Cowdery, Signey Rigdon, Frederick G. Williams* (Kirtland, Ohio, 1835), revelation given to Joseph Smith, Jr, and Sidney Rigdon, December 1830

10. Journal History of the Church of Jesus Christ of Latter-day Saints, unpublished, in Church Historians Office in Salt Lake City (hereafter cited as "Journal History"), May 16, 1831

11. Lucy Mack Smith, *Biographical Sketches of Joseph Smith the Prophet, and His Progenitors for many Generations* (Liverpool, 1853), p. 179

12. Ibid.

13. DHC, Vol. I, pp. 177-179

14. Ibid., p. 191

15. Emily M. Austin, *Mormonism; or Life Among the Mormons* (Madison, Wisconsin, 1882), p. 65

   Deseret News, August 31, 1935

16. *Utah Genealogical and Historical Magazine,* Vol. XXVI, p. 154

17. DHC, Vol. I, p. 273

18. Thomas Bullock, compiler, CHD, "A List of Saints in Jackson County"

19. Journal History, September 27, 1832

20. Circuit Court of Independence, Missouri, Record B, pp. 197-198

21. DHC, Vol. I, p. 336

22. *Times and Seasons* (Commerce and Nauvoo, Illinois), Vol. I, No. 2 (December 1839)

23. David Pettegrew, "A History of David Pettegrew," MS, p. 15

24. *Evening and Morning Star* (Independence, Missouri; Kirtland, Ohio), Vol. II, No. 14 (July 1833), and EXTRA, July 16, 1833

25. Ibid., Vol. II, No. 15 (December 1833), p. 114

26. Pettegrew, "History," MS, pp. 15-16

27. *Western Monitor,* Fayette, Missouri, August 2, 1833

28. John P. Greene, *Facts Relative to the Expulsion of the Mormons from the State of Missouri, Under the "Exterminating Order"* (Cincinnati, 1839), pp. 10-11

   Times and Seasons, Vol. I, No. 2 (December 1839), pp. 17-20

29. *Times and Seasons,* Vol. I, No. 2 (December 1839), p. 18

30. Testimony of Rockwell dated February 3, 1840, sworn before B.K. Morsell, Justice of the Peace, District of Columbia, submitted May 10, 21, 1842, U.S. House of Representatives (hereafter cited as "D.C. Testimony")

31. Andrew Jenson, *Church Encyclopaedia,* Book I (consisting of Volumes V, VI, VII, and VIII of *The Historical Record, A Monthly Periodical, Devoted Exclusively to Historical, Biographical, Chronological and Statistical Matters* (Salt Lake City, 1889), p. 640

   Greene, *Facts Relative,* pp. 10-11

Times and Seasons, Vol. I, No. 2 (December 1839), p. 18

32. Greene, *Facts Relative,* pp. 10-11

33. *Times and Seasons,* Vol. I, No. 2 (December 1839), p. 18

34. Daniel Dunklin, letter to Joel H. Haden, August 15, 1834, Western Historical Manuscripts Collection, University of Missouri

35. Lyman Wight, affidavit, *Deseret News,* December 24, 31, 1856

36. DHC, Vol. I, p. 426

37. D.C. Testimony

38. DHC, Vol I, pp. 426-427
    Pettegrew, "History," MS, pp. 16-25

39. *Times and Seasons,* Vol. I, No. 2 (December 1839), p. 18

40. Ibid.

41. Parley Parker Pratt, *Autobiography of Parley P. Pratt* (New York, 1874), p. 103

42. Pettegrew, "History," MS, p. 18

43. D. C. Testimony

44. DHC, Vol. I, pp. 429-430

45. Jenson, *Church Encyclopaedia,* Book I, p. 643

46. D.C. Testimony

47. Pettegrew, "History," MS, p. 19

48. *Times and Seasons,* Vol. I, No. 3 (January 1840), p. 33

49. Lyman Wight testimony, DHC, Vol. I, p. 428n,
    Times and Seasons, Vol. I, No. 3 (January 1840), p. 34

50. John Corrill testimony, DHC, Vol. I, p. 428n

51. Jenson, *Church Encyclopaedia,* p. 643

52. DHC, Vol. I, p. 430

53. Op. cit.

54. DHC, Vol. I, pp. 429-430

55. Ibid., p. 430

56. Jenson, *Church Encyclopaedia,* pp. 643-644

57. D. C. Testimony
    DHC, Vol. I, p. 430

58. DHC, Vol. I, p. 431

59. Jenson, *Church Encyclopaedia,* pp. 644

60. Ibid., pp. 643-644
    DHC, Vol. I, pp. 432-433

61. Op. cit.

62. *Times and Seasons,* Vol. I, No. 3 (January 1840), p. 34

63. Ibid.

64. DHC, Vol. I, p. 432

Times and Seasons, Vol. I, No. 3, January 1840, p. 34

65. *Times and Seasons,* Vol. I, No. 3, January 1840, p. 35

Chapter Two

1. *Times and Seasons,* Vol. I, No. 3, January 1840, p. 35

2. Lyman Wight testimony before municipal court of Nauvoo, Illinois, July 1, 1843

   The Latter-Day Saints' Millennial Star (Liverpool, England, 1840), Vol. XXI, p. 506

   DHC, Vol. I, p. 435n

   Deseret News, 24 December 1856

3. DHC, Vol. III, p. 439

   Millennial Star, Vol. XXI, p. 506

4. Pettegrew, "History," MS, pp. 18-20

5. *Times and Seasons,* Vol. I, No. 3 (January 1840), p. 36

6. Austin, *Life Among the Mormons,* p. 72

7. Chapman Duncan, "Biography," MS, pp. 8-9, 39

   D.C. Testimony

8. Austin, *Life Among the Mormons,* pp. 72-73

9. DHC, Vol. II, pp. 99-100.

10. Pettegrew, "History," MS, pp. 23-25

11. Ibid., pp. 25-26

12. *Times and Seasons,* Vol. I, No. 3 (January 1840), p. 36

13. Pettegrew, "History," MS, pp. 26

14. *History of Santa Clara County, California* (Los Angeles, 1922), p. 407

    History of Santa Clara County, California (San Francisco, 1881), p. 622

15. Records, Genealogical Society of Utah, Salt Lake City

16. *History of Caldwell and Livingston Counties, Missouri, Written and Compiled from the Most Authentic Official and Private Sources, Including a History of Their Townships, Towns and Villages, Together With A Condensed History of Missouri; A Reliable and Detailed History of Caldwell and Livingston Counties -- Their Pioneer Record, Resources, Biographical Sketches of Prominent Citizens; General and Local Statistics of Great Value; Incidents and Reminiscences* (St. Louis, 1886), pp. 120-122

17. Brigham H. Roberts, *A Comprehensive History of the Church of Jesus Christ of Latter-day Saints* (Salt Lake City, 1930), six volumes, Vol. I, pp. 438-439

18. James A. Little, "Biography of Lorenzo Dow Young," *Utah Historical Quarterly,* Vol. XIV, Nos. 1-4 (January-October, 1946), pp. 54-55, extensive quotes from diary of Lorenzo Dow Young

Sect, With an Examination of the Book of Mormon; also, Their Troubles in Missouri, and Final Expulsion from the State (St. Louis, 1844)

20. T. B. H. Stenhouse, *The Rocky Mountain Saints: A Full and Complete History of the Mormons, from the First Vision of Joseph Smith to the Last Courtship of Brigham Young, Including the Story of the Hand-Cart Emigration, the Mormon War, the Mountain-Meadow Massacre, the Reign of Terror in Utah, the Doctrine of Human Sacrifice, the Political, Domestic, Social, and Theological Influences of the Saints, the Facts of Polygamy, the Colonization of the Rocky Mountains, and the Development of the Great Mineral Wealth of the Territory of Utah* (New York, 1873; Salt Lake City, 1904)

21. John Whitmer, *History of the Church of the Latter-day Saints From 1831-1846* (Independence, Missouri, 1908)

22. John Whitmer's affidavit, *Document Showing the Testimony Given Before the Judge of the Fifth Judicial Circuit of the State of Missouri, on the Trial of Joseph Smith, Jr., and Others, for High Treason, and Other Crimes Against That State, February 15, 1841; Copy of the Testimony Given Before the Hon. Austin A. King, Judge of the Fifth Judicial Circuit in the State of Missouri, At the Court-House in Richmond, in a Criminal Court of Inquiry Begun November 12, 1838,* 26th Congress, 2d Session, Circuit Court, 5th Circuit

23. Dr. Sampson Avard's affidavit, Ibid.

24. Oliver Cowdery, *Defence in a Rehearsal of My Grounds for Separating Myself from the Latter Day Saints* (Norton, Ohio, 1839) (Likely a 1906 forgery published by R. B. Neal)

25. John Hyde, Jr., *Mormonism: Its Leaders and Designs* (New York, 1857)

26. William A. Hickman, *Brigham's Destroying Angel: Being the Life, Confession, and Startling Disclosures of the Notorious Bill Hickman, The Danite Chief of Utah* (New York, 1872) (nowhere in the volume does Hickman refer to the Danites)

27. John Corrill's affidavit, *Document Showing, etc.*

28. John Cleminson's affidavit, *Document Showing, etc.*

29. William Swartzell, *Mormonism Exposed, Being a Journal of a Residence in Missouri From the 28th of May to the 20th of August, 1838* (Pekin, Ohio, 1840)

30. William Hall, *The Abominations of Mormonism Exposed; Containing Many Facts and Doctrines Concerning That Singular People, During Seven Years' Membership With Them; From 1840 to 1847* (Cincinnati, 1852)

31. John C. Bennett, *The History of the Saints; an Exposé of Joe Smith and Mormonism* (Boston, 1842)

32. John D. Lee, *Mormonism Unveiled; Including the Remarkable Life and Confessions of the Late Mormon Bishop, John D. Lee; and Complete Life of Brigham Young, Embracing A History of Mormonism From Its Inception Down to the Present Time, With An Exposition of the Secret History, Signs, Symbols, and Crimes of The Mormon Church. Also the True History of the Horrible Butchery Known as The Mountain Meadows Massacre* (St. Louis, 1877; Lewisburgh, Pennsylvania; 1882)

33. Reed Peck, "Mormons So Called" (Quincy, Adams County, Illinois, September 18, 1839), MS

34. Oliver Boardman Huntington, "Diaries," MSS, three volumes, Vol. I, p. 36

35. DHC, Vol. VI, p. 165

36. *Journal of Discourses, by Brigham Young, President of the Church of Jesus Christ of Latter-day Saints, His Two Counselors, and the Twelve Apostles, and Others* (Liverpool, England 1854-1886), twenty-six volumes, Vol. V, p. 6.

37. *Document Showing, etc.*

38. "Answers To Questions," *Improvement Era*, Vol. V (February 1901), p. 309

39. Swartzell, *Mormonism Exposed*, pp. 27-28

40. *An Appeal to the American People: Being An Account of the Persecutions of the Church of Latter Day Saints; and of the Barbarities Inflicted on Them by the Inhabitants of the State of Missouri* (Cincinnati, 1840), pp. 17-19

41. Ibid., pp. 17-24

42. Lee, *Mormonism Unveiled*, pp. 58-60

43. DHC, Vol. III, pp. 59-60

44. Ibid.

45. Marsh's affidavit, *Document Showing, etc.*, pp. 57-59, also in DHC, Vol. III, p. 167

46. Pratt, *Autobiography*, p. 177

47. Little, "Biography of Lorenzo Dow Young," p. 54

48. Op. cit., p. 178

49. Op. cit., p. 54

50. Op. cit., p. 179

51. *History of Caldwell and Livingston Counties*, p. 130

Chapter Three

1. Pratt, *Autobiography*, p. 179

2. Little, "Biography of Lorenzo Dow Young", pp. 55

3. Pratt, *Autobiography*, pp. 177-180

4. Joseph Dickson and Sashiel Woods, letters in DHC, Vol. III, pp. 168-169
   Document Showing, etc. p. 60

5. *Document Showing, etc.* p. 61

6. Major Reburn S. Holcombe, *St. Louis Globe-Democrat*, October 6, 1887; reprinted in the series by Rollin J. Britton, "Early Days on Grand River and the Mormon War," *The Missouri Historical Review*, Columbia, Missouri, Vol. XIII, No. 3 (April 1919), pp. 298-305
   DHC, Vol. III, pp. 183-187
   Jenson, *Church Encyclopaedia*, pp. 671-184

History of Caldwell and Livingston Counties, pp. 145-159

Times and Seasons, Vol. I, No. 10 (August 1840), pp. 145-150

7. *History of Caldwell and Livingston Counties,* pp. 145-159

8. Amanda Smith, affidavit, Ibid., p. 158

9. Ibid.

10. Ibid.

11. *Times and Seasons,* Vol. I, No. 10 (August 1840), pp. 146-147

12. Ibid., p. 149

13. Lee, *Mormonism Unveiled,* pp. 81-83

14. Ibid.

15. Op. cit., pp. 83-84

16. *Document Showing, etc.,* pp. 97-151

17. DHC, Vol. III, pp. 251-254

Jensen, *Church Encyclopaedia,* pp. 713-714

18. DHC, Vol. III, pp. 251-254

19. Ibid.

20. DHC, Vol. III, p. 292

21. Ibid., p. 375

22. DHC, Vol. IV, p. 19

23. Ibid., p. 440

Millennial Star, Vol. XXIII, p. 770

24. DHC, Vol. IV, p. 80

25. *Utah Genealogical and Historical Magazine,* Vol. XXVI, pp. 155-156.

26. Charles J. Scofield, *History of Hancock County* (Chicago, 1921), three volumes, Vo. II, pp. 834-835

Newton Bateman, J. Seymour Currey, Paul Selby, editors, *Historical Encyclopedia of Illinois,* same volume as ibid., Vol. II (Chicago, 1921)

27. Edward Tullidge, *Life of Brigham Young; Or, Utah and Her Founders* (New York, 1876) pp. 30-31

28. *Sangamo Journal* (Springfield, Illinois), as quoted in *The Wasp* (Nauvoo, Hancock County, Illinois), June 18, 1842

29. "Abstract of the Census of 1840, Jackson County, Missouri," p. 52

30. William F. Switzler, *Illustrated History of Missouri From 1541 to 1877* (St. Louis, 1879), p. 251

31. *Quincy Whig,* July 16, 1842

Bennett, *History of the Saints,* p. 281

32. *The Weekly Inter Ocean* (Chicago), October 26, 1886

Burlington Hawkeye, May, 1842

Oliver H. Olney, *The Absurdities of Mormonism Portrayed, A Brief Sketch* (Hancock County, Illinois, 1843), p. 19

Joseph H. Jackson, *A Narrative of the Adventures and Experience of Joseph H. Jackson; Disclosing the Depths of Mormon Villainy Practiced in Nauvoo* (Warsaw, Illinois, 1844), p. 7

Warsaw Signal and Agricultural, Literary and Commercial Register (Warsaw, Illinois, newspaper), June 5, 1844

Thomas Gregg, *The Prophet of Palmyra* (New York, 1890), p. 198

Fitz Hugh Ludlow, "Among the Mormons," *The Atlantic Monthly,* Vol. XII (April 1864), p. 492

William Alexander Linn, *The Story of the Mormons, From the Date of Their Origin to the Year 1901* (New York, 1923)

33. Charles W. Dilke, *Greater Britain: A Record of Travel in English-Speaking Countries During 1866 and 1867* (London, 1868), two volumes, Vol. I, p. 184

Sangamo Journal, July 15, 1842

34. Bennett, *History of the Saints,* p. 283

The Wasp--Extra, July 27, 1842

35. *The New York Watchman,* July 30, 1841

36. Hall, *Abominations of Mormonism Exposed,* p. 30

37. Wilhelm W. Wymetal, *Mormon Portraits, Joseph Smith the Prophet, His Family and His Friends* (Salt Lake City, 1886), p. 255

38. Wymetal, interview with William Law, *Salt Lake Tribune,* July 31, 1887

39. John Whitmer, "History of the Church of the Latter Day Saints From 1831 to 1846," Chapter xxi, from publication in *Journal of History,* Vol. I (Independence, Missouri, 1908) by The Reorganized Church of Jesus Christ of Latter Day Saints (along with chapters xx, xxii and part of xix)

40. *The Weekly Inter Ocean,* October 26, 1886

41. Hoffman Birney and Charles Kelly, *Holy Murder, the Story of Porter Rockwell* (New York, 1934), p. 204

42. *Jeffersonian Republican* (Jefferson City, Missouri) May 14, 1842

43. Ibid., May 21, 1842

44. Monte B. McClaws, "The Attempted Assassination of Missouri's Ex-Governor, Lilburn W. Boggs," *Missouri Historical Review,* Vol. LX (October 1965), pp. 50-62

45. U. S. Bureau of Census, "Seventh Census of the United States: 1850. Jackson Co. Missouri," Vol. VII, p. 562

46. Duane Meyer, *The Heritage of Missouri -- A History* (St. Louis, 1963), pp. 261-262

47. *Laws of the State of Missouri,* 9th General Assembly, 1st Session, 1838-1839, pp. 29-30

48. Ibid., 10th General Assembly, 1st Session, 1838-1839, pp. 14-15

49. Missouri Senate Journal, 11th General Assembly, 1st Session, 1840-1841, pp. 446-447

50. Missouri House Journal, 11th General Assembly, 1st Session, 1840-1841, pp. 530-531

51. *Missouri Argus* (St. Louis)

52. *Jeffersonian Republican,* May 14, 1842

53. Ibid.

54. Stenhouse, *Rocky Mountain Saints,* p. 140

55. *Niles' National Register* September 30, 1843

56. Charles T. Stanton, letter to Sidney Stanton, July 12, 1846, *New York Herald,* November 4, 1846

57. *Missouri Whig* (Palmyra, Missouri), June 4, 1846

58. *Lee County Democrat,* March 18, 1843

59. Joseph Smith and Heman C. Smith, *History of the Church of Jesus Christ of Latter Day Saints,* by the Reorganized Church (Lamoni, Iowa, 1911), Vol. II, p. 580

60. Nicholas Van Alfen, "Porter Rockwell and the Mormon Frontier, A Thesis Submitted to the Department of History of Brigham Young University in Partial Fulfillment of the Requirements for the Degree of Master of Fine Arts" (Provo, 1938), p. 23, used by permission

61. Bennett, *History of the Saints,* p. 285

62. *Quincy Whig,* August 13, 1842

63. George A. Smith, Church Historians Record Book, Entry for Monday, August 8th, 1842

64. DHC, Vol. V, pp. 86-87

65. *Millennial Star,* Vol 19, p. 630
    Jenson, *Historical Record,* Vol. I, p. 499

66. *Lee County Democrat,* August 13, 1842

67. *Quincy Whig,* August 20, 1842

68. Oliver H. Olney Papers, 46 documents, Document 17
    See also Document 24 on Joseph Smith and Porter Rockwell
    William Decatur Kartchner, "Expedition of the Emmett Company," MS
    James Hold, diary, "Reminiscences of James Hold, A Narrative of the Emmett Company," edited by Dale L. Morgan, *Utah Historical Quarterly,* Vol. XIII (1955)
    Millennial Star, Vol. XXIII, p. 519

69. *Quincy Whig,* May 22, 1842

70. Brigham H. Roberts, *The Rise and Fall of Nauvoo* (Salt Lake City, 1900), p. 145

71. DHC, Vol. V, p. 92

72. Boggs, "Sketch of Lilburn W. Boggs," *Missouri Historical Review,* Vol. IV, p. 108

73. DHC, Vol. V, p. 125

74. S. Armstrong letter, *Millennial Star,* Vol. XX, p. 215

75. Op. cit., p. 230
    The Wasp, January 28, 1843

Chapter Four

1. *Millennial Star,* Vol. XXII, pp. 517-520, 535-536

2. *Lee County Democrat,* July 1, 1843

3. Ford, *History of Illinois,* pp. 68-69

4. Matthew C. Field, *Prairie and Mountain Sketches,* collected by Clyde and Mae Reed Porter, edited by Kate L. Gregg and John Francis McDermott (Norman, Oklahoma, 1957), pp. 18-20

   Matthew C. Field, letter to the *New Orleans Daily Picayune,* June 7, 1843

5. Field, *Prairie and Mountain Sketches,* pp. 18-20

6. Circuit Court Records, Jackson County, Missouri, Book I, 1827-1833, p. 133

7. Op. cit.

8. Circuit Court Records, Jackson County, Missouri, August Term, Book E. 1843, p. 166

9. Fifth Judicial District Court of Missouri, Record Book G, No. 4, p. 228

10. *Warsaw Signal,* June 5, 1844

    Joseph H. Jackson, *A Narrative of the Adventures*

11. *Millennial Star,* Vol. XX, p. 806, letter of April 7, 1843

12. DHC, Vol. V, p. 439

13. Ibid., p. 440

    Times and Seasons, Vol. IV, No. 16 (July 1843), p. 242

14. Wandle Mace, "Journal," MS, p. 62

15. DHC, Vol. V, p. 445

16. Ibid.

17. Ibid.

18. Ibid.

19. Mace, "Journal," MS, p. 63

20. Ibid., p. 64

21. DHC, Vol. V, p. 539

22. Ibid.

23. *Millennial Star,* Vol. XXI, p. 172

24. Mace, "Journal," MS, pp. 67-68

25. Fifth Judicial District Court of Missouri, Record Book G, No. 4, p. 236

26. DHC, Vol. VI, pp. 134-135

27. DHC, Vol. V, p. 305

28. James Jepson, "Memories and Experiences," MS, pp. 9-10

    George Washington Bean, *Autobiography of George Washington Bean, A Utah Pioneer of 1847 and His Family Records,* compiled by Flora Diana Bean Horne (Salt Lake City, 1945), p. 175

    Stenhouse, *Rocky Mountain Saints,* p. 140n

Elizabeth D. E. Roundy, "Porter Rockwell" letter, Jenson's Biographical Manuscripts, CHD, unpublished

29. Gilbert Belnap, "Autobiography of Gilbert Belnap," MS, p. 30

30. Joseph Smith III, *Joseph Smith III and the Restoration,* edited by Mary Audentia Smith Anderson, condensed by Bertha Audentia Anderson Holmes (Independence, 1952), pp. 74-75

31. Ibid., pp. 74-76

Belnap, "Autobiography," MS, p. 30

32. *Doctrine and Covenants* (Salt Lake City, 1981) pp. 175-176

33. Belnap, "Autobiography," MS, pp. 30-31

34. Patriarchal Blessings, Vol. IX, p. 272, No. 819, CHD

35. *Times and Seasons,* Vol. I, No. 2 (December 1839), p. 32

36. *Deseret News,* August 31, 1935

37. Patriarchal Blessings, Vol. IX, p. 272, No. 820, CHD

38. DHC, Vol. VI, pp. 149-152

39. Ibid., p. 164

40. Ibid., pp. 162-165

41. Ibid., p. 170

42. Ibid., pp. 280n-281n

43. Ibid., pp. 278-280

Chapter Five

1. DHC, Vol. VI, p. 333

2. Ibid., p. 341

3. *The Neighbor* (Nauvoo, Illinois), May 1, 1844

4. Op. cit., p. 344

5. Ibid.

6. Journal History, September 15, 1868

7. *Nauvoo Expositor,* June 7, 1844, reprinted

8. *Millennial Star,* Vol. XXIII, p. 673

9. Gregg, *The Prophet of Palmyra,* pp. 296-297

10. DHC, Vol. VI, p. 414

11. Ibid., p. 399

12. Ibid., p. 424

13. Ibid.

14. Ibid., p. 440

15. Ibid., pp. 456-457

16. Ibid.

17. Ibid.

18. Ibid.
19. Ibid., p. 458
20. *Warsaw Signal,* June 19, 1844
21. Steven Markham, letter, June 17, 1844, Op. cit., p. 492
22. DHC, Vol. VI, p. 495
23. Ibid., p. 497
24. Ibid., pp. 498-500
25. *Doctrine and Covenants,* P. 164
26. Ibid.
27. DHC, Vol. V, p. 394
28. *Deseret News,* September 24, 1856
29. Huntington, "Diaries" MSS, Vol. 2, pp. 205-206
30. DHC, Vol. VI, p. 509
31. Ibid., pp. 511-512
32. Ibid.
33. Ibid., p. 513
34. Ibid.
35. Ibid., pp. 507, 511, 516
36. Ibid., p. 521
37. Ibid., pp. 538-540

Chapter Six

1. DHC, Vol. VI., p. 543-544
2. Ibid., p. 545
3. Ibid., p. 546
4. Ibid., p. 547
5. Ibid., p. 548
6. Ibid.
7. Mace, "Journal," MS, p. 88
8. Op. cit., p. 549
9. Mace, "Journal," MS, p. 88
10. DHC, Vol. VI, p. 551
11. Ibid., p. 555
12. Ibid., p. 558
13. Ibid.,
14. Ibid., p. 559
15. Ibid., pp. 562-563
16. Ibid.

17. Ibid.
18. DHC, Vol. VII, p. 130
19. *Millennial Star,* Vol. XXIV, p. 358
   DHC, Vol. VI, p. 565
20. Ibid., p. 566
21. Ibid.
22. Ibid.
23. Ibid.
24. Ibid., p. 568
25. Ibid., p. 574
26. Allen Joseph Stout, "Allen Joseph Stout Journal," MS, p. 19
27. Stenhouse, *Rocky Mountain Saints,* p. 164n
28. DHC, Vol. VI, p. 570
29. Ibid., p. 592
30. Ibid.
31. Ibid.
32. Ibid.
33. Ibid., p. 608
34. *Randolph Co. Record* (Randolph County, Illinois), June 1844
35. Op. cit., pp. 613-614
36. Ibid., p. 614
37. Jenson, *Church Encyclopaedia,* Book I, p. 569
38. Scofield, *History of Hancock County,* Vol. II, p. 847
39. Ibid.
40. DHC, Vol. VI, p. 617
41. Jenson, *Church Encyclopaedia,* Book I, p. 570
42. Ibid., p. 590
43. Ibid., p. 570
   DHC, Vol. VI, p. 619
44. DHC, Vol. VI, p. 620
45. *History of Hancock County,* p. 847
46. Eyewitness account of William M. Daniels, *Correct Account of the Murder of Generals Joseph and Hyrum Smith, At Carthage, On the 27th Day of June, 1844* (Nauvoo, Illinois, 1845), p. 15
47. Ibid., p. 18
   Jenson, *Church Encyclopaedia,* Book I, p. 571
48. Littlefield, *The Martyrs,* p. 71
49. Jenson, *Church Encyclopaedia,* Book I, p 27
50. *Atlantic Monthly,* 1869

51. Testimony of O. P. Rockwell, April 14, 1856, to Thomas Bullock, Salt Lake County Recorder, DHC, Vol. VI, pp. 588-589

Daniels, *A Correct Account,* p. 18

Jenson, *Church Encyclopaedia,* Book I, p. 571

52. DHC, Vol. VI, p. 623

53. Ibid., p. 625

54. Anson Call, "Life and Record," MS, p. 27

55. Mace, "Journal," MS, p. 90

56. Ibid., p. 30

57. Jenson, *Church Encyclopaedia,* Book I, p. 27

58. George Q. Cannon statement, Tullidge, *Life of Brigham Young,* pp. 115-116

Wilford Woodruff, *Deseret News,* March 12, 1892

59. Ford, *History of Illinois,* p. 364

60. *Sangamo Journal,* October 10, 1844

Burlington Hawkeye, October 3, 1844

61. Bennett, *History of the Saints*, p. 92

62. *Times and Seasons,* Vol. VI, No. 1 (January 1845), pp. 773-776; Vol. IV, No. 12 (May 1843), pp. 183-184; Vol. III, No. 3 (December 1841), pp. 615-618

63. Ibid., Vol. VI, p. 775

64. DHC, Vol. VII, p. 380

65. Dallin H. Oaks, Marvin S. Hill, *Carthage Conspiracy; The Trial of the Accused Assassins of Joseph Smith* (Urbana, Illinois; Chicago, Illinois; London, England; 1975)

66. DHC, Vol. VII, p. 428

67. Ibid., p. 444

68. Ibid., p. 447

69. Ibid.

Journal History, September 16, 1845

70. Jesse W. Crosby, "History and Journal," MS, p. 28

71. DHC, Vol. VII, pp. 446-447.

See George Miller, letter of June 28, 1855, *Northern Islander* (Beaver Island, Lake Michigan), September 6, 1855

See Backenstos, "Proclamation II," *The Neighbor,* September 17, 24; October 1, 1845

72. Frank Eshom, *Pioneers and Prominent Men of Utah* (Salt Lake City, 1913)

73. Peter Wilson Conover, "Autobiography," MS, p. 20

Gregg, *History of Hancock County,* pp. 340-341

Illinois State Register, December 19, 1845

John Harper testimony, *Warsaw Signal,* October 15, 1845

74. Bean, *Autobiography,* p. 175

75. DHC, Vol. VII, p. 447

76. *Proceedings of a Convention, Held at Carthage, in Hancock County, Ill., on Tuesday and Wednesday, October 1st and 2nd,* 1845 (Quincy, 1845), p. 9, reports of the *Quincy Whig*

77. Joseph Smith III and Heman C. Smith, *History of the Church of Jesus Christ of Latter Day Saints* (The Reorganized Church, Iowa, 1911), Vol. III, p. 147

78. George Miller, letter of June 28, 1855, *Northern Islander,* September 6, 1855
    Journal History, September 18, 1845

79. *The Missouri Whig,* September 24, 1845
    Ford, *History of Illinois,* P. 408

80. DHC, Vol. VII, pp. 448

81. Ibid.

82. Ibid., p. 439

83. Ibid., p. 449

84. Ibid., p. 481

85. Journal History, October 9, 1845

86. *Warsaw Signal,* December 10, 1845

87. Hall, *Abominations of Mormonism Exposed,* p. 28

88. Ford, *History of Illinois,* pp. 356-357
    Warsaw Signal, December 10, 1845

89. *Warsaw Signal,* December 24, 1845

90. Ibid.

91. Hall, *Abominations of Mormonism Exposed,* p. 28

92. *St. Louis Daily New Era,* February 18, 1846

93. Hall, *Abominations of Mormonism Exposed,* p. 48

94. DHC, Vol. VII, pp. 549-551
    See *Springfield Journal,* December 25, 1845

95. Lee, *Mormonism Unveiled,* p. 175

96. *Burlington Hawkeye,* May 7, 1846
    People's Daily Organ (St. Louis) May 7, 1846

97. *Quincy Whig,* April 22, 1846, quoting from *Warsaw Signal*

98. *Quincy Whig,* May 6, 1846

99. *Daily Missouri Republican,* May 5, 1846

100. *St. Louis American,* May 4, 1846

101. *The People's Daily Organ,* May 7, 1846

102. *Lee County Democrat,* May 9, 1846

103. Ibid.
     Quincy Whig, May 6, 1846

104. *Burlington Hawkeye*, May 7, 1846

105. Hall, *Abominations of Mormonism Exposed*, p. 29

106. *The Republican* (St. Louis), May 16, 1846

107. *Quincy Whig*, May 6, 1846
    Missouri Whig, May 14, 1846
    The People's Daily Organ (St. Louis), May 5, 1846

108. *Quincy Whig*, May 6, 1846

109. *Missouri Whig*, May 14, 1846
    The People's Daily Organ, May 5, 1846

110. *Warsaw Signal*, May 6, 1846

111. *St. Louis Daily New Era*, June 1, 1846
    St. Louis American, May 30, 1846
    Quincy Whig, May 27, 1846
    Missouri Whig, June 4, 1846
    St. Louis American, May 30, 1846; June 17, 1846
    St. Louis Daily New Era, June 1, 1846
    Weekly American (St. Louis), June 5, 1846

112. *Quincy Whig*, May 27, 1846
    St. Louis American, May 28, 1846
    Weekly American, May 29, 1846

113. *St. Louis American*, June 17, 1846

114. *Quincy Whig*, June 17, 1846; June 24, 1846
    Republican, September 7, 1846; September 26, 1846

115. *Sangamo Journal*, January 18, 1847
    Republican, September 7, 1846
    Quincy Whig, July 29, 1846

116. Joseph Smith III, *Joseph Smith III and the Restoration*, pp. 76-77

117. William Clayton, *William Clayton's Journal, A Daily Record of the Journey of the Original Company of "Mormon" Pioneers from Nauvoo, Illinois, to the Valley of the Great Salt Lake* (Salt Lake City, 1921), pp. 61-62.

118. *Journal History*, August 19, 1846

119. *Quincy Whig*, July 29, 1846
    St. Louis Daily New Era, July 25, 1846

120. Clayton, *Journal*, p. 63

121. Journal History, August 22, 1846

122. Journal History, August 25, 1846

123. Ibid., December 29, 1846

124. Ibid.

125. Ibid.

126. Erastus Snow, "Journal," MSS, eight volumes, Book 3rd (June 1841 - February 1847), pp. 56-57

127. Ibid.
   Little, "Biography of Lorenzo Dow Young", p. 156

128. Little, "Biography of Lorenzo Dow Young", p. 156

129. Clayton, *Journal*, p. 82

130. Amasa M. Lyman, "Amasa M. Lyman's Journals," MSS, 1847, p. 9

131. William M. Egan, editor, *Pioneering the West 1846 to 1878, Major Howard Egan's Diary, Also Thrilling Experiences of Pre-Frontier Life Among Indians; Their Traits, Civil and Savage, and Part of Autobiography, Inter-Related to His Father's,* (Richmond, Utah, 1917), pp. 23-24

132. Ibid.

133. Ibid., pp. 29-30

134. Clayton, *Journal*, pp. 109-110
   See Egan, *Pioneering the West 1846 to 1878*, p. 30

Chapter Seven

1. Clayton, *Journal*, pp. 109-110
   Egan, *Pioneering the West 1846 to 1878*, p. 30

2. Clayton, *Journal*, pp. 118-119

3. Ibid., p. 120

4. Ibid., p. 134

5. Egan, *Pioneering the West 1846 to 1878*, p. 35

6. Ibid
   Appleton Milo Harmon, *Appleton Milo Harmon Goes West* (Berkeley, 1946), p. 18
   Clayton, *Journal*, pp. 134-135
   Little, "Biography of Lorenzo Dow Young," p. 157
   See also Lyman, "Journals," MSS, 1847, p. 22

7. Appleton Milo Harmon, "Diary," MS, May 8, 1847
   Appleton Milo Harmon, *The Journals of Appleton Milo Harmon, A participant in the Mormon Exodus from Illinois and the early settlement of Utah 1846-1847,* edited by Maybelle Harmon Anderson (Glendale, 1946)

8. Lyman, "Journals," MSS, 1847, p. 22

9. Clayton, *Journal*, p. 36

10. Little, "Biography of Lorenzo Dow Young," p. 85

11. Egan, *Pioneering the West 1846 to 1875*, p. 35

12. Brigham Young, *Manuscript History of Brigham Young, 1846-1847*, p. 553

13. Lyman, "Journals," MSS, 1847, p. 23

14. Ibid., p. 27

15. Hand-written note to Porter Rockwell, May 26, 1847, CHD

16. Clayton, *Journal,* p. 176

17. Lyman, "Journals," MSS, 1847, p. 37

18. Orson Pratt, *The Orson Pratt Journals,* compiled by Elden J. Watson (Salt Lake City, 1975), p. 389

19. Little, "Biography of Lorenzo Dow Young," p. 159

20. Clayton, *Journal,* pp. 189-201

21. Harmon, "Diary," MS, pp. 274-275

   Harmon, *The Journals of Appleton Milo Harmon,* edited by Maybelle Harmon Anderson

22. Clayton, *Journal,* pp. 234-235

23. William H. Russel, letter to the *Missouri Statesman,* "Nebraska or Big Platte River, About 400 Miles West of Independence," June 13, 1846

   See also George L. Curry, letter "South Fork of Platte River" to the *St. Louis Reville,* June 16, 1846

   See James Clyman, *American Frontiersman, 1792-1881, The Adventures of a Trapper and Covered Wagon Emigrant As Told In his Own Experiences and Diaries,* edited by Charles L. Camp (San Francisco, 1928), p. 230

24. *Weekly Reville,* June 8, 1846

25. *Missouri Republican,* June 6, 1846

26. Clayton, *Journal,* pp. 234-235

27. Ibid., p. 289

28. Ibid., p. 290

29. Ibid.

30. Lyman, "Journals," MSS, 1847, p. 69

31. Orson Pratt, "Extracts From Orson Pratt's Private Journal," *Millennial Star,* Vol. XII, p. 178

32. Erastus Snow, "Autobiography of Erastus Snow, Dictated to his son Franklin R. Snow, in the year 1875," *The Utah Genealogical and Historical Magazine,* Vol. XIV, No. 3 (July 1923), p. 112

33. Journal History, August 29, 1847

34. Ibid.

35. Egan, *Pioneering the West 1846 to 1875,* p. 134

36. Journal History, September 9, 1847

37. Lyman, "Journals," MSS, 1847, p. 85

38. Journal History, October 5, 1847

39. Ibid., October 12, 1847

40. Ibid., November 16, 1847

41. John Hunt, quoted extensively in article, " 'Mormon' Pathfinders Guests of Senator Clark, Startling Story of the First Trip From Salt Lake to Los Angeles," *Deseret News,* October 7, 1905

42. Ibid.

43. Ibid.

44. Frank Alfred Golder, *The March of the Mormon Battalion, from Council Bluffs to California, taken from the Journal of Henry Standage* (New York, 1928), pp. 260-264

Journal History, January 25, 1848

45. Journal History, June 5, 1848

46. Daniel Tyler, *A Concise History of the Mormon Battalion in the Mexican War, 1846-1847* (Salt Lake City, 1881), pp. 331-332

Henry W. Bigler, "Day Book and Diary," MS, p. 79

Findla, "Statistics," MS, pp. 4-6

Ross, "Statistics," MS, p. 12

Oregon Bulletin, May, 1848

Hubert Howe Bancroft, *The Works of Hubert Howe Bancroft, Vol. XXIII, History of California* (San Francisco, 1886-1890), seven volumes; Vol. VI, 1848-1859 (San Francisco, 1888), p. 56

47. Claire Noall, "Mormon Midwives," *Utah Historical Quarterly,* Vol. X (1942), p. 103, journal quote of Patty Bartlett Sessions

48. Journal History, June 9, 1848

49. John D. Lee, *A Mormon Chronicle: The Diaries of John D. Lee, 1848-1876,* edited by Juanita Brooks and Robert Glass Cleland (San Marino, California, 1955), two volumes, Vol. I, pp. 39-40

Egan, *Pioneering the West 1846 to 1875,* p. 140

50. Lee, *A Mormon Chronicle,* Vol. I, pp. 68-69

51. J. Cecil Alter, "In the Beginning," *Salt Lake Tribune,* January 10, 1935, Catharine E. Mehring Woolley journal entry of September 20, 1848

52. Lee, *A Mormon Chronicle,* Vol. I, p. 75

53. Isaac Chauncey Haight, "Journal," MS, September 19, 1848

Journal History, September 15, 1848

54. Salt Lake County Abstracts, Plats and Surveys, Book A2

55. J. Cecil Alter, "In the Beginning," *Salt Lake Tribune,* January 10, 1935, Catherine E. Mehring Woolley, journal entry of October 15, 1848

56. Lee, *A Mormon Chronicle,* Vol. I, p. 82

57. Ibid., p. 86

58. Bean, *Autobiography,* p. 49

Journal History, January 6, 1849

59. Bean, *Autobiography,* p. 86

60. Journal History, November 26, 1848

61. Ibid., March 3, 1849

   Lee, *A Mormon Chronicle,* Vol. I, p. 99

62. Lee, *A Mormon Chronicle,* Vol I, p. 99

   Journal History, March 12, 1849

63. Van Alfen, "Thesis," p. 54, used by permission

64. Bean, *Autobiography,* pp. 175-176

65. Ibid., pp. 53-54

66. Ibid.

67. Ibid., p. 55

68. Ibid., pp. 175-176

69. Journal History, March 31, 1849

   Lee, *A Mormon Chronicle,* Vol. I, p. 104

70. *Scientific American,* October 13, 1849

71. Ibid.

72. Journal History, April 11, 1849

73. Interview with John Rockwell, Lehi, Utah; known family information, used by permission

74. Lyman, "Journal, 1848-1850," MSS, January 8, 1850

75. Journal History, April 5, 1849

76. Asbury Harpending, *The Great Diamond Hoax and Other Stirring Incidents in The Life of Asbury Harpending,* edited by James H. Wilkins (San Francisco, 1913), p. 169

77. Journal History, July 23, 1850

78. Parley Parker Pratt, "A Mormon Mission to California in 1851, From the Diary of Parley Parker Pratt," edited by Reva Holdaway Stanley and Charles L. Camp, *California Historical Society Quarterly,* Vol. XIV (June 1935), p. 176

79. Ibid.

80. Ibid.

81. Eliza R. Snow, "Diary," MS, April 13, 1849

   Eliza Marie Partridge Lyman, "Autobiography and Diary, 1820-1885," MS, p. 37

82. Amasa Lyman, letter to J. H. Flanigan, dated from San Francisco, April 11, 1850, published in *Millennial Star,* Vol. XII, pp. 214-215

83. Paolo Sioli, *Historical Souvenir of El Dorado County, California* (Oakland, 1883), p. 201

   Joseph Cain and Arieh C. Brower, *Mormon Way-Bill, To the Gold Mines from the Pacific Springs* (Salt Lake City, 1851), pp. 16-17

   Achilles [Samuel D. Sirrine], *The Destroying Angels of Mormondom; or a Sketch of the Life of Orrin Porter Rockwell, the Late Danite Chief* (San Francisco, 1878), p. 14

Nelson Slater, *Fruits of Mormonism* (Coloma, California, 1851), pp. 77n-78n

84. Joseph F. Smith, *Gospel Doctrine,* 5th Ed. (1st Ed. 1919), p. 365

85. Wendell Robie, "Murderer's Bar and Gold Rush on the Middlefork," *The Pony Express,* Vol. XXV (July 1958), p. 5, reprinted address to the California Historical Society, March 10, 1955

86. Lyman, "Journal, 1848-1850," MS, February 3, 1850

87. Ibid., May 19, 1850

88. Louisa Barnes Pratt, "Journal of Louisa Barnes Pratt," *Heart Throbs of the West, A Unique Volume Treating Definite Subjects of Western History,* compiled by Kate B. Carter, Vol. VIII (1947), p. 256

Achilles, *Destroying Angels of Mormondom,* p. 14

Slater, *Fruits of Mormonism,* pp. 77n - 78n

John M. Letts, *California Illustrated: Including a Description of the Panama and Nicaragua Routes. By a Returned Californian* (New York, 1852), p. 95

89. Switzler, *Illustrated History of Missouri,* p. 251

90. Letts, *California Illustrated,* p. 95

91. Interview with John Rockwell, Lehi, Utah; known family information, used by permission

92. Ibid.

93. Letts, *California Illustrated,* p. 96

94. Ibid., p. 95

95. Caroline Barnes Crosby, "Journal," MS, July 17, 1850

Jonathan Crosby, "Biographical Sketch," MS, July 17, 1850

Thomas Orr, Jr., *Life History of Thomas Orr Jr., Pioneer Stories of California and Utah,* edited by Lillie Jane Orr Taylor (privately published, 1930), p. 21

96. Caroline Barnes Crosby, "Journal," MS, July 17, 1850

Jonathan Crosby, "Biographical Sketch," MS, July 17, 1850

97. Caroline Barnes Crosby, "Journal," MS, July 17, 1850

Jonathan Crosby, "Biographical Sketch," MS, July 17, 1850

98. Journal History, September 29, 1850

99. Ibid.

100. Achilles, *Destroying Angels of Mormondom,* p. 14

101. Ibid.

102. Ibid.

103. *Salt Lake Herald,* August 6, 1878

104. Op. cit.

105. Journal History, November 12, 1850

Deseret News, Vol. I, No. 155 (November 1850)

106. Goudy E. Hogan, "History of Goudy E. Hogan," MS, p. 21

107. Ibid.

108. George A. Smith, letter to Orson Pratt, July 31, 1850, *Millennial Star,* Vol. XII, pp. 349-350

109. *Saint Louis Daily Journal,* May 24, 1851

110. William P. Bennett, *The Sky-Sifter* (Gold Hill, Nevada, 1892), pp. 285-286

111. Lyman, "Journal, 1848-1850," May 31, 1850

112. See Henry W. Bigler, "Extracts from the Journal of Henry W. Bigler," *Utah Historical Quarterly,* Vol. V (1932), p. 138

113. Slater, *Fruits of Mormonism,* pp. 78-79

114. Captain William H. Kimball's Life Guards, payroll records, Military Records Section, Utah State Archives

115. Daniel H. Wells' orders to Captain Wright, April 21, 1851, Military Records Section, Utah State Archives,

116. Edward W. Tullidge, *Tullidge's Histories, Vol. II, Containing the History of all the Northern, Eastern and Western Counties of Utah; Also the Counties of Southern Idaho. With A Biographical Appendix of Representative Men and Founders of the Cities and Counties; Also a Commerical Supplement, Historical,* (Salt Lake City, 1889), p. 83

Peter Gottfredson, editor and compiler, *History of Indian Depredations in Utah* (Salt Lake City, 1919), p. 38

117. W. R. Dickinson, letter to his parents, May 29, 1851, Utah State Historical Society Library

118. Ibid.

119. Ibid.

120. Ibid.

121. Ibid.

122. Journal History, April 23, 1850 (mis-recorded by the clerk, as it should have been dated 1851)

123. Tullidge, *Histories,* Vol. II, p. 84

Gottfredson, *Indian Depredations,* p. 39

Hosea Stout, *On the Mormon Frontier, The Diary of Hosea Stout, 1844-1866,* edited by Juanita Brooks (Salt Lake City, 1965), two volumes, Vol. II, p. 398

124. Slater, *Fruits of Mormonism,* p. 37

Hoffman and Birney, *Holy Murder,* p. 104

125. Hoffman and Birney, *Holy Murder,* p. 104

126. Ibid.

Gottfredson, *Indian Depredations,* p. 39

Tullidge, *Histories,* Vol. II, p. 84

Hosea Stout, "Journal," MSS, eight volumes, Vol. IV, p. 283

127. Journal History, June 3, 1851

128. Bean, *Autobiography,* p. 175-176

129. Journal History, Nov. 20, 1851

Chapter Eight

1. Journal History, January 3, 1852

2. Orson F. Whitney, *History of Utah, Comprising Preliminary Chapters on the Previous History of Her Founders, Accounts of Early Spanish and American Explorations in the Rocky Mountain Region, the Advent of the Mormon Pioneers, the Establishment and Dissolution of the Provisional Government of the State of Deseret, and the Subsequent Creation and Development of the Territory* (Salt Lake City, 1892-1904), four volumes, Vol. I, p. 502

3. Petition of Porter Rockwell and Franklin Neff, March 22, 1853

4. Daily Alta California, July 6, 1853

5. *Deseret News,* December 4, 1853

   Journal History, November 28, 1853

   Utah Executive Papers, 1850-1855, Territorial Secretary Correspondence, Utah State Archives

   Almon W. Babbitt, letter to Secretary of the Treasury, December 17, 1853, Utah State Archives

6. George McKenzie, "Cause and Origin of the Walker War," in Gottfredson's *Indian Depredations,* pp. 43-46

7. Bean, *Autobiography,* pp. 93-100

8. Thomas D. Brown, "Journal of the Southern Indian Mission," MS, April 26, 1854

9. Op. cit.

10. "A Record of Marriages (Solemnized) (Alphabetically Arranged) 1853-1856," p. 36

11. Journal History, May 10, 1854

12. S. N. Carvalho, *Incidents of Travel and Adventure in the Far West; with Col. Fremont's Last Expedition* (New York, 1857), pp. 213-214

13. Also see Journal History, May 11, 1854

14. Ibid., May 12, 1854

15. Andrew Love, "Journal," MS, p. 45

16. George W. Bradley, letter to Lieutenant General Daniel H. Wells, June 17, 1854, Military Records Section, Utah State Archives

17. U. S. State Department, Territorial Papers, Utah Series, April 30, 1853 - December 24, 1859, National Archives

18. Nelson Winch Green, *Fifteen Years Among the Mormons, Being the Narrative of Mrs. Mary Ettie V. Smith* (New York, 1860), p. 318

19. Birney and Kelly, *Holy Murder*

20. Op. cit., p. 368

21. James S. Brown, *California Gold, An Authentic History of the First Find* (Oakland, 1894)

22. Bigler, "Day Book and Diary," MS

    Erwin G. Gudde, *Bigler's Chronicles of the West* (Berkely, 1962), p. 111

Brown, *California Gold*

James S. Brown, *Giant of the Lord* (Salt Lake City, 1960)

Azariah Smith, "Azariah Smith's Journal," Journal History, January - April 1848

Paul W. Rodman, *California Gold Discovery* (1966)

23. James S. Brown, *Life of a Pioneer, Being an Autobiography* (Salt Lake City, 1900), pp. 345-346

24. *Journal of Discourses,* Vol. I, p. 187

25. Mrs. C. V. Waite, *The Mormon Prophet and His Harem* (Chicago, 1867), pp. 27-28.

J. H. Beadle, *Life in Utah, or the Mysteries and Crimes of Mormonism* (Philadelphia, 1870), p. 171

26. Bean, *Autobiography,* p. 110

27. See also Josiah F. Gibbs, "Gunnison Massacre — 1853 — Millard County, Utah — Indian Mareer's Version of the Tragedy — 1894," *Utah Historical Quarterly,* Vol. I (July 1928), p. 72

28. Bean, *Autobiography,* p. 112

29. Love, "Journal," MS, p. 70

30. *Deseret News,* October 26, 1854

31. Steptoe, letter to Cooper, Office of Indian Affairs, National Archives, September 14, 1854

32. Oliver Boardman Huntington, "A Trip to Carson Valley," *Eventful Narratives* (Salt Lake City, 1887), p. 78

For details of the journey see also:

Huntington, "Diaries," MSS, Vol. II, p. 84

Jacob H. Holeman, Indian Agent for Utah Territory, letter report to Luke Lea, Commissioner of Indian Affairs, "Utah Expedition," *Executive Documents Printed by Order of The House of Representatives During the First Session of the Thirty-Fifth Congress,* 1857-'58, fourteen volumes, Vol. X, No. 71, p. 141

U. S. House of Representatives, Office of Indian Affairs, *Executive Document No. 1* (1856), p. 778

Garland Hurt, in Captain J. H. Simpson, "A Memoir on the Indians of Utah Territory," *Report of Explorations Across the Great Basin of the Territory of Utah, for a Wagon-Route from Camp Floyd to Genoa, in Carson Valley* (Washington, D.C., 1876), p. 461

Deseret News, December 7, 1854

33. Bean, *Autobiography,* p. 114

34. Captain Rufus Ingalls, letter to Major General Thomas S. Jesup, "Report to the Quartermaster General," *Executive Document No. 1,* U. S. Senate, 34th Congress, 1st Session, 1855, p. 161

Captain J. H. Simpson, "A Memoir on the Indians of Utah Territory," *Report of Explorations Across the Great Basin of the Territory of Utah, for a Wagon-Route from Camp Floyd to Genoa, in Carson Valley* (Washington, D.C., 1876), pp. 24-25

See also Steptoe, letter of recommendation regarding Rockwell, Historical Record Book, p. 196, CHD

35. *Utah Genealogical and Historical Magazine,* Vol. XXVI, p. 156

36. Bean, *Autobiography,* p. 113

37. Joseph L. Heywood, letter to George A. Smith, *Deseret News,* September 19, 1855

Chapter Nine

1. Her move to California is described in Raymund Francis Wood and Josephine Dewitt Rhodehamel, *Ina Coolbirth, Librarian and Laureate of California* (Provo, 1973), pp. 24-25

2. Mrs. Elizabeth D. E. Roundy, letter to CHD, Jenson's Biographical Manuscripts

3. *Deseret News,* October 10, 1855

4. U. S. Population Census, Seventh (1850), Utah

"Box Elder County," *Heart Throbs of the West,* Vol. IX (1948), p. 241

5. John Bennion, "Journal," MSS, five volumes, Book I, p. 18

6. *Deseret News,* October 3, 1855

7. Jules Remy, *A Journey to Great-Salt-Lake City* (London, 1861), two volumes, Vol. II, pp. 314-315

8. *Deseret News,* September 12, 1855

9. Journal History, January 12, 1856, p. 2

Deseret News, January 23, 1856

10. Journal History, February 2, 1856

Deseret News, February 6, 1856

See also Hyde, *Mormonism,* p. 105

11. Edwin Ward Stout, "Journal," MS, p. 8

12. *Deseret News,* April 23, 1856

13. James Ure, company clerk, Journal History, June 8, 1856

14. U. S. House of Representatives, "Engagement Between United States Troops and Sioux Indians," *House of Representatives Report No. 63,* 33rd Congress, 2d Session, 1855, pp. 1-27

15. Eugene Bandel, *Frontier Life in the Army 1854-1861,* (Glendale, 1932), pp. 28-35

General Richard C. Drum, "Reminiscences of the Indian Fight at Ash Hollow, 1855," *Nebraska State Historical Society, Collections,* Vol. XVI (1911), pp. 143-150

16. Journal History, June 8, 1856

17. Ibid., p. 7

18. George A. Smith, letter, *Deseret News,* June 11, 1856

Journal History, June 8, 1856

19. Journal History, June 8, 1856, p. 8

20. *Deseret News,* July 2, 1856

21. *Frontier Guardian* (Kanesville, Iowa), May 2, 1851

Journal History, May 2, 1851

22. Sarah Hollister Harris, *An Unwritten Chapter of Salt Lake 1851-1901* (New York, 1901), pp. 55-56

23. George Bird Grinnel, *The Fighting Cheyennes* (Norman, 1955), p. 113

24. John Jaques, "Some Reminiscences," *Salt Lake Herald,* December 8, 1878

Journal History, November 30, 1856, p. 14

25. U. S. House of Representatives, "Report of the Secretary of Interior," *Executive Document No. 1,* 34th Congress, 3rd Session, December 1, 1856 - March 3, 1857, p. 650

26. Captain H. W. Wharton's reports, *Transactions of the Kansas State Historical Society, Embracing the Fifth and Sixth Biennial Reports, 1886-1888* (Topeka, 1890), Vol. IV, pp. 492-493

Council Bluffs Bugle, September 9, 1856

Millennial Star, Vol. XVIII, p. 686

27. U. S. Senate, "Report of the Secretary of the Interior," *Executive Document No. 5,* 34th Congress, 3rd Session, December 1, 1856 to March 3, 1857, p. 650

Op. cit.

28. Rockwell, testimony before W. I. Appleby, clerk of the Supreme Court of the United States for the Territory of Utah, dated February 11, 1857, Utah Executive Papers, 1856-1858, "Governor (Miscellaneous Correspondence) 1857," Utah State Archives

29. "Secretary of Territory (Miscellaneous Correspondence) 1857," Utah Executive Papers, 1856-1858, Utah State Archives

30. Jaques, "Some Reminiscences," *Salt Lake Herald,* December 29, 1878

31. Journal History, October 4, 1856

32. Captain H. W. Wharton, letter to Major G. Deas, Assistant Adjutant General, in *Transactions of the Kansas State Historical Society,* Vol. IV, pp. 494-495

Julia Ann Babbitt, "Letter to the Editor," *New York Herald,* July 25, 1857

The Mormon, August 1, 1857

33. Journal History, October 4, 1856

34. Journal History, October 4, 1856

35. Julia Ann Babbit, *New York Herald,* July 25, 1857

The Mormon, August 1, 1857

36. *Council Bluffs Bugle* article reprinted in *The Mormon,* April 18, 1857

Millennial Star, Vol. XIX, p. 443

Crescent City Oracle, May 22, 1856

37. Ibid.

38. Achilles, *Destroying Angels of Mormondom,* pp. 16-17

39. "Utah Expedition," *Executive Document No. 71,* U. S. House of Representatives, 35th Congress, 1st Session, 1858, pp. 212-214

"Resignation of Associate Justice W. W. Drummond," *New York Herald,* April 1, 1857

The Mormon, April 18, 1857

40. Hungtington, "Journal," MSS, three volumes, Vol. II, p. 106

41. Hosea Stout, "Journal," MSS, Vol. VI, p. 48

Journal History, November 4, 1856

Stout, *On the Mormon Frontier, The Diary of Hosea Stout,* Vol. II, p. 604

42. *Utah Genealogical and Historical Magazine,* Vol. XXVI, p. 156

43. Brigham Young, letter to Horace Eldredge, St. Louis, March 27, 1857

44. John M. Bernhisel, letter from Washington, D.C. to John Taylor, Great Salt Lake City, *Deseret News,* January 14, 1857

45. Hickman, *Brigham's Destroying Angel,* p. 113

46. *Burlington Hawkeye,* October 3, 1844

Sangamo Journal, October 10, 1844

47. Whitney, *History of Utah,* Vol. I, pp. 637-638

48. Hickman, *Brigham's Destroying Angel,* pp. 114, 116

49. Daniel W. Jones, *Forty Years Among the Indians, A True Yet Thrilling Narrative of the Author's Experiences Among the Natives* (Salt Lake City, 1890); p. 99, reprinted version

Joseph M. Tanner, *John Riggs Murdock, A Biographical Sketch* (Salt Lake City, 1909), pp. 114-120

Deseret News, May 20, 1857

50. M. M. Long and O. H. O'Neill, "Journals of the Eastern and Central Divisons of the Fort Kearney, South Pass, and Honey Lake Wagon Road, June 4, 1857, to October 8, 1859," MSS, Records of the Secretary of the Interior, National Archives

51. John I. Ginn, "Mormon and Indian Wars: the Mountain Meadows Massacre and Other Tragedies and Transactions Incident to the Mormon Rebellion of 1857. Together With the Personal Recollection of a Civilian Who Witnessed Many of the Thrilling Scenes Described," MS, p. 15

52. *Deseret News,* June 3, 1857

53. Remy, *A Journey to Great-Salt-Lake City,* Vol. I, p. 208

54. W. I. Appleby, Supreme Court clerk for Territory of Utah, *The Mormon,* May 23, 1857

Ibid., June 13, June 20, July 4, 1857

Millennial Star (reprint), Vol. XIX, p. 401

55. Mrs. W. Drummond, letter to Mr. and Mrs. Silas Richards, September 4, 1856, *Deseret News* May 20, 1857

56. Remy, *A Journey to Great-Salt-Lake City,* Vol. I, p. 469

57. Hickman, *Brigham's Destroying Angel,* p. 111

58. Ibid.

59. Remy, *A Journey to Great-Salt-Lake City,* Vol. II, p. 343

60. *Executive Document No. 71,* U. S. House of Representatives, 35th Congress, 1st Session, 1858, pp. 212-214

61. *New York Times,* April 1857

New York Sun, April 1857

National Intelligencer, April 1857

New York Herald, April 1857

New York Tribune, April 1857

62. *New York Times,* May 21, 1857

63. Vaux [Junius Wells], "The Echo Canyon War," *The Contributor,* 1882, Vol. III, p. 84

64. *New York Herald,* February 23, 1858

Deseret News, May 12, 1858

65. Julia Ann Babbitt, *New York Herald,* July 25, 1857

66. *Crescent City Oracle,* May 22, 1857

67. Vaux, *The Contributor,* Vol. III, p. 54

68. Ibid.

69. *New York Times,* May 21, 1857

70. Ibid., May 18, 1857

71. Vaux, *The Contributor,* Vol. III, p. 84

72. Samuel Bowles, *Our New West; Records of Travel Between the Mississippi River and the Pacific Ocean* (Hartford, 1869)

William Chandless, *A Visit to Salt Lake; Being a Journey Across the Plains and a Residence in the Mormon Settlements at Utah* (London, 1857)

Waite, *The Mormon Prophet and His Harem*

Sir Richard Francis Burton, *The City of the Saints and Across the Rocky Mountains to California* (London, 1861; New York, 1862)

73. *Journal of Discourses,* Vol. III, pp. 234-235

Chapter Ten

1. Vaux, *The Contributor,* Vol. III, p. 86

2. Albert G. Browne, "The Utah Expedition," *The Atlantic Monthly, A Magazine of Literature, Art, and Politics,* Vol. III (1859), p. 367

Colonel Edmund B. Alexander, letter to Brigham Young, Military Records Section, Utah State Archives, October 12, 1857

3. Abraham O. Smoot, letter to Edward W. Tullidge, February 14, 1884

Edward W. Tullidge, *The History of Salt Lake City and Its Founders* (Salt Lake City, 1886), p. 157

4. Vaux, *The Contributor*, Vol. III, p. 104

5. *Deseret News*, September 23, 1857

   Journal of Discourses, Vol. V, pp. 226-227

   Hubert Howe Bancroft, *The Works of Hubert Howe Bancroft, History of Utah 1540-1887* (San Francisco, 1890), p. 505

   Linn, *Story of the Mormons*, p. 483

   Vaux, *The Contributor*, Vol. III, p. 146

   Stenhouse, *Rocky Mountain Saints*, p. 351

6. Vaux, *The Contributor*, Vol. III, p. 105

7. Music: *Minstrel Songs, Old and New* (1882), pp. 94-95

   See also J. H. Beadle, *Polygamy* (Philadelphia, 1904), pp. 159-160

   Stenhouse, *Rocky Mountain Saints*, pp. 370, 372

8. Vaux, *The Contributor*, Vol. III, pp. 216-217

9. Hickman, *Brigham's Destroying Angel*, pp. 123-124

10. Roberts, *Comprehensive History of the Church*, Vol. IV, pp. 246-247

11. Vaux, *The Contributor*, Vol. III, p. 217

12. *Deseret News*, August 12, 1857

13. *Journal of Discourses*, Vol. V, pp. 77-78

14. Daniel H. Wells, letter to officers, Nauvoo Legion, August 1, 1857, Military Records Section, Utah State Archives

   Vaux, *The Contributor*, Vol. III, p. 177

15. Vaux, *The Contributor*, Vol. III, pp. 215-216, delivered September 15, 1857, *Deseret News*

16. U. S. House of Representatives, *Executive Documents*, 35th Congress, 1st Session, ii, Part 2, pp. 35-37

   Captain Stewart Van Vliet, letter to Captain Alfred Pleasanton, Assistant Adjutant General, United States Army Expedition to Utah, letter dated September 16, 1857, Fort Leavenworth, Kansas, "Utah Expedition," *Executive Document No. 71*, U. S. House of Representatives, 35th Congress, 1st Session, 1858, pp. 24-26

17. Ibid.

18. Brigham Young, Brigham Young Letter Book No. 23, September 14, 1857

19. *Deseret News*, September 16, 1857

   Journal History, September 14, 1857

20. Vaux, *The Contributor*, Vol. III, p. 147

21. Ibid., September 20, 1857

22. George Alfred Townsend, "Interview With the Mayor of Salt Lake," *The Mormon Trials at Salt Lake City* (New York, 1871), p. 33

23. Ibid., pp. 24-27, 37-38

24. Van Vliet, letter to Pleasanton, "Utah Expedition," *Executive Document No. 71*

25. Vaux, *The Contributor,* Vol. III, p. 148

26. Tullidge, *History of Salt Lake City,* p. 214

27. *The Savannah News,* as Reprinted July 27, 1857 in the *Valley Tan*

28. *Daily Telegraph,* January 20, May 25, 1865

29. *Deseret News Weekly,* December 5, 1880

30. Vaux, *The Contributor,* Vol. III, pp. 178-179

31. *San Francisco Herald,* November 25, 1857

Sacramento Daily Herald, November 25, 1857

Executive Documents, U. S. House of Representatives, 35th Congress, 1st Session, ii, part 2, pp. 32-33

Vaux, *The Contributor,* Vol. III, pp. 178-179

San Francisco Alta, November 25, 30, 1857

Pomeroy Tucker, *Origin, Rise, and Progress of Mormonism* (New York, 1867), pp. 232-237

Waite, *The Mormon Prophet And His Harem,* pp. 43-45

Stenhouse, *Rocky Mountain Saints,* pp. 358-359

Chapter Eleven

1. Wilford Woodruff, "Wilford Woodruff Journal," MS, September 25, 1857

2. Townsend, *Mormon Trials at Salt Lake City,* p. 33

3. Vaux, *The Contributor,* Vol. III, p. 271

4. Jesse A. Gove, *The Utah Expedition 1857-1858, Letters of Capt. Jesse A. Gove, 10th Inf., U. S. A., of Concord, N. H., to Mrs. Gove, and special correspondence of the New York Herald,* Otis G. Hammond, editor (Concord, Massachusetts, 1928), p. 217

5. Jesse W. Crosby, "The History and Journal of the Life and Travels of Jesse W. Crosby," *Annals of Wyoming,* Vol. XI (July 1939), p. 90

6. Gove, *Utah Expedition 1857-1858,* p. 64

7. Ibid.

8. Hosea Stout, "Journal," MSS, Vol. VII, p. 48

9. Gove, *Utah Expedition 1857-1858,* p. 64

10. Vaux, *The Contributor*

11. Crosby, "The History and Journal," pp. 90-91

12. Ginn, "Mormon and Indian Wars," MS, pp. 9-10

13. William F. Cody, *The Life of Hon. William F. Cody, Known as Buffalo Bill, the Famous Hunter, Scout, and Guide* (Hartford, 1879), pp. 69-70

14. Gove, *Utah Expedition 1857-1858,* p. 66

15. Newton Tuttle, "A Territorial Militiaman in the Utah War; Journal of Newton

Tuttle," edited by Hamilton Gardner, *Utah Historical Quarterly,* Vol. XXII (October 1954), pp. 306-307

16. Journal History, October 25, 1857, p. 11

    Tuttle, "A Territorial Militiaman," pp. 306-307

17. Crosby, "The History and Journal," p. 92

18. Ibid.

19. Ibid.

20. Salt Lake County Mortgage Records, Book B, pp. 125-127, Salt Lake County Recorder's Office, Lewis Robison (for purchase on October 18, 1858 for final payment of $4,000)

21. Ibid., p. 128, August 3, 1855, for down payment of $4,000

22. Op. cit.

23. Hickman, *Brigham's Destroying Angel,* p. 118

24. Brigham Young, *Manuscript History of Brigham Young,* p. 715

25. Henry Ballard, "Private Journal of Henry Ballard, 1852-1904," MS, pp. 4-5

26. Ibid.

    Tuttle, "A Territorial Militiaman," pp. 306-307

27. Vaux, *The Contributor,* Vol. III, pp. 272-274

28. Ibid., Vol. IV, pp. 27-28

29. Ibid., Vol. III, pp. 272-274

    Ibid., Vol. IV, pp. 27-29

30. "Utah Expedition," *Executive Document No. 71,* U. S. House of Representatives, 1858, p. 63

31. Journal History, October 25, 1857, p. 17

    Wells, letter to McAllister, October 8, 1857, Military Records Section, Utah State Archives

32. Vaux, *The Contributor,* Vol. IV, p. 48

33. Ibid., pp. 48-50

34. George A. Smith, "Church Historians Record Book," October 14, 1857

35. Ibid.

36. Tuttle, "A Territorial Militiaman," p. 309

37. Journal History, October 25, 1857, p. 17

    New York Times, December 28, 1857

    Ballard, "Private Journal," MS, p. 7

38. Vaux, *The Contributor,* Vol. III, p. 48

39. Ibid., Vol. IV, pp. 167-168

40. Ibid., pp. 168-169

41. Ibid., pp. 225-226

42. Townsend, *Mormon Trials at Salt Lake City,* pp. 33-34

43. Colonel Alexander, letter to the Adjutant General of the Army, October 9, 1857

44. Crosby, "The History and Journal," p. 93

45. Ibid.

46. Vaux, *The Contributor,* Vol. IV, p. 381

47. Ginn, "Mormon and Indian Wars," MS, pp. 85-89

48. Ibid., p. 89

49. Crosby, "The History and Journal," p. 94

50. William Inman and William F. Cody, *The Great Salt Lake Trail,* 1898, p. 130

51. Albert Tracy, "Journal of Captain Albert Tracy," edited by J. Cecil Alter and Robert J. Dwyer, *Utah Historical Quarterly,* Vol. XIII (1945), p. 23

52. Vaux, *The Contributor,* Vol. III, p. 148

53. Ibid., p. 270

54. Ebenezer Crouch, "Autobiography of Ebenezer Crouch" (1850-1923), MS completed September 12, 1923, p. 21

55. Ginn, "Mormon and Indian Wars," MS, pp. 16-19

56. John R. Young, letter to Henry W. Bigler, January 31, 1858, in Bigler, "Incidents (1857-1858)," *Union,* (St. George, Utah, newspaper), November 21, 1896

57. Journal History, November 3, 1857

58. Lee, *A Mormon Chronicle,* Vol. II, p. 644

59. Ibid.

60. Ibid.

61. Hosea Stout, "Journal," MSS, Vol. VII, p. 57

62. Stout, *On the Mormon Frontier, The Diary of Hosea Stout,* Vol. II, p. 645

63. Op. cit., p. 59

64. Ibid.

65. *New York Times,* March 16, 1858

66. Inman and Cody, *The Great Salt Lake Trail,* pp. 141-142

67. Murray Averett, "The Averett Narrative," MS, p. 21

68. William Marsden, "Journal and Diary of William Marsden," *Daughters of Utah Pioneers, Lesson for January, 1951,* p. 157

69. *New York Weekly Tribune,* March 6, 1858
    Journal History, August 30, 1859

70. Randolph B. Marcy, *Thirty Years of Army Life on the Border* (New York, 1866), pp. 224-250

71. A. R. Mortensen, editor of letter, "The Governor's Lady; A Letter from Camp Scott, 1857," *Utah Historical Quarterly,* Vol. XXII (April 1954), pp. 165-173

72. *New York Herald,* February 23, 1858
    Deseret News, May 12, 1858
    Journal History, February 23, 1858

73. Gove, *Utah Expedition 1857-1858,* p. 218

74. Brigham Young, letter to Thomas L. Kane, January 14, 1859, Thomas L. Kane Papers, MS, Stanford University Library

75. John Wolcott Phelps, "Diary," MS, March 13, 1858

76. John Kay, letter to Thomas Williams, Journal History, May 10, 1858

Alfred Cumming, letter to Lewis Cass, Secretary of State, May 2, 1858, U. S. State Department, Territorial Papers, Utah Series, April 30, 1853, to December 24, 1859.

Bancroft, *History of Utah,* p. 526n

77. Gove, *Utah Expedition 1857-1858,* p. 147

78. Cumming, letter to Cass, May 2, 1858, U. S. State Department, Territorial Papers, Utah Series

Bancroft, *History of Utah,* p. 526n

Stenhouse, *Rocky Mountain Saints,* pp. 289-390

Waite, *The Mormon Prophet and His Harem,* pp. 53-55

79. Crosby, "The History and Journal," p. 94

80. Inman and Cody, *The Great Salt Lake Trail,* p. 131

81. Cumming, letter to Cass, May 2, 1858. U. S. State Department, Territorial Papers, Utah Series

82. Tracy, "Journal," p. 27

83. Cumming, letter to Cass, May 2, 1858, U. S. State Department, Territorial Papers, Utah Series

84. U. S. Senate, Senate Document, 35th Congress, 2nd Session, ii, p. 161

85. U. S. House of Representatives, *Executive Document No. 2,* 35th Congress, 2nd Session, 1858, pp. 165-166

86. Joseph Fielding Smith, as quoted in Jenson, *The Historical Record,* p. 189

87. Jenson, *Church Encyclopaedia,* p. 189

88. U. S. Senate, Senate Document, 35th Congress, 2nd Session, ii, pp. 175-177

Deseret News, June 23, 1858

89. Tullidge, *History of Salt Lake City,* p. 215

90. Ibid., pp. 215-216

91. Ibid., p. 216

92. Ibid.

93. Ibid., p. 217

94. Ibid.

Chapter Twelve

1. Cumming, letter to Cass, June 18, 1858, U. S. State Department, Territorial Papers, Utah Series

Bancroft, *History of Utah,* p. 532n

Tullidge, *History of Salt Lake City,* p. 215

2. Tullidge, *History of Salt Lake City,* pp. 220-224

3. *New York Times,* as quoted in ibid., pp. 421-422

   Reynolds' Newspaper, as quoted in Tullidge, History of Salt Lake City, p. 422

4. *The London Times,* as quoted in Tullidge, *History of Salt Lake City,* p. 221

5. Tullidge, *History of Salt Lake City,* p. 223

6. Ibid, p. 217

7. Ibid, p. 224

8. Burton, *City of the Saints,* as quoted in Tullidge, *History of Salt Lake City,* p. 223

9. Op. cit., p. 223

10. Ibid., p. 224.

11. Inman and Cody, *The Great Salt Lake Trail,* p. 130-131

12. Vaux, *The Contributor,* Vol. III, p. 179

13. Utah County Deeds, 1851-1864, Book G, p. 169; Lot 4, Block 44 on the American Creek Survey of Meadow Land; Lot 2, Block 2, on Dry Creek, Plat B, p. 308

14. Ibid., p. 362

15. William Marsden, clerk of Utah County Recorder's Office, Inspector of Spirituous Liquors and Beer, "Journal and Diary," p. 174

16. Journal History, August 29, 1860

17. *Valley Tan,* July 27, 1857, see article, for example, on Mormon Church leaders' reception of Horace Greeley

18. *Valley Tan,* July 20, 1859

19. *The Mountaineer,* January 7, 1860

20. Ibid.

21. Ibid.

22. Church Historian's Office Journal, Vol. XXIV, October 20-21, 1860

23. Ibid.

24. *Utah Genealogical and Historical Magazine,* Vol. XXVI, p. 156

25. Rockwell, letter to Colonel Kane, November 20, 1858, Coe Collection (MS 279, Yale University)

   Journal History, November 20, 1858

26. Journal History, June 3, 1859

27. *Deseret News,* September 21, 1859

28. Wilford Woodruff, letter to George A. Smith, Journal History, July 12, 1859

29. *Deseret News,* September 21, 1859

   Hosea Stout, "Journal," MSS, Vol. VIII, p. 21

   Stout, *On the Mormon Frontier, The Diary of Hosea Stout,* Vol. II, p. 703

30. Crosby, "The History and Journal," p. 96

31. *Extra* of the *Leavenworth Daily Times,* June 4, 1859
  Valley Tan, July 20, 1859

32. Horace Greeley, *An Overland Journey From New York to San Francisco in the Summer of 1859* (New York, 1860), p. 234

33. Young, *Manuscript History of Brigham Young,* November 4, 1858, p. 1067

34. Stenhouse, *Rocky Mountain Saints,* p. 417

35. George Morris, "Autobiography," MS, pp. 86-87

36. Crosby, "The History and Journal," pp. 98

37. Ibid., pp. 96-97

38. Ibid.

39. Vaux, *The Contributor,* Vol. III, p. 54

40. Op. cit., p. 96

Chapter Thirteen

1. *The Mountaineer,* October 8, 1859

2. Hosea Stout, "Journal," Vol. VII, p. 93
  Stout, *On the Mormon Frontier, The Diary of Hosea Stout,* Vol. I, p. 665

3. Achilles, *Destroying Angels of Mormondom,* p. 31

4. George Laub, "Diary No. 2 of George Laub, 1814-1880," MSS, three volumes, Vol. II (1858-1870), pp. 58-59

5. Lee, *A Mormon Chronicle,* Vol. I, p. 222

6. Ibid.

7. *Deseret News,* February 1, 1860

8. *The Mountaineer,* February 4, 1860

9. Op. cit.

10. Op. cit.

11. *Utah Genealogical and Historical Magazine,* Vol. XXVI, p. 156

12. Lee, *A Mormon Chronicle,* Vol. I, pp. 241-242

13. Young, *Manuscript History of Brigham Young,* August 29, 1860

14. *Deseret News,* September 5, 1860

15. *Deseret News,* May 7, June 11, 1862

16. Burton, *City of the Saints,* pp. 448-450

17. Tracy, "Journal," p. 84

18. Laub, "Diary," MSS, Vol. II, p. 83
  Charles L. Walker, "Journal," MSS, twelve volumes, p. 199
  Charles Lowell Walker, *Diary of Charles Lowell Walker,* edited by A. Karl Larson and Katherine Miles (Logan, Utah, 1980), two volumes, Vol. I, p. 160

19. Crouch, "Autobiography," MS, pp. 14-16

20. Journal History, July 23, 1861

21. Op. cit., pp. 18-20

22. Orson Twelves, "Early History of Charles Twelves and Family," MS, p. 2

23. Charles A. Scott, "Charles A. Scott's Diary of the Utah Expedition, 1857-1861," edited by Robert E. Stowers and John M. Ellis, *Utah Historical Quarterly,* Vol. XXVIII (1960), p. 395

24. Hickman, *Brigham's Destroying Angel,* p. 148

25. Francis B. Heitman, *Historical Register and Dictionary of the United States Army, from Its Organization, September 29, 1789, to March 2, 1903* (Washington, 1903), two volumes, Vol. I, pp. 577-578

William Preston Johnston, *The Life of Gen. Albert Sidney Johnston* (New York, 1878), p. 229

26. Austin Gudmundsen, "Journal," MS at Lehi, Utah in possession of his widow, Myrl Gudmundsen; used by permission

27. Israel Bennion, "Incidents relating to Orrin Porter Rockwell," Document, 3 pp, Ms d 4125, CHD, p. 3

28. Ibid., p. 2

29. "In Early Times. A Narrative of Old 'Uncle Porter Rockwell.' After the Horse Thieves. A Pueblo Man Who Found 'Port' Anything but a Destroying Angel," dated Pueblo, Colorado, July 20, 1885, *Salt Lake Herald,* July 30, 1885

30. Whitney, *History of Utah,* Vol. II, p. 38

Tucker, *Origin, Rise, and Progress of Mormonism,* p. 239

Tullidge, *History of Salt Lake City,* p. 249

Deseret News, January 1, 1862

31. Waite, *The Mormon Prophet and His Harem,* p. 76

Stenhouse, *Rocky Mountain Saints,* p. 592

Beadle, *Life in Utah,* p. 201

32. Stenhouse, *Rocky Mountain Saints,* p. 592

Whitney, *History of Utah,* Vol. II, p. 38

33. *Deseret News,* January 22, 1862

34. Ibid.

35. Elias Smith, "Journal, January 1, 1859 -- August 24, 1864," MS

Elias Smith, "Elias Smith, Journal of a Pioneer Editor, March 6, 1859 -- September 23, 1863," edited by A. R. Mortensen, *Utah Historical Quarterly,* Vol. XXI (1953), p. 150

36. *Deseret News,* January 22, 1862

37. Glynn Bennion, "The Best Laid Schemes," *Salt Lake Tribune,* March 9, 1924

38. Journal History, January 16, 1862

See George Morris, "Autobiography," MS, p. 89

39. Egan, *Pioneering the West 1846 to 1878,* pp. 217-218

40. *Deseret News,* January 22, 1862
41. Ibid.
42. Stenhouse, *Rocky Mountain Saints,* p. 419
43. *Deseret News,* December 18, 1861; June 18, 1862
44. *Chicago Tribune,* June 20, 1862
45. Tullidge, *History of Salt Lake City,* p. 252
46. *Deseret News,* May 7, 1862
   Op. cit., p. 255
47. Daniel H. Wells, letter to Porter Rockwell, April 28, 1862, Military Records Section, Utah State Archives
48. *Deseret News,* August 6, 1862
49. Ibid., September 24, 1862
   Fred B. Rogers, *Soldiers of the Overland, Being Some Account of the Services of General Patrick Edward Connor & His Volunteers in the Old West* (San Francisco, 1938), pp. 29- 31
50. Ibid., p. 29
51. *Deseret News,* September 25, 1862
52. Logan Branch recorder, January 28th, 1863, as quoted in Tullidge, *History of Salt Lake City,* p. 289
53. William D. Ustick, First Lieutenant and Adjutant, Third Infantry, California Volunteers, Acting Assistant Adjutant General, By order of Patrick Edward Connor, Colonel 3rd California Volunteers, Com'd District, at Headquarters District of Utah, Camp Douglas, letter February 6, 1863 to Lieutenant Colonel R. C. Drum, Assistant Adjutant General, U. S. A., Department of the Pacific
54. Colonel Martineau, as quoted in Tullidge, *History of Salt Lake City,* p 289
55. *Deseret News,* December 17, 1862
56. Ibid., December 31, 1862
57. Whitney, *History of Utah,* Vol. II, p. 78
58. Op. cit., January 28, 1863
59. Verite, Letter No. 1, "The Battle of Bear River," penned February 7, 1863, Salt Lake City, Utah, published in *Daily Alta Californian* (San Francisco)
   Edward W. Tullidge, editor, *Tullidge's Quarterly Magazine* (Salt Lake City, 1881), Vol. I, p. 191
   Fred B. Rogers, *Soldiers of the Overland,* p. 69
60. Tuttle, "A Territorial Militaman"
61. *Deseret News,* February 4, 1863

Chapter 14

1. Captain Charles H. Hempstead, "Anniversary Oration," *Union Vedette,* January 30, 1864

Rogers, *Soldiers of the Overland,* pp. 69-70

2. Verite, Letter No. 3, "Official List of Killed and Wounded At the Battle of Bear River," penned February 9, 1863, Salt Lake City, Utah, published in the *Daily Alta Californian*

Tullidge, editor, *Tullidge's Quarterly Magazine,* Vol. I, p. 194

Richard H. Orton, Brigadier-General, *Records of California Men in the War of the Rebellion, 1861-1867* (Sacramento, 1890), pp. 176-179

3. Whitney, *History of Utah,* Vol. II, pp. 78-79

4. *Deseret News,* February 11, 1863

5. Patrick Edward Connor, Colonel 3rd California Volunteers, Com'd. District, at Headquarters District of Utah, Camp Douglas, letter February 6th, 1863 to Lieutenant Colonel R. C. Drum, Assistant Adjutant General, U. S. A., Department of the Pacific

Tullidge, *History of Salt Lake City,* pp. 284-285

See also Rogers, *Soldiers of the Overland,* p. 71

6. *Deseret News,* February 11, 1863

Tullidge, editor, *Tullidge's Quarterly Magazine,* Vol. I, p. 192

Orton, *Records of California Men,* pp. 176-179

7. *Deseret News,* February 11, 1863

8. Harmon Zufelt, "The Battle of Bear River," *The Utah Monthly Magazine,* Vol. IX, No. 3 (December 1892), p. 84, part of *The Utah Magazine, an Illustrated Monthly Journal of Free Discussion and General Current Intelligence,* Vol. IX: October, 1892 to September, 1893 (Salt Lake City, 1893)

9. Verite, Letter No. 1, February 7, 1863, *Daily Alta Californian*

Tullidge, editor, *Tullidge's Quarterly Magazine,* Vol. I, p. 192

Orton, *Records of California Men,* pp. 176-179

Rogers, *Soldiers of the Overland,* p. 71

10. Crouch, "Autobiography," MS

11. "Observer," *Army and Navy Journal,* December 15, 1866

Union Vedette, January 29, 1867

12. Verite, Letter No. 1, February 7, 1863, *Daily Alta Californian*

Tullidge, editor, *Tullidge's Quarterly Magazine,* Vol. I, p. 192

Orton, *Records of California Men,* pp. 176-179

13. Connor, letter February 6th, 1863 to Lt. Col. R. C. Drum

Tullidge, *History of Salt Lake City,* pp. 284-285

14. Verite, Letter No. 1, February 7, 1863, *Daily Alta Californian*

Tullidge, editor, *Tullidge's Quarterly Magazine,* Vol. I, p. 192

Orton, *Records of California Men,* pp. 176-179

15. *San Francisco Bulletin,* February 10, 1863

16. *Daily Alta Californian,* quoted in Orton, *Records of California Men,* pp. 175-181

17. Verite, Letter No. 1, February 7, 1863, *Daily Alta Californian*
    Tullidge, editor, *Tullidge's Quarterly Magazine*, Vol. I, p. 192
    Orton, Records of California Men, p. 176
18. Connor, letter February 6th, 1863 to Lt. Col. R. C. Drum
    Tullidge, *History of Salt Lake City*, p. 285
19. *Deseret News*, February 11, 1863
20. Verite, Letter No. 1, February 7, 1863, *Daily Alta Californian*
    Tullidge, editor, *Tullidge's Quarterly Magazine*, Vol. I, p. 193
    Orton, *Records of California Men*, p. 176
21. *Deseret News*, February 11, 1863
22. Connor, letter February 6th, 1863 to Lt. Col. R. C. Drum
    Tullidge, *History of Salt Lake City*, p. 285
23. Whitney, *History of Utah*, Vol. II, p. 79
24. Connor, letter February 6th, 1863 to Lt. Col. R. C. Drum
    Tullidge, *History of Salt Lake City*, p. 286
25. Colonel James H. Martineau, report quoted in Tullidge, *History of Salt Lake City*, p. 290
    Tullidge, editor, *Tullidge's Histories*, Vol. II, pp. 367-368
26. Ibid.
27. Hiram S. Tuttle, "Account," MS
    Rogers, *Soldiers of the Overland*, p. 74
28. Young, *Manuscript History of Brigham Young*, February 7, 1863
29. Harmon Zufelt, *The Utah Monthly Magazine*, Vol. IX, No. 3, p. 84
30. Connor, letter February 6th, 1863 to Lt. Col. R. C. Drum
    Tullidge, *History of Salt Lake City*, p. 285
31. *Army and Navy Journal*, December 15, 1866
32. John Kelly, affidavit to Abraham C. Anderson, *Daily Bulletin* (Blackfoot, Idaho), January 19, 1929
33. *Deseret News*, February 4, 1863
34. H. W. Halleck, General-in-chief, letter to Brigadier-General George Wright, Commanding Department of the Pacific, San Francisco
    Tullidge, *History of Salt Lake City*, p. 287
35. Whitney, *History of Utah*, Vol. II, p. 80
36. Verite, Letter No. 2, "The Return of the Wounded Volunteers to Camp Douglas," penned February 9, 1863, Salt Lake City, Utah, published in the *Daily Alta Californian*
37. Rogers, *Soldiers of the Overland*, p. 75
    Alexander Stalker, letter in Journal History, January 29, 1863
    William G. Nelson, letter in Journal History, January 29, 1863

38. Tullidge, editor, *Tullidge's Quarterly Magazine,* Vol. I, p. 196
39. Whitney, *History of Utah,* Vol. II, p. 80
40. Colonel James H. Martineau, report quoted in Tullidge, *History of Salt Lake City,* p. 290
41. Crouch, "Autobiography," MS, p. 33
42. Connor, letter February 6th, 1863 to Lt. Col. R. C. Drum
    Tullidge, *History of Salt Lake City,* p. 286
43. *Deseret News,* February 11, 1863
44. Rogers, *Soldiers of the Overland,* p. 73
    Deseret News, August 5, 1863
    A. Stalker, letter in Journal History, February 8, 1863
    S. Roskelly, letter in Journal History, February 8, 1863

Chapter Fifteen

1. Crouch, "Autobiography," MS, pp. 26-28
2. Tullidge, *History of Salt Lake City,* p. 316
3. Journal History, March 9, 1863
4. *Deseret News,* March 11, 1863
5. Journal History, March 9, 1863
6. Stenhouse, *Rocky Mountain Saints,* p. 607n
7. Lyman, "Journals," MSS, March 27, 1863
8. *Deseret News,* April 8, 1863
   Journal History, April 2, 1863
9. Crouch, "Autobiography," MS, p. 23
10. *Deseret News,* April 1, 1863
11. Ibid.
12. Ibid.
13. Crouch, "Autobiography," MS, p. 25
14. Rogers, *Soldiers of the Overland,* p. 91
    Gottfredson, *Indian Depredations in Utah,* p. 117
15. Gottfredson, *Indian Depredations in Utah,* pp. 115-117
16. Ibid., p. 116
17. Ibid., p. 117
18. Ibid., p. 118
19. *Deseret News,* April 22, 1863
20. Ibid.
21. *Utah Genealogical and Historical Magazine,* Vol. XXVI, p. 156
22. Journal History, May 19, 1863

23. Ibid.

   Ibid., September 4, 1862

   Ibid., September 25, 1862

24. Hamilton Gardner, *History of Lehi* (Salt Lake City, 1913) p. 163

25. *Deseret News,* June 17, 1863

26. Ibid.

27. Gardner, *History of Lehi,* pp. 163-164

28. *Deseret News,* June 17, 1863

29. Ibid.

30. Crouch, "Autobiography," MS, p. 24

31. Gardner, *History of Lehi,* p. 164

32. *Deseret News,* June 17, 1863

33. John Bennion, "Journal," MSS, Book 3, p. 19

34. Tooele County Recorder's Office, Patent Record Book 1, Patent 1311, p. 442,

35. Van Alfen, "Thesis," p. 54, quoting John Bennion, used by permission

36. Fitz Hugh Ludlow, "Among the Mormons," *The Atlantic Monthly,* Vol. XIII (April 1864), p. 492

37. Fitz Hugh Ludlow, *The Heart of the Continent: A Record of Travel Across the Plains and in Oregon, With an Examination of the Mormon Principle* (New York, 1870), pp. 353-356

38. Ibid., p. 357-358

39. Ibid., pp. 360-361

40. Ibid., pp. 361-364

41. Ibid., pp. 364-375

42. Ludlow, "Among the Mormons," p. 492

43. Feramorz Little, "Letterbook, 1863 - 1877," MS, p. 39

44. Journal History, December 24, 1864

45. *Deseret News,* December 28, 1864

46. Utah Territory, Records of Marks and Brands, December 29, 1849, to December 9, 1874, pp. 37, 113

47. Samuel Bowles, *Across the Continent: A Summer's Journey to the Rocky Mountains, The Mormons, and the Pacific States, With Speaker Colfax* (Springfield, Massachusetts, 1866), pp. 128-129

48. *Utica Morning Herald And Daily Gazette,* August 21, 1865

49. *Springfield Republican,* August, 1865

50. Albert D. Richardson, *Beyond the Mississippi: From the Great River to the Great Ocean. Life and Adventure on the Prairies, Mountains, and Pacific Coast* (Hartford, Connecticut, 1869), pp. 468-469

51. Van Alfen, "Thesis," p. 96, used by permission

52. Whitney, *History of Utah,* Vol. II, p. 146

53. Birney and Kelly, *Holy Murder,* pp. 226-228,

54. quoted in op. cit.

55. Interview with John Rockwell, Lehi, Utah; known family information, used by permission

56. Ibid.

57. *Union Vedette,* October 25, 1866

58. Stenhouse, *Rocky Mountain Saints*

59. *Investigation Into the Murder of Dr. J. K. Robinson, Who Was Assassinated On the Night of October 22d, 1866, near the corner of East Temple and 3d South or Emigration Streets, had before Jeter Clinton, Coroner for the County of Great Salt Lake, Chief Justice Titus, and Judge McCurdy, commencing Tuesday, October 23d, at 11 o'clock A.M.* (Salt Lake City, 1866)

60. Birney and Kelly, *Holy Murder,* p. 230

61. *Union Vedette,* December 13, 1866

62. Salt Lake County Death Records, No. 2897

63. Op. cit.

64. Achilles, *Destroying Angels of Mormondom,* p. 34

65. Hosea Stout, "Journal," Vol. VIII, p. 21
Stout, *On the Mormon Frontier, the Diary of Hosea Stout,* Vol. II, pp. 695, 702

66. *Valley Tan,* April 19, 1859
Stout, *On the Mormon Frontier, the Diary of Hosea Stout,* Vol. II, p. 695

67. Achilles, *Destroying Angels of Mormondom,* p. 34
Bancroft, *History of Utah,* p. 629n
Beadle, *Life in Utah,* p. 212

68. Phil Robinson, *Sinners and Saints* (London, 1883), pp. 235-238

69. Ibid., p. 245

70. *New Republic,* May 30, 1934, Vol. LXXIX, p. 82

71. Van Alfen, "Thesis," p. 117, used by permission

72. Salt Lake County Abstracts, Plats and Surveys, Book A2, p. 73
Salt Lake County Deeds and Transfers, Book C, pp. 579-580

73. Alexander Toponce, *Reminiscences of Alexander Toponce, Pioneer, 1839-1923* (Salt Lake City, 1923), p. 142

74. Ibid., pp. 142-143

75. Robert A. Griffen, "Introduction" to 1971 Edition, Ibid., pp. vii-viii

76. Ibid., p. vi

77. C. G. Coutant, *The History of Wyoming From The Earliest Known Discoveries* (Laramie, 1899), three volumes, Vol. I, pp. 647-648

78. Hickman, *Brigham's Destroying Angel,* pp. 174-175

79. Op. cit.

80. Volney King, "Millard County, 1851-1875," *Utah Humanities Review,* Vol. I, No. 1 (October 1947), pp. 381-382

81. [William Elkanah Waters,] An Officer of the U. S. Army, *Life Among The Mormons, And A March To Their Zion: To Which is Added a Chapter on the Indians of the Plains and Mountains of the West* (New York, 1868), pp. 186-187

82. Herman Francis Reinhart, *The Golden Frontier; The Recollections of Herman Francis Reinhart,* 1851-1869, edited by Doyce B. Nunis, Jr. (Austin, Texas, 1962)

83. Reinhart, *The Golden Frontier,* pp. 280-281

84. Gardner, *History of Lehi,* pp. 204-205

85. *Deseret News,* December 12, 1868

86. Op. cit., p. 205

87. Op. cit.

88. Gardner, *History of Lehi,* pp. 204-205

89. *Deseret News,* December 17, 1868

90. Ibid., December 18, 1868

91. Gardner, *History of Lehi,* p. 206

92. *Deseret News,* January 29, 1869

93. Ibid., July 8, 1869

94. *Hamilton Empire,* July 1869, paraphrased in *Deseret News,* July 8, 1869

95. Deseret Agricultural and Manufacturing Society, Record, p. 109
    Journal History, October 5, 1869

96. Van Alfen, "Thesis," p. 74, used by permission

97. *Salt Lake Tribune,* February 24, 1924

98. James P. Sharp, "The Old Man's Story," *Improvement Era,* Vol. XLVI (1943), pp. 85, 100-101

99. James P. Sharp, "Singing Wires," *Improvement Era,* Vol. XLVII (1944), pp. 754, 794

100. Op. cit., p.101

101. Ibid., p. 85

102. Sharp, "Singing Wires," *Improvement Era,* Vol. XLVII, p. 794

103. Nicholas Van Alfen, *Porter Rockwell, Mormon Frontier Marshal and Body Guard of Joseph Smith* (Salt Lake City, 1971), p. 53, used by permission from the author

104. O. J. Hollister, *Life of Schuyler Colfax* (New York, 1886), p. 342

105. *Deseret News,* May 3, 1870
     Tullidge's Histories, Vol. II, pp. 101-102

106. *Deseret News,* May 4, 1870
     Deseret News Weekly, May 11, 1870

107. Tooele County Recorder's office, Ophir Mining District, Record Book A, p. 182

    See Tooele County Deeds, Book D, p. 445

    Also Tooele County Deeds, Book E, pp. 153-154, 429

108. *Salt Lake Herald,* October 9, 1870

109. *Cincinnati Commercial,* October 27, 1871

    Townsend, *Mormon Trials at Salt Lake City,* pp. 17-19, 39

110. Townsend, *Mormon Trials at Salt Lake City,* pp. 17-19, 39

111. Ibid.

112. Ibid.

113. Hickman, *Brigham's Destroying Angel,* p. 191

114. *Salt Lake Tribune,* October 30, 1871

115. Walker, "Journal," p. 541

116. Bean, *Autobiography,* p. 158

117. *Cincinnati Commercial,* October 27, 1871

    Townsend, *Mormon Trials at Salt Lake City,* pp. 17-19, 39

118. Ibid.

119. Young, *Manuscript History of Brigham Young,* 1871, Vol. II, pp. 2101-2102

120. Whitney, *History of Utah,* Vol. II, p. 658n

121. Ibid., p. 658

122. John Codman, *The Round Trip By Way of Panama Through California, Oregon, Nevada, Utah, Idaho, and Colorado with Notes on Railroads, Commerce, Agriculture, Mining, Scenery, and People* (New York, 1881), pp. 195-196

123. *Utah: A Guide to the State,* compiled by Workers of the Writers' Program of the Work Projects Administration for the State of Utah (New York, 1941), p. 288

124. Olive W. Burt, collector and editor, *American Murder Ballads and Their Stories* (New York, 1958), pp. 114-115

125. W. G. Tittsworth, *Outskirt Episodes* (Avoca, Iowa, 1927), pp. 31-32

126. *Salt Lake Tribune,* June 11, 1878

127. James T. Harwood, "A Basket of Chips (1860-1940)," MS

128. Glynn Bennion, "Suggestion and the Quick Draw," *Salt Lake Tribune,* February 24, 1924

129. John F. Everet, Springville, Utah, interview with Nicholas Van Alfen in 1938, used by permission

130. Austin Gudmundsen, "Journal," MS, used by permission

131. Bennion, "Suggestion and the Quick Draw," *Salt Lake Tribune,* February 24, 1924

132. Interview with Glen Trane, Lehi, Utah, relating story of Susan Trane, his grandmother; used by permission

133. Ibid.

134. Bennion, "Suggestion and the Quick Draw," *Salt Lake Tribune,* February 24, 1924

135. "Leaves from Old Albums," *Deseret News,* December 21, 1918

136. Van Alfen, "Thesis," p. 89, used by permission

137. Bennion, "Suggestion and the Quick Draw," *Salt Lake Tribune,* February 24, 1924

138. Van Alfen, "Thesis," p. 55, used by permission
139. Ibid., p. 84
140. Ibid., pp. 71-73
141. Ibid., p. 73
142. Ibid.
143. Ibid., p. 90A
144. Ibid., p. 73
145. *Utah Genealogical and Historical Magazine,* Vol. XXVI, p. 156
146. Elijah Averett; transcribed by Murray Averett, his son; "The Averett Narrative," MS, p. 21
147. *Utah Genealogical and Historical Magazine,* Vol. XXVI, p. 156
148. William Clayton, "Letterbook, 1860-1879," MS, p. 287, June 22, 1873
149. Gottfredson, *Indian Depredations in Utah,* p. 330
150. Bean, *Autobiography,* p. 171
151. Ibid., p. 178
152. Gottfredson, *Indian Depredations in Utah,* pp. 330-332
153. Ibid., p. 331
154. Bean, *Autobiography,* p. 179
155. Ibid., p. 180
156. Van Alfen, "Thesis," p. 83, used by permission
157. Ibid.
158. *Journal of Discourses,* Vol. XIX, p. 37
159. Tooele County Deeds, Deed Book X, pp. 494-495, 517-518
160. Ibid.
161. Interview with John Rockwell, Lehi, Utah; known family information, used by permission

Chapter 16

1. Utah County and Territorial Criminal Records, File 81, File 82 (The People vs. O. P. Rockwell, etc.), Utah County Clerk's Office, Provo, Utah

Andrew Jenson, *Church Chronology* (Salt Lake City, 1914), p. 101

2. *Salt Lake Tribune,* September 30, 1877, p. 4

3. Ibid., October 6, 1877

4. Ibid., June 12, 1878, p. 2

5. Ibid., June 11, 1878

6. Ibid.

7. "Court Answer, Third District Court, Territory of Utah, County of Salt Lake, Horace Rockwell, Pltf, vs. Orin (sic) p. Rockwell, Defendant," October 13, 1877, CHD

8. *Utah Genealogical and Historical Magazine,* Vol. XXVI, p. 156

9. *Salt Lake Tribune,* June 11, 1878

10. Ibid.

11. *Deseret Evening News,* June 10, 1878
    Deseret News Weekly, June 12, 1878
12. *Salt Lake Tribune,* June 11, 1878
13. *Deseret News Weekly,* June 12, 1878
14. *Salt Lake Daily Herald,* June 11, 1878
15. *Salt Lake Tribune,* June 12, 1878
16. Op. cit.
17. Ibid.
18. *Salt Lake Tribune,* June 13, 1878
19. Ibid., June 18, 1878
20. Ibid., June 13, 1878
21. Ibid., June 18, 1878
22. Ibid.

References to Notes

Note 1

Deseret News, August 31, 1935

Note 2

Cited in text.

Note 3

1. DHC, Vol. III, pp. 178-182
2. Allen Joseph Stout, "Journal," MS, p. 7
3. Cowdery, *Defence in a Rehearsal of My Grounds,* p. 2
    Chad J. Flake, *A Mormon Bibliography, 1830-1930* (Salt Lake City, 1978), pp. 182, 455
    Richard Lloyd Anderson, "I Have A Question," *The Ensign,* Vol. XVII, No. IV (April, 1987), pp. 23-25
4. *Document Showing,* etc., pp. 111, 114, 117, respectively
5. Ibid., pp. 97-102
6. Swartzell, *Mormonism Exposed,* pp. 17-18
7. John Whitmer, "History of the Church," Chapter XX (unpublished chapter)
8. Luman Andros Shurtliff, "Biographical Sketch," MS, p. 33.
9. Ibid.
10. Allen Joseph Stout, "Journal," MS, pp. 101-102
    "Items of Personal History of the Editor," *The Return* (October 1889), Vol. I, pp. 145-146

11. Bennett, *History of the Saints*, p. 267

    Achilles, *Destroying Angels of Mormondom,* pp. 8-9

12. Reed Peck, "Mormons So Called," MS, pp. 49-50

Note 4

1. *History of Caldwell and Livingston Counties,* pp. 145-159
2. Ibid.
3. Roberts, *Comprehensive History of the Church*
4. Jenson, *Church Encyclopaedia,* Book I, p. 672
5. Ibid., p. 671
6. *Times and Seasons,* Vol. I, No. 10 (August 1840), pp. 146-149
7. Ibid., p. 148
8. Op. cit.
9. Jenson, *Church Encyclopaedia,* Book I, p. 673
10. *Times and Seasons,* Vol. 1, No. 10 (August 1840), pp. 146-149
11. DHC, Vol. III, pp. 186-187
12. Amanda Smith, affidavit, *History of Caldwell and Livingston Counties,* p. 156
13. *Times and Seasons,* Vol. I, No. 10 (August 1840), pp. 148-149
14. Jenson, *Church Encyclopaedia,* Book I, p. 673
15. Op. cit., p. 150
16. Ibid., p. 147
17. Lee, *Mormonism Unveiled,* pp. 79-81
18. Jenson, *Church Encyclopaedia,* Book I, p. 676
19. Wilford Woodruff, *History of His Life and Labors as Recorded in his Daily Journals,* edited by Mathias F. Cowley (Salt Lake City, 1909), p. 103

    Tullidge, editor, *Tullidge's Quarterly Magazine,* Vol. III, p. 123

20. Amanda Smith, as quoted in *History of Caldwell and Livingston Counties,* p. 158
21. Jenson, *The Historical Record,* Vol. VIII, p. 675
22. *History of Caldwell County,* p. 158
23. Op. cit., pp. 674-681
24. Ibid., p. 682
25. Ibid., p. 683
26. *The Missouri Historical Review,* Vol. XIII, No. 3 (April, 1919), pp. 298, 303-305

    Amanda Smith, as quoted in *History of Caldwell and Livingston Counties,* p. 156

Note 5

Cited in text.

Note 6

Monte B. McClaws, "The Attempted Assassination of Missouri's Ex-Governor Lilburn W. Boggs," *The Missouri Historical Review,* Vol. LX (October 1965) pp. 59-60, 62

Note 7

DHC, Vol. VI, pp. 446-447

Note 8

1. DHC, Vol. VI, p. 490
2. Ibid., p. 491
3. Ibid., pp. 457-458

Note 9

DHC, Vol. VI

Note 10

Clayton, *Journal,* pp. 234-235

Note 11

1. DHC, Vol. VI, p. 571
2. Ibid., pp. 571-572
3. Ibid., p. 574
4. Ibid., p. 586
5. Ibid., p. 592

Note 12

DHC, Vol. VI, p. 600

Note 13

DHC, Vol. VI, pp. 602-603

Note 14

Tullidge, *Life of Brigham Young, p. 115*

Note 15

1. *Times and Seasons,* Vol. IV, pp. 183-184
2. Ibid., Vol. III, pp. 615-618
3. Ibid.
4. Ibid., p. 617
5. Ibid., p. 618
6. Ibid., Vol. VI, pp. 773-774
7. Ibid., pp. 774-775
8. Ibid., pp. 775-776

Note 16

1. DHC, Vol. IV, p. 549
2. J. B. Backenstos, clerk of District Court, District Court Records of Nauvoo, November 29, 1842, CHD
3. Ibid.
4. DHC, Vol. V, p. 197
5. Op. cit.
6. Op. cit., p. 199
7. Op. cit.
8. "Historical Research File C14-3 Amos Davis -- Miller, Rowena, J., Study 30, Oct 1965, Rev. 1967," MS, CHD
9. Ibid.
10. Ibid.

Note 17

Joseph Smith III, *Joseph Smith III and the Restoration,* pp. 77-79

Note 18

Clayton, *Journal,* pp. 189-201

Note 19

1. Clayton, *Journal,* pp. 210-211
2. Appleton Milo Harmon, "Diary," MS, p. 275

Note 20

Clayton, *Journal,* p. 234

Note 21

1. Bancroft, *History of California,* Vol. VI, p. 56
2. Gillespie, "Vigilante Committee," MS, p. 4
3. J. H. Carson, *Early Recollections of the Mines, and a Description of the Great Tulare Valley* (Stockton, 1852), p. 4
4. Bancroft, *History of California,* Vol. VI, p. 57

Henry G. Boyle, "Diary," MS, p. 41

Journal History, June 5, 1848

Jenson, *Church Encyclopedia,* p. 934

Bigler, "Day Book and Diary," MS, p. 78-79

Oregon Bulletin, May 12, 1851

John Augustus Sutter, *New Helvetia Diary,* p. 56

John Augustus Sutter, *A Nation's Benefactor: Gen'l John A Sutter. Memorial of His Life and Public Services, and An Appeal to Congress, to Citizens of California, and the People of the United States, by His Fellow Pioneers of California* (New York, 1880)

Frank Soule, John H. Gihon, and James Nisbet, *The Annals of San Francisco; Containing a Summary of the History of the First Discovery, Settlement, Progress, and Present Condition of California, Complete History of All the Important Events Connected With Its Great City; To Which Are Added, Biographical Memoirs of Some Prominent Citizens* (New York, 1855), pp. 203, 220

Mariano Guadalupe Vallejo, "Documentary History of California," MS, Vol. XXXV, p. 47

Bassham, letter to Cooper, May 15, 1848, in Vallejo, "Documentary History of California," MS, Vol. IV, Vol. XII, p. 344

Mariano Guadalupe Vallejo, *Report on the Derivation and Definition of the Names of the Several Counties of California* (San Jose, 1850)

Coutts, "Diary," MS, p. 113

Charles L. Ross, "Experiences of a Pioneer of 1847 in California," MS, pp. 11-12

Larkin, "Documentary History of California," MS, Vol. VI, pp. 74, 111, 116, 144

Larkin, letter to Mason from San Jose, in Larkin, "Documentary History of California," Vol. I, p. 505

D. L., *The Digger's Hand-Book and Truth About California* (Sydney, 1849), p. 53

George McKinstry, *Lancaster Examiner; Stockton Independent,* October 19, 1875

Barstow, "Statistics," MS, pp. 3-4

Franklin Tuthill, *The History of California* (San Francisco, 1866), pp. 235-244

Henry I. Simpson, *The Emigrant's Guide to the Gold Mines. Three Weeks in the Gold Mines, Adventures with the Gold Diggers of California in August, 1848* (New York, 1848), p. 4

Benjamin Hayes, *Pioneer Notes from the Diaries of Judge Benjamin Hayes, 1849-1875* (later privately published at Los Angeles, 1929)

Revue des Deux Mondes, February 1, 1849, p. 469

Quarterly Review, No. 91, 1852, p. 508

John Shertzer Hittell, *Mining in the Pacific States of North America* (San Francisco, 1861), p. 17

Overland Monthly, Vol. VI, pp. 12-13

Ryan, *Judges and Criminals,* pp. 72-77

American Quat. Reg., Vol. II, pp. 288-295, with reports of Larkin, Mason, Jones, and Paymaster Rich

Samuel Hopkins Willey, *Two Historical Discourses Occasioned by the Close of the First Ten Years' Ministry in California, Preached in the Howard Street Presbyterian Church* (San Francisco, 1859), pp. 12-17

Samuel Hopkins Willey, *Thirty Years in California, A Contribution to the History of the State from 1849 to 1879* (San Francisco, 1879)

Samuel Hopkins Willey, *The Transaction Period of California from a Province of Mexico in 1846 to a State of the American Union in 1850* (San Francisco, 1901)

William Gleason, *History of the Catholic Church in California* (San Francisco, 1859), Vol. II, pp. 175-193

William Tecumseh Sherman, *Memoirs of General William T. Sherman* (New York, 1875), two volumes, Vol. I, pp. 46-49, 56-57

San Francisco Directory, 1852-1853, pp. 8-9

San Francisco News, Vol. II, pp. 142-148, with extract of letter from San Francisco, May 27, 1848

Vallejo Recorder (Vallejo, California), March 14, 1848

Gillespie, "Vigilante Committee," MS, pp. 3-4

Findla, "Statistics," MS, pp. 4-6

John A. Swan, "A Trip to the Gold Mines," MS, p. 2 (reprint of 1849 California original: San Francisco, 1960)

Adam Treadwell Green, *Seventy Years in California* (San Francisco, privately printed 1923), original MS: p. 11

Frisbie, "Reminiscences," MS, pp. 30-32

Hypolite Ferry, *La California* (Venezia: Dalla Tipografia Fontana, 1851), pp. 325-326

Edward E. Dunbar, *The Romance of the Age; or, the Discovery of Gold in California* (New York, 1867), p. 102

Fourgeaud, "The Prospects of California" (serialized article), *California Star,* April 1, 1848

E. Gould Buffum, *Six Months in the Gold Mines: From a Journal of Three Years Residence in Upper and Lower California, 1847-8-9* (Philadelphia, 1850), p. 68

History of Sacramento County, California (Oakland, 1880)

Alexander Forbes, *California: A History of Upper and Lower California from Their First Discovery to the Present Time, Comprising An Account of the Climate, Soil, Natural Productions, Agriculture, Commerce, &c.*, pp. 17-18

George Quayle Cannon, writings from the *Western Standard* (Liverpool, 1884)

G. Lauts, *Kalifornia door den hoogleeraar G Lauts* (Amsterdam, 1849), pp. 24-31

William Redmond Ryan, *Personal Adventures in Upper and Lower California, in 1848-9; with the Author's Experiences at the Mines* (London, 1850)

Zoeth Skinner Eldredge, *The Beginnings of San Francisco from the Expedition of Anza, 1774, to the City Charter of April 15, 1850* (San Francisco, 1912)

Zoeth Skinner Eldredge, *History of California* (New York, 1915), five volumes

John Shertzer Hittell, *A History of the City of San Francisco* (San Francisco, 1878)

John Shertzer Hittell, *Marshall's Gold Discovery. A Lecture Before the Society of California Pioneers* (San Francisco, 1893)

An Illustrated History of Sonoma County, California (Chicago, 1889)

R. N. Willcox, *Reminiscences of California Life. Being an Abridged Description of Scenes Which the Author Has Passed Through in California, and Other Lands. With Quotations from Other Authors* (Avery, Ohio, 1897)

Henry K. Norton, *The Story of California From the Earliest Days to the Present* (Chicago, 1913)

Northern California; A Memorial and Biographical History of Northern California. Containing a History of This Important Section of the Pacific Coast from the Earliest Period of its Occupancy to the Present Time, Together with Glimpses of its Prospective Future (Chicago, 1891)

Edmund Randolph, *Address on the History of California, From the Discovery of the Country to the Year 1849, Delivered Before the Society of California Pioneers, At Their Celebration of the Tenth Anniversary of the Admission of the State of California into the Union, by Edmund Randolph, Esq.* (San Francisco, September 10, 1860)

Josiah Royce, *California From the Conquest in 1846 to the Second Vigilance Committee in San Francisco* (Boston, New York, Cambridge, 1886)

Robert T. Greenhow, *The History of Florida, Louisiana, Texas, and California, and of the Adjacent Countries, Including the Whole Valley of the Mississippi* (New York, 1856), Vol. 1

James Miller Guinn, *Coast Counties. Histories of the State of California. Biographical Record of Coast Counties. An Historical Story of the State's Growth from Its Earliest Settlement to the Present Time, Containing the Biographies of Well Known Citizens of the Past and Present* (Chicago, 1904)

James Miller Guinn, *A History of the State of California, and Biographical Record of Oakland and Environs, Also, Containing Biographies of Well-Known Citizens of the Past and Present* (Los Angeles, 1907), two volumes

James Miller Guinn, *History of the State of California and Biographical Record of the San Joaquin Valley, California* (Chicago, 1905)

Theodore Henry Hittell, *History of California,* (San Francisco, 1898), four volumes

William Kelly, *An Excursion to California Over the Prairie, Rocky Mountains, and Great Sierra Nevada. With a Stroll Through the Diggings and Ranches of That Country* (London, 1851), two volumes

E. S. Kelly, *A Stroll Through the Diggings of California* (London, 1852)

Charles Nordhoff, *Northern California, Oregon, and the Sandwich Islands* (New York, London, 1877)

Lucia Norman, *A Youth's History of California from the Earliest Period of Its Discovery to the Present Time* (San Francisco, 1867)

Oscar Tully Shuck, *Bench and Bar California; History, Anecdotes, Reminiscences* (San Francisco, 1889)

Oscar Tully Shuck, *California Anthology; Or, Striking Thoughts on Many Themes, Carefully Selected from California Writers and Speakers* (San Francisco, 1880)

Oscar Tully Shuck, *The California Scrap-Book: A Repository of Useful Information and Select Reading. Comprising Choice Selections of Prose and Poetry, Tales and Anecdotes, Historical, Descriptive, Humorous, and Sentimental Pieces, Mainly Culled From the Various Newspapers and Periodicals of the Pacific Coast* (San Francisco, 1869)

Oscar Tully Shuck, *Historical Abstract of San Francisco* (San Francisco, 1897), three volumes

Oscar Tully Shuck, *History of the Bench and Bar of California, Being Biographies of Many Remarkable Men* (Los Angeles, 1901)

Oscar Tully Shuck, *Representative and Leading Men of the Pacific: Being Original Sketches of the Lives and Characters of the Principal Men, Living and Deceased, of the Pacific States and Territories — Pioneers, Politicians, Lawyers, Doctors, Merchants, Orators, and Divines — to Which Are Added Their Speeches, Addresses, Orations, Eulogies, Lectures, and Poems, Upon a Variety of Subjects* (San Francisco, 1870)

Octavius Thorndike Howe, *Argonauts of '49; History and Adventures of the Emigrant Companies from Massachusetts, 1849-1850* (San Francisco, 1870)

Henry Howe, *Historical Collections of the Great West: Containing Narratives of the Most Important Events in Western History* (Cincinnati, 1854)

John Williamson Palmer, *The New and Old; Or, California and India in Romantic Aspects* (New York, London, 1859)

Charles Edward Pancoast, *A Quaker Forty-Niner; The Adventures of Charles Edward Pancoast on the American Frontier,* edited by Anna Paschall Hannum (Philadelphia, London, 1930)

Jessie Heaton Parkinson, *Adventuring in California, Yesterday, Today, and Day Before Yesterday* (San Francisco, 1921)

R. R. Parkinson, *Pen Portraits. Autobiographies of State Officers, Legislators, Prominent Business and Professional Men of the Capital of the State of California; Also of Newspaper Proprietors, Editors, and Members of the Corps Reportorial* (San Francisco, 1878)

George Frederick Parsons, *The Life and Adventures of James W. Marshall, The Discoverer of Gold in California* (Sacramento, 1870)

Lawson B. Patterson, *Twelve Years in the Mines of California; Embracing General View of the Gold Region, With Practical Observations on Hill, Placer, and Quartz Diggings; and Notes of the Origin of Gold Deposits* (Cambridge, 1862)

George Payson [Ralph Raven, pseudonym], *Golden Dreams and Leaden Realities* (New York, 1853)

Robert A. Thompson, *Historical and Descriptive Sketch of Sonoma County, California* (Philadelphia, 1877)

John Whipple Dwinelle, *The Colonial History of the City of San Francisco, Being A Synthetic Argument in the District Court of the United States for the Northern District of California, for Four Square Leagues of Land Claimed by that City* (San Francisco, 1863)

Gertrude Atherton, *California, an Intimate History* (New York, London, 1914)

Gertrude Atherton, *The Californians* (New York, London, 1898)

John Woodhouse Audubon, *Audubon's Western Journal: 1849-50, Being the MS. Record of a Trip from New York to Texas, and an Over-Land Journey Through Mexico and Arizona to the Gold-Fields of California* (Cleveland, 1906)

John Woodhouse Audubon, *Illustrated Notes of an Expedition through Mexico and California* (New York, 1852)

James J. Ayres, *Gold and Sunshine; Reminiscences of Early California* (Boston, 1922)

Chauncy L. Canfield, *The Diary of a Forty-Niner* (San Francisco, New York, 1906)

Elisha Smith Capron, *History of California, from Its Discovery to the Present Time* (Boston, 1854)

Robert Glass Cleland, *A History of California: The American Period* (New York, 1922)

George B. Crane, *A Life History Consisting of Incidents and Experiences in the Life of George B. Crane, with Comments on a Variety of Topics. Written by Himself for the Information and Entertainment of His Family and Descendants* (San Jose, 1886)

James M. Crane, *The Past, the Present and the Future of the Pacific* (San Francisco, 1856)

William Heath Davis, *Sixty Years in California; A History of Events and Life in California: Personal, Political, and Military, Under the Mexican Regime; During the Quasi-Military Government of the Territory by the United States, and After the Admission of the State into the Union, Being a Compilation By a Witness of the*

Events Described (San Francisco, 1889; updated in 1929 as *Seventy-Five Years in California*)

Jennett Blakeslee Frost, *The Gem of the Mines. A Thrilling Narrative of California Life. Composed of Scenes and Incidents Which Passed Under the Immediate Observation of the Author During Five Years Residence in That State in the Early Days* (Hartford, Connecticut, 1866)

John Frost, *History of the State of California, from the Period of the Conquest by Spain, to her Occupation by the United States of America; Containing An Account of the Discovery of the Immense Gold Mines and Placers* (Auburn, New York, 1850)

Burton B. Porter, "One of the People; His Own Story," MS, 1907

5. *California Star*, May 27, 1848

6. Gudde, *Bigler's Chronicles of the West*, p. 111

7. J. Tyrwhitt Brooks, *Four Months Among the Gold-finders in California: Being the Diary of an Expedition from San Francisco to the Gold Districts* (Philadelphia, 1849), pp. 14-15

8. Bancroft, *History of California*, Vol. VI, p. 60

9. Op. cit.

10. Larkin, letter from San Francisco to Secretary Buchanan, June 1, 1848, "Documentary History of California"

11. Bancroft, *History of California*, Vol. VI, p. 61

Hypolite Ferry, *La California* (Venezia: Dalla Tipografia Fontana, 1851), pp. 306-313

Fayette Robinson, *California and Its Gold Regions; With A Geographical and Topographical View of the Country, Its Mineral and Agricultural Resources* (New York, 1849), pp. 23-30

Joseph Warren Revere, *A Tour of Duty in California; Including a Description of the Gold Region and An Account of the Voyage Around Cape Horn; With Notices of Lower California, the Gulf and Pacific Coasts, and the Principal Events Attending the Conquest of California* (New York, 1849), p. 254

12. Bancroft, *History of California*, Vol. VI, p. 61

13. George McKinstry, *Lancaster Examiner, Stockton Independent*, October 19, 1875

14. *Californian* (newspaper), August 4, 5, 14; September 5, 1848

Albert Gallatin Brackett, *History of the United States Cavalry* (New York, 1865), pp. 125-127

15. Elisha O. Crosby, Statistics, MS, p. 12

16. *First Steamship Pioneers*, p. 124

17. *San Jose Pioneer*, January 27, 1877

Bancroft, *History of California*, pp. 62-63, 62n

18. C. L. Ross, "Experiences from 1847," MS

19. J. Belden, letter to Larkin, in Larkin, "Documentary History of California," MS, p. 219

20. Bancroft, *History of California,* Vol. VI, p. 64-65, 65n

21. J. D. Borthwick, *Three Years in California* (Edinburgh, London 1857), pp. 247-248

    Reverend Walter Colton, *Three Years in California* (New York, 1850)

    Revue des Deux Mondes, February 1, 1849, p. 469

22. Vallejo's Oration at Sonoma, July 4, 1876, reported in *Sonoma Democrat,* July 8, 1876

Note 22

1. Interview with John Rockwell, Lehi, Utah; information from family tradition, used by permission

2. Journal History, April 11, 1849

Note 23

    Captain Rufus Ingalls, letter to Major General Thomas S. Jesup, U. S. Senate, "Report to the Quartermaster General," *Executive Document No. 1,* 34th Congress, 1st Session, 1855, p. 161

Note 24

1. *Council Bluffs Bugle,* 1857
    The Mormon, April 18, 1857

2. *Millennial Star,* Vol. XIX, p. 443
    Crescent City Oracle, May 22, 1856

3. *Council Bluffs Bugle,* 1857
    The Mormon, April 18, 1857

4. Jacques, "Some Reminiscences," *Salt Lake Herald,* December 8, 1879

5. *Crescent City Oracle,* May 22, 1856

6. Wharton, letter to Deas, *Transaction of the Kansas State Historical Society,* Vol. IV, pp. 494-495

7. *New York Herald,* July 25, 1857, Julia Ann Babbitt

8. Jacques, "Some Reminiscences," *Salt Lake Herald,* December 8, 1879

9. Ibid.

10. Joel Hills Johnson, "Journal," MS, p. 53
    Joseph L. Heywood, "Diary," MS, p. 30

11. *Millennial Star,* Vol. XIX, p. 443
    Crescent City Oracle, May 22, 1856

12. Journal History, October 4, 1856

13. Johnson, "Journal," MS, p. 41

14. Ibid., pp. 50, 53

15. U. S. Senate, "Report of the Secretary of the Interior," *Executive Document No. 5,* 34th Congress, 3rd Session, 1856, pp. 650-654

U. S. House of Representatives, "Report of the Secretary of the Interior," *Executive Document No. 1,* 34th Congress, 3rd Session, 1856, pp. 650-654

Note 25

Vaux, *The Contributor,* Vol. III, p. 54

Note 26

1. Ginn, "Mormon and Indian Wars," MS, Forward by Newbern I. Butt

2. Richard E. Lingenfelter, *1858-1958 The Newspapers of Nevada, A History and Bibliography* (San Francisco, 1964), pp. 80, 83, 88, 90, 91, 93

3. Ibid.

See also Thomas H. Thompson and Albert A. West, *History of Nevada, with Illustrations and Biographical Sketches of Its Prominent Men and Pioneers* (Oakland, 1881), p. 326

Wells Drury, *An Editor of the Comstock Lode* (Palo Alto, 1948), p. 272

Note 27

1. *Union* (St. George, Utah), November 21, 1896

2. Ginn, "Mormon and Indian Wars," MS, p. 22

3. John I. Ginn, letter to editor of *Valley Tan,* April 26, 1859

4. Op. cit.

5. Hickman, *Brigham's Destroying Angel,* Appendix F, p. 207

6. Ginn, "Mormon and Indian Wars," MS, p. 22

7. John Cradlebaugh, *Utah and the Mormons; Speech of Honorable John Cradlebaugh, of Nevada, on the Admission of Utah as a State. Delivered in the House of Representatives, February 7, 1863,* pp. 64-65

8. Anthony Metcalf, *Ten Years Before the Mast. Shipwrecks and Adventures at Sea! Religious Customs of the People of India and Burma's Empire. How I Became a Mormon and Why I Became an Infidel!* (Malad City, Idaho, 1888)

9. Ann Eliza Young, *Wife No. 19* (Hartford, Connecticut, 1876), pp. 272-273

10. R. N. Baskin, *Reminiscences of Early Utah* (Salt Lake City, 1914), p. 151

11. R. DeWitt Talmage, *"Mormonism." A Sermon Preached by the Rev. R. DeWitt Talmage, D.D., in the Tabernacle, Brooklyn, N.Y., on the 26th of September, 1880* (Brooklyn, 1880), p. 8

12. *Salt Lake Tribune,* October 10, 1878
    Salt Lake Daily Herald, October 11, 1878
13. *Salt Lake Tribune,* October 11, 1878
    Salt Lake Daily Herald, October 11, 1878
14. *Salt Lake Tribune,* October 12, 1878
    Salt Lake Daily Herald, October 12, 1878
15. *Salt Lake Tribune,* October 10, 1878
16. Guy Foote testimony, *Salt Lake Daily Herald,* October 10, 1878
17. William Skeen testimony, *Salt Lake Herald, Salt Lake Tribune,* October 11, 1878
18. *Salt Lake Tribune,* October 10, 1878
19. Reuben Down testimony, *Salt Lake Tribune,* October 11, 1878
20. Hickman, *Brigham's Destroying Angel,* pp. 128-129
21. Utah County and Territorial Criminal Records, File 81, File 82 (The People vs. O. P. Rockwell, etc.), Utah County Clerk's Office, Provo, Utah
22. Orson F. Whitney, *History of Utah* (Salt Lake City, 1893), Vol. III, pp. 27-35
23. *Salt Lake Tribune,* October 12, 1878
    Salt Lake Herald, October 12, 13, 1878
24. *Salt Lake Tribune,* October 13, 1878
    Salt Lake Daily Herald, October 13, 1878
25. *Salt Lake Tribune,* October 13, 1878
    Salt Lake Daily Herald, October 13, 1878
26. *Salt Lake Daily Herald,* October 15, 1878
    Salt Lake Tribune, October 15, 1878
27. *Salt Lake Tribune,* October 10, 1878
28. *Daily Alta Californian,* January 25, 1858

Note 28

1. *The London Times,* as quoted in Tullidge, *History of Salt Lake City,* p. 421
2. *Reynolds Newspaper,* as quoted in ibid., p. 422
3. *New York Times,* as quoted in ibid., pp. 421-422

Note 29

The Mountaineer, October 8, 1859

Note 30

Burton, *City of the Saints,* pp. 448-450

Note 31

Burton, *City of the Saints,* pp. 237-245

Note 32

Burton, *City of the Saints,*

Note 33

1. Chandless, *Visit to Salt Lake*
2. Remy, *Journey to Great Salt Lake City*
3. Ludlow, *Heart of the Continent,* pp. 375-377

Note 34

1. *London Times,* September 4, 1855
2. Frederick Hawkins Piercy, *Route from Liverpool to the Great Salt Lake Valley* (Liverpool, 1855)
3. Charles Dickens, "Bound for Great Salt Lake," *The Uncommerical Traveller* (1863)

Note 35

1. Achilles, *Destroying Angels of Mormondom,* pp. 31-32
2. Smith, "Journal," pp. 128-129
3. Charles E. Griffin, "History," MS
   Charles L. Walker, "Journal," p. 249
   Journal History, August 31, 1861
4. Elias Smith, "Journal," *Utah Historical Quarterly,* Vol. XXII, pp. 128-129
5. Journal History, August 31, 1861
6. "Muster Roll of Captain Michael E. Van Buren, Co. A, Reigment of Mounted Rifles, Commanded by Bvt. Gen. Persifor F. Smith, December 31, 1853, to February 28, 1854," Record Group 94, National Archives
7. *New York Times,* May 20, 1857
8. Hyde, *Mormonism,* p. 106
9. S. George Ellsworth, *Dear Ellen. Two Mormon Women and Their Letters* (Salt Lake City, 1974), pp. 34, 39
10. *New York Times,* May 20, 1857
11. Andrew Jenson, "History of Las Vegas Mission," *Nevada State Historical Society Papers,* Vol. V (1926), p. 276

12. *The Millennial Star,* Vol. XXIII (1861), p. 508
    The Mountaineer, September 3, 1859
13. *The Salt Lake Tribune,* November 12, 1875
14. Achilles, *Destroying Angels of Mormondom,* pp. 17-18
15. Ibid., pp. 18-19
16. Whitney, *History of Utah,* Vol. I, p. 710n
    Cradlebaugh, *Utah and the Mormons,* p. 64
    Stout, *On the Mormon Frontier, The Diary of Hosea Stout,* Vol. II, p. 653
    Deseret News, April 6, 1859
    Stenhouse, *Rocky Mountain Saints,* p. 405
    Valley Tan, April 19, 1859
17. Stout, *On the Mormon Frontier, The Diary of Hosea Stout,* Vol. II, p. 653
18. Milo Andrus affidavit, sworn November 23rd, 1934; including letter from Serena G. Andrus; affidavit sent as letter to CHD
19. Ibid.
20. Ibid.
21. Ibid.
22. *Richard Wilds,* "Travel Diary," MS, p. 32
23. Ibid.
    Tracy, "Journal," *Utah Historical Quarterly,* Vol. XIII, p. 71
    Linn, *Story of the Mormons,* p. 536
    Stenhouse, *Rocky Mountain Saints,* pp. 410-412
24. *Deseret News,* May 23, 1860
25. Ibid.
26. Stenhouse, *Rocky Mountain Saints,* p. 418
27. Birney and Kelly, *Holy Murder,* p. 198

Note 36

    Tullidge, *History of Salt Lake City*

Note 37

    Fitz-Hugh Ludlow, *Heart of the Continent,* pp. 364-375

Note 38

    Coutant, *The History of Wyoming,* Vol. I, pp. 647-648

Note 39

1. George Alfred Townsend, letter from Utah to the *Cincinnati Commercial,* October, 1871

Townsend, *Mormon Trials at Salt Lake City*

2. *Pittsburgh Leader,* March 17, 1875

3. Tullidge, *History of Salt Lake City,* p. 623

4. Ibid., pp. 590-591

5. Ibid., p. 596

6. Ibid., pp 595-596

Note 40

1. Van Alfen, "Thesis," MS, p. 49, used by permission

2. Ibid., p. 75

3. Ibid., p. 2

4. Ibid., p. 3

5. Ibid., pp. 3-4

6. Interview with Glen Trane, Lehi, Utah; used by permission

7. Interview with A. Ralph Curtis, Tucson, Arizona; used by permission

8. Interview with John Rockwell, Lehi, Utah; used by permission

9. Interview with Beverly B. Thompson, Draper, Utah; used by permission

Zelma S. Thompson, "The Brass Kettle," from *Grandma's Pioneer Stories* (to be published), compiled and edited by Beverly B. Thompson, used by permission

10. Ty Harrison, letter to author from Sandy Utah; used by permission

Interview with Ty Harrison, resident of Sandy, Utah; used by permission

11. Zelma S. Thompson, "The Brass Kettle," from *Grandma's Pioneer Stories* (to be published), compiled and edited by Beverly B. Thompson, used by permission

12. Ty Harrison, letter to author from Sandy Utah; used by permission

Interview with Ty Harrison, resident of Sandy, Utah; used by permission

13. Russell Stocking, "Andrus Half Way House," MS (Midvale, Utah), used by permission

Interview with Russell Stocking, Midvale, Utah; used by permission

Note 41

Peter Gottfredson, *History of Indian Depredations in Utah,* pp. 330-332

Bibliography

Books, Manuscripts, Documents, Articles, Letters

Abstract of the Census of 1840, Jackson County, Missouri, MS.

Achilles [Sirrine, Samuel D.]. *The Destroying Angels of Mormondom; or a Sketch of the Life of Orrin Porter Rockwell, the Late Danite Chief* (San Francisco, 1878).

Alexander, Colonel Edmund B. Letter to the Adjutant General of the Army, October 9, 1857.

——————. Letter to Brigham Young, Military Records Section, Utah State Archives, October 12, 1857.

Alter, J. Cecil. "In the Beginning," Salt Lake Tribune, January 10, 1935, Catharine E. Mehring Woolley journal entry of September 20, 1848.

American Quat. Reg., Vol. II, pp. 288-295, with reports of Larkin, Mason, Jones, and Paymaster Rich.

An Appeal to the American People: Being An Account of the Persecutions of the Church of Latter Day Saints; and of the

Barbarities Inflicted on Them by the Inhabitants of the State of Missouri (Cincinnati, 1840).

An Illustrated History of Sonoma County, California (Chicago, 1889).

Anderson, Richard Lloyd. "I Have A Question," *The Ensign*, Vol. XVII, No. IV (April, 1987).

Andrus, Milo. Affidavit, sworn November 23rd, 1934; including letter from Serena G. Andrus; affidavit sent as letter to Church Historical Department, Salt Lake City, Utah.

"Answers To Questions," Improvement Era, Vol. V (February 1901).

Appleby, W. I, Supreme Court clerk for Utah Territory. *The Mormon,* May 23, 1857.

Armstrong, S. Letter to *Millennial Star,* Vol. XX, p. 215.

Atherton, Gertrude. *California, an Intimate History* (New York, London, 1914).

——————. *The Californians* (New York, London, 1898).

Audubon, John Woodhouse. *Audubon's Western Journal: 1849-50, Being the MS. Record of a Trip from New York to Texas, and an Over-Land Journey Through Mexico and Arizona to the Gold-Fields of California* (Cleveland, 1906).

——————. *Illustrated Notes of an Expedition through Mexico and California* (New York, 1852).

Austin, Emily M. *Mormonism; or Life Among the Mormons* (Madison, Wisconsin, 1882).

Avard, Dr. Sampson. Affidavit in *Document Showing the Testimony Given Before the Judge of the Fifth Judicial Circuit of the State of Missouri, on the Trial of Joseph Smith, Jr., and Others, for High Treason, and Other Crimes Against That State, February 15, 1841; Copy of the Testimony Given Before the Hon. Austin A. King, Judge of the Fifth Judicial Circuit in the State of Missouri, At the Court-House in Richmond, in a Criminal Court of Inquiry Begun November 12, 1838,* 26th Congress, 2d Session, Circuit Court, 5th Circuit.

Averett, Elijah, transcribed by Murray Averett, his son. "The Averett Narrative," MS.

Ayres, James J. *Gold and Sunshine; Reminiscences of Early California* (Boston, 1922).

Babbitt, Almon W. Letter to Secretary of the Treasury, December 17, 1853, Utah State Archives.

Babbitt, Julia Ann. "Letter to the Editor," *New York Herald,* July 25, 1857.

Backenstos, J. B., clerk of District Court. District Court Records of Nauvoo, November 29, 1842, Church Historical Department, Salt Lake City, Utah.

——————. "Proclamation II," *The Neighbor,* September 17, 24; October 1, 1845.

Ballard, Henry. "Private Journal of Henry Ballard, 1852-1904," MS.

Bancroft, Hubert Howe. *History of California* (San Francisco, 1886-1890), seven volumes; Vol. VI, 1848-1859 (San Francisco, 1888).

——————. *The Works of Hubert Howe Bancroft, History of Utah 1540-1887* (San Francisco, 1890).

Bandel, Eugene. *Frontier Life in the Army 1854-1861* (Glendale, 1932).

Barstow. "Statistics," MS.

Baskin, R. N. *Reminiscences of Early Utah* (Salt Lake City, 1914).

Bassham. Letter to Cooper, May 15, 1848, in Vallejo, "Documentary History of California," MS, Vol. IV, Vol. XII, p. 344.

Bateman, Newton; Currey, J. Seymour; Selby, Paul, editors. *Historical Encyclopedia of Illinois,* Vol. II (Chicago, 1921).

Beadle, J. H. *Life in Utah, or the Mysteries and Crimes of Mormonism* (Philadelphia, 1870).

——————. *Polygamy* (Philadelphia, 1904).

Bean, George Washington. *Autobiography of George Washington Bean, A Utah Pioneer of 1847 and His Family Records,* compiled by Flora Diana Bean Horne (Salt Lake City, 1945).

Belden, J. Letter to Larkin, in Larkin, "Documentary History of California," MS, p. 219.

Belnap, Gilbert. "Autobiography of Gilbert Belnap," MS.

Bennett, John C. *The History of the Saints; an Expose of Joe Smith and Mormonism* (Boston, 1842).

Bennett, William P. *The Sky-Sifter* (Gold Hill, Nevada, 1892).

Bennion, Glynn. "The Best Laid Schemes," *Salt Lake Tribune,* March 9, 1924.

_____. "Suggestion and the Quick Draw," *Salt Lake Tribune,* February 24, 1924.

Bennion, Israel. "Incidents relating to Orrin Porter Rockwell," Document, 3 pp, Ms d 4125, Church Historical Department, Salt Lake City, Utah.

Bennion, John. "Journal," MSS, five volumes.

Bernhisel, John M. Letter from Washington, D.C. to John Taylor, Great Salt Lake City, *Deseret News,* January 14, 1857.

Bigler, Henry W. "Day Book and Diary," MS.

_____. "Extracts from the Journal of Henry W. Bigler," *Utah Historical Quarterly,* Vol. V (1932).

Biographical History of Northeastern Ohio, Embracing the Counties of Ashtabula, Geauga and Lake (Chicago, 1893).

Birney, Hoffman and Kelly, Charles. *Holy Murder, the Story of Porter Rockwell* (New York, 1934).

Boggs. "Sketch of Lilburn W. Boggs," *Missouri Historical Review,* Vol. IV.

Borthwick, J. D. *Three Years in California* (Edinburgh, London 1857).

Bowles, Samuel. *Across the Continent: A Summer's Journey to the Rocky Mountains, The Mormons, and the Pacific States, With Speaker Colfax* (Springfield, Massachusetts, 1866).

_____. *Our New West; Records of Travel Between the Mississippi River and the Pacific Ocean* (Hartford, 1869).

"Box Elder County," *Heart Throbs of the West,* Vol. IX (1948).

Boyle, Henry G. "Diary," MS.

Brackett, Albert Gallatin. *History of the United States Cavalry* (New York, 1865).

Bradley, George W. Letter to Lieutenant General Daniel H. Wells, June 17, 1854, Military Records Section, Utah State Archives.

Brooks, J. Tyrwhitt. *Four Months Among the Gold-finders in California: Being the Diary of an Expedition from San Francisco to the Gold Districts* (Philadelphia, 1849).

Brown, James S. *California Gold, An Authentic History of the First Find* (Oakland, 1894).

_____. *Giant of the Lord* (Salt Lake City, 1960).

_____. *Life of a Pioneer, Being an Autobiography* (Salt Lake City, 1900).

Brown, Thomas D. "Journal of the Southern Indian Mission," MS, April 26, 1854.

Browne, Albert G. "The Utah Expedition," *The Atlantic Monthly, A Magazine of Literature, Art, and Politics,* Vol. III (1859).

Buffum, E. Gould. *Six Months in the Gold Mines: From a Journal of Three Years Residence in Upper and Lower California, 1847-8-9* (Philadelphia, 1850).

Bullock, Thomas, compiler. "A List of Saints in Jackson County," Church Historical Department, Salt Lake City Utah.

Burt, Olive W., collector and editor. *American Murder Ballads and Their Stories* (New York, 1958).

Burton, Sir Richard Francis. *The City of the Saints and Across the Rocky Mountains to California* (London, 1861; New York, 1862).

Butt, Newbern I., writer of Forward to John I. Ginn, "Mormon and Indian Wars," MS.

Cain, Joseph; and Brower, Arieh C. *Mormon Way-Bill, To the Gold Mines from the Pacific Springs* (Salt Lake City, 1851)

California, Oregon, Nevada, Utah, Idaho, and Colorado with Notes on Railroads, Commerce, Agriculture, Mining, Scenery, and People (New York, 1881).

Call, Anson. "Life and Record," MS.

Canfield, Chauncy L. *The Diary of a Forty-Niner* (San Francisco, New York, 1906).

Cannon, George Quayle. Statement in Tullidge, *Life of Brigham Young.*

_____. Writings from the *Western Standard* (Liverpool, 1884).

Capron, Elisha Smith. *History of California, from Its Discovery to the Present Time* (Boston, 1854).

Carson, J. H. *Early Recollections of the Mines, and a Description of the Great Tulare Valley* (Stockton, 1852).

Carvalho, S. N. *Incidents of Travel and Adventure in the Far West; with Col. Fremont's Last Expedition* (New York, 1857).

Chandless, William. *A Visit to Salt Lake; Being a Journey Across the Plains and a Residence in the Mormon Settlements at Utah* (London, 1857).

Church Historian's Office Journal, Vol. 24, October 20-21, 1860.

Circuit Court of Independence, Missouri, Record B, pp. 197-198.

Circuit Court Records, Jackson County, Missouri, Book I, 1827-1833, p. 133.

Circuit Court Records, Jackson County, Missouri, August Term, Book E. 1843, p. 166.

Clayton, William. "Letterbook, 1860-1879," MS, p. 287, June 22, 1873.

_____. *William Clayton's Journal, A Daily Record of the Journey of the Original Company of "Mormon" Pioneers from Nauvoo, Illinois, to the Valley of the Great Salt Lake* (Salt Lake City, 1921).

Cleland, Robert Glass. *A History of California: The American Period* (New York, 1922).

Cleminson, John. Affidavit in *Document Showing the Testimony Given Before the Judge of the Fifth Judicial Circuit of the State of Missouri, on the Trial of Joseph Smith, Jr., and Others, for High Treason, and Other Crimes Against That State, February 15, 1841; Copy of the Testimony Given Before the Hon. Austin A. King, Judge of the Fifth Judicial Circuit in the State of Missouri, At the Court-House in Richmond, in a Criminal Court of Inquiry Begun November 12, 1838*, 26th Congress, 2d Session, Circuit Court, 5th Circuit.

Clyman, James. *American Frontiersman, 1792-1881, The Adventures of a Trapper and Covered Wagon Emigrant As Told In his Own Experiences and Diaries*, edited by Charles L. Camp (San Francisco, 1928).

Codman, John. *The Round Trip By Way of Panama* (New York, 1881).

Cody, William F. and Inman, Henry. *The Great Salt Lake Trail* (New York, 1898).

Cody, William F. *The Life of Hon. William F. Cody, Known as*

Buffalo Bill, the Famous Hunter, Scout, and Guide (Hartford, 1879).

Colton, Reverend Walter. *Three Years in California* (New York, 1850).

Connor, Patrick Edward, Colonel, 3rd Infantry, California Volunteers, Com'd. District, at Headquarters District of Utah, Camp Douglas. Letter February 6th, 1863 to Lieutenant Colonel R. C. Drum, Assistant Adjutant General, U. S. A., Department of the Pacific.

_____. Letters to Lewis Cass, Secretary of State, May 2, 1858, June 18, 1858, U. S. State Department, Territorial Papers, Utah Series, April 30, 1853, to December 24, 1859.

Conover, Peter Wilson. "Autobiography," MS.

Corrill, John. Affidavit in *Document Showing the Testimony Given Before the Judge of the Fifth Judicial Circuit of the State of Missouri, on the Trial of Joseph Smith, Jr., and Others, for High Treason, and Other Crimes Against That State, February 15, 1841; Copy of the Testimony Given Before the Hon. Austin A. King, Judge of the Fifth Judicial Circuit in the State of Missouri, At the Court-House in Richmond, in a Criminal Court of Inquiry Begun November 12, 1838,* 26th Congress, 2d Session, Circuit Court, 5th Circuit.

_____. Testimony in DHC, Vol. I, p. 428n.

Coutant, C. G. *The History of Wyoming From The Earliest Known Discoveries* (Laramie, 1899), three volumes.

Coutts. "Diary," MS.

Cowdery, Oliver. *Defence in a Rehearsal of My Grounds for Separating Myself from the Latter Day Saints* (Norton, Ohio, 1839) (Probably a forgery, first published in 1906 by R. B. Neal).

Cradlebaugh, John. *Utah and the Mormons; Speech of Honorable John Cradlebaugh, of Nevada, on the Admission of Utah as a State. Delivered in the House of Representatives, February 7, 1863.*

Crane, George B. *A Life History Consisting of Incidents and Experiences in the Life of George B. Crane, with Comments on a Variety of Topics. Written by Himself for the Information and Entertainment of His Family and Descendants* (San Jose, 1886).

Crane, James M. *The Past, the Present and the Future of the Pacific* (San Francisco, 1856).

Crosby, Elisha O. "Statistics," MS.

Crosby, Caroline Barnes. "Journal," MS, July 17, 1850.

Crosby, Jesse W. "The History and Journal of the Life and Travels of Jesse W. Crosby," *Annals of Wyoming,* Vol. XI (July 1939).

Crosby, Jonathan. "Biographical Sketch," MS, July 17, 1850.

Crouch, Ebenezer. "Autobiography of Ebenezer Crouch," (1850-1923) MS completed September 12, 1923.

Curry, George L. Letter "South Fork of Platte River" to the *St. Louis Reville,* June 16, 1846.

D. L. *The Digger's Hand-Book and Truth About California* (Sydney, 1849).

Daniels, William M. *Correct Account of the Murder of Generals Joseph and Hyrum Smith, At Carthage, On the 27th Day of June, 1844* (Nauvoo, Illinois, 1845).

Davis, Amos: "Historical Research File C14-3 Amos Davis — Miller, Rowena, J., Study 30, Oct 1965, Rev. 1967," MS, Church Historical Department, Salt Lake City, Utah.

Davis, William Heath. *Sixty Years in California; A History of Events and Life in California: Personal, Political, and Military, Under the Mexican Regime; During the Quasi-Military Government of the Territory by the United States, and After the Admission of the State into the Union, Being a Compilation By a Witness of the Events Described* (San Francisco, 1889; updated in 1929 as Seventy-Five Years in California).

Deseret Agricultural and Manufacturing Society, Record, p. 109.

Dickens, Charles. "Bound for Great Salt Lake," *The Uncommerical Traveller* (1863).

Dickinson, W. R. Letter to his parents, May 29, 1851, Utah State Historical Society Library.

Dickson, Joseph and Woods, Sashiel. Letters in DHC, Vol. III, pp. 168-169.

Dilke, Charles W. *Greater Britain: A Record of Travel in English-Speaking Countries During 1866 and 1867* (London, 1868), two volumes.

Doctrine and Covenants of the Church of the Latter Day Saints, Carefully Selected From the Revelations of God, and Compiled by Joseph Smith, Jr., Oliver Cowdery, Sidney Rigdon, Frederick G. Williams (Kirtland, Ohio, 1835), revelation given to Joseph Smith, Jr, and Sidney Rigdon, December 1830.

Drum, General Richard C. "Reminiscences of the Indian Fight at Ash Hollow, 1855," Nebraska State Historical Society, *Collections,* Vol. XVI (1911).

Drummond, Mrs. W. Letter to Mr. and Mrs. Silas Richards, September 4, 1856, *Deseret News,* May 20, 1857.

Dunbar, Edward E. *The Romance of the Age; or, the Discovery of Gold in California* (New York, 1867).

Duncan, Chapman. "Biography."

Dunklin, Daniel. Letter to Joel H. Haden, August 15, 1834, Western Historical Manuscripts Collection, University of Missouri.

Dwinelle, John Whipple. *The Colonial History of the City of San Francisco, Being A Synthetic Argument in the District Court of the United States for the Northern District of California, for Four Square Leagues of Land Claimed by that City* (San Francisco, 1863).

Egan, William M., editor. *Pioneering the West 1846 to 1878, Major Howard Egan's Diary, Also Thrilling Experiences of Pre-Frontier Life Among Indians; Their Traits, Civil and Savage, and Part of Autobiography, Inter-Related to His Father's,* (Richmond, Utah, 1917).

Eldredge, Zoeth Skinner. *The Beginnings of San Francisco from the Expedition of Anza, 1774, to the City Charter of April 15, 1850* (San Francisco, 1912).

_____. *History of California,* five volumes (New York, 1915).

Ellsworth, S. George. *Dear Ellen. Two Mormon Women and Their Letters* (Salt Lake City, 1974).

Eshom, Frank. *Pioneers and Prominent Men of Utah* (Salt Lake City, 1913).

Ferry, Hypolite. *La California* (Venezia: Dalla Tipografia Fontana, 1851).

Field, Matthew C. Letter to the *New Orleans Daily Picayune,* June 7, 1843.

_____. *Prairie and Mountain Sketches,* collected by Clyde and Mae Reed Porter, edited by Kate L. Gregg and John Francis McDermott (Norman, Oklahoma, 1957).

Fifth Judicial District Court of Missouri, Record Book G, No. 4, p. 228.

Findla. "Statistics," MS.

First Steamship Pioneers.

Flake, Chad J. *A Mormon Bibliography, 1830-1930* (Salt Lake City, 1978).

Forbes, Alexander. *California: A History of Upper and Lower California from Their First Discovery to the Present Time, Comprising An Account of the Climate, Soil, Natural Productions, Agriculture, Commerce, &c.*

Ford. *History of Illinois.*

Fourgeaud. "The Prospects of California," (serialized article), *California Star,* April 1, 1848.

Frisbie. "Reminiscences," MS.

Frost, Jennett Blakeslee. *The Gem of the Mines. A Thrilling Narrative of California Life. Composed of Scenes and Incidents Which Passed Under the Immediate Observation of the Author During Five Years Residence in That State in the Early Days* (Hartford, Connecticut, 1866).

Frost, John. *History of the State of California, from the Period of the Conquest by Spain, to her Occupation by the United States of America; Containing An Account of the Discovery of the Immense Gold Mines and Placers* (Auburn, New York, 1850).

Gardner, Hamilton. *History of Lehi* (Salt Lake City, 1913).

Gibbs, Josiah F. "Gunnison Massacre — 1853 — Millard County, Utah — Indian Mareer's Version of the Tragedy — 1894," *Utah Historical Quarterly,* Vol. I (July 1928).

Gillespie. "Vigilante Committee," MS.

Ginn, John I. Letter to editor of *Valley Tan,* April 26, 1859.

_____. "Mormon and Indian Wars: the Mountain Meadows Massacre and Other Tragedies and Transactions Incident to the Mormon Rebellion of 1857. Together With the Personal Recollection of a Civilian Who Witnessed Many of the Thrilling Scenes Described," MS.

Gleason, William. *History of the Catholic Church in California* (San Francisco, 1859), Vol. II.

Golder, Frank Alfred. *The March of the Mormon Battalion, from Council Bluffs to California, taken from the Journal of Henry Standage* (New York, 1928).

Gottfredson, Peter, editor and compiler. *History of Indian Depredations in Utah* (Salt Lake City, 1919).

Gove, Jesse A. *The Utah Expedition 1857-1858, Letters of Capt. Jesse A. Gove, 10th Inf., U. S. A., of Concord, N. H., to Mrs. Gove, and special correspondence of the New York Herald,* Otis G. Hammond, editor (Concord, Massachusetts, 1928).

Greeley, Horace. *An Overland Journey From New York to San Francisco in the Summer of 1859* (New York, 1860).

Green, Adam Treadwell. *Seventy Years in California* (San Francisco, privately printed 1923), also original MS.

Green, Nelson Winch. *Fifteen Years Among the Mormons, Being the Narrative of Mrs. Mary Ettie V. Smith* (New York, 1860).

Greene, John P. *Facts Relative to the Expulsion of the Mormons from the State of Missouri, Under the "Exterminating Order"* (Cincinnati, 1839).

Greenhow, Robert T. *The History of Florida, Louisiana, Texas, and California, and of the Adjacent Countries, Including the Whole Valley of the Mississippi,* Vol. I (New York, 1856).

Gregg, Thomas. *The Prophet of Palmyra* (New York, 1890).

_____. *History of Hancock County, Illinois, Together With an Outline History of the State and a Digest of State Law* (Chicago, 1880).

Griffen, Robert A. "Introduction" to 1971 Edition, in Alexander Toponce, *Reminiscences of Alexander Toponce, Pioneer, 1839-1923* (Salt Lake City, 1923).

Grinnel, George Bird. *The Fighting Cheyennes* (Norman, 1955).

Gudde, Erwin G. *Bigler's Chronicles of the West* (Berkeley, 1962).

Gudmundsen, Austin. "Journal," MS at Lehi, Utah in possession of his widow, Myrl Gudmundsen; used by permission.

Guinn, James Miller. *Coast Counties. Histories of the State of California. Biographical Record of Coast Counties. An Historical Story of the State's Growth from Its Earliest Settlement to the Present Time, Containing the Biographies of Well Known Citizens of the Past and Present* (Chicago, 1904).

_____. *A History of the State of California, and Biographical Record of Oakland and Environs, Also, Containing Biographies of Well-Known Citizens of the Past and Present* (Los Angeles, 1907), two volumes.

_____. *History of the State of California and Biographical Record of the San Joaquin Valley, California* (Chicago, 1905).

Haight, Isaac Chauncey. "Journal," MS.

Hall, William. *The Abominations of Mormonism Exposed; Containing Many Facts and Doctrines Concerning That Singular People, During Seven Years' Membership With Them; From 1840 to 1847* (Cincinnati, 1852).

Halleck, H. W., General-in-chief. Letter to Brigadier-General George Wright, Commanding Department of the Pacific, San Francisco.

Harmon, Appleton Milo. *Appleton Milo Harmon Goes West* (Berkeley, 1946).

_____. "Diary," MS.

_____. *The Journals of Appleton Milo Harmon, A participant in the Mormon Exodus from Illinois and the early settlement of Utah 1846-1847,* edited by Maybelle Harmon Anderson (Glendale, 1946).

Harpending, Asbury. *The Great Diamond Hoax and Other Stirring Incidents in The Life of Asbury Harpending,* edited by James H. Wilkins (San Francisco, 1913).

Harper, John. Testimony in *Warsaw Signal,* October 15, 1845.

Harwood, James T. "A Basket of Chips (1860-1940)," MS.

Hayes, Benjamin. *Pioneer Notes from the Diaries of Judge Benjamin Hayes,* 1849-1875 (later privately published at Los Angeles, 1929).

Heitman, Francis B. Historical Register and Dictionary of the United States Army, from Its Organization, September 29, 1789, to March 2, 1903 (Washington, 1903), two volumes, Vol. I.

Hempstead, Captain Charles H. "Anniversary Oration," *Union Vedette,* January 30, 1864.

Harris, Sarah Hollister. *An Unwritten Chapter of Salt Lake 1851-1901* (New York, 1901).

Heywood, Joseph L. Letter to George A. Smith, *Deseret News,* September 19, 1855.

Hickman, William A. *Brigham's Destroying Angel: Being the Life, Confession, and Startling Disclosures of the Notorious Bill Hickman, The Danite Chief of Utah* (New York, 1872).

Historical Encyclopedia of Illinois, Vol. II (Chicago, 1921).

History of Caldwell and Livingston Counties, Missouri, Written and Compiled from the Most Authentic Official and Private Sources, Including a History of Their Townships, Towns and Villages, Together With A Condensed History of Missouri; A Reliable and Detailed History of Caldwell and Livingston Counties — Their Pioneer Record, Resources, Biographical Sketches of Prominent Citizens; General and Local Statistics of Great Value; Incidents and Reminiscences (St. Louis, 1886).

History of Santa Clara County, California (Los Angeles, 1922).

History of Santa Clara County, California (San Francisco, 1881).

Hittell, John Shertzer. *A History of the City of San Francisco* (San Francisco, 1878).

_____. *Marshall's Gold Discovery. A Lecture Before the Society of California Pioneers* (San Francisco, 1893).

_____. *Mining in the Pacific States of North America* (San Francisco, 1861).

Hittell, Theodore Henry. *History of California* (San Francisco, 1898), four volumes.

Hogan, Goudy E. "History of Goudy E. Hogan," MS.

Holcombe, Major Reburn S. *St. Louis Globe-Democrat,* October 6, 1887; reprinted in the series by Rollin J. Britton, "Early Days on Grand River and the Mormon War," *The Missouri Historical Review.* Columbia, Missouri, Vol. XIII, No. 3 (April 1919), pp. 298-305.

Hold, James. Diary: "Reminiscences of James Hold, A Narrative of the Emmett Company," edited by Dale L. Morgan, *Utah Historical Quarterly,* Vol. XIII (1955).

Holeman, Jacob H, Indian Agent for Utah Territory. Letter report to Luke Lea, Commissioner of Indian Affairs, "Utah Expedition," *Executive Documents Printed by Order of The House of Representatives During the First Session of the Thirty-Fifth Congress, 1857-'58,* fourteen volumes, Vol. X, No. 71, p. 141.

Hollister, O. J. *Life of Schuyler Colfax* (New York, 1886).

Howe, Henry. *Historical Collections of the Great West: Containing Narratives of the Most Important Events in Western History* (Cincinnati, 1854).

Howe, Octavius Thorndike. *Argonauts of '49; History and Adventures of the Emigrant Companies from Massachusetts, 1849-1850* (San Francisco, 1870).

Hunt, James H. *Mormonism; Embracing the Origin, Rise and Progress of the Sect, With an Examination of the Book of Mormon; also, Their Troubles in Missouri, and Final Expulsion from the State* (St. Louis, 1844).

Hunt, John. Quoted extensively in article, "'Mormon' Pathfinders Guests of Senator Clark, Startling Story of the First Trip From Salt Lake to Los Angeles," *Deseret News,* October 7, 1905.

Huntington, Oliver Boardman. "A Trip to Carson Valley," *Eventful Narratives* (Salt Lake City, 1887).

——————. "Diaries," MSS, three volumes.

Hurt, Garland. In Captain J. H. Simpson, "A Memoir on the Indians of Utah Territory," *Report of Explorations Across the Great Basin of the Territory of Utah, for a Wagon-Route from Camp Floyd to Genoa, in Carson Valley* (Washington, D.C., 1876).

Hyde, John Jr. *Mormonism: Its Leaders and Designs* (New York, 1857).

"In Early Times. A Narrative of Old 'Uncle Porter Rockwell.' After the Horse Thieves. A Pueblo Man Who Found 'Port' Anything but a Destroying Angel," Pueblo, Colorado, *Salt Lake Herald* July 20, 1835.

Ingalls, Captain Rufus. Letter to Major General Thomas S. Jesup, "Report to the Quartermaster General," *Executive Document No. 1,* U. S. Senate, 34th Congress, 1st Session, 1855, p. 161.

Investigation Into the Murder of Dr. J. K. Robinson, Who Was

Assassinated On the Night of October 22d, 1866, near the corner of East Temple and 3d South or Emigration Streets, had before Jeter Clinton, Coroner for the County of Great Salt Lake, Chief Justice Titus, and Judge McCurdy, commencing Tuesday, October 23d, at 11 o'clock A.M. (Salt Lake City, 1866).

Jackson, Joseph H. *A Narrative of the Adventures and Experience of Joseph H. Jackson; Disclosing the Depths of Mormon Villainy Practiced in Nauvoo* (Warsaw, Illinois, 1844).

Jaques, John. "Some Reminiscences," *Salt Lake Herald,* December 8, 1878.

Jenson, Andrew. *Church Chronology; A Record of Important Events Pertaining to the History of the Church of Jesus Christ of Latter-day Saints* (Salt Lake City, 1914).

_____. *Church Encyclopaedia,* Book I, (consisting of Volumes V, VI, VII, and VIII of *The Historical Record, A Monthly Periodical, Devoted Exclusively to Historical, Biographical, Chronological and Statistical Matters* (Salt Lake City, 1889).

_____. "History of Las Vegas Mission," *Nevada State Historical Society Papers,* Vol. V (1926), p. 276

_____. *The Historical Record, A Monthly Periodical, Devoted Exclusively to Historical, Biographical, Chronological and Statistical Matters* (Salt Lake City, 1889)

Jepson, James. "Memories and Experiences," MS.

Johnson, Joel Hills. "Journal," MS.

Johnston, William Preston. *The Life of Gen. Albert Sidney Johnston* (New York, 1878).

Jones, Daniel W. *Forty Years Among the Indians, A True Yet Thrilling Narrative of the Author's Experiences Among the Natives* (Salt Lake City, 1890, also reprinted version).

Journal History of the Church of Jesus Christ of Latter-day Saints, unpublished, in Church Historians Office, Salt Lake City.

Journal of Discourses, by Brigham Young, President of the Church of Jesus Christ of Latter-day Saints, His Two Counselors, and the Twelve Apostles, and Others (Liverpool, England, 1854-1886), twenty-six volumes.

Kartchner, William Decatur. "Expedition of the Emmett Company," MS.

Kay, John. Letter to Thomas Williams, Journal History, May 10, 1858.

Kelly, E. S. *A Stroll Through the Diggings of California* (London, 1852).

Kelly, John. Affidavit to Abraham C. Anderson, *Daily Bulletin,* Blackfoot, Idaho, January 19, 1929.

Kelly, William. *An Excursion to California Over the Prairie, Rocky Mountains, and Great Sierra Nevada. With a Stroll Through the Diggings and Ranches of That Country* (London, 1851), two volumes.

Kimball's Life Guards, Captain William H. Payroll records, Military Records Section, Utah State Archives.

King, Volney. "Millard County, 1851-1875," *Utah Humanities Review,* Vol. I, No. 4 (October 1947).

Larkin. "Documentary History of California," MSS, Vol. VI.

——————. Letter to Mason from San Jose, in Larkin, "Documentary History of California," Vol. I, p. 505.

——————. Letter to Secretary Buchanan, from San Francisco, June 1, 1848, "Documentary History of California."

Laub, George. "Diary No. 2 of George Laub, 1814-1880," MSS, three volumes, Vol. II (1858-1870).

Lauts, G. *Kalifornia door den hoogleeraar G Lauts* (Amsterdam, 1849).

Laws of the State of Missouri, 9th General Assembly, 1st Session, 1838-1839, pp. 29-30.

Laws of the State of Missouri, 10th General Assembly, 1st Session, 1838-1839, pp. 14-15.

"Leaves from Old Albums," *Deseret News,* December 21, 1918.

Lee, John D. *A Mormon Chronicle: The Diaries of John D. Lee, 1848-1876,* edited by Juanita Brooks and Robert Glass Cleland (San Marino, California, 1955), two volumes.

——————. *Mormonism Unveiled; Including the Remarkable Life and Confessions of the Late Mormon Bishop, John D. Lee; and Complete Life of Brigham Young, Embracing A History of Mormonism From Its Inception Down to the Present Time, With*

An Exposition of the Secret History, Signs, Symbols, and Crimes of The Mormon Church. Also the True History of the Horrible Butchery Known as The Mountain Meadows Massacre (St. Louis, 1877; Lewisburgh, Pennsylvania, 1882).

Letts, John M. *California Illustrated: Including a Description of the Panama and Nicaragua Routes. By a Returned Californian* (New York, 1852).

Lingenfelter, Richard E. *1858-1958 The Newspapers of Nevada, A History and Bibliography* (San Francisco, 1964).

Linn, William Alexander. *The Story of the Mormons, From the Date of Their Origin to the Year 1901* (New York, 1923).

Little, Feramorz. "Letterbook, 1863 - 1877," MS.

Little, James A. "Biography of Lorenzo Dow Young," *Utah Historical Quarterly,* Vol. 14, Nos. 1-4 (January-October, 1946), pp. 54-55, extensive quotes from diary of Lorenzo Dow Young.

Littlefield, Lyman Omer. *The Martyrs* (Salt Lake City, 1882).

Long, M. M. and O'Neill, O. H. "Journals of the Eastern and Central Divisons of the Fort Kearney, South Pass, and Honey Lake Wagon Road, June 4, 1857, to October 8, 1859," MS, Records of the Secretary of the Interior, National Archives.

Logan Branch recorder. January 28th, 1863, as quoted in Tullidge, *History of Salt Lake City,* p. 289.

Love, Andrew. "Journal," MS.

Ludlow, Fitz Hugh. "Among the Mormons," *The Atlantic Monthly,* Vol. XII (April 1864).

_____. *The Heart of the Continent: A Record of Travel Across the Plains and in Oregon, With an Examination of the Mormon Principle* (New York, 1870).

Lyman, Amasa M. "Amasa M. Lyman's Journals," MSS, 1847.

_____. "Journal, 1848-1850," MS.

_____. Letter to J. H. Flanigan, dated from San Francisco, April 11, 1850, published in *Millennial Star,* Vol. XII, pp. 214-215.

Lyman, Eliza Marie Partridge. "Autobiography and Diary, 1820-1885," MS.

Mace, Wandle. "Journal," MS.

Marcy, Randolph B. *Thirty Years of Army Life on the Border* (New York, 1866).

Markham, Steven. Letter from, June 17, 1844, DHC, Vol. VI, p. 492.

Marsden, William. "Journal and Diary of William Marsden," *Daughters of Utah Pioneers, Lesson for January,* 1951.

Marsh. Affidavit, *Document Showing the Testimony Given Before the Judge of the Fifth Judicial Circuit of the State of Missouri, on the Trial of Joseph Smith, Jr., and Others, for High Treason, and Other Crimes Against That State, February 15, 1841; Copy of the Testimony Given Before the Hon. Austin A. King, Judge of the Fifth Judicial Circuit in the State of Missouri, At the Court-House in Richmond, in a Criminal Court of Inquiry Begun November 12, 1838,* 26th Congress, 2d Session, Circuit Court, 5th Circuit.

Martineau, Colonel. As quoted in Tullidge, *History of Salt Lake City,* p. 289.

McClaws, Monte B. "The Attempted Assassination of Missouri's Ex-Governor, Lilburn W. Boggs," *Missouri Historical Review,* Vol. LX (October, 1965).

McKenzie, George. "Cause and Origin of the Walker War," in Gottfredson's *Indian Depredations.*

McKinstry, George. Articles in *Lancaster Examiner; Stockton Independent,* October 19, 1875.

Metcalf, Anthony. *Ten Years Before the Mast. Shipwrecks and Adventures at Sea! Religious Customs of the People of India and Burma's Empire. How I Became a Mormon and Why I Became an Infidel!* (Malad City, Idaho, 1888).

Meyer, Duane. *The Heritage of Missouri — A History* (St. Louis, 1963).

Miller, George. Letter of June 28, 1855, *Northern Islander* (Beaver Island, Lake Michigan), September 6, 1855.

Missouri House Journal, 11th General Assembly, 1st Session, 1840-1841, pp. 530-531.

Missouri Senate Journal, 11th General Assembly, 1st Session, 1840-1841, pp. 446-447.

Morris, George. "Autobiography," MS.

Mortensen, A. R., editor (of letter). "The Governor's Lady; A Letter from Camp Scott, 1857," *Utah Historical Quarterly,* Vol. XXII (April 1954), pp. 165-173.

Music: Minstrel Songs, Old and New (1882).

"Muster Roll of Captain Michael E. Van Buren, Co. A, Regiment of Mounted Rifles, Commanded by Bvt. Gen. Persifor F. Smith, December 31, 1853, to February 28, 1854," Record Group 94, National Archives.

Nelson, William G. Letter in Journal History, January 29, 1863.

New Republic. Vol. 79 (May 30, 1934).

Noall, Claire. "Mormon Midwives," *Utah Historical Quarterly,* Vol. X (1942), p. 103, journal quote of Patty Bartlett Sessions.

Nordhoff, Charles. *Northern California, Oregon, and the Sandwich Islands* (New York, London, 1877).

Norman, Lucia. *A Youth's History of California from the Earliest Period of Its Discovery to the Present Time* (San Francisco, 1867).

Northern California; A Memorial and Biographical History of Northern California. Containing a History of This Important Section of the Pacific Coast from the Earliest Period of its Occupancy to the Present Time, Together with Glimpses of its Prospective Future (Chicago, 1891).

Norton, Henry K. *The Story of California From the Earliest Days to the Present by Henry K. Norton* (Chicago, 1913).

Oaks, Dallin H. and Hill, Marvin S. *Carthage Conspiracy; The Trial of the Accused Assassins of Joseph Smith* (Urbana, Illinois; Chicago, Illinois; London, England; 1975).

"Observer," *Army and Navy Journal,* December 15, 1866.

Olney, Oliver H. *The Absurdities of Mormonism Portrayed, A Brief Sketch* (Hancock County, Illinois, 1843).

_____. Papers, 46 documents, Document 17, Document 24 (on Joseph Smith and Porter Rockwell), Church Historical Department, Salt Lake City, Utah.

Orr, Thomas Jr. *Life History of Thomas Orr Jr., Pioneer Stories of California and Utah,* edited by Lillie Jane Orr Taylor (privately published, 1930).

Orton, Richard H., Brigadier-General. *Records of California Men in the War of the Rebellion, 1861-1867* (Sacramento, 1890).

Palmer, John Williamson. *The New and Old; Or, California and India in Romantic Aspects* (New York, London, 1859).

Pancoast, Charles Edward. *A Quaker Forty-Niner; The Adventures of Charles Edward Pancoast on the American Frontier*, edited by Anna Paschall Hannum (Philadelphia, London, 1930).

Parkinson, Jessie Heaton. *Adventuring in California, Yesterday, Today, and Day Before Yesterday* (San Francisco, 1921).

Parkinson, R. R. *Pen Portraits. Autobiographies of State Officers, Legislators, Prominent Business and Professional Men of the Capital of the State of California; Also of Newspaper Proprietors, Editors, and Members of the Corps Reportorial* (San Francisco, 1878).

Parsons, George Frederick. *The Life and Adventures of James W. Marshall, The Discoverer of Gold in California* (Sacramento, 1870).

Patriarchal Blessings, Vol. IX, p. 272, No. 819, Church Historical Department, Salt Lake City, Utah.

Patterson, Lawson B. *Twelve Years in the Mines of California; Embracing General View of the Gold Region, With Practical Observations on Hill, Placer, and Quartz Diggings; and Notes of the Origin of Gold Deposits* (Cambridge, 1862).

Payson, George [Ralph Raven, pseudonym]. *Golden Dreams and Leaden Realities* (New York, 1853).

Peck, Reed. "Mormons So Called" (Quincy, Adams County, Illinois, September 18, 1839), MS.

Pettegrew, David. "A History of David Pettegrew," MS.

Phelps, John Wolcott. "Diary," MS.

Piercy, Frederick Hawkins. *Route from Liverpool to the Great Salt Lake Valley* (Liverpool, 1855).

Porter, Burton B. "One of the People; His Own Story," MS (1907).

Pratt, Louisa Barnes "Journal of Louisa Barnes Pratt," *Heart Throbs of the West, A Unique Volume Treating Definite Subjects of Western History,* compiled by Kate B. Carter, Vol. VIII (1947).

Pratt, Orson. "Extracts From Orson Pratt's Private Journal," *Millennial Star,* Vol. XII.

_____. *The Orson Pratt Journals,* compiled by Elden J. Watson (Salt Lake City, 1975).

Pratt, Parley Parker. "A Mormon Mission to California in 1851, From the Diary of Parley Parker Pratt," edited by Reva Holdaway Stanley and Charles L. Camp, *California Historical Society Quarterly,* Vol. XIV (June 1935).

_____. Autobiography of Parley P. Pratt (New York, 1874).

_____. "Discourse by Parley P. Pratt" (of September 7, 1856), *Deseret News,* December 24, 1856.

Proceedings of a Convention, Held at Carthage, in Hancock County, Ill., on Tuesday and Wednesday, October 1st and 2nd, 1845 reports of the Quincy Whig (Quincy, 1845).

Randolph, Edmund. *Address on the History of California, From the Discovery of the Country to the Year 1849, Delivered Before the Society of California Pioneers, At Their Celebration of the Tenth Anniversary of the Admission of the State of California into the Union, by Edmund Randolph, Esq.* (San Francisco, September 10, 1860).

"A Record of Marriages (Solemnized) (Alphabetically Arranged) 1853-1856," Church Historical Department, Salt Lake City, Utah.

"Records of Early Church Families," *Utah Genealogical and Historical Magazine,* Vol. XXVI (Salt Lake City, 1935).

Records, Genealogical Society of Utah, Salt Lake City.

Reinhart, Herman Francis. *The Golden Frontier; The Recollections of Herman Francis Reinhart,* 1851-1869, edited by Doyce B. Nunis, Jr. (Austin, Texas, 1962).

Remy, Jules. *A Journey to Great-Salt-Lake City* (London, 1861), two volumes, Vol. II.

"Resignation of Associate Justice W. W. Drummond," *New York Herald,* April 1, 1857.

Revere, Joseph Warren. *A Tour of Duty in California; Including a Description of the Gold Region and An Account of the Voyage Around Cape Horn; With Notices of Lower California, the Gulf and Pacific Coasts, and the Principal Events Attending the Conquest of California* (New York, 1849).

Revue des Deux Mondes, February 1, 1849.

Richardson, Albert D. *Beyond the Mississippi: From the Great River to the Great Ocean. Life and Adventure on the Prairies, Mountains, and Pacific Coast* (Hartford, Connecticut, 1869).

Roberts, Brigham H. *A Comprehensive History of the Church of Jesus Christ of Latter-day Saints* (Salt Lake City, 1930), six volumes.

—————. *The Rise and Fall of Nauvoo* (Salt Lake City, 1900).

Robie, Wendell. "Murderer's Bar and Gold Rush on the Middlefork," *The Pony Express,* Vol. XXV (July 1958), reprinted address to the California Historical Society, March 10, 1955.

Robinson, Fayette. *California and Its Gold Regions; With A Geographical and Topographical View of the Country, Its Mineral and Agricultural Resources* (New York, 1849).

Robinson, Phil. *Sinners and Saints* (London, 1883).

Rockwell, Orrin Porter. Hand-written note to, May 26, 1847, Church Historical Department, Salt Lake City, Utah.

—————. Letter to Colonel Kane, November 20, 1858, Coe Collection (MS 279, Yale University).

—————; and Neff, Franklin. Petition, March 22, 1853.

—————. Testimony dated February 3, 1840, sworn before B. K. Morsell, Justice of the Peace, District of Columbia, submitted May 10, 21, 1842, U.S. House of Representatives.

—————. Testimony before W. I. Appleby, clerk of the Supreme Court of the United States for the Territory of Utah, dated February 11, 1857, Utah Executive Papers, 1856-1858, "Governor (Miscellaneous Correspondence) 1857," Utah State Archives.

—————. Testimony of April 14, 1856, to Thomas Bullock, Salt Lake County Recorder, DHC, Vol. VI, pp. 588-589.

Rodman, Paul W. *California Gold Discovery* (1966).

Rogers, Fred B. *Soldiers of the Overland, Being Some Account of the Services of General Patrick Edward Connor & His Volunteers in the Old West* (San Francisco, 1938).

Roskelly, S. Letter in Journal History, February 8, 1863.

Ross, Charles L. "Experiences of a Pioneer of 1847 in California," MS.

Ross. "Statistics," MS.

Roundy, Elizabeth D. E. "Porter Rockwell" letter, Jenson's Biographical Manuscripts, Church Historical Department, Salt Lake City, Utah.

Royce, Josiah. *California From the Conquest in 1846 to the Second Vigilance Committee in San Francisco* (Boston, New York, Cambridge, 1886).

Russell, William H. Letter to the *Missouri Statesman,* "Nebraska or Big Platte River, About 400 Miles West of Independence," June 13, 1846.

Ryan. *Judges and Criminals.*

Ryan, William Redmond. *Personal Adventures in Upper and Lower California, in 1848-9; with the Author's Experiences at the Mines* (London, 1850).

Salt Lake County Abstracts, Plats and Surveys, Book A2.

Salt Lake County Death Records, No. 2897.

Salt Lake County Deeds and Transfers, Book C, pp. 579-580.

Salt Lake County Mortgage Records, Book B, pp. 125-127, Salt Lake County Recorder's Office, Lewis Robison (for purchase on October 18, 1858).

San Francisco Directory, 1852-1853.

Scofield, Charles J. *History of Hancock County* (Chicago, 1921), three volumes, Vol. II.

Scott, Charles A. "Charles A. Scott's Diary of the Utah Expedition, 1857-1861," edited by Robert E. Stowers and John M. Ellis, *Utah Historical Quarterly,* Vol. XXVIII (1960).

"Secretary of Territory (Miscellaneous Correspondence) 1857," Utah Executive Papers, 1856-1858, Utah State Archives.

Sharp, James P. "The Old Man's Story," *Improvement Era,* Vol. XLVI (1943).

_____. "Singing Wires," *Improvement Era,* Vol. XLVII (1944).

Sherman, William Tecumseh. *Memoirs of General William T. Sherman* (New York, 1875), two volumes, Vol. I.

Shuck, Oscar Tully. *Bench and Bar California; History, Anecdotes, Reminiscences* (San Francisco, 1889).

——————. *California Anthology; Or, Striking Thoughts on Many Themes, Carefully Selected from California Writers and Speakers* (San Francisco, 1880).

——————. *The California Scrap-Book: A Repository of Useful Information and Select Reading. Comprising Choice Selections of Prose and Poetry, Tales and Anecdotes, Historical, Descriptive, Humorous, and Sentimental Pieces, Mainly Culled From the Various Newspapers and Periodicals of the Pacific Coast* (San Francisco, 1869).

——————. *Historical Abstract of San Francisco* (San Francisco, 1897), three volumes.

——————. *History of the Bench and Bar of California, Being Biographies of Many Remarkable Men* (Los Angeles, 1901).

——————. *Representative and Leading Men of the Pacific: Being Original Sketches of the Lives and Characters of the Principal Men, Living and Deceased, of the Pacific States and Territories — Pioneers, Politicians, Lawyers, Doctors, Merchants, Orators, and Divines — to Which Are Added Their Speeches, Addresses, Orations, Eulogies, Lectures, and Poems, Upon a Variety of Subjects* (San Francisco, 1870).

Shurtliff, Luman Andros. "Biographical Sketch," MS.

Simpson, Henry I. *The Emigrant's Guide to the Gold Mines. Three Weeks in the Gold Mines, Adventures with the Gold Diggers of California in August, 1848* (New York, 1848).

Simpson, Captain J. H. "A Memoir on the Indians of Utah Territory," *Report of Explorations Across the Great Basin of the Territory of Utah, for a Wagon-Route from Camp Floyd to Genoa, in Carson Valley* (Washington, D.C., 1876).

Sioli, Paolo. *Historical Souvenir of El Dorado County, California* (Oakland, 1883).

Slater, Nelson. *Fruits of Mormonism* (Coloma, California, 1851).

Smith, Amanda. Affidavit, *History of Caldwell and Livingston Counties*, p. 158.

Smith, Azariah. "Azariah Smith's Journal," Journal History, January - April 1848.

Smith, Elias. "Journal, January 1, 1859 — August 24, 1864," MS.

_____. "Elias Smith, Journal of a Pioneer Editor, March 6, 1859 — September 23, 1863," edited by A. R. Mortensen, *Utah Historical Quarterly,* Vol. XXI (1953).

Smith, George A. Church Historians Record Book, Entry for Monday, August 8th, 1842.

Smith, George A. Letter to Orson Pratt, July 31, 1850, *Millennial Star,* Vol. XII, pp. 349-350.

Smith, Joseph F. *Gospel Doctrine,* 5th Ed. (1st Ed. 1919).

Smith, Joseph Fielding. As quoted in Jenson, *The Historical Record,* p. 189.

Smith, Joseph Jr. *History of the Church of Jesus Christ of Latter-day Saints. Period I. History of Joseph Smith, the Prophet, by Himself* (Salt Lake City, 1902-1912), six volumes, elsewhere in Bibliography referred to as "DHC," for "Documentary History of the Church."

Smith, Joseph III. *Joseph Smith III and the Restoration,* edited by Mary Audentia Smith Anderson, condensed by Bertha Audentia Anderson Holmes (Independence, 1952).

_____. and Smith, Heman C. *History of the Church of Jesus Christ of Latter Day Saints,* published by the Reorganized Church (Lamoni, Iowa, 1911), Vols. II and III.

Smith, Lucy Mack. *Biographical Sketches of Joseph Smith the Prophet, and His Progenitors for many Generations* (Liverpool, 1853).

Smith, Mrs. M. C. R. Article in *Naked Truths About Mormonism* (Smith's section) Vol. 1, No. 2 (April 1888, Oakland, California).

Smoot, Abraham O. Letter to Edward W. Tullidge, February 14, 1884.

Snow, Eliza R. "Diary," MS.

Snow, Erastus. "Autobiography of Erastus Snow, Dictated to his son Franklin R. Snow, in the year 1875," *The Utah Genealogical and Historical Magazine,* Vol. XIV, No. 3 (July 1923).

_____. "Journal," MSS, eight volumes, Book 3rd (June 1841 - February 1847).

Soule, Frank; Gihon, John H.; and Nisbet, James. *The Annals of San Francisco; Containing a Summary of the History of the First Discovery, Settlement, Progress, and Present Condition of California, Complete History of All the Important Events Connected With Its Great City; To Which Are Added, Biographical Memoirs of Some Prominent Citizens* (New York, 1855).

Stafford, C. M. Article in *Naked Truths About Mormonism,* Vol. 1, No. 2 (April 1888).

Stalker, Alexander. Letters in Journal History, January 29, February 8, 1863.

Stenhouse, T.B.H. *The Rocky Mountain Saints: A Full and Complete History of the Mormons, from the First Vision of Joseph Smith to the Last Courtship of Brigham Young, Including the Story of the Hand-Cart Emigration, the Mormon War, the Mountain-Meadow Massacre, the Reign of Terror in Utah, the Doctrine of Human Sacrifice, the Political, Domestic, Social, and Theological Influences of the Saints, the Facts of Polygamy, the Colonization of the Rocky Mountains, and the Development of the Great Mineral Wealth of the Territory of Utah* (New York, 1873; Salt Lake City, 1904).

Steptoe. Letter of recommendation regarding Rockwell, Historical Record Book, p. 196, Church Historical Department, Salt Lake City, Utah.

_____. Letter to Cooper, Office of Indian Affairs, National Archives, September 14, 1854.

Stocking, Russel. "Andrew Half Way House," MS (Midvale, Utah).

Stout, Allen Joseph. "Allen Joseph Stout Journal," MS.

Stout, Edwin Ward. "Journal," MS.

Stout, Hosea. "Journal," MSS, eight volumes.

_____. *On the Mormon Frontier, The Diary of Hosea Stout, 1844-1866,* edited by Juanita Brooks (Salt Lake City, 1965), two volumes.

Sutter, John Augustus. *A Nation's Benefactor: Gen'l John A Sutter. Memorial of His Life and Public Services, and An Appeal to Congress, to Citizens of California, and the People of the United States, by His Fellow Pioneers of California* (New York, 1880).

_____. *New Helvetia Diary.*

Swan, John A. "A Trip to the Gold Mines," MS, p. 2 (reprint of 1849 California original: San Francisco, 1960).

Swartzell, William. *Mormonism Exposed, Being a Journal of a Residence in Missouri From the 28th of May to the 20th of August, 1838* (Pekin, Ohio, 1840).

Switzler, William F. *Illustrated History of Missouri From 1541 to 1877* (St. Louis, 1879).

Talmage, R. DeWitte. *"Mormonism." A Sermon Preached by the Rev. R. DeWitt Talmage, D.D., in the Tabernacle, Brooklyn, N.Y., on the 26th of September, 1880* (Brooklyn, 1880).

Tanner, Joseph M. *John Riggs Murdock, A Biographical Sketch* (Salt Lake City, 1909).

Thompson, Beverly B., compiler and editor. *Grandma's Pioneer Stories* (to be published).

Thompson, Robert A. *Historical and Descriptive Sketch of Sonoma County, California* (Philadelphia, 1877).

Thompson, Thomas H. and West, Albert A. *History of Nevada, with Illustrations and Biographical Sketches of Its Prominent Men and Pioneers* (Oakland, 1881).

Tittsworth, W. G. *Outskirt Episodes* (Avoca, Iowa, 1927).

Tooele County Deeds, Books D, E, and X, Tooele, Utah.

Tooele County Recorder's Office, Ophir Mining District, Record Book A, p. 182.

Tooele County Recorder's Office, Patent Record Book 1, Patent 1311, p. 442.

Toponce, Alexander. *Reminiscences of Alexander Toponce, Pioneer, 1839-1923* (Salt Lake City, 1923).

Townsend, George Alfred. *The Mormon Trials at Salt Lake City* (New York, 1871).

Tracy, Albert. "Journal of Captain Albert Tracy," edited by J. Cecil Alter and Robert J. Dwyer, *Utah Historical Quarterly,* Vol. XIII (1945).

Tucker, Pomeroy. *Origin, Rise, and Progress of Mormonism* (New York, 1867).

Tullidge, Edward W. *Life of Brigham Young; Or, Utah and Her Founders* (New York, 1876).

_____. *The History of Salt Lake City and Its Founders* (Salt Lake City, 1886).

_____. *Tullidge's Histories, Vol. II, Containing the History of all the Northern, Eastern and Western Counties of Utah; Also the Counties of Southern Idaho. With A Biographical Appendix of Representative Men and Founders of the Cities and Counties; Also a Commercial Supplement, Historical* (Salt Lake City, 1889).

_____, editor. *Tullidge's Quarterly Magazine* (Salt Lake City, 1885).

Tuthill, Franklin. *The History of California* (San Francisco, 1866).

Tuttle, Hiram S. "Account," MS.

Tuttle, Newton. "A Territorial Militiaman in the Utah War; Journal of Newton Tuttle," edited by Hamilton Gardner, *Utah Historical Quarterly,* Vol. XXII (October 1954).

Twelves, Orson. "Early History of Charles Twelves and Family," MS.

Tyler, Daniel. *A Concise History of the Mormon Battalion in the Mexican War, 1846-1847* (Salt Lake City, 1881).

U. S. Bureau of Census, "Seventh Census of the Un..ed States: 1850. Jackson Co. Missouri," also for Utah, 1850.

U. S. House of Representatives, "Engagement Between United States Troops and Sioux Indians," *House of Representatives Report No. 63,* 33rd Congress, 2d Session, 1855.

U. S. House of Representatives, Office of Indian Affairs, *Executive Document No. 1* (1856).

U. S. House of Representatives, "Report of the Secretary of Interior," *Executive Document No. 1,* 34th Congress, 3rd Session, December 1, 1856 - March 3, 1857.

U. S. Senate, "Report to the Quartermaster General," *Executive Document No. 1,* 34th Congress, 1st Session, 1855, p. 161.

U. S. Senate, "Report of the Secretary of the Interior," *Executive Document No. 5,* 34th Congress, 3rd Session, December 1, 1856 to March 3, 1857, p. 650.

U. S. Senate, Senate Document, 35th Congress, 2nd Session, ii, p. 161.

U. S. State Department, Territorial Papers, Utah Series, April 30, 1853 - December 24, 1859, National Archives.

Ure, James, company clerk. Journal History, June 8, 1856.

Ustick, William D., First Lieutenant and Adjutant, Third Infantry, C. V., Acting Assistant Adjutant General, By order of Colonel Connor, headquarters District of Utah, Camp Douglas. Letter of February 6, 1863 to Lieutenant Colonel R. C. Drum, Assistant Adjutant General, U. S. A., Department of the Pacific.

Utah: A Guide to the State, compiled by Workers of the Writers' Program of the Work Projects Administration for the State of Utah (New York, 1941).

Utah County and Territorial Criminal Records, File 81, File 82 (The People vs. O. P. Rockwell, etc.), Utah County Clerk's Office, Provo, Utah.

Utah County Deeds, 1851-1864, Book G, p. 169; Lot 4, Block 44 on the American Creek Survey of Meadow Land; Lot 2, Block 2, on Dry Creek, Plat B, p. 308.

Utah Executive Papers, 1850-1855, Territorial Secretary Correspondence, Utah State Archives.

Utah Genealogical and Historical Magazine, Vol. XXVI.

The Utah Magazine, an Illustrated Monthly Journal of Free Discussion and General Current Intelligence (Salt Lake City, 1893).

Utah Territory, Records of Marks and Brands, December 29, 1849, to December 9, 1874, pp. 37, 113.

Vallejo, Mariano Guadalupe. *Report on the Derivation and Definition of the Names of the Several Counties of California* (San Jose, 1850).

_____. "Documentary History of California," MS.

Van Alfen, Nicholas. "Porter Rockwell and the Mormon Frontier, A Thesis Submitted to the Department of History of Brigham Young University in Partial Fulfillment of the Requirements for the Degree of Master of Fine Arts" (Provo, 1938), used by permission.

_____. *Porter Rockwell, Mormon Frontier Marshal and Body Guard of Joseph Smith* (Salt Lake City, 1971), used by permission from the author.

Van Vliet, Captain Stewart. Letter to Captain Alfred Pleasanton, Assistant Adjutant General, United States Army expedition to Utah, September 16, 1857, "Utah Expedition," *Executive Document No. 71,* U. S. House of Representatives, 35th Congress, 1st Session, 1858, pp. 24-26.

Vaux [Wells, Junius]. "The Echo Canyon War," *The Contributor* (Salt Lake City, 1882).

Verite, Bear River correspondent. Letter No. 1, "The Battle of Bear River," penned February 7, 1863, Salt Lake City; Letter No. 2, "The Return of the Wounded Volunteers to Camp Douglas," February 9, 1863, Salt Lake City; Letter No. 3, "Official List of Killed and Wounded At the Battle of Bear River," February 9, 1863, Salt Lake City; published in *Daily Alta Californian.*

Waite, Mrs. C. V. *The Mormon Prophet and His Harem* (Chicago, 1867).

Walker, Charles Lowell. *Diary of Charles Lowell Walker,* edited by A. Karl Larson and Katherine Miles (Logan, Utah, 1980), two volumes.

_____. "Journal," MSS, twelve volumes.

[Waters, William Elkanah], An Officer of the U. S. Army. *Life Among The Mormons, And A March To Their Zion: To Which is Added a Chapter on the Indians of the Plains and Mountains of the West.* (New York, 1868).

Wells, Daniel H. Letter to Porter Rockwell, April 28, 1862, Military Records Section, Utah State Archives.

_____. Orders to Captain Wright, April 21, 1851, Military Records Section, Utah State Archives.

_____. Letter to McAllister, October 8, 1857, Military Records Section, Utah State Archives.

_____. Letter to officers, Nauvoo Legion, August 1, 1857. Military Records Section, Utah State Archives.

_____. Letter to Major G. Deas, assistant adjutant general, in *Transactions of the Kansas State Historical Society, Embracing the Fifth and Sixth Biennial Reports, 1886-1888* (Topeka, 1890), Vol. IV.

Wharton, Captain H. W. Reports, *Transactions of the Kansas State Historical Society, Embracing the Fifth and Sixth Biennial Reports, 1886-1888* (Topeka, 1890), Vol. IV.

Whitmer, John. *History of the Church of the Latter-day Saints From 1831-1846* (Independence, Missouri, 1908).

————. "History of the Church of the Latter Day Saints From 1831 to 1846," Chapter xxi, deleted from publication in *Journal of History,* Vol. I (Independence, Missouri, 1908) by The Reorganized Church of Jesus Christ of Latter Day Saints (along with chapters xx, xxii and part of xix).

————. Affidavit in *Document Showing the Testimony Given Before the Judge of the Fifth Judicial Circuit of the State of Missouri, on the Trial of Joseph Smith, Jr., and Others, for High Treason, and Other Crimes Against That State, February 15, 1841; Copy of the Testimony Given Before the Hon. Austin A. King, Judge of the Fifth Judicial Circuit in the State of Missouri, At the Court-House in Richmond, in a Criminal Court of Inquiry Begun November 12, 1838,* 26th Congress, 2d Session, Circuit Court, 5th Circuit.

Wight, Lyman. Affidavit, *Deseret News,* December 24, 31, 1856.

————. Testimony, DIIC, Vol. I, p. 428n.

————. Testimony before municipal court of Nauvoo, Illinois, July 1, 1843.

Whitney, Orson F. *History of Utah, Comprising Preliminary Chapters on the Previous History of Her Founders, Accounts of Early Spanish and American Explorations in the Rocky Mountain Region, the Advent of the Mormon Pioneers, the Establishment and Dissolution of the Provisional Government of the State of Deseret, and the Subsequent Creation and Development of the Territory* (Salt Lake City, 1892-1904), four volumes.

Willcox, R. N. *Reminiscences of California Life. Being an Abridged Description of Scenes Which the Author Has Passed Through in California, and Other Lands. With Quotations From Other Authors* (Avery, Ohio, 1897).

Willey, Samuel Hopkins. *Two Historical Discourses Occasioned by the Close of the First Ten Years' Ministry in California, Preached in the Howard Street Presbyterian Church* (San Francisco, 1859).

—————. *Thirty Years in California, A Contribution to the History of the State from 1849 to 1879* (San Francisco, 1879).

—————. *The Transaction Period of California from a Province of Mexico in 1846 to a State of the American Union in 1850* (San Francisco, 1901).

Wood, Raymund Francis and Rhodehamel, Josephine Dewitt. *Ina Coolbirth, Librarian and Laureate of California* (Provo, 1973).

Woodruff, Wilford. *History of His Life and Labors as Recorded in his Daily Journals,* edited by Mathias F. Cowley (Salt Lake City, 1909).

—————. Letter to George A. Smith, Journal History, July 12, 1859.

—————. "Wilford Woodruff Journal," MS, September 25, 1857.

Wymetal, Wilhelm W. *Mormon Portraits, Joseph Smith the Prophet, His Family and His Friends* (Salt Lake City, 1886).

—————. *Deseret News,* March 12, 1892.

—————. Published interview with William Law, *Salt Lake Tribune,* July 31, 1887.

Young, Ann Eliza. *Wife No. 19* (Hartford, Connecticut, 1876).

Young, Brigham. Brigham Young Letter Book No. 23, September 14, 1857.

—————. Letter to Horace Eldredge, St. Louis, March 27, 1857.

—————. Letter to Thomas L. Kane, January 14, 1859, Thomas L. Kane Papers, MS, Stanford University Library.

—————. *Manuscript History of Brigham Young, 1846-1847.*

Young, John R. Letter to Henry W. Bigler, January 31, 1858, in Bigler, "Incidents (1857-1858)," published in *Union* (St. George, Utah, newspaper), November 21, 1896.

Zufelt, Harmon. "The Battle of Bear River," *The Utah Monthly Magazine, Vol. IX, No. 3 (December 1892); part of The Utah Magazine, an Illustrated Monthly Journal of Free Discussion and General Current Intelligence,* Vol. IX: October, 1892 to September, 1893 (Salt Lake City, 1893).

Newspapers

Alton Telegraph, Alton, Illinois.

Army and Navy Journal.

Daily Alta Californian, San Francisco, California.

Weekly American, St. Louis, Missosuri.

Daily Bulletin, Blackfoot, Idaho.

Burlington Hawkeye, Burlington, Iowa.

California Star, San Francisco.

Californian, San Francisco.

Chicago Tribune, Chicago, Illinois.

Cincinnati Commercial, Cincinnati, Ohio.

Corinne Reporter, Salt Lake City, Utah.

Council Bluffs Bugle, Council Bluffs, Iowa.

Crescent City Oracle, Crescent City, Iowa.

Deseret Evening News, Salt Lake City, Utah.

Deseret News, Salt Lake City, Utah.

Deseret News Weekly, Salt Lake City, Utah.

Evening and Morning Star, Independence, Missouri, and Kirtland, Ohio.

Frontier Guardian, Kanesville, Iowa.

Hamilton Empire, Nevada.

Index, Placerville, California.

Illinois State Register.

Inter Ocean, The Weekly, Chicago, Illinois.

Jeffersonian Republican, Jefferson City, Missouri.

Lancaster Examiner, Lancaster, California

The Latter-Day Saints' Millennial Star, Liverpool, England.

Leavenworth Daily Times - Extra, Leavenworth, Kansas

Lee County Democrat, Lee County, Missouri.

The London Times, London, England.

Missouri Argus, St. Louis, Missouri.

Daily Missouri Republican, St. Louis, Missouri.

Missouri Statesman.

Missouri Whig, Palmyra, Missouri.

The Mormon, New York, New York.

The Mountaineer, Salt Lake City, Utah.

National Intelligencer.

Nauvoo Expositor, Nauvoo, Illinois.

The Neighbor, Nauvoo, Illinois.

New Orleans Daily Picayune, New Orleans, Louisiana.

New York Herald, New York, New York.

New York Sun, New York, New York.

New York Times, New York, New York.

New York Tribune, New York, New York.

New York Weekly Tribune, New York, New York.

The New York Watchman, New York, New York.

Niles' National Register, Baltimore, Maryland.

Northern Islander, Beaver Island, Lake Michigan.

Oregon Bulletin.

Overland Monthly.

The People's Daily Organ, St. Louis, Missouri.

Pittsburgh Leader, Pittsburgh, Pennsylvania.

Quarterly Review.

Quincy Whig, Quincy, Illinois.

Randolph Record, Randolph County, Missouri

The Republican, St. Louis, Missouri.

Review, Salt Lake City, Utah

Weekly Reville, St. Louis, Missouri.

Reynolds' Newspaper, Great Britain

Sacramento Daily Herald, Sacramento, California.

St. Louis American, St. Louis, Missouri.

St. Louis Globe-Democrat, St. Louis, Missouri.

St. Louis Daily Journal, Saint Louis, Missouri.

St. Louis Daily New Era, St. Louis, Missouri.

St. Louis Reville, St. Louis, Missouri.

Salt Lake Herald, Salt Lake City, Utah.

Salt Lake Daily Herald, Salt Lake City, Utah.

Salt Lake Tribune, Salt Lake City, Utah.

San Francisco Alta, San Francisco, California.

San Francisco Bulletin, San Francisco, California.

San Francisco Herald, San Francisco, California.

San Francisco News, San Francisco, California.

San Jose Pioneer, San Jose, California.

Sangamo Journal, Springfield, Illinois.

The Savannah News, Savannah, Georgia.

Scientific American.

Sonoma Democrat, Sonoma, California.

Springfield Journal, Springfield, Illinois

Springfield Republican, Springfield, Illinois

Stockton Independent, Stockton, California

Daily Telegraph.

Times and Seasons, Commerce and Nauvoo, Illinois.

Union, St. George, Utah.

Union Vedette, Camp Douglas, Utah.

Utica Morning Herald And Daily Gazette.

Vallejo Recorder, Vallejo, California.

Valley Tan, Salt Lake City, Utah.

Warsaw Signal and Agricultural, Literary and Commercial Register, Warsaw, Illinois.

The Wasp — Extra, Nauvoo, Illinois.

Western Monitor, Fayette, Missouri.

Index

Rockwell: U.S. Marshal, by Richard Lloyd Dewey

—Autographed copies available—

Historically accurate fiction of America's premier gunfighter. A compelling, non-stop action story, and study of his rocky relationship with the woman who loved him most.

Cloth, 212 pages. ISBN: 0-9616024-2-2. $15.95, plus $1.00 shipping. Prices subject to change. Send check or money order to Paramount Books, Western Distributing Office, P.O. Box 1371 Provo, UT 84603-1371.